Reluctant Race Men

Reluctant Race Men

Black Challenges to the Practice of Race in Nineteenth-Century America

JOAN L. BRYANT

OXFORD
UNIVERSITY PRESS

Oxford University Press is a department of the University of Oxford. It furthers
the University's objective of excellence in research, scholarship, and education
by publishing worldwide. Oxford is a registered trade mark of Oxford University
Press in the UK and certain other countries.

Published in the United States of America by Oxford University Press
198 Madison Avenue, New York, NY 10016, United States of America.

© Oxford University Press 2024

All rights reserved. No part of this publication may be reproduced, stored in
a retrieval system, or transmitted, in any form or by any means, without the
prior permission in writing of Oxford University Press, or as expressly permitted
by law, by license, or under terms agreed with the appropriate reproduction
rights organization. Inquiries concerning reproduction outside the scope of the
above should be sent to the Rights Department, Oxford University Press, at the
address above.

Chapters two, three, and five use material that has been adapted from Joan L. Bryant,
"Race and Religion in Nineteenth-century America," in *Perspectives on American
Religion and Culture*, edited by Peter W. Williams, 1999. Used with permission of Blackwell
Publishers, permission conveyed through Copyright Clearance Center, Inc.

Chapters two and three use material that appears in a different form in "Colored Conventions,
Moral Reform, and the American Race Problem," published in *The Colored Conventions
Movement: Black Organizing in the Nineteenth Century*, edited by P. Gabrielle Foreman, Jim Casey,
and Sarah Lynn Patterson. Copyright © 2021 by the University of North Carolina Press.
Used by permission of the publisher. www.uncpress.org

Some material has been published in a different form in "Les Réformateurs Africains-Américains
et la Lutte contre la Marginalisation Raciale," trans. in *Histoire en Marges: Les Périphéries de
L'Histoire Globale*, ed. Hélène Le Dantec-Lowry et al. Tours: Presses Universitaires
François-Rabelais, 2018. pp. 49–73.

You must not circulate this work in any other form
and you must impose this same condition on any acquirer.

Library of Congress Control Number: 2023045525

ISBN 978–0–19–531297–3 (pbk.)
ISBN 978–0–19–531296–6 (hbk.)

DOI: 10.1093/oso/9780195312966.001.0001

For Linda and Kay
in memory of our parents

Contents

Acknowledgments	ix
Notes on Terminology	xi
Introduction	1
1. "Not a Difference of Species": Nationality and the Question of Representation	11
2. "That Odious Distinction": Moral Reform and the Language of Obligations	41
3. "One Common Family": Equality and the Logic of Authority	72
4. "Humanology": Difference and the Science of Humanity	118
5. "One Color Now": Freedom and the Ethics of Association	180
6. "Race-ship": Citizenship and Imperatives of Progress	233
7. "The Whole Question of Race": Jim Crow and the Problem of Consciousness	275
Conclusion: "Along the Color Line"	315
Notes	329
Bibliography	393
Index	425

Acknowledgments

The kindness, encouragement, generosity, and companionship of many people supported my efforts to think clearly about race in writing this book. My gratitude is deeper than I can express in acknowledgments.

Susan Ferber, my editor at Oxford University Press, offered unflagging support for my efforts over the many years it took me to finish. I am thankful for her incisive feedback and patience.

Former advisors, commentators at conference presentations, and long-standing conversation partners helped me develop and refine my analysis of race. I am grateful for past and present input, advice, moral support, and collegiality from Sheila Briggs, Jon Butler, John Ernest, Evelyn Higginbotham, Reginald Hildebrand, Jacqueline Jones, Melissa Nobles, Carla Peterson, James C. Scott, and Harry Stout.

I appreciate the contributions of current and former colleagues and friends who were willing to listen, question, and encourage. Thanks to William Carrigan, Jacqueline Goldsby, LaVerne Gray, Diane Grimes, Stephen G. Hall, Johnnie Hamilton-Mason, Kathryn Jackson, Serene Jones, Lucy Mulroney, Kendall Phillips, Romita Ray, Marcia Robinson, Michele Ronnick, William Seraile, and Judith Weisenfeld.

Several fellowships supported my research for this book. I am grateful to the Institute for Citizens & Scholars (formerly the Woodrow Wilson Foundation) for the Mellon Career Enhancement Fellowship, Harvard University's W. E. B. Du Bois Institute for African and African American Research, the former Institute for the Race and Social Division at Boston University, and the former Institute for the Advanced Study of Religion at Yale University.

Conversations with students in the classroom and while serving as a research advisor kept me mindful of the importance of diverse configurations of race. I appreciate the gratifying exchanges I had with Liora Cobin, Lauren Doamekpor, Rob Heinrich, Miriam Hurwitz, H. Muoki Mbunga, David Mwambari, Charmane Perry, Reuven Sunshine, Enkeshi Thom El-Amin, Travis Watson, Roy Whitaker, and Robert Yufer.

X ACKNOWLEDGMENTS

The generosity of librarians, curators, archivists, faculty, administrators, and collectors eased the process of securing images and permissions. I gratefully acknowledge the assistance of David Broda, Regina Cole, Nicolette Dobrowolski, and Brenda Muhammad, all of Syracuse University; Jacqueline Brown (Wilberforce University); Teresa Fry Brown (AME Church Department of Research and Scholarship); Hélène Le Dantec-Lowry (Université Sorbonne Nouvelle, Paris 3); David Grinnell (University of Pittsburgh Library System); William Hart (Middlebury College); Connye Richardson and Robert Woodson (Thomas Woodson Family Association); George R. Rinhart and Francis DiMauro (Rinhart Collection); Dale Sauter (Joyner Library, East Carolina University); Deborah Sisum (National Portrait Gallery); Jason E. Tomberlin (UNC Libraries); and Tehra Williams (NAACP).

Friends, who walked, talked, and broke bread with me, helped bring "my race men" to life and print. Thanks to Brett Flamm, Albert Kelly, Linda Littlejohn, Langston McKinney, Myron Miller, Lynn Shields, Mary Slechta, Matej Slechta, Sibyll Wiggins, and Vita Williams for steadfast interest in my well-being and curiosity about my work.

My family's unconditional love nurtured me throughout this project. My nieces and nephews, Tamara, Lionell, Lamont, Valerie, Kayla, and Kieran, inspired me to occasionally turn from the past and look hopefully to the future. My sisters, Linda and Kay, saw me through our many losses. Their faith and wit sustain me.

Notes on Terminology

Throughout this book, I employ racial references used in nineteenth-century contexts. Terms such as "colored" and "mulatto" are routinely left uncapitalized, while I capitalize "Negro." I also capitalize "Black" and "White" and use them to refer to people across historical periods, acknowledging the convention of labeling human populations as colors. Capitalization highlights the fact that the terms are titles rather than descriptions of physical qualities. My usage patterns are not intended to suggest logical or "right" ways to name people as races.

I understand that the term "enslaved person" is widely used to affirm the humanity of people living in bondage. Nevertheless, I use the more capacious reference, "slave," noting that slaves are by definition human beings. "Enslaved" defines individuals solely from the vantage point of people who own them. The passive voice privileges the perspective of enslavers. I think it limits the conceptual space needed to contend with the historical fact that people living in slavery defined, interpreted, and contested the institution and what it meant to be a slave.

Introduction

In his inaugural address to the American Negro Academy, W. E. B. Du Bois set out to make race a basis of collective consciousness among Black people. He reasoned that races were foundational elements of human history. As such, they were the only sure units of progress. This "natural law" of advancement applied even in the United States in spite of its acclaimed individualism. Thus, the academy had to help its constituents recognize that human beings are "divided into races" and inspire them to identify themselves accordingly.[1]

This 1897 initiative might seem curious in contexts where it is customary to treat race and identity as inseparable, particularly with reference to Black Americans. Media discussions about Black people typically proceed as if they are, by definition, conversations about race. In everyday parlance, racial designations typically function as self-evident mirrors of constitutive properties, despite scientific uncertainty about their coherence as scientific modes of classification. It is commonplace to characterize interactions among people distinguished by different racial names as "race relations." Conflicts over how the US Census Bureau tracks the nation's population have centered on the accuracy with which its racial categories match individuals' sense of themselves. Similarly, race has figured in affirmative action controversies as an inherent element of identities that wrongfully disadvantages or privileges people. Such conventional scenarios construe race as an inescapable personal quality that defines who a person is. They suggest that Du Bois's endeavor was an unnecessary attempt to convince people simply to be themselves.[2]

Yet Du Bois understood his task as essential and new. Translating race into identity entailed contending with ideas long embedded in Black American reform discourse. He described the situation at the start of his address, *The Conservation of Races*, as if he were eulogizing a position that might have been noble but was ultimately untenable. He observed that Negroes had always been skeptical about talk of races because they believed it advanced inaccurate propositions about their innate moral, mental, and political capacity. They tended to "deprecate and minimize race distinctions," he observed, clinging to a belief that "out of one blood God created all nations."[3]

Reluctant Race Men. Joan L. Bryant, Oxford University Press. © Oxford University Press 2024.
DOI: 10.1093/oso/9780195312966.003.0001

2 RELUCTANT RACE MEN

For his part, it was a mistake to use ideals of "human brotherhood" to navigate social and political realities. Anyone who proposed such undertakings apparently failed to grasp what it meant for Negroes to be American.

Reluctant Race Men reconstructs the tradition Du Bois sought to displace. It traces nineteenth-century challenges to race in reform initiatives largely among Northern Black men. It thus situates the equation of race and identity at the end of a long trajectory of collective action. Repudiations of race developed as a critical dimension of antebellum reform work and persisted through the turn of the century. A broad assortment of reformers issued challenges to the logic and ethics of race practices, condemning their configurations of difference, sameness, and rank for destabilizing bases of public authority, contracting the boundaries of duty and association, and eroding the foundations of citizenship, freedom, manhood, and humanity. Race was a construct that distorted identities and thwarted progress.

Judgments of this sort informed a host of reform endeavors before and after emancipation. Records of race challenges appear in religious and secular periodicals, convention proceedings, sermons, ethnological treatises, literature, and political speeches—sources familiar to scholars of African American history. Such materials reveal that race was central to Black American reform endeavors in ways that prevailing accounts of activism have not clearly delineated. The sources include a spectrum of actors— abolitionists, emigrationists, educators, temperance campaigners, lawyers, church leaders, anti-colonizationists, missionaries, writers, physicians, and voting rights advocates—who devoted aspects of their work to questioning the coherence of dividing, grouping, and ranking people into races.

Prominent antebellum and Reconstruction-era figures were in the forefront of questioning the construct. Minister and newspaper editor Samuel Cornish, Philadelphia businessman James Forten, Sr. abolitionists Frederick Douglass and Robert Purvis, physician James McCune Smith, and African Methodist Episcopal (AME) Church leaders Daniel Payne and Benjamin Tucker Tanner were among the many vocal race critics. Joining them were individuals whose prominence diminished over time. William Whipper and ministers Hosea Easton, Theodore Wright, and Samuel Ringgold Ward raised oppositional voices, along with such pseudonymous reformers as "Americanus," "PENN," "EUTHYMUS," and "VIATOR," whose ideas are the only certain aspects of their identities.

As age and death muted the voices of early challengers, a rising generation of reformers reinterpreted the concept's significance. In the wake of

INTRODUCTION   3

Reconstruction, Du Bois was among the individuals who formulated agendas for progress as "race men"—reformers committed to developing a collective racial consciousness as a foundation for advancing "the race." Their initiatives did not eradicate race challenges. Affiliates of the Negro Academy and similar venues continued to express misgivings. Writer Charles Chesnutt, scholars Kelly Miller and William Scarborough, and ministers Theophilus Steward and John P. Sampson were among the men who continued to question the veracity and validity of race practices. As "reluctant race men," they extended the tradition of interrogating, contesting, interpreting, and denouncing race into the early twentieth century.

This book helps to explain how people of African descent became a putative American race. It reconstructs reform discourses that counter the notion that race is a self-evident, transhistorical site of collective identity for Black Americans that expressed itself most clearly in religious and secular reform endeavors. It analyzes the myriad repudiations and disavowals of race that emanated from forums organized and operated by Black people. Black-controlled newspapers, societies, churches, and conventions—arenas popularly construed as manifestations of race consciousness—provided the principal loci and resources for questioning race. In these contexts, people of African descent generated a lexicon for refuting race, debated its logic, and, ultimately, reinterpreted it. Divergent sites of reform fostered multiple modes of contesting race. Questions about morality, nationality, rights, scientific standards, and the terms of association gave rise to discrete race challenges. Taken together, however, they comprise a reform tradition in which individuals questioned the validity of grouping Americans, free men, citizens, Christians, and humans into essentially different and unequal classes.

Nineteenth-century American freedom shaped the evolution of race. Slavery does not tell the whole story.[4] Race challenges emerged with the expansion of freedom in the decades after gradual emancipation statutes took effect in Northern states. By 1830, rising numbers of free people of African descent vastly overshadowed the North's slave population. This group comprised at least 99 percent of the 1830 colored populations in every Northern state, except New Jersey, where two-thirds of all Northern slaves resided. Even there, the last state to enact a gradual emancipation statute,

4 RELUCTANT RACE MEN

free people comprised 89 percent of the colored population. They had grown to 97 percent by 1840.[5] Increases in the freeborn population, individual manumissions, and migration among escaped slaves made free people of color recognizable as a distinct class in antebellum America. This Northern population was a new phenomenon. Unlike small communities of free people that had dotted the northeast since the seventeenth century, it could not be reflexively absorbed into the existing social fabric or dismissed as an anomaly. It destabilized the axiomatic connection between slavery and racial categories denoting African descent. Officially, such designations as Black, Negro, colored, and mulatto were no longer sufficient proof of a person's eligibility for enslavement. Despite this shift, the terms of American freedom for people who were not White remained undeveloped. Conceptions of freedom had not evolved to accommodate them. This situation lends currency to characterizations of Southern and Northern free people as "slaves without masters," "quasi-free," and "almost free."[6] Such notions vividly capture the extent to which legal, economic, civil, and religious restrictions circumscribed the liberties of free people of color. They highlight the fact that White Americans subjected people of African descent—enslaved and free— to assorted forms of subjugation and exclusion. However, they have limited use as analytic tools because they imbue the claims and power of privileged White men with a seemingly natural authority over what freedom meant and how Americans experienced it.

This authority was hardly a given. White people in many sectors of American society responded to changes in the parameters of Northern slavery by recalibrating how race labels marked difference and inequality. They expanded the varieties of subjugation associated with African descent and codified justifications for claiming citizenship and rights exclusively for themselves. They tried to guarantee that, even if people of African descent were not slaves, they could not be free and equal Americans. As the free colored population expanded over the course of the antebellum period, White reformers and statesmen diligently worked to ensure that citizenship and rights, two hallmarks of American freedom, became the exclusive property of White men. Colonization schemes to remove free people of color from the United States; state legislative enactments restricting the franchise to White men; systematic discrimination in public accommodations, education, churches, and employment; efforts to strengthen the scientific legitimacy of race classifications; and Roger Taney's infamous dictum in the *Dred Scott* decision denying Negroes' rights all served this function.[7] Such innovations reconfigured how race categories gauged claims to American identity, political rights, civil liberties, religious authority, and even membership in the human family. Thus, navigating American freedom meant confronting the landscape of race that defined it.

Mapping race challenges requires tracking a moving target. It means explicating reformers' engagement with diverse ethical, legal, political, religious, and scientific activities that configured or sustained difference, sameness, hierarchy, or consciousness. The process generates a new conception of race as a set of disparate practices that constituted multiple realities. Race challenges operated from three vantage points. The most fundamental inquiries targeted the existence of taxonomies that purported to represent naturally occurring differences among humans, sameness within populations, or a hierarchies of people grouped with such terms as Negroid, Mongoloid, and Caucasoid. Other queries involved attacks on methods of assigning people to population categories. In such instances, reformers took aim at laws and customs that invoked appearance, ancestry, behavior, or birthplace to render people Negroes, mulattoes, Caucasians, or another supposedly natural category. Illogical classification schemes sometimes exposed the incoherence of the entire race enterprise. However, some individuals sought only to modify the rules of race assignment, stopping short of questioning whether categories were logical ways of dividing, grouping, or ranking people. A third action entailed questioning what it meant to inhabit a racial classification. Reformers contested the meanings of being labeled "Negro," for example—of *being* Black. Engagements of this sort addressed traits, behaviors, sensibilities, and loyalties that presumed to define and regulate blackness as a basis of personal or collective consciousness.[8]

This work occupies an anomalous place in the expanding body of scholarship on race in the history of the United States.[9] A long tradition of examining Black American struggles against discrimination and racist ideologies has devoted scant attention to their challenges to race. A preoccupation with paradigms of assimilation, integration, separatism, and nationalism that reduce reform endeavors to political strategies has dominated discussions of Black reform discourse related to race. The consensus that emerges from this literature is that, even as they fought racism, Black people subscribed to a notion that fundamental differences and similarities distinguished and comprised races. As practitioners of what historian George Frederickson has termed "romantic racialism," they were apparently content to ascribe positive racial traits to Black people.[10]

6 RELUCTANT RACE MEN

This book offers an alternative interpretation. It abandons conventional paradigms that parse reform endeavors into competing strategic gestures. Instead, it probes concerns about ethics and truth that shaped the logic and mechanics of opposing race. It explains how individuals with varied ideological perspectives participated in this reform tradition. Their activism and misgivings blur lines that demarcate tactical differences among people labeled assimilationists, integrationists, separatists, and nationalists.[11]

Attacks on race began as part of the culture of "voluntaryism" that shaped antebellum reforms. Voluntary associations enabled people customarily barred from participating in American politics to assert moral authority. They effectively expanded the spheres of public discourse and political action by recognizing popular opinion as an arbiter of public virtue. Reform societies, conventions, and benevolent organizations thrived on trying to shape this opinion and claiming to represent it. Through speeches, the press, pamphlets, and other publications, they claimed an auxiliary role in defining the public good. Associations fostered agency among people denied access to official modes of authority. As alternate loci of public discourse, they aroused suspicion among some Americans, who thought that they could undermine the authority of the state and churches. For example, in 1829, Unitarian minister William Ellery Channing counseled his contemporaries never to give these groups the deference due to constitutional governments and religious institutions recognized as "arrangements of God." Associations, he warned, constituted "irregular" forms of governance and "contrived" social relations. They required close monitoring to prevent them from wielding public power that they had no authority to exercise. This result, he feared, would be tyranny.[12]

Channing's dire cautions point to possibilities for private associations to function as venues for social change. This potential was not lost on free Black people seeking freedom, justice, and equality. Voluntaryism provided a framework within which they forged identities as reformers and developed a reform tradition that evolved through successive generations of activism. They used this cultural milieu to envision and promote a "moral revolution." Theirs was an "age of reform," insisted Presbyterian minister Samuel Cornish, who helped launch the reform press among free people of color. He and his allies believed they possessed the moral authority, right, and responsibility to try to shape the terms of free manhood and citizenship.[13]

INTRODUCTION 7

Everyday experiences of oppression also fueled faith in the power of public opinion. Reformers understood that inequality was not solely the creation of state officials. Popular biases against Northern free colored populations allowed injustices to flourish. Examples of this awareness abound in the press and in convention proceedings. They are replete with accounts of harm resulting from "corrupt public sentiment" and of the necessity of altering "the public mind." James McCune Smith dubbed public opinion "the King of today" that antebellum reformers could and must conquer. Echoing this judgment, New Yorker Thomas Hamilton, editor of the *Anglo-African Magazine*, bemoaned the fact that free people of color failed to hold annual national conventions to disseminate their messages. Lapses meant missed opportunities to affect "the living law of the land." He perceived public opinion as a "malleable, ductile entity" that stood in contrast to institutionalized bureaucratic and legal practices. Any group could mold it, he reasoned, by earnestly broadcasting its ideas.[14]

Race challenges were embedded in struggles among free Black men to ground their humanity and identity as citizens on gendered platforms of equality. They reflect an evolving discourse of manhood. Although voluntaryism expanded access to public spheres, there was nothing democratic or egalitarian about its venues. The press and associations that facilitated opposition to race were fraught with some of the same hierarchies, conflicts, and inconsistencies that typified broader social and political initiatives. They were not open to all. Most excluded women from their deliberations or severely circumscribed their roles. Mary Ann Shadd Cary was one of the few women to contest "complexional distinctions" in public arenas. She controlled her medium by editing the *Provincial Freeman* in Canada. In their near universal exclusion of women, the men who questioned race practices largely adhered to conventions of equating reform with manliness. As Baltimorean William J. Watkins asserted, the courage, potency, and nerve of "true Reformers" lay beyond the reach of the "unmanly."[15]

The chapters that follow explore opposition to race in reform initiatives concerned with bases of representation, parameters of mutual obligations, grounds for claiming authority, the science of identifying humans, the ethics of defining associations, the meaning of progress, and the foundations of group consciousness for people of African descent. They map race challenges

8 RELUCTANT RACE MEN

that were integral to the course of nineteenth-century African American reform. Thus, they present two distinct phenomena—a history of Black people's actions and ideas and a history of a concept that configured them as a discrete population. They show that the historical meanings of race extend beyond the forces that constructed and sustained it; they encompass the ideas lodged against it.

The first chapter traces the foundations of race challenges. It explains how arguments against American Colonization Society efforts to resettle free people of color in Liberia evolved from disavowals of Africa to forthright assertions of American nationality. This process began in local venues, where groups denounced the flawed reasoning of claims that native-born Americans belonged on a foreign continent. It developed in national conventions of the 1830s where delegates tried to resolve tensions between colonization and emigration projects. They forged identities as reformers in these contexts, grappling with whether reform called for collective self-improvement to prove colored people worthy of American freedom or a commitment to improving a corrupt nation. As they pondered the terms of their citizenship, declarations of membership in the human family inspired misgivings about racial constructions of difference.

Opposition to race expanded in initiatives that followed the first series of antebellum national conventions. The second chapter explores this development and the debates it inspired. Competing and shifting reform coalitions argued over the language that should define the parameters of moral obligations among citizens and Christians. The American Moral Reform Society, spearheaded by former national convention delegates, was at the center of conflicts. The conviction that reform was a sacred undertaking intensified conflicts over repudiations of racial distinctions. Clerics, such as Samuel Cornish and Lewis Woodson, and "unchurched" reformers Robert Purvis and William Whipper were in the forefront of contentious exchanges that curtailed the Reform Society's initiatives but set the terms for enduring race challenges.

Challenges to race spread to diverse reform venues in the 1840s and 1850s. Reformers who decried discrimination in political and civil arenas for creating "unnatural" distinctions struggled to deflect charges that their own endeavors inscribed notions of race difference. Chapter 3 analyzes such paradoxes in efforts to secure equal political and civil rights, debates over colored churches and segregated schools, antislavery activism, and emigration campaigns. It explores race challenges and conflicts embedded in reformers' efforts to exercise public authority as Americans and members of the human race.

Scientific theories of race raised unique sorts of concerns. While social and political race practices circumscribed freedom, race science disputed the humanity of people of African descent. Mid-nineteenth-century scientific innovations exacerbated the situation as the American School of ethnology advanced the theory of polygenesis that conceived of people of African descent as a nonhuman species. Chapter 4 analyzes how reformers moved beyond political and moral discourse to refute scientific claims. Without altogether dismissing human variation, they devised alternative explanations for differences that race categories allegedly signified. The chapter explicates the historical, religious, political, and scientific ideas they employed to draw their own conclusions about human nature and the causes of difference and inequality.

The indignation that characterized antebellum attacks on race gave way to widespread optimism on the heels of the Civil War. The expansion of freedom appeared to disrupt the role race categories played in regulating access to civil and political participation. Some surmised that classification practices had been abolished. Taking stock of emancipation, Frederick Douglass declared that the "race condition" of Black people was finished. Chapter 5 analyzes how reformers engaged questions about the validity of using race categories as bases of secular and religious association as they navigated a new political landscape that recognized Black citizenship. Conventions, newspapers, freedom celebrations, suffrage campaigns, "class legislation" proposals, and "race churches" offer a window into reflections and conflicts over the ethics of race practices in the "new era" of freedom.

Persistent misgivings about race complicated the work of rising race men intent on cultivating group consciousness. Chapter 6 explores how post-Reconstruction political developments and changes in scientific discourse fueled attempts to link race to human progress and American identity. It shows how cultivating "the race" became integral to notions of progress for reformers as diverse as Martin Delany, W. E. B. Du Bois, Alexander Crummell, and others who worked to make a virtue and a necessity of racial identity. The chapter analyzes how campaigns to foster a collective race consciousness coexisted with ongoing denunciations of race practices and inspired questions about the politics and ethics of making race a site of identity.

The spread of discriminatory Jim Crow enactments and generational shifts among reformers framed challenges to race at the close of the century.

Chapter 7 maps divergent forms of opposition that flourished amid the period's competing social and political forces. Although the racial hierarchy of Jim Crow was an obvious target, the notion of discrete races continued to provoke scorn even among proponents of race consciousness. Efforts of race men to instill a collective identity founded on race became another phenomenon to interrogate. Proposals for a group designation for people of African descent also raised questions about the phenomena that constructed race. Legal claims, literature, religious pamphlets, political speeches, and philosophical essays display the varied conceptualizations that comprised race challenges as reformers sought stable foundations for collective endeavors.

The conclusion reflects on the enduring significance of race challenges as the push to cultivate race consciousness came to dominate reform endeavors. It explains how race men forged discursive space "along the color line" to foster a collective racial consciousness and continue the practice of condemning Jim Crow racial configurations that restricted opportunities for Black Americans to flourish in the early twentieth century.

Race challenges expand the nation's complex genealogy of race. Although they can tell only a partial story of Black reform thought, they reveal sustained confrontations with laws, public policies, reform initiatives, scientific theories, political activities, religious organization, and social interactions that illuminate how race functioned. They feature a broad set of practices that configured difference, hierarchy, sameness, and consciousness. The changing actions and aims that defined this under-explored dimension of race history help explain what it meant for Black reformers to be men and citizens in nineteenth-century America.

1

"Not a Difference of Species"

Nationality and the Question of Representation

The project that Samuel Cornish and John Russwurm launched in 1827 seemed modest. Cornish, a former teacher turned Presbyterian minister, and Russwurm, a recent graduate of Bowdoin College, intended to offer the public "a simple representation of facts."[1] Yet the undertaking of these New Yorkers—the first known colored editors of an American newspaper— was an innovation with far-reaching goals. Heretofore, free people of color possessed no established medium for publicly representing themselves. They felt "incorrectly represented" by friends and enemies alike who misapprehended the truth of their condition. *Freedom's Journal* promised to be an instrument of reform that would enable them to confront "misrepresentations" by speaking for themselves.[2] The editors were confident that their intervention would help to eliminate bigotry and the many injustices it inspired. It would thereby strengthen the colored population's hold on American freedom.

For two years, *Freedom's Journal* provided reformers with a venue in which to counter derogatory images of colored people. Yet, the project was more complicated than Cornish, Russwurm, and the paper's patrons initially imagined. An independent publication for self-expression did not resolve problems of representation. The shared menace that spurred collaboration offered no ready-made or obvious basis for asserting a collective identity. Instead, with the expansion of reform endeavors, questions about how colored people should represent themselves as a group became as complicated as contesting how others characterized them.[3]

Freedom's Journal's truncated career suggests how elusive viable terms of representation could be. The paper collapsed amid dissension over whether free people of color were truly American. Subscribers and supporters of the paper forced Russwurm from his post when he ridiculed assertions of American citizenship as a "waste of words" and declared the American Colonization Society's (ACS) colony in West Africa "our promised Land."[4]

Reluctant Race Men. Joan L. Bryant, Oxford University Press. © Oxford University Press 2024.
DOI: 10.1093/oso/9780195312966.003.0002

12 RELUCTANT RACE MEN

Shortly thereafter, he settled in Liberia under the auspices of the Maryland Colonization Society.

Colonization projects lent immediacy and complexity to the problem of how to be known. White American efforts to relocate free people of African descent to West Africa inspired denunciations throughout the antebellum period.[5] In his address to the 1834 national convention of colored people, New Yorker William Hamilton observed that, in the absence of any other concerns, the mere existence of the ACS would be reason enough for collective action.[6] The removal campaign provided an impetus for delineating forthright claims to American freedom among colored people. It fueled their efforts to forge identities as reformers. *Freedom's Journal* was one step in the development of an infrastructure to bolster this work. Along with mutual aid societies, churches, conventions, and ad hoc gatherings, the press was a venue through which free people of African descent could contend with political, religious, ethical, and scientific claims used to justify depriving them of membership in the nation.

The institutional initiatives that facilitated Russwurm's shift reflect the daunting forces surrounding early collective endeavors. They announced that freedom disqualified people of African descent from being American. Colonizationists worked to protect the republic's boundaries by broadcasting the message that the Black population could not function in America as free. This dispatch helped place the representation problem at the core of early African American reform. Establishing a hold on freedom required reformers to engage and contest racial configurations of American identity. The ambitions and demise of *Freedom's Journal* signal this process and its complicated negotiations, which laid foundations for the development of a tradition of race challenges. Reformers pondered and debated resettlement, moral improvement, and assaults on American structures of immorality as they grappled with the significance of ancestry and the terms of freedom, nationality, citizenship, and human rights.

Colonization agendas that ruled out Black citizenship emerged with the founding of the republic. White statesmen and reformers proposed settling emancipated slaves outside of the United States as early as the 1780s. Thomas Jefferson offered a famous articulation of the idea in his *Notes on the State of Virginia,* which characterized removing Black people as necessary to the goal of ending slavery. He perceived a "difference of race" in Negroes' skin color, hair texture, facial features, sweat, sleep patterns, body shape, emotions, letters, mental ability, odor, heat tolerance, poetry, sexual desires, and capacity for love—factors he believed made it impossible to incorporate them into the nation.[7] The formation of the American Colonization Society in 1816 gave institutional weight to such suggestions and transformed resettlement ideas into a reform measure that promised to protect and advance the new nation. The scheme brought together Northern and Southern politicians, clergy, slaveholders, opponents of slavery, entrepreneurs, and philanthropists. Such prominent statesmen as James Madison, James Monroe, Andrew Jackson, John Marshall, Henry Clay, and Daniel Webster endorsed it, along with officials of many Protestant denominations—Baptists, Congregationalists, Dutch Reformed, Episcopalians, Lutherans, Methodists, Moravians, Presbyterians, and the Society of Friends.[8] Through national and local alliances, individuals and groups created a full-fledged crusade to cleanse the nation of its free colored population. The ACS program was far more complex than Jefferson's sketch and addressed a broader array of concerns. However, racial notions of difference, hierarchy, and sameness were central to a shared vision of whitening the republic.

Colonization became many things as its advocates tried to convince people of its virtues. Explanations of the undertaking reflected the interests of a diverse group of subscribers. The colored population's alleged characteristics fluctuated with the changing claims about what colonization would accomplish. Free people were variously depraved and dangerous outsiders, budding Christian imperialists, a class wronged and injured by slavery, the key to abolition, potential African trade partners, and redeemers of Africa. The one constant was that they could not be simultaneously free and American.

The scorn that infused colonization rhetoric might have been reason enough for colored people to denounce the project. Proponents lauded its potential to rid the nation of an immoral pestilence. Princeton attorney James Green invoked a typical image in his description of the population as a "mass of ignorance, misery and depravity, . . . revolting wretchedness and deadly pollution."[9] Such sentiments suggested that moral impairments put free people beyond the reach of all conceivable domestic interventions. Hopelessness prevailed even among colonization advocates who attributed the degraded status of free people to bigotry among White Americans. Reverend Frederick Freeman described their alleged moral deficits as "the natural consequence of their condition and not the result of any inherent depravity in their natural

14 RELUCTANT RACE MEN

constitution, or of deficiency of mental faculties."[10] Similarly, Dutch Reform minister William McMurray told White congregants that, faced with similar oppressive circumstances and prejudices, they would be as slothful as colored people appeared to be.[11] Nevertheless, because colored depravity appeared to be so great and White bigotry seemed indestructible, colonization presented itself as the only sensible course of action. The perceived magnitude of the problem led Lucius Elmer, US district attorney for New Jersey, to champion it as a benevolent and virtuous undertaking. Removing free people offered an opportunity to improve their prospects for achievement, which appeared to be nil in America.[12]

The merits of eliminating the free population went well beyond securing the nation's moral fabric. Removal also promised to neutralize a threat to its social and political stability. Supreme Court justice John Marshall was hardly alone in his judgment that free colored people embodied the dangers that had been realized in the Haitian Revolution.[13] The possibility that an "African sceptre" could rule on US soil was a horror that colonizationists could not stress enough. Their project promised to minimize this risk because it would promote a peaceful end to slavery and eliminate a group whose freedom would inevitably create futile expectations. Slaveholders might be more readily disposed to manumitting their slaves if they could be certain that they would not have to live with them as free people. Colonization offered such certainty.[14]

Ultimately, it mattered little whether colonization was a manifestation of White bigotry or benevolence. Opponents of the plan acknowledged various factors at work in the initiative, ranging from malevolence to charity. They rejected it in any case because neither contempt nor concern got to the heart of the matter. The critical issue was the claim that people of color were not and could not be free and equal American citizens. It rested on the premise that national boundaries and citizenship had to conform to distinctions marked by racial classifications. In short, race was a critical facet of the ideological foundations of removal. The "natural" distinctions White colonizationists saw between them and people of African ancestry guided their determinations of membership in the republic and the parameters of American freedom. These connections were self-evident. As the ACS periodical *African Repository and Colonial Journal* reported, the "insurmountable barrier of color" made free people "a distinct and inferior race, repugnant to our republican feelings and dangerous to our republican institutions." Even when they acknowledged prejudice as the obstacle to equal participation, colonization advocates found its root cause in differences *"beyond the control of human will.*" The most altruistic proponents displayed similar convictions and made unflinching assertions that emancipation could not yield freedom for colored people. Frederick Freeman observed that colored individuals had "the *name* of being free," nothing more. Connecticut minister Leonard Bacon put the natural incompatibility of American freedom and blackness in equally stark terms. "You may call him free," he sneered, "but you cannot bleach him into the enjoyment of freedom." Eliphalet Nott, president of Union College, echoed this opinion, arguing that, colored people, whether free or enslaved, would forever be "a distinct, a degraded, and a wretched race."[15]

Colonizationists generally stopped short of identifying moral degradation as an innate, unalterable race trait. Yet they maintained that natural differences between races made the degradation of the free population inevitable and intractable. As Lucius Elmer argued, the "indelible mark" of African descent was not the cause of inferiority; nevertheless, it destined colored people to subservience by precluding citizenship.[16] Similarly, although moral depravity made removal the remedy of choice for Reverend William McMurray, "colour and blood" made it logical and necessary. For Reverend Richard Fuller, free people of color were not merely "an inferior caste"; they comprised "a separate and distinct race." The "Anglo-Saxon race" was acting according to a divine plan by sending Negroes to the land "assigned their race by God."[17] ACS officials believed that they had no real choice in the matter because Africa was the divinely ordained home of colored people. Christian charity could do nothing to address their condition in America; it could aid them only in Africa. To emphasize this limitation, they explained that it was "not the fault of the colored man, nor of the white man, nor of Christianity; but an ordination of Providence, and no more to be changed than the laws of nature."[18]

ACS supporters typically rejected the notion that the alleged distinctiveness of colored people placed them outside the boundaries of humanity. Instead, African identity was proof of membership in the human race. An *African Repository* essay "Observations on the Early History of the Negro Race" tried to demonstrate that people of color had a glorious African past, despite the fact that they had become a "despised and persecuted race."[19] It extolled the biblical Cushites from whom Negroes presumably descended as having been enlightened. This commonplace invocation of antiquity highlighted noble origins to disprove popular claims that people of color were a subhuman link to monkeys.[20]

A presumed inherent otherness offered proof that free people of color belonged in Africa. Officially, the ACS was willing to send them anywhere

Congress identified as suitable.[21] However, race distinctions made it seem reasonable and just to send them to their ancestral continent. One of the purported virtues of colonization was that it would resettle people in their natural habitat. Leading colonists, such as Baptist preacher Lott Cary, who helped build Liberian institutions, embraced this formulation. A former Virginian slave who purchased his freedom, he explained his desire to go to Liberia by professing a commitment to his race and declaring, "I am an African."[22] James Hall, general agent of the Maryland Colonization Society, drew on this tradition to make the simplest of appeals for colored audiences to take their place in Africa: "Africa is your fatherland." It followed then that they were foreigners who should go home. The maxim that Africa should be for Africans thus guided colonizationists long before Black nationalists asserted this connection to fuel emigration. ACS officials celebrated the achievement of having, with God's help, "rendered unto Africa that which is Africa's." Scientific parlance lent credence to the idea that "the temperature of his blood, the chemical action of his skin, the very texture of his wool hair" fit the Negro for Africa. The plan to send Negroes to the only place they could find happiness and respectability justified removal and turned colonization into a gesture of goodwill. It promised to restore the freedom that American bigotry denied former slaves and descendants of slaves. An African homeland held out possibilities for social mobility and political agency associated with being "real freemen."[23] There, colored people would be able to exercise citizenship rights they could not possess in America.

Missionary aims gave weight to the notion of restoration, rendering free people of color—the ostensible beneficiaries of colonization—American emissaries. By volunteering for removal, colored people would enable the nation to provide reparations to Africa for enslaving its people.[24] They would also help to share the glories of Christian civilization that allegedly made America great. This civilizing mission would rescue Africa from "ignorance and sin," including the evils of the ongoing illegal slave trade. It would repay a "moral debt" owed the continent and, in the process, absolve America. Christianizing Africa would enable the ACS to fulfill the biblical passage in Psalms 68:31: "Ethiopia shall soon stretch forth her hand unto God." Free colored people could carry out the restoration mission because they imbibed American civilization and thereby earned the qualifications of colonizers.[25] Every individual the ACS sent to Africa could be a missionary.

Concerns about inaccuracy that inspired *Freedom's Journal* animated opponents of colonization. They countered the movement's logic with appeals to facts to demonstrate that the project relied on perversions of truth, errors of judgment, and, as New York Episcopal minister Peter Williams concluded, "scandalous misrepresentations."[26] On one hand, denunciations of the enterprise reflected anxieties over the prospects of moving to unfamiliar territory. On the other, opponents were confident about the validity of their criticisms. They were certain that they did not belong in Africa even if their civil and political status was precarious. Baltimore minister and teacher William Watkins ventured that facing death in a ruthless and unjust America was more appealing than the prospect of being "driven like cattle to the pestilential clime of Liberia."[27]

Strident rejections of colonization arose on the heels of enthusiasm about prospects for voluntary emigration initiatives among such prominent Philadelphia figures as wealthy sailmaker James Forten Sr. and AME Church founder Richard Allen. They supported the work of Massachusetts seaman Paul Cuffe, who transported a small group to the British colony of Sierra Leone before the ACS was established. Forten offered financing to help Cuffe establish a colony for Americans in West Africa. However, his connection to Africa initiatives changed as news circulated about the Colonization Society's launch. Within a month of its founding, free communities in Philadelphia, the District of Columbia, and Richmond, Virginia, opposed it. Forten and Allen became spokespersons for some three thousand Philadelphians who gathered at Allen's church to voice fears and hostility about the plan. Forten sympathized with their apprehensions, but he worried about possibilities for self-determination in the United States. As he confided to Cuffe, he was concerned that "they will never become a people until they com[e] out from amongst the white people."[28]

The earliest ACS opponents were nonconfrontational. In Philadelphia, colored people implored White residents to oppose the organization's plan on their behalf because of the harm it would do in dividing families and depriving people of education and Christianity. Anti-colonizationists in Richmond showed more restraint as well as a willingness to cooperate with the ACS. They deemed colonization appropriate and advantageous and were willing to relocate. Nevertheless, they opposed settling in Africa. They requested that Congress designate a region along the Missouri River for colored people because they preferred the most isolated corner of their native land to foreign exile.[29]

18 RELUCTANT RACE MEN

Modest opposition gave way to widespread denunciations after 1829, the year of John Russwurm's highly visible defection to colonization ranks and of the publication of David Walker's *Appeal*, which named colonization as one of the principal evils afflicting colored people.[30] By then, early support for resettlement ventures had been expunged from public memory. Paul Cuffe had died in 1817. Forten and Allen had remained in the forefront of anti-colonization forces and their past support for emigration to Africa was forgotten. In an 1831 letter to William Lloyd Garrison, Forten betrayed nothing of his judgment that there could be some merit to leaving the United States. He maintained that no "intelligent man of color" would think of abandoning his home in America for Africa.[31] When he died just over a decade later, his son-in-law Robert Purvis praised him as one who had stood with Allen against colonization from the very start. Even colonizationists overlooked his early support for an African colony. The *African Repository* eulogized him as an "upright and virtuous" man, who, nonetheless, had erred on the colonization issue.[32] Although it was not unanimous, by the 1830s, anti-colonization sentiment had become orthodoxy in Northern reform discourse. It was so widespread that lectures against colonization were occasions to raise funds for other causes. With support from William Lloyd Garrison, who converted from colonization, opposition gained structure and visibility. Over a twelve-month period in 1831 and 1832, groups of colored people in nineteen cities Garrison visited issued condemnations of the scheme, which he collected and published in *Thoughts on Colonization*.[33]

Forums for denouncing colonization displayed complex and multifaceted connections to Africa. "African" churches and schools hosted anti-colonization meetings that included people who designated themselves "Afric-Americans." Despite public acknowledgment of African ties, refusals to settle in Africa often meant denying being African, repudiating natural obligations to or affinity with people in Africa, challenging the desirability of living on the continent, and claiming the mantle of true American reformers. Ultimately, it meant rejecting colonizationists' assumption that the label "African" signified an inherited racial and continental identity and designated the natural homeland of America's free colored population.[34]

Nearly every aspect of colonization came under the scrutiny of early opponents. Denunciations often began with the charge that the ACS was duplicitous. Although it stipulated that resettlement was to be consensual, critics assumed that colored people could be removed through coercion and force. The prominence of the society's proponents, coupled with endorsements from all levels of government, gave the initiative the appearance and authority of a state action. James Forten lamented to William Lloyd Garrison that "the weight, numbers, and unbounded influence of the colonizationist make me almost despair."[35] Others likened their plight to the situation of Cherokee people expelled from Georgia. Critics in New York and Providence chided Justice John Marshall for championing the ACS agenda, which was as coercive as the Cherokee removal requirement he had opposed.[36] Anti-colonizationists in Wilmington, Delaware, believed the ACS inspired antipathy against them to force departures for Liberia. Even without experiencing overt threats of physical violence, they denounced the organization for human rights violations that subverted freedom of choice.[37] Months later, the accusation's credence became clear as 350 Virginians looked to colonization to escape White people's backlash following the Nat Turner revolt. That situation, along with the fact that, for many, resettling in Africa was a condition of manumission from slavery, reinforced the sense that relocation was anything but voluntary. Over time, colonization assumed an aura of a grand conspiracy that pervaded every aspect of American society. Samuel Cornish saw its coercive dimensions in the daily experiences of discrimination that free people faced. He complained that the ACS orchestrated exclusion. "The churches, the schools, the steamboats, the rail roads, the stage coaches, the public houses, and the highways—the priests and the people—all, all are apparatus of torture, *set in motion*, to drive colored Americans to Liberia."[38]

ACS accounts of its aims were as suspect as its representations of colored people. A record of deception undermined colonizationists' presentation of themselves as agents of positive change. George Willis and Alfred Niger of Providence spoke for many when they declared it oxymoronic for the ACS to represent itself as an American missionary agency given its "unchristian and anti-republican" program. William Watkins denounced ACS members as "retrograde reformers."[39] Their efforts to send colored people to Africa violated the principles of citizenship, human rights, and Christian tenets by placing individuals outside the sphere of human reciprocity. Despite their proponents' assertions, colonization initiatives were inimical to the welfare of the colored population, Africa, and America. David Walker helped set the tone for this line of criticism in his attack on Kentucky senator Henry Clay's claim that colonization would promote national prosperity. More implausible was the idea that Clay was concerned about the welfare of colored people and Africa. Walker asked Americans, "Do you believe that Mr. Henry Clay . . . is a friend to the blacks. . . . Does he care a pinch of snuff about

20   RELUCTANT RACE MEN

Africa—whether it remains a land of Pagans?"[40] Reformers from Nantucket to Pittsburgh shared this distrust and called it a lie to label colonization "philanthropy." They believed that no one with the interests of colored Americans at heart would consign them to Africa and cited accounts of Liberian settlers suffering in a land of sickness and death. AME churchman George Hogarth impressed this point upon Brooklyn's Colored Association, decrying colonizationists' duplicity in promising freedom while plotting to sacrifice colored people to Africa's "barbarian despots."[41]

The stated goal of halting the illegal slave trade was further proof that the ACS was not qualified for the work of reform. Anyone truly concerned about slave trafficking, critics reasoned, would condemn American slavery. ACS officials were instead strengthening the link between blackness and servitude by working to remove free people from the country. Members of Boston's ACS investigative committee—John Hilton, James Barbados, Reverend Hosea Easton, Thomas Dalton, and Thomas Cole—had the temerity to declare that they, not colonizationists, were the true American reformers. Since they advocated abolition and Black citizenship rights, it was evident that they were working on behalf of the nation's welfare.[42]

Critics shared colonizationists' opinion that Africa needed to be enlightened. Despite rebuking the project, Peter Williams encouraged Russwurm's mission and praised Paul Cuffe's desire to extend "the light of science and religion" to Africa. Yet evangelical sympathies also strengthened convictions that colonization was a flawed reform undertaking. ACS charges about moral depravity among colored people highlighted its distorted logic and the instability of its missionary endeavor. "If we are as vile and degraded as they represent us," Williams argued, "and they wish the Africans to be rendered a virtuous, enlightened, and happy people, they should not *think* of sending *us* among them, lest we should make them worse instead of better."[43] New Haven's Peace and Benevolent Society of Afric-Americans, which shared the hope of seeing Africa "civilized," was equally skeptical about the perverse plan to send "a nation of ignorant men to teach a nation of ignorant men."[44]

Sweeping allegations of Black inferiority gave critics of colonization a clearer view of the bigotry guiding the enterprise and the racial notions of hierarchy at its foundations. The idea that natural deficiencies made it impossible for the population to thrive in America with White people was one of the many "false representations" in ACS discourse. Citing the dearth of evidence for the group's assertions about difference, New Yorkers ridiculed the argument that an inability to display trappings of respectability proved that colored people comprised "an inferior part of the human family." Such specious claims about Negro character demonstrated that colonization was not truly a reform endeavor. As Wilmington, Delaware, residents observed, the zeal with which ACS proponents worked to remove the people they refused to help in their home country displayed a rejection of basic Christian standards of human kindness. New Bedford residents concluded that, in sanctioning the treatment of colored people as if they were "unnatural and illegal residents," the Colonization Society showed that it was an agent of terror spouting the rhetoric of goodwill.[45]

The idea that physical characteristics justified removal highlighted grave flaws in ACS conceptions of nationality and human difference. There was no logical basis for the assumption that a dark complexion turned Americans into Africans. The notion failed to convince critics that there were any biological, political, cultural, or ethical grounds for designating Africa as their home. "A Colored Philadelphian," possibly sailmaker James Forten, reasoned that colored people were no better suited for living in Africa than White Americans were. Writing in the *Liberator*, he insisted that birthplace, not color, determined where individuals could live. Comparing colored Philadelphians with their White counterparts, he asked, "How is it that we, who are born in the same city or state with themselves, can live any longer in Africa than they?"[46] New Yorkers likewise stressed the futility of using appearance to map human differences in order to disqualify colored people from American citizenship. The facts of nature illustrated the illogic of efforts to render colored people ineligible for inalienable human rights guaranteed in the US Constitution. "There are different colors among all species of animated creation," they explained; "difference of color is not a difference of species."[47] ACS critics in Massachusetts and Delaware also insisted that African and American identities were established by birth. As "American born citizens," they could not be Africans. How, they asked, could a person be born in two countries? American nativity meant that they had no shared interests with Africans. Instead, their concerns and rights were akin to those of "other Americans."[48] Even critics who sympathized with ACS missionary aims questioned the supposition of natural moral ties to Africa. As William Watkins argued, skin color created no special affinity between colored Americans and Africans; it would give colored missionaries no advantages in evangelizing Africans. Moreover, he was certain that complexion created no "exclusive moral obligation" for colored people to save Africans.[49] Cultural differences highlighted dissimilarities between Americans and Africans.

22   RELUCTANT RACE MEN

Spokesmen for Delaware's free population—Abraham Shadd, William Thomas, and African Union Church founder Peter Spencer—insisted that Africa was neither their "nation nor home" because their "language, habits, manners, morals, and religion" all differed from those of Africans. If they settled in Africa, they would remain a "distinct people."[50] They shared the position of "Afric-Americans" in Connecticut and Pennsylvania who denounced all efforts to remove them from the "true and appropriate" home they inherited from their fathers. While identifying themselves as descendants of Africa, Delawareans interpreted ties to the continent as strictly voluntary. They opted to sever such links with the pronouncement, "We disclaim all connexion with Africa."[51]

Citizenship created a moral obligation to condemn colonization. Despite being denied its privileges, ACS opponents invoked their responsibilities as citizens to further counter suppositions that colored people belonged in Africa. New Haven "Afric-Americans" denounced everyone who planned to settle in Africa as enemies of their country.[52] Remaining in America was not simply a right; it was a duty. John Vashon and other Pittsburgh residents declared every colored man who colonized Africa "a traitor to our cause," which they defined by their identity as American free men. They were "brethren," "countrymen," and "fellow-citizens" with all other American men and entitled to equal protection by the federal government.[53] They were obliged to oppose any plan that entailed leaving America, regardless of whether departure was coerced or voluntary or whether the destination was Africa, Canada, or Haiti.

ACS critics who had no qualms about leaving the United States found common ground with anti-colonizationists in rejecting Africa. Richard Allen, for instance, presided over Philadelphia's Haytian Emigration Society while condemning colonization. In the 1820s, he enlisted five hundred prospective émigrés to Haiti under a subsidized settlement program of President Jean Pierre Boyer. Anti-colonizationists in Baltimore and New York operated similar projects. Historian Julie Winch reports that, by 1825, such efforts were instrumental in sending an estimated six thousand emigrants to Haiti.[54] Other colonization opponents organized moral and financial support for emigration. David Walker advised those who felt compelled to leave the country to take refuge among the British or with Haitians rather than surrender to colonization. Likewise, anti-colonization meetings throughout the Northeast— in Brooklyn and Rochester, New York; Wilmington, Delaware; Trenton, New Jersey; and Harrisburg, Lewistown, and Columbia, Pennsylvania—declared their bias against Africa by admonishing individuals fleeing US oppression to settle in Canada or Mexico. They pledged support for the Wilberforce Colony—the Canadian settlement of free people who fled Cincinnati in 1829 to escape mob violence and enforcement of Ohio's Black Codes. In addition to recruiting emigrants to Haiti, Peter Williams used his opposition to African colonization to support emigration to Canada. His 1830 Fourth of July anti-colonization speech doubled as a fundraising event for the new Canadian settlement.[55]

Distinctions between Africa and other settlement options meant that there was no necessary contradiction in endorsing emigration while opposing colonization. ACS proponents and opponents cited destination to differentiate between colonization from emigration. Anti-colonizationists praised emigration for shielding colored people from Africa's dangers, and ACS proponents broadcast their program as a means of protecting colored people from outrages that compelled some to emigrate. Without irony, colonizationist Mathew Carey declared that fleeing to Canada was a flawed solution for colored Ohioans forced to forsake their birthplace in the face of anti-Black violence. Settling in Africa was the only way free colored people could find real fulfillment, he reasoned, because it was their true homeland.[56]

National conventions succeeded local anti-colonization meetings as sites for interrogating questions about American identity. Reformers launched the new reform initiative in 1830 armed with a sharp distinction between colonization and emigration. However, it ultimately became difficult to reconcile opposition to the former project with simultaneous support for the latter enterprise. Vehement anti-colonization sentiment marked early gatherings that pledged aid to individuals seeking refuge in places other than Africa. The twofold commitment became unsustainable because of its divergent messages about the nationality of free people of color. The issue created divisions that made the first six national conventions occasions for struggles over the nature of claims to being American among individuals who strove to institutionalize and nationalize broad reform initiatives.

The structure of the conventions complicated matters. A typical gathering included formally and informally educated Northern men who could afford or solicit from others the costs of travel, lodging, and dues.[57] However, a new slate of participants and constituents at each meeting brought shifting

24 RELUCTANT RACE MEN

concerns and priorities to the arena. Only one person was a delegate at the inaugural convention and each of the five annual meetings that followed. This lone constant was William Whipper, a Columbia, Pennsylvania, native who built lumber and real estate businesses there and in Philadelphia. He is a relatively insignificant figure in traditional accounts of Black American activism, known primarily as a pacifist and advocate of moral improvement, who was something of an outlier for repudiating race. Historians Jane and William Pease cite his rejection of racial designations as a sign that his vision was out of step with their view of the conventions' purpose of promoting "race pride and cohesion."[58] Yet Whipper attended the first forum as a twenty-six-year-old Pennsylvania representative and went on to play a critical role in the course of the decade's subsequent national gatherings. The evolution of the conventions and his participation illustrate how doubts about notions of human difference propelled opposition to race beyond attacks on the ACS. They provide a window into how race challenges that emerged in anti-colonization forums unfolded in the unwieldy process of forging American freedom and nationality.

The gathering that launched the national conventions exposed some of the challenges associated with claiming American identity in the face of colonization campaigns and discrimination. Delegates denounced the ACS, advocated emigration, and proposed reforms within the United States. They inscribed their multiple perspectives in the title, American Society of Free Persons of Colour for Improving their Condition in the United States; for Purchasing Lands; and for the Establishment of a Settlement in Upper Canada. Despite this multifaceted agenda, the twenty-six delegates devoted their energies to facilitating emigration.[59] The meeting, convened at the behest of Philadelphians Richard Allen, Cyrus Black, James Cornish, Junius Morel, and Benjamin Paschal, planned a settlement in the British province of Upper Canada, the region that would become Ontario. The proposal was, in part, a response to Black Codes and violence that prompted Cincinnati, Ohio, residents to flee the city during the previous year. Convention organizers also wanted to provide a haven for the growing population of destitute individuals who flocked to northeastern cities in search of freedom and safety. Although immediate developments provided the occasion for the gathering, the proposed purchase of Canadian land was not an ad hoc response to an isolated crisis. It was the basis for a mutual aid organization with auxiliaries and dues-paying members committed to financing a settlement for people seeking refuge or opportunities to improve their lives. At the time,

Philadelphia was home to more than forty such groups supporting diverse causes. In 1778, Richard Allen had helped found one of the earliest, the Free African Society, to support ill members and their families.[60]

Upper Canada was appealing because its culture, environment, and economy made it seem similar to the United States. However, its chief virtue was the apparent absence of race distinctions. The convention's "Address to the Free People of Colour of these United States" reports that province officials recognized "no invidious distinction of colour." Thus, colored settlers would be "entitled to all the rights, privileges, and immunities of other citizens."[61] This idealized characterization inspired Junius Morel and Peter Gardiner to praise individuals who fled Ohio for being authors of their own freedom. They urged the ACS to turn its sights to Canada because the promise of freedom in a healthy environment might induce colored people to emigrate.[62]

Some were unconvinced that Upper Canada was a more enlightened and congenial version of the United States. Baltimorean Hezekiah Grice, credited with being the first to suggest national conventions, reported that there were lengthy arguments over how to characterize the territory. For two days, delegates debated whether Junius Morel was accurate in portraying it as comparable to life in Northern states. At issue were the intimate linkages some reformers made between free manhood and American identity. They worried that support for emigration to Canada or elsewhere compromised claims that American freedom was an essential element of birthright citizenship. They sensed that the group could not function as a credible representative of anti-colonization if it endorsed emigration.[63]

Romantic images of Canadian freedom also made it hard to address the circumstances of people who had no intention of migrating. Delegates paid scant attention to the stated objective of improving their condition. The natural rights that made Upper Canada appealing did not factor into Richard Allen's conception of free manhood in the United States. Here, rights had to be earned. Accordingly, reform meant changing colored people rather than challenging the discrimination they faced. It meant helping them attain the "rank" of freeman by promoting education in agriculture, the mechanical arts, and science. Such training, Allen reasoned, would improve the moral status of free colored people and demonstrate that they were worthy of citizenship rights. Instead of introducing programmatic measures, he lamented that such endeavors exceeded the convention's capacity because, despite operating numerous independent churches and societies, colored people apparently lacked the unity required to advance their collective mental development and standard of living.[64]

The idea that American equality and citizenship rights required moral improvement became critical to subsequent conventions. In the wake of Richard Allen's death, the Philadelphians who announced the second convention were poised to act on this precept. They minimized the importance of emigration at the outset. Belfast Burton, who had once migrated to Haiti, joined William Whipper in calling for participation only from men who had no interest in exchanging stability in their native land for unfamiliar destinations.[65] They saw no need to facilitate emigration, because the Ohio crisis had long subsided and migrants had purchased land and built houses. Even Junius Morel no longer encouraged support for the Canadian settlement. Instead, he sought the convention's endorsement for the *American*, a forthcoming weekly he was co-editing to promote abolition, education, and moral elevation. The prospectus promised to refrain from polluting the paper with anything that endorsed colonization, because there was "no other home for the native born man of color than these United States."[66] This stance set the stage for the sixteen delegates to the 1831 convention to devote their attention to improving the status of free colored people in their own land. It also meant abandoning the mutual aid model to develop a national forum representing free colored people in efforts to secure rights.

Ongoing support for emigration jeopardized the shift. A majority of the delegates believed that a Canadian settlement remained necessary and needed financial support. Although the organizers felt pressured into accepting this position, they tried to curtail its significance by engineering changes in the forum's structure. The meeting was ostensibly an extension of the prior year's proceedings; however, organizational modifications subsumed the structure for supporting a Canadian settlement under the First Annual Convention of the People of Colour. In theory, the society created under Allen's leadership continued to exist as an auxiliary of the convention, but, in practice, emigration would not define the purpose of future annual gatherings.[67]

Although additional innovations made the convention a more representative body, it was not an egalitarian gathering. Recognized delegates comprised less than one-fourth of the seventy-two men in attendance and fewer than half of the states from which they hailed.[68] Men who had traveled to Philadelphia from Connecticut, the District of Columbia, Massachusetts, New Jersey, Ohio, and Rhode Island had no official say in deliberations. Philadelphians tried to control the proceedings by stipulating that convention officers had to reside in their city.[69] Nevertheless, there were signs of change. A Committee of Inquiry—Junius Morel of Philadelphia, Abraham Shadd of Wilmington, William Duncan of Virginia, Robert Cowley of Baltimore, and Henry Sipkins and Thomas Jennings of New York—had the job of assessing the needs of the free population to facilitate the development of an appropriate convention agenda. Local committees and officers further expanded the base of participation, albeit largely for fundraising purposes. A provision allowing localities without auxiliaries to send delegates to the next convention was also a step toward inclusivity. Ultimately, the presence of individuals from various parts of the country forced delegates to democratize the proceedings and address diverse opinions.[70]

Moral issues posed a dilemma for reform proponents. They hoped to devise a program of uplift without suggesting that depravity was a trait common among colored people. A complicating factor was that some delegates shared ACS judgments that decadence was prevalent among free people. They had a distressing sense that a sizeable segment of the colored population was "dissolute, intemperate, and ignorant," which made moral reform initiatives a priority. Furthermore, some individuals who deemed themselves part of a representative body recoiled at the idea that they were part of an undifferentiated mass of colored people. They explained that race designations and morality should not be conflated because degradation stemmed from systematic denials of opportunities to advance. Ignorance among people who suffered from deprivation was not an accurate indicator of mental capacity. Still, they took pains to distinguish themselves from such people, insisting that similarities in skin color did not translate into a common moral sensibility or level of intelligence. Indeed, they declared it unreasonable and improper to "class the virtuous of [their] colour with the abandoned."[71] Nevertheless, they deemed themselves qualified to guard the interests of debased members of the free population and felt obligated to uplift them.

The efficacy of reform lay in its potential to change depictions of colored people. The virtues of education, temperance, and thrift were key to accomplishing this outcome because they promised to enhance social standing. Education became a focus of deliberations after delegates endorsed a recommendation to establish a college in New Haven for colored men—an idea Samuel Cornish had suggested years earlier. The new proposal came from White visitors to the convention—William Lloyd Garrison; Arthur Tappan, who had purchased land for the school; and New Haven minister Simeon Jocelyn, who led a colored congregation in the city.

The college was to offer a classical education, as well as agricultural and mechanical training on the manual labor system. Following the examples of Lane Theological Seminary, Oberlin College, and Oneida Institute, which were open to colored men, poor students would earn an education by working at the institution. Several factors made the plan viable and desirable. Proponents attested to the friendliness of New Haven residents and to the administration of local laws "without regard to complexion."[72] Garrison predicted that the college would prove beneficial to the students and colored people as a whole. It would do for them what Yale College did for White people. Delegates imbued education with the capacity to eliminate prejudice, even as they valued it for its own sake. They were careful to point out, however, that neither their moral condition nor lack of education caused the discrimination they faced. It originated in erroneous notions of human difference. The convention's publishing committee—Belfast Burton, Junius Morel, and William Whipper—maintained that prejudice and exclusion were the real causes of degradation among colored people, not the other way around. Moreover, deleterious effects were just one dimension of bigotry's evils. The notion that "accidental diversities of colour" were valid bases for determining worth displayed corrupt and illogical ideas that had no place in reform initiatives.[73]

Advancement entailed more than moral improvement. Delegates sensed that efforts to gain public esteem were no substitute for questioning policies that infringed on their rights. However, they made only small gestures in this direction. They recognized a wide chasm between their self-understanding as citizens and their circumstances. To mark the disparity between the rights they claimed and their reality, they designated the Fourth of July as a day of prayer and fasting. Nevertheless, they clung to the idea that American birth guaranteed colored people "the rights and immunities of citizenship." This conviction grounded calls for other citizens to condemn the ACS for infringing on their citizenship. However, it failed to inspire explicit political demands. Instead, delegates counseled individuals to seek legal redress through appeals to local officials.[74]

Attempts to shift the convention's focus to moral reform proceeded haltingly in the 1832 national convention. The presence of ACS officials forced delegates to contend with emigration and citizenship claims. Reverend Ralph Gurley and other ACS representatives had come to the meeting to correct misperceptions about the society and were allowed to speak despite numerous objections. Their attempts to communicate the virtues of colonization provided an opportunity for critics to reaffirm their opposition. After each presentation, William Lloyd Garrison, Junius Morel, and Pittsburgh delegate John Vashon offered rebuttals and reasserted the citizenship claims of free people.[75] Support for emigration faded in this setting. As if to reaffirm their place in the United States, delegates denounced emigration to Haiti, even though it was no longer a popular option. They placed it in the same category as following colonizationists to Liberia. Both divided "the whole colored family," which apparently did not include people of African descent outside of the United States.[76]

The ACS presence altered interpretations of Canadian emigration. Delegates had to contend with practical limitations of establishing a settlement and ongoing conflicts about how free people should collectively relate to the United States. Some individuals considered it essential to facilitate emigration. Junius Morel renewed his support for the cause in his convention announcement because he believed persistent threats might compel many free people to flee the country.[77] Others felt differently. William Hamilton of New York; John Peck of Carlisle, Pennsylvania; and William Whipper led opposition to the plan. The initial question for debate was whether to support a permanent settlement or a temporary asylum in Canada. The latter aim appealed to individuals who saw emigration only as a last resort for people in desperate circumstances. Without settling this distinction, however, delegates moved to the question of whether to support emigration at all. The ensuing debate created two camps: those who differentiated between support for a Canadian settlement and defense of African colonization and those who refused to distinguish among actions that entailed leaving the United States. Complicating matters was the fact that Upper Canada was beginning to appear less idyllic as White Canadians petitioned the provincial government to stem the flow of colored immigrants. Yet citizenship remained the central concern of emigration opponents. They interpreted emigration and reform efforts in the United States as mutually exclusive and argued that they could quell the desire to leave only by correcting the nation's problems. They reasoned that promoting emigration would threaten reform by suggesting that colored people had surrendered claims to their native land.[78] Concerns about appearances returned the convention's focus to domestic issues. However, it did not settle debate. In a final compromise, the delegation designated Austin Stewart, who was already at the Wilberforce Colony, as an agent who would oversee land purchases and give financial assistance to new settlers on the convention's behalf.[79]

30 RELUCTANT RACE MEN

As they reasserted a collective American identity, delegates invoked the principle that rights required moral development and stressed the importance of moral reform with new vigor. However, they faced formidable obstacles. Organizing schools, for example, was difficult even with the support of White benefactors. Public opposition forced the abandonment of the proposed college in New Haven. The mayor and Yale officials, prominent colonizationists among them, led White residents in denouncing the proposal.[80] Remaining sanguine, proponents planned to continue fundraising and to find a new location. The convention address celebrated their prospects. Authors Hamilton, Shadd, and Whipper ventured that "an *oppressed people*, deprived of the rights of citizenship" could nonetheless affect their "personal and mental elevation by *moral suasion alone*."[81] This commitment reflected a deep conviction that reformers could advance social change outside of official political channels.

Some individuals favored campaigns for legal rights over moral reform. Conflicts arose when Hezekiah Grice urged delegates to support his recently formed Legal Rights Society. However, after debating the issue, the majority opposed organizing around any collective political campaign, agreeing only to support individuals who tried to secure legal rights. It demurred on forming any official alliances with the society.[82] Legal appeals and political activism were incompatible with the premise that colored people should demonstrate their fitness for rights through moral rectitude. Even antislavery activism remained a personal undertaking, as individuals were simply encouraged to use products made with free labor.

Despite persistent conflicts at convention proceedings, localities continued to express confidence in their utility by sending increasing numbers of representatives. In 1833, official participation reached an all-time high of fifty-eight delegates. Questions about self-definition remained unresolved, and the specter of colonization continued to be the most stable source of unity. It energized claims to American citizenship even as the group continued to ponder its collective identity. Delegates at the new convention lodged both standard and novel complaints against colonization. It no longer presented a serious threat; however, it remained the cornerstone for a host of misrepresentations that prevented them from freely exercising their rights as Americans. They mused that free men of color would be accorded these rights once reformers disseminated the truth about colonization; accordingly, they were intent on exposing its racial fallacies. Veteran delegates William Whipper, Robert Cowley, and Henry Sipkins, along with Richard Johnson of New Bedford and John Stewart of Albany shouldered this task, using the convention's public address to assail the ACS for trying to turn American citizens into Africans. The authors echoed earlier arguments and insisted that a "difference in complexion" was an unsound criterion for concluding that individuals were not American. They argued that, if the ACS consistently used this standard to define citizenship in Africa, many of its colonists would have to return to the United States because their complexions starkly differed from those of African natives.[83] Color designations were as baseless as phenotype in adjudicating political membership. Delegates continued to ridicule colonizationists for advancing the senseless idea that the label "coloured" made Africans of people born in the United States. Their conviction that citizenship stemmed from birth made it illogical and deceptive to link it to racial classifications. Being labeled "coloured" meant only that one was "not white."[84] It communicated nothing about nationality or citizenship.

While delegates rallied around the idea that Africa was not their home, renewed conflicts over emigration betrayed a tenuous unity. The convention address explained "a great difference of feeling, as well as judgment" on the matter.[85] The fragility of prior compromises on Canada paved the way for dissension. Robert Cowley and others who insisted on establishing a settlement demanded that the group revisit the issue. As a result, delegates resumed earlier debates about whether support was necessary and, if so, what it should entail. Initially, with a majority of just over 50 percent, the group decided to continue funding an agent for the settlement. However, opponents provoked further rounds of voting until even the modest measure was abandoned in favor of unspecified assistance. A final resolution opposing the settlement came from William Whipper and Frederick Hinton, proprietor of Gentlemen's Dressing Room, a Philadelphia hair salon. It admonished the colored population to devote its energies to improvement in the United States, while promising to support individuals who felt compelled to flee. Help in settling in Canada would save them from Liberia. Although this was not a new consensus, opponents and supporters of emigration again found common ground by using Canadian emigration to express contempt for colonization.[86]

A new way of defining the place of free people of color in the United States emerged. They could enact American identities as moral reformers. The idea was among the least contentious proposals of the convention because it promised to counter allegations of depravity. A census of conditions in Northern colored communities promised to showcase collective moral

32 RELUCTANT RACE MEN

agency with tallies of churches, Sunday schools, day schools, student enrollment, temperance and benevolent societies, mechanics, and entrepreneurs. A proposed Coloured American Conventional Temperance Society to coordinate existing local societies served a similar function. Although temperance committee members considered drinking not as great a problem among colored people as it was among other groups, pervasive bigotry made it essential to promote total abstinence and public decorum. Temperance campaigns also had the potential to unite colored reformers with other advocates of moral reform. They offered an avenue to fuller participation in the country's civic arena.[87]

Grounding American identity in moral activity further marginalized legal and political dimensions of citizenship. It pushed demands for rights outside the convention's purview. When Hartford residents called for a protest of Connecticut's ban on nonresident colored students in its schools, delegates took no action. They simply reasserted their hope that the manual labor college would somehow become a reality. Although formal learning was an important moral undertaking, most delegates did not perceive educational discrimination as a basis for demanding equality.[88]

Efforts to strengthen the foundations of reform intensified at the 1834 convention. There was a push to make the forums more representative and to create a solid basis from which to devise reforms. The location of the meeting set the tone for greater inclusivity. The forty-nine delegates met in New York to follow through on the previous year's agreement to expand participation and influence beyond Philadelphia. They accepted John Peck's suggestion to transform annual conventions into a permanent national society. Institutionalizing the forums promised to systematize delegate selection and ensure continuous accountability to local constituents.

Concerns about programmatic clarity were evident from the start. William Hamilton, Conventional Board president, opened the proceedings by delineating distinctive features of the free colored population to frame their collective endeavors. His optimistic peroration cited gradual emancipation in the British Caribbean as a sign of growing international opposition to slavery and bigotry. It was a small indicator of possibilities for freedom and rights for colored people in the United States. However, conditions in the nation were bleak. It had no conception of "the common good of the whole." It was instead a "community of castes," each with distinct concerns. The scorn White people directed at people of African descent helped structure this

"NOT A DIFFERENCE OF SPECIES" 33

hierarchy. However, racial categories were not the sole basis of distinctions. Freedom mattered. It made it necessary for free people of color to attend to the peculiarities of their own situation, which were markedly different from concerns slaves faced. As he saw it, the convention's task was to identify and advance their distinct interests. It was essential to the ongoing work of exposing the artifice of the ACS as it garnered greater public support. Moral development was equally critical. Even if it failed to generate material benefits, virtue could promote happiness.[89]

Hamilton's framework invited more decisive, if not more substantive, assertions of American citizenship. Delegates decided to publish Andrew Jackson's call for Louisiana's free colored men to join in the fight against the British in the War of 1812. The documents were significant because they recognized colored people as "fellow citizens" and identified the United States as their "native country." Since the former general was president and a prominent colonizationist, his pronouncements carried weight.[90] Interest in the welfare of Liberian settlers replaced concerns about emigrants to Canada. The group voted to correspond with them to ascertain their actual circumstances, consider ways to assist them, and explore means for helping them to return to "their own country." In an effort to weaken the ACS, delegates urged colored people to circulate petitions demanding that the organization cease its operations.[91]

Familiar problems hobbled efforts to translate claims to American freedom into positive reform measures. Hamilton's insistence that collective interests derived from a shared class standing rekindled ambivalence about identifying as a discrete group and colored efforts to address routine experiences of injustice. Participants considered ways to fight discrimination in voting, transportation, schools, employment, and churches. However, the undertaking seemed to exceed their capacity, and they opted to monitor unjust legislation, seek greater involvement from colored clergy, and advise individuals to restrict patronage to conveyances that assured equal accommodations.[92] In contrast, recommendations about duties were concrete. They exposed class distinctions among colored people and concerns about being identified as "people distinct from other portions of the community."[93] Public decorum and vice were easy targets. Boarding houses that permitted gambling deserved censure along with detrimental street processions that impoverished colored people and invited derision. There was broad agreement that condemnations of such activities should be submitted to local newspapers.[94]

34   RELUCTANT RACE MEN

Although delegates distinguished their interests from the concerns of slaves, there was a push to use the venue to speak out on their behalf. This action made the convention the first to engage in sustained discussions of antislavery activism. Some individuals were wary. After Carlisle, Pennsylvania, delegates Frederick Hinton and Samuel Hutchins raised the issue, it took two further interventions by prominent Philadelphia Freemason Samuel Van Brackle for the delegation to put antislavery on the agenda. Three more days passed before it rendered a judgment. Despite the aid individual participants offered fugitive slaves through local vigilance committees, they were fearful about public declarations and preferred to treat abolition as a personal matter. Two awkwardly worded resolutions offered support to antislavery societies, "individually or collectively." Although there is no reference to debate, the next day, the convention recommended that colored people refrain from participating in public forums sponsored by abolitionists and colonizationists. Concerns about reprisals apparently kept some men from voicing commitments to antislavery work. Anti-Black violence in Northern cities validated such worries. Just one month after the convention, White mobs in New York and Philadelphia attacked colored people and abolitionists.[95]

Before Hamilton's idea of discrete castes could be developed, a Declaration of Sentiment presented delegates with a different paradigm for activism. It mapped new foundations for the convention by reinterpreting the status and obligations of colored people and changing the meaning of reform. Although it expanded on ideas from the previous year's proceedings, it marked a turning point. It was the first of several developments that would disrupt the course of national conventions. Yet reformers would unwittingly applaud the document for its display of "noble sentiments—a Christian spirit—for expansive philanthropy, and . . . a forcible and manly style."[96]

The convention minutes identify the declaration as the work of a committee that included Hamilton. However, Whipper recalled drafting the document alone in the grip of sorrow over the condition of colored people. When he arrived at the convention, he decided to forgo the evening parties where other delegates socialized and isolated himself in his room. He struggled to articulate his ideas, weeping as he wrote.[97] He divided the political landscape into antislavery and colonization. This division framed colored people's reform options. History established the mandate for choosing the former cause and guided Whipper's reasoning. It provided grounds on which to indict the nation and call for the immediate abolition of slavery because it showed no precedent comparable to the situation facing colored people in America. It was an anomaly with no coherent justifications. To demonstrate that their sufferings were unwarranted, Whipper evoked the glorious past of ancestral Africa as a place with unrivaled artistic, literary, and scientific attainments. It showed that the lineage of colored people did not destine them to the degradations of American enslavement and discrimination. It discredited statutes governing slavery for supporting human trafficking in violation of nature's laws. This was grounds for their repeal.[98]

Reflections on history led Whipper to portray the convention's commitment to reform as a righteous cause. He cast delegates as God's agents charged with shaping the course of human destiny. Their initiatives were revolutionary and quintessentially American because they embodied ideals of equality and natural rights inscribed in the Declaration of Independence. Their goals were nobler than the American Revolution because they were trying to achieve "divine justice." The principle of liberty equipped them with the potential to transcend notions of freedom that accommodated slavery and injustices against colored people. However, they could achieve this end only if they annihilated self-interest and opportunism—traits that fueled slavery. As these tendencies waned, reformers would be able to influence governments to act "without distinction of nation or complexion," and colored people could become integral and equal members of a national union.[99]

Delegates reportedly accepted the document without debate even though it outlined a vision that diverged from prevailing conceptions of reform. Whipper disregarded the idea that colored people needed to improve themselves to demonstrate their fitness for freedom and rights. He believed they could and should enact their status as free Americans by repairing their corrupt nation. He charged them with carrying out the moral duties of citizens and Christians. From this vantage point, the decisive answer to the question of how people of color should be known was as American reformers.

The project's premise was that racial constructions of difference were logically and ethically flawed. The proposition also framed Whipper's goal for colored reformers to rally Americans "without distinction of caste or complexion." This novel endeavor admonished individuals traditionally targeted for needing improvement to reform the nation that oppressed them. The unprecedented call to eschew racial categories relied on familiar claims that race was a fallacy. It held reformers to standards of truth they used to condemn colonization and discrimination.[100]

36   RELUCTANT RACE MEN

The declaration highlights perfectionist tendencies that guided Whipper's commitments. Like other utopian reformers, he believed human agency could eliminate evil from American society and establish a just and harmonious social order. Glimpses of his orientation appear in an 1834 address to Philadelphia's Colored Temperance Society. He confessed his faith in the power of reform to eradicate bigotry, believing that widespread abstinence could transform dark skin from a "badge of degradation" into something honorable.[101] The point of promoting abstinence was not to show that colored people deserved rights. Rather, it gave them a decisive role in defining and maintaining standards of public morality. The obligation to carry out temperance work was not limited to colored people. All reformers had a duty to God and society to promote the well-being of the species. Interventions were critical because intemperance knew no social distinctions. The scope of its injury was broader than the slave regime. Everyone needed to fight it because it heaped evils upon all members of "the human race."[102]

Personal writing further displayed ideals that framed Whipper's reform endeavors. His reflections in the personal album of Amy Matilda Cassey, wife of his reform associate Joseph Cassey, a wealthy Philadelphia hairdresser and perfumer, explain in stylized prose that light and love were the central elements of moral reform. Light was a metaphor for the principle that people created in God's image should make human history reflect God's character. Love defined how individuals should view and relate to others. As an outgrowth of these forces, moral reform recognized the humanity and kinship of all people. Its advocates had a duty to regard everyone "as having descended from the same common parent, possessing the same natural rights."[103] This recognition required them to promote civic and political goals to secure equal privileges for all.

The conviction that colored people could practice freedom and citizenship through reform endeavors set the tone for deliberations of the thirty-five delegates to the 1835 convention in Philadelphia. Whipper and his allies were intent on implementing this vision by creating an organizational structure that would alter the course of activism among colored people. Their recommendation to form a new society was among the meeting's first proposals. Washington, DC, delegate Augustus Price and AME preacher Stephen Smith, Whipper's partner in a flourishing lumber business, moved that the convention form the American Moral Reform Society to improve humankind. Although they linked the suggestion to the popular Declaration of Sentiment, it prompted such heated debate that Price withdrew it. Frederick

Hinton immediately followed with a successful recommendation, which Smith seconded, to form a *National* Moral Reform Society. This dispute over names signaled differences over whether to prioritize the scope of the organization's constituency or the goal of representing the nation's ideals and principles. It foreshadowed future tensions over the terms on which colored reformers should claim authority and who could define them. In the end, proponents of an "American" society simply ignored the vote.[104] Such politics marked previous conventions; however, the outcome in this case was far more significant. By design or disorganization, the Moral Reform Society disabled national conventions for seven years.[105]

Whipper and other proponents of the society saw themselves as participants in a broad movement of "liberal and enlightened philosophy" that they hoped would one day take hold throughout America and the world. They tried to advance the trend by modifying the meaning of moral reform and offering new foundations for its efficacy. This entailed embellishing ideas that were familiar to convention participants. They were poised to challenge slavery and bigotry because they had faith in the power of facts to change minds, even if they could not change hearts. Social elevation of free colored people and a commitment to uplifting freed slaves could diminish opposition to emancipation by giving the lie to allegations that people of African descent were naturally depraved. Truth was central to their reasoning that a "clear and discriminating mind" could not tolerate slavery or other injustices once it became aware of "the structure" of prejudice.[106]

Faith in the power of facts harkened back to beliefs that had inspired *Freedom's Journal*, which also drew on Whipper's long-held ideas about reform and philosophy. In an address to fellow members of Philadelphia's Colored Reading Society for Mental Improvement seven years earlier, he shared his delight that intellectual developments of the time had set the "philosophy of mind" on firmer foundations. Popular reliance on speculation and conjecture seemed to be yielding to an insistence on truth. This intellectual shift meant that "mere hypotheses" could no longer pass as explanations. Instead, "fixed principles and matters of fact" would serve as the basis of knowledge. The focus on truth and the efficacy of broadcasting evidence was a new facet of Whipper's interpretation of reform and his commitment to moral suasion. Framing moral exertions in scientific terms meant that reform was not merely an expression of feelings. It was a field of inquiry founded on logic and carried out with rational and systematic methods. This perspective sheds light on the praise Maryland's 1852 Free Colored People's

38 RELUCTANT RACE MEN

Convention issued for improvements in "moral sciences." It explains the decision of the Phoenixonian Literary Society of New York to host a lecture on "the elements of moral science" in a program featuring presentations on astronomy, geography, and physiology.[107]

Against the backdrop of change, assertions of American identity at the convention became more decisive. Anti-colonization still provided a rallying point. Contempt for the ACS remained intense. The group accepted Junius Morel's call for colored people to condemn and refrain from attending "proslavery farces and apelike exhibitions, commonly known as Colonization meetings."[108] They added Whipper's insistence that colored people petition state legislatures to abolish their Colonization Society auxiliaries. Robert Purvis and Frederick Hinton were to reach out to Liberian settlers who felt deceived by ACS promises of true freedom.

Yet rebuke of colonization gave way to assertions of American citizenship and claims to political and civil rights. On the recommendation of Washington, DC, delegates Dr. James Fleet and AME preacher John Cook, the convention called on colored people to petition Congress and state legislatures demanding the "rights and privileges of American citizens," including equal legal protections. Citizenship also encompassed civil issues. As delegates encouraged people to seek education and renewed their commitment to establishing a college, they reinterpreted schooling. It was no longer simply a means for improving the colored population's moral status. Instead, equal access to education required recognizing the rights of adult and child citizens. Colored organizations had to adapt to the new emphasis on citizenship by changing how they represented themselves. Delegates reportedly endorsed a proposal from Whipper and Purvis calling on colored people to "remove the title African from their institutions." Not surprisingly, "animated and interesting" debate ensued. Members of African Methodist and African Episcopal churches had played prominent leadership roles in the conventions from the very start. Nevertheless, the minutes report that the recommendation passed unanimously.[109]

Modified interpretations of citizenship rejected the idea that colored people had to prove themselves worthy of American freedom. Their collective identity as free people was a fact that compelled them to act on behalf of slaves. The previous year's ambivalence about publicly identifying with antislavery was replaced by outspoken opposition to slavery. Delegates praised antislavery societies and abolitionists, especially the Lane Theological Seminary students in Ohio known as the "Lane Rebels," who condemned the sinfulness of slavery and denounced colonization. They were voted honorary members of the convention.

New appeals called for a permanent boycott of products made with slave labor. This action was so essential to promoting human rights that it could not be framed as a matter of personal choice. Whipper and Robert Purvis argued that everyone who was committed to freedom had a duty to use material made with free labor and refuse to cooperate in efforts to capture fugitives. Acting on behalf of slaves fulfilled an obligation to God that trumped any responsibility to obey corrupt American laws.[110]

The most significant departure from prior conventions appeared in the new premise of reform that Whipper and his allies formulated. Ethical foundations replaced conventional notions of charity and benevolence. The need to address the circumstances of free colored people and slaves was an imperative of being human. The convention's address to Americans crystallized the change. The speech was a group assignment for Whipper, Augustus Price, and Rhode Islander Alfred Niger. However, Whipper's ideas about religion, American identity, and human distinctions were apparent in its message.[111] High-minded and earnest in its explication of reform goals, the discourse assumed a sardonic tone. It betrayed an acute awareness of the audacity of positing a national reform program in which colored people played a leading role. The authors confronted presumed skepticism about their efforts by questioning the legitimacy of standard racial distinctions and hierarchies. They asserted the humanity of colored people and ridiculed linkages between whiteness and genius. There was no correlation between intelligence and skin complexion, they reasoned, because the Bible's account of creation proved the humanity and equality of all. Furthermore, history, science, philosophy, and common sense demonstrated that there was no natural connection between mental acuity and "a fair complexion." Having dispensed with racial conventions, the men grounded their efforts in a commitment to the "human race."[112] This shift meant that Christian duty, universal love, and human rights were to be the imperatives for activism. Reform thus became a fundamental human obligation—an activity in which all rational beings should participate.

This modification gave rise to a call to eradicate appeals to race categories among colored people. According to the convention address, reformers planned to purge from the affairs of the colored population "hateful and unnecessary distinctions" that divided the human family. The idea of common descent was an essential component of this reform mission aimed at

40 RELUCTANT RACE MEN

highlighting the fallacy of race categories. The last day of the convention proceedings marked the start of this effort when Whipper and Purvis declared that, to the extent possible, colored people should "abandon the use of the word 'colored,' when either speaking or writing concerning them."[113] Despite debate, delegates reportedly agreed that the term did not accurately represent them or their constituents. Whatever unanimity prevailed on that final afternoon quickly evaporated, however. Conflicts over the meaning and use of color designations persisted amid misgivings about the legitimacy of race practices.

The 1835 proceedings brought Northern reform efforts to a crossroads. Activists with new ideas had made significant changes to the reform landscape since the first groups of colored men gathered to protest colonization. The initial endeavors had morphed into plans for a full-blown reform agenda. Although the annual conventions had a broader scope than anti-colonization meetings, they did not function as national forums. They continued to address concerns and interests of changing groups of Northern men and were dominated by Philadelphians and New Yorkers.[114] Nevertheless, they were self-consciously American. The forums enabled reformers to press beyond the position that colored people were merely not African. This development set the stage for ongoing negotiations of collective identity. William Whipper, Robert Purvis, and James Forten stood at the center of change. They and their American Moral Reform Society colleagues believed their conception of reform settled the meaning of American identity. However, it remained to be seen whether they could implement the idea that citizenship entailed repudiating race. Realizing this vision hinged on their ability to provide concrete ways for people to represent themselves as American reformers. A protracted and contentious process for working out this issue lay ahead.

2

"That Odious Distinction"

Moral Reform and the Language of Obligations

With raised hands, nearly all the worshippers at a Troy, New York, interfaith revival accepted the speaker's entreaty to embrace the principles of moral reform. Thus launched a new auxiliary of the American Moral Reform Society (AMRS) in the spring of 1837. In Pittsburgh and in the small New Jersey towns of Burlington, Cranberry, and Bordentown, members of the group regularly gathered to reaffirm their commitment to its aims, pledging to "shun every sinful way." When Reform Society president James Forten Sr. made an altar call at the organization's annual meeting in Philadelphia, inspired listeners made their way to the front of the assembly to express their dedication to its work.[1]

Evangelical rituals befitted endeavors to eradicate society's evils. The goal required spiritual convictions to undergird strict adherence to moral precepts. Accordingly, religious leaders were among the first recruits when the organization initiated its work in 1836. Early AMRS affiliates included such prominent Presbyterian clergy as Samuel Cornish, Stephen Gloucester, and Daniel Payne, along with AME ministers Morris Brown, John Cook, Lewis Woodson, and Reuben Cuff, a cofounder of the denomination. Participation on the part of such figures signaled the sanctity of moral reform.[2]

In short order, however, ministerial distrust in how leading AMRS representatives interpreted race and its significance in reform fractured alliances, transforming allies into vociferous critics. Some church officials came to view the group's project as a disruption of efforts to improve colored people and a hindrance to the cause of expanding freedom. Such judgments reframed the society's rituals of piety. Instead of symbolizing spiritual leadership, they became signs of hubris among unchurched men making illegitimate claims to the mantle of moral reform.

Criticism stemmed from a refusal to use racial designations in defining the obligations of Christian American reformers. The stance should not have

Reluctant Race Men. Joan L. Bryant, Oxford University Press. © Oxford University Press 2024.
DOI: 10.1093/oso/9780195312966.003.0003

42 RELUCTANT RACE MEN

been surprising, as it stemmed from ideals that shaped the society's inception. Having repudiated race labels in proposing the initiative, William Whipper, Robert Purvis, and other AMRS stalwarts continued to deny their validity in framing reform endeavors. Their position fueled quarrels among a diverse set of individuals who grappled with configurations and meanings of race for much of the society's six-year career. Dissension thus made challenges to race a focal point of reform.[3]

The Reform Society's contentious evolution occasioned the first sustained collective inquiry in Black American reform history about "color"—the primary metaphor for racial conceptions of human difference, rank, and sameness. The discord that dogged the process reflected divergent perspectives on the meanings of race as well as the fact that organization supporters and critics had no clear maps to guide their interrogations of the construct and its significance for visions of progress. AMRS appeals to spiritual convictions further complicated debates by pushing reform issues beyond strategic concerns and tactics for navigating White domination. The idea that reform endeavors were sacred undertakings that needed to be free of racial constructions in order to develop ethical spheres of obligation raised challenging questions. What principles should guide confrontations with race practices? Who were the rightful arbiters and targets of reform projects? What was the appropriate lexicon for explaining moral duties? The contentious and halting steps with which Reform Society adherents and detractors navigated unfamiliar terrain gave rise to enduring conceptual parameters for interpreting and contesting race in reform initiatives.

———

Competing perspectives shaped the emergence of the AMRS. Founders perceived it as a venue in which to fulfill the goals of national conventions. They also hoped it would foment a "moral revolution." The visions converged at the 1836 inaugural meeting. In his first report as chairman of the society's board, Philadelphia barber John Burr—son of US vice president Aaron Burr and a servant in his household —bemoaned the fact that the public had yet to realize the "newness and greatness" of the group's undertaking. Having presided over the 1835 national convention board, Burr was apparently able to discern innovations in the opening AMRS agenda that others did not see. It promoted education, temperance, economy, universal freedom, and other reform issues that had been regularly addressed in convention gatherings and *Freedom's Journal.* Concerns about improving the decorum of colored people and education remained prominent. Baltimore minister William Watkins won support for sanctions against extravagant funeral processions and for advising servants to adopt a strong work ethic. He and James Forten Jr. delivered lengthy speeches on the virtues of education, extolling its ability to make "useful citizens and enlightened Christians."[4]

A proposal to improve American churches highlighted how AMRS leaders sought to wield moral authority. Warrants for the undertaking stemmed from a pledge in the 1835 convention address to help churches "rid themselves of the sin of slavery and immorality."[5] Implementation would widen the gap between the group's reform ideals and aims that gave rise to national conventions. The measure entailed publishing two open letters to churches in Benjamin Lundy's *National Enquirer, and Constitutional Advocate of Universal Liberty.* The first item instructed churches operated by free people of color concerning their duty to oppose slavery. The second admonished White Christians to abandon "prejudice against color."[6] Both communications condemned the immorality of complexional categories.

The message to "colored churches in the free states" tethered the goal of weakening slavery's economic vitality to the belief that reform required individuals to act on convictions. It aimed to convince colored Christians to refrain from using items produced with slave labor. The measure reflected actions some individual members and their families had already taken. In 1831, John Burr's wife, Hester, became an officer in the Colored Female Free Produce Society of Pennsylvania. That same year, Frederick Hinton and Robert Purvis joined the newly formed Colored Free Produce Society. In 1834, Whipper began promoting products made without the exploitation of slaves by opening a "free labor" and temperance store in Philadelphia. These individual commitments did not represent the sensibilities that prevailed among society adherents. James Forten Jr. pled with his colleagues to act as a principled body, insisting that, as defenders of human rights, they had a responsibility to use their spending power to advance freedom. His reasoning was no match for the high prices, limited options, coarse fabrics, and flavorless confections commonly associated with "free produce," making it an impractical and unattractive option. After lengthy deliberations, a majority agreed to encourage patronage of such enterprises, but, as an organization, they could not carry out actions members expected of churches.[7]

Responsibility for drafting the call for congregations to boycott slave-produced items fell to Philadelphia cemetery operator Jacob C. White and

44 RELUCTANT RACE MEN

Baltimoreans William Watkins and Jacob Moore. They implored church members to make sacrifices by framing the use of commodities created with slave labor in ethical terms. The appeal characterized the consumption of such products as a "spiritual and moral, as well as a political evil" that deprived people of God-given freedom. All Christians had an obligation to fight it. The letter derided the excuse that colored people were powerless against the slave system, insisting that they had the capacity and duty to resist immorality. The logic was simple. Consumers nurtured slavery, and Christians who used slave-made products were complicit in depriving people of their rightful liberty. The culpability of free people of color was palpable. The group estimated that 150,000 colored people in free states spent an average of ten dollars per year on cotton, tobacco, rice, sugar, and molasses produced with slave labor. Assuming a 10 percent profit, these purchases generated an annual net yield to slaveholding planters of $150,000. Incredulously, the letter asked, "Is this doing nothing for the support of slavery? Can the colored churches wink at this?" Colored people were not exempt from the Christian duty to fight slavery because there was no valid basis for correlating moral obligations with skin color. God, reformers argued, made "no distinction in complexion." On Judgment Day, no one would be able to justify negligence by pleading, "We are *Colored*."[8]

The letter to "PROFESSED FOLLOWERS OF JESUS CHRIST" in White Protestant churches, further questioned the notion that physical differences were valid bases on which to ground moral judgments about relationships. The reasoning in this undertaking was not novel. Jacob Oson confronted the issue in his 1817 address, *A Search for Truth; or An Inquiry for the Origin of the African Nation*. Reflecting on biblical injunctions for Christians to love their neighbors as themselves, he wondered whether physical traits of people of African descent disqualified them from consideration as neighbors by White American believers. He considered the moral significance of appearance with the simple question of "whether the tincture of the skin can destroy the validity of the commands."[9] Convinced that scripture settled the matter, he left the decision of whom to embrace as a neighbor to individual conscience. In contrast, the Reform Society's probe into the meanings ascribed to complexion led to a sweeping critique. Its letter acknowledged at the outset that the group might be deemed presumptuous for addressing White people, given disparaging verdicts about everything originating from people with African origins. This observation gave way to an attack on the bigotry that fueled such conclusions and propagated false notions of difference.

"THAT ODIOUS DISTINCTION" 45

The appeal became an indictment and an admonition for churches to promote "primitive holiness" by eradicating prejudices that created "invidious distinctions" out of mere "physical peculiarities." It condemned efforts to attach moral meanings to phenotype. Such ascriptions distorted reality and human relations by making appearance acceptable grounds for determining merit and narrowing the parameters of sympathy. The standard of skin color had become so potent, reformers argued, that it disempowered the most logical arguments for justice. As the colonization scheme showed, appeals to "color" enabled even the cruelty of exile to be cloaked in the language of benevolence.[10]

Moral reformers rejected the idea that ethnological factors explained anti-Black biases. Convinced that racial differences were illusory, they saw no point in analyzing the source of phenotypic traits White Christians viewed as signs of inferiority. What mattered was the moral basis of prejudice, which had to be understood in light of human relations outlined in the Bible. The apostle Paul's declaration that God made all nations "of one blood" provided evidence of "the identity of the human race—our common origin, and natural equality."[11] This principle of the unity of the human species meant that discriminatory distinctions in churches and political institutions violated nature. It was thus sinful for Christian leaders to perpetuate the idea that there were essential differences among humans. In doing so, they sent the false message that it was impossible for White Christians to include colored people in their spheres of obligation and love. Routine injustices illustrated the injurious effects of the sins churches abetted and showed the urgent need for corrective action.[12]

The implications of the Reform Society's opening assault on race practices became clear after its second meeting in 1837. Members who endorsed criticism of churches opposed a drive to exclude color designations from the society's endeavors because such a step might mean abandoning a commitment to colored people. A refusal to name them as the specific beneficiaries of reform appeared to be an unconscionable attempt to shirk a primary obligation. Vehement reactions to this prospect sparked debates that transformed the premise of the AMRS into the core of its reform agenda. Notwithstanding its array of measures, the group gained a reputation for one thing—repudiating color designations. As its leading spokesperson, Whipper became a crusader against racial classifications and distinctions.[13]

The ensuing strife was a sharp departure from the spirit that marked the start of the AMRS. Despite disappointment over the demise of the national

conventions, initially, there had been a measure of optimism and hopefulness about the Reform Society's prospects. In the recently launched *Colored
American*, Samuel Cornish had endorsed the enterprise in laudatory terms
and encouraged attendance from people throughout the country. The noble
aim of extending "moral principle and action" among colored people was
such that no one could refuse to support it. When he arrived at the 1837
meeting, he observed that it seemed poised to generate beneficial outcomes.[14]
Others shared his positive interest. Approximately one hundred people were
among its initial members and delegates. Forty individuals from this group—
a number comparable to the size of the 1830 national convention—officially
participated in the meeting.[15] Yet, by the close of the five-day session, signs of
goodwill had dissipated. The question of using color designations became so
contentious that it overshadowed other agenda items. Advocacy for popular
reform issues—antislavery, education, public decorum, temperance, and
skilled labor opportunities—failed to build a cohesive coalition.

The official account of the Reform Society meeting offers a glimpse of the
events that pushed the issue of color distinctions to the fore. Tensions surfaced in exchanges after the meeting when parties on all sides argued about
their ideas in the press. Conflicts developed with efforts to delineate agenda
items. A group resolution from John Cook, Reuben Cuff, Daniel Payne, and
Philadelphian Frederick Hinton urged free people of color to form societies
that promoted education. Unnamed participants objected to the reference to
free people of color, and debate ensued among Whipper, Hinton, Purvis, and
others. After two days of arguing, James Forten Sr. exercised his presidential
prerogative and ordered delegates to abandon the term. Although his directive ended the meeting's discussion, it marked the start of extended quarrels
in the press.[16]

Controversy rapidly extended beyond the AMRS resolution to broader
questions about the significance of color classifications and distinctions. It
persisted largely through letters and editorials in reform newspapers, especially the *Colored American*. Individuals frequently talked past each other,
such that even the terms of debate were a point of contention. Whipper was
largely a solitary voice speaking for the AMRS; virtually all correspondence that referred to him and to the AMRS as a group was negative. Despite
overwhelming criticism of the AMRS, debates persisted, in part, because
Whipper was so tenacious in arguing against the use of color designations.
Just as important, however, was the fact that others deemed his ideas worth
engaging. Even though they disagreed with his conception of reform, critics

were unable or unwilling to disregard him. In addition, the magnitude of hostility toward the AMRS might have been exaggerated. Although the press expanded opportunities for people to participate in public debate, it was not a purely democratic forum. Not everyone had access to print. A chief critic of Whipper and the AMRS, Cornish refused to publish many letters he received concerning the society, insisting that they were unsuitable for the paper. He acknowledged excluding one letter simply because it mentioned the Reform Society and warned the writer to confine future comments to national conventions.[17]

The protracted debate surrounding the AMRS suggests that its defenders were not alone in harboring doubts about racial distinctions. Moreover, it was difficult for reformers to speak coherently about the meanings and import of color designations. With no solid discursive tradition on which to draw, many struggled to factor clear conceptions of race into their understanding of reform obligations. Yet the notion that color labels were benign, useful, or malleable signifiers did not trump misgivings about their validity as markers of essential difference and rank.

Divergent aims of integrationists and separatists fail to explain conflicts over the AMRS. Individuals who disparaged segregated associations and welcomed the participation of White people in their forums were among the group's harshest critics. For instance, in castigating the Reform Society, Frederick Hinton assailed the idea that colored reformers had any obligation to assist White people. Such a notion was "absurd and preposterous," he argued, because that group possessed all the advantages that colored people were trying to secure. Hinton was no separatist. He had urged the Reform Society to invite presidents of antislavery societies and "other friends of our cause" to participate in its meetings. Even AMRS critics who advocated a return to national conventions were not necessarily advocating segregated forums. A former New York delegate, distressed that national conventions had lapsed, appealed to leading AMRS members to redirect their energies to revive them. The pseudonymous "Hamilton" acknowledged that the conventions had not been perfect. Inexperience had compromised delegates' ability to manage authority, convince colored people of the need to unite, and wring coherence out of the "discordant elements" in the colored population. Despite these limitations, he extolled the arenas as fruitful sites of integration because they had fostered friendships with "the white brethren."[18]

Early critics of the AMRS focused attention on how to name the objects of reform. It appeared obvious to them that the society's principal aim was

48 RELUCTANT RACE MEN

to improve free people of color. Thus, it was logical and necessary to identify them as such. The matter seemed so straightforward that the refusal of Whipper, Forten, Purvis, and their allies to identify free people of color "by name" was inexplicable and morally indefensible. There was, however, a broad spectrum of ideas about the term "colored" among the society's detractors. It was variously a phenotypic description, a designation of social circumstances, and a caste label. Its multiple meanings complicated debate.

Hinton, who had proposed that the AMRS promote education specifically for free colored people, interpreted "colored" as a description of characteristics. He assumed it was a given that colored people were the society's focus. Upon leaving the Reform Society over its rejection of racial classifications, he explained to *Colored American* readers that he had referred to free people of color to distinguish them from slaves, since it would be useless to include the latter group in the reform agenda. He equated reformers' opposition to the designation with a refusal to identify with "the peculiarities of their people." This was a moral shortcoming. Discarding the label "colored" amounted to rejecting the skin God created. Those who scorned it as a "*badge of . . . degradation*" slighted people for acts of nature.[19] They could not be trusted to lead the cause of reform.

The conviction that the free population faced unique circumstances explained some of Samuel Cornish's frustrations with moral reformers. Despite his initial praise, he confessed to harboring doubts about their measures from the start. Their concerns about such a trivial matter as color categories confirmed his fears. He insisted that he was "as much opposed to complexional distinctions as brother Whipper, or any other man." However, pragmatic considerations about the colored population's "SPECIAL" needs meant that reformers should specify for whom they were promoting moral principles. It was ludicrous to suggest that they could serve everyone. Defining the focus of one's initiatives was not at odds with a commitment to universal principles.[20]

In belittling concerns about names, Cornish overlooked his own struggles to characterize the status of the free colored population. He had once opposed the idea that there was anything distinctive about colored people. As editor of the short-lived *Rights of All*, which succeeded *Freedom's Journal*, he decried the suggestion that they comprised a "*separate people, [possessing] separate interests.*" The formulation was an evil akin to colonizationist actions that treated them as an "*extraneous mass.*"[21] Outside of the anti-colonization arena, however, he discerned unique contours of the colored population's circumstances and a need for distinctive measures. The term "colored" denoted this situation. When establishing the *Colored American*, he insisted that names mattered. The designations "*Negroes, Africans,* and *blacks*," he argued, were all "names of reproach" that compromised the legitimacy of colored people's claims to being American. He acknowledged that some might dismiss the title of his paper as yet another signifier of Black subjugation. "Why draw this cord of caste?" he asked. The "peculiarity" of colored people's circumstances and needs supplied the answer. A reader's comments validated his decision. The correspondent reported that, at first glance, the paper's name was so repugnant that its merits seemed dubious. However, careful consideration of other distasteful alternatives showed that the term had the potential to create bonds among people subjected to similar persecutions and proscriptions. The reader came to see the word as a trope for a common social experience and espoused the editor's faith in its power to unite people, "whatever their hue."[22]

Although he perceived color designations as markers of stratification, Cornish suggested that some labels could function as a benign way of distinguishing among Americans. He believed that everyone, including moral reformers, should welcome being called "colored" because it was superior to being "nothing else but NEGROES, NEGROES." This bias was not new. More than two decades earlier, Jacob Oson condemned "that fictitious name *Negro*" as a scandalous epithet. The term stigmatized people of African descent as wretches, whether used in ignorance or with the intent to disgrace. He believed it was an appropriate reference to fallen humanity's wretchedness; however, it was unjust to "brand" one group of people with a trait inherent in "all mankind."[23]

Cornish's preferred alternative was popular. White observers noted that the free population viewed the label "colored" as radically different from and superior to other titles. Methodist minister John Watson complained that after they secured authority and autonomy in their own churches, Philadelphia's free people forgot "their place" and, with it, their names. Once, he recalled, they had willingly submitted to being called "servants, Negroes, or blacks." However, they now insisted that they were "colored people" and greeted each other as ladies and gentlemen.[24] Cornish viewed color designations as characteristically American. They conformed to the logic that made Indians "RED AMERICANS" and White people "WHITE AMERICANS." Such labels were not rankings of essentially different beings; no group was better or worse than any another group. Customary proof of their shared humanity was in the biblical assertion that all derived from the same blood.[25]

Critics of the Reform Society considered varied justifications for using racial terms even as they harbored misgivings about them. Philadelphian Junius Morel is a case in point. He formulated an elaborate defense of the designation "Colored Man" as he entered the fray against moral reformers. He initially suggested that the label was an empty signifier since it did not equate colored people with monkeys or connote "inherent degradation," criminal activity, mental incapacity or inferiority, physical impairment, or immorality. His objections to the Reform Society mirrored Hinton's reasoning that the group was rejecting the normalcy of dark skin. Bible stories persuaded him that there was sound historical precedent for the label's appropriateness. Citing "Adam, the red, Cush, the black, and Luban, the white man," he argued that since "the ancients" saw fit to name people by skin color, the custom was sound. He added sarcastically that it was crucial to use color designations to make moral distinctions between White and colored Americans. The term "colored," he argued, distinguished "the sinning and the sinned against."[26]

Ultimately, none of Morel's justifications overcame his discomfort with a label he perceived as reproachful. Yet he continued to insist that there were warrants for using it. Advising moral reformers to follow the example of the Religious Society of Friends, he noted that when that group navigated disrepute, it did not reject the name "Quaker." Virtuous actions among its members transformed the word's meaning. Morel suggested that if colored people followed this example, they could change the significance of "colored" and perhaps eliminate the need for it altogether. Like Cornish, he saw the term as a social designation, albeit a temporary one. He was convinced that when people of color became free of constraints, they would no longer have to contend with labels that distinguished them as a class.[27]

Concerns about the accuracy and practicality of naming colored people as beneficiaries of reform obscured the conceptual basis of the Reform Society's objections to color designations. Contrary to critics' assumptions, the stance did not arise from the question of how to name the objects of reform. Nor was it a pragmatic judgment about how to implement reforms effectively. It flowed from the same belief about the unity of the human species that shaped the society's critique of churches. In short, the group embraced the idea that a common origin determined human relations and thus fixed the boundaries of obligation. This principle of human unity, routinely invoked to protest discrimination, defined the society's reform platform. Moral reformers transposed the logic of human equality into foundations for moral reform.

Conceptually, the group's position mirrored anti-colonization rhetoric. It drew on earlier reform endeavors as well. For instance, in 1813, Reform Society president James Forten invoked the principle of species unity to challenge the legitimacy of differential treatment for White and Black Philadelphians. Writing as a "Man of Colour," he issued a series of letters denouncing a proposal to ban colored migration to Pennsylvania and require free colored people already living in the state to register their presence. The injustice of the proposal lay in its assumption that Black people were fundamentally different from White people. He asked, "Has the God who made the white man and the black, left any record declaring us a different species?"[28]

Although his alliance with Forten likely informed Whipper's ideas, he attributed his stance to the example of radical abolitionists who, in principle, looked beyond whiteness in defining their spheres of obligation. His conviction about the immorality of color designations arose from something akin to a conversion experience. He told Cornish that, when he began his reform work, he interpreted the task using the same "narrow compass" that his critics employed. However, the motto of William Lloyd Garrison's *Liberator* gave rise to an epiphany. His "moral vision awoke," he recalled, upon reading, "My country is the world—my countryman are all mankind."[29] He felt liberated by the realization that all people were connected by descent from a single divine source. This experience gave rise to his belief in universal moral principles that applied to all.

Whipper's insight sheds light on the stakes for moral reformers in trying to alter the terms of reform. He and his allies deemed it essential to calibrate reform initiatives with the nature of humanity. Skin complexion and color designations were of no moral consequence; they neither created nor defined obligations. The only valid categories for understanding human difference were "virtues and vices." Whether viewed in terms of ethics or nature, a "color" was not something a person could be; it was not an identity.[30]

In practice, moral reformers premised their opposition to race categories as much on the obligations they associated with American citizenship as on the idea of a common humanity. They believed the nation's founding documents inscribed the religious principle that all were "of one blood." Thus, they had a duty to reject color distinctions. Citizenship claims informed their understanding of the content of reform endeavors, its targets, and the incompatibility of racial distinctions and American identity. A pseudonymous member of the society, "REMEMBER THAT," tried to elucidate these connections in a letter to the *National Enquirer, and Constitutional*

52   RELUCTANT RACE MEN

Advocate of Universal Liberty. He explained that the group's position derived from members' shared belief that God created human nature and endowed humans with varied complexions. They were certain, however, that God had not designated anyone "by the term 'colored.'" Convinced that this same reasoning applied to American citizenship, the writer insisted that the Declaration of Independence was similarly averse to color designations because it also failed to reference anyone "by his color."[31] To mark the designation as a label of inferiority, he contrasted it with the founding document's affirmation that all people were equal.

As the public voice of the Reform Society, Whipper further distilled its position. He attempted to situate the identities of free people of color in their status as Christian citizens. This meant that they should understand themselves as part of a national body of Americans and promote Christian morality. He reasoned that the nation was a geopolitical entity that could not be legitimately divided into "complexional domains." Any national society that defined its aims by skin color was unworthy of the title "American." The American Bible Society was a clear example. Whipper accused the organization of restricting its mission by making distinctions according to "complexion and condition" because it withheld Bibles from slaves. In contrast, the Reform Society's agenda of education, temperance, economy, peace, and universal freedom simultaneously specified its aims and identified the targets of reform as "the uneducated, the intemperate, the luxurious, the quarrelsome, and the abettors of slavery." Adamant about the primacy of citizenship, Whipper put a positive slant on accusations that he and his allies had lost sight of their oppressed status as colored people. With an air of moral superiority, he pled guilty. Moral reformers had indeed failed to perform the degradation that others heaped upon them. This was hardly a cause for lament because refusing to accept subjugation enabled them to assume their noble undertaking.[32]

The Reform Society attempted to ground reforms in an ethic that fused a religious notion of humanity with American citizenship. This effort reframed the terms of debate with critics. The focus on naming gave way to the question of how reformers should define their obligations. For AMRS members, reformers' responsibilities were rooted in citizenship claims. Whipper declared that it was illogical for critics to distinguish the duties of citizens from those of colored people while insisting that colored people were citizens. For moral consistency, he argued that reformers needed to act and refer to themselves as American men. They had to reject color designations because the labels artificially contracted the sphere of human obligations. They were unacceptable guides for ethical and religious activism.[33]

Critics of the AMRS made similar claims about the moral significance of being American in their ongoing repudiations of colonization. In that context, the moral imperatives of citizenship were decisive. For instance, Philip Bell, one-time editor and owner of the *Colored American*, cited loyalty to slaves as a reason to reject colonization. He declared that, as Americans, free people of color could not abandon slaves to their oppressors. "Leaving color out of the question," he argued, they must stand by their "country and countrymen" to see that the nation overcame dishonor and accorded redress and rights to injured Americans.[34] This commitment arose from patriotism that inspired love for the nation, despite its profound and numerous flaws.

There was little agreement on how American identity should inform the duties of moral reformers. The issue of defining the terms of association in America remained unanswered. Like convention delegates before them, Reform Society members and their critics remained at odds over the ethical implications of citizenship claims. Whipper framed the conflict as a matter of principle versus expediency. His opponents disparaged him as an idealist who was incapable of formulating practical aims. They interpreted expedient measures as principled actions. Cornish and Morel ridiculed the Reform Society as a reckless innovation among "MODERN ELEMENTS" who shunned pragmatic interventions in favor of specious claims to spiritual authority. The work of reform rightfully belonged to churches and "exemplary, self-denying, practical Christians." Unable to discern any virtue in Whipper's position, Cornish found it difficult to reconcile himself to the fact that the venerable James Forten, an exemplar of colored people's achievement, associated with the moral reformers. He argued that Forten's refined sensibilities made him ill suited for such an alliance and urged him to relinquish his leadership position and resign from the group. He acknowledged Whipper and his allies as cultured and intelligent men, but they were misguided and "as visionary as the winds." Prudent reformers were not visionary. Whipper had scorned this sensibility early in his career, assuring prospective patrons of the Philadelphia Reading Room Society for Men of Colour that the collections would be free of such material.[35]

The dichotomy between idealism and pragmatism obscured the fact that critics of the AMRS ultimately met the group on its own moral ground. They responded to its efforts to formulate ethical bases for reform with competing ideas about the foundations of duty. In the process, they framed the AMRS

54 RELUCTANT RACE MEN

position as a refusal to target colored people in its agenda rather than a rejection of race labels. Cornish insisted that the only legitimate question was whether colored people should devote their energies to improving the nation or improving themselves. Arguing that the Reform Society focused on the former goal, he asked, "Is it truly benevolent for colored men to overlook the immediate disabilities and suffering of their own people, and aim, in their efforts, indefinitely, to effect the good of the whole nation?"[36] His logic held that a shared social experience should define obligations. A common reality created a duty that voided any responsibility to refrain from making "complexional distinctions." Moreover, it pointed to a moral obligation to aid other colored Americans, as such. This meant a willingness to act "irrespective of color" but not "irrespective of condition," which skin color signified.[37] He dismissed the notion that colored reformers should or could ignore the exigencies of oppression in defining their duties. Shared social circumstances, he insisted, created "peculiar relations" among colored people that stemmed from their collective oppression. Henry Highland Garnet later lodged similar arguments against the society's unyielding position. Writing under the name "SIDNEY," he also maintained that duties arose from relationships. As if sealing his defection from the society, he repudiated the doctrine concerning the universal character of morality and obligations. He insisted, "What is morally right for one man to do may be morally wrong for another."[38] This notion of contingent morality meant that obligations stemmed from discrete relations in particular contexts.

The religious and political principles that framed their agenda did not void the social realities that grounded the stand Whipper and his allies took against race categories. Everyday experiences that clashed with their visions of American citizenship fueled condemnations of racial categories. They gave substance to arguments that color designations were antithetical to Christian and American principles. The constructs were central to the oppression colored people faced. According to the pseudonymous moral reformer "REMEMBER THAT," the society's rejection of color labels was a refusal to endorse ideologies of inferiority. It tried to avoid the suggestion that people of color had an inherent need for moral improvement, for they were "no more morally degraded" than any other people were, including individuals with greater opportunities. Moral reformers refrained from labeling their endeavors "colored" because doing so would be tantamount to asserting that colored people were, by definition, categorically inferior to others. Inequality could then be justified. The writer postulated that immorality prevailed only where colored people lacked access to resources necessary for moral development. There was no reason to use labels that implied otherwise.[39]

Whipper cared more about the social functions of American race distinctions than about negative messages linked to the word "colored." His opposition to the term reflected the evils he perceived in constructions of whiteness. His suspicions were longstanding. In 1832, he joined Robert Purvis and James Forten in challenging the logic of race categories in Pennsylvania's plan to repeal protections for escaped slaves and bar free colored people from migrating to the state. Their protest to the state legislature argued that the pursuit of fugitives compromised Pennsylvania's status as a free state. The proposed ban on migrants was worse. Its reliance on the arbitrary and dubious criteria of color differences violated the very principle of liberty. The attempt to regulate autonomy using "wavering and uncertain shades of white" placed freedom on unstable and illusory foundations.[40]

Experience taught Whipper that race distinctions were not benign or self-evident descriptors. A litany of wrongs exposed their role in orchestrating injustice. "Now what is it," he asked,

> that deprives us of the benefit of institutions of learning—churches—the social circles—schools—the mechanic arts—elective franchise—the privileges and protection of government—the favor of just and equitable laws—trial by jury—mercantile employments—riding in stages and steamboats on equal footing with "white people," but that odious distinction in language, principle, and practice, that confers the boon of favor on those that are known by the distinctive appellation of "white people."[41]

In this formulation, race categories were linguistic, ideological, and behavioral mechanisms that regulated access to intellectual, social, political, economic, legal, and religious resources by inventing whiteness. Even without a full-blown scientific theory about races, reformers perceived clear empirical warrants for rejecting racial terms. Inequality was intrinsic to the discourse of "color," not merely a product of individual prejudice. Moral reformers had a duty to reject designations based in false notions of difference and hierarchy that configured unjust treatment.

Whipper stopped short of concluding that colored people could make the concept of race disappear by rejecting it. Standards of rectitude compelled reformers to act on accurate principles. Using a baseless racial taxonomy of difference and rank would make them culpable in sustaining discourses

56 RELUCTANT RACE MEN

that structured oppression. As long as the race categories functioned as part of everyday speech, there could be no hope of abolishing the color-coded injustices they framed and justified. Language would sustain them until "all the different SHADES mingle into ONE."[42]

Experiential arguments for opposing race did nothing to change opinions of Reform Society critics who associated race designations with physical or social facts. The "condition vs. color" debate, which exposed divergent interpretations of linkages between bigotry and reform, set this impasse in sharp relief. Historical analyses of this phenomenon typically adopt the arguments of Whipper's adversaries and ascribe to him the notion that skin color caused prejudice. They credit his opponents with the practical insight of addressing the moral condition of colored people because it was a factor they could influence.[43] This interpretation overlooks the fact that, in addition to routinely misrepresenting each other's opinions, opposing groups of reformers were rarely discussing the same thing. Whipper tried to understand how conceptions of human difference structured discrimination, while his critics searched for its causes in colored people's behaviors and appearance.

Cornish and other critics translated Whipper's ideas into a claim that the complexions of colored people inspired prejudice. They countered with the assertion that the moral condition of colored people inspired and perhaps justified bigotry. Surveying poverty, ignorance, and "want of enterprise" among colored city dwellers, Cornish pinpointed these factors as the chief cause of disparaging attitudes among White people. It followed that moral initiatives specifically for colored people were essential. Improved conduct would enable colored people to prove themselves "worthy to be freemen." Familiarity also seemed to reduce antipathy toward dark skin. Observations of daily contact between free colored and White urban dwellers convinced Cornish that revulsion toward dark skin that might have inspired mistreatment in the past had abated.[44]

Observations from *Colored American* readers gave force to the position that colored reformers should devote their energies to improving colored people. The commentator "ECONOMY" stressed the efficacy of such endeavors. The writer insisted that, if colored Americans became "more religious, more moral, more industrious" and economical, they would earn respect, even from those who oppressed them. "PHILOS" offered similar predictions about the power of reform to quell misrepresentations. The sight of colored people working to elevate themselves promised to "correct public opinion, and consequently, public feeling and public action" toward them. To ensure this outcome, it was critical to designate reform endeavors "colored." Otherwise, PHILOS concluded, in a climate of rampant misrepresentations, the wrong people might get credit for successful uplift efforts.[45]

White sympathizers agreed that colored reformers should improve their moral condition. Their perspectives lent legitimacy to judgments that moral reformers were misguided in opposing color designations. They supported Cornish's stance that ignorance and immorality explained the negative connotations of the term "colored." He reported that Charles Ray, the Congregational minister who published the *Colored American*, won accolades for shifting attention away from skin color in discussing prejudice. White audiences praised Ray's insight that prejudice was merely a response to immorality. They insisted that bigotry would vanish when free colored people collectively reached a higher moral standard. An unidentified "distinguished Quaker lady" who was sympathetic to AMRS leaders reinforced this point. Cornish recounted that she advised them to develop "EMINENCE in moral, intellectual, and social virtues" among colored people. She assured them that, if they succeeded in this endeavor, White people would "lose sight of [their] color," which signified their alleged inferiority. Presumably, citizenship rights would follow. Another Reform Society sympathizer, Benjamin Lundy, also questioned the wisdom of renouncing color designations. He agreed that labels should not be "unnecessarily prominent." However, he explained that designating oneself "colored" was not necessarily the same as confessing inferiority. Like the Quaker advisor, he insisted that, if colored people worked to improve their hearts and minds with "ever increasing zeal," the term would become a "title of honor" instead of a "badge of disgrace." He argued further that designating reform efforts as "colored" was appropriate because the word denoted "actually existing things." The things would endure even if they went unnamed. In short, moral reformers could not eliminate natural differences color labels purported to designate, but they could change their meanings.[46]

Others who had severed ties with moral reformers helped to broaden criticism of the organization. Lewis Woodson, a Pittsburgh minister whose family claimed descent from Thomas Jefferson, responded to an appeal from Cornish to help refute the group's position. Although he admittedly shared moral reformers' loathing of oppressive racial distinctions, Woodson thought it was necessary to contend with the lamentable fact that generations of prejudice made colored Americans a "distinct class." Writing under the moniker

58 RELUCTANT RACE MEN

"Augustine," he cited ignorance as the cause of degradation. Observations of the ease with which individuals displaying stellar ethical behavior and mental acuity gained acceptance into "polite" society illustrated his point. It was thus clear that colored reformers should concentrate on moral improvement and that the AMRS was promoting futile attacks on prejudice.[47] His commentary "Moral Work for Colored Men" maintained that the task was more essential than any other reform endeavor, even antislavery. To communicate its importance, he observed that, if prejudice and slavery suddenly vanished, colored people would still occupy the "lowest depths of moral degradation."[48] Being free from slavery and bigotry would not make them worthy of equal participation in American society. Special measures were necessary to raise their standing.

Woodson rejected the notion that efforts to reform colored people entailed moral compromises. However, he struggled to reconcile his stance with the principle of a common humanity. He explained that God established the "sameness of the whole human family" by making all people "of one blood." Yet, in creating the first humans separately, God made everyone responsible for their individual care. By extension, colored people had a duty to reform themselves without depending on assistance from others. Neglecting to improve their low moral condition would affirm allegations of their intellectual inferiority.[49]

A principle of self-reliance resolved Woodson's concerns about the quality of life for colored residents of crowded cities. Cornish suggested that colored people should live among White people. However, Woodson saw a remedy to urban problems in the promise of land and economic independence that pulled Americans westward in the 1820s and 1830s. He proposed separate settlements for colored people. Inspiration came from his father's experiences in rural Ohio and the suggestion of Quaker spiritualist Augustus Wattles, who campaigned for the development of farm communities in Ohio, Michigan, Wisconsin Territory, Canada, and other areas offering acres of fertile uncultivated land. They confirmed Woodson's long-standing position that colored people would have better opportunities for advancement in independent communities. Such arrangements would ensure unfettered access to schools, churches, and all other social privileges. Religious and political history showed the wisdom of such a project. It was analogous to denominational divisions that produced the Society of Friends, Methodists, and Presbyterians. It bore a resemblance to the decision of the biblical figures Lot and Abraham, who divided their property and parted ways. These examples framed separation as a morally sound means of avoiding and overcoming strife. It was, moreover, consistent with American ideals because the nation owed its political existence to separatist actions. He was not advising anyone to abandon the citizenship rights earned by birth on United States soil. Individuals could be equal citizens, he explained, with no social interactions. Colored people could maintain "an identity of interest" with other Americans without "an identity of community." The fact that individual states united in managing and defending slavery showed that communities could function as distinct entities while maintaining shared concerns.[50]

Responses to Woodson's platform exposed a tenuous commitment to race categories among critics of the AMRS. They reveal the narrow parameters within which Cornish and others accepted race categories as valid. Although Woodson's advocacy of agricultural pursuits had broad appeal, for some, the reliance on race categories to make permanent social divisions went too far. Virtually no support for the idea of separation appeared in the *Colored American*. The specter of colonization and wrongs that hinged on racial distinctions made the proposal largely unacceptable to other commentators Cornish published. Even the rare letter that applauded Augustine's wisdom measured the potential benefits of a separate settlement in terms of its ability to overcome color distinctions. The correspondent "OGLER" agreed that a separate settlement would enable colored people to develop independence from White people. It would foster the formation of a colored professional class of physicians, lawyers, and merchants, an outcome that would likely please colonizationists. The central benefit would be the framework it provided for a parallel society that White Americans would have to engage as an equal partner. It could make colored and White people "reciprocally dependent" and produce the same sort of "community of interest" that Woodson identified among American states. OGLER imagined separate entities as means to ends that might be their undoing. He believed that, over time, shared interests would create indissoluble bonds that would make Americans "one common people."[51]

Woodson's proposal forced Cornish to voice his misgivings about race categories. He led the charge against what he saw as a morally defective scheme that relied on faulty reasoning. He insisted that the logical outcome of shared interest between colored people and their "white brethren" was not separation but "social intercourse." He countered Woodson's appeals to the past with his own historical examples of the efficacy of social interaction. Contact, he asserted, alleviated prejudice against Jews, Catholics, Quakers,

60 RELUCTANT RACE MEN

and Black West Indians. Churches, schools, and colleges that fostered social intercourse between colored and White people demonstrated the benefits of forging broad alliances. He suggested that these types of arenas exemplified the ideals of such White reformers as Beriah Green, Theodore Weld, Lydia Maria Child, and the Grimké sisters, all of whom defended the humanity of slaves and free people of color.[52]

Cornish rallied opposition to Woodson's plan by highlighting its reliance on racial distinctions and parallels with colonization. He contrasted the proposal with the principle that all people possessed "the same blood" and belonged to "the same family." This physical unity provided a natural basis for association and common interests. It meant that people of varied complexions could develop together "in the same place." To suggest otherwise, he asserted, was to defame God's wisdom and providence. The use of race categories to make colored people a socially and geographically distinct group was at odds with this perspective. Separate settlements were morally unsound, and it was difficult to distinguish their logic from colonization, whose proponents might interpret such a proposal as an endorsement of their project. Woodson's historical examples failed to sway Cornish because they provided no justifications for the racial distinctions the project would require. They supplied no warrants for relying on the "cord of caste." When Woodson and Wattles ignored appeals to qualify their ideas, Cornish assured readers that they actually shared his contempt for separation and suggested it only for individuals in dire circumstances.[53]

Commentators who followed Cornish's lead in assessing Woodson's proposal variously praised its promise of economic autonomy, supported the idea of farming in the West, and rejected everything it represented. The plan made economic sense to the pseudonymous New Yorker "VIATOR." The writer mused that a settlement organized for business purposes would offer lucrative individual and collective benefits to colored people. While adamantly opposed to colonization, VIATOR was open to exploring prospects for business-related settlements, even outside of the United States. Canada, the British West Indies, Haiti, and Africa were deemed worthy of investigation. Yet the mass character of Woodson's plan was suspect. It was apparently a fine thing for individual farmers, "commercial men," and other professionals to explore forming a settlement in an economic alliance. However, Woodson's attempt to forge separate societies of colored people seemed like a prescription for the entire colored population. Ultimately, its similarity to despised colonization initiatives rendered it "heretical."[54]

Writing from Geneva, New York, James W. Duffin, an ally of abolitionist Gerrit Smith, celebrated the genius of the suggestion that many colored people could improve themselves by becoming western farmers. However, he shared Cornish's opinion of the virtues and efficacy of living among White people. He instructed colored people who could move westward to disperse themselves among "white brethren" and rear their children together in order to dispel prejudice. He protested Woodson's proposal because it conceived of colored people as a discrete entity. It would be both impolitic and harmful, Duffin argued, for colored people to try to become "a distinct and separate body." Would such an attempt validate the claims of their enemies by implying that they could not live as equals with White people? Would separate settlements be anything other than "colonization at home?" Duffin reduced these questions to identity. He concluded that colored people should ignore racial labels and claim their citizenship rights "as men and as Christians."[55]

The pseudonymous "Americanus" denounced Woodson's proposed settlements as the culmination of wrongheaded reasoning. The plan was little more than an extension of the flawed notion that there was reform work peculiar to colored people. Americanus praised Cornish for repudiating the proposed settlements, while pointing out that they were perfectly consistent with Woodson's broader perspective, which Cornish endorsed. He perceived Woodson as a budding colonizationist because no reformer who truly opposed the scheme would have insisted that colored people had a "special moral work." He periodically perused the *Colonization Herald* expecting to find letters from Woodson advancing its agenda.[56]

Woodson defended separate settlements by confronting critics' qualms about race categories, which he believed could have multiple meanings and serve varied functions. Judgments about them needed to consider the motives that inspired their use. His aim was to foment a "moral revolution" among colored people. This noble and formidable undertaking required him to accept the reality of social distinctions in order to eradicate the "wicked spirit" that produced them.[57] He dismissed Cornish's claim that social separation consigned colored people to degradation as tantamount to an assertion that they were inherently inferior to White people. If the "moral tendency" of colored people was "naturally downward" when they were alone, he observed, it could not be otherwise when they mixed with others. Social intercourse would be physiologically impossible. Thus, Cornish should either withdraw his criticism or confess that he believed in the "natural inferiority" of colored people.[58]

62 RELUCTANT RACE MEN

Woodson concluded his defense by explaining the significance of skin color. He argued that prejudice would persist because the complexions of colored people were "too obvious" a contrast with white complexions. Since slavery was linked to everyone deemed "colored," they would be tied to the institution's degradation for as long as their appearance could distinguish them from White people. He reasoned, presciently, that even if the institution ended, the memory of it would forever stigmatize colored people. The social meanings of phenotype made separation the only path of escape from the contempt and pity of White bigots and sympathizers.[59]

Parallels between the Reform Society's stance and arguments against Woodson's proposal gave Whipper fodder to charge his critics with inconsistency. He felt vindicated in observing that Cornish's critique of Woodson echoed the society's objections to color distinctions. This was just one of several occasions in which Cornish expressed sentiments that seemed to affirm moral reformers' principles. While castigating the society for its refusal to label proposed educational facilities "colored," Cornish denounced separate churches and schools for colored people. They were "the curses of our country," he argued, and separate settlements were even worse.[60]

Frederick Hinton's opinions came under similar scrutiny. Months after he belittled the society's position, Hinton joined Presbyterian minister Charles Gardner, a member of the AMRS, in drafting a political petition that denounced "distinctions of color." The document issued on behalf of Philadelphia's free people of color protested a legislative proposal to restrict the Pennsylvania franchise to White men. Its central arguments concerned the process of disenfranchisement. Heading the objections was the claim that the proposal violated the principle of natural equality by making distinctions that God did not acknowledge. Although the circumstances Hinton was attempting to redress were radically different from those confronting the Reform Society, Whipper saw the issues as morally indistinguishable. He argued that the "same principle" guided all deployments of color labels. Identifying eligible voters as "white" was thus no different from designating the sphere of moral obligations as "colored."[61]

Repudiations of Woodson's stance failed to diminish censure of the AMRS. Rapprochement with critics seemed impossible. Weary of public scorn, the group tried to remove itself and Whipper from the *Colored American*'s shadow. To assert greater control over the society's image, moral reformers launched a monthly paper of their own at their 1838 meeting. Like Cornish and Russwurm, they saw an independent press as the answer

"THAT ODIOUS DISTINCTION" 63

to misrepresentations and mistreatment. They had faith in the power of "ungarnished truth" to advance the goals of reform. They hypothesized that the lack of a means through which to present their principles had allowed misrepresentations to proliferate. The *National Reformer*'s prospectus complained that, because the society had no medium for explaining its initiatives, observers "grossly misunderstood" its objectives. Whipper disavowed the "silly doctrines" attributed to the society, arguing that it was not true that the group neglected the morality of colored people in favor of elevating White people. It simply refused to rally under the "complexional flag."[62]

From the start, it was apparent that an autonomous press would not shield the AMRS from attacks. Cornish used the occasion of welcoming the paper to cast barbs at Whipper, who remained an agent for the *Colored American*. He assured readers that they would encounter an able editor in Whipper, who might even "soar like an eagle" when he recovered from "mistiness." Cornish predicted that the experiences of moral reformers would ultimately prove the wisdom of Woodson's maxim that there was a peculiar moral work for colored reformers, even for those who adorned their tasks with "national colors."[63]

Cornish's attack was just one instance of ongoing conflicts surrounding the Reform Society. Although the group was still viable in its third year, to the delight of critics, its remaining members fought over the use of color categories in defining the basis and content of reform. Accounts of the 1838 meeting that authorized the new periodical show ongoing support for the society as well as dissension within its ranks. Observers reported to *Colored American* readers that the meeting was well attended and that "a considerable number of ladies" were in the audience. Although the minutes of the meeting do not disclose the numbers of visitors or members in attendance, they suggest that there were at least thirty delegates, which was comparable to participation at the third national convention. An observer noted that the meeting also drew new members into the society's ranks.[64] The pseudonymous "Origen," an AMRS loyalist, added to this positive picture with a report to his congregation that the proceedings were inspiring and productive. The "virtuous" James Forten continued to preside over the group's deliberations, which were intellectually stimulating and of "thrilling interest to the human race." The piety, modesty, and mental acumen of the participants were apparently impressive. Andrew Harris, a recent graduate of the University of Vermont, was especially noteworthy.

64 RELUCTANT RACE MEN

He was a "discriminating logician" who displayed a refined moral character throughout the meeting. A less sympathetic "PENN" countered Origen's rosy image by highlighting the forum's disagreements. According to his recollections, the gathering was small, and a "large minority" of the participants opposed the group's "ultra measures."[65]

As with debates of the previous year, the disputes to which PENN alluded appeared in the press after the society's meeting. The *National Reformer's* account of the proceedings offered scant evidence of discord and only a glimpse of opposition to color designations. It suggests that the group was trying to convey a more moderate sensibility. Were it not for a prefatory statement to the public reflecting Whipper's style and perspective, readers would have seen little of the opinions critics found so objectionable. Affirming the common descent of humanity, the address called for the abolition of "complexional preferences" and the "heathenish spirit of caste" in defining moral duties. The only other hints of this sentiment were Whipper's resolutions questioning color distinctions in ways that even Cornish could have advanced. The first resolution condemned racially segregated churches. The second encouraged loving interactions among Christians "irrespective of color or condition." Both resolutions reportedly passed without debate. However, there were signs that the society's Board of Managers found uncomfortable truths in critics' accusations. Its annual report cited the necessity of delineating a concrete agenda; the managers confessed that the hubris of purporting to reform the entire nation would only alienate people who otherwise shared their views. This sentiment fueled efforts to revive the aims of the national conventions. Members deliberated over such familiar issues as a manual labor school and the use of "free labor" products. Neither issue won broad support. The group agreed only to general resolutions citing the importance of education and praising White abolitionists and emancipation in the British West Indies.[66] Anti-colonization and moral rectitude were successful rallying points. The most concrete public statement addressed the latter issue. It reported data on the "state of the Colored Population" collected by members and correspondents in forty-four cities, towns, and counties in ten states. This statistical table, however rudimentary and inaccurate, tallied churches; clergy; real estate; reform, literary, and benevolent groups; schools; and the incidence of poverty and crime as measures of the moral status of free people of color. Its data refuted charges that colored people were depraved.[67]

The *Colored American* exposed disagreements about color categories that the *National Reformer's* report of the proceedings omitted. Cornish took pleasure in reprinting a letter from the *Pennsylvania Freeman* in which AMRS member William Watkins criticized the group. The document was potentially damning as evidence of dissent and because it suggested that moral reformers were trying to silence him after he missed the annual meeting. In his ongoing attack on the AMRS, Cornish contrasted the letter's "orthodox philosophy" with the society's "defective" views.[68] Despite the fuss surrounding it, the communication was congenial and expressed dissenting opinions that were familiar to his audience. It was, moreover, a sympathizer's suggestions about the society's position and direction since Watkins still identified as part of the group. Yet it is clear that he opposed focusing on the structure of discrimination. He construed the society's fundamental purpose as indistinguishable from that of the national conventions—namely, improving the moral and mental condition of colored people. In his eyes, misplaced discomfort over the term "colored" and with "exclusive" action prevented Whipper and others from declaring this purpose. He attempted to bring philosophical and ethical clarity to the issue. In a didactic style he might have used with pupils in his Baltimore school, he reflected on two related aspects of the group's approach. Although he objected to its "prodigal" use of the word "colored," he concluded that it was appropriate. The designation was far superior to the label "African" and was "philosophically correct" because there was an obvious link between it, "the sign," and "the thing signified." The connection had been established by custom. The moniker, however arbitrary, was no different from other forms of speech that derived their logic and efficacy from usage.[69]

Ultimately, the legitimacy of the label "colored" was incidental to Watkins's understanding of how the Reform Society should identify its objectives. He was concerned about the exclusion of colored people from institutions promoting moral and intellectual development. His colleagues needed to confront this problem. He appreciated their attempts to distinguish moral action from race categories and insisted that "being *colored*" was not a reason for targeted reforms. However, it was a reliable proxy for identifying who lacked resources for sound ethical judgment and behavior. Reformers could name colored people as the exclusive objects of their efforts and remain true to universal principles. This focus would make the society more practical and offer a corrective to its far-reaching designation as "American." The title betrayed a lack of propriety among individuals "just emerging from darkness" purporting to reform a nation of people fully immersed in the ideals of universal liberty.[70]

Watkins's letter made opposition to race a more conspicuous facet of the AMRS. His critique prompted further explanations of the group's official position. Whipper denied that any AMRS members had ever been so fanatical as to advocate the wholesale eradication of the word "colored" from general speech. Yet he insisted on the need to envision reform in universal terms. Since, as Watkins argued, social customs gave meaning to the word "colored," it was evident that long-standing discriminatory practices identified the term with caste. The connection strengthened his resolve to reject racial labels because they narrowed the boundaries of Christian duty and sustained the system of inequality.[71]

The society's modest reform endeavors reflected its ongoing refusal to deploy racial distinctions. Its antislavery platform treated all Americans as equals in needing to understand the principle of universal liberty. In a recapitulation of the society's letter to colored churches, Whipper argued that all free consumers of products made with slave labor helped to deprive people of freedom. Complexion did not mitigate or heighten guilt. In forging an antislavery alliance with freed people in the British West Indies, Whipper, Robert Purvis, and Andrew Harris urged their allies to avoid all "complexional banners." The cause of universal emancipation, they admonished, demanded adherence to universal moral principles.[72]

Lessons on "economy" pointed to the need for moral reform among White and colored people. Whipper observed that the nation's racial caste system ensured that Americans received constant exposure to claims about the "natural inferiority" of colored people. This experience eroded appreciation for human equality. It was thus imperative for reformers to confront the material benefits and moral debts that race practices bestowed upon individuals "distinguished by the term 'white.' " He denounced the structures that protected the interests of White men as a "complexion tariff" that deprived others of the opportunity to participate in society as equals. He derided the misguided sense of superiority he witnessed among men who benefitted from the "protective system" of White privilege. If they were unwilling to abolish caste arrangements, he argued, they should at least be honest enough to abandon their prattle of superiority over African intelligence.[73]

The high moral and psychological toll of subjugation presented reformers with another problem. They wanted to help colored people overcome the "moral stupor" that resulted from race practices. A report of distorted reasoning shed light on the problem. A widespread preference for light complexions and straight hair, the assumption that whiteness was a "badge of merit" and standard of goodness, a reluctance to lead moral reform initiatives, and submissive attitudes in interactions with White people were prevalent among individuals who accepted the logic of race. Overcoming these defects required colored people to shun "every vestige of distinction." They had to reject the idea that skin color and racial designations were indicators of meaningful and legitimate human differences.[74]

In its fourth year, the AMRS still clung to its ambition of instituting reforms through local temperance and moral reform societies, schools, and alliances with churches and antislavery networks. However, persistent criticism and internal tensions made implementation of such initiatives impossible. Reform endeavors remained largely confined to its newspaper commentaries. Although the group held annual meetings through 1841, after it discontinued its paper in 1839, there was little chance that it could continue to function as a viable reform association. Its existence was precarious despite reported participation levels that suggest it was thriving. Attendance at its annual proceedings peaked at fifty-eight. Yet the meeting was largely a local affair. Daniel Payne of Troy, New York, was the only delegate from outside of Pennsylvania, and he was considering migrating to Trinidad. Whipper publicly lamented that the meeting was flawed because it had not attracted people of different regions, complexions, antislavery societies, and churches. He boasted, nevertheless, that it had upheld principle and avoided expediency.[75]

A decision to espouse a universal moral code that meant abandoning gender distinctions expanded the group's base of support. On the final evening of the society's fall meeting, members amended their constitution to stipulate that individuals would be accepted "without regard to sex." Seventeen Philadelphia women were immediately included in the roster of delegates. This enactment was logically consistent with the society's position that moral distinctions were the only legitimate way of dividing humans. It mirrored the policy of the Philadelphia auxiliary of admitting women, which led to Hester Burr's election several months earlier. Moreover, it resonated with the idea of gender equality Whipper expressed in refusing to create a separate women's section in the *National Reformer* on the grounds that women and men were equal. Although these convictions justified the inclusion of women, the ad hoc manner of the change at the close of the forum suggests that fears about a dwindling constituency inspired it.[76]

An expanded membership base failed to ensure conformity with the society's creed regarding color designations. The platforms of local affiliates

68 RELUCTANT RACE MEN

reflected the same divergent opinions on this matter that led some members to defect. Samuel Cornish reveled in this fact. He printed the constitution of the reform society in Cranberry, New Jersey, to show that AMRS members disagreed with the group's leaders. He praised the local association's "definite" objectives, which named colored people as its beneficiaries. Although it was Cornish's only example, Cranberry was not an isolated phenomenon. At least three other societies, in Pittsburgh, Pennsylvania, and Burlington and Bordentown, New Jersey, indicated that they existed to carry out moral reforms among colored people.[77] If Whipper was chagrined by deviations from his standard, he masked it. He vacillated between using the Cranberry case to rebut charges that the Reform Society had no local applicability and defending the auxiliary's orthodoxy by insisting that specificity made the group's principles no less "pure" than the aims of associations with universal perspectives. He explained that the society's universal principles sparked the impulse to initiate reforms "among those with whom we are identified by complexion, by suffering, and by wrong." Lest he appear to be imparting a "complexional standard," he used the occasion to restate his opposition to all initiatives that transformed skin color into qualifications. Such arrangements were "unchristian, anti-moral, and anti-republican."[78]

———

The constitutional disenfranchisement of Northern colored men proved to be a more formidable threat to the viability of the AMRS than diminished numbers and deviations in aims of local affiliates. In 1838, Pennsylvania joined Connecticut and New York in adopting a constitutional amendment that restricted the vote to White men. Connecticut had enacted such a provision in 1818. New York effectively disenfranchised its colored population in 1821 by subjecting it to a $250 property requirement that was abolished for White men. This change meant that only sixteen colored New Yorkers were eligible voters in 1826, and no more than 3 percent of the state's free colored population was ever eligible to vote before the Civil War. New Jersey had barred colored people from voting in 1807 and made this restriction a constitutional reality in 1844.[79]

The effect of state-by-state denial of political rights was twofold. It undermined a fundamental premise of the AMRS. Although its designation as "American" expressed a nationalist sentiment rather than a claim about its geographic reach, the group's reform vision was expansive. Claims to American citizenship created the imperatives for Whipper's activism, grounding his insistence that "moral power" transcended complexional and state boundaries. Disenfranchisement confronted him and others with a diminished sphere of citizenship and, hence, of moral action. They had to contend with the fact that states regulated the terms of citizenship; it was not a national phenomenon. Outraged by the reform implications of this situation, Whipper decried the fact that colored people could make no claims on the American government. There was "no federal union" that could link their diverse experiences across individual states. The long-standing problem of finding a stable basis for reform actions had mutated and become more intractable.[80]

Political exclusion undermined the logic of reformers' appeals to citizenship more directly and profoundly than did colonization efforts. Their claims seemed groundless without the rights associated with free men, even if they confined their notions of citizenship to states. The situation brought moral reformers face to face with the reality that political participation defined nationality and freedom. This complex connection became a popular cant among White men who pronounced the right to vote "the only true badge of the freeman."[81] Colored men shared this sentiment. Charles Ray, who replaced Cornish at the *Colored American*, declared it a disgrace to live as a political "cypher" when political rights were the "bulwark" of freedom. "Coloured Citizens" in slaveholding Washington, DC, observed that "Franchise Liberty" was a distinguishing trait of citizens.[82] Without it, reformers had to reinterpret the character of their freedom. Even if they managed to fend off wholesale colonization, their status as citizens was unstable. The idea that colored reformers would forever enact citizenship solely through reform associations was untenable.

Yet disenfranchisement did nothing to diminish Whipper's belief in grounding reform in the concept of American citizenship. It hardened his stance on the immorality of color distinctions. Moreover, it disabused him of any lingering attachment to the idea that moral improvement was a key to rights. Since it had not been aborted at conception, he argued, the notion "should have been annihilated at its birth." If anything needed improvement to remove barriers to rights, it was White people's hearts, not colored people's morals. He surmised that the imposition of moral standards for rights would disenfranchise "half the white population." His conviction that birth was the sole qualification for citizenship rights was unwavering. To suggest that religion, morality, or mental ability was a condition for exercising political privileges was to commit a "fatal error." Immorality, wickedness, ignorance, and a lack of piety did not cause disenfranchisement. It arose from the "wicked principle" of color distinctions.[83] The notion that the franchise was a moral issue gave undue credence to individual prejudice and obscured the structure of injustice. While assuring *National Reformer* readers of the power of religion, humanity, and even legislation to overcome bigotry, he urged them to jettison the false idea that elevation could earn rights for colored people.

Disenfranchisement and the decline of the Reform Society brought Whipper and his opponents to a turning point. He made conciliatory gestures toward critics. Calling for "new terms" for addressing inequality, he conceded that the society had failed to translate its principles into a viable basis of association. As a result, free people were bereft of the broad base of representation they had in national conventions. A revisionist assessment of the disputes over the past four years turned conflicting moral visions into "minor differences." Nevertheless, Charles Ray, Junius Morel, and others were open to reconciliation and concurred with Whipper that their conflicts amounted to small disputes over "method of organization." Morel reestablished ties with the society through a letter that praised the *National Reformer* and declared, "I am with you." Ray observed that a combined struggle of White and colored reformers to bring about social equality was the primary task ahead. Because he thought that the AMRS shared this belief, he insisted that it needed to say as much by naming colored people as the objects of its agenda. This simple modification could secure the group's popularity and effectiveness.[84] However sincere, attempts at reconciliation failed because the conflicts were not merely about tactics. Disparate perspectives on color classifications and divergent views of the terms of association and authority resulted in seemingly irreconcilable ethical positions. Whipper's closing words to *National Reformer* readers suggest how little he was willing to compromise. The paper expired with his renunciation of "all COMPLEXIONAL ALLEGIANCE with every class of mankind."[85]

A fractured reform discourse set the stage for ongoing tensions among people who shared misgivings about race categories. From this impasse, it was impossible for anyone to anticipate the scenario of the next two decades, when individuals who defended "exclusive" reform endeavors would expand opposition to race practices. Increased attention to political matters would shift concerns away from defining obligations to establishing authority. The fervor of race challenges would shape the claims of growing ranks of reformers and infuse a broader range of endeavors.

3

"One Common Family"

Equality and the Logic of Authority

The 1841 New York County convention stood deadlocked for five days. Delegates could not settle on a rationale for extending suffrage to colored men. At issue was whether it was more appropriate to base their claim to the franchise on contributions to the nation's independence or on membership in a "common humanity" and the principle of human equality. Supporters of the first proposition maintained that sacrifices of colored Revolutionary War soldiers justified political rights for subsequent generations of colored men. Theodore Wright, a Princeton Theological Seminary graduate, defended entitlements to the military legacy by noting that such claims were common among other groups. Opposing delegates rejected the idea of inheriting collective rights based on a shared racial designation, asserting that only the biological sons of soldiers could truthfully make such appeals. Furthermore, they refused to construe citizenship rights as compensation. Charles Ray and physician James McCune Smith argued that suffrage demands had to rest on "more impregnable grounds" than service. They viewed the natural characteristics colored men shared with fully enfranchised citizens as the only stable foundation for their rights. Put simply, they deserved the vote because they were men.

On the final day of the convention, the fifty-six-member delegation was still at an impasse, with an equal number of participants supporting each option. All agreed that New York's property requirement for colored voters abrogated republican tenets because it imposed a price on rights that were intrinsic to manhood. Furthermore, participants deemed it undemocratic to make the privileges of freemen a function of racial classifications. Despite common aims and shared convictions about rights, the factions could not agree on what constituted a valid basis for their collective bid for political authority. Thus, the proceedings closed with the demand for equality unexplained.[1]

Reluctant Race Men. Joan L. Bryant, Oxford University Press. © Oxford University Press 2024.
DOI: 10.1093/oso/9780195312966.003.0004

The local stalemate reflected broader ideological divisions and concerns about building logical foundations for pursuing equality and rights. A commitment to rational and ethical arguments was critical to reformers' sense of mission and their drive for public influence. It helped fuel misgivings about race practices, such that principles previously associated with the American Moral Reform Society informed a range of undertakings. They shaped efforts to secure political rights, advance civil and religious equality, sustain antislavery alliances, and assess warrants for emigration. Activism on each of these fronts entailed grappling with disparate interpretations and configurations of race to construct sound bases of authority.

An ongoing push for change inspired fresh race challenges, as experienced and novice reformers joined forces to launch local and state conventions, reconstitute national conventions, and nurture existing reform networks. Such enterprises brought old and new discursive patterns to bear on deliberations over rights, freedom, the morality of racially exclusive institutions, causes of discrimination, and US citizenship. A wide array of initiatives rendered queries about race diffuse, ad hoc, and inconsistent. They flourished in independent conventions, churches, and newspapers and defied neat distinctions between integrationist and separatist agendas. An ideologically diverse set of individuals confronting disparate issues shared concerns about the potential effects of race practices on their quests for authority as freemen who identified as citizens, Christians, and reformers.

The issues that inspired race challenges reflect the broad scope of efforts to contest limitations on freedom and citizenship. The myriad phenomena that structured American inequality reduced the nation to what Samuel Ringgold Ward dubbed a "pseudo-republic." It required diverse interventions. Political disenfranchisement, combined with exclusion from schools, employment restrictions, unequal access to public space, discrimination in reform circles, and "negro-pewism" in Christian churches compromised the colored population's ability to participate in American society as free people and citizens. The deadlock over voting initiatives was just one of the factors complicating the reform terrain of the 1840s and 1850s. The landscape was marked by challenges to notions of human difference and hierarchy, repudiations of racialized notions of sameness, questions about appropriate racial designations, and appeals to a common ground of human existence.

74   RELUCTANT RACE MEN

The New York County debate grew out of controversies surrounding state conventions in the 1840s. Northern disenfranchisement prompted a heightened sense of urgency about organizing to secure rights. Political exclusion made conventions logical arenas for group action. It also reinforced convictions that racial configurations of difference were ethically and logically unsound. State officials did not try to justify voting prohibitions with evidence that colored men were mentally incompetent or morally depraved, nor did voting legislation stipulate that only intelligent and virtuous men could exercise the franchise. Color designations sufficed to justify and implement measures to deprive certain free men of voting rights. Simply by inserting the term "white" into state constitutions, officials indicated which men could not have access to the franchise without having to explain the logic or ethics of inclusion and exclusion. Such actions accentuated connections between racial categories and configurations of injustice.

The impulse to organize for rights collided with ambivalence about reviving national conventions. Lewis Woodson, writing as "Augustine," along with the pseudonymous "Americanus" worried that colored reformers had no coherent platform for collective interstate endeavors despite the widespread discrimination they faced. They argued that a national forum needed to have a clearly delineated "common object," which they did not believe existed.[2] David Ruggles, secretary for the New York Vigilance Committee, disagreed. He cited colonization, repressive Black Codes, and disenfranchisement as issues that could frame a broad initiative. He proposed a "National Reform Convention of the Colored Inhabitants of the United States of America" to be held in New Haven, Connecticut, in the fall of 1840. Many dismissed the undertaking as too hasty. Not surprisingly, William Whipper, Robert Purvis, and Junius Morel criticized the plan for relying on false "badges of distinction" that could not function as truly national bases of authority.[3]

The concept of race and ideas about skin color created practical difficulties for coalitions, even after the re-establishment of conventions. Optimistic pronouncements that they were united as "one people" did little to minimize difficulties of forming and sustaining collective initiatives. In 1854, when the sustainability of annual national conventions seemed dim, physician James McCune Smith, using the pseudonym "Communipaw," considered the source of disunity. Scientific and statistical interests and six years of study for three University of Glasgow degrees informed his perspectives on activism. He concluded that the great impediment to establishing coherent bases of reform was the fact that colored people confronted different "species

"ONE COMMON FAMILY" 75

of oppression." He could enumerate "two thousand distinct forms" of discrimination against them. Biases regarding variations in skin color further complicated matters. Complexional distinctions and caste were not solely matters of White people versus other groups. There was a correlation between the magnitude of subjugation and darkness of complexion within the colored population. He believed the many facets of "unequal oppression" required reformers to realize the necessity of combatting public opinion—a foe that injured them all—and denounce injustices in all realms.[4]

Controversy plagued Northern state and regional conventions from the very start. The forums sparked immediate objections to "exclusive" initiatives. For some, the issue was a straightforward matter of whether to include White people in their deliberations. Others questioned the validity of race categories as bases of reform. White reformers' input presented additional considerations. For example, Nathaniel Rogers, editor of the *National Anti-Slavery Standard*, opposed colored reformers operating independent forums because he believed they should act under the auspices of the American Anti-Slavery Society. He worried that conventions would prevent White people from forgetting "color"—a step he deemed necessary. "You cannot be free," he admonished, until White people "see and feel that you are *men*. They do not feel it yet." Although he thought segregated colored schools, churches, and benevolent associations were essential, he viewed exclusive campaigns for rights as unsound for people who were politically debased. They were also unnecessary because "thousands of whites" stood ready to help. He urged reformers to follow the example of their White counterparts, reasoning disingenuously that White reformers did not maintain exclusive associations; "such a thing in the struggle for principles is unheard of," he declared, "save among the colored people."[5]

Other White reformers simply expressed a desire to participate in promoting equal political rights. Speaking on their behalf, James McCune Smith questioned the wisdom of holding an exclusive colored convention in New York. He reported that Isaac Hopper, founding president of New York State's interracial vigilance committee, along with abolitionists William Chace and James Gibbons wanted to aid the push for equal suffrage. Although Charles Ray dismissed Smith's appeal and criticized Nathaniel Rogers as despotic, he defended holding a convention only for colored men by arguing that White people supported the idea. It mattered little that the endorsement came from people who accepted the legitimacy of slavery. The two "respectable" newspapers he named that "indirectly" commended the

76 RELUCTANT RACE MEN

initiative opposed universal freedom.[6] Concerns about exclusivity and distinctiveness remained so thorny and entrenched that, as late as 1859, William Wells Brown opened the New England convention by confessing ambivalence about proceedings solely for colored people. He seemed to concur, in part, with Nathaniel Rogers that the independent convention would be unnecessary if colored people had participated more fully with White people in antislavery societies. The gathering and other initiatives that appeared to take "separate action from ... white fellow-citizens" unsettled him.[7]

Debates that prefaced and followed the 1840 New York state convention in Albany displayed shifting alliances and divergent perspectives on using color categories in organizing for rights. Theodore Wright and Charles Ray played prominent roles at the gathering, whereas James McCune Smith and his allies were conspicuously absent. Ray and Smith, who shared editorial responsibilities for the *Colored American*, were opponents in the discordant prelude to the meeting. One year later, they would be allies in the New York County conflict. Smith opposed the state convention because it was "distinguished by complexion" instead of being based on principle. The "separate action," he argued, sent a message that there was a logical correlation between rights and racial designations. He reasoned further that using "complexional distinctions" to set the parameters of participation contradicted the ideal of equality that colored reformers were trying to realize. The exclusion of abolitionists who identified with disenfranchised people and felt "oppressed from *the same cause*" enraged him because its sole reason was that "their complexion is different." Echoing moral reformers' sentiments, Smith likened independent reform arrangements to the strictures used to oppress colored people. The former seemed to validate the latter.[8]

Charles Ray was indignant about the suggestion that the convention undermined standards of equality. He declared that he had "always been opposed ... to exclusive action." Necessity, however, compelled him to support a convention of colored citizens, which he pointedly distinguished from a "Colored Convention." Because the group acted out of need and had no explicit intention to exclude any prospective participants, it was impossible to claim that it deviated from principle. Furthermore, it appeared nonsensical for Smith to equate a meeting of disenfranchised citizens with color-coded political rights. Ray argued that the convention had universal foundations, even though it restricted participation to colored men. Its demands for equal access to the franchise stemmed from a belief in "the rights of man." This reasoning was consistent with Ray's broader views on how colored reformers should relate to the United States. He insisted that they were part of the nation and identified with other Americans and American interests. Nevertheless, as long as caste arrangements blocked equality, it was essential for reformers to acknowledge and address the "special interests" of colored people. Exclusive conventions stemmed from an obligation to confront this reality.[9]

Old conflicts resurfaced after the Albany gathering adjourned. William Whipper used the meeting and the debate it inspired to stake out an offensive position, attacking the state convention in the *Colored American*. The discord was another occasion for him to offer lessons on the tenets of true reform. He continued to worry about the logic of "complexional distinctions" in defining the terms of inclusion. Disenfranchisement reinforced his conviction that legitimate reform organizations must refuse to sanction the idea that skin color was a coherent and valid index of sameness or difference. He pushed for a "reformation" that would foster moral authority needed to effect political and social change. Although he did not express Smith's preference for inviting White participants, he echoed his conclusion about the significance of exclusive organizations. Associations whose parameters relied on "complexional variations," he reasoned, fortified justifications for slavery and disenfranchisement. Feigned praise for the Albany convention suggested that it affirmed this position. The convention had declared that all laws and systems "founded on the SPIRIT OF COMPLEXIONAL CAST [*sic*]" violated divine decrees and should be destroyed. Conflating a denunciation of hierarchy with his opposition to all racial configurations of difference, Whipper declared the group's pronouncement tantamount to a condemnation of "complexionally distinctive organizations." It appeared to simultaneously indict delegates for wrong-headed action and broadcast a message for others to refrain from basing associations on "the complexion of the human form."[10]

Ray dismissed Whipper's arguments and deflected criticism by elaborating on how color distinctions configured inequality. He pointed out that Whipper failed to acknowledge the term "spirit" that qualified the reference to "complexional caste." To expose the groundlessness of Whipper's accusations, he explained that a caste spirit was a "false assumption" that there was "some natural arrangement" that rendered certain men inferior and justified discrimination and hatred. Disposition and intent thus distinguished virtuous projects from corrupt actions. In other words, even if some people used color categories to structure rank, reformers could deploy the terms for just ends. They could signify multiple things because motivations

78   RELUCTANT RACE MEN

and aims shaped their meanings. Such ideas were untenable to Whipper. In his mind, racial categories, by definition, forged unjustifiable differences and hierarchies of complexion and ancestry. His moral and conceptual framework disallowed the possibility that reformers could reconfigure them or use them without affirming the logic of injustice and subjugation.[11]

The New York state convention's insistence on operating without White participation did not translate into a categorical defense of race. Yet clashes over the "colored" label that referenced segregated reform actions obscured the fact that the group's condemnations of race practices extended beyond assaults on caste. The language used to denounce color categories targeted all configurations of racial difference, suggesting that they could have no merit. It provided fodder for Whipper to gloat that the convention's position was compatible with the American Moral Reform Society's platform. New York's property requirement was flawed, delegates argued, because it used erroneous conceptions of difference to make distinctions among citizens. They decried the mere "toleration of complexional difference" for defiling constitutional values. Neither skin color nor race categories were valid grounds for rights, they reasoned, because the former was a product of chance and the latter was solely a matter of custom.[12] The legislature erred in making rights a function of "arbitrary" and "unnatural" distinctions. It violated the ideals of equality in the Declaration of Independence by relying on "accidental circumstances" and "factitious arrangements" in conceptions of rights. The imputation of difference was unjust "not because it restricts us socially," delegates asserted, but because it was not a logical basis for barring men from political participation.[13]

Charles Ray, Theodore Wright, and other outspoken delegates took pains to frame their actions as the work of native-born Americans and descendants of natives who fully imbibed the nation's political culture. They pointed out that the blood of "dark browed" men infused the soil of the country's battlefields. These factors were only "considerations," they argued, not suffrage justifications, for they would not "fall into the error of basing rights on grounds so untenable." They added that they would never predicate rights on skin complexion or other features of the human body, asserting that no ethical standards would sanction such claims.[14]

Challenges facing the New York state convention resonated across time and regions. It became commonplace to interpret disenfranchisement and civil rights injustices as artificial restrictions on the boundaries of humanity, manhood, freedom, and citizenship. Typical petitions assailed state reliance on "color" for dividing "freemen into castes." The "odious distinction" was all the more despicable, reformers argued, because states required colored people to perform the duties of citizens. Using such logic, participants in the 1841 Albany County convention argued that their claims to suffrage were identical to the claims of citizens "of a different hue." The legislature's construction of "arbitrary and invidious distinctions" violated principles of republican governance and Christian standards of human equality. It robbed men of their rightful standing as members of the political community.[15] New York conventions held after 1840 also assailed such denials as contrary to "the very essence" of republicanism and citizenship, because they singled out individuals from "the mass" of equals to subject them to differential and abusive treatment. The use of race categories to limit the franchise thus undermined the collective sovereignty of citizens and turned the republic into a theater of tyranny. In 1858, the final antebellum convention delegation of New Yorkers echoed the cry against political castes by condemning state race practices that violated the constitutional rights that were theirs "as part of the people."[16]

Other state conventions joined the chorus that criticized color distinctions as antithetical to free manhood. The conviction that political discrimination was at odds with human kinship guided the campaign for rights at the 1849 Connecticut convention in New Haven. Spokespersons Amos Beman, George Francis, and Samuel Gray prefaced their appeal with a profession of faith in voters' commitment to truth, reason, and honor. They conjectured that the only way to make sense of disenfranchisement would be to inscribe "hypocrite" on the gravestones of the nation's founders. Citing eighteenth-century British jurist Sir William Blackstone, they presented their push for redress as a sign of loyalty to principles that shielded a man's access to rights from such "accidents of his birth" as complexion. "Ours is a claim of humanity," they argued, characterizing the franchise as recognition of natural relations among men. Withholding it scorned nature by denying the existence of "common brotherhood."[17] As if anticipating charges that ignorance, immorality, or subjugation made them unfit to vote, delegates insisted that skin color was not an indicator of an individual's virtues, intelligence, capacity for just action, or "personal degradation." As evidence, they cited steady increases in schooling and literacy, property ownership, temperance initiatives, and religious institutions—feats the colored population accomplished in spite of discriminatory obstacles to its advancement. These tokens of worthiness were not substitutes for the fact that manhood sufficed as

80 RELUCTANT RACE MEN

grounds for rights. Participants emphasized this point by contrasting their status with classes they thought were justifiably barred from political participation—"women, minors, aliens, criminals, the insane, and idiots." They treated the designations as self-evident reasons for exclusion.[18]

In New Jersey, small-town residents urged reformers to organize for manhood suffrage at the state capital. Leaders of the delegation were pioneering AME minister and former American Moral Reform Society member Joshua Woodlin, newly established Presbyterian minister William Catto, physician John Rock, and his fellow Salem County native Ishmael Locke—grandfather of Harlem Renaissance philosopher Alain Locke. The specter of colonization loomed over their push for citizenship rights. Locke remained in poor health after abandoning a Quaker-sponsored teaching post in Liberia. Catto had recently fled north, eluding retaliation from Southern sponsors for aborting preparations to migrate to Liberia for missionary work.[19] Nevertheless, unlike many other delegations, the group maintained a singular focus on the franchise. They explained to citizens of the state that, as possessors of the same "rationality, knowledge, and feelings" held by privileged segments of "civilized mankind," they were not ignorant of their manhood. They had heard endless declarations of the nation's founding principles concerning men's "natural and inalienable rights" and learned the precept: "Political power is inherent in the people." These factors, along with their audience's accountability to God and claims to justice, patriotism, intelligence, and honesty indicated that the duty to contest voting prohibitions did not belong solely to the victims. Individuals committed to practicing "good citizenship" should petition the legislature to remove the word "white" from state voting provisions. Because manhood explained their right to suffrage, delegates gave little notice to the notion of "color" that structured their disenfranchisement beyond speculating that it reflected conservatism, ignorance, or bigotry.[20]

Rock extended appeals for rights in calls for petitions after the convention. With assertions of manhood, he sought state acknowledgement of a natural phenomenon. The inconsistency of withholding equal rights from colored men while requiring them to pay taxes and obey the law highlighted legislators' defective thinking and bogus conceptions of justice. He reviled their reasoning as indistinguishable from the "sophistry" of colonizationists. Insisting that birth, not lineage, determined a person's homeland, he decried actions that distorted nature to consign free colored populations to select parts of the world and declare "*any place the white man chooses to go, HIS country."* The custom of treating "color" as valid grounds for refusing to aid other human beings and upholding White supremacy exposed the failure of lawmakers and "titular philanthropists" to meet the ethical demands of manhood. They did not deserve "the name of man."[21]

Ohioans contested disenfranchisement by taking aim at their state's convoluted configurations of difference. The 1856 convention address to the legislature from a committee chaired by abolitionist editor Peter Clark expanded on a memorial to lawmakers that attorney John Langston prepared two years earlier. Representing twenty-five thousand "half freeman," Langston staked franchise claims on a shared humanity, society's obligations, and birthright citizenship. "We possess . . . the attributes common to humanity," he declared. "We have the same feelings, desires and aspirations that other men have; and we are capable of the same high intellectual and moral culture. As men then, we have . . . inherent rights, which civil society . . . is bound to protect and defend." He explained that disenfranchisement deprived colored men of the citizenship they possessed as a matter of "established principle," as well as "reason and common sense."[22] When he and nine other delegates drafted the state convention address, they lampooned the idea that "difference of race" provided coherent warrants for excluding colored people from political membership. Conflating race with nationality, they insisted that colored people did not comprise a different race because they were Americans, "not Africans." Disenfranchisement was unjustified because, in consigning them to an alien race, the state failed to acknowledge their rightful identity. The men further pointed out that colored people's attachment to this country was like that of other human beings to their homes. Alluding to eighteenth-century scientific racial taxonomies, they compared their fidelity to the land of their birth to the supposed innate characteristic that made Laplanders prefer "snows and skins" to Italian silks. For the sake of argument, however, they entertained the possibility that White and colored people did constitute divergent races and concluded that such a scenario would necessitate equal access to the franchise because it would make White people incapable of advocating on their behalf. Standards of group representation would require colored men to participate in the polity in order to speak for themselves.[23]

A law allowing Ohioans with Black and White ancestors to vote further displayed illogical constructions of difference. It extended the franchise to "a large portion" of the state's colored population. The provision stemmed from an 1842 state supreme court decision in *Jeffries v. Ankney*, which ruled that men whose ancestry was "more than half white" were eligible to

82 RELUCTANT RACE MEN

vote.[24] Delegates observed that members of this favored class were no better equipped to wield the franchise than other colored men. Even the "most obtuse intellect," they argued, could discern that this statute granting preferential treatment was but a feeble attempt to lend precision to the illogical practice of basing rights on the "accident of color." It failed to obscure the state's irrational and unjust actions that created and sustained distinctions among freemen.[25]

Questioning racial designations in suffrage campaigns was hardly a universal practice. Some defenders of "exclusive" conventions insisted on labeling collective endeavors as "colored." "A Friend" writing in the *Colored American* perceived the term as a designation for a phenotypic reality. Thus, critics of the label were guilty of disparaging God-given complexions. "Friend" conjectured that only people who found dark skin loathsome would object to the word "colored." The bias showed a need to eradicate bigotry instead of avoiding words.[26] Henry Highland Garnet agreed. Writing as "Sidney," he defended using "colored" in general speech because it captured the "undeniable fact" of ancestral ties to "the negro race." The term was also necessary to label targeted initiatives to contend with long-standing experiences of oppression. The name and the need it signified were inseparable. In a similar vein, Lewis Woodson invoked the rules of language to assess the validity of racial designations. He insisted that it was appropriate to refer to citizens and their associations as "colored" because a word that conveyed a "true idea of the quality of the thing named" fulfilled a function of language.[27]

Woodson's reasoning, coupled with the premium he placed on moral improvement to promote political advancement, guided him in initiating Pennsylvania state conventions. By spearheading a gathering to advance suffrage for colored men, he and allies in Pittsburgh and elsewhere supplanted American Moral Reform Society aims to make the faltering organization a leading force in demanding voting rights for "all the citizens of the free States."[28] He reported that a "citizen of Columbia"—a likely reference to Whipper—advised the planning committee that he would rather waive his right to suffrage "than obtain it by holding a Convention distinguished by complexion!" The *Colored American* reported that a "GREAT MEETING" of Philadelphians dissented from Whipper and other Reform Society leaders and applauded the "complexional distinction" used to set Pennsylvania's convention parameters. The group selected fifteen men to represent them at the convention, including some former AMRS members. Although they did not attend the gathering, delegates added their names to the official roster to acknowledge their support.[29]

The Pittsburgh convention announcement suggested that it would follow the pattern of contesting disenfranchisement as an act premised on false racial notions of difference. It denounced the baseless "political annihilation" enacted by Pennsylvania officials by pointing out that it arose from "no other cause" than the fact that God created some people "with a dark hue." Participants echoed this stance at their meeting, decrying all state constitutional restrictions "founded upon complexion," labeling them "impolitic, oppressive, and wrong."[30] Proposed remedies for the situation made it clear that, although delegates perceived the actions as unjustly punitive, harmful to colored people, and damaging to the state's honor, they did not view racial constructs undergirding disenfranchisement as the real problem. Political exclusion, they reasoned, was an expression of understandable biases against degradation and immorality in the free colored population. Woodson and his colleagues declared, "It is a mistake to suppose that there is any prejudice against mere color." Evidence lay in the observation that elite men and women, "distinguished alike for their learning, their virtues, and their taste," acquired furniture and clothing made with black fabric, a color "universally considered . . . rich and magnificent."[31] This interpretation placed the burden for change on people of African descent. Accordingly, "Colored Freemen" comprised the target audience of the convention address. With an eye toward improving their conduct and lifestyles, delegates admonished them to avoid claiming public space with parades and extolled the virtues of education, temperance, paying taxes, and farming. They suggested that these steps would change the group's condition in ways that would destroy White people's prejudices.[32] Presumably, they would facilitate the dismantling of barriers to rights.

Although the Pittsburgh delegations' ideas about blackness were distinctive among responses to disenfranchisement, the group's priorities were not novel. On one hand, they reflected the sorts of concerns that shaped the initial national conventions. They were also in sync with persistent reform struggles over balancing demands for rights with commitments to rectitude and worries about popular perceptions of free people of color. Such tensions were on display at the 1853 Illinois state convention as it tried to carry out a broad reform agenda. It demanded the elimination of all state statutes that distinguished people by complexion and condemned the "unnatural prejudice" against the colored population. Yet it declared that American bigotry

84 RELUCTANT RACE MEN

was "not against color" and thus admonished colored people to improve aspects of their condition that inspired it. Amassing wealth, acquiring property, practicing temperance, gaining education, and becoming "respectable" promised to pave the way to equality. Similar sentiments prevailed among delegates to California's 1855 convention, organized to protest the exclusion of court testimony from individuals deemed to possess "one-half or more of negro blood." Mifflin Gibbs, who would become the nation's first elected municipal judge, protested a resolution attributing the ban to White people's misperceptions of colored people's "intellectual and social condition." He refused to accept the "undignified" and futile burden of presenting evidence of colored people's capacity to participate in civic affairs.[33] A majority of the delegation disagreed with him.

Seven years passed before Pennsylvanians launched another state convention. It marked the resumption of leadership efforts by Whipper and other members of the defunct Reform Society. They had not been idle. Antislavery and other reform endeavors claimed their attention as they continued to question the assumption that colored people, by definition, needed to be elevated to deserve rights. Whipper, Purvis, and James Bias admonished Pennsylvania abolitionists to expunge the language of improving the free colored population from their missions and agendas. They rejected enduring correlations between color classifications and moral condition and urged their antislavery allies to battle social privileges "founded on complexion" and demand equal civil rights.[34]

The 1848 gathering was, for Whipper and other AMRS loyalists, a venue in which to carry out moral obligations of free men committed to republicanism. It was also an occasion to try to institutionalize control over endeavors to secure the franchise. Two of the meeting's earliest actions reflect the latter goal. The first was the creation of a new organization—the Citizens' Union of the Commonwealth of Pennsylvania. Its constitution, which delegates reportedly adopted, expanded the objectives and participant base of suffrage campaigns beyond men. Its goal was to secure "all the Rights and Immunities of Citizenship" for "the colored people" of the state. "Any person," eighteen or older, who was or aspired to be a state citizen and paid fifty cents in annual dues could be a member. Although there is no indication that this entity developed, the convention record of its endorsement indicates that organizing as "coloured citizens" to extend rights to colored men did not quell the desire to avoid using racial categories as bases of reform initiatives. It also implies that some participants supported women's rights.[35]

"ONE COMMON FAMILY" 85

The second action, the formation of a Philadelphia-based conventional board that would function as a state parent organization, signals a bid for power. Administrative responsibilities would rest with the unit, which would coordinate operations with local affiliates. Robert Purvis was elected board president. Other officers included young reform partners—Vice President Isaiah Wears, son of a vigilance committee ally, and physician David Jones Peck, a corresponding secretary whose father presided over the 1841 state convention. As a board manager, Mifflin Gibbs was building on alliances he established with Purvis, Wears, and others through the Philadelphia Library Company of Colored Persons, successor of the Reading Room Society. There, as an untutored apprentice, he learned to appreciate the "acumen and eloquence" of discussion. It nurtured his manhood by helping him understand "the inseparable relations of man to man and the mutuality of obligation."[36]

The presence of Reform Society critics made it impossible to dismiss their viewpoints. John Vashon, one of the men charged with drafting the 1841 convention address with Lewis Woodson, became convention president. Martin Delany, Woodson's one-time protégé, participated in the meeting as an honorary member. The Philadelphia delegation included men who protested moral reformers' objections to the Pittsburgh meeting; namely, John Bowers, Samuel Van Brackle, and James McCrummell, who was also a conventional board member. The resolution concerning convention addresses reflects the delegation's divergent perspectives. A call to address Pennsylvania voters was consistent with suffrage campaigns in other conventions, but the rationale for an appeal to the state's colored citizens was at odds with sentiments among Reform Society stalwarts. It reflected the ethos of the 1841 convention in citing a need for them to "vindicate their right to the enjoyment of citizenship" through good conduct. The burden of negotiating the competing sentiments fell to seven delegates—James Bias, Mifflin Gibbs, Isaac Dickson, Robert Purvis, Abraham Shadd, Samuel Van Brackle, and William Whipper.[37] The published addresses display compromises and irreconcilable differences regarding the significance of racial classifications in political reform.

The address to voters warns that suffrage demands were not pleas for new foundations of government. They were consistent with religious and political principles touted throughout the nation. The issue is "solely a question of rights," delegates advised, and it sprang from voters' "own republican creed."[38] Despite the conviction that their objectives were logical and just, they insisted that submitting petitions and calling on others to do so were the only actions they could take to promote change. This assertion countered the assumption that moral improvement would earn rights. Instead, it reflected an attempt to indict the legislature for implicating God and nature in disenfranchisement by referring to the natural phenomenon of complexion as the basis for recognizing rights. This stance meant that intellectual achievements, economic successes, and moral pursuits that reflected the purity of Jesus would be powerless to make colored men politically equal to any man classified as "white." It was thus essential for the voting audience to petition state officials. Colored men's arguments might touch a legislator's "humanity," whereas voters had the authority to issue directives specifying "a course of action."[39]

The address to colored Pennsylvanians accomplished more and less than called for in the convention resolution. The exercise created an opportunity for Whipper and his allies to refine and broadcast their conceptions of reform and citizenship. It also suggests that the rhetorical power of identifying as citizens was not a stable basis for claiming the franchise.[40] Unable to base arguments on the state constitution that legalized their disenfranchisement, the authors created a scenario to validate appeals to principle. They numbered free colored people among "the governed" whose consent, according to the Declaration of Independence, made a government just. On this ground, they argued, "every principle of republican justice" vindicated their push for equal rights. They likened their campaign to a lawsuit to portray disenfranchisement as wrong. The framework made republican principles akin to laws. The legislature and governor comprised "the Court," and voters represented the jury. Manhood was the premise of their complaint; they were suing "as men."[41]

This legal imagery inspired an alternate conceptualization of rights to confront a social and political equation linking blackness and chattel slavery. The writers sharply distinguished their status as freemen from enslavement. On one hand, they highlighted their "new position" by assessing their endeavors in light of the work of forbears. "Our fathers sought personal freedom," they explained, attributing their circumstances to successful struggles of enslaved ancestors even though many reformers had been born into slavery themselves. In contrast, they worked toward "political freedom." They confronted slavery's dominance in their own time by distinguishing their position from limitations and presumed sensibilities among their contemporaries living in bondage. Dissimilarities aimed to validate suffrage demands. "Slaves have learned to lick the dust and stifle the voice of free inquiry," they declared, "but we are not slaves."[42] They assumed that, as legally free men, they possessed a capacity and license for unfettered intellectual explorations that slaves lacked. They believed that their freedom "vindicated" claims to the franchise because foremost scholars of government cited civil and political freedoms as the "only true safeguards of individual liberty." Rights were thus a necessary feature of their status as freemen. The contrast between their identities and their depiction of slaves aimed to disrupt popular linkages between political standing and race designations.

The address acknowledges the importance of upright behavior for collective advancement. In the process, however, it refutes the notion that rectitude was required to render colored people worthy of suffrage. Speculations about the sensibilities of White voters who comprised the fictive jury weighing their case for suffrage shaped the discussion. That group would surely treat conduct as evidence. Biases that upheld discrimination and distorted their vision would transform "petty jealousies and bickerings" among colored people into "lawless invasions." Drunkenness, "the essence of fashionable folly among the whites," would prove colored people's "degeneracy." Instead of counting as ordinary human weakness, vices would showcase an "inherent quality" of the population. In this milieu, rectitude was a necessary tactic to evade scorn. A tactic was not a remedy, however, nor did it capture the logic of disenfranchisement. Preaching that improvements in "condition" were the key to securing rights would mean accepting the fallacy that immorality and ignorance caused the subjugation colored populations experienced at the hands of White people who claimed superiority over others. The address challenges this thinking, explaining that "cunning logicians" understood that invoking "condition" would not enable them to justify discriminatory legal action. "They knew that the period had long since passed," the delegates reasoned, for citing "a standard of condition that would separate the white from the colored people."[43] The case of the late James Forten, former AMRS president and father-in-law of Robert Purvis, illustrated the point. His widely recognized respectability and prosperity did not exempt him from laws that barred colored Pennsylvanians from participating as equals in political and social arenas. The established practice of referencing "color" as a self-evident mark and metaphor of difference and rank meant that legislators "did not need reasons."[44] The classification scheme enabled them to restrict the franchise and inscribe a "color" hierarchy in the state constitution.

While acknowledging benefits of improving moral, intellectual, and material conditions among free colored people, the authors were intent on

88   RELUCTANT RACE MEN

disabusing readers of the idea that such deficiencies caused disenfranchisement. Global religious history helped them shed light on the situation. They
observed that groups responsible for significant human developments—
Protestants, Catholics, Quakers, and Jews—had suffered persecution at the
hands of authorities who objected to their doctrines, faith practices, and
identities. "Our cause is analogous," they argued. The older phenomena
were acts of "religious intolerance," while they faced the despotism of
"complexional intolerance." They found inspiration in figures who refused
to abandon their principles amid attacks while noting that colored people
did not have the option of changing the features lawmakers cited to target
them and justify their oppression. They were "forced to meet the issue . . . on
complexional grounds."[45] Nevertheless, principles prepared them for combat
against barriers to equal rights.

Proposed actions and appeals to the past reveal how the authors perceived
the terms and scope of their struggle. The planned Citizen's Union made
it clear that ongoing suffrage campaigns would try to avoid the racial
distinctions that premised disenfranchisement and refrain from operating
exclusive domains. The authors used excerpts from Whipper's 1839 editorial
in the final edition of the AMRS *National Reformer* to stand against tethering
suffrage rights to improvements in condition. As the previous chapter
explains, the piece denounces the claim that morality was a prerequisite for
equality and calls for "new terms" to vindicate citizenship rights. The need to
reissue this message nearly a decade after its original delivery points to the
unrelenting struggle to explain and contest race practices shaped injustices
and reform.[46]

Qualms about race kept pace with the evolution of national conventions.
Proceedings of the 1840s and 1850s displayed some of the same wariness evident in state and local venues about framing endeavors in terms of "color."
If titles are indicative of their tenor, reconstituted initiatives sought to avoid
appearing to sanction racial distinctions and tried to juggle concerns about
moral improvement and discrimination. The 1843 national forum espoused
a familiar commitment to morality and rights with its framing as a convention of "colored citizens" who gathered to consider "their moral and political condition as American citizens." More pointed was the 1847 gathering of
"Colored People and their Friends." Both delegations were more outspoken
about slavery than those at prior conventions. Yet their agendas drew from
traditional reform issues involving decorum, farming, the press, and colored
people's social status. The latter group unhinged the need for reform from

race classifications in advocating temperance for all, "without a thought of color."[47] Apologetic gestures aimed to assure the public that autonomous endeavors did not mean that colored people were different from other human beings. The 1848 national convention address, issued by Frederick Douglass, Henry Bibb, William Day, Abner Francis, and one D. Jenkins, asserted that "general complexion," shared subjugation, and popular perception brought disparate elements of the colored population together as "one people." This melding inspired uneasiness, as if it was at odds with practicing "human brotherhood." Delegates confessed that they had no alternative and lamented that circumstances would compel them to meet in this manner for some time. They urged other colored people to take up the cause of reform "without exclusiveness" and act "without distinction of color."[48] Five years later, the 1853 national convention in Rochester issued a wholesale repudiation of color distinctions to pinpoint the wrongs of disenfranchisement and establish citizenship claims. The address submitted by Frederick Douglass, Amos Freeman, George Vashon, H. O. Wagoner Sr., and J. Whitfield argued that distinctions in the political rights of citizens were indefensible because they rested on an incoherent conception of difference. The men averred that their physical, moral, mental, and spiritual needs demonstrated that they were "members of the human family." As such, they required the same means to meet those needs as other humans. An array of sources substantiated their citizenship claims, including the Constitution's provision on the "privileges and immunities" of citizens, politicians' references to colored people as citizens, and the proclamation of Andrew Jackson to the colored people of Louisiana that many reformers cherished. To drive home the point that citizenship was not the province of a select population, they suggested that the term "white" was antithetical to American identity. It was a "modern word" devised by "modern legislators" whose actions were at cross-purposes with the spirit of the American Revolution and founding principles of the republic.[49]

Repudiations of the idea that colored people were "a distinct and separate class" continued as delegates tried to establish a permanent forum of representation. Championing rights, unity, morality, and intellectual development through the National Council of the Colored People was a means of promoting equality among all Americans, they argued. This push for broad "Human Rights" won the endorsement of a diverse set of actors, including individuals known for standing against all racial distinctions. Junius Morel and Syracuse minister Jermain Loguen subscribed to the project, insisting

90 RELUCTANT RACE MEN

that rights could not be defined with racial or sex categories. Former Moral Reform Society members James Bias, Robert Purvis, and William Whipper, along with Lewis Woodson, joined the organization as the "Anti-Colonization and Woman's Rights Ticket" in a bid to serve as Pennsylvania representatives.[50] Despite fervent efforts to premise equal political rights on the common humanity of all Americans, the council faltered after two fitful years of dissension among constituencies whose shared hopes of transcending racial designations failed to establish a common ground of authority or unity.[51]

Support for women's rights was a glaring but short-lived departure from the gender culture of convention initiatives. The equation of citizenship and rights with manhood, along with the popular notion that women had no rightful role in political affairs, made exclusion from proceedings standard. The National Council opened a small window for women's participation. At a Geneva, New York, convention to form a local council auxiliary, Barbara Ann Steward served as secretary for the group while her father, Austin Steward, presided. Another woman, a Mrs. Jeffrey, was a vice president. Two years later, possibilities for this sort of input and leadership had virtually disappeared. The 1855 New York convention summarily removed Steward's name from the delegate roster after "several gentlemen" opposed her inclusion. They complained that the group was not hosting "a Woman's Rights Convention." Mary Ann Shadd fared better at the national convention Philadelphians hosted that year. She was an exception. Charles Remond's motion to admit her prompted "spirited discussion" before passing. Frederick Douglass won reconsideration of the vote, and after further discussion, more than half of the male delegates, including Douglass, endorsed her participation. Writing as "Ethiop," William J. Wilson reported that Shadd proved to be a "superior woman" at the proceedings. She presented what he recalled as "one of the most convincing and telling speeches in favor of Canadian emigration" he had ever heard. Entranced by her delivery, convention leaders extended her speaking time to more than double the allotment for others.[52] Nevertheless, her impressive showing did not diminish reformers' gender biases or the widespread commitment to American manhood as a foundation for mapping progress.

The rituals of rallying against political exclusion failed to unify divergent reform factions. Although competing conceptions of its causes, arguments for contesting it, and the parameters of participation in reform initiatives were not insurmountable barriers to organizing discrete events, they interfered with the viability and implementation of convention proposals. Common experiences of discrimination generated some comparable modes of asserting authority among reformers who opposed racial notions of human difference. Yet they led to starkly different propositions among individuals who accepted race designations as accurate reflections of diverse natural populations or social groups even as they acknowledged their role in structuring disenfranchisement.

The significance of divergent reform perspectives and the conflicts they inspired extended beyond the conventions. The strife that rendered Pennsylvania's 1848 convention a "splendid failure," for example, was tied to phenomena in other reform sites. The pseudonymous "Observer," possibly Bostonian Charles Remond, who attended the Philadelphia meeting, described the proceedings as properly organized, declaring "their rules particular and correct; their deliberation orderly and harmonious; the speeches able, spirited, eloquent and worthy[of] the occasion." However, he chronicled factors outside of the gathering that undermined the execution of its plans and contributed to its undoing after the fact. Preachers and laity opposed alliances with critics of pro-slavery churches. Fraternal orders would not cooperate with detractors of secret societies. The "morally fastidious" refused to collaborate with individuals of "doubtful moral character."[53] Although no single venue was a model of reform, initiatives overlapped, converged, and depended on partners that faced similar challenges in trying to develop and execute reforms on a social and political terrain complicated by an array of race practices and divergent conceptions of their meanings.

Concerns about equality beyond political arenas gave rise to further questions about notions of difference and rank that circumscribed freedom. Public and private spaces of social interaction—transportation networks, schools, and churches—were primary targets of criticism. In addition to attacking the injustice of unequal access, reformers continued to grapple with the logic of voluntary segregation in private spaces. They worried that inconsistent actions compromised the authority they claimed as American reformers.

Inequalities in mass transit prompted condemnations of contrived differences and hierarchies for creating invalid restrictions. Charles Remond presented arguments to this effect in testimony before a Massachusetts legislative committee. He called for an end to discrimination in public conveyances by questioning the ethics of assigning color labels to citizens. The wrong was not simply that colored people suffered. He argued that structuring rights by color variations would be equally reprehensible if used against White people, because complexion was an illegitimate "criterion of rights." The institutionalization of "concocted" distinctions in everyday life meant that injustice could not be isolated or dismissed as the caprice of individual actors. The treachery that was embedded in the national language disgraced the entire country.[54]

Similar logic armed critics of school policies that used racial designations to apportion children's educational access. They denounced the practice for creating unsound and unjust social arrangements. Such reasoning guided the 1848 lawsuit *Roberts v. the City of Boston*, which stemmed from Benjamin Roberts's efforts to enroll his daughter in a school restricted to White children. The Boston School Committee's explanation for separation gave reformers explicit warrants for opposing race. Officials declared that the policy was not merely to uphold color differences; it rested on a distinction "of race." It stemmed from what the committee perceived to be divinely ordained differences in the "physical, mental, and oral natures of the two races."[55] Neither legislation nor custom could eliminate these facts. The response of abolitionist Charles Sumner and his Black co-counsel Robert Morris, who represented Roberts, was customary. They insisted that there was nothing natural about the racial distinction. It was simply the creation of a caste system among schoolchildren. As such, it violated the principle of equality in the Massachusetts constitution.

Ohio and New York reformers shared these views. One A. J. Anderson complained to the *North Star* that Ohio authorities were incapable of fulfilling their responsibility of educating children because they made distinctions "on account of color." He acknowledged that many viewed segregation as a positive development because it provided schooling for even the poorest colored children. However, he could not reconcile the work of instruction with "invidious distinctions" of color and caste that denied the fundamental precept of human equality.[56] In Rochester, Frederick Douglass echoed the charge that it was wrong to invoke "unnatural" color distinctions in schools. Like others, he saw a necessary connection between conceptual and legal distinctions and the denial of rights. In this case, it meant depriving people of education. Arrangements for segregated schools were evil because they contradicted the natural unity of members of the human family and forged a path to other social evils. Foreshadowing arguments in *Brown v. Board of Education*, Douglass observed that appeals to color caused colored children to "undervalue themselves" and view White children as "their oppressors." School authorities were thus creating conditions for perpetual hostilities that had no natural foundations. When plans for separate schools advanced, protests began at the courthouse. Protesters threatened to remove school board members who supported color distinctions that degraded and separated citizens. They were poised to denounce anyone who invoked differences even if they extended special privileges to colored children. They wanted "RIGHTS," not "favors." Color distinctions, regardless of their intent, undermined the basis of claims to manhood and citizenship.[57]

Despite limited prospects for success, some reformers championed "mixed" schools as logical and desirable institutions. Delegates to the 1851 New York state convention resolved that "every good citizen" had an obligation to oppose the formation and maintenance of schools specifically for colored children. A lone dissenting voice from Brooklyn confessed to supporting the measure's intent, but he questioned its value. The resolution thus passed with little discussion. Even with no expectation of material consequences, the group believed it was important to denounce such schools because they were yet another instance in which public authorities invoked color differences. The convention followed precedent in condemning such distinctions as baseless attempts to rank human beings. It equated schooling organized around color categories with teaching children to believe in the "superiority of races." This action compromised the public good by promoting the "false notions" of natural dominance and subjection among human beings.[58]

Reformers' proposals to create schools on their own did not settle questions about equal access. Faced with intolerance for racial distinctions, proponents of independent education projects tried to deflect charges of exclusivity with apologetic assertions that they were not upholding unnatural notions of difference. Disavowals of abetting race practices accompanied a National Council plan to build a manual labor school. Charles Ray, William J. Wilson, and William Whipper, members of the Committee of Social Relations that advanced the idea, argued that prevailing circumstances compelled colored people to operate their own schools. The issue was not that colored youth were "different from the white youth." It was widespread discrimination. Wilson assured council members who opposed the plan that the proposal did not advocate separate education facilities for colored children. New Yorker

94   RELUCTANT RACE MEN

Charles Reason elaborated, denouncing race constructions on the group's behalf and explaining that the proposed school would not promote "the principle of complexional exclusiveness." He was an apt spokesperson, having recently left his position as a literature professor at an interracial manual labor school, New York Central College, in McGrawville. Founded by the American Baptist Free Mission Society in 1849, it admitted students without racial or gender distinctions, proclaiming "the unity, common origin, equality and brotherhood of the human race."[59] Reason espoused the school's creed, but he found that officials' actions fell short of their ideals. He thus left for Philadelphia to lead the Quaker-sponsored Institute for Colored Youth.

Assurances failed to allay fears that the proposed education project would reinforce race distinctions. After it became clear that the manual labor school would not materialize, delegates to the 1855 national convention promoted an industrial education project. Philadelphians protested, arguing that it would be "necessarily (if not in theory, yet in fact) a complexional institution." As such, it would reinforce the very conceptions of difference that reformers were trying to eradicate. This claim was consistent with the principles of Whipper and his Philadelphia allies; however, it was disingenuous. The committee responsible for devising plans for the proposed American Industrial School—Frederick Douglass, James McCune Smith, Amos Beman, John Peck, John Jones, and J. Bonner—stipulated that students and teachers be selected "without reference to sex or complexion." Given struggles for control over the planned school, conflicts likely stemmed from the choice of Frederick Douglass as the school's agent and from plans to locate the school in northwestern Pennsylvania or upstate New York. Even though the Philadelphia accusation was untrue, reformers knew that the charge of "complexional distinctions" had the power to discredit.[60]

Concerns about valid bases of authority made churches a conspicuous target of race challenges, inspiring worries about Christian complicity in perpetuating racial distinctions. While outsiders criticized churches for compromising their moral standing, church leaders struggled with their own uneasiness about how their institutions engaged race constructions. Although they were the most established and prominent institutions operated by free people of color, churches occupied an unstable place in reform landscapes.

Several factors combined to make them vulnerable to criticism. Some reprimands echoed abolitionist disparagement of all American churches for failing to lead attacks on slavery and other forms of oppression. Whipper observed that even "distinguished divines" found churches guilty of protecting wrongs and undermining moral progress. There was a consensus at the 1849 New England Anti-Slavery Convention that slavery would not endure for more than six months without the ongoing support of churches. Perceived moral failures elicited more targeted attacks. For instance, Philadelphia's St. Thomas Episcopal Church and the "misnamed" Free Church of Scotland drew scorn when well-founded fears of attacks led them to curtail open support for abolitionists. Whipper accused them of betraying Christianity "in the temple" by failing to fight social ills. Douglass added that such churches and any others that charged abolitionists fees to use their buildings were so obsessed with "getting religion" that they forgot God's will. A delegate to the 1850 Ohio convention condemned the African Methodist Episcopal *Christian Herald* for promoting Methodist interests at the expense of the abolitionist cause. Charles Ray observed that many AME leaders were "men of worth and piety," but their silence on slavery reflected a dearth of "public spirit" that hampered their religious mission. A *North Star* correspondent from Ohio lodged a sweeping critique of the "demoralizing and damning influence" of colored churches resulting from their ties to proslavery institutions. Such connections undermined trust in their capacity to lead reforms.[61]

The actions and opinions of AME churchmen both invalidated and lent credence to accusations. Clergy and laypeople were active promoters of "free produce" and refrained from buying or consuming products made with slave labor. Such preachers as Paul Quinn earned the wrath of some colored people for denouncing slavery. Some individuals refused to hear him preach because he would not be silent about abolition. They complained, "it is something that we colored folks have nothing to do with, and it only makes it worse for us by stirring it up."[62] Others avoided taking any risks. David Smith boasted that White people in Maryland thought well of him because he said nothing about freedom to his slave congregation. He advised them only on "becoming free from the devil."[63] Daniel Payne did not hesitate to preach against the sin of bondage, but he acted cautiously. He privileged prayer over "unprincipled" agitation and vehement denunciations against slavery and other "moral evils."[64] Denomination officials feared that loud protests for changes would put congregations and buildings in danger.

Biases against racially exclusive reform endeavors meant that virtually all antebellum churches were subject to criticism regardless of their social and political activism. Segregation was the norm, whether by domination or congregation. Yet assaults on colored churches are paradoxical, given their aim of overcoming impediments to religious authority in White-dominated institutions. Founders had sought to transcend oppressive race practices by associating along racial lines. Speaking for himself and his allies as they quit the Methodist Episcopal Church, Richard Allen explained the purpose of organizing an independent church: "to secure to our selves our rights and privileges, to regulate our affairs, temporal and spiritual, the same as if we were white people."[65] As entities created to exercise religious authority unfettered by racial restrictions, colored churches became an unanticipated focus of reform efforts to abolish racial barriers to freedom and equality.

Fears that the very existence of these organizations upheld false notions of difference and rank guided some critics. Delegates to the 1847 national convention condemned all sects that adhered to "caste" distinctions as "synagogues of Satan." Samuel Cornish, William Whipper, and Frederick Douglass, along with abolitionist Henry Bibb and the youthful Delaware reformer Mary Ann Shadd found common cause on this point. Cornish was perhaps an unlikely critic. He ministered to segregated congregations; defended exclusive political organizations and reform periodicals, such as his *Colored American* newspaper; and insisted on using color designations. Still, he used his paper to condemn religious institutions led by colored people. Some of his commentaries suggest that he simply privileged inter-racial partnerships. However, his stand on colored churches went deeper. He judged the mere fact of separation by "color" to be at odds with biblical teachings and "true religion," supporting unnatural hierarchies and reinscribing unjust political and social inequalities. He worried that independent denominations, in particular, implied that colored people, as a group, were inherently different from and inferior to White people. They thereby justified social and political inequality.[66]

Personal experiences inspired some of Cornish's complaints. He reported that, after serving as a Presbyterian minister for seventeen years, he could not find one church in the denomination that would admit his sons to its school. He planned to leave New York to shield his family from the Christian bigotry that might transform them into "haters of God and of man." The "separate churches" maintained by colored people could not escape perpetuating the "caste" structure that restricted fellowship and ecclesiastical authority. He was thus appalled when Lewis Woodson defended the organizations. The gesture seemed tantamount to sanctioning discrimination and giving White people license to bar citizens from churches "with the same impunity with which they do it from the social circle!" Worse, separation seemed grounded in anti-Black sentiment that drove colonization. The "same spirit that would drive us from our country," he cried, "colonizes us in the churches."[67]

Because biblical truths and Christian ideals supplied arguments against discriminatory race practices, religious institutions were logical objects of scrutiny. Their visibility and their roles in providing institutional resources for colored people earned them special consideration. Some of the harshest criticism expressed skepticism about the capacity of any Protestant entity to provide moral leadership. Whipper, vexed by the pervasiveness of American Protestantism among colored people, was convinced that it robbed religion of its moral authority. It thwarted collective action by depriving reformers of coherent conceptual tools with which to advance change. Colored churches were a serious stumbling block in his eyes, as he struggled to identify ethical grounds from which to demand justice. In a squabble with Frederick Douglass over a proposed organization dubbed the National League, he complained that colored people had no legitimate basis of authority for broad reform initiatives because they had no national citizenship. If asked, "From whence do you hail?" they would be unable to identify a clear and just basis for collective action. They would have no evidence with which to refute the inevitable charge that they were making a "complexional issue" and perpetuating the very notions of difference they opposed. He believed the problem stemmed from the fact that so many colored people espoused American Protestantism. The tradition was antithetical to the freedom, morality, and welfare of colored people. It was too corrupt to generate valid reform standards. The pro-slavery sentiments it abetted convinced him that caste was intrinsic to its theology, making it worse than "no religion at all." Adherents who subscribed to the notion that colored people were a naturally "distinct and inferior people" were proof. Methodists, Presbyterians, Baptists, and Episcopalians were all guilty of supporting or accommodating a pro-slavery constituency. Their belief in "the natural inferiority of the colored people" appeared to be as central to their creed as their faith in God. William Lloyd Garrison's call to leave pro-slavery churches offered a remedy. It would facilitate Christian efforts to establish nonsectarian religious bases of reform.[68]

Whipper perceived no fundamental differences between religious units operated by colored people and those led by White people. Indeed, similarity was the problem. He believed that all churches that reflected the dogma that people with different complexions should worship separately were "unworthy of Christian patronage." Colored churches could not maintain proper

98 RELUCTANT RACE MEN

ethical standards, he believed, because they practiced the same morally bankrupt religion espoused by people who abetted slavery and denied colored
people authority and equal fellowship. He was troubled to see that, despite
segregated congregations, colored and White believers shared a common
orthodoxy. A distinct ecclesiology among colored people failed to generate
a theology that upheld the natural, religious, civil, and political equality of
White and colored people. He lamented that this was perhaps a logical outcome of planting institutions in "slave-cursed soil."[69] Thus, he could not hold
colored clergy and laity fully accountable for defects embedded in their religious traditions.

Because colored churches could never fulfill his vision of what free people
needed, Whipper sketched a path for change. Religious and secular history
showed him possibilities for redeeming American Christianity and republicanism from a corrupt Protestant ethos. Donning a revivalist mantle, he
called on reformers to embrace an undefiled doctrine—a civil religion that
upheld universal equality and freedom tied to ideals of the Revolution.
He believed Protestantism distorted the republic's founding principles by
validating the "divine right of complexion" and imposing a "complexional
tariff" that allowed White privilege to trump the birthright of other citizens.
He was certain that colored Christians could not be free and equal unless
they repudiated Protestant sectarianism. Only then could they establish
institutions that reflected the fact that humans comprised "one common
family."[70]

American churches had ceased being places of true worship. For
Whipper, the reverence surrounding their edifices merely lent a sacred
aura to race distinctions. They seemed destined to become "prison houses
of complexional pride," he feared. If left unchecked, they would lure colored people into making complexion a "VIRTUE." The prospect of a fallacy
about difference becoming a spiritual principle was distressing. He imagined
institutions ostensibly committed to spreading wisdom trafficking in the
morally bankrupt doctrine of "complexional merit." Yet he could not think
of any intelligent way to explain "why the different shades of the human form
should inculcate in us feelings of glory or shame."[71]

Concerns about logical inconsistency added fuel to criticism of racial
distinctions. They made Boston's colored churches a target of scorn from
William J. Watkins for circumscribing free association among Christians. He
could see no rational way to contest "complexional distinctions" in schools
while colored people perpetuated them in churches. Their mere existence,

"ONE COMMON FAMILY" 99

he argued, affirmed the "proscriptive principle" that subjected people to discrimination and lent currency to allegations of inferiority.[72] Using a national reform lens, Whipper extended such criticism to "colored" and "African" institutions throughout the country. He stopped short of declaring that their leaders had simply reaped what they had sown. However, he bitterly observed that disenfranchisement should not have surprised them. Colored people "must have *free churches*," he reasoned, if they were to be truly free. This outcome required shunning groups engaged in "distinctive" practices. Even if they had not "defaced" their names with racial terms, he believed they perpetuated a form of "religious despotism" that was morally indistinguishable from the broader phenomenon of "civil tyranny."[73]

Colored churches drew further attacks for failing to reflect the unity of the human species. This was a sign that they neglected Christian tenets. The accusation formed the core of Frederick Douglass's rebuke shortly after he launched the *North Star*. What began as an isolated response to Massachusetts AME preacher Leonard Collins provided fodder for editorials and speeches, as well as commentary from Henry Bibb and Mary Ann Shadd, who supported Douglass's stance. The critique was a sign of how far Douglass had come since his escape from slavery. To inspire audiences who gathered for his tirades against colored churches, he liked to recount the lessons in literacy and freedom he gained from William Lloyd Garrison's *Liberator* when he arrived in New Bedford. Like Whipper, he felt a moral transformation upon reading the paper's "noble and sublime" motto "My country is the world—my countrymen are all mankind." This life-changing moment reportedly led him to question the legitimacy of colored churches. His actual path from slave to abolitionist critic of churches was more circuitous. Following his 1838 escape, he had become a licensed preacher in New Bedford's African Methodist Episcopal Zion (AMEZ) Church. Yet, nearly a decade later, having quit the pulpit for the abolitionist circuit, he tried to convince *North Star* readers that institutions like the one he once served were evil.[74]

Douglass marshaled arguments others had lodged against race practices over the course of the previous decade and applied them to colored churches with his own rhetorical flourish. A host of factors made them immoral. Their membership relied on "artificial and conventional distinctions" that separated humans into classes. As such, they disregarded human brotherhood and the "essential oneness of the human family." They falsely implied that colored people possessed moral and religious needs that differed from the needs of other people. In making skin color a condition of Christian ministry, they upheld distinctions that were at odds with the principle of human equality stemming from a common creation. In sum, they reinforced notions of difference used by "every negro hater" who invoked complexional distinctions to exclude colored people and deprive them of equal status in hotels, steamboats, railroad cars, schools, and churches. Douglass derided Leonard Collins's defense of the "propriety" of colored people worshipping with their "own kind." It showed colored churches to be "a mere counterpart of colonization," morally indistinguishable from the "negro pew." The only differences were scale and location. Going beyond other critics, he concluded that, collectively, they issued arguments on behalf of discrimination and injustice.[75]

Henry Bibb repeated Douglass's perspective, while Mary Ann Shadd focused on the manner in which churches operated. Bibb affirmed the point that exclusive colored churches were morally identical to segregated White churches. They were in sync with the fanciful imagery of "a colored heaven and a colored God." The demeanor of colored church leaders added to their most despicable character. After disparaging their distinctiveness, Shadd decried the corruption and "frightfully wretched instruction" of the men who presided over them. She complained that they made a duty of ignorance and bred superstition in place of "true religion." She was convinced that these factors contributed more to the degradation of the colored population than slanderous public discourse. For Douglass and Bibb, the solution was for colored people to abandon their own churches. Douglass, certain that their necessity had long passed, was curiously optimistic about prospects for equal access to religious rites and authority elsewhere. He placed churches in the same category as the railroad cars in which colored travelers demanded non-discriminatory seating. Colored people had to follow this example, he admonished, and insist on participating as equals in organizations that White people controlled. Similarly, Bibb envisioned demands for religious equality as simple appeals to "the natural equality of the human family." They were part of a broad push for justice that entailed eradicating ignorance, sectarianism, bigotry, colored schools, and slavery—"the mother of all these abominations."[76]

Leaders of colored churches variously ignored and dismissed the idea that they should not exist. Persistent discrimination in White churches made critics' concerns inconsequential. Lewis Woodson snubbed reformers who expressed anxieties about colored churches and rejected the assumption that the right to worship bore any resemblance to political or civil rights. There was no question that the churches had a right to exist, and there was no need for angst about the possibility that they reinscribed caste. They violated "NO MORAL PRINCIPLE." Independent colored churches were a matter of religious freedom, he reasoned, because Americans had the right to privately associate with people they chose. The public moral authority churches exercised did not change the fact that they were private voluntary associations subject to rules governing private property. "The inherent freedom and undoubted right which everyone has to worship God according to the dictates of their own conscience," Woodson explained, "must not be confounded with an unqualified right to worship in every particular place." The Constitution created no "moral or legal" right for colored people to inhabit churches other people built for themselves.[77]

In practice, Woodson's stance did not require limiting affiliations to the churches colored people organized. After sixteen years as an AME minister, he joined the Wesleyan Methodist Connection, a group that split from the Methodist Episcopal Church over its tolerance for slavery and church governance restrictions. Woodson became secretary of the organization's inaugural General Conference in 1844 and served its congregations for eight years before resuming pastoral duties in his original denomination. During this period, he muted his former message about the necessity for moral improvement to eradicate prejudice. Instead, he admonished his Wesleyan brethren that discrimination caused immorality and degradation and implored them to assist in educating and converting colored people because they could not always secure resources for enlightenment on their own.[78]

Leonard Collins's challenge to the call for colored churches to disband extended the issue to other independent ventures. After charging that the proposed step would force colored Christians into the churches of the "man-stealers" Douglass claimed to despise, he accused him of hypocrisy. "Shall we have Mr. Douglass set the first example?" If he truly opposed colored establishments, it seemed reasonable to Collins that he would halt his media enterprise and demand equality as an editor of a newspaper controlled by White people.[79]

The suggestion touched a sore point. The press invited scrutiny because it was vital to reform efforts. It was a vehicle for reshaping disparaging popular portrayals of the free colored population. Delegates to Pennsylvania's 1841 convention declared an independent press "absolutely necessary" to enable colored people to advance their own cause. Yet, they also envisioned it as

102 RELUCTANT RACE MEN

a mechanism for creating a future of unity for "the whole family of man." Citing the role of the media in justifying colored people's subjugation, the 1848 national convention declared, "The means which have been used to destroy us must be used to save us."[80] Some were, nevertheless, wary of making "complexional issues" in carrying out such work. William Day launched his Cleveland, Ohio, paper with the announcement that its actions on behalf of "Colored Americans" would not rest on such unsound measures of manhood as hair, nose shape, or "the accident of color." The title, *Aliened American*, explained its concern for "native-born citizens" rendered aliens by laws and "Public Opinion" that deprived them of their rights. "We speak for Humanity," Day argued, and committed the paper to serve "wherever the rights common to human beings are infringed."[81] Douglass, in contrast, justified operating "colored newspapers," as such, well before Collins criticized him. Shortly after issuing the *North Star*, he countered charges that the paper perpetuated "an odious and wicked distinction." He protested that divergent social experiences demanded different interventions. It was dangerous to ignore the fact that "white is not black, and black is not white," he argued. There was "neither good sense, nor common honesty" in suggesting otherwise.[82] In the end, however, he tempered his strident talk and confessed that his ultimate aim was to eliminate distinctions. When he revisited the issue, he prefaced his comments with the affirmation that all humans comprised a "common family" made of "one blood." He acknowledged that this doctrine suggested a degree of impropriety in designating the *North Star* a "colored" journal. However, peculiar circumstances provided him with a defense. Using logic Samuel Cornish deployed in the *Colored American*, he explained that it was appropriate to represent colored people in ways that designated their "distinct and peculiar condition."[83]

No defense managed to silence the detractors. Yet concerns about the titles of collective endeavors signaled possibilities for compromise. Names stood as evidence that colored organizations were at odds with claims to American citizenship. The term "African" in the titles of Black-led denominations and churches drew censure as the label "colored" grew popular among colonization opponents. Whipper insisted that "African" churches fostered artificial divisions among American citizens. Echoing this sentiment, Episcopalian Prince Loveridge, Agent of the Schools for Colored Children in New York City, counseled AME churchmen to remove the lie from their name. Adopt the name "colored," he advised; "there are no Africans in your connection." An anonymous editorial in David Ruggles's *Mirror of Liberty* applied the same logic to New York's African schools. The writer was unable to comprehend the "metamorphosis" that transformed "native born *American* citizens" into Africans but speculated that colonizationists could likely shed light on the phenomenon.[84]

The term "African" troubled some church leaders. An African Baptist Boston congregation took a decisive step to eliminate the appearance of inconsistency and renamed itself the First Independent Church of the People of Color. Members believed that the former title "ill applied to a church composed of American citizens." They were an exception. The term endured in denominations led by colored men. Tradition kept some African Methodists from making changes in spite of discomfort. George Hogarth, editor of the *A.M.E. Church Magazine*, echoed the Baptists' sentiment. "It is true," he wrote in response to objections to his denomination's name, "we are not Africans." This apparent truth was less compelling than other factors. Hogarth defended the institutional use of "African" with appeals to biblical history and American practices. He first compared the situation of colored people to that of enslaved Israelites. Rejecting the implication that a slave past should be a source of shame, he noted that mistreatment in Egypt had not caused Jews to discard the name that signified their national origins. Lest the analogy imply that he ceded claims to American citizenship, he explained that people of color could not expect to claim possession of a promised land. Moreover, he saw no reason for them to abandon their "native land." However, they could do what other Americans did. People of English descent boasted of their "Saxon blood," and descendants of the French celebrated their "Norman and Gaulish blood." If these "other races" were proud to preserve the names of their ancestral countries, he reasoned, "why should not we be?" The term "African" was thus perfectly compatible with American citizenship. It was not an assertion of nationality but a remembrance of origins.[85]

Interdenominational competition raised additional concerns about tradition. The AME Church almost lost a Rahway, New Jersey, congregation as a result of "intrigues and misrepresentation" by other African Methodists. In recounting the situation, church officials described themselves as "the first and only society of Methodists under the general supervision of a colored Bishop in this country." They denounced all others who used the name as frauds unworthy of public confidence.[86] The reference was probably to members of the group who became the AMEZ Church. Until 1848, it had several different designations. Its claims to rightful ownership of the name African Methodist Episcopal Church in America raised the stakes associated

104 RELUCTANT RACE MEN

with the title for the other AME Church. Within a year of the Rahway property dispute, its bishop, Dempsey Kennedy, called on the *Colored American* to print an open letter to his connection objecting to a name change. His quarrel was not with the AME Church but with fellow denominational leaders who published new church manuals under two different names— "Wesleyan Zion Episcopal Church in America" and "Colored Methodist Church in America." They thought that "African" discredited their organization. Like Hogarth, Kennedy appealed to tradition, arguing the change would destroy the church by effectively banishing people who had gathered under the established name.[87]

Disagreements over using race categories did not plague antislavery endeavors with the intensity that they affected conventions and churches. Appeals to a common humanity were part of an antislavery tradition rooted in the eighteenth century. In 1776, before beginning a long career as a Congregational minister to White New Englanders, Lemuel Haynes condemned slavery by asserting that Africans were equal members of the human race and thus possessed a natural right to freedom. In England, former slave Ottobah Cuguano drew from British abolitionist rhetoric to assert the unity of humankind in his 1787 treatise *Thoughts and Sentiments on the Evil and Wicked Traffic of the Slavery and Commerce of the Human Species.* The following year, his friend Olaudah Equiano relied on the same discourse in his popular autobiography to conclude that all people shared a common blood.[88] Antebellum reformers extended the tradition of invalidating claims of racial hierarchy and difference that cast slaves outside the sphere of humanity. James McCune Smith was one of many whose appeals to a shared humanity formed the core of a stand against slavery. His 1855 convention address stated simply that slaves were "persons, not things." This fact, he argued, proved that slavery violated the constitutional guarantee that no one can be deprived of freedom without due process. The umbrella of personhood also meant that infringements on one individual's liberty compromised the freedom of other human beings. The bondage of slaves convinced him that no American was truly free.[89] Connections of a different sort guided Henry Highland Garnet's call for slaves to resist bondage. His 1843 address assured them that "a common humanity" bound them to free people. It made them "Fellow-men," "Brethren," and "Fellow-Citizens." These ties authorized him to admonish slaves of a "moral obligation" to stand for freedom even if it meant dying.[90]

The importance of human relations in antislavery endeavors was popularized by the iconic sketch of a kneeling slave posing the plaintive question, "Am I Not a Man and a Brother?" A later version depicted a kneeling woman with a query about sisterhood. Originally, the male image was the seal for Britain's Society for Effecting the Abolition of the Slave Trade. As it spread, it was absorbed into the material culture of abolition in England and the United States. Patrons at antislavery fairs could find both images on jewelry, stationary, decorative boxes and bags, dishes, and fireplace accessories. The queries in the images issued a challenge. Acknowledging enslaved individuals as men and women entailed embracing them as brothers and sisters.[91]

The ideal of a shared humanity was tested as reformers forged coalitions with White abolitionists. The tenet of natural equality that helped support the cause was no match for the premium on White skin. Antislavery poetry for children reflects the phenomenon's pervasiveness and a corresponding condescension toward blackness. Two examples illustrate. The first appeared in the American Anti-Slavery Society's magazine for children, *The Slave's Friend*, which tried to inspire sympathy for slaves with tales of hardships arising from family separation, violence, and prohibitions on education. The unidentified author of *The Little Colored Boy* promoted this aim by dramatizing the sorrow of a child confronting the inescapability of dark skin. Having imagined the joy he would feel if he were "pure and white" like his owner's child, he goes to the river to wash away his color. His repeated cry, "I cannot, cannot wash it off," captures his heartbreak. Although his "sable" skin appears to be an understandable and untreatable source of sorrow, young readers receive the comforting news that his mind is "pure and fair" and that heaven can cleanse the blackness of sin from anyone.[92] In contrast, *Difference of Color* put all complexions on the same level because God created them. The unequivocal message from Lydia H. Sigourney, one of antebellum America's most famous poets and an ardent colonizationist, is that God does not tolerate bigotry. Divine wrath is certain for anyone who "despises a brother's darker brow" because God has equal regard for people marked with "sable dye" and those formed "Of fairer, whiter clay." Although Sigourney accepted European descent as a valid criterion for regulating access to American citizenship, she presented skin color as an un-Christian basis for determining worth. What is the basis of divine judgment? It is "the hue of deeds," "the

106 RELUCTANT RACE MEN

complexion of the heart," and "the color of the soul." All these things were, of necessity, white.[93]

The popular trope of whiteness as a sign of beauty, goodness, and intelligence created difficulties for Black reformers in dealings with White allies.[94] An unchecked sense of superiority burdened alliances among abolitionists. Lampooning "negrofobia" in reform circles showed the limitations of White sympathy as a reform platform. In "Caste among Quakers," David Ruggles mocked the spectacle of White members of the Society of Friends encountering an individual in their meetings "who differs from them in complexion." There was a stark contrast between their pity for slave supplicants and the terror that seized them upon meeting a Black guest who was not kneeling in tattered clothes. Ruggles could only marvel at such scenarios. They displayed members' inability to discern that Negroes bore a striking likeness to the species to which they belonged.[95] Sarcasm also shaped Samuel Ringgold Ward's interpretation of whiteness in confronting Christian condescension toward blackness. As a minister to White congregations, he knew well the Sunday school lessons that promised white souls to obedient Black children and taught that all would "be white" in Heaven. Described as "black as ink" by his neighbor and fellow abolitionist, Gerrit Smith, he saw no virtue in getting a white soul, especially if it resembled morally stunted "'white' bodies" plagued by "color-phobia." If heavenly whiteness were anything like being "'White' on earth," he mused, he would forgo the blessings of "complexional change."[96]

It was difficult to find humor in the smugness of White reformers who believed personal interactions with people of African descent were a feat. Such sentiment in testimony at a Pennsylvania Anti-Slavery Society meeting compelled Robert Purvis to assail abolitionist condescension toward colored people. He became irate when a Long Island minister boasting of freedom from "prejudice against color" offered as proof that he had eaten and slept with a Black man and declared the experience "as severe a test as a man's antislavery character could be put to." Purvis took umbrage at the supposition that White men bestowed "favor" upon colored men with whom they had personal interactions. He scoffed, moreover, at the "novel antislavery doctrine" that reduced the work of freedom to a taxing "social intimacy" that ignored principle and "the question of human rights."[97]

Disdain for associating with Black people seemed more noticeable in antislavery circles as they expanded. An inadequate appreciation for the unity of the human species appeared to be the root of the problem. Theodore

Wright, a founding member of the New York State Anti-Slavery Society, complained that a rush of new converts compromised the cause by blurring what it meant to be an abolitionist. Once, he argued, such figures were identifiable as individuals who acknowledged "the identity of the human family." This standard receded as people with diverse political commitments joined the movement. He feared that, with "everybody an abolitionist," discrimination against colored reformers would flourish. As a preventative measure, aspiring activists needed to be catechized to ensure that they understood that human beings were "of one blood and one family."[98] This principle, typically invoked in protests against discrimination and slavery, had to be taught to regulate relations among allies. Without it, antislavery initiatives could not proceed with moral certainty. The aim of ending slavery would mean little as long as abolitionists accepted race designations as legitimate markers of human difference and worth.

Revulsion toward the servile position of slaves complicated how reformers acted on their platform of a common humanity. The principle sometimes receded as individuals struggled to solidify their own citizenship claims. It gave way to other grounds for condemning racial categories. Disavowals of servitude and subjection exposed uneasiness with race designations that grouped and labeled people as the same. Strident rhetoric scorned slaves, with whom reformers purportedly sympathized, in order to distinguish them from free people claiming political rights. Although none displayed more contempt than the 1848 Pennsylvania state convention, the empathy reflected in fervent calls for abolition faded amid dramatic protests of the injustice of subjecting free people to the "spirit of slavery." Theodore Wright, for instance, railed against discrimination in schools, churches, and public accommodations with indignation over the failure to distinguish free people from individuals held in bondage. The "degrading distinction" that consigned all free people to "an inferior caste" judged them "irrespective of their morals or intellectual cultivation."[99] He experienced the bigotry as so violent and devastating that he believed it rivaled the physical brutality meted out by slaveholders.

Status anxieties fueled efforts to control the meanings of race classifications. Delegates to the 1848 national convention confronted the issue when Martin Delany, Frederick Douglass, and Henry Bibb urged colored people to shun menial labor and restrict their employment to "respectable" pursuits. Delany maintained that he would prefer to have relatives afflicted with a "loathsome disease" than to see them working as servants—positions that carried "a badge of degradation." From Canada, H. Ford Douglas concurred that it was demeaning for individuals to accept positions "set apart exclusively for colored men."[100] Doing so fortified the distinctions that reformers were trying to obliterate.

Calls to avoid lowly positions reflected a desire to avoid contempt by shifting the odium of race classifications from unwarranted privileges of whiteness to the degradation ascribed to blackness. The concern led John Hamilton, one of the first colored Americans to migrate to Trinidad, to discourage unskilled workers from settling on the island. Within months of his arrival in the fall of 1839, he established himself as a successful mechanic and carpenter. He cautioned individuals without a trade, education, or money from making the journey because they would be relegated to agricultural pursuits requiring labor formerly performed by slaves. He explained that everyone who did such work was designated "negro"—a label that placed them outside the boundaries of desirable associations. To be a Negro, he observed, was to be "no fit companion for other men."[101]

New legal enactments increased obstacles to freedom and citizenship. The 1850 Fugitive Slave Act undermined the security and stability of free communities. The obligation of all the nation's residents, even individuals in free states, to aid in the return of alleged escaped slaves expanded the institution's reach and threatened to implicate reformers in aiding it. The 1857 opinion of Supreme Court justice Roger Taney in *Dred Scott v. Sanford* signaled more formidable barriers in declaring that the mere fact of African descent was disqualified a group from rights and participation in the national polity. The combination of these developments further diminished prospects for Black American citizenship. It framed another context for race challenges. Some reformers tried to navigate the new landscape by revising conceptual foundations for claims to American identity. Restauranteur George Downing, a veteran of New York City's Underground Railroad and champion of equal education in his adopted state of Rhode Island, tackled the issue as president of the 1859 New England convention of "colored citizens" in Boston. He was optimistic that colored people would withstand the Fugitive Slave Act and the *Dred Scott* decision just as they resisted wholesale colonization and emigration initiatives. These dangers, however distressing, were not permanent setbacks. Underlying his prediction was a belief that colored people possessed an "inseparable, providential identity" with America and had a pivotal role to play in its mission. He explained that Negroes introduced diversity to American life, imparting vigor to a nation that would otherwise be uniform. His allusion to racial differences aimed to highlight their illusory character. Phenotypic and ancestral diversity were not at odds with human brotherhood, he argued, because perceived dissimilarities between Negroes and White people were not constitutional differences. Instead, they were a basis for demonstrating the essential commonalities that linked human beings. Colored Americans thus offered the nation an opportunity to affirm "the fraternal unity of man."[102]

In contrast to efforts to shore up American identity, emigration campaigns called on colored people to place their hopes for belonging and rights elsewhere. Some proponents of leaving the country stressed the futility of efforts to realize the principle of a common humanity in the United States. Others pressed for progress with an eye toward Black autonomy and self-determination. Appeals to settle in Canada, South and Central America, and the Caribbean resurfaced with a new urgency. Interest in establishing settlements in Africa that were not part of Colonization Society initiatives, also flourished. The options hinged on divergent conceptions of human difference. The ideas of reformers who promoted migrating to Canada stood in stark contrast to visions of individuals seeking a "Black Nationality." Advocates of the former option sought to overcome racial notions of difference, while the latter group construed uplift as an endeavor to make the colored population "a distinct people and a homogeneous nation."[103] Mary Ann Shadd and Martin Delany exemplified the contrasting viewpoints. Although they maintained congenial relations, they issued competing interpretations of the coherence of race categories. Shadd opposed "complexional distinctions," while Delany invoked them as grounds for developing a distinct nationality.[104] They shared opposition to colonization proposals and hopes for spreading Christianity in Africa, there was no common ground for the discrete rationales they developed to promote emigration.

Intolerance for race practices grounded Shadd's emigration advocacy and attempts to shape settlement patterns and education in Ontario, then known as Canada West. Her initiatives extended a family tradition of reform that began in the United States. Her father, Abraham Shadd, had been active in Delaware anti-colonization efforts, and, in Pennsylvania, he had allied himself with William Whipper and Robert Purvis to promote moral reform and voting rights while aiding escaping slaves. The Shadd family was drawn

110   RELUCTANT RACE MEN

into the first wave of emigration following passage of the Fugitive Slave Act. Mary Ann Shadd left her teaching post in New York in 1851 and joined several of her siblings in Canada West. As an emigrationist, she traded long-standing hopes for American citizenship rights for the prospect of freedom and equality in Canada.

Within a year of settling in Windsor, Shadd began a campaign to encourage widespread migration. She published a lengthy tract—*A Plea for Emigration or Notes on Canada West, in its Moral, Social, and Political Aspect, with Suggestions Respecting Mexico, W. Indies and Vancouver Island, for the Information of Colored Emigrants.* The work mixed the genres of travelogue, guidebook, political treatise, and propaganda to explain and exaggerate the virtues of the province, especially concerning the absence of racial distinctions. Her claims on this point were part of her overall stand against race practices. She celebrated a refusal to deploy color labels as a characteristic that made Canada the best destination for colored people. Prospective emigrants received her assurances that there was "no legal discrimination whatever." To illustrate how oblivious the province was to race categories, she observed, "Even in the slight matter of taking the census, it is impossible to get the exact number of whites or coloured, as they are not designated as such." Strictly speaking, this claim was true. Unlike the United States, which began counting the population with racial categories at the inception of the census, Canadian provinces enumerated people according to origin, birthplace, and language. As historian Robin Winks explains, even when "Negro" was an option for respondents, the category was an undefined reference to "national origin" rather than a term to sort inhabitants into races. In Shadd's telling, this practice was evidence of liberal social norms. It offered assurances that emigrants would encounter no obstacles to making a living. Everyone's work, she announced, stood or fell "according to merit."[105]

The *Provincial Freeman* equipped Shadd with a medium for expanding the reach of her message. She edited the weekly paper from 1852 to 1860 with assistance from Ohio emigrant and antislavery lecturer H. Ford Douglas, Baptist minister William P. Newman, and her siblings Isaac and Amelia.[106] Editorials in the paper describe the province as an entity that avoided turning "peculiarities of feature, complexion, &c." into legislative topics. A survey of the region's legal codes and social landscape showed it was devoid of the familiar "distinction of color." There were no linguistic practices identifying people as Black "in contradistinction to white." The bigotry Shadd witnessed in Canada arose from encounters with people who were typically "under

American influence" or members of "an inferior class."[107] Even injustices were infrequent and of a different sort. She likened Canadians' discriminatory treatment of colored people to the condescension many Americans expressed toward impoverished immigrants. Such distinctions seemed more logical and acceptable to her since they did not seem to rest on racial notions of human difference.

Idealized depictions of Canadian egalitarianism contributed to a moral imperative for migrants to eschew color distinctions. H. Ford Douglas helped instill this lesson, which had taken him some time to learn. Before allying himself with Shadd, he had argued that a "COLORED NATIONALITY" on the North American continent was necessary to conduct an effective assault against slavery.[108] This nationalist orientation yielded to condemnations of color classifications. To reinforce the message that Canada was caste-free, Ford Douglas advised migrants to become "as thoroughly British" as possible. This meant rejecting "relics of Yankee negrophobia"—colored schools and churches—that created a "line of demarcation" among British subjects.[109]

Additional backing for Shadd's campaign against distinctions came from the Provincial Union. The fifty-seven Toronto residents that Shadd helped organize staked their authority on functioning as an "associated" body of citizens. The group tried to ensure that Canadians avoided "complexional considerations" that were at odds with the nation's character. One of its first actions was to condemn settlements that housed colored migrants for reinscribing caste arrangements that fugitives from the United States had fled. Its constitution denounced the formation of "exclusive communities" for supporting the "dangerous doctrine" that the only way people "of different complexions" could live together was in a relationship of domination and subservience.[110]

Equating color distinctions with caste was critical to Shadd's efforts to secure funding for her school in Windsor. Her appeal to American Missionary Association secretary George Whipple insisted that there was no excuse for "exclusive institutions" in Canada West. Thus, her school was open to children "of all complexions." Since it was clear that the school would primarily serve children of colored migrants, Shadd tried to balance the need for the school with her claim that colored children could attend government-supported schools. Her solution was to blame parents for a lack of concern about their legal rights. She preferred this account to an acknowledgment that discrimination was an ordinary aspect of Canadian life. She was silent about the 1850 Separate School Act, which allowed groups of colored

112   RELUCTANT RACE MEN

families to petition for separate public schools. In practice, it offered White Canadians an excuse to exclude colored children from existing schools.

Unwilling to abet the "spirit of caste," Shadd discontinued her membership in the African Methodist Episcopal Church after she settled to Canada. The "distinctive character" of independent colored churches violated her principles. She believed that they distorted Christianity and made it impossible for colored people to adequately appreciate their status as British subjects. Their "caste character" was out of sync with a social environment that did not sanction separation via the "negro pew."[111]

Exaggerated accounts of equality in British Canada were not new. More than a decade earlier, Charles Ray had campaigned against "separate churches and separate schools" in Canada West (then known as Upper Canada) at the same time he defended independent conventions of colored people.[112] In 1841, he published editorials criticizing the establishment of schools for colored children in Canada. The complaint targeted Hiram Wilson, one of the "Lane Rebels" and a former agent of the American Anti-Slavery Society. He helped organize escaped slaves into the communities Shadd disparaged as "caste settlements." He gained greater visibility while trying to raise money for educational projects and for soliciting funds for a manual labor school. Ray judged Wilson as unqualified to enlist support from Christians and called for proof that the schools, like segregated conventions, were necessary. Ray's image of Canada as a place with no color distinctions made it impossible for anyone to meet this standard. He insisted that the schools were not essential, out of step with government policy, and ruinous.[113]

Wilson did not advocate schools exclusively for colored children. He defended his work by pointing out that he had never established a separate colored church or school. He organized schools where none existed, was committed to teaching students "on equal terms," and reported that half of the students in some schools were White. Although he seemed to accept Ray's moral standard, he challenged the idea that schools specifically for colored children were unnecessary in Canada. Samuel Ward, who would later migrate to Canada and assisted in editing the *Provincial Freeman*, helped Wilson explain. The men cited residents' and visitors' accounts of widespread bigotry, identified churches operating on "the negro pew system," and observed that government-supported schools denied equal access to colored children. In view of the facts, Ward chided Ray for misrepresenting the civil and political situation in Canada, which harbored the same distinctions that prevailed in the United States. He reminded Ray that many of the

"ONE COMMON FAMILY" 113

inhabitants of Canada West were not "the English" but "Yankees" whose bigotry crossed the border with them. In addition to undermining the truth of Ray's claims, Ward charged him with hypocrisy, insisting that if he opposed color distinctions, he should abandon the *Colored American* and colored conventions.[114]

Shadd questioned the "theory and practice" of using racial categories as bases of unity and authority. She presented her ideas in response to an affront from Frederick Douglass. He took notice of the *Provincial Freeman* in an editorial that disparaged her reform efforts while pretending to praise them. She felt slighted, wounded, and exploited by the "certificate" he bestowed upon her character as he maligned it. He applauded Shadd as a woman who had no equal "among the colored ladies of the United States." Given the unqualified praise Douglass offered for Harriet Beecher Stowe, whom he cited in the same editorial, the compliment diminished Shadd's stature as a reformer. The Stowe reference was all the more problematic for Shadd because Douglass failed to distinguish individuals who migrated to Canada from people represented by characters in Stowe's novel who colonized Liberia. This elision of differences appeared to be part of an attempt to curry favor with Stowe and other White reformers who were sympathetic to colonization. In Shadd's eyes, it sullied the Canadian emigration project. It made matters worse that he ridiculed Shadd's social commentary as mere "complaining" that was sometimes too abrasive for his tastes.[115]

Complimentary portions of Douglass's commentary also perturbed Shadd. His recognition of her editorial work seemed to serve as a means to boost his own prominence. He claimed credit for bringing Shadd into public view. She sarcastically mused that perhaps she should be flattered at being "brought 'to light'" by Douglass.[116] Instead, she bristled at his condescension and at being used in a self-promotion enterprise. She navigated the problem by making the editorial an occasion to further contrast British Canadian ideals and US realities. It enabled her to broadcast the shortcomings of framing collective authority with racial labels. Differences between the needs of colored people in the United States and those in Canada shaped her argument. For example, her father's activism, which would lead to his election to the Town Council in Raleigh, West Canada, demonstrated that Canadians could participate in politics, whereas colored people in the United States faced nearly wholesale political exclusion. The divergent circumstances of the two populations showed why it was illogical to ground collective endeavors solely on race categories; a shared racial designation was not evidence of identical ideas.

Rejecting what she perceived as a popular expectation that colored people "should agree upon one course of action," she reasoned that only a bigot or an idiot would insist on grouping colored people into an undifferentiated mass simply because they all shared the designation "colored." The notion that "color must be a bond of union among colored" was anathema to her. She was indignant that Douglass—presumed "writer-in-chief for the colored people of America"—sought to assert authority over the interests of Canadians. As someone who lived in a society riven by racial categories, he was not equipped, in her estimation, to address concerns of British subjects who had escaped the specter of "complexional distinctions." She resented attempts to incorporate Canadians into any group represented by "colored leaders" because appeals to "complexional distinctions" relied on the fiction that they were naturally a distinct racial unit. The effort implied that the "colored" label should displace citizenship and national allegiances as grounds of belonging. It was tantamount to a call for treason because it directed loyalties to "an imaginary power."[117]

Proponents of a "Negro Nationality" labored to adapt racial conceptualizations of political authority for collective advancement. Martin Delany, "father" of Black nationalism, pressed this aim forward with the insistence that colored people possessed features that were unique to them. "We have then inherent traits, attributes—so to speak—and native characteristics, peculiar to our race."[118] This was a critical facet of his six-hour speech "The Political Destiny of the Colored Race on the American Continent," delivered at the 1854 emigration convention in Cleveland. He admonished listeners that race traits revealed the unavoidable "truth" that colored people were "not identical with the Anglo-Saxon." Accordingly, they required a nationality beyond the United States that was compatible with their racial characteristics.[119]

Forthright appeals to race constructions distinguished Delany's project from Henry Highland Garnet's emigration endeavor, the African Civilization Society. The men consulted on their respective projects, each accepted financial support from the American Colonization Society, and, like Delany, Garnet touted his plan to develop "a grand centre of Negro nationality" that would generate worldwide respect for colored people. Yet justifications for their endeavors differed. Ridiculed for operating nothing more than a variant of colonization, Garnet was accused of merely echoing the ACS message that Black people did not belong in America. His defense emphasized the project's missionary aims and the antislavery potential of competing with slavery by producing African cotton with free laborers. Indeed, the organization's constitution named these factors and the eradication of Africa's slave trade in defining its objectives.[120] In contrast, Delany looked to turn racial taxonomies into a rationale for national political differences that justified.

Embracing race categories entailed a shift in Delany's thinking. It bore little resemblance to his apologetic tone in the *Mystery*, the reform paper he launched in 1843. He introduced the periodical by disavowing race constructions as he announced its commitment to the "Moral Elevation of the Africo American and African race." He assured readers that he rejected "distinctive principles of race" and, instead, devoted the paper to the "universal benefit of man." Despite the specificity of his objectives, he was guided by a vision of common and "inseparable" human interests that were odds with notions of essential human difference and rank.[121]

There was precedent among reformers for premising emigration projects on racial constructions of difference. John Mercer Langston made similar connections before abandoning emigration campaigns for a career in law and American politics. He had insisted that Black people "must have a nationality" if they were to become "any body." The claim that there was a "natural repellency between the two races" gave legitimacy to his vision of building a separate Black nation. He had repudiated this platform by the time Delany began broadcasting his plans. New ideals of a destiny "in common" with White men supplanted his once dire warnings of the "absorption and extinction" of colored people. Yet his work contributed to a conceptual framework for connecting the existence of races to nationality.[122]

Delany had difficulty explaining the two phenomena. When considering emigration to Central or South America and the Caribbean, he sidestepped straightforward assertions about essential differences and characteristics among races. Instead, he sought historical warrants to justify ascribing traits to colored people. The history of nations revealed the importance of collective identity and a sense of common origin. He learned that Egypt, Carthage, and Rome had collapsed as each lost its "original identity." The contemporary political landscape proved the ongoing importance of sustaining such connections across time. Nations that displayed strength and endurance—the United States, Great Britain, Russia, Turkey, and France—were all true to a foundational identity. Hungary, however, did not become a viable nation after its 1849 bid for independence from Austria because its population lacked a "unity of interests," which meant they had no "identity of origin."[123] Failure was predictable.

116 RELUCTANT RACE MEN

Adapting a theory of national development to warrants for emigration was complicated. It entailed transforming some nations into races. Delany's method for determining what constitutes a race is ambiguous. For instance, he questioned the appropriateness of identifying Hungary's "Magyars, Celts, and Sclaves" as distinct races, despite the fact that they identified themselves as such. Yet he had no reservations imputing an "identity as a distinct race" to colored people. He equated them with nations posing as races and used this equation as the basis for a Black nation. He reasoned that if "all other races," including the English, French, Irish, Germans, Italians, Turks, Persians, Greeks, and Jews, possessed "native or inherent peculiarities," then "why not our race?" He did not address the question of what made colored people a race comparable to national groups.[124]

The list of "inherent traits" Delany ascribed to colored people suggests that he viewed races and race traits as social and cultural factors, rather than essential phenomena. For example, he described the "colored races" as "civil, peaceable, and religious" groups that could teach the world languages, poetry, music, painting, ethics, metaphysics, theology, and jurisprudence. Instruction would take place in the future because the "traits" had to be developed through social and cultural practices. They were "inherent" qualities that did not automatically express themselves.[125]

Conceptions of race became more muddled in Delany's explanations of Africa as the rightful home of "the African race." He mocked colonizationist assertions that colored people were especially suited to warm African climates. To parody their ideas, he cited a "physiological fact" of his own. Unlike the "white race," the "colored race" could adapt to every climate. Not all members of the race exhibited this trait, however; it was characteristic of people with dark skin. This subset constituted a "black race" on which God bestowed "natural properties" of adaptability. These factors justified African emigration and explained the basis for building an African nation. They demonstrated that Black people had a natural "right and duty" to live anywhere they chose. Choice was a supplementary facet of Delany's configuration of races; it determined which members of the "colored race" had a legitimate claim to Africa. Loyalty appeared to trump physical traits. Only men of African descent who "claim an identity with the race" had a right to rule the planned nation.[126]

The ideas grounding Delany's emigration program distinguish his reform platform from the agendas of many of his antebellum contemporaries who engaged race. Yet, the juxtaposition of his theory to his admiration for spaces that lacked state-regulated racial distinctions complicates his stance and exposes common difficulties in conceptualizing justifications for collective authority. In 1856, as he worked to finalize plans for developing an independent nation, he temporarily relocated his family from Pittsburgh to Canada West. The praise he heaped on the region suggests that a Negro nationality was not the sole component of his vision of an ideal society. "We love the Canadas," he declared, because "there is no difference known among the people—no distinction of race."[127] Despite the utility of racial constructs in his work, their virtues, like their logic, were apparently mutable. In any case, his declaration shows an ungainly convergence of contempt for prevailing constructions of human difference, sameness, and hierarchy and the complicated quest for coherent grounds for collective advancement. It highlights the diverse array of antebellum reform perspectives on race practices.

———

Questions about the logic and ethics of race complicated antebellum reform initiatives. Exclusion and hierarchy helped sustain qualms about the legitimacy of racial concepts even among reformers who tried to reframe them. Misgivings would deepen and harden as scientists advanced theories to justify everyday wrongs and structural inequalities that sustained the American "pseudo-republic." As scholarly speculations about races flourished, reformers would rely on established media networks of newspapers, pamphlets, petitions, and tracts to broadcast arguments against innovations in American racial practices. Their ideas would extend race challenges into a new arena.

4

"Humanology"

Difference and the Science of Humanity

William Whipper launched his 1839 reform endeavors with a scientific innovation dubbed "humanology."[1] He presented the project as akin to phrenology and thus ventured that it would have popular appeal. His confidence was well founded. Fascination with phrenology was widespread. Advertisements for treatments and instruction were common in reform newspapers. Profits from lucrative practices helped finance colored conventions. Even individuals esteemed for their formal scientific training had difficulty convincing audiences of the scheme's fallacies.[2] Whipper, however, derided the enterprise as a specious technique that structured an invalid hierarchy. He ridiculed the proposition that anyone could discern mental capacities by scrutinizing the contours of human heads. Nevertheless, he surmised that the audacious fad would persist and erode appreciation for the "natural equality" of human beings. Disgust with phrenology's allure prompted him to propose a science that would contrive an anatomical basis for excluding people from the sphere of humanity. "Humanology" promised to explain once and for all "what organs a man ought to have to render him a slave."[3]

Whipper's critique of phrenology was a steppingstone to condemnations of race science, specifically, the theory of polygeny that was taking shape in professional scientific arenas. The idea that people naturally fell into essentially different and unequal populations exasperated him. He decried the contention that there were "different species and races in the human family," dismissing it as an attempt to prop up the pro-slavery cant against amalgamation. He mused that, "strictly speaking," this notion of mixing did not exist among human beings. The term was a misnomer because a single origin constituted everyone in the same way. Scripture offered proof. He found no evidence of multiple creations; all people descended from Adam. Polygenesis, which deviated from the biblical tenet that humanity was "of one blood," was thus unsound science.[4]

Reluctant Race Men. Joan L. Bryant, Oxford University Press. © Oxford University Press 2024.
DOI: 10.1093/oso/9780195312966.003.0005

This terse repudiation of race science captured a pervasive sensibility among colored reformers. Scorn for its prevailing theories was commonplace. Episcopal minister James Theodore Holly, for example, deemed it a waste of time to delve into the field. He celebrated Haiti's achievement of sovereignty as a sign that there was no need for "long drawn out arguments to defend negro-Ethnography against the Notts and Gliddons"—two preeminent theorists of Black inferiority. The existence of the independent nation sufficed to show the fallacious pretensions of the science. An anonymous colored contributor to the *Liberator* was equally skeptical. The writer ridiculed the absurd conclusions of anatomists who dissected bodies to demonstrate that colored people belonged to "the race of Oran Outangs." Such bigoted speculations did not warrant confrontation. Instead, they paved the way for future generations to mock the self-assured "enlightened" thinkers of 1830s for fostering the same type of "ignorance and superstition" that condemned Copernicus and Galileo for heresy and sorcery.[5]

Unbridled contempt for scientific pretense left few reformers willing to contend with race science in a sustained or systematic manner. Most collective endeavors targeted arguments about human bodies in terms of imminent social and political hazards. They assailed barriers to freedom and citizenship with the assertion that physical attributes of people of African descent were natural, normal, and even desirable. The insistence that God's original and benevolent design explained phenotype became ubiquitous in reform arenas. A well-worn script chastised White people for discrimination by reminding them that people of color were their "fellow creatures" and explaining that a wise God thought it appropriate to endow some people with dark skin. It was thus irreverent and "insulting to humanity" to equate the appearance of colored people with natural deficiencies that were grounds for oppression. Such declarations generally concluded with the affirmation that all humans were "of one blood," despite differences in size, shape, and color.[6]

Efforts of a select set of men extended beyond conventional reform milieus to engage the claims of race science. The treatises, editorials, letters, and speeches that frame their confrontations stand apart from the dialogue and debate that characterized collective initiatives. Through largely solitary undertakings, such figures as *Freedom's Journal* editor John Russwurm, New England ministers Hosea Easton and James W. C. Pennington, and New York physician James McCune Smith countered the scientific credibility of assertions and assumptions that people of African descent were indistinguishable from each other, essentially different and innately inferior

120   RELUCTANT RACE MEN

to White populations, and permanently incapacitated. Taken together, individual challenges comprise a shared effort to delineate natural warrants for a common humanity and inborn equality among the world's peoples.[7]

———

The science of human variation was in flux in the antebellum period. As phrenology was capturing the popular imagination, professional scientists—polygenists, craniologists, and some environmentalists—were concocting and debating new theories of inequality and constitutional differences among human populations. This landscape reinforced reformers' convictions that race classifications were, as Frederick Douglass asserted, merely "artificial" constructs invented to support the contention that nature required separating White and colored people into separate and unequal spheres.[8] The theory of polygenesis and the practice of craniology were the most conspicuous innovations of the era. They were hallmarks of the American School of ethnology spearheaded by prominent scientific professionals. Samuel Morton, whose 1839 *Crania Americana* spurred the group's research, was a medically trained president of Philadelphia's Academy of Natural Sciences. He also dabbled in phrenology. Swiss naturalist Louis Agassiz was a Harvard professor and founder of its Museum for Comparative Zoology. George Gliddon, an Egyptologist, served as US vice consul in Cairo. Josiah Nott, a Mobile, Alabama, slaveholder, operated a successful medical practice. These men—all apologists for American slavery—divided humans into unequal populations, variously labeled races, types, and, ultimately, species. The final term encapsulated their dream of proving that each of the populations they differentiated as a race was a "primordial organic form." American race science thus assumed a leading role in mapping variations in physical, intellectual, and moral traits that distinguished these forms. The dissimilarities were purportedly "independent of external causes" and indicated separate origins. Craniology generated empirical evidence of the essential character of differences and of a fixed hierarchy among human populations. Morton and his colleagues used skull measurements to prove that White people's claims to social superiority reflected an immutable natural order. Cranium size provided a proxy for intellectual capacity. Skulls that Morton distinguished as Caucasian, Mongolian, Malaysian, American, and Negro grounded his conclusion that brains became "successively smaller" in each successive race. The "primeval attributes of mind" explained this finding and gave his race "a decided and unquestionable superiority over all the nations of the earth."[9] American School scientists used such logic to render people of African descent a discrete and inferior species. They created physical warrants for permanent social and political subjugation and exclusion.

Morton credited physician Charles Caldwell, a devotee of anthropology and phrenology, with inspiring his work on craniology. Caldwell paved the way for American School assaults on environmentalism, a theory that had grown popular among scientists in the late eighteenth century. Its adherents insisted on the unity of the human species and attributed physical differences to environmental factors. Caldwell, who taught natural history at the University of Pennsylvania and medicine in Kentucky schools, launched his first salvo at environmentalism and the doctrine of a single human origin in an 1811 book review. His target was *An Essay on the Causes of the Variety of Complexion and Figure in the Human Species*, a work of Presbyterian minister Samuel Stanhope Smith, president of Princeton University's precursor, the College of New Jersey. An 1830 monograph, *Thoughts on the Original Unity of the Human Race*, further developed Caldwell's critique. The text used an assessment of British anthropologist James Cowles Prichard's study *Researches into the Physical History of Mankind* as a springboard for discrediting arguments for the unity of the human species. Alleged differences in virtually every facet of the body—blood, toes, bones, muscles, knees, heads, genitals, and fingernails—led Caldwell to conclude that "the Caucasian race" and "the African race," comprising "the Hottentots, the Boschesemen, and the Papuas, or negroes of Oceanica," were different species.[10]

Environmentalism offered colored reformers potentially commanding weapons against charges that physical differences reflected natural inequalities and divergent origins. However, critics had to be judicious in their use of the theory. Adherence to monogenism did not prevent proponents from theorizing about innate Black inferiority. Natural historian John Bachman was a case in point. The Lutheran minister and professor at the College of Charleston was a staunch critic of polygeny. He acknowledged the existence of a single human species, but he was convinced that profound natural differences separated Negroes and White people. He posited that Negroes were an inferior "permanent variety." This meant that mental, moral, and physical attributes that allegedly made them lesser beings remained unchanged in the face of environmental forces. Only a "revolting" biological process of "amalgamation," he argued, could modify them.[11]

The concept of degeneration accommodated environmentalist speculations that inherent inequality could coexist with a common origin. It provided a framework for the position that some groups had deteriorated from humans' initial state. Invariably, the darkest complexions correlated with the greatest measures of decline. Even environmentalists who were sympathetic to the circumstances of colored people judged dark skin as abnormal. Samuel Stanhope Smith hoped that their complexions would become lighter in North America's moderate climates. Such a transformation would bring them closer to the "original" human variety from which they purportedly had degenerated. Philadelphia physician Benjamin Rush, a former mentor to Charles Caldwell, held more extreme views. Long after his death, Rush, a founding member of the Pennsylvania Society for Promoting the Abolition of Slavery, won praise from antebellum reformers for his kindness to colored people. Nevertheless, the medical case of Henry Moss betrayed his conviction that dark skin was neither natural nor healthy. Moss was one of several men of African descent who gained notoriety in the early republic for a skin condition that made him appear to be turning white. Caldwell, Smith, and Rush all took an interest in his situation. Caldwell diagnosed "morbid albinism." Smith read the phenomenon as an example of climate's ability to change phenotype. After his examination of Moss, Rush concluded that dark skin among Negroes was a sign of a heritable form of leprosy. The case convinced him that "spontaneous cures" could turn dark skin into "natural white flesh." Moreover, it illustrated the need for benevolent scientific interventions, such as bleeding, to relieve the colored population of its complexional affliction.[12]

Tackling scientific developments expanded the terrain on which reformers confronted the meaning of race. The stakes associated with race science were obvious, even if they seemed more remote than consequences of other conceptions of difference and hierarchy. Theories and empirical methods constructed purportedly natural foundations for myriad forms of exclusion and domination. As Frederick Douglass observed:

> Let it be once granted that the human race are [sic] of multitudinous origin, naturally different in their moral, physical, and intellectual capabilities, and at once, you make plausible a demand for classes, grades and conditions, for different methods of culture, different moral, political, and religious institutions, and a chance is left for slavery, as a necessary institution.[13]

"HUMANOLOGY" 123

Critics of race science confronted its claims within parameters governing scientific methods. They exhibited the same regard for scientific knowledge that prevailed in endeavors to promote progress and civilization. Individuals with divergent reform visions extolled it. Whipper's 1834 Declaration of Sentiment cited scientific genius for distinguishing ancient Africa as one of the world's great civilizations. He perceived the founding of Philadelphia's Colored Reading Society as a scientific advancement for privileging principles and facts over hypotheses. Similarly, *Colored American* editors Samuel Cornish and Charles Ray called for elevating free people of color by developing their mastery of science. To this end, colored Bostonians of all ages flocked to the Adelphic Union's programs on scientific topics. The New York Philomathean Society sponsored debates, recitations, and readings on scientific questions and lionized individuals who labored up the "Hill of Science." The group praised scientific instruction for inspiring goodness and preventing misconduct. As Lewis Woodson reasoned, the "sun of science" dissipated "moral gloom." New York's Phoenixonian Literary Society acted on such sentiments by devoting nearly half of its 1841 forums to scientific lectures on astronomy, blood circulation, genius, the laws of "mind and matter," morality, and phrenology. A decade later, conceptual linkages among science, analytic rigor, and enlightenment persisted. AME Church bishop Daniel Payne urged the denomination's clergy to educate themselves "by the light of science" as the first step in exercising Christian leadership. Maryland's convention of free colored people optimistically hailed scientific inquiry as the outstanding feature of the age, as demonstrated by advances in all the sciences—"physical, political, intellectual, and moral." Even gender conventions wavered in the face of concerns about science. On the one hand, Maria Stewart transgressed antebellum gender norms by publicly chastising Boston's colored male leadership for lacking "the man of science." This deficiency, she warned, would cause the entire community to languish. Philip Bell, on the other hand, believed that all "civilized communities" required scientific understanding of human bodies. He criticized the exclusion of women from a Pacific Museum exhibition on anatomy, pronouncing men and women equals in their need for accurate knowledge of this subject and its methods. Northern free people of color exhibited such enthusiasm over the virtues of scientific inquiry that the American League of Colored Laborers worried that they might forget the utility of "the ARTS of Agriculture, Manufacture, and Commerce."[14]

Challenging race science required reformers to replace conventional assertions about civil and political equality with explanations of developments

124   RELUCTANT RACE MEN

in human history. The task entailed alternative accounts of the allegedly inherent disparities that race categories signified. Two sets of issues structured the undertaking. The first concerned the nature of history. Reformers interpreted it as an aggregation of contingent factors. Lessons from the ancient past and the Bible helped them distinguish human populations using lineage and geography to track experiences over time. They scoured the historical record for insights into discrete social and political situations that explained why the fortunes of various populations differed. This approach defied polygenists' assumptions that observable human differences and divergent historical experiences were temporal manifestations of primordial traits and rank.[15]

The second group of issues involved procedures for identifying and interpreting differences. Critics charged race science with using flawed assumptions and methods, specious evidence, and faulty logic, all of which violated scientific strictures. They refuted its claims with empirical observations, biblical narratives, historical data, and their own theories about human difference and characteristics of people of African descent.

Investigations validated the contempt for race science expressed by individuals who refused to engage it as a science. They confirmed that it was an illegitimate means for interpreting human difference and sameness. Its inability to demarcate accurate boundaries for the human species made it a poor arbiter of national membership. Only true scientific principles could offer reliable means for understanding humanity, equality, and citizenship.

———

Confrontations with race science emerged with the development of antebellum reform initiatives. John Russwurm took on the issue in 1827, just after launching *Freedom's Journal* with Samuel Cornish. Reverend Hosea Easton, a contributor to national conventions and anti-colonization forums, followed in the 1830s. Their analyses laid the groundwork for subsequent challenges to American School ideas about human difference and rank.

Russwurm was unconvinced that scientific evidence showed that the world's populations were essentially different and naturally unequal. He was intent on unseating the idea that there was "a superior and an inferior race." Christian teachings and observable facts helped him challenge speculations of such "visionary philosophers" as Swiss taxonomist Carolus Linnaeus, French naturalist Georges Louis Leclerc, Comte de Buffon, British naturalist

Charles Darwin, and Scottish philosopher Henry Home, Lord Kames, all of whom he denounced by name. Although he found polygeny particularly loathsome, a sweeping condemnation lumped the environmentalism of Linnaeus and Buffon with Kames, who rejected the unity of the human species before the rise of the American School. Darwin warranted a special denunciation for allegedly privileging oysters as a superior life form. Russwurm determined that all the theories were "devoid of sense" and violated the fundamental principle of human equality reflected in biblical history that traced human descent from Adam.[16]

An editorial on the downfall of Egypt launched Russwurm's quarrels with scientific ideas about human inequality, particularly claims about the "intellectual inferiority of the African race." He confessed that people of African descent were a degraded class in America. The circumstances of slaves and free colored people were obvious indicators. However, the Egyptian mummy that became a New York City spectacle in 1826 was a glaring example of the problem's magnitude. After viewing the mummy in Rubens Peale's New York museum, he lamented that such an extraordinary cultural and scientific achievement had been reduced to a commodity for "a gazing world." The depths to which Africa's people had fallen were apparent in the fact that the tombs of royalty had been plundered and their bodies "bought and sold."[17]

Russwurm linked Egypt's downfall to historical forces to demonstrate that African debasement did not stem from innate inferiority. Environmentalist arguments and interpretations of the past guided his efforts in an essay entitled "The Mutability of Human Affairs." To connect colored Americans to Egypt, he insisted that Egyptians and Ethiopians descended from the biblical Cush, a son of Ham. As such, the groups comprised a single ancestral people who once shared physical attributes. The genealogical connection enabled Russwurm to sidestep a tradition that mapped Negro descent from Canaan, Ham's other son, whom Noah condemned to servitude. The observation of Greek philosopher Herodotus that ancient Egyptians possessed "black skins and frizzled hair" further linked them to Ethiopians. To account for differences in skin color between Egyptians and Ethiopians of his day, Russwurm recast the populations as "two races" whose color variations resulted from climatic differences among various geographic areas. He reasoned that the darkest skin was confined to the hottest climates, while people with copper-colored skin lived throughout the globe, including temperate regions of hot environments. Reports of Portuguese settlers in Africa whose complexions became indistinguishable from the dark skins of some

126 RELUCTANT RACE MEN

indigenous Africans showed that phenotype was a geographically variable characteristic. It established neither essential differences nor worth. Although environmentalist logic supported his argument for the unity of the species, Russwurm credited first-century Roman scholar Pliny the Elder for the insight that the sun made the complexion of Africans dark.[18]

Political connections between Egypt and Ethiopia offered additional proof that dark-skinned Ethiopians were not an intellectually inferior race. Such ties provided historical grounds for identifying oppressed people of African descent in America with the magnificence of ancient Egypt. Citing Herodotus and the Bible, he placed Ethiopians among the Egyptian monarchs. Their status as rulers made it was impossible for him to see "any great difference" between the state of culture and science in the two nations.[19]

Religious tenets and biological facts supplemented historical evidence against scientific misrepresentations. The belief that God designed no differences in the core nature of human beings meant that there was no correlation between variations in appearance and "moral and intellectual worth." The insignificance of complexion was clear; it did not correspond to intellectual differences or situate Africans between humans and beasts. Russwurm noted that the coloring of dark skin comprised only a "thin mucous stratum" located between the cuticle and the cutis, or "true skin"—layers that varied "LITTLE" among human beings.[20] This explanation had prevailed since the late seventeenth century, when Italian anatomist Marcello Malpighi and Dutch anatomist Johann Pechlin published experiments on Ethiopian cadavers. After applying Malpighi's dissection methods, Pechlin reported in 1677 that, when he removed the dark mucus between upper and lower skin layers, "a whiteness came forth immediately of the sort seen often enough in Europe."[21] Such evidence enabled Russwurm to assure readers that there was no complexional basis for differences in achievement between colored and White Americans. He thus dismissed craniologist charges that Africans suffered from natural incapacity and concluded that limited opportunities explained the low social status of colored people.

Egypt's fate reinforced the judgment that colored people's oppression was not a natural or permanent phenomenon. As historian Wilson Moses observes, Russwurm believed in cyclical history that rendered human fortunes unstable. This concept, evident in Herodotus's *Histories*, became popular in the wake of Constantin-François Volney's 1791 reflections on the ascent and decline of empires in *The Ruins, or Meditations on the Revolutions of Empires and the Law of Nature*. It provided a template for situating experiences of Africans and their descendants in broader currents of human history. Russwurm argued that, although dire, their circumstances were consistent with world developments. War, for example, explained Egypt's decline. A single defeat at the Battle of Actium resulted in Roman domination, population decreases, loss of wealth, and ultimately the decline of Egyptian civilization. Egypt's hardships, like the misfortunes of Greece, Rome, and Spain, demonstrated that the degradation of Ethiopia and, by extension, of colored Americans, represented discrete transitory phases in "continually revolving" human affairs.[22]

The following year, a new essay, "On the Varieties of the Human Race," aimed to explain causes of phenotypic variations. It set out to counter the polygenist assertion that physical differences were evidence of multiple human origins and a natural hierarchy. Climate again supplied the decisive explanation, showing that differences in appearance resulted from exposure to different environments and were not visible at creation. Food and lifestyle had "equally astonishing" effects on physical makeup. This formulation stemmed from Samuel Stanhope Smith's arguments about the effects of customs. Smith theorized that a group's "habits of living" could either intensify or mitigate the effects of climate on appearance. To illustrate, he observed that the routines of American Indians made their brown complexions even darker. Working long hours in the sun inhaling gases from decaying vegetation at waterside camps gave a "deep bilious tinge" to their skins. The theory convinced Russwurm that phenotype was so unstable that climate, diet, and lifestyle could alter an individual's appearance in the course of decades. The case of "the Moorish prince" Abduhl Rahahman showed that changing these factors could dramatically transform features. Rahahman, who had been a slave in Mississippi, gained public notoriety when the American Colonization Society supported his efforts to return to Africa. Russwurm noted that, before Rahahman's enslavement, his skin was "copper coloured," and his hair was "long and straight, like our Indians." Slavery wrought such striking changes in his appearance that they were "perceptible to all."[23]

In the short term, Russwurm's commentaries did little to inspire comparable initiatives. Three years after they appeared, the pseudonymous "EUTHYMUS" made tentative efforts to employ similar methods. However, he did so only after declaring race science an unworthy opponent. The "colored subscriber" from Columbia, Pennsylvania, announced at the start of his letter to the *Liberator* that it was useless to engage in "philosophical speculation" about color variations. Nevertheless, he was intent on using the biblical

128   RELUCTANT RACE MEN

record of ancient history, modern history, and environmentalism to discredit the use of complexion to group, divide, and rank human beings. He reasoned that the Bible undermined efforts to correlate dark skin with inferiority or opprobrium because it portrayed Solomon as an eminent colored leader and presented white skin as divine punishment for wrongdoing. Observations of modern-day Jews further demonstrated that variations in complexion were unsound grounds for making distinctions among people. Their appearance lent credibility to the environmentalist stance that "climate and mode of life have produced the diversification of color in the human species." Jews' complexions were white, olive, copper, or swarthy, depending on the regions they inhabited. Yet color variations failed to diminish their identity or status as one "distinct people."[24]

Failure to contend with the historical subjugation colored people faced compromised the logic of scientific judgments. The insistence that Negroes were akin to monkeys displayed ignorance about basic anatomical and spiritual facts. EUTHYMUS explained that, in addition to being quadrupeds, monkeys lacked the "gizzard of musculous stomach" that was characteristic of humans. They also lacked souls—another feature that distinguished people from other life forms.[25] After attempting to engage race science seriously, he expressed the same intolerance that left other reformers silent in the face of its claims. He concluded that, even if people of color were physically or intellectually inferior to White people, there were no valid warrants for slavery and discrimination. Such modes of subjection violated natural and divine laws, as well as the nation's founding ideals of equality.[26]

———

Nearly a decade passed between Russwurm's editorials and another comprehensive effort to engage race science. During this interval, reformers became increasingly aware of polygenist claims that phenotypic variations connoted innate difference and rank. In 1837, Hosea Easton expressed concerns about such ideas in a fifty-four-page tract that historian Bruce Dain has identified as the first monogenist race theory formulated by a Black American. The publication, *A Treatise on the Intellectual Character, and Civil and Political Condition of the Colored People of the U. States; and the Prejudice Exercised towards Them*, was the most extensive scientific explication of race to appear among colored reformers before 1840. The title candidly announces the political and social considerations at the core of the project. Like Russwurm,

"HUMANOLOGY" 129

Easton engaged race science as part of his involvement with broader reform endeavors. In addition to anti-colonization and national convention activities, he ministered to spiritual and social concerns of colored people in Congregational and Methodist churches in Massachusetts and Connecticut and participated in Boston's General Colored Association, its Adelphic Union, and the Hartford Literary and Religious Institution. These commitments guided his attempts to explain circumstances facing colored people.[27]

Easton set out to demonstrate what he thought learned people should have known—that there were "no constitutional differences" among human beings. He accepted this principle as a Christian truth. However, the treatise offered empirical foundations for his convictions that phenotypic variations among humans were insignificant and no population was naturally inferior or superior to another. Initially, Easton echoed Russwurm. He deployed environmentalist reasoning to show that variations in human skin color and hair texture conformed to the same laws that diversified the rest of the natural world. He observed that, contrary to the claims of polygenists, innumerable colors and textures comprised individual species of plants and animals. Visible differences were thus poor indicators of "intrinsic" differences. He was further convinced that skin color had no permanent physical substance and played no essential role in constituting human bodies. As proof, he observed that dissecting organs did not reveal a person's complexion. Moreover, after a corpse decomposed, there was no way to isolate color as a body part in a way that was comparable to identifying hands or legs. The apparent disappearance of skin color after death rendered it inconsequential.[28]

This unusual interpretation of physical features buttressed Easton's view that skin color had no inherent meaning or power. It did not constitute bodies, it was an unreliable marker of human difference, and it had no natural connection to social relations. Its purported social significance and influence were figments of biased American imaginations.[29]

A sharp distinction between questions of difference and the issue of hierarchy guided Easton's attempt to show that the inferiority ascribed to slaves had no "original hereditary cause." His undertaking involved separating the mind from the physical world because he was convinced that nature had no bearing on intellectual ability. As craniologists worked to measure intellectual capacity through skull size, he severed intellectual ability from bodily attributes. "I cannot believe," he declared, "that nature has anything to do in variegating intellect." His sense that intelligence was a social construct led to

130   RELUCTANT RACE MEN

a search for the source of mental differences between Europeans and Africans in divergent customs or "habits of life." The course of their populations' respective histories through barbarity, civilizations, conquest, commerce, religion, and fraud compelled him to ascribe "true greatness" to "the descendants of Ham," progenitor of the "African race." He saw no need to delineate ancestral ties or phenotypic similarities to specific regional populations. African origins apparently gave people of color in the United States a claim to developments on the entire continent. He discerned evidence of Africa's intellectual and cultural prowess in libraries, mathematicians, astronomers, and philosophers of Egypt and Carthage. In contrast, the "motley" pasts of Europe and America confirmed that favorable circumstances and avarice, not natural superiority, explained their dominant positions. The conquests that led to Africa's loss of people and wealth crystallized the depravity of Europe's preeminence and showcased "the rapacity of the great minds of European bigots."[30]

Africa's history inspired Easton, nonetheless. Past achievements nurtured his conviction that Africans and their descendants would experience a resurgence and lead Christians into the millennium. The trajectory he imagined mirrors the biblical prophecy of Psalms 68:31: "Princes shall come out of Egypt and Ethiopia shall soon stretch forth her hands unto God." Historian Albert Raboteau has argued that nineteenth-century Black theologians "read their future" in this text.[31] Although Easton did not cite the passage as the source of his prediction, its promise complements his sense of historical contingency by providing warrants for belief in Africa's ultimate salvation and spiritual ascendancy.

Greatness was just one dimension of the African past. Degradation was also a critical aspect of the story. Easton confessed that changing historical circumstance had produced "as much difference" between colored Americans and their "noble" ancestors as existed between them and any contemporary "race or nation."[32] Nevertheless, he took comfort in the idea that contingent factors explained the decline from past achievement to present ignominy as he struggled to explain the moral and mental capacity of people living in slavery. He rejected popular and scientific projects that failed to consider the institution's mechanisms in issuing judgments about slaves' "intellectual and physical inferiority." The "approbrious [sic] terms" that described "negro character"—"sloped foreheads; prominent eye-balls; projecting under-jaw . . . no taste for high and honorable attainments"— offered empirical evidence of slavery's "lineal effects."[33] The arduous labor and physical privations of slave life did not fully explain such pronounced attributes. Instead, Easton believed that the psychological trauma of violent subjugation also produced adverse outcomes and undesirable characteristics. His concerns presaged later insights that generations of enslavement could have persistent mental, emotional, and material consequences for slaves' descendants. In his analysis, psychological experiences had profound physical manifestations. Enslaved women who repeatedly witnessed physical brutality were traumatized and produced children who exhibited the same "distended" facial muscles displayed by victims of whipping.[34]

This argument resonates with antebellum medical opinions that attributed the appearance of offspring to psychological factors. For example, in an 1839 case of albinism, New Jersey physician Samuel Marcy took seriously a mother's insistence that a scare from witnessing the fall of a white mare she was driving caused her to produce an albino child. Marcy initially rejected the explanation because he believed that God's operations could not be so volatile as to allow a woman's imagination to "alter or determine form or color of her children." However, after pondering the fact that the woman bore three albino children after her frightening experience, he conjectured that "the mind of the mother may affect the fetus in utero."[35]

A biblical event explained Easton's thinking. He recalled that, in the Genesis story of Jacob and Laban, mating sheep and goats produced streaked offspring after they gazed at streaked rods. Although trauma is missing from the narrative, it suggested the possibility for mental phenomena to produce material results, thus validating his maxim, "mind acts on matter."[36]

Empathy with victims of slavery's trauma shaped Easton's interpretation of the situation facing colored people. He attempted to explain it with an argument about heredity using a concept analogous to the early nineteenth-century biological theory of French scientist Jean-Baptiste Lamarck, who posited an evolutionary system driven by the inheritance of individually acquired traits. Emphasizing the acute effects of slavery, Easton insisted, "Unnatural causes produce unnatural effects. The slave system is an unnatural cause." A psychological version of Lamarckian reasoning made the case that slavery's perverse effects were heritable. They were analogous to a "complicated disease" that damaged characters, deformed bodies, and distorted normal habits. They were so powerful and devastating that Easton marveled at the fact that, as someone who was merely three generations removed from enslavement, he was truly "a man."[37]

132 RELUCTANT RACE MEN

An analysis of why colored people had a rightful claim to American civil, religious, and social privileges brought Easton's project to its culmination. At the beginning of the treatise, he simply asserted that colored people were American. Arguments from anti-colonization meetings and conventions established that birth, habits, and language grounded colored people's nationality. Scientific reasoning strengthened his contentions. Armed with the environmentalist proposition that climate affected bodies, he took the unique step of devising biological foundations for birthright citizenship. He argued that all children born in the United States were American, even if their parents had been born in Africa and they resembled Africans. The food, atmosphere, and climate of the United States affected the composition of the blood parents transmitted to their children, making them Americans by birth and blood. The implications of this physical reality were clear. National recognition of it would accord colored people their freedom and rights. When this happened, the effects of slavery would recede, and sound health would gradually replace the deformities that marked souls, minds, and bodies.[38]

This novel logic of citizenship endured. Two decades after Easton's death, the Massachusetts colored convention cited his argument in accusing churches and governments of murder for denying colored people privileges they were due as Americans. Delegates decreed that rights were constitutive elements of their lives. They reasoned that, since the nation's climates, foods, governance, and customs sustained their "American bodies and minds," to deprive an American of any of these factors was tantamount to "taking away his life."[39]

Although Easton died within months of publishing his treatise, he and Russwurm left models for the spate of challenges to race science that emerged in the shadow of expanding American School endeavors.[40] Traces of their logic appear in the arguments of a diverse group of reformers in the two decades preceding the Civil War. They included New York classics professor William Allen; abolitionist editors Henry Bibb and Frederick Douglass; Presbyterian minister and emigrationist Henry Highland Garnet; Baptist minister John Lewis; Congregational minister James Pennington; physician John Rock; James McCune Smith; Congregational minister and editor Samuel Ringgold Ward; and an *Anglo-African Magazine* editorialist known only as S.S.N. These men used three broad themes to defend the equality and unity of human populations to establish grounds for the humanity of colored Americans. Charges of innate African inferiority remained a persistent target. To combat American School allegations of inherent differences, reformers invoked a common human origin, exposed the illogical character of race classifications, and reconfigured categories of human variation. James McCune Smith took challenges further by reinterpreting the nature and significance of difference. Finally, critics assailed ethical problems that compromised the methodological and conceptual validity of race science.

Claims about the innate inferiority of people of African descent became more concrete and elaborate as the American School sought a wider circulation for its opinions. Intellectual capacity became a focal point for arguments that there was a natural hierarchy among human beings. James Pennington mapped this development as he initiated a new phase of reform challenges to race science. He explicated the charge of inferiority in his 1841 *Text Book of the Origin and History, &c. &c. of the Colored People*, a work that *Colored American* editors recommended for the enlightenment of their readers. After escaping bondage in Maryland, Pennington secured an education, a teaching position on Long Island, and informal ministerial training at Yale Divinity School, which denied him admission, and he became a licensed preacher for Congregational and Presbyterian churches. He was a ten-year veteran of reform endeavors when he published his text. He had helped draft Brooklyn's earliest anti-colonization address and was a regular New York delegate to the national colored conventions. His treatise is the only extant comprehensive confrontation colored reformers launched against race science during the 1840s. It appeared eight years before he wrote about his life in a more conventional genre of slave narratives.[41]

Pennington prefaced his refutation of inferiority with an explanation of what he would not attempt to do. Questions about whether colored American attainments were lower than what White people achieved, whether circumstances could diminish prospects and desires for "enlightened education," or whether human populations possessed different degrees of talent were not part of his agenda. Although he confessed ignorance about the precise meaning of assertions that colored people were inferior, his description of the allegation he aimed to contest meshed with polygenist conceptions of fixed traits. He summarized it as follows: "There is an *inferior order of intellect and . . . those of this order are radically and constitutionally inferior, so that no means can change that constitution or raise them from that order*."[42]

134   RELUCTANT RACE MEN

Refuting this proposition entailed denying the existence of constitutional differences among humans. Like Russwurm and Easton, he initially garnered evidence of historical greatness by linking the colored American population to Ethiopia and the glories of Egypt. Reliance on the Bible and Herodotus enabled him to amplify Russwurm's account of descent from Cush along with blood and political ties between Ethiopia and Egypt. These connections once again challenged the conclusion that heredity or nature consigned colored people to subjugation. Theology offered the true explanation. Pennington insisted that the "grand error" of polytheism, which had spread from Ethiopia and Egypt to the rest of the continent, caused the degradation of once great peoples. It undermined moral codes, blinded people to religious truths, and created divisions and animosities that, ultimately, accommodated the Atlantic slave trade.[43]

Despite evidence of moral degradation, achievements showed that allegations of African intellectual inferiority to people of European descent were spurious. Pennington assailed Thomas Jefferson's speculations in *Notes on the State of Virginia* for lending credibility to such notions by claiming that "mixture with whites" produced immediate physical and mental improvements in Negroes. This assertion meant that inferiority did not arise from circumstances. Jefferson concluded, "Different species of the same genus, or varieties of the same species, may possess different qualifications."[44] Pennington countered with examples of intellectual accomplishments by "full-blood Africans," including African-born artists Higiemondo and Ottobah Cugoano; math savant Thomas Fuller; Anton Wilhelm Amo, a philosophy professor in Germany; and Latinist cleric James Eliza John Capitein. Readers were likely familiar with Pennington's choices. With the exception of Higiemondo, all the names appear on a longer list of talented Negroes and mulattoes in the work of the French Catholic priest and activist Henri Gregoire, *On the Cultural Achievements of Negroes*. Ethical and political considerations made Capitein a dubious candidate for Pennington's roster of notables because his University of Leiden dissertation argued that slavery was compatible with Christian ideals of liberty. Pennington addressed this problem with the wry observation that slaveholders would likely cede the talents of "the apologist of slavery" for his use, since they owned his "principles." Such considerations notwithstanding, the selections buoyed Pennington's confidence that he successfully nullified charges of natural African inferiority and discredited attempts by adherents of "the

"HUMANOLOGY" 135

Jefferson School" to attribute colored Americans' achievements to European ancestry.[45]

A theory of intelligence augmented biographical anecdotes. Pennington rejected Easton's model of a non-material mind and reasoned instead that intellect was as much a product of creation as was the body. It followed that, because there was a common physical basis for the human race, there was a common foundation of intelligence. This reasoning paved the way for the conclusion, "Human intellect is identical." It was thus illogical to argue that any group of people was naturally more or less intelligent than another.[46]

Religious views further developed this position. Pennington reasoned that God created human intelligence to distinguish people from "brute creatures." Whereas instinct caused other animals to heed the demands of nature, God's moral law regulated human action. A universal ethical code demonstrated that God endowed the entire human race with the mental capacity to comprehend and follow divine strictures. Intelligence rendered people capable of ethical action in accordance with God's law.[47] Reconciling this argument with Africa's perceived downfall was complicated. Faith in a just and rational God made Pennington loath to invoke innate incapacity to explain the moral laxity he associated with the continent's declining fortunes. It did not stem from ignorance or stupidity, he reasoned, for African leaders tolerated polytheism knowing that it was a false doctrine. Although their personal religious practices were likely "rational and true" and adhered to orthodox precepts, quests for popularity led to their failure to uphold moral standards in their communities. Ultimately, God was just and good. A rhetorical question affirming his faith settled the question of Africa's intellectual equality. "Is it credible to say that he has put a difference between men in point of intellect, while he has put none in point of obligation?"[48]

Pennington's ideas provided tools for others who attempted to refute the existence of natural hierarchies. Invocations of past greatness guided even terse condemnations of such claims. Henry Highland Garnet and his cousin Samuel Ringgold Ward tied Egypt's intellectual reputation to Negroes. Garnet trusted that the sacred character of the Bible rendered the connection true. Ward averred that Herodotus undoubtedly "knew black from white." North African Christian divines—Augustine of Hippo, Tertullian, and Cyprian—whom readers of reform periodicals would have recognized as exemplars of African achievement, showed Black people's leadership in early ecclesiastical affairs. Euclid's prowess offered grounds for ridiculing Thomas

136   RELUCTANT RACE MEN

Jefferson's insistence that Negroes were incapable of understanding mathematical calculations.[49]

Ward's personal history contained additional data to challenge the supposed natural correlation between physical appearance and intellectual capacity. He had been educated at New York City's African Free Schools. Nevertheless, he contrasted an unpromising youth of roaming city streets being derided as a "nigger" with his adulthood achievements. If he, "one of the poorest specimens of my race," was capable of improvement in the face of social obstacles, other colored people must be similarly able. Years of teaching children of "all complexions" in New Jersey and New York further advanced this case. White children with limited academic ability and Black children with "the finest" mental powers proved that Black and White people possessed equal intellectual potential.[50]

Unequal levels of achievement were unreliable indicators of innate inferiority and superiority. Henry Bibb set out to make this case in an 1851 editorial directed at slave owners. In exploring determinants of differences in "the character and capabilities" of human beings, he ruled out the possibility that they arose from divergent human origins and, instead, looked to historical conditions. A theory of human development in which circumstances were "all powerful" was key to understanding variations in character formation. Bibb argued that "unphilosophical" and "superficial" methods blinded scientists to this truth and resulted in erroneous judgments about human differences. To elucidate, he described conditions guaranteed to produce "degraded intellect," impaired moral sensibilities, and physical deformities in any segment of "the human family." The structure of forced labor was sufficient to explain deterioration. To illustrate, Bibb proposed the following experiment for any group of people: "Cut off from society its most highly cultivated minds; let education cease; enslave the mass; let toiling, eating, and sleeping constitute their only employment; let their whole time be devoted to ministering to the . . . animal portion of their nature."[51] Such conditions assured destructive outcomes in just "a few generations." The damage could be profound even in situations where the labor was not excessive.

> The forehead will become low and retiring, while the back of the head—the seat of the animal passions—will be increased in proportion to the decrease in the anterior region; they will become groveling in their ideas; of morals, they will have a very imperfect conception; and anything of an intellectual character, they will be unable to appreciate.[52]

This sketch aims to explain labor's effects on agricultural workers in England and southern Ireland's "lower class." Bibb's population choice underscored the message that circumstances determined human development and phenotypic variations and undermined the coherence of race classifications and hierarchies. Support for the idea that environmental forces reduced workers to brutes appeared in the popular work *Vestiges of the Natural History of Creation*, published anonymously by British naturalist Robert Chambers. It argues that some Irish populations developed "repulsive" features as a direct result of forced settlement in a bleak coastal region. Thin, bowed limbs and "projecting jaws" were signs of "barbarous" living conditions. Buffon's assertion that poor nutrition gave human beings a "degenerate" appearance gave Bibb further confidence in his judgments.[53]

Scientists were to blame for perpetuating false views of rank embedded in race categories. Bibb suggested that, simply by virtue of being classified as "white," the most degraded populations escaped the sorts of disparaging judgments that race scientists heaped on colored Americans. If they stopped equating intellectual gifts with whiteness, investigators would have to face the fact that many of their English and Irish brothers ranked with "lower animals."[54] The failure of race science to draw such logical conclusions from empirical evidence showed that it was a defective source of knowledge about human capacity.

The effects of deprivation helped Freewill Baptist preacher and teacher John Lewis rebut charges of inherent inferiority in his "Essay on the Character and Condition of the African Race." He explained that a population's superior social standing was simply a sign of favorable historical opportunities, not innate virtues. If White English and American people had been subjected to four centuries of military, political, and civil tyranny, he ventured that they would surely be as low as the most abject colored people and lower than their degraded Gaulish ancestors. He marveled that despotism had not completely obliterated African manhood or thwarted accomplishments of Africans and their descendants. A roster of worldwide achievers that began with Euclid and ended with the lawyers, physicians, clergy, professors, and editors among his contemporaries provided evidence that the "natural intellect" of Africa's peoples and their descendants put them "side by side with the European race." Industrious colored farmers undermined charges that Negroes, as a group, were morally debased. Examples of Black achievement showed that Haiti's political instability was not a reflection of a depraved "African character."[55] It was no different from unrest in European nations and, thus, offered no

138 RELUCTANT RACE MEN

basis for claims about wholesale incapacity or inferiority. No group had a monopoly on achievement or ignorance.

An invitation to deliver the 1854 commencement address at Western Reserve College gave Frederick Douglass an occasion to confront scientific questions about mental capacity. Worried about developing an analysis for an academic setting, he enlisted the aid of educated friends and studied James Prichard's *Natural History of Man*. Nevertheless, he thought that he was not fully equipped to challenge American School theorists. "The Claims of the Negro Ethnologically Considered" thus supplemented ethnological evidence with personal observations and "common sense."[56]

As the son of a slave woman and an unknown White man, he found the contention that mulatto intelligence stemmed from the mental superiority of "the white race" irksome. He countered by asserting that mental capacity "uniformly derived from the maternal side." The presumption that the women who produced the American mulatto population were Black linked intellect to "Negro blood." Egyptians provided historical evidence. Without explicitly identifying them as Negroes, he noted physical resemblances that pointed to "a strong affinity and a direct relationship" between them and the genius that erected pyramids. Philological evidence of similarities in languages spoken throughout the continent reinforced the connection. It strengthened the likelihood that all African populations and, by extension, their American descendants comprised "one people."[57] Their noble past proved that, as a class, Negroes were not intellectually stunted.

Circumstances explained the inferiority Douglass and others perceived in Black bodies. Ireland's "common people" shed light on the coarse qualities associated with "the plantation negro." They displayed the ruinous physical and mental effects that typically arose from grim material conditions. His travels gave him firsthand knowledge of the "open, uneducated mouth—the long, gaunt arm—the badly formed foot and ankle—the shuffling gait—the retreating forehead and vacant expression—and . . . petty quarrels and fights." These features were the loathsome signs of low rank. The "handsome" physiognomy of learned and refined Irish gentlemen, however, offered a stark and welcome contrast, leading Douglass to conclude that inferiority among Negroes was not innate: "May not the condition of men explain their various appearances? Need we go behind the vicissitudes of barbarism for an explanation of the gaunt, wiry, ape like appearance of some of the genuine negroes?"[58]

"HUMANOLOGY" 139

The contention that races were constitutionally different was as disquieting as charges about Negro inferiority. Over time, this claim, which was embedded in the theory that Negroes comprised a distinct species, became an increasingly prominent part of American School pronouncements against the unity of the human race and its repudiation of a common origin for the world's populations. Samuel Morton, Louis Agassiz, and Josiah Nott refined their judgments in exchanges with environmentalists. Morton confessed his belief that multiple origins caused differences in physical attributes as well as in mental and moral capabilities. A group's capacity for development was fixed at its inception along with its ability to adapt to geographic environments. Accordingly, attempts to overcome the limits of original "endowments" were doomed to fail, and people of African descent could never become mentally capable and equal Americans.[59]

Perspectives on difference assumed a provocative edge when Agassiz tailored them to audiences that used the Bible to understand human origins. In an 1850 essay for the *Christian Examiner*, he drove a wedge between the principle of species unity and common origins. The former, he argued, was perfectly compatible with polygeny because it concerned ethical responsibilities to others, not physical connections. The "true unity of man," he quipped, was "consciousness of the higher moral obligations." On one hand, Agassiz assumed the voice of religious orthodoxy to discredit environmentalists. He argued that they unwittingly granted climate more creative power than God possessed when they insisted that differences in human appearances developed after creation. On the other hand, orthodoxy fell by the wayside as he tried to establish human diversity as a "primitive" feature of multiple creations. He called into question the Bible's utility in efforts to track a universal human history, claiming that its creation account referred only to "branches of the white race" and provided no insight into the origins of "colored races." To reinforce the subordinate status of Negroes, Agassiz arrogantly dismissed reformers' long-standing argument that Egyptian accomplishments were Negro achievements. Morton's *Crania Americana* had paved the way for this claim. It reported no Negro bones in Egyptian tombs. This outcome was consistent with Georges Cuvier's refutation of the popular "error" that Negroes produced Egypt's civilization. Regardless of their skin color, Morton argued, Egyptians were members of his race. He later satisfied himself with the less definitive conclusion that they were not strictly Negroes. Agassiz, however, did not waver. With naked condescension, he asked, "Have men who do not know that Egypt and Northern Africa have never been inhabited by Negro tribes, but always by nations of the Caucasian race, any right to express an opinion on this question?" Egypt thus became proof of innate White superiority. Its ancient monuments showed that primeval differences between Negroes and "the white race" consistently revealed themselves in historical developments. American slavery was just another manifestation of such foundational differences.[60]

Josiah Nott presented the American School argument that human differences were immutable and permanent. The "Jewish race" illustrated the supposed truth of this proposition because the original "type" of that group remained unchanged through four thousand years of "every possible variety of moral and physical influences." Migrations resulting in climate-induced complexion variations and intermarriages that adulterated "blood" were of little consequence. Nott determined that "Jewish features" withstood climate change and other forces. Heads thus replaced skin color as the trait that marked decisive differences. Despite observable variations in complexions, a mummified "Israelite" head that Gliddon contributed to Morton's skull collection established the permanence of the undefined Jewish type. The sample was a "characteristic specimen" of features that only "Jewish blood" could produce. The preservation of Jewish distinctiveness confirmed for Nott the existence of multiple origins and divergent species. It rendered possibilities for a common humanity baseless.[61]

Nott's speculations about Jews culminated in arguments about the permanence of differences between Negroes and White people. He prefaced his claims by musing that "arbitrary terms" designated the races and failed to account for the "*many* types" and possibly divergent origins within the "so-called" Caucasian and Negro races. Despite admittedly "forced divisions," he concluded that the heads typifying "each race" remained unchanged across time and space. This was a crucial determination, since Morton's skull specimens showed that, compared to Caucasians, Negroes possessed "nine cubic inches less of brain!" The persistence of such stark differences seemed to confirm the existence of multiple origins and highlighted the mistake of treating races as equal members of a single species. It reinforced Morton's admonition that it was futile to form "fixed laws of nature."[62]

The assertion that Negro skulls bore a closer resemblance to those of simians rather than to Caucasian heads added fodder to claims of innate difference. The basis for this craniological connection lay in the mid-eighteenth-century work of Dutch anatomist Petrus Camper. He devised a measurement for facial angle that extended from the top of the forehead to the front of the

"HUMANOLOGY" 141

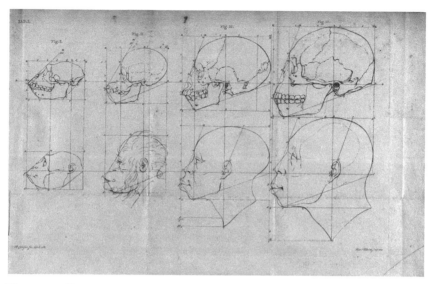

Figure 4.1 Petrus Camper, Orangutan to Moor, 1791. From *Dissertation physique... sur les différences réelles que présentent les traits du visage chez les hommes de différents pays et de différents âges: Sur le beau qui caractèrise les statues antiques et les pierres gravées. Suivie de la proposition d'une nouvelle méthode pour déssiner toutes sortes de têtes humaines /* ... Published by Adrien Gilles Camper. Translated by Denis Bernard Quatremere d'Isjonval. Wellcome Collection.

lips to gauge prognathism—the degree to which the jaw juts forward. A set of profiles illustrated the progression of the angles. Lower angle measurements corresponded with more forward jutting of the jaw. Monkey and orangutan skulls totaled forty-two and fifty-eight degrees, respectively; African and Asian skulls each measured seventy degrees; a European skull totaled eighty degrees; and the head of a Greek statue reflecting the highest standard of beauty measured one hundred degrees. A monogenist, Camper criticized individuals who "wrongly" consigned Black populations to "some particular kind of species which did not descend from Adam." He compared simians with Negroes—"our fellow men"—as part of a challenge to philosophers who insisted "with some rhetorical flourish" that Negroes emerged from mating between White people and orangutans. His human dissections revealed that "everything" about Negroes was "the same as for a white man." According to his biographer Miriam Meijer, Camper produced the profiles to illustrate the proximity of this relationship, not to liken Negroes to apes. Nevertheless, the

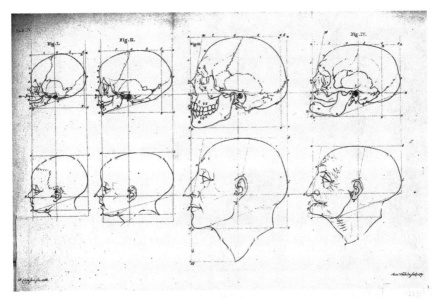

Figure 4.2 Petrus Camper, European male, 1791. From *Dissertation physique... sur les différences réelles que présentent les traits du visage chez les hommes de différents pays et de différents âges: sur le beau qui caractèrise les statues antiques et les pierres gravées. Suivie de la proposition d'une nouvelle méthode pour déssiner toutes sortes de têtes humaines /* ... Published by Adrien Gilles Camper. Translated by Denis Bernard Quatremere d'Isjonval. Wellcome Collection.

comparisons provided nineteenth-century race science with a convenient tool for illustrating essential difference.[63]

The most straightforward way to address arguments about constitutional differences was to underscore a common beginning for all populations. A single origin connoted one human species. Making this connection entailed an almost reflexive invocation of scriptural authority. In principle, the task united colored reformers and White biblicists in a shared rebuke of polygeny. Both classes judged the theory as heretical and snubbed Agassiz's claim that the Bible recounted an exclusive history of White people.[64]

This orientation simplified the question of origins for Pennington. He flatly announced that colored people descended from the first humans named in the Bible. Scripture made Africans part of a single historical creation and thus settled the issue of species difference between colored and White peoples.[65] Henry Highland Garnet expanded on this argument when analyzing people of African descent as a discrete race. He thought it prudent to distinguish his exploration of the historical trajectory of "the colored race" from practices of race scientists. He thus prefaced his 1848 address to a Troy, New York, audience with an apology. It was necessary to use "improper terms" in order to identify his subject clearly. He had to "speak of races, when in fact there is but one race." The existence of "but one Adam" from whom all humans descended proved this singularity.[66] Although he acknowledged that dissimilarities in skin color warranted an explanation, he did not offer one, trusting that the God that varied their complexions created them as equals.

Science training made Samuel Ward confident that physical variations were of no essential consequence. Having "studied dead men's bones" while briefly enrolled in medical school, he was certain that craniological measurements were insignificant. "It makes no odds," he concluded, "if the chin protrudes or the forehead retires." Even Euclid must have possessed "the elliptical head, the protruding jaw" that signified Black people's purported inferiority and dubious humanity. "If he was not a man, then there are no men."[67]

This stance also informed Ward's analysis of Negro origins. His 1852 address to the Cheltenham Literary and Philosophical Institution, "Origin of the Negro Race," cautioned British listeners not to expect a treatise on the relationship of Negroes to the human race. It was a logical conclusion and a historical fact that all races shared the same origin. Accordingly, he would not "stoop to discuss whether the Negro belongs to the human family or not; or whether they are essentially inferior."[68] Religion provided mooring for Ward's stance that wrongdoing among "ancient Negroes" showed Africa's humanity. Although it caused the degradation of colored people, sin showed that they behaved as other people did and thereby illustrated their "oneness with the human race." Virtue supplemented this evidence. The presence of Simeon "called Niger" among early Christian teachers was an indicator of the "propinquity" of Black and White people. Collaboration among people of different regions in spreading the gospel challenged the supposed "natural instinct" of aversion between the groups. It suggested that bigotry between groups did not spring from inborn traits or divergent origins. It was merely a "Yankee invention."[69]

John Lewis concurred that prejudice against dark skin was unnatural. Religious judgments and physical observations demonstrated that there was no physical evidence to support the existence of essential distinctions among

144 RELUCTANT RACE MEN

human beings. If bigotry arose from natural differences, then God would have instilled an innate hatred of dark complexions in White people, and they would be justified in heaping injuries upon colored people. However, divine goodness disallowed this possibility. Furthermore, empirical evidence showed that complexion was an anatomically insignificant detail of the body's covering in contrast to "the flesh, blood, bones, or the muscles, of which the human body is composed."[70] This meant that the basic physical structure of all humans was the same, and geography, temperature, and regional customs accounted for variations in appearance.

Polygenist claims ranked with bootleg liquor for Frederick Douglass. He insisted that humanity was a discrete entity that could not be plotted on "a sliding scale" between orangutans, presumably Black, and angels, undoubtedly White. Like others, he explained differences in complexion by repeating accounts of Jews and similar discrete populations whose appearance varied with changes in climate. Such empirical observations challenged the theory of multiple origins by highlighting the capacity for "countless variations in form, feature, and color" in a single unit of creation. They demonstrated that multiple creations were not needed to produce each variation in the human population. Hence, complexional variety failed to prove the existence of "distinct species" with divergent origins.[71]

The question of human difference prompted James McCune Smith's denunciations of race science. In an 1841 speech on colored people's destiny, he affirmed his belief in a single origin with the time-honored credo that God created all people "of one blood." This biblical tenet corresponded to scientific methods. Data obtained through systematic observations substantiated it and established species unity as a fact. The microscope showed that the "globules" in all human blood were identical. It also distinguished human blood from that of other animals. Further verification came from investigations of fertility. The scientific dictum that offspring of different species do not reproduce was critical to Smith. He concluded that, since mulattoes are not sterile, Black and White people must comprise a single species with all other humans.[72]

This simple observation struck at a key polygenist tenet. Charles Caldwell's repudiation of species unity partially hinged on the claim that mulattoes would lose the capacity to reproduce. American School scientists grappled with this issue in a more complex fashion. Morton harbored doubts that measures of mulatto fecundity could actually substantiate the theories of difference he tried to establish in craniological studies. He thus worked to minimize fertility's importance in his claims about Negro inferiority. Historian Brad Hume reports that, in 1846, Morton began canvasing other naturalists for examples of fertile offspring produced by mating between different animal species. His investigation in the *American Journal of Science and Arts* concluded that fertility among offspring of different human races was insufficient proof that they comprised a single species. By labeling putative races as "proximate species"—species that produce fertile offspring—Morton allowed for the possibility of limited reproduction among mulattoes without abandoning his stand against the unity of the species.[73]

Morton's caution failed to temper Nott's conviction that mulattoes were hybrids who would lose their reproductive capacity and become extinct. Nott found mulattoes to be mentally superior to "pure" Negroes. His view of "crossing" races thus promised some positive outcomes for "negro races" because the process infused them with the blood of White people. However, the alleged species difference between races made such benefits unsustainable. The title of Nott's twice-published article, "The Mulatto a Hybrid—Probable Extermination of the Two Races if the Whites and Blacks are Allowed to Intermarry," summarizes his speculations about the inevitable physical decline that would result from interracial mating. Nott was intent on tracking this decline statistically and lobbied Congress to include a mulatto category on census questionnaires. North Carolina senator Thomas Clingman publicized the proposal and urged the Census Bureau to adopt it. He argued that monitoring would reveal that mulattoes had more limited longevity and weaker reproductive powers than "pure races" possessed. A *North Star* correspondent railed against the perverse underpinnings of the plan that displayed the sensibilities of the "American negro-hater" awaiting the "ultimate extinction" of colored people. The mulatto category was added to census forms in 1850 and remained through 1920.[74]

The increasing importance of skulls in claims about human difference compelled Smith to investigate the significance of heads. Heads had framed the beginning of his reform career, when, upon returning to New York from medical school in Glasgow, he assumed a prominent role in campaigns against the "science, falsely so called," of phrenology. Despite its professional garb, craniology warranted no more esteem than phrenologists' "Bumpification" theories.[75] He wryly expressed his disdain for the practice through a series of essays entitled "Heads of the Colored People," published in *Frederick Douglass' Paper*. Each segment features a tale of a nameless Black worker—a newspaper vendor, a teacher, a bootblack, a sexton,

146 RELUCTANT RACE MEN

a washerwoman, an inventor, and an editor, among others. The narratives are at turns poignant, witty, astute, and acerbic. They often stray from the ostensible subject to unrelated matters—Robert Purvis's Pennsylvania estate; Thomas Jefferson's "shouting Methodist" granddaughter in Liberia who showed that his "mixed blood" progeny were as widespread as his ideas; condolences upon the death of Samuel Ward's mother; or ineffective Christian missions in New York City's Five Points district.[76] One such digression in the narrative about a New York bootblack brought uncharacteristic levity to the defense of a common human origin. Smith conferred humanity on his hero by recounting the passion of his courtship—"the close grappling of iron arms round substantial waists and that positive contact of 'lips that are lips.'" The lighthearted account presents physical affection as a manifestation of species unity because, according to Orville Dewey's "Problems of Human Destiny," kissing is "peculiar to the human species." A pastime "reveled in by colored folks" was indisputable evidence "of the unity of the human race."[77]

There was no place for humor in the critique of John Augustine Smith, a naturalist and former president of William & Mary College who adapted the Camper scale to prove innate Negro inferiority. McCune Smith's rebuttal of Augustine Smith targeted flawed methods and illogical premises of skull measurement. Unbeknown to McCune Smith, Augustine Smith increased a conventional simian facial angle; he reported that it was only six degrees smaller than the angle for Negro skulls. McCune Smith's twofold methodological challenge targeted Camper's measurements for referring to young simian skulls. This choice would produce angles closer to human skulls than adult simian skulls would show. McCune Smith attempted to counter the suspected distortion with zoological measures of adult apes. The result was a larger difference between Negroes and apes that exceeded the difference between Negroes and White people. He also questioned the extent to which the human skulls used for the endeavor were representative. Casual observations of the profiles of Henry Clay, figures on European coins, and congregants in colored churches revealed that extreme jaw angles were common among White people and that the Negro skulls in Camper's measures were uncommon. The use of unusual skulls to prove the existence of a distinct Black race or "type" showed that polygenists were engaged in a specious enterprise. It was as baseless as categorizing gray-eyed White men as a race.[78]

McCune Smith sharpened his critique of craniology when he questioned the utility of measuring head shapes. He observed that there was no support for the assumption that facial angle was an indicator of intelligence. Because it ascertained "the position of the upper jaw in regard to the orifice of the ear," it revealed nothing about the size, shape, or functioning of the brain. It offered no evidence about mental capacity or degrees of intelligence. The "best anatomists," McCune Smith argued, discerned no size, weight, consistency, or color differences between the brains of Black people and those of White people. Furthermore, accurate measurements showed uniformity in the bone structure of skulls in various populations. Instead of proving the existence of fundamental differences, human skulls established "the unity of the human race."[79]

———

Commentaries on racial classifications expressed widespread contempt for polygenist interpretations of difference. Reformers with little tolerance for contrived racial designations tried to redefine categories of human variation. For some individuals, this undertaking included challenging the contention that Africans and their descendants comprised a discrete race or species. Such challenges coexisted with ancestral claims to Africa that deflected charges of inferiority. John Lewis and James Pennington criticized the view that Africans possessed natural traits permanently distinguishing them from others. Although Lewis referred to "the African race," he rejected the idea that its peoples possessed innate characteristics that suited them only for hot climates. His personal experience as a Rhode Island native living and lecturing throughout New England proved otherwise. The fact that he had developed normally in cold regions showed that people were suited to climates as the result of acclimation, not because of innate race traits. Moreover, within Africa, varying environmental conditions produced vast phenotypic differences. The "jet black" inhabitants of Madagascar, for example, presented a stark contrast to the "white African Albino race." This phenomenon highlighted a fundamental reality that the "diversity of the human appearance" derived from climate, geography, and other circumstances.[80]

Pennington scoffed at Pechlin and anatomists who probed the flesh and brains of colored people in search of the cause of their complexions. With reluctance, he also disparaged the theory of the beloved Benjamin Rush that dark skin was diseased. He opted for "common sense" and the perspectives of other prominent environmentalists, particularly the "learned and humane Stanhope Smith," to echo the conclusion that climate caused variations in skin color.[81] This factor explained why populations in Africa's

148 RELUCTANT RACE MEN

torrid western regions were darker than some eastern populations. Striking physical differences made it impossible to label African populations using a single racial designation. Citing British naval and travel records, he observed that the continent was home to "more than forty separate and distinct families of nations." Together, these groups contained "all the varieties of races." The complexions of some native populations, he argued, looked the same as those of White colonizationists who named Africa the natural and appropriate home for colored people. He believed the diverse complexions of African peoples rendered prevailing categories of difference incoherent.[82]

Similar problems plagued classification schemes in the United States. Pennington named the shortcomings in his presidential address to the 1852 New York colored convention. The crux of the problem was that the complexions of colored people were becoming lighter because of climatic influences, rising intermarriages between colored and White people, and "illicit intercourse." Appearance and the "natural desire" of people to be "ranked" as White complicated official racial designations, making it "extremely difficult and dangerous" to rely on color as the basis of classifications.[83]

Audiences at John Rock's popular lectures on slavery and "the unity of the human race" heard sweeping condemnations of the irrationality of all race classifications. Although the texts of his speeches have not survived, sketches of a lecture in *Frederick Douglass' Paper* show Rock rejecting the contention that there was any rational way to divide human beings into groups. He acknowledged significant differences within the human species. Yet, like other environmentalists, he attributed physical variations to "known and unknown" natural causes, "local circumstances," and time. These factors, he explained, generated new varieties of human populations in the past and had the potential to produce future changes. He ridiculed scientists who were so intent on categorizing people that they ignored this reality and created race classifications that defied "reason and the facts." He poked fun at the standards for assigning people to the "regular" Caucasian race or to the "irregular" African race. Strict adherence to these standards would make Africans of White men whose features deviated from the norm of whiteness and create Caucasians out of Black men with supposed "regular" features. Physical features were not the problem; the classifications themselves were fictions. "In undertaking to prove too much," he concluded, "they prove nothing." In the end, it was "utterly impossible to classify mankind into races."[84]

"HUMANOLOGY" 149

Efforts to impart veracity to race categories could be the stuff of farce. The editorialist S.S.N. led readers of the *Anglo-African Magazine* through a labyrinth of absurdities to illustrate the incoherence of ethnological labels. The writer was not content to impugn professional scientists for the artifice of race designations. Ordinary people were also accountable for using such illogical and erroneous terms as "Anglo-Saxon" and "Anglo-African." The romantic notion that White Americans were Anglo-Saxons defied historical and biological facts; the "conglomeration" of Celts, Teutons, Spaniards, Greeks, Poles, French people, "and their multiplied varieties" embodied in the White American population made the precious designation nonsensical. It demonstrated that the criterion of "pure blood" that supposedly grounded race classifications was a fiction. Consanguinity between White Americans and Anglo-Saxons was as tenuous as the position that, because Saxons "were once slaves," enslaved Americans must be Saxons.[85] Unchecked sarcasm gave rise to the conjecture that Anglo-Saxons must have fallen under a harsh divine judgment because it was otherwise inconceivable that "so superior a race" could have been reduced to servitude. Writing long after Morton and Agassiz decreed that Egyptians were Caucasian, S.S.N. predicted that grand achievements of ancient Egyptian people would eventually transform them all into Anglo-Saxons, retrospectively.[86]

The irrationality of the term "Anglo-Saxon" paved the way for ridiculing the newly coined label "Anglo-African," which had equally dubious historical foundations. The allusion to people with "pure African blood" was a serious matter that prompted S.S.N. to admonish individuals who praised or derided this population that there was "no such race." Ethnological evidence exposed the flawed logic of attempts to create precise classifications by showing a hopelessly blurred boundary between the Negro and Caucasian races. Numerous authorities facilitated the task, including the German theorist of human difference Johann Blumenbach; *Calmet's Dictionary of the Holy Bible*; the Rome lectures of Catholic priest Nicholas Wiseman that linked science and religion; and a monogenist critique of Agassiz entitled *The Unity of the Human Races Proved to be the Doctrine of Scripture, Reason, and Science*, by Thomas Smyth, a Charleston Presbyterian minister and member of the American Association for the Advancement of Science. Five critical observations emerged from these sources. S.S.N. reported that Blumenbach identified Negroes as Ethiopians. Smyth, along with Josephus, cited Egyptian hieroglyphic studies showing that Cush's name applied to Ethiopians. The *New American Cyclopedia* named Abyssinians as descendants of Cush.

150 RELUCTANT RACE MEN

Calmet's Dictionary equated Ethiopia and Abyssinia as a "mixture of nations." Finally, Wiseman described Abyssinians as "perfectly black" members of "the Semitic family," which made them "a white race." These observations translate into the following propositions:

1. Negroes are Ethiopians.
2. Ethiopians are Cushites.
3. Abyssinians are Cushites.
4. Ethiopians and Abyssinians are mixed and alike.
5. Abyssinians are black.
6. Abyssinians are Semitic.
7. Semitic peoples are members of a white race.
8. Ethiopians must be members of a white race.

S.S.N. summed up this admittedly "curious chain of evidence" with the pronouncement, "*we* belong to a white race." This conclusion offered a satirical twist to observations that Africa was a continent of "mixed people." It supported Smyth's calculation that the "intermixture of races" was so widespread that there was no such thing as a "pure Caucasian."[87]

Having dispensed with conventional race classifications and ethnological distinctions, S.S.N. targeted popular invocations of Egyptian ancestry. The argument for abandoning the practice required leaving the scientific realm and resorting to reform efforts that urged colored people embrace the term "American" if they needed a collective designation. As "poor as it is," S.S.N. confessed, it had the modest value of being true. In contrast, the Egyptian and African labels were misnomers. "Because some of our foreparents, one or two hundred years ago, were brought from Africa, does it prove *us* to be Africans, and our posterity such, forever?" the writer asked. Did appeals to an ancient Egyptian past render anyone "Egyptian today?" Doubts about the merits of race and national classifications led to the editorial's final admonition: the truest way for readers to proclaim their humanity was to assert their manhood.[88]

Concerns about scientific accuracy compelled James McCune Smith to reconfigure categories of difference. A focus on complexion framed the start of his scrutiny of distinctions among human populations. James Prichard's research provided him with categories for grouping everyone into three "great varieties" that dispensed with strict correlations to specific continents. Populations comprising the "melanocomous" or "melanic" variety, possessing dark skin and hair, included peoples of southern Europe and most of Asia, Africa, Australia, and the Americas. They ranged from Italians with "bright brunette" complexions to Negroes with "jet black" skin and represented the largest percentage of humans. The predominance of this variety was at odds with the concept of degeneration because it showed dark complexions as part of a norm. Groups with lighter complexions comprised the "xanthous" variety, which included populations in northern Europe, northern Asia, and the "Highlands of Africa." The only people designated as White, or members of the "leucos" variety, were albinos. Whiteness was not the "distinctive type of any race." It was a deformity among all putative races.[89] This formulation thwarted attempts to classify Africans or Black Americans as a distinct type. Prichard's observations as well as evidence from other scholars and travel writers demonstrated that a dark complexion was not unique to Negroes. Native Americans and populations in various parts of India displayed complexions that were "perfectly black." Like Pennington, Smith observed that the complexions of some sub-Saharan African populations, presumptuously called "black," were actually "a tawny color." All the evidence pointed to the conclusion that there was no basis for distinguishing Negroes as a "special variety of the human race" or as a distinct component of the "melanic race."[90]

The view that Negroes comprised a distinct species inspired further denunciations as Smith tried to show that variations in skin color did not reflect constitutional differences. He cited the latest scientific investigations to discredit anatomists' claims that the source of dark skin was a membrane peculiar to Negroes. Microscopic evidence, he observed, revealed no differences in the cell structures of light- and dark-colored skin. Environmentalism pushed the argument further. If skin color was mutable and changed with climate and terrain, migrations could subject populations to climactic influences capable of altering their complexions. The biblical suggestion that skin color was permanent was thus incorrect. The Ethiopian, like all other people in the world, could in fact "change his skin" by relocating to a new environment. The unstable index of color undermined the logic of assigning racial groups to different species.[91]

Experiences of living in varied climates demonstrated Negroes' membership in the human race. This issue was featured in a serialized analysis, "A Statistical View of the Colored Population of the United States—from 1790 to 1850." Although it appeared anonymously in 1859 *Anglo-African Magazine* editions, its substance and style mirror Smith's other work. Comparisons of birth and death rates for enslaved Negroes in tropical and temperate regions show that, in the hot area of Louisiana, they succumbed to the climate "to which popular science holds him to be specially adapted." However, they thrived in the more temperate regions of Maryland and Virginia, which Smith found well suited for human development. The ability to thrive in an ideal climate, even under conditions of slavery, confirmed that Negroes were part of "THE GREAT HUMAN RACE."[92]

The lengths to which American School theorists were willing to go in their quest for distinctions vexed Smith. He was bewildered by the notion that size and hair texture proved essential differences. He wondered that a lone calf muscle could inspire "earnest speculation" and make "the black race" essentially different from fairer populations. Josiah Nott's assertion that hair differences were grounds for declaring Black and White people "distinct species" gave him further pause. How did it create the "insurmountable difficulty" of incorporating the populations into a single nation? Scientific reasoning and circumstantial factors discredited such ideas. Heavy labor and poor nutrition affected the condition and size of calf muscles. If they were criteria for barring people from the human race, he mused, "many who have a white complexion" would be excluded. He assured all who gaped at wooly hair that textures varied with changing climatic conditions and that grooming could straighten the strands.[93]

Smith single-handedly pushed refutations of polygenist claims beyond questions of origins and classifications. He devised a theory in which difference became the centerpiece of a "philosophy of human progress" that recognized intercourse among diverse populations as a key to the development of civilization.[94] One of its central tenets held that prospects for advancement were best when the degree of intermingling among populations was extensive and the variety among the populations was high. This premium on difference raised the specter of polygeny, a pitfall Smith worked to elude through two decades of exploring comparative anatomy, physiology, and geography for insights into human variations. The result was a conceptual framework that simultaneously explained difference and affirmed the unity, equality, and common origin of the human species. Philosophy, climatology, statistics, history, and anecdotal observations steered his efforts to delineate "a science" of civilization that refuted the logic of associating difference with separate creations and fixed hierarchies.[95]

Environmentalism gave Smith empirical grounding to explain the causes and nature of physical variations in a monogenist paradigm. He went further, however, by making difference a starting point for understanding how civilizations progressed. His investigations into how environmental factors affected populations began with two analyses focusing on climate—"Civilization: Its Dependence on Physical Circumstances" and *A Dissertation on the Influence of Climate on Longevity*, produced in 1844 and 1845, respectively, and subsequently revised.[96] He later noted that the principles explained in the works were "mainly the same" as views Henry Buckle expressed in his 1857 study, *History of Civilization in England*, which considers the significance of climate in world developments. Smith also concurred with Belgian statistician Lambert Adolphe Quetelet whose research determined that, within a single climatic region, life span and quality of life varied with occupation, access to food, and "mode of living." Yet, even as Smith acknowledged that climate was not the sole determinant of variation, he insisted that its influence was decisive. Phenotypic observations along with statistical data on age distribution, mortality, population size, and temperature fluctuations offered vital clues about climatic and topographic effects on populations throughout the world. Such information emboldened Smith. He ventured beyond modest claims concerning influence to hypothesize that mental and constitutional differences "arise from climatic or geographical causes."[97]

The first phase of exploring this proposition entailed examining the significance of climatic variability. To demonstrate that climate was a critical factor in the growth of civilization, Smith presented data suggesting that extremely cold and hot climates diminished physical vigor and, hence, stunted mental development. Age statistics for populations in cold regions indicated that frigid temperatures curtailed human longevity. This outcome pointed to limitations on the aggregate physical vitality and mental development in such places. The records indicated that many people in cold climates died before attaining their full intellectual stature. The small percentages of people with long lives in these regions, in theory, had longer opportunities for intellectual development. However, the effects of aging made them less likely to possess the physical stamina that mental exertion required.[98] In contrast, it was unlikely that extreme heat significantly limited longevity, although Smith lacked measures of precise effects. Yet he believed that tropical climates tended to curb physical vigor throughout the life span because humid atmospheric conditions diminished oxygen availability. This effect was not nearly as dire as outcomes in cold regions. Nevertheless, even small reductions in strength had negative implications for intellectual development and

154 RELUCTANT RACE MEN

civilization growth because, as experience taught him, "mind-work" was difficult. Physical energy was "a necessary condition" for individuals to withstand the "wear and tear" of strenuous thinking.[99]

The diverse attributes of Americans who smugly placed themselves within "the Anglo-Saxon race" enabled Smith to further demonstrate how climate mattered. Correlations between climatic variation and physical and mental "peculiarities" challenged Samuel Morton's conclusion that each population's peculiar endowments were fixed. Smith argued that stark phenotypic differences existed among White Americans and that they differed from English groups who shared their ancestry. Inhabitants of Vermont, for example, displayed light features characteristic of "the Xanthous race," whereas dark hair and eyes of "the Melanic variety" were common among Georgians. Such developments were visible throughout the country. They proved that members of "the same stock" experienced changes in their "mental and physical endowments" as a result of exposure to divergent geographical conditions.[100]

Environmental forces could also produce dramatic effects on bone structure. Smith recounted that a sculptor identified a skull shape typically associated with Native Americans in depictions of Daniel Webster and Henry Clay. These White American statesmen apparently exhibited environmental changes in bone structure that could occur across generations. "Indian blood" was not necessary. Smith's own observations found such a pronounced "depth of chest and symmetry of form" among colored natives of the Chesapeake that he claimed the ability to identify men from the region through cursory examinations of their upper bodies. This example of transformations that American descendants of diverse groups of enslaved Africans experienced over the course of two centuries displayed the profound impact of changes in "geological position."[101]

An analysis of terrain increased his theory's complexity. It forestalled any rush to the conclusion that temperate climates pushed civilization growth to its peak. On one hand, Smith accepted James Prichard's assertion that Africa's Mandingo and Fulah populations were "more intelligent" than maritime groups because they enjoyed moderate temperatures in the mountainous regions they inhabited. However, he also maintained that such prized settings were only able to fuel aspects of civilization peculiar to the region. Local occurrences could not produce multifaceted large-scale advancement. The ideal site for maximizing progress would be a geopolitical territory with a varied terrain, one "interspersed with mountains, plains, rivers, and sea coasts." Inhabitants of such an area would display a broad array of physical and mental characteristics because of their exposure to diverse climatic conditions. Interactions among such differently endowed peoples would push progress to its zenith. Yet no single location in the world possessed the topographical and climatic variations needed to create a population of differently endowed inhabitants. Thus, civilization could not advance optimally in any single territory.[102]

History revealed ways of transcending geographic limitations on the growth of civilization and showed that migrations were key components of progress. Global developments illustrated this solution. Smith observed that Anglo-Saxons exhibited great vitality and had been responsible for broad and profound advances in civilization. The explanation for this feat lay in an alternative account of difference and race. He pointed out that it would be a mistake to attribute Anglo-Saxon achievements to the "assumed superiority of certain so-called 'races' of mankind." Just as no lone territory could push civilization to its fullest, a "single variety" was incapable of generating maximum development. This principle set no limits on the advancement of Anglo Saxons, however, because they were not a discrete race in the polygenist sense, that is, "a separate and distinct creation of the genus *homo*." Such phenomena did not actually exist. They did not even comprise a discrete population or "breed" of people in terms that environmentalists could accept, despite the claims of many White Americans. This collection of peoples was "an admixture of all the Indo-European races." In addition to Low Dutch peoples and Celts, it encompassed "the Germanic race or Bersekers," who had previously experienced a "thousand and one admixtures" during migrations from Asia to Europe. Anglo-Saxon prominence thus sprang from mixtures and movements facilitated by "fortunate accidents" of climate and geography. This outcome was consistent with Smith's premise that human progress depended on blending the "varieties of the species."[103]

Other historical developments reinforced the Anglo-Saxon lesson. Smith found a parallel example in John Stuart Mill's explanation of broader European progress rising from the great diversity among its "family of nations," not from any inherent superiority of its peoples. Mill also saw dissimilarities as requirements for human advancement.[104] Although Smith did not reference them, American School scientists made similar observations. In 1853, Nott attributed Caucasian superiority to mixture, and, in 1854, he and Gliddon attributed human progress to the "new blood and novel influences" resulting from "the war of races" in world history. Their theory could not advance

156 RELUCTANT RACE MEN

Smith's project because their historical observations were not prescriptions for advancement. In keeping with the polygenist tenet of incompatible essential differences among races, they cautioned that the process of improvement through mixture did not apply to "the lowest types," such as the Negroes that concerned Smith.[105]

Negative phenomena enabled Smith to develop his position further. The nations of Haiti and Liberia, which polygenists referenced as proof of innate Negro incapacity and "natural African barbarism," highlighted the importance of mixture among varied populations. Smith had praised Haiti in 1841, insisting that, under the brief leadership of Toussaint Louverture, the nation exposed the error of those who believed in "the natural inferiority of the Negro race." Its self-governance demonstrated the "artificial nature" of caste distinctions. A decade later, he shared the perception that, along with Liberia, Haiti was retrograde. Hot climates and insufficient diversity in its population accounted for the nations' inability to thrive. Hence, James Theodore Holly's stipulation that Haiti's inhabitants and migrants should be "homogenous" to facilitate assimilation was a recipe for chronic stagnation. Smith focused on a diagnosis. He summarized conditions in both countries with the dictum, "Admixture is progress; Isolation is retrogression." These correlations were matters of historical fact. Lessons from the past showed that a failure to maintain the process of admixture impeded a population's progress. Haiti was just one instance of this outcome. The Celts, Chinese, and isolated tribal territories around the globe suffered from the same limitation during various periods of their development.[106]

Smith's theory had positive implications for the future of the United States. It suggested that the country possessed prerequisites for progress and, thus, had the potential to produce an advanced culture that could rival anything Europe could produce. The Atlantic slave trade, along with migrations from diverse regions, made the United States home to the largest assemblage of "variously endowed" peoples in world history. The nation's terrain offered sufficient variety to assure the ongoing reproduction of diverse populations, and climatic conditions across regions were conducive to physical and intellectual growth. Technological advances with steam engines eased travel and thus guaranteed present and future populations, "races if you will," opportunities for sustained interactions. Lest anyone liken his sense of diversity to polygeny, Smith repeated the point that, in referencing different endowments, he was not inferring "difference of race." He reaffirmed his monogenist credentials with the insistence, "there is but one human race made *ekeinou aimatos* 'of the same blood.' The difference we mean is such as springs from the difference in climate or geographical position."[107]

The persistence of caste structures that subjugated enslaved and free people in the United States posed formidable barriers to growth. This problem elicited more than a denunciation of injustice. Adhering to his scientific paradigm, Smith argued that bondage and exclusion contravened the natural order and thereby threatened the development of civilization. Paradoxically, the artificiality of caste made him sanguine about its ultimate demise and the role colored people would play in human advancement. He was convinced that they could make a decisive contribution to progress. Through free and equal interactions, he argued, each American group could offer "its particular bent and modifications to the general stream." The stream metaphor illustrated the blurring of prevailing distinctions. It indicated that the peculiarities distinguishing discrete populations would become obscure in the march of civilization. It did not, however, spell the destruction or disappearance of differences. Smith insisted that it would be a gross error to assume that the characteristics distinguishing any civilization could simply vanish even though he was unable to identify the factors enabling them to persist in changing environments. He knew of no scientific theory of inheritance that could explain how genetic substances retained their distinctive properties when mixed with other material. The American School notion of permanent racial "types" that withstood mixture and climatic influences was not an intelligible or ethical option. However, a basic scientific principle provided him with grounding. The precept that matter cannot be destroyed supported his proposition that colored people could contribute to America as full and equal participants without losing their distinctiveness.[108]

Music, poetry, oratory, and a drive to realize a "common brotherhood" were the contributions Smith anticipated. He observed that slaves had already created "the only music which the country has produced." Reform endeavors in the arena of "moral science" would generate additional offerings. Because campaigns for freedom and rights exemplified "true oratory," he predicted that they would heighten public appreciation for the values that inspired colored poets. Continuous messages about humanity's common foundation could help the nation realize its own founding ideals and transform an oligarchy into a true republic.[109]

Colored people's participation in human development would demonstrate the equality of "all members of the human species." Even rudimentary formulations of this theory displayed certainty about its prospects.

158 RELUCTANT RACE MEN

Smith believed equality was a logical extension and necessary consequence of the "unity of the human race." He underscored this conviction by distinguishing it from a prediction by Boston abolitionist Lydia Maria Child that people of African descent would make a distinct contribution to the nation's progress. Smith linked her anticipation to an erroneous belief in constitutional differences between Black and White people, which resulted in misidentifying characteristics that developed from circumstances as essential traits. In contrast, he maintained that colored people would help fuel civilization because they inhabited a country in which this outcome was physically possible and because it was consistent with the unitary nature of human existence.[110]

Linguistic and philosophical tenets provided additional warrants for Smith's hopes. They enabled him to build on the precept that difference was critical to the growth of civilization. They shed additional light on why he placed a premium on intercourse among differently endowed groups instead of attributing progress to particular characteristics. The etymology of the term "civilization" suggested a causal relationship between difference and advancement. He explained that the root "co-ivis" signaled the mechanism by which varied populations united and lived together, thereby fulfilling "an essential condition" for civilizations to thrive. A philosophical principle further developed this point by connecting the process of uniting different groups to an underlying physical reality. Henry James's views of society helped Smith validate his perspective. James argued that free association among divergent social elements manifested the "unity of human nature." It followed that a society's capacity for perfection or the enactment of this unity hinged on intercourse within its boundaries. Interactions were indicators of progress because they instantiated the species unity at the root of humanity. This logic highlighted the prescriptive nature of Smith's philosophy of advancement. It was a "Higher Law" that demanded the "free admixture of human kind."[111]

The process of engaging race science was generally free of disputes. However, Smith's work was an exception. Muddled accounts of human difference and progress from an aspiring scholar sparked a clash resembling the discord that plagued other reform initiatives. More importantly, however, it exposed conceptual difficulties reformers negotiated in trying to make sense of difference in the glare of American School propositions.

On the surface, William Allen was an unlikely object of scorn. A self-identified quadroon born free and orphaned in Virginia, he occupied a stable place among radical abolitionists. Environmentalist tenets and appeals to a common human history shaped his lectures on the popular topic of the origin and destiny of people of African descent. With the aid of abolitionist Gerrit Smith, he had enrolled in the Oneida Institute and, after graduating, studied law in Boston. He quickly abandoned that career path to assume the faculty position vacated by Charles Reason in Greek, German, rhetoric, and belle-lettres at New York Central College. By his own account, Allen studied James McCune Smith's work, including press submissions authored under the pen name "Communipaw." He felt confident that he and Smith held "precisely the same opinion" about races.[112] Smith believed otherwise. Succinct dismissive queries showcased his disrespect for Allen's understanding of human difference and the logic of progress.

Limited science education only partially explains Allen's failure to meet Smith's standards for sound thinking. He unwittingly stumbled into the arena of race science when writing a review of Harriet Beecher Stowe's *Uncle Tom's Cabin*. Once there, he tried to stake out a position. The otherwise stirring novel lapsed into "sheer nonsense," he thought, when it presented the quest to develop an "African nationality."[113] In trying to articulate his misgivings about Stowe's celebratory characterization of the phenomenon, he struggled to interpret race, difference, and progress. Their complexities confounded his efforts.

The first sign of difficulty appeared in his analysis of successful and unsuccessful races. Upon considering the distinctive traits of Saxons, Romans, Danes, Normans, Americans, Asiatics, and "the bona fide African race," he determined that a discrete African civilization would be "almost good for nothing." To explain the conclusion, he tried to adapt Smith's theory of progress, noting that nations "worthy of the name" arose solely from "a fusion of races." Saxons, Americans, and Jews met the test, but they obscured what constituted a race. He reasoned that Saxons had been merely "a clever people" until they mixed with other races, including the Romans, Normans, and Danes. Americans—"of all the races, the most amalgamated"—distinguished themselves by their energy and power. In contrast, Jews had virtually no engagement with science, literature, or art, which were fundamental to civilization. These examples showed that failure to intermingle in accordance with the "rule" that humans were created of common blood sent races on a backward course. Obedience to the stipulation meant progress.[114]

160 RELUCTANT RACE MEN

Allen appeared to follow Smith's lead by interpreting isolation as contrary to the original and essential unity of the species. However, he privileged traits over the imperatives of species unity. His perspective became clearer as he supplemented his initial analysis in response to queries about its coherence. Apparently satisfied with the cogency of his ideas, he dismissed flaws identified in his logic, advising critics to be mindful of the distinction between nations and races. However, he neither explained how the divergent populations he cited functioned as races nor indicated how they compared to nations. The revised analysis, in which Americans were no longer a race, embellished his initial examples. It presented the traits that disqualified a race from greatness and concluded that mixture, along with climate and unspecified beneficial conditions, ensured greatness. The eminence that mixture guaranteed was not merely a testament to the virtue of uniting various members of the human species; it was the means for producing particular traits associated with great civilizations. Allen explained that the African race, which was "superior to other races" in musical ability, religious sentiment, and kindness, could not produce a great nation because these traits did not connote greatness. A nation of Africans would develop "too little of physical force, calculating intellect, daring enterprise, and love of gain" needed for greatness. The "calculating intellect and physical force" of the Anglo-Saxon race would produce a nation with an excess of fierce warlike activity and insufficient "kind, gentle, charitable, and merciful" practices. Greatness, Allen concluded, required uniting the qualities of the mind with those of the heart.[115]

Smith reacted with a mixture of exasperation and condescension. "Professor Allen overwhelms me," he declared. His terse remarks bypassed the attempt to fuse divergent perspectives of human difference and progress. Instead, he addressed two issues within Allen's broader conceptual framework. Initially, he targeted the logic of progress and difference. He charged Allen with ignoring history and knowing nothing about Jews since he failed to acknowledge the accomplishments of such prominent figures as composer Felix Mendelssohn, statesman and novelist Benjamin Disraeli, and banker Mayer Rothschild. He also questioned references to ancient Jews as "a mixed race" and contemporary Jews as a "single race." What, he asked, was "a single race of mankind, in contradistinction to any other, or all other races of mankind?" Despite suggesting that Allen was flirting with polygeny, Smith seemed more intent on accentuating incoherent interpretations of difference and their logical pitfalls.[116]

Allen's response was shrill. He was convinced that Smith was spiteful toward him because he had condemned a reception Smith and other reformers attended for Louis Kossuth, leader of the Hungarian independence struggle.[117] He believed, moreover, that his conclusions about Jews and Africans were logical. He made the provocative suggestion that Smith had sufficient "sense and science" to know that his propositions were valid. Nevertheless, he provided further explanations, some of which he adapted from Smith without acknowledgment. Achievements of individual Jews and of such figures as Benjamin Banneker, Samuel Ward, and Henry Highland Garnet were exceptions that proved the lack of greatness among the masses of both races. This reasoning represented a departure from his judgment that individual achievements exemplified African capability. Two years earlier, he published a pamphlet celebrating the intellectual prowess of Benjamin Banneker, Phillis Wheatley, and George Horton to refute claims about the intellectual inferiority of Africans. His new fascination with traits rendered this logic obsolete. He suggested that people who ceased to embody the traits of their assigned race no longer belonged to that race. Race-defining traits inexplicably trumped individual action in explaining difference and prospects for progress. He argued that renowned Jews and Africans thrived because living among other groups enabled them to develop traits that differed from those associated with their respective races. Once again, the merits of mixture resided in specific traits. Jewish accomplishment required transcending the "money-gathering faculty," which Allen did not consider a feature of greatness. Africans had overcome a record of achieving "next to nothing."[118]

Environmentalist ideas supported Allen's claim that individuals could change by interacting with people of other races. As if challenging Smith on this point, he asked, "Does not Communipaw know that folks conform (and without admixture of blood either) to the influences ... which surround them?" Lamarckian reasoning enabled him to predict that such influences had a lasting impact. Once acquired, new attributes could be "transmitted from generation to generation." Although the explanatory power of environmentalism impressed him, Allen's attachment to race-defining traits prevented him from integrating it into his understanding of human difference. He continued to cite blood as the factor that explained broad human developments and distinctions. It determined whether a population was a "single race" or a "mixed race." Any race that failed to "mingle its blood" with that of other races would become a single race over time, even if, previously, it had been mixed.[119]

162   RELUCTANT RACE MEN

Accusations likening him to polygenists pushed Allen to reassert monogenism. He rehearsed conventional affirmations of one human race, apologizing that the scientific nature of his inquiry required him to speak of races. Nevertheless, he remained convinced that peculiar characteristics divided humans into discrete groups. The notion of race traits continued to shape his conception of human difference long after his encounter with Smith. It enabled him to accept charges of Negro inferiority and criticize people who believed otherwise. When colored reformers in New Bedford disparaged Horace Mann for making such claims, Allen came to his defense. Mann, who espoused monogenism and phrenology, perceived inherent "physiological and psychological differences" among the "families" of the human race. After consulting the literature on "characteristics of the different races," he reported that "the Caucasian," created for cold climates, exceeded other groups in mental capacity. In contrast, the African, whom God adapted to warm regions, surpassed all others in emotion. Allen argued that Mann's critics were wrong to dismiss the claims as bigotry because a scientific interpretation would show that they were not demeaning.[120]

Such ideas resurfaced when Allen began speaking on the British lecture circuit. Central New York mobs, incensed over his courtship with the White student he ultimately married, prompted him to flee to England in 1853. In a speech to the Leeds Anti-Slavery Society on the likely future of "the coloured race of mankind," he repeated his conclusion that morality, kindness, and submissiveness were the distinguishing traits of "the African race." These characteristics promised to lead the race to a high civilization, although it would lack the "intellectuality" of Anglo-Saxon civilization. His views on mixture also framed his predictions about colored people in the United States. Because they possessed "Anglo-Saxon blood" and almost all were born in America, their future lay in further assimilation with White Americans. He predicted that this mixture would increase their intelligence, power, and wealth. Some African traits would endure, however. For instance, colored people would remain in America because the African race was "preeminently distinguished" for its attachment to home.[121]

A postscript to Smith's encounter with Allen displayed enduring antagonism. Months after their exchanges ended, Smith noted a "very curious" scientific occurrence in a British region frequented by US ships. A number of children born in the area had brown complexions and "semi-woolly" hair despite records of White parentage. Smith amused himself with the quip,

"Perhaps the learned Professor Allen might elucidate this subject; it is decidedly too knotty for poor Communipaw."[122]

—

The rigor with which reformers defended human equality and unity failed to transform race science into a respected opponent. It was difficult to separate flaws that eviscerated its scientific credibility from its ethical limitations. Douglass and Smith, whose knowledge and commitments to scientific standards sharply diverged, formed a notable pair in assailing the ethics of race science. Theirs was not a simple retreat to the familiarity of moral injunctions. Rather, the linkages they made between bigotry and claims about innate difference and rank tried to expose the source of logical and methodological flaws in race science. They endeavored to elucidate why it was an unsuitable arena in which to interpret human difference.

Douglass vilified the aims of American School scientists. He argued that their basic orientation betrayed a quest for a theory to support "a foregone conclusion." Partnerships that Nott, Gliddon, Morton, Augustine Smith, and Agassiz maintained with pro-slavery forces reflected their anti-Black sentiment. Only distortions could emerge from such an immoral alliance. Conspicuous "contempt for negroes" in Samuel Morton's *Crania Americana* substantiated this judgment. According to Douglass, it was the work of someone guided by bigotry instead of facts. The methodological consequences of unprincipled scientific undertakings were easy to discern. They generated "infamously distorted" characterizations of human difference and Negro intellect and made deceptive comparisons between "the *highest* type of the European and the *lowest* type of the negro."[123]

Despite his conviction that immoral objectives produced unreliable conclusions, Douglass was reluctant to dismiss American School claims altogether. He was convinced that "the weight of the argument" proved the existence of a common origin of the human species. Nevertheless, he cautiously entertained the possibility that polygeny had merit and considered potential implications. The practical question was whether it was just to degrade Negroes. Justice was a matter of fundamental human rights, which turned on the question of human nature. He argued that there was a natural basis for equal rights because a "common nature" gave all people the same "essential characteristics." Although he offered no evidence, he deemed the proposition unassailable because divergent origins did not disprove or rule out

164 RELUCTANT RACE MEN

commonality. Inconclusiveness freed Douglass to invoke the political philosophy of Irish statesman John Curran and conclude that all human claims to life, freedom, Christianity, social intercourse, civilization, and knowledge were just. Race science thus failed to diminish the natural claim that Negroes had to human rights even if some of its assertions turned out to be true.[124]

Concerns about the ethics of dividing "the human species" into different races guided Smith's critiques of race science from the start. Motives were the source of the problem. Summarizing what other reformers assumed, he perceived the "rage for classification" as little more than an attempt to make science fit "popular prejudices." Such commitments doomed colored people to "the very lowest rank." If this status were natural, subjugation would exist without volumes of exclusionary statutes. "There is no law," he observed, "to prevent dogs & monkeys from voting at the polls."[125]

Errors in the 1840 US census offered a graphic display of how the enterprise of classifying people pandered to bigotry and pro-slavery sentiment. This census marked the first time that the federal government collected data on mental illnesses. It showed rates of insanity among Northern free colored people to be more than ten times higher than rates for southern slaves. Smith spearheaded a campaign to correct the erroneous data that suggested freedom drove colored people mad. Statistical tabulations for 115 towns in eleven states reported the presence of 186 insane colored people where no colored people resided. An additional 133 White inmates at a Worcester, Massachusetts, asylum were counted as colored people. Smith might have been unaware of the intimate connection between American School efforts and Secretary of State John C. Calhoun's refusal to correct the flawed census data. However, consultations among Calhoun, Gliddon, and Morton to deploy the data as ethnological evidence supporting slavery's expansion would have hardly surprised him. He understood that such individuals spread misinformation and ignored scientific standards because they were "hindered by their prejudices." Morally challenged experts would have no qualms about presenting data based on a glance at "specimens" in New York's notorious crime-ridden, impoverished, and overcrowded Five Points district.[126]

A study of Nicaragua reinforced Smith's judgment that biases hobbled race science. It was the work of Ephraim Squirer, an ally of Gliddon and Morton and a member of the New York Ethnological Society. He was, according to Smith, a product of "filthy American prejudice and nasty Negro hate" who exemplified the ease with which scientific standards fell prey to ignorance. What was ostensibly a review of Squirer's study became an occasion for a wholesale condemnation of the bigotry and distorted perceptions that rendered race science unable to contend with empirical evidence. Squirer was fascinated by Nicaraguans whose appearance he could liken to European peoples, particularly the offspring of Indian and Negro unions. In describing their beauty, he reported that Nicaraguan Negroes were nothing like American Negroes. The contrast suggested to Smith that Squirer knew nothing about African populations or Negroes in the US Biases seemed to cloud his ability to make credible ethnological observations. Squirer candidly expressed his prejudices in a letter to his parents that announced his intolerance of slavery and his "precious poor opinion of niggers or any of the darker races."[127] Anti-Black sentiment was apparently evident in his study, along with thinly veiled lasciviousness. Smith perceived that, for men like Squirer, the American Negro was "not an actual physical being of flesh and bones and blood, but a hideous monster of the mind, ugly beyond all physical portraying." This artificial Negro, "utterly and ineffably monstrous," banished reason, integrity, and justice from judgments about colored people. It was so distorted that evidence of humanity in "an actual negro" transformed the person into "anything but a negro."[128]

Smith persisted in engaging race science on scientific grounds even as its "stale anti-negroisms" wearied him. A notable exception appeared at the end of his 1859 essay "On the Fourteenth Query of Thomas Jefferson's Notes on Virginia." His discussion strayed from science only after a "tedious array of facts" undermined the physical basis of Jefferson's assertion that differences prevented Negroes and White people from "equal and harmonious participation" in American society. The political focus of the claim required engagement with the language of politics and popular sentiment. Citing French statesman Comte de Mirabeau's insistence that words were "things," Smith reported that media outlets—"sure indices of public opinion"—identified Negroes as people. It was thus fitting to place them among "the people" endowed with "inalienable rights" acknowledged in the nation's founding documents. This conclusion complemented Smith's stance that the contrived physical differences Jefferson and American School scientists assembled as warrants for exclusion had no logical bearing on the common citizenship of colored and White Americans.[129] He believed that a scientific understanding of difference might have saved Jefferson from wallowing in the "philosophy of negro hate."[130] Had he appreciated the law of human progress, he might have refrained from making unsound claims about the composition of the

166 RELUCTANT RACE MEN

citizenry. Its dubious reasoning was further proof that race science was an illegitimate means of adjudicating citizenship.

Charles Darwin's *On the Origin of Species* provided McCune Smith with tools for a final strike against polygeny. In a droll essay, "A Word for the 'Smith Family,'" he celebrated innovative scientific grounds for establishing the existence of a common human family. Discrediting "Nott & Co." meant revising some of his own views. He readily accepted Darwin's position that offspring of different species in the same genus were commonly fertile. He contrasted this outcome with the polygenist contention that mulattoes were doomed to poor health, imbecility, and truncated lives because they were products of unlike species. If they did suffer from such disorders, he reasoned, it would not prove species difference between White and Negro people. Instead, it could signal the dreadful effects of "in-breeding" among closely related individuals—a practice whose deleterious health effects he discerned among European royalty and isolated Quaker communities. Accordingly, evidence of compromised constitutions among mulattoes would affirm the "absolute consanguinity" of Negroes and White people.[131]

The mulatto question was a small indicator of the scientific advance that Darwin represented. The most exciting news for Smith was that, after two decades of research, a "profoundly learned naturalist" observed that humans shared a single common origin that rendered them all members of the same species. He delighted in summarizing the findings:

> Instead of . . . manufacturing each separate genus and each separate species by a separate and peculiar manipulation, and then setting them down in pairs, . . . (or perchance making up a separate pair for each locality)—the Creator simply set in motion the earliest form of organism . . . and out of this . . . grew a higher and higher organism.[132]

He was satisfied that this modern theory of human development annihilated "the American School of Ethnology with its . . . bungling philosophers."[133]

American School prominence was waning when Smith's sketch appeared in 1860. Morton and Gliddon had died. Agassiz endured as the leading defender of polygenesis. His ongoing search for proof of essentially different racial types comprising separately created species relegated him to the margins of professional scientific practice as Darwin's ideas gained scholarly importance.[134] Reformers' engagement with race science subsided without disappearing altogether. As Civil War battles began, the AME *Christian*

Recorder published an eighteen-part series on ethnology that rehearsed historical developments linking Negroes to Egyptian achievements.[135] As the combat was ending, Agassiz set sail for Brazil on a quest for data to shore up his besieged theory. A dearth of evidence at the end of his trip left him undaunted. He asserted that it did not matter whether the varied races originated from multiple creations because "constant permanent features" showed enough differences to justify likening them to divergent species. Unwilling to abandon polygenesis, he ventured further that claims to a common human origin were inconsistent with the facts and that differentiating races from species was at odds with "scientific principles." He hoped for future discoveries and concluded that the common parlance of the term "races" needed to continue "only . . . till the number of human species is definitely ascertained and their true characteristics fully understood."[136]

———

Configurations of freedom wrought by military might would change the immediate contexts in which reformers confronted race. Ethical concerns would come to overshadow science as the primary lens through which to interrogate the character and significance of difference and rank. Nevertheless, as they anxiously awaited a Union victory, delegates to the 1864 National Convention of Colored Men were mindful of the stakes associated with race practices. They introduced their "Declaration of Rights and Wrongs" with the pronouncement that they were part of "the human family."[137] Such assertions would echo throughout the decades following the Civil War as reformers navigated moral and political complexities of equality and belonging in a new era of freedom.

Richard Allen (1760–1831). African Methodist Episcopal Church founder and organizer of the meeting that launched the national conventions of free people of color. Library of Congress.

Benjamin Arnett (1838–1906). African Methodist Episcopal Church minister and representative in the Ohio legislature. Library of Congress.

Henry Bibb (1815–1854). Fugitive slave and editor of *Voice of the Fugitive* (Canada). Courtesy of Joyner Library, East Carolina University.

John Wesley Bowen (1855–1933). Methodist Episcopal Church minister, professor of historical theology and president of Gammon Theological Seminary, and co-editor of *Voice of the Negro*. Library of Congress.

Richard Cain (1825–1887). African Methodist Episcopal Church minister and South Carolina congressional representative. Library of Congress.

Mary Ann Shadd Cary (1823–1893). Teacher and emigrationist editor of *Provincial Freeman* (Canada). Library and Archives Canada.

Charles Chesnutt (1858–1932). Writer and lawyer. Print Collection, Miriam and Ira D. Wallach Division of Art, Prints and Photographs, New York Public Library, Astor, Lenox and Tilden Foundations.

Samuel Cornish (1795–1858). Presbyterian minister and editor of *Freedom's Journal*, *Rights of All*, and *Colored American* reform newspapers. Photographs and Prints Division, Schomburg Center for Research in Black Culture, New York Public Library, Astor, Lenox and Tilden Foundations.

John Wesley Cromwell (1846–1927). Teacher, lawyer, and editor of *People's Advocate*. New York Public Library.

Alexander Crummell (1819–1898). Episcopal priest, missionary to Liberia, and founder of the American Negro Academy. Manuscripts, Archives and Rare Books Division, Schomburg Center for Research in Black Culture, New York Public Library, Astor, Lenox and Tilden Foundations.

Martin Delany (1812–1885). Emigrationist, race theorist, and first Black US Army major. Special Collections Research Center, Syracuse University Libraries.

Frederick Douglass (c. 1818–1895). Library of Congress.

George T. Downing (1819–1903). Caterer and manager of the US House of Representatives dining room. Courtesy of Olivia Rice Collection, Rhode Island Black Heritage Society.

W. E. B. Du Bois (1868–1963). Library of Congress.

James Embry (1834–1897). African Methodist Episcopal Church minister. New York Public Library.

James Forten Sr. (1766–1842). Sailmaker and American Moral Reform Society president (unverified image). Courtesy of George R. Rinhart.

T. Thomas Fortune (1856–1928). Founding editor of the *New York Globe*. New York Public Library.

Henry Highland Garnet (1815–1882). Presbyterian minister, emigrationist, and president of the African Civilization Society. National Portrait Gallery.

Richard Greener (1844–1922). Attorney and president of the short-lived Negro American Society. National Association for the Advancement of Colored People.

James Holly (1829–1911). Protestant Episcopal bishop of Haiti. Library of Congress.

John T. Jenifer (1835–1919). African Methodist Episcopal Church minister. Library of Congress.

Benjamin F. Lee (1841–1926). African Methodist Episcopal Church minister, editor of the *Christian Recorder*, and president of Wilberforce University. Library of Congress.

Kelly Miller (1863–1939). Essayist and Howard University mathematician, sociologist, and dean. Library of Congress.

Daniel Payne (1811–1893). African Methodist Episcopal Church minister and first president of Wilberforce University. Library of Congress.

James Pennington (c. 1807–1870). Fugitive slave, abolitionist, and Congregational minister. National Portrait Gallery, UK.

Robert Purvis (1810–1898). Founding member of the American Moral Reform Society and the American Anti-Slavery Society and president of the Pennsylvania Anti-Slavery Society. Digital Commonwealth, Massachusetts Collections Online.

Charles Ray (1807–1886). Congregational minister and publisher of the *Colored American*. Special Collections Research Center, Syracuse University Libraries.

John B. Reeve (1831–1916). Presbyterian minister and founder of Howard Univesity's theology department. New York Public Library.

Hiram Revels (1827–1901). Methodist minister and first African American in the US Senate. Library of Congress.

John Rock (1825–1866). Teacher, physician, and attorney who became the first African American admitted to argue before the Supreme Court. Library of Congress.

Charles Roman (1864–1934). Physician, professor of medical history and ethics at Meharry Medical College, and first editor of the *Journal of the National Medical Association*. Library of Congress.

John Russwurm (1799–1851). Co-editor of *Freedom's Journal* before resettling in Liberia. Special Collections Research Center, Syracuse University Libraries.

John P. Sampson (1837–1928). Daguerreotypist, attorney, editor of the *Colored Citizen*, and African Methodist Episcopal Church minister. Library of Congress.

William S. Scarborough (1852–1926). Classics professor and president of Wilberforce University. Library of Congress.

James McCune Smith (1813–1865). Physician, pharmacist, and journalist. Special Collections Research Center, Syracuse University Libraries.

Theophilus Gould Steward (1843–1924). African Methodist Episcopal Church minister and US Army chaplain. Library of Congress.

Benjamin Tucker Tanner (1835–1923). African Methodist Episcopal Church minister and editor of the *Christian Recorder* and *A. M. E. Church Review*. Library of Congress.

Henry McNeal Turner (1834–1915). African Methodist Episcopal Church minister, Georgia legislative representative, and first African American US Army chaplain. Library of Congress.

Samuel Ringgold Ward (1817–c. 1866). Fugitive slave, Congregational minister, and editor of the *Impartial Citizen*. Special Collections Research Center, Syracuse University Libraries.

Everett J. Waring (1859–1914). First African American attorney admitted to the Maryland bar. Library of Congress.

Booker T. Washington (1856–1918). Library of Congress.

William Watkins (1803–1858). Teacher and Methodist minister. Courtesy of Department of Research and Scholarship. African Methodist Episcopal Church.

William Whipper (1804–1876). Lumber merchant and founding member of the American Moral Reform Society. Special Collections Research Center, Syracuse University Libraries.

Lewis Woodson (1806–1878). African Methodist Episcopal Church minister. Courtesy of Robert Woodson.

Theodore Wright (1797–1847). Presbyterian minister and first African American graduate of Princeton Theological Seminary. Yale Collection of American Literature. Beinecke Rare Book and Manuscript Library.

5

"One Color Now"

Freedom and the Ethics of Association

Robert Fitzgerald faced the abolition of slavery with optimism and pity. The ratification of the Thirteenth Amendment convinced the Pennsylvania navy veteran that the nation had embarked on a path toward equality that would undermine the logic of dividing Americans into races. Inspired, he headed to Virginia to teach freed people. As he worked to prepare them for new opportunities, he encountered White Southerners who regarded Black freedom as merely a temporary disruption in the established racial order. Their speculations did not discourage him. He felt sorry for individuals who could not see that "those days of distinction between colors" were nearly finished in this "(now) free country."[1]

Another veteran despaired that some South Carolina freedmen believed the Fifteenth Amendment fulfilled Fitzgerald's vision of America's future. The Civil War had made Martin Delany so sanguine about the potential for Black advancement that he suspended his emigration campaign and devoted his energies to the Union army; he became its first Black major. On the heels of Union victory, he joined AME churchmen in welcoming religious freedom to the South, delivering a speech entitled "Unity of the Races" at the conference inaugurating their missions to freed people.[2] He pressed for political power when suffrage expanded to include Black men by registering former slaves for the Republican Party. His recruits dampened his enthusiasm when they rebuffed his appeals to unite as a bloc of colored voters. Exuberant over their transformation from chattel to citizens, they surmised that the racial taxonomy of difference and rank had also been abolished. Delany lamented that mentioning color "in any manner" among the "simpleminded" folk provoked the angry response, "We don't want to hear that; we are one color now!"[3]

Civil rights legislation appeared to offer decisive proof that race designations were being stripped of customary meanings. The prospect enraged North Carolina senator August Merrimon. The imminent passage of

Reluctant Race Men. Joan L. Bryant, Oxford University Press. © Oxford University Press 2024.
DOI: 10.1093/oso/9780195312966.003.0006

the 1875 Civil Rights Act, which would mandate equal access in cemeteries, juries, public accommodations, and transportation, threatened to force him into sharing social space with Black people. It would thus subvert the status he ascribed to whiteness. "Why did God make our skins white?" he railed. Who gave Republicans "authority to change the color God has blessed us with? Where can any authority be found to make my skin black and corrupt my blood?"[4]

Constitutional and legislative modifications in criteria for national belonging aroused hopes, joys, frustrations, and anxieties in the aftermath of the Civil War. Expanded parameters of freedom and rights seemed to subvert the conventional role racial designations played in delimiting citizenship. The apparent removal of race from legal concepts that structured the nation presented Black reformers with peculiar challenges. New standards for public membership prompted inquiries into the bases of affiliation in private initiatives. Did all American associations have a duty to shun race practices? Was it unethical for groups to use racial terms in naming their organizations? Such concerns generated further scrutiny of race as reformers strove to stabilize voluntary collective endeavors on a shifting political terrain.

The impact of Reconstruction enactments was not nearly as acute for colored reformers who had known antebellum freedom as it was for newly liberated individuals. However, in demographic terms, it was similarly pivotal. Freed people had the unique experience of learning that the US Constitution eradicated their existence as slaves. Yet the abolition of the slave designation meant that the former free colored population also ceased to comprise a discrete social entity. This transformation gratified and concerned William Whipper. He took stock of the development after the Fourteenth Amendment validated reformers' longstanding insistence that American birth constituted citizenship. Contrasting this new political reality with former legal divisions among " 'citizens, slaves and free blacks,' " he observed, "now all have been absorbed into the term American citizen, and all these invidious distinctions are being removed from our civil codes. The class termed 'free people of color' . . . no longer exists."[5] This reconfiguration further complicated questions about the terms of association for reformers who, before emancipation, labored to create a distinct social and political space for free colored people while battling slavery. In their ongoing quests for equality, they struggled to find sure footing on the common ground they now occupied with a population whose circumstances many had pitied and scorned and with White people, with whom they continued to claim a

182   RELUCTANT RACE MEN

shared humanity and citizenship. Whipper likened the situation to that of a shipwrecked mariner adrift in the aftermath of a storm. Unsettled, he issued an alert through the era's most widely circulated colored weekly—the AME *Christian Recorder*—calling for "fresh soundings" in order to chart a forward course.[6]

Despite unprecedented freedoms, there was no reason for anyone to expect an easy surrender of entrenched race practices that had long helped regulate the manner and degree to which individuals could exercise citizenship. Nevertheless, perceived linkages between legal developments and broad societal shifts buoyed hopes. Months before his death, as the Thirteenth Amendment was being ratified, James McCune Smith marveled that Henry Highland Garnet had been invited to deliver a sermon to the House of Representatives. It was one of "the most prominent proofs of the change" he discerned in "public sentiment."[7] This "glorious thing" was surely a sign of a new day. A slave-born preacher was ushered into the "hell of hells" to lead worship with legislators whose time-honored "rites" had callously seared the manhood of "God's poor" and denied their "Common Humanity."[8] In addition to the magnitude of political transformations, a relentless drive for progress and persistent misgivings about the logic and ethics of racial categories inspired interrogations of their role in structuring membership and association in a free America. Reformers in religious and secular venues questioned, condemned, refuted, and reinterpreted these phenomena as they tried to turn the promise of statutory changes into tangible experiences.

The sense that freedom and rights might be within reach reignited opposition to race well before the Emancipation Proclamation. Rising hopes occasioned by the Civil War sparked challenges. Boston physician and attorney John Rock hurled an early attack. With faith in "God and gunpowder," he perceived war as the mechanism through which slavery would end.[9] The presumed inevitability of freedom wrought by divine forces or military necessity compelled him to denounce ideas that appeared to compromise it. Amid a boisterous crowd at the Massachusetts Anti-Slavery Society's 1862 gathering, he excoriated self-proclaimed humanitarians who invoked colonization as a commonsense counterpart of any initiative to emancipate slaves. The plan to banish people from their native country once they could no longer be treated as commodities and cheap labor revealed a morally

"ONE COLOR NOW" 183

corrupt vision of liberty among statesmen who claimed to be civilized. The premise that racial differences prevented freed people from continuing to live in the United States displayed a distortion of logic. An allegedly natural race aversion made the ongoing coexistence of Southern freed people and former slaveholders inconceivable. Moreover, the supposition that Negroes' innate physical capacity enabled them to thrive only in tropical regions ruled out life in northern climes. Rock met the first contention by observing that the nation's mulatto population totaled nearly one million people. As a sign of physical, if not emotional, intimacy, the group's existence countered colonizationist claims. High mortality rates among colored Northerners who migrated to Haiti, the strain of adjustment among Black and White Caribbean immigrants to mainland North America, the ability of colored Bostonians to tolerate cold temperatures, and the ease with which generations of White people endured the South's intense heat further undermined racial justifications for colonization. It was noteworthy, he added, that pundits who invoked climate to justify removing colored people did not find Northern White men unsuited for citizenship even though many of them withstood factory temperatures that rivaled the heat in some tropical zones. Specious reasoning made it difficult for him to escape the conclusion that colonizationists were simply trying to controvert the human right to liberty that arose from a common creation.[10]

Presidential plans for Negro removal elicited the same types of denunciations. Abraham Lincoln's declaration that free colored people had no coherent place in America because they constituted "a different race" suggested that their freedom created self-evident warrants for exclusion. It rendered Black American citizenship an oxymoron. This stance prompted an indignant Robert Purvis to invoke the resentment of Shakespeare's Shylock at having to contend with rampant disregard for Black men's humanity among individuals committed to shoring up a "bogus Democracy." He bewailed all talk of "the 'two races'" and their antipathies. Such notions exposed the nation's highest leaders as incapable of comprehending simple facts; namely, "there is but one race and that is the human race."[11] New York activists issued their claims to America in a more moderate tone; however, they were just as decisive. The unity of the species, native birth, and ties of blood and affection to "white kindred" bound them to their fatherland, its peoples, and its climate.[12] Leaving was not a logical option.

Signs of a possible reversal in wartime progress toward freedom and rights highlighted the necessity of advocating for "the welfare of the human race."[13]

184 RELUCTANT RACE MEN

Even as they anticipated a Union victory, delegates to the 1864 National Convention of Colored Men perceived and underscored dangers, including disheartening indicators that Republicans were poised to reconcile with the Confederacy and with slavery. The peril gained clarity in Secretary of State William Seward's announcement that, when combat ended, "war measures" would lose their force. The fate of the slaves Lincoln declared free through the Emancipation Proclamation would devolve to legislators and courts.[14] Because the Thirteenth Amendment had twice failed to pass in the House of Representatives before the fall convention, delegates could not trust that Congress would continue the process of ending slavery. Furthermore, "invidious distinctions, based upon color," in wages, work, and promotion opportunities of Union soldiers showed that Republican officials shared the bigotries of their Confederate enemies.[15] The convention faced this dismal situation with claims to "manhood and justice" that linked freedom, suffrage, and citizenship as "natural rights" unjustly withheld from colored members of the human family.[16] The long history of Black men being denied "ownership" of their bodies, wives, children, homes, and the fruits of their labors illustrated violations of a collective birthright. It grounded delegates' demands for "unconditional abolition" and the franchise. These outcomes were essential to state recognition of their status as men and Americans who were entitled to political membership on equal terms with other male citizens.[17]

After passage of the Thirteenth Amendment, appeals to a shared humanity fortified campaigns to secure the entitlements of being American. Reformers continued to interpret rights as a corollary of liberty, insisting that it would remain incomplete without means to fight injustice. It was a betrayal for government officials to withhold the ballot from men they supplied with bullets to defend the Union. George Downing, the highly regarded director of the US House of Representatives Members' Dining Room, confronted this moral inconsistency when he led a delegation of thirteen men to present their case for the franchise to President Andrew Johnson. His success in securing an audience with the nation's leader signaled Black men's potential for wielding political authority as American citizens. Representing thirteen states and the District of Columbia, the group, which included Frederick Douglass and William Whipper, spoke on behalf of freed people as well as individuals who had long been subjugated by "class legislation" in free states.[18] United as native-born citizens, they claimed the franchise as their due. Anything short of comprehensive rights violated the nation's codes of justice, which, they believed, no longer sanctioned racial configurations of rank.

Johnson ignored the fact that the spokesmen had lived as free men before emancipation. He contrasted the liberty Black people gained as a result of war with damages suffered by poor White Southerners who now found it difficult to distinguish their ranks from the social status of Black people. Pairing this calculus with his belief that a natural hatred separated racial groups, he determined that universal manhood suffrage would be unfair to the White population and incite a race war. A Black emigration program, however, would resolve the situation.[19] Downing denounced Johnson's arguments as flawed and treacherous and dismantled the notion of racial antipathy with an analysis of power. Planters, he observed, incited antagonism between poor Whites and Black people in order to dominate them all.[20] The idea of deporting Negroes because they were free heaped further disgrace on the president's leadership. *Christian Recorder* editor Jabez Pitt Campbell echoed the outrage, assuring the paper's readers that colored people would never submit to exile. They would uphold the "*unity of races—the brotherhood of man*," principles he deemed essential to the elevation of all Americans.[21]

The common blood of humankind established Black men's eligibility for political and civil rights. This argument was a linchpin of the push for suffrage. William Steward, Theodore Gould, and Abijah Gould—spokesmen for the New Jersey Equal Rights League and active African Methodist churchmen—condemned disenfranchisement as an unholy distinction that robbed them of the divinely ordained equality among human beings acknowledged in the Declaration of Independence. They believed the league exemplified the principles of a common humanity and democracy because neither race classifications nor gender defined membership criteria, even though its goals excluded women's rights.[22]

Stirred by the possibility that freedom signaled the nation's repudiation of "all distinctions founded upon caste or color," some espoused a broad conception of unnatural political differences.[23] Robert Purvis, for one, turned his joy over prospects for citizenship rights into work with the American Equal Rights Association, a group that was open to all and sought the franchise for men and women. He also participated in launching the voting rights campaign of the Social, Civil, and Statistical Association of the Colored People of Pennsylvania. However, he quickly withdrew his support for the project and rejected appeals for financial assistance, criticizing initiatives that appeared to use "a distinctive principle" in agitating for rights.[24] Not only did autonomous colored organizations seem unnecessary, in his eyes it was illogical to frame suffrage initiatives in racial terms because the issues facing the colored

186 RELUCTANT RACE MEN

population were circumstantial; they would be the same for any people in their condition. Moreover, phenotypic features arising from chance were unsound bases on which to organize for rights that belonged to all "by virtue of a common humanity."[25] Reformers thus needed to do away with separate associations in demanding citizenship rights and act on their status as Americans.

———

Denunciations of racial constructs in campaigns for rights offered little guidance to individuals casting about for ways to structure and manage reforms. Political concerns, social pressures, and new objectives led to different considerations about the significance of race for private collective endeavors. In some cases, they pointed to a need to ground united action in race designations that specified the bases of collective advancement. They thus highlighted the limits of appealing to a common humanity and citizenship in carrying out the work emancipation required.

William Whipper's evolution offers a glimpse of the extent to which freedom altered conceptions of race and reform. Removed from skirmishes that had saddled his attempts to lead national reform campaigns, he carefully surveyed the social and political scene to determine appropriate terms of association and advancement. His reflections on unforeseen challenges and murky prospects that accompany freedom generated new ethical principles, transforming his approach to reform. After years of developing initiatives that eschewed a diverse set of racial constructs, he became an unlikely advocate of their virtues.

Gradual shifts in his orientation that began before emancipation accelerated in the wake of the Union victory. The triumph validated Whipper's resolute struggles for freedom. In addition to denouncing slavery and promoting free labor products for more than a decade, he had contributed approximately $1,000 per year to antislavery causes and sheltered hundreds of fleeing slaves in his Columbia, Pennsylvania, home before escorting them North in carts supplied by the Smith & Whipper lumber company that he owned with Stephen Smith.[26] Despite his dedication, he was sometimes uncertain about the potential for equality in the United States. After passage of the 1850 Fugitive Slave Act, circumstances appeared to be so bleak that he took steps to migrate to Canada. Others he knew, including his siblings, former Moral Reform Society members Abraham Shadd and

William Watkins, and nearly half of Columbia's colored population, had already resettled there. In 1854, he and Smith began purchasing land in Dresden, Ontario, accumulating at least seven plots. He erected a home and a warehouse and established a flour mill and a lumberyard. He and his wife, Harriet, were still maintaining their residence in Columbia in 1860; however, a census placed her in Dresden the following year.[27] The move prompted a confrontation with abolitionist Gerrit Smith, who charged "black men" who left the United States with deserting "their own bruised and bleeding people to identify themselves with another people." By emigrating, he argued, they disgraced "themselves and their race, and . . . human nature" in order to "better their fortunes."[28] Incredulous, Whipper called on Smith to explain why he condemned individuals for leaving a country besieged by "republican despotism" and "moral, civil, and religious" influences calibrated to extinguish their manhood. He questioned the ethics of defaming efforts to secure equal rights and broader opportunities for antislavery work. Canada was not a refuge. Whipper viewed it as a space from which he could expand the work of promoting freedom and "the progress of civilization."[29]

War interrupted Whipper's relocation plans. It raised his hopes that the country was on the brink of a "new civilization." Doubtful at first, he debated optimists who perceived the nation's conflict as an opportunity for freedom. In time, however, it became a "sacred cause" that inspired him to set aside his pacifist principles and donate $1,000 annually to support Union military efforts.[30]

A reassessment of colonization was among the first modifications in his reform ethos. His antagonism subsided once the initiatives were no longer associated with maintaining slavery. He observed that the civilizing aims of the American Colonization Society had always been admirable, noting that even its staunchest antebellum critics had championed Christianity and education in Africa. This mission, he argued, was now a central focus of colonization advocates, making their cause worthy. It meant that activists who disparaged the project in their reflexive rejection of "everything African" needed to check their prejudices lest they deprive the continent of civilization's benefits.[31]

Although *Christian Recorder* editor Benjamin Tanner praised Whipper's loyalty to Africa as part of a "new era of thinking" that accompanied abolition, seeds for change had taken root years earlier through encounters with White Quaker colonizationist Benjamin Coates.[32] A successful Philadelphia dry goods merchant, Coates had devoted his energies to colonization, antislavery, and educating students at the Institute for Colored Youth since

188 RELUCTANT RACE MEN

the 1830s. He monitored the views of prominent figures in the press and at conventions and reached out to them in hopes of gaining their support for colonization. Whipper was among his targets, along with Mary Ann Shadd Cary, Martin Delany, Frederick Douglass, and Robert Purvis. In 1858, after reading Coates's pamphlet *Cotton Cultivation in Africa*, Whipper and Shadd Cary championed his proposal to produce cotton in Africa's Niger Valley region using paid African labor.[33] This ACS venture delegated to Henry Highland Garnet, the African Civilization Society representative, engaged Whipper's animus toward the consumption of products made with slave labor. Furthermore, because production costs and prices for African cotton would be cheaper than for American cotton, he believed an African cotton trade with Britain could undermine markets for slave-grown cotton. Thus, the outcome would be as Coates predicted; slavery would become so unprofitable that masters would end up "running away from the slave."[34] Individuals who exercised their "moral right" to migrate and oversee the African enterprise would be undertaking "practical anti-slavery work," and their influence would enable Africa to be "baptized afresh on the altar of civilization."[35] In response to Coates's letter of gratitude for endorsing his plan, Whipper thanked the philanthropist for his endeavors on behalf of "the Colored race" but offered no hint that he was interested in settling in Africa.[36]

Emancipation failed to dampen Coates's colonizationist zeal. He assured colleagues that he had no desire to "get rid of the Negro" and secure the nation exclusively for White people. However, his belief in the existence of essentially different races—each innately suited for a separate region of the world—convinced him that the "African race" did not belong in the United States. Although, at emancipation, the majority of the nation's Negroes were native born, he believed that they had not fully adapted to the country's climates. They were "children of the Tropics," inclined by "the laws of their nature" and God's design to settle in warm regions of Africa, South America, or the Caribbean.[37] To stimulate interest in this supposedly natural arrangement, he distributed material on opportunities in Africa to churches and schools and continued supporting Black education to prepare future migrants to spread US cultural practices in new environments. He was confident that, within four years of emancipation, a sizable Black vanguard would be ready to launch commercial, agricultural, and missionary enterprises in Liberia. He tried to realize his vision by tracking ideas Black reformers expressed in the press and plying them with colonizationist literature. He took a special interest in Whipper's avowed allegiance to Africa

"ONE COLOR NOW" 189

and circulated his commentaries among ACS allies, identifying him as a potential candidate for US minister to Liberia, a financial resource for Liberian education, and an exemplar who could inspire other wealthy colored men to support their cause.[38]

Coates's hopes were misplaced. Whipper's endorsement of missionary ventures did not lessen his commitment to reform work in the United States. As Alexander Crummell observed in praising Whipper's stance, a concern for humanity on Africa need not translate into support for emigration or colonization. A native New Yorker serving as an Episcopalian missionary in Liberia, Crummell saw no inconsistency in having a "*special* interest in Africa . . . and a tenacious grasp upon your birthright as a denizen of the U.S.A."[39] Whipper's focus was clear as he immersed himself in local and national political, educational, economic, and religious endeavors to bolster Black American freedom. He joined Robert Purvis as an officer in the American Equal Rights Association and helped finance the Philadelphia suffrage campaign of the Social, Civil, and Statistical Association of the Colored People.[40] He spearheaded a group effort to purchase a building where Black Philadelphians could conduct reform business. A dedicated community space to deliberate and unite, he argued, would enable them to apply the "true theory" of progress and self-preservation and demonstrate the efficacy of "organized power" and "free discussion." It promised to be a venue for planting "seeds of a revolution . . . in their moral, material, and civil condition."[41]

Whipper's concerns about American education and religious institutions ran deep. Missives to graduating students at Lincoln University (Pennsylvania) cheered those who chose to labor among freed people at a time when shame and fear kept many Black Northerners from venturing south. Financial contributions to Howard University earned him a place on its Honorary Board. For four years, he was the only Black member of the group, made up of the institution's largest benefactors, including wealthy New York reformer Gerrit Smith.[42] Although he never joined the AME Church, he counseled its leaders on developing the denomination to meet modern standards, advised them on the acquisition of Wilberforce University, and, by invitation, wrote regular commentaries for the *Christian Recorder*. He was the only nonmember with official oversight of the publishing wing. As the unit developed during Reconstruction, he served as one of the general managers of the Book Concern, an Executive Committee member for the Board of Publication, and a member of the Publication Department Committee. Editorial contributions and personal relationships

190 RELUCTANT RACE MEN

led to an expansive role that included strategizing to increase the *Recorder's* circulation and admonishing ministers of their duty to lead as "Statesmen, Christians, and Citizens."[43] Such commitments framed his reconsideration of race and the ethical basis for reforms that could advance American citizenship and human welfare.

Reflections on the past guided Whipper through the era's social and political transformations and provided warrants for reinterpreting race practices. His keen understanding of the utility of racial classifications in configuring artificial human differences and ranks had led him to steadfastly repudiate distinctions that rendered "white" a privileged designation. However, Reconstruction required different ways of thinking; "we *must* change our habits and theories," he argued, "to suit the new order of things."[44] History suggested appropriate adjustments. It showed that prosperous nations developed through self-help and by adopting measures to protect their priorities. He ventured that, even without geographical boundaries to demarcate concerns peculiar to colored people, divisions isolating their rights and interests from those of other Americans were no less visible than the rivers and mountain ranges that separated territories. Mindful of his former renunciation of "complexional allegiance," he explained that independent reform initiatives would make it possible to distinguish enemies from supporters of Black advancement. Moreover, a "complexional standard" already prevailed in church and state institutions. If reformers erred in espousing it, they would be acting in concert with the nation's esteemed religious, political, and legal leaders.[45]

The work of pioneering reformers offered a template for this new orientation. AME Church founder Richard Allen, whose antebellum convention agenda Whipper had jettisoned, became a model for Reconstruction-era endeavors. The survival and growth of the religious and reform initiatives Allen helped inaugurate were a testament to the virtues of the impulse that fostered them—namely, "love of race." Not only had the principle proven to be efficacious; it met Whipper's standard of basing reform on truth, for it was, he reasoned, a divinely ordained instinct—a "dictate of nature." It affected everyone except "hybrids," a category he once decried as contrary to the principle of species unity.[46] It established a "law of affinity" that drew people together for self-preservation and the collective exercise of power. Allen's undertakings thus illustrated an established fact of human history, whereby success and organization followed the cultivation of racial kinship. Through this process, Whipper argued, "the 'white race' in this country" helped make

"Anglo-Saxon" a term that signified invincible might. Conversely, the fall of Africa into the barbarity of the slave trade showed the evils resulting from a failure to develop the innate "affinity of race."[47] The lesson for colored Americans was that if they hoped to succeed and determine their own destiny, they must heed historical precedent.

Race love was a capacious phenomenon that could bridge differences among people of African descent. For Whipper, it meant using the needs of destitute, uneducated individuals to define the condition of the colored population. Despite his standing as a learned reformer and successful lumber merchant and real estate investor whose lifestyle included vacations at the New Jersey shore, he believed colored Americans should represent themselves "as a class" lacking "elements of modern civilization."[48] This call to reckon with slavery and discrimination as experiences resulting in collective deficiencies aimed to forge common ground from which to pave the way for advancement of the whole.

Global loyalties stemmed from race love. The sentiment transcended national and continental borders. The motto of the antislavery *Liberator*, "Our country is the world—our countrymen mankind," which once inspired Whipper to renounce "complexional" allegiances, now referenced the need for colored people to reject geographical boundaries in mapping the scope of their sympathies.[49] It framed his advocacy of racial ties connecting the prospects of Africans and people of African descent throughout the world. If Africa remained "uncivilized," he warned, its degradation would threaten "our 'race' in this country."[50] Similarly, he reasoned that the persistence of Cuban slavery demanded that, as lovers of their race and as citizens, reformers must call for US action against it. Embracing Africa and the Caribbean was a necessary step toward constructing a comprehensive history that would illustrate the claims of the entire race to natural equality.[51]

The call to foster unity using race categories muted Whipper's former message that theories delineating the existence of divergent races advanced false conceptions of human difference. Yet the new framework did not quiet his anxieties about the dangers of race practices. When AME Church bishops issued a public address declaring that Indians lacked the capacity to tolerate "American Civilization," he chastised them for nurturing the same sentiments White people aired in asserting superiority over others. Condescension toward "any portion of human kind," he cautioned, perpetuated the "despotic spirit of caste."[52] Abiding apprehensions about how race practices functioned also fortified his belief in the necessity of developing racial affinity. He

192 RELUCTANT RACE MEN

reflected on the improbability of broad White support for colored people's claims to equal citizenship. Personal experiences of barriers to progress—witnessing Andrew Johnson rebuff calls for Black voting rights and the American Equal Rights Association's fatal conflicts over whether to demand the franchise for women or colored men—sharpened his perspective.[53] Johnson's sentiment was a fitting barometer of popular hostility toward Black freedom, expressed in rising mob violence and such spiteful retaliatory acts as a White Georgian's quest to reclaim land he donated to a Black congregation after nearly two decades because he had given it to slaves, not to "free negroes." Rumor held that he acted at Johnson's behest.[54] In any case, it was clear that there would be no outpouring of sympathy for the destitute masses who received nothing to establish their freedom. Instead, Whipper foresaw a resurgence of "the ancient pride of the 'white race' " that would spur vigorous efforts to sustain social, economic, and political supremacy. Initiatives to ensure that whiteness remained a site of privilege meant that colored people had to protect themselves and carry out their own advancement. They were duty bound to promote "pride of race."[55]

While broad uncertainties about navigating freedom gave rise to Whipper's concerns, developments at the 1869 National Convention of the Colored Men of America created an additional impetus for the *Christian Recorder* commentaries that sketched his new outlook. They might have prompted the question that framed his editorial series: "Where are we drifting?" It cited the Washington, DC, proceedings to illustrate the need for change. His participation was largely limited to the finance committee, whose members covered shortfalls in dues payments; however, he closely observed the meeting. The gathering continued to trouble him when the proceedings were finally published, two months after it ended.[56] He believed that decades of protesting for justice, exhausting "every form of prayer and the whole vocabulary of denunciation," should have solidified commitments to forbearance and free discussion. However, this gathering to promote manhood suffrage had displayed intolerance, duplicity, and mob rule on the part of "the most intellectual body of colored men ever assembled on this continent."[57]

His complaint targeted delegates' refusal to extend honorary membership to Joseph Jenkins Roberts, president of Liberia College and former president of the Republic of Liberia. The denial came amid courteous bestowals of the distinction upon visiting White politicians and military officers—men whose attainments fell below Roberts's rank. In addition, a group of Philadelphians had pressed others to endorse the exclusion at a late-night session that did not allow time for discussion. Roberts's American Colonization Society ties offered sufficient grounds for delegates to oppose his presence at a gathering claiming citizenship rights. Indeed, some invoked a tradition of rejecting colonization proposals that emerged with the founding of the ACS. They repeated the old claim that their duty to Africa was no greater than the obligations of any other Americans. The United States was their legitimate home. Affirming anti-colonization sentiments helped deflect potential criticism from observers who might contrast Roberts's exclusion with the honors extended to White men. A special resolution addressed the issue, explaining that it would be a mistake for anyone to interpret their actions as a sign that they believed White men to be superior to other men or that delegates lacked respect for one another. Instead, they argued, they acted to display their enduring contempt for the ACS.[58]

Isaiah Wears reviled Roberts for deserting colored people by fleeing to "the swamps of Liberia." A person who had surrendered American identity had no right to impose a "foreign odor" upon an initiative of citizens. George Downing was more diplomatic in attributing his rejection of Roberts to Liberia's "Negro nationality." In keeping with his creed that the colored population comprised an "inseparable part of the American people," he opposed "any nationality based on color."[59]

For Whipper, the exclusion of Roberts displayed delegates' willingness to act with the same malevolence and bigotry that incited White attacks. It was a glaring example of the "hatred of race" that threatened to keep colored people disorganized and undermine their prospects for advancement. Accordingly, it was at odds with the convention's core aim to foster progress. The practical significance of the issue lay in his judgment that, in addition to having to demand equal rights, it was necessary to contend with the demoralizing effects of oppression that, on their own, neither religious ministrations nor legislative enactments could effectively address. Black and White audiences alike needed to hear the message that no population held a monopoly on endowments that God meted out with impartiality. Reformers could ill afford to look solely to people recovering from slavery for evidence of accomplishments or to limit accounts of Black capacity to American soil.[60]

The spectacle of a prominent figure's ceded citizenship was just one of the factors that burdened the 1869 convention. Delegates grappled with ethical

194 RELUCTANT RACE MEN

questions regarding gender and racial distinctions in trying to structure a campaign for equality. Their struggles further highlighted the complicated work of conceptualizing the contours of progress on a new political terrain.

Deliberations about women's membership created a moral calamity. They highlighted reformers' narrow conceptions of injustice and progress. When AME minister Henry McNeal Turner initiated the proceedings as the temporary convention chair, he stressed the importance of demanding universal manhood suffrage. The freeborn South Carolina native who served in the Civil War as the first Black US Army chaplain urged the group to strike a mighty blow against "the spirit of caste" to secure the franchise.[61] The principles needed to carry this work forward were not self-evident. The presence of a woman, Harriet Johnson, representing Allegheny City, Pennsylvania, forced men to consider the scope of their opposition to caste structures. Johnson, an 1864 graduate of Philadelphia's Institute for Colored Youth, was principal of the preparatory and ladies departments at Avery College, where Henry Highland Garnet served as president.[62] Although convention guidelines assured the admission of individuals elected by their localities, debates arose over whether to recognize "the learned and accomplished lady" as a delegate. Challengers cited no ethical grounds for her exclusion. They were simply content to claim that the convention was "expressly for colored men" and that they should retain exclusive control. Others countered that reformers calling for change needed to act in accordance with the "progressive" tenor of the era, which suggested that women would ultimately secure the franchise. They felt a need to push beyond conventional American ideas and their own personal prejudices to acknowledge that they had no right to exclude any representative. The term "men" in the convention's title thus had to include women. Individuals who admitted that they would prefer not having to deal with the issue felt compelled to confess that there was no valid basis for excluding women. One delegate framed his support for admitting Johnson as part of his obligation to act on behalf of the fifty women in his home community who elected him to be their convention representative.

Isaiah Wears, an advocate of women's suffrage, made an explicit connection between racial caste and gender hierarchy. Although he had opposed admitting Mary Ann Shadd to the 1855 national convention, he now interpreted bans on women delegates as "too much like" the actions of politicians who deprived "the colored race" of their rights. He insisted on a vote to approve all delegate credentials, which carried and formally admitted Johnson.[63] Nevertheless, the issue stoked further acrimony when John

W. Menard arrived with a Louisiana delegation. He had been a clerk in the Department of the Interior during the Lincoln administration and had recently fought, unsuccessfully, to claim a seat in the House of Representatives after a contested election. His prominence did not spare him from heckling and hisses as he declared support for Johnson's participation, chided delegates on their silence concerning women's suffrage, criticized their disorder, and admonished them to fight all distinctions "of color and sex."[64]

Discussions about Johnson's inclusion did not alter how delegates grounded appeals for equal rights. After citing descent from "a common Father," they invoked manhood, American birth, generations of uncompensated labor, and principles of republican government to justify receiving the same entitlements White male citizens possessed.[65] Calls for "systematic organization" of franchise campaigns sparked debate about racial distinctions. It centered on a proposal to revive the National Equal Rights League formed at the 1864 national convention.[66] A committee led by William Forten, James Forten's youngest son and a leader of Philadelphia's league, was charged with planning the process. However, apart from explaining the necessity for such an entity, he was unable to present the group's plan. Instead, delegates aired individual perspectives.[67] The most vocal participants, who spoke after the group welcomed Massachusetts senator Charles Sumner, William Lloyd Garrison, and Wendell Phillips as honorary delegates, opposed relying on race distinctions to define political associations. Physician Charles Purvis, son of Philadelphia reformer Robert Purvis, denounced "colored" coalitions and insisted on forming "leagues of American citizens."[68] Tennessee delegate William Watkins championed unity among colored people, but he refused to endorse any national body designated solely for colored individuals. Dr. John Brown of Maryland expanded on this challenge in denouncing the pervasive American bigotry that forced colored people into "distinctive places" for worship, travel, entertainment, and other daily activities. White people's participation in the convention convinced him that it was an interracial undertaking and a model for forming political leagues that avoided race distinctions. Isaiah Wears, George Downing, and John Langston added unqualified denunciations of the league idea. Downing complained that its supporters created the harmful impression that delegates were planning unilateral actions. Langston condemned the scheme as indistinguishable from segregated schools. The outcry prompted Wears to call for a comprehensive assessment of the league option in a revised committee report. Perhaps the new charge and the dissension overwhelmed Forten, for he apparently

196 RELUCTANT RACE MEN

abandoned the task. The matter was tabled, and the proceedings ended without a plan for organized collective action to secure the franchise.[69]

The work of outlining the grounds on which the convention sought voting rights ultimately fell to a delegation chaired by Isaiah Wears. An invitation to present the group's claims to the House of Representatives Judiciary Committee gave him an opportunity to call for suffrage as a basic right. His didactic style betrayed his judgment that, despite achievements in the arts and sciences, his audience knew "nothing about human rights." He cautioned the committee not to envision the extension of the franchise as an act of benevolence. To think in this manner would be analogous to a thief presuming to have granted him traveling privileges by releasing him after a highway robbery. If the government ceased withholding citizenship rights, the gesture would not constitute a gift, he explained. Such an interpretation, along with popular drivel about Black men owing gratitude to politicians who spoke in favor of entrusting them with the vote, misconstrued a simple fact. The franchise "is ours," he declared, "because it is yours and for the same reason that it is yours."[70] He expressed astonishment that White men whose undemocratic actions defied "fundamental principles of the Government" had the audacity to label Black men "too ignorant" to vote. White voters and the White representatives they elected had driven the nation to the brink of destruction in a war requiring the aid of thousands of Black men. If the ballot was necessary to White men's success, he asked, how were Black men to protect their rights and thrive without it? If they were indeed mentally deficient, what genius should they summon to enact the citizenship that voting bestowed upon White men?[71]

William Forten tried to influence the terms of suffrage on his own after the convention. He appealed to Charles Sumner for new language when he learned that the draft of the Fifteenth Amendment stipulated that the vote could not be denied on the basis of race, color, or previous condition of servitude. He opposed permanently marking American citizens with the contrived categorization scheme that had structured their oppression and rendered them ineligible for rights. "We want no reference to Race or Color, or . . . previous condition, engrafted on the National Charter," he argued. "There must be no *Color* known to *Americans* but the National one."[72] Inscribing taxonomies of race, color, and servitude in the constitution apparently implied that they were objective and innocuous ways of distinguishing among Americans. It cast them as naturally occurring phenomena that had to be overlooked in according rights, thereby obscuring their status as social and political classifications deployed to maintain inequality. He wanted the franchise to be a national acknowledgment of manhood and citizenship, long withheld from Black men. Thus, he proposed eliminating the draft amendment's offending references and making suffrage an affirmative right for adult male citizens, with a proviso that excluding convicts required fair application of laws.[73] A configuration of rights that validated flawed conceptions of human difference and rank fell far short of the equality he envisioned.

Passage of the Fifteenth Amendment sparked widespread joy. Voting access overshadowed concerns about the terms of political inclusion that troubled Forten. It seemed to confirm freedom's conquest over racial distinctions. Victory celebrations echoed strident race denunciations that marked calls for rights. The conviction that the franchise was, in the words of Bishop Jabez Campbell, God's "final seal" on the abolition of slavery, compelled churchmen to broadcast it as a religious feat.[74] Officials in the AME Church assumed prominent roles in organizing observances of this development as part of their commitment to civic leadership. When AME ministers James Pierce and Stephen Smith spearheaded New Jersey celebrations, they credited heaven for developments that eradicated the nation's caste system. Emancipation and the franchise proved the heresy of long-standing appeals to the "divine right of complexion." Daniel Payne took the phenomena as signs that "the American mind" was finally recognizing "the unity of the human race" and the evils of sustaining hierarchy among Christians.[75]

Appeals to a common creation helped defend access to the franchise. Trenton, New Jersey, minister William Walker invoked the phenomenon to address backlash to the Fifteenth Amendment. He met calls for colored people should go back to "their native soil" if they wanted to exercise rights with the rejoinder that a return to origins would transport Black and White Americans to the biblical garden of Eden together. Exasperated by references to skin color in initiatives to deprive citizens of rights he asked, "What is color but nature? And what is nature but an effect, whose cause is God?" Basing the ability to exercise rights on "form, features, or complexion" was sacrilegious and tantamount to atheism.[76]

Despite pervasive optimism, everyday experiences made it difficult to ignore the importance of race categories in setting reform parameters. New Yorkers confronted this issue at a celebratory Colored Voters Convention, where they faced competing concerns among constituents who were jubilant about achieving rights and wary about navigating a new

198 RELUCTANT RACE MEN

social landscape. As they reveled in the abolition of "political proscription," some triumphant participants declared that their meetings should cease because they had secured legal recognition as equals to other American men. Dissenters objected that the fight for equality could not end with constitutional provisions for voting privileges. Discrimination in workplaces and leisure venues required civil rights protections from private corporations. Although he had once argued that national conventions should meet until Black men attained the franchise, Henry Highland Garnet, chair of the gathering, now stressed the importance of learning to fend off deception and bribery attempts by political parties seeking colored votes. After weighing such factors, delegates compromised. They conceded that there was "no further necessity" for citizens to form political associations based on color classifications. However, it was "absolutely necessary" to continue annual colored conventions because they offered a resource for new voters to master the duties of citizenship.[77] New Jersey residents sidestepped this dilemma by organizing themselves as a convention of "new citizen voters," whom the Fifteenth Amendment acknowledged as "part of the body politic." William Whipper, a delegate from New Brunswick, where he maintained a second home, and a host of ministers and county representatives united to develop principles ensuring exclusive support for politicians who defended equal rights "without distinction of race or color." In planning the gathering, William Walker noted that the delegation affirmed the era's ethical tenets by eschewing racial designations. Because "the word white is stricken from the constitution of the State," he explained, "we should also drop the word colored."[78]

Frederick Douglass found himself in a struggle to balance elation over the apparent end to the state-sponsored "injustice of complexional distinctions" and his awareness that color designations signified palpable social differences. He maintained that separate initiatives on the part of colored people flouted "true republicanism" and the nation's emerging moral standards because they sustained racial distinctions. Yet, the *New Era* newspaper he edited with Presbyterian minister J. Sella Martin was dedicated specifically to the moral, intellectual, and political development of the colored population. Acknowledging racial differences offered a means to promote colored men as self-sufficient dignified citizens who deserved all the citizenship privileges White men exercised. A letter that he, George Downing, William J. Wilson, and other supporters circulated to enlist financial assistance from Republican congressmen described the paper as a vehicle to rally and publicize colored people's support for the Republican Party. Wary of circumscribing the endeavor with racial categories, they explained their venture as a necessary initiative to address the needs and serve the interests of colored Americans, "not as a separate Class, but as part of the WHOLE PEOPLE."[79] Such disclaimers were not unique among reformers pressing citizenship clams. Philip Bell framed the 1865 launch of his San Francisco reform paper, *Elevator*, declaring, "While we shall, as colored men, battle for the rights of our race, we shall do it on the broad principles of humanity, not because we are colored."[80] Douglass presented similar ideas to critics who insisted that freedom and rights meant that colored Americans no longer constituted a discrete class. He defended the paper against accusations that it presented colored people as "a peculiar variety of the human family" by stressing the need to use racial classifications in proving that they were capable of fully participating in American civilization.[81] The *New Era*, which earned him congressional press credentials, promised to provide such evidence. Ultimately, however, the editors were unconvinced of the merits of the paper's most prominent racial references. In the first six months of publication, they changed the subtitle describing their endeavor from *A Colored American National Journal* to *A National Journal Edited by Colored Men* and finally settled on *A National Journal*.[82]

Questions about the significance and ethics of race practices in the newly free nation proved to be especially thorny in churches. As the most established and prominent colored voluntary organizations, they were critical to negotiations of freedom. The AME Church, which boasted of its status as the "largest body of organized colored men in all the world," was in the forefront of this process.[83] In addition to addressing social and political issues through its widely circulated newspaper, church officials and lay people used their spiritual authority, ideals, and facilities to promote freedom and rights in a host of venues. As Bishop Daniel Payne explained to delegates of the 1869 national convention meeting, which convened at Israel Bethel AME Church, religion could not be severed from secular issues because God connected them. He believed the church had a duty to make colored people a "civilizing power in the Republic and an enlightening force in the world."[84] Accordingly, any minister who failed to fulfill this obligation in a systematic manner was unworthy of the public trust.

Churchmen took this injunction to heart. Historian Eric Foner determined that more than 22 percent of some 240 Black ministers who held political office during Reconstruction were African Methodists, making the institution the single largest denominational source of clerical politicians. The convictions of Reverend Charles Pearce of Florida help to explain the phenomenon. He insisted that no minister could perform "his whole duty" unless he tended to the political needs of his parishioners. Georgia preachers embodied this sentiment; every AME minister in the state worked as an organizer of voters for the Republican Party.[85] Reverend Richard Cain went further, bringing his oratorical skill and wit into the US House of Representatives. Citing physical characteristics common to people throughout the world, he urged his colleagues to pass the civil rights legislation introduced by Charles Sumner. He observed that a single act of creation made human beings homogeneous. This event alone created an imperative for equal rights. Invoking God and Shakespeare's Shylock, he declared, "I have two eyes, two nostrils, one mouth, two feet. I stand erect like you. I am clothed with humanity like you."[86] In short, there was no valid physical basis for unequal treatment of Black people in civil arenas. They had a natural right to associate with others in public spaces. Such activism, taken on behalf of a diverse constituency that extended beyond congregations, exemplified wide-ranging civic and political commitments that made the denomination a vibrant site of inquiry and debate over the terms of association.

Framing political achievements as acts of God imbued them with a degree of spiritual gravity that could render other interpretations heretical. Frederick Douglass encountered the depth of this sentiment when he ridiculed the "hackneyed cant about thanking God" for voting rights. He viewed the discourse as an example of a mindless tendency to privilege scriptural wonders over "scientific truth." This dismal effect of slavery hampered preachers' leadership. His anticlerical scorn reflected worries that exaggerated praise for the amendment as miraculous obscured the tremendous work required to address centuries of subjugation and the historical gap between American law and practice.[87] Nevertheless, indignant churchmen joined Jabez Campbell in a mock trial that judged Douglass unfit to lead because he seemed intent on hurling the Bible and morality from the courts and churches, thus threatening the nation with ruin.[88] Apart from the theatrics it inspired, invocations of divine intervention increased the stakes associated with navigating freedom. If God eliminated race practices in political arenas, how could they be justified in churches?

Confrontations with race constructions arose as Northern preachers and former slaves met on the common ground of religious liberty. Church leaders seized new opportunities to increase the denomination's membership by proselytizing freed people who were exercising unprecedented autonomy in choosing church affiliations. This encounter set in motion a complex discourse of ambivalence, apology, and dissent about race and African Methodism. It situated race practices among key factors that shaped the religious work of Reconstruction.

Daniel Payne, who joined the denomination after cutting ties with Lutherans and Presbyterians, spearheaded endeavors to expand church ranks in the South. In the spring of 1865, he led a delegation to Charleston to extend work begun during the Civil War by his Baltimore protégé James Lynch. With pledges of support from the American Missionary Association, a cadre of preachers—Richard Cain, James Handy, James Johnson, Anthony Stanford, and Theophilus Steward—set out to develop African Methodist roots in the city and throughout South Carolina. The project was a homecoming on two fronts. Payne was returning to Charleston after migrating to the North thirty years earlier, when state officials closed his school. The group was also re-establishing the denomination's presence in the region. It had been banished after Black church members were named as leaders of the 1822 Denmark Vesey conspiracy to mount a slave revolt.[89]

Race practices were among the first issues the group had to address. At the founding of the African Methodist South Carolina Conference, former slaves who were wary of racial distinctions confronted church leaders with charges that they circumscribed religious freedom by basing church membership on skin color. Cain and Payne took the lead in defending the denomination against accusations that it excluded White people and mulattoes. Cain feared that this rumor would impede efforts to elevate people of color "as a race." Such an outcome would be calamitous for an organization that claimed to have done more than any other body to elevate colored people and was intent on doing much more. He argued that the church's actions and regulations proved the charges unfounded. The denomination had an established tradition of rejecting "distinctions of color" and welcoming all Christians who dedicated themselves to elevating people of African descent.[90] The need to address the conditions of freed people trumped any inclination to reject race categories altogether in defining the purpose of Southern missions.

Payne shared Cain's commitment to evangelizing freed people, but he deflected the suggestion that the church subscribed to color distinctions.

202 RELUCTANT RACE MEN

He insisted that its effort to save humanity encompassed individuals of all complexions, a mission that distinguished it from the Methodist Episcopal Church (MEC), North. The predominantly White organization, which Payne accused of misrepresenting African Methodism, maintained an unambiguous caste structure based on race categories that exacted a high price from the denomination's colored membership. A seat in a Northern Methodist "negro pew" demanded that a colored man yield "half his own manhood," Payne argued. In Charleston, he had witnessed worshippers possessing "what is falsely called African blood" pulled from the Methodist altar to satisfy the conceit of "what is falsely called Anglo-Saxon blood." A pattern of discrimination based on the notion of races showed his fellow Methodists' refusal to acknowledge that there were "no such things in existence" and their failure to accept the common humanity of all people.[91] This charge shaped Payne's perspective on reunification of American Methodism. While he and other church officials expressed interest in a merger, they understood that it would never succeed unless their White counterparts forswore bigotry and learned to conceive of union "on terms of perfect equality."[92]

A desire for religious unity as a counterpart of the expansion of freedom and citizenship led some AME clergy to leave their denomination for the Methodist Episcopal Church. Preachers who proselytized Southern freed people were among the first to defect. Their experiences occasioned a loss of faith in the utility of churches organized specifically for people of color. Reverend Charles Smith left the AME Church while working in Tennessee, believing that effective missionary work demanded more than the denomination could offer. He was concerned the church would compromise the elevation of people it aimed to help because it lacked educational resources needed to properly train ministers. Moreover, "the power of association" convinced him that freed people would flourish by becoming part of the MEC community.[93] He gleefully reported that he faced no slights in his new denomination. Instead, a feeling of spiritual fellowship confirmed his sense that the possibilities for freedom and equality in the church could enhance colored people's experience of citizenship.

James Lynch, editor of the *Christian Recorder*, acted on a perception that colored churches could not effectively navigate the expansion of freedom. His 1867 departure was especially noteworthy because it coincided with his increased prominence in the denomination. He had just received a prestigious pastoral appointment to the original Bethel Church in Philadelphia. Yet he was struggling with a personal crisis about serving in a religious institution that appeared to sustain racial distinctions. Relating his decision to MEC bishop Matthew Simpson, he explained that African Methodism thrived on the "idea of exclusiveness on account of color" as its *vitalizing force*." However, he believed that freedom and rights eradicated the logic of racial distinctions and affirmed "the grander idea of human brotherhood."[94] This perception reinforced his conviction that the necessity for African Methodism was fading. Continuing his affiliation with the church would require him to act contrary to the era's progressive currents and his principles. He imagined that distancing himself from the AME Church would enable him to promote true freedom and advancement. Conscience demanded the break, he argued, "for seperate [*sic*] church organizations on account of color have the sympathy of democrats, conservatives and Southern Methodists only."[95] He could not remain in the AME Church because he believed it reinscribed a concept that defined people of color as an inferior caste.

Lynch's interpretation of the needs of people of color highlighted his discomfort with invoking racial distinctions for any social arrangements. He envisioned Southern freed people living in community with White people and applied that ideal to institutions. Just as slaves did not single-handedly free themselves from slavery, he reasoned, Black people could not overcome its degrading effects by themselves. Agency had to include partnering with White people who were willing to assist. Denominational union did not appear to be forthcoming, and he understood that African Methodists would resist losing their institutional integrity in a merger. Their cooperation with Southern Methodists to relieve the latter group of its colored members further convinced him that his decision was right. The AME alliance with an organization that supported the subjugation of colored people showed him that it lacked a proper appreciation of the times and could not adequately address the moral needs of its primary constituents.[96]

Hiram Revels, who left a temporary affiliation with Presbyterians to help preach Methodism in the South, agreed with Lynch that the success of Protestant missionary efforts to uplift Southern freed people demanded what African Methodists lacked. He was drawn away from the organization for a second time by the belief that the MEC could do more for colored people than any other denomination. Its resources were not strictly material. Principles were critical, especially what he saw as the MEC refusal to make "distinctins [*sic*] on account of race or color." This flawed proposition held practical import for Revels because he linked the effectiveness of Southern missions to freed people's ability to witness, firsthand, "true principles of church

204 RELUCTANT RACE MEN

government."[97] An environment defined by immoral race distinctions could not foster such an experience.

The promise of deliverance from stratification in the Methodist Episcopal Church proved to be illusory. This outcome had clear warning signs. Missionary work among freed people that appeared to strike a blow at prevailing race constructions coincided with the creation of segregated jurisdictions. The denomination sidestepped the tradition of geographical conferences in 1864 by creating the Delaware and Washington Conferences as separate districts for Northern colored members. Less than a decade later, a similar arrangement threatened to take hold throughout the South. Former African Methodist preachers found themselves battling to keep their new denominational home from further codifying racial distinctions. At the General Conference before his sudden death in 1872, James Lynch worked to stave off the formation of colored conferences.[98] When officials proposed them again four years later, Hiram Revels helped mount protests with New England preacher and abolitionist Gilbert Haven. Perhaps the most outspoken opponent of "colorphobia" in the Methodist Episcopal Church, Haven had a long record of condemning the notion that race designations were morally valid markers of difference. He rejected the racial apportionment of religious authority and admonished coreligionists to "let the word and idea of black and white be expelled from the heart of the church."[99] Yet he was a minority voice. As missions to freed people progressed, his views became increasingly marginal. Revels thus tried a different tack and framed separate jurisdictions as a threat to the reputation of the Methodist Episcopal Church. If it officially invoked "the color line," he argued, it would appear that critics had been right all along. Moreover, missionary endeavors would fail if the church did not oppose caste. The denomination would be culpable for the dangerous social consequences that would inevitably result from leaving newly freed citizens in ignorance about responsible use of their political rights.[100]

Warnings and tirades about the immorality of race practices were ineffective. Bigotry held far greater sway than commitments to equality or the public good. Northern Methodists gave their local conferences the option of creating separate jurisdictions for colored members; they all quickly exercised it. Appeals for the denomination to heed the principle of "the Brotherhood of Man" persisted into the twentieth century. However, instead of continuing to assail the organization's jurisdictional color line, Black ministers resorted to calls for access to church authority. They fought for the right to become bishops in the denomination while boasting of its ability to

advance the Negro race and contrasting its equality with the marginaliza-
tion and segregation they perceived among other Protestants, especially "colored Methodisms."[101] Although the institutionalization of racial difference
and rank blunted MEC criticism of Black churches, its officials continued to
compete with the AME Church using forceful rhetoric about the immorality
of racial categories in religious associations. They charged it with building
institutional strength on a sinful caste system and compromising its moral
authority by relying on the "mere distinction of complexion."[102] In the end,
however, denominational leaders were unwilling to adhere to the principles
they advertised and applied in judging others.[103]

The MEC path to internal division signals lofty ideals of equality and a
competing investment in social distinctions and hierarchies that marked
broad adjustments to emancipation and rights. Even denominations not popularly regarded as venues for nurturing Black people's religious experiences
confronted this issue. Controversy among Congregationalists is instructive
of how notions of racial difference and sameness informed efforts to contend
with new parameters of religious freedom.

Conflicts burdened the process of expanding the Southern reach of the
Congregational Church after emancipation. Efforts to establish a church in
Washington, DC, turned contentious when a group of colored people sought
membership. Among them was Oberlin College graduate John Hartwell
Cook, chief clerk for the Freedmen's Bureau, who called upon General O. O.
Howard—head of the bureau and fellow Congregationalist—to try to ensure that the new church welcomed "any and all of God's creatures." It was
a tenet of his faith and in the "interest of humanity," he explained, to promote "comingling of the races in State and church."[104] His appeal to Howard
stemmed from a rebuff by the budding congregation's pastor, Charles
Boynton, chaplain of the House of Representatives and inaugural president of
Howard University. In addition to personally dissuading Cook from joining
the congregation, he preached and circulated a sermon, *The Duty which the
Colored People Owe to Themselves*, mapping a theory of race separation and
advancement. The point, as Cook understood it, was to justify making the
congregation "a white man's church" and sanction "the old state of things."[105]

Boynton's sermon describes the division of the human race into diverse
nations at the biblical Tower of Babel as a providential dictate for the world
to develop as discrete races. It praises the biblical Moses for embodying the
virtue and obligation of separate race development by choosing to live as
"a Jew among Jews, rather than leave his people to associate with another

race"—namely, the Egyptian royals who reared him.[106] Numerous cases of persistent national identities feature a seemingly natural occurrence whereby "race everywhere separates from race, and each seeks an independent and Separate life." Boynton observed that "Arabs have preserved their race distinct," and God held the "Greek race" apart from the Turks.[107] Eleven additional races showed the persistence of difference, demonstrating that racial segregation was the normal order of things as ordained by God. Chinese, Japanese, Indians, Moors, Castilians, Francs, Teutons, Italians, Scandinavians, Celts, and "Sclavs" were separate races that heeded the imperative of self-preservation. Their integrity was historical evidence of God's will and the "race affinities" embedded in human nature. The Civil War showed the phenomenon in the American context. Boynton found validity in the Southern boast that the battles reflected a "conflict between the Norman blood of the South and the Saxon race of the North" and concluded, "the North and the South descended from different races."[108] This factor allegedly nurtured regional hostilities among White Americans.

The upshot of the narrative was that the religious fellowship Cook believed would promote human welfare was at odds with the discrete racial development God required to advance human civilization. Boynton imagined a Black racial purity that withstood all manner of "unnatural intermingling" wrought by two centuries of American slavery as he posited that Negroes remained "a distinct race, not in color alone but in their mental and spiritual character, preserving the original traits of their people."[109] Although genetic mixture was inconsequential when most Black people were property, interracial worship as equals threatened "too close a contact." He warned that it would thwart Negroes' capacity to survive as a race by altering their culture and disrupting the formation of "their own proper black manhood." His hope was for Negroes to cultivate a "true black humanity" through cultural undertakings. This work promised to foster "an African civilization" when they migrated to "their native Africa." He explained that "when prepared," they would "carry back . . . a type of Christianity better fitted to the millions there than even our own."[110] Negroes would then contribute to human advancement.

O. O. Howard had helped launch the church with the understanding that the congregation would make "no distinctions" in the new era of freedom. The initiative was an extension of his Freedmen's Bureau work on behalf of "*the manhood of the black man*" in political and educational arenas.[111] He and a minority of church members protested the exclusion campaign for well over a year, during which newspapers editorialized about the strife,

Boynton resigned from his Howard University post, and Congregationalist leaders from around the country tried to settle matters. The battle ended with Boynton and his supporters—roughly two-thirds of the membership—uniting with Presbyterians.[112] The departures paved the way for Cook to join the First Congregational Church, which subsequently drew prominent colored individuals who often visited without joining. His victory did not alter the established pattern of segregated congregations.[113]

The inability or unwillingness of White Protestant leaders to develop denominational structures that reflected their professions of human equality did not stop them from disputing the validity of churches led by colored men. Like Methodists, Congregationalist leaders lodged criticisms. One D. M. Wilson called for an intervention to eliminate the "ecclesiastical monstrosity" of colored churches. He believed a welcome atmosphere in White congregations would stifle the "senseless noise" that passed for worship among colored people.[114] Minister and social reformer Washington Gladden was less charitable. He accused colored churches of race practices that promoted false conceptions of religious difference. The institutions were unworthy of interdenominational partnerships because they violated Christian tenets of oneness. A fictional account of ecumenical alliances, "The Christian League of Connecticut," popularized his judgment. Duty required the proposed organization to exclude colored churches from "Christian union" as a first step toward destroying them. Their sin, the protagonist explains, entailed "the meanest kind of sectarianism" that used skin color as a basis for religious association. Despite a commitment to ensuring that there was "no color-line in Christianity," Gladden's character overlooked racial distinctions in predominantly White denominations.[115] The story suggests that churches led by Black clergy used racial classifications to determine membership and thus deserved eradication. It is silent about the ethics of the common practice of organizing congregations along racial lines in denominations administered by White people.

White criticism posed no compelling ethical challenge to colored churches, and defections of prominent AME clergy failed to spark a sizable exodus. Nevertheless, the developments signaled broad concerns about the denomination's status as a discrete entity. Church leaders and outside observers claimed a stake in whether and how colored churches should exist. Questions about caste, sectarianism, educational equality, configurations of races, citizenship, and Christian manhood were critical to attempts to clarify the issue.

208 RELUCTANT RACE MEN

Colored churches reflected contrived notions of difference and hierarchy. For some, this was a self-evident fact. Ohio educator and political activist Peter Clark made a straightforward observation that the name of the African Methodist Episcopal Church signified that it was "founded upon the color line." A defender of colored schools, he interpreted such structures as logical and "manly" responses to inequalities that plagued all sectors of American society.[116] Others observed colored churches with the understanding that stratification was a primary function of racial taxonomies. Frederick Douglass expressed this view while defending his newspaper as necessary to progress. He objected to colored churches for allegedly sustaining caste arrangements. He stopped short of his antebellum call for the organizations to disband. However, he admonished them to surrender designations that suggested racial bases of association, warning that voluntarily use of such terms provided fodder for "color proscribers" who sought to deprive Black people of equal access to authority and citizenship privileges. His assumption that race classifications were, by definition, exclusionary, took aim at the nomenclature that upheld claims of White purity and privilege. As *New Era* correspondent William Walker argued, the term "negro" was not a benign reference to a fact. It did not function merely as a sign that an individual's appearance differed from that of a White person. Noting that the complexions of thousands who were classified as "negroes" were lighter than the skin of many White individuals, he flagged the term as part of the apparatus of White supremacy. The label's purpose was to degrade colored people to distance them from an allegedly higher and purer class of Americans. It followed that organizations intent on overcoming hierarchical structures and improving the group's status should not name themselves with racial terms.[117]

Before signing on as a *Christian Recorder* contributor, George Downing added his voice to criticism, disparaging colored churches as unfit for the work of advancement. He and Massachusetts activist Charles Remond reportedly stormed a meeting at Washington's Union Bethel AME Church with a "tirade of abuse" against the organizations, equating them with the colored schools they had long despised and protested.[118] Although colored people might have launched separate churches with laudable aims, Downing was convinced that the institutions now injured their cause. The nature of the harm was nonspecific; however, animus toward institutionalized racial distinctions was consistent with his ideas about caste. He avoided ascribing any inherent virtue to Black membership in White-controlled churches. Experience taught him that affiliations with White people were not necessarily better options than organizations of colored people. He fled the Episcopal Church of his childhood, even though its leaders preached "the common brotherhood of man, and the common fatherhood of God." Unequal access to fellowship and rites for colored seminarians and laity demonstrated that some preachers of commonality despised the "brother" created by the "common Father" they worshipped.[119] In contrast, the inclusivity he found in the Roman Catholic Church convinced him that the masses of colored people should join its ranks. His optimism about the benefits that would accrue if they cast their lot with American Catholics was not dampened by the fact that, at emancipation, the only men of African descent in the priesthood were the Healy brothers—James, Alexander, and Patrick—who were not deemed Black. The welcome colored people received upon entering the fold bolstered his faith that identifying with the church would strike a "killing blow against color caste in America."[120] Catholic associations promised to facilitate intimate relationships that could further blur phenotypic distinctions between colored and White people. In theory, this physical "absorption" would undermine notions of difference and rank embedded in prevailing race classifications. Religious bonds would thus help realize what he believed to be the nation's ultimate mission and destiny of forging a unified race out of its diverse inhabitants.[121]

The dreams and disapprovals of reformers who struggled with or ignored race practices in their own initiatives presented no fundamental threat to African Methodism. Its leaders found no reason to worry about the possibility that White-led denominations were operating on a higher moral plain than they occupied. Benjamin Lee, one of several AME leaders from a rural New Jersey clan, dismissed criticism from coreligionists as foolish and inaccurate. He explained that the "exclusively colored" conferences and churches Northern Methodists created in areas where White congregations and conferences already existed demonstrated that they were operating a "race-protecting" institution. He dared colored members of ME churches and the Colored Methodist Episcopal Church, which reportedly limited membership to colored people, to do "manly and Christian" self-assessments to get a true picture of "raciness" among Methodists.[122] Washington Gladden's high-minded talk of a war on colored churches elicited a similarly pointed denunciation. Its hypocrisy irritated Benjamin Tanner, who ventured, "A church in which all are white is as much a color church as one where all are black."[123] He surmised that the latter was less guilty of being a "race church" because all colors likely comprised its membership—people "in whose veins is not only

210 RELUCTANT RACE MEN

negro, but white blood."[124] Gladden's imagination might have been better used to explore how his Christian League could address the sin of caste that threatened all American churches.

African Methodist leaders understood that they had a right to configure their institutions as they saw fit and that membership in voluntary associations was a matter of choice. Accordingly, standards that applied to public entities did not determine their legitimacy. The sense of civic responsibility that informed their efforts to shape public policies did not trump their claims to religious freedom. Stressing the legal status of churches, Benjamin Tanner declared that if the state financed and prescribed membership standards for American religious institutions, he would insist that there should be "but one class of Churches." However, this was not the case, and Black Americans possessed the same rights of other citizens to religious freedom. It followed that a colored church had "just as much right to exist as a white Church." Separation between religious and government functions enabled him to distinguish the valid option of maintaining Black-led churches from the illegitimate practice of operating colored public schools. If the churches were "of the State," he argued, "then I would say abolish them, just [as] I say abolish colored schools."[125]

This distinction was critical among African Methodist leaders who protested, sued, and lobbied against separate public schools for colored children. Delegates to the 1878 session of the AME Philadelphia Conference unanimously adopted Theophilus Steward's resolution denouncing the "sad spectacle of Colored Schools." They condemned the operations as a product of "class legislation" that flouted "the idea of a common humanity" and cautioned that there was no contradiction in maintaining colored churches while protesting colored schools. Because "a church is a purely voluntary association," they reasoned, no one is forced to attend or join. In contrast, the state required colored people to send their children to colored schools—a stipulation that highlighted the stark difference "between choice and compulsion."[126] In Burlington, New Jersey, AME minister Jeremiah Pierce successfully sued the school district for barring his children from the local school reserved for White children. He explained that his action was not a question concerning skin color or a request for "special provisions." It was a claim for recognition of his rights as an American citizen in light of school officials' apparent failure to realize that he and his children "belonged to the human race."[127] Benjamin Arnett used his position in the Ohio House of Representatives to secure prohibitions against colored public schools. Noting that even the Democratic governor criticized school segregation as "compulsory non-association," he railed against continuing the "law of distinction." His demands rested on "principles of common humanity" that created a moral imperative for all people to rally against evil.[128] Allies who helped push the endeavor forward won his praise for being exemplars of modern reform. He recognized African Methodist colleagues Jabez Campbell, Benjamin Lee, Benjamin Tanner, Henry McNeal Turner, James Shorter, and William Scarborough, along with Frederick Douglass and former Mississippi senator Blanche K. Bruce for sharing his vision of "wiping out the color line in State and Church" in the name of human brotherhood.[129] Tanner's hopes for an end to "race churches" were cast into the distant future. He believed such organizations would endure "for years and years to come" and took comfort in the belief that they did not impinge on the free exercise of faith.[130]

While asserting their right to exist, African Methodist churchmen confronted misgivings about race practices within their ranks. They grappled with the extent to which the bases of their organizations were consistent with principles that should guide Christian American citizens as they navigated novel experiences of freedom and rights. The impulse to defend their spiritual and social initiatives generated apologetic justifications for the existence of independent colored organizations. While "race churches" appeared to lack intrinsic virtues, a diverse set of factors pointed to the necessity for colored Christians to structure religious associations using race classifications and validated their moral authority and worth.

A traditional narrative that presented African Methodism as a reaction to a "color line" drawn by White Christians suggested that it needed no defense. The mere existence of congregations of colored people was not a sound basis for concluding that they operated as a collective "race church." Benjamin Tanner drew on this view in citing White people's ongoing refusal to worship on equal terms with colored Christians as the impetus and justification for maintaining separate churches.[131] Widespread experiences of discrimination made their operations perfectly consistent with structures that typified America's religious and political networks. Benjamin Lee elaborated on the significance of bigotry against colored Christians, calling it a power beyond the control of "Afro-American" Christians. It required operating organizations in which they could practice their faith and perform their religious duties. He agreed that "race churches" were at odds with Christian tenets. However, the AME Church could not be numbered among such entities "in the unchristian and culpable sense" because hateful actions of

212 RELUCTANT RACE MEN

others forced it into existence and it did not have a racial caste structure.[132] To Black and White observers who questioned the "propriety, the reason and the righteousness" of the church as it expanded its ministry among domestic servants and manual laborers, Lee explained that he would apologize for sustaining "a seeming race church" when its members gained full ecclesiastical equality and fraternity with other Christians, "not before."[133] He scoffed at a call for unity from White Methodists that suggested maintaining the distinction between Northern and Southern White-led denominations while consolidating Black Methodism. Instead of fostering solidarity, the proposal was a scandalous "mock cosmopolitanism" that would ensure that the whole of American Methodism remained a "race church forever."[134]

One of the denomination's first itinerants, Texas preacher Molson Clark, expressed the popular view that colored churches were essential to the development of "Christian manhood." The ethos informed his ministry to promote religious rehabilitation among freed people. As if moral uplift and spiritual development were not adequate justifications, he praised the agency and authority independent colored churches fostered. Their autonomy enabled even the most subjugated individuals to live as God's people.[135] Scripture supported this perspective. New Jersey native William Dickerson explained the idea in a sermon entitled "The Reasons for the Existence and Continuance of Race Churches." It featured a biblical promise dear to African Methodists, ensuring everyone a place of safety under their own vine and fig tree.[136] The autonomy the church fostered showed that it was fulfilling prophesy. Accordingly, African Methodists needed to resist the seductive appeals of defectors who had exchanged manliness for subjection. "Let our ranks not be depleted or our cause weakened by desertions," he declared.[137] Self-sufficiency was part of a divine purpose that permitted "race churches." God used them to bring about freedom from White hostilities and to promote egalitarian and harmonious human relations. Critics who blamed colored churches for making invidious distinctions and undermining social equality failed to acknowledge that the institutions were working to end bigotry.

Logical connections between upholding the necessity of independent colored religious associations and affirming species unity received a lucid elaboration from AMEZ bishop James Hood. Like many of his AME counterparts, the Pennsylvania native journeyed to the South on the heels of emancipation to engage in missionary work. He competed with White Methodists in North Carolina to minister to freed people and expand the reach of his denomination. As a senior church official, he concurred with Henry Chandler Bowen, the White editor of the Congregationalist paper the *Independent*, that no church should be organized "on the color line." He praised Bowen's willingness to treat the common humanity of Black and White people as a principle that guided his social interactions. Nevertheless, he felt compelled to expose the flawed logic and ethical blind spots that informed condemnations of colored churches. Critics ignored the resentment and resistance most White Christians would likely express if Negroes presumed to share their pews without having received a "special patronizing invitation" because they lacked the desire and spiritual capacity to worship in community with Black people. Injunctions for colored ministers to remedy the "low down" moral condition of freed people overlooked the fact that, for more than two centuries, "the most enlightened race on earth" systematically degraded them. Such scenarios made him marvel that Black people managed to display any virtues at all and that fault-finders failed to notice that White Christians needed instruction in the rudiments of "divine etiquette." The fact that White officials in Methodist churches who "kept back" enslaved Negroes now refused to allow colored ministers to become bishops demonstrated that Black people had to advance themselves. It signaled the longstanding and widespread problem of unequal access to authority for Black men in denominations historically controlled by White people. There would be no Black bishops, he argued, without the "African Church," which developed skills for use in and beyond the pulpit. Its divinely inspired achievements and leadership promised to help disabuse White Americans of erroneous conceptions of Black capacity that were akin to forces that molded the Israelites into a "peculiar people." Notwithstanding their virtues, separate "African" denominations would not be needed, Hood argued, if American churches as a whole followed Bowen's enlightened example and lived out the truth that God made all people "of one blood."[138]

The juxtaposition of merit and necessity in accounting for African Methodism reflected a persistent uneasiness about racial distinctions in religious undertakings. Noble values failed to settle qualms about their use even though officials did not seriously consider dismantling the organization and worked to expand it. A new church in Washington, DC, prompted Benjamin Arnett to extoll the fact that the denomination had "no color-line test" for membership and highlight its campaign for rights "on a basis of common humanity." Until the political ideals it promoted became a reality, he argued, the organization would serve an essential function.[139] Some colleagues contested the assumption among members and outsiders that the AME Church was a "colored" institution. Ministers Benjamin Lee, John Jenifer, and Benjamin Tanner, among others, asserted that White preachers and parishioners in the denomination's ranks presented a different picture. Jenifer boasted that their "so-called" colored church included "some of the ablest and most cultured of both races" in its pulpits and pews. Its inclusivity and achievement aligned it with the ideals of "a free republic and a homogenous nation."[140] On their own, such virtues apparently did not adequately refute charges that the church—led by colored people and principally for colored people—was at odds with American citizenship. Jenifer resorted to the familiar claim that African Methodism was "a creature of emergency and necessity" in a society beset with bigotry.[141]

As a novice itinerant minister, Theophilus Steward sought to validate African Methodism by portraying its use of race categories as honorable. He was convinced that religious and philosophical principles justified employing them to structure Christian associations. At the start of a sermon on Southern missions, he observed that racial designations inscribed oppression. However, there was no way to avoid the social reality that people of African descent were "uniformly denoted 'colored people'" and constituted a "distinct class" of Americans.[142] This situation bore no resemblance to gradations in the complexity of life forms displayed in the natural environment. Unlike those sorts of phenomena, which Steward accepted as normal, hierarchies tied to racial categories rested on "accidents, such as color, race, [and] previous condition." In place of these objectionable grounds for stratification, he insisted that "manhood—moral and intellectual worth—be the basis of classification" to promote unrestrained mental exploration and free association.[143] Prohibitions on interracial marriage illustrated his point that racial labels were complicit in proscriptive laws and customs that incorrectly treated variations in appearance as signs of "essential differences." He explained that such statutes served the express purpose of relegating colored people to an inferior social position "as a peculiar class."[144]

Instead of using this perspective as grounds for eschewing associations founded on race categories, Steward formulated a theology of love upholding the maxim that races should stick with "their own kind" and justifying religious endeavors organized along racial lines. He argued that colored preachers had a "special, indisputable, and heaven-born right" to save colored people's souls because salvation work required ministers to love their congregations and promote their welfare. Love, he explained, was a force of nature that extended outward from the individual to "family, kindred, nation or race, and thence to all mankind," diminishing in intensity the further it traveled from its origins.[145] This formula supported the moral authority of African Methodist ministers doing missionary work among colored people and accounted for ongoing spectacles of White hatred and domination. It also reflected a practical challenge Steward navigated as a twenty-two-year-old missionary among freed people in South Carolina. The organizing theme of his first sermon, "I Seek My Brethren," signaled conceptual limitations in racial notions of difference, deployed race to reference affective ties, and acknowledged that a shared classification did not necessarily translate into commonality. He invoked the biblical story of the youthful Joseph to explain why he had come South from his New Jersey home. When a stranger asked what he was looking for as he wandered through fields, Joseph replied that he was seeking his brothers.[146] The answer encapsulated Steward's quest. Like Joseph, he claimed the offspring of various mothers as his brothers—people "of different races and nations" yet of "one blood." It did not matter if individuals were born to European, African, or Asian mothers; all were children of the same divine father.[147] Yet he was on a mission to forge ties with "brethren by virtue of race." His focus, he argued, did not mean that he or church leaders gave any credence to "races or nations," for his search encompassed humankind. It recognized shared afflictions marked by slavery for some and "partial freedom" for others. It affirmed that African Methodist missionaries were bound to them by "sympathy for the oppressed and love of man."[148] Steward was mindful of the fact that his appeal to race and love might not bridge social, regional, cultural, and educational differences between AME preachers and newly freed people and did not void individuals' right to select their associates. He closed his sermon with a plea for listeners to receive and stand with him "as brethren." Acknowledging that he knew nothing of their lives and thoughts and that the choice was theirs, he confessed, "I am at your mercy."[149] Thus began seven years of service among Southern freed people and reflections on race that would persist throughout his ministerial career.

Institutional vitality failed to dispel worries about abetting false notions of difference. Concerns about modern ethics and progress led church leaders, laity, and outside observers to rethink the appropriateness of the "African" title and the need to broadcast the "savor of Americanism." Questions about the name became increasingly common in the wake of freedom and rights. Henry Highland Garnet noticed a rising "Anti-African class" in American churches. A *Christian Recorder* correspondent sensed that the label inspired more frequent challenges and defections in religious and secular venues. "Men have clamored to have the name expunged," A.F. observed.[150] The AME Church and the African Grand Lodge of Ancient and Honorable York Masons earned the writer's esteem for refusing to yield to demands for change even though their stand diminished their membership. As he praised the expansion of the franchise for striking "white" from the "Legislative, Municipal, Corporative, and Religious" landscape, James Handy determined that the denomination's "African" reference was unwarranted and called for its removal.[151] These sentiments informed African Methodist efforts to balance religious obligations and political commitments. They sparked debates involving divergent considerations. Was "African" an accurate racial, ethnological, or theological descriptor of denominational membership and eligibility? Was it compatible with American citizenship or Christian identity? Such issues reflected ongoing concerns about the use and meanings of racial designations and distinctions.

A name change was among the reforms James Lynch recommended several years before he decamped to the MEC fold. The idea was not simply a prelude to defection. As Civil War battles raged, his proposal came with a caution for colored people not to join the Northern Methodist denomination because it failed to heed "the law of universal brotherhood."[152] His rationale for a new title was that the "African" label was illogical and inconsistent with the times. Who, he wondered, would name a denomination "European Church" simply because forefathers of its members came from Europe? Loath to criticize AME founders, he characterized their choice as a "protest against American prejudice" at a moment that offered no reason to hope that conditions would improve. However, the war pointed to a destiny of "religious, social and political equality" for colored people. Its "crimsoned streams and piles of the slain," issued a forceful message that the United States was their country. The organization's status and influence created an obligation to present this truth in its name.[153]

Tradition strengthened his case. Throughout Christendom, churches used names to reference their doctrines or polity. The African Methodist allusion to "physical characteristics" raised ethical concerns. "If we are right" in implying an organizational preference for no association "with those who are not of our own color," he asked, "are the whites right in acting as they do?"[154]

Rumors that respected congregational leaders wielded the "African" title as a license to bar White people from church office and membership highlighted its potential moral hazards. The name seemed to justify actions that were out of sync with right principles and growing prospects for egalitarianism.

The progress of the war bolstered his optimism that colored people might enjoy equal rights as American citizens and deepened his conviction that the word "African" was inappropriate. The political scene suggested that the significance of complexion was fading. Yet the church name announced a commitment to operating on "the basis of color," which had no logical or ethical rationale. It put the denomination at risk of becoming "a waning power . . . a decaying hulk" for suggesting that colored people comprised a "separate nationality." The need for an accurate descriptor of people who were "a mixed race, mingling Saxon, Indian, and African blood," further justified a new name.[155] Future prospects created a "sacred duty" for the church to remove anything that could diminish colored people's political identification with America. Revising the title would enable conceptions of membership that made colored men draft eligible to evolve and render them eligible to cast ballots and hold elective office.[156]

Henry McNeal Turner declared himself "a devotee" when he read Lynch's "irrefutable arguments" about the denomination's name.[157] He confessed to having contemplated change for some time, but concerns about contemptuous reactions from individuals who had not carefully considered the matter kept him from suggesting it. His endorsement was not a sign of qualms about racial categories or of shame about his African ancestry—a sentiment he perceived in many. To the contrary, he felt a "peculiar exaltedness" when walking city streets and hearing a stranger say, "there goes a negro preacher."[158] His objections were practical and hopeful. He worried that the existing name circumscribed membership by sending a false message that the church welcomed only Africans. The title "Methodist Episcopal Church of Color" would not remedy the problem because it was at odds with his belief that religious and moral institutions designating themselves with such "local terms" were "destined to die out" as unity flourished amid God-ordained progress.[159] "Allen Methodist Episcopal Church" would be ideal. It preserved the church's initials and followed the sensible examples of Lutherans and Wesleyans who graced their organizations with founders' names. If the group merged with a sister denomination, together, they could identify as the "United Methodist Episcopal Church." Even "Acceptable ME

Church" would work, he reasoned, because it announced the acceptance of everyone "irrespective of color or cast[e]."[160]

The Pittsburgh Annual Conference sidestepped media discussion and presented a request directly to the governing church body for administrative action. The group's petition to the 1876 AME General Conference included a letter from delegate John G. Mitchell explaining the rationale for calling the denomination the "American ME Church." He linked his vote to African Methodist history and the unprecedented expansion of "civil and religious freedom" after 1860.[161] He recalled that the institution was founded to promote a brand of Christianity that had no complexional or racial divisions. Reconstruction's opportunities created an imperative to vindicate the founding faith and prepare for reunion with the Methodist Episcopal Church. The denomination had a duty to exercise leadership by eschewing all names that implied "a distinction on account of mere color or previous enslavement."[162] Even if circumstances required it to continue functioning as a discrete entity for some time, he argued, a name change would demonstrate readiness for unity.

Political and scientific principles further grounded Mitchell's position. Freedom and rights prompted him to echo long-standing claims that colored Americans were not Africans. The organization's label was "a *misnomer*," he argued, because "we the people of the United States, citizens by birth, citizens by law, *are Americans, not Africans*."[163] African ancestry could not outweigh the significance of American citizenship. Environmentalist ideas helped build a case that divine will, "revealed in nature," also required setting aside the African title. He ventured that the course of natural history undermined the ethnological credence of applying the term to Americans because it fostered "homogeneity" among populations within discrete geopolitical boundaries. A hypothetical scenario illustrated his point. "Let an American family or an English family migrate to Ethiopia . . . and within less than a thousand years their descendants will be Ethiopians, not simply by birth or civil law, but Ethiopians in color, in features, in habits."[164] The influence of climate, food, lifestyles, education, and intermarriage promised to have the same impact on people of African descent in the United States by transforming "the color of the blackest Ethiopian to that of the whitest American." He supposed that the latter represented the country's autochthonous population and predicted that a new denominational name would be a harbinger of a time, "one hundred and fifty or two hundred years" hence, when descendants of existing church members would be "Americans in complection [*sic*]."[165]

Membership in "the Church universal" gave James Theodore Holly, Protestant Episcopal Bishop of Haiti, a stake in denominational titles. Although he did not join the public debates, his views on appropriate church names for Christians appeared as authoritative judgments for African Methodists. Daniel Payne publicized the ideas by sharing personal correspondence in which Holly endorsed his stand against incorporating "fourteen millions of foreigners of African descent"—Caribbean and South American members of the British Methodist Episcopal Church—into the AME fold. Payne presented the letter to *Christian Recorder* readers as "nothing more nor less than a development of my opinions." It summarily condemned the proposed annexation as imperialist in its effort to group "different nationalities occupying distinct territories under one common government."[166] Such actions were at odds with the teachings of the gospel. Holly reasoned that early Christian practices illustrated the importance of accurately configuring and designating the parameters of association in churches. They grounded his forthright opposition to the "African" name. He observed that "the only qualification" the ancients made to the Christian designation was the name of the countries where their churches operated. References to "a whole continent, such as Asiatic, African, or European," he argued, displayed the same "idea of imperialism" that plagued international annexations. It would be presumptuous for the Church of England to call itself "the *European* Church" or for a Christian church in Liberia to claim the name "African," because "Egypt, Abyssinia and many other nations also occupy that continent."[167] It was morally indefensible to employ continent titles "in an *ethnological* sense" because doing so violated the scriptural principle that rendered believers "one in Christ Jesus," for whom there is no "Jew or Greek, Barbarian or Scythian, bond or free."[168] This creed discredited racial designations and distinctions in Christian churches. In contrast, biblical references to churches being inventoried through a roll call of nations on the ancient Day of Pentecost and at the future advent of Christ illustrated the appropriateness of national monikers.

Political developments inspired ministers to support calls for a denominational name change. A. Johnson interpreted Reconstruction enactments as a command to substitute "American" for "African." He believed this step would fulfill a duty to join the national "march of progress." Chronicles of the shift would explain how slaves and political outcasts who developed the

220 RELUCTANT RACE MEN

church joined the national body as citizens in an age of "true manhood."[169] Even after Reconstruction's decline, and H. C. C. Astwood, consul to San Domingo, cited the victories of emancipation and the Fourteenth and Fifteenth Amendments as bases for a new title. He feared that ongoing use of the "African" prefix would compromise the denomination's capacity to spread the gospel and hoped that eliminating it would facilitate Methodist unity. Removing it was part of a Christian duty to shun designations that structured the "odious discrimination" reformers fought to destroy. It would exhibit the church's faith that heaven would not accommodate "Africanism or any other nationalism" and demonstrate that the aims linked to the original name had been fulfilled.[170]

Justifications for keeping the "African" designation ranged from worries about African ties to questions about the status of American churches and the racial, political, and spiritual meanings of the denomination's title. Distinctions between private affiliations and political identity were critical to the defense. The observation that it was a common and valid American practice to acknowledge ancestral origins united African Methodist critics and Presbyterian minister Henry Highland Garnet in opposing a new name for the church. Reflections on the identities and obligations of Black people framed their stance. Garnet felt compelled to chide those who were uncomfortable with their African lineage. He asserted that the only people of whom everyone, "white or colored, should be ashamed" were those embarrassed about "their natural descent and their identity with their own race." The "latter day negro" was abnormal in despising "his own name" because of a misguided belief that Black people were inferior beings.[171] John Jenifer insisted that African Methodists were no different from Americans who publicly acknowledged their German, English, French, or Irish "blood."[172] G. E. Boyer refuted the claim that the African designation did not apply to a "mixed race." Because African descent contributed to the mix, the church "might as well be called an African organization as any thing else." Even if it lacked theological significance, its use was justified as a statement of love.[173] Anthony Stanford, perhaps drawing on studies at Philadelphia's Eclectic Medical College, cited the error of equating the word "African" with color and assuming that it did could not accurately designate "mixed" people. He explained that the label referred to populations whose complexions ranged from dark to light. Probing Lynch's notion of mixture, he asked whether the term designated a "kind of blood peculiar to a certain race of men." If so, the apostle Paul lied to the Athenians when he assured them that God created all people "of one blood." He shared Lynch's hope that the nation's obsession with color would soon pass. However, he disputed the notion that providence destined African descent to disappear in the United States while "other races" thrived. The persistence of Black people indicated that there was no need to abandon the reference to African ancestry.[174]

Flawed conceptions of religion's place in America were among the presumed culprits that inspired calls for a name change. A denomination's name, Garnet explained, had no effect on the nationality of its constituents. To illustrate, he asked, "Do Americans attempt to blot out 'Dutch' or 'German' from other Reformed Churches?"[175] Other *Christian Recorder* correspondents concurred, distinguishing the denomination's ecclesiastical character from state functions to make the point that its designation referenced spiritual associations that had no political significance. "The Roman Catholic in this country," the pseudonymous "HAM" explained, "rejoices in being a citizen, in a political sense, but in a spiritual sense, he rejoices more in being a member of the Roman Catholic Church." The same held for African Methodists, whose name aimed to distinguish their "spiritual government" from the Methodist Episcopal Church, not from their American political identity.[176]

New meanings for "the *significant A*" that identified the church helped deflect calls for a title change. John Jenifer and Benjamin Lee argued that the term "African" should not be read as "Africanized" Methodism or as a venue solely for people of African descent. Instead, it signified the denomination's sympathy with Christians other Americans "almost universally repulsed."[177] Tanner embellished the position, insisting that the "African" title issued a creedal statement that affirmed "the Negro's humanity." It was comparable to German Reformed congregations that welcomed all who understood the German language. "It is precisely thus with the African ME Church," he declared, "where the Negro language is spoken." Notwithstanding claims to the contrary by the likes of British novelist Anthony Trollope—"slave to American prejudice"—the Negro had a language. It was the "broad language of humanity, . . . which says to men of every race, 'All we are brethren.'" The church embraced everyone who spoke its "Pauline tongue." The admission of a White member at the founding of the denomination demonstrated that there was no historical basis for charges that the name was proscriptive.[178]

Obligations to tradition, concerns about organizational stability, and logistical complexities limited prospects for an institutional name modification. As the promise of Reconstruction faltered, African Methodist reformers stressed the utility of Black collective initiatives. Deferred prospects for civil and political arrangements that affirmed common membership in a single human family focused attention on present needs. For Daniel Payne, this meant advocating national advancement through the moral improvement of families. He formulated guidelines on domestic education for all families, reasoning that, if "the races" of the country became "intelligent, virtuous, and Christian," the nation would be likewise.[179] The denomination's work to advance colored people via educational institutions, moral guidance, literary programs, and the operations of "republican government" demonstrated its value. A comparison of resources and achievements of Methodist institutions showed no differences in their social benefits. Methodism as practiced by the AME Church improved Negro lives just as Methodism of other denominations improved Anglo-Saxon and Anglo-American life. Payne anticipated this outcome because scientific research proved "the unity of the human race." Moreover, scripture characterized individuals comprising so-called "distinct races" as "one man," signaling no essential physical or moral differences among them that required peculiar remedies.[180] The usefulness of Methodism across diverse social contexts challenged the ethics of questioning the AME Church when no comparable objections were made to White organizations.

Prophetic messages about a future in which no religious entity would be "a race church" helped quiet concerns about the issue. Benjamin Tanner advised that the Bible foretold a time when separate arrangements would no longer be necessary. His objections to changing the denomination's name came with the disclaimer that they were not intended to be forever binding. He admitted to longing for the elimination of the "African" designation. However, it needed to be retained as a sign of Christian liberty until American churches recognized that all people belonged to a common humanity. He doubted that this outcome would occur in his lifetime.[181] Daniel Payne, who was similarly anxious to see the "African" prefix "give place to a broader term," reportedly took comfort in the conviction that it was "less objectionable to have the odious name without the odious thing, than to have the odious thing without the odious name."[182] In short, African Methodism was not as offensive as Northern and Southern Methodist denominations because it had no policy of associating on the basis of race classifications. Acknowledging that all American churches fostered false notions of human difference and rank, he outlined a utopian vision of the future. He believed universal laws of progress would inevitably enable the AME Church to heed a principle of humanity that dispensed with race constructs. All "non-progressive" churches that threatened this destiny with "the miserable, puerile and heathenish question of color" would be annihilated. Ultimately, he averred, "*Races perish.*"[183]

———

Although he was an established contributor to African Methodist administrative operations with ready access to its media, William Whipper steered clear of debates about the denomination's existence and name. Work related to his new ethos consumed his attention. His diverse commitments did not always translate into consistent interpretations of racial constructs. The cogency with which he traced warrants for race love in self-help endeavors waned as he tried to configure race practices to engage government affairs.

A rumor prompted him to push beyond the aim of cultivating racial affinity and stress the imperative of functioning as a political class. In the days following Ulysses S. Grant's presidential re-election, there was widespread media speculation that he would create a cabinet post for a representative of colored citizens. Frederick Douglass was a prime prospect; he had served on Grant's commission to explore US annexation of San Domingo and campaigned for his re-election.[184] When Whipper heard about the position, he fired off a letter to Douglass's *New National Reformer* and to the *Christian Recorder* condemning it. The rationale for the post was not his concern. Instead, he targeted Black men's duty to act in a manner that was consistent with the terms of citizenship and identify with the masses of uneducated Black people. He disparaged the notion of a Black cabinet member with admonitions against using race designations to seek political office and instructions on the necessity of class alliances.

His opening claim evoked the optimistic view that emancipation and suffrage invalidated race distinctions. The Fifteenth Amendment prohibition against denying voting rights based on "race, color, or previous condition of servitude" became, in his formulation, a stipulation that citizens could not exercise their rights on these grounds. They had to stake political advancement on personal qualifications and merit, he argued, not on foundations that had been "rejected by the fundamental laws of the land."[185] These assertions suggest a concern that Douglass or some other unelected colored man might attempt to become a political representative based on race membership. Yet the potential for illegitimate appeals to racial designations was not the primary source of Whipper's apprehension. He devoted the remainder of his letter to other factors that explained why no colored person should seek or accept the position. In the process, his logic faltered, and he rested his case on the very distinctions he identified as invalid. He ventured that, as a matter of principle, Americans chose representatives only from a set of individuals whose education made them fit for public office. By his reckoning, this standard disqualified all colored people. A history of denied educational opportunities made it impossible for them to secure the "knowledge of statesmanship" he deemed necessary for a cabinet post. His vision of progress required that they first seek political experience in lower positions. Moreover, because oppression had rendered colored people a class, they "must *rise as such*."[186] Previously, his class concept was a tool to inspire colored people to admit to inferior attainments in order to move forward. Now, it was a mandate to limit individual progress.

This proposed restriction prompted criticism from Henry Wagoner Jr. The Howard University student agreed that "personal merits" should be the basis of individual attempts to advance. However, he saw a contradiction in Whipper's attempt to couple this principle with the insistence that colored people must elevate themselves en masse. The class idea placed stultifying constraints on personal initiative, he argued. It was tantamount to a directive to set aside all aspirations of excelling beyond "the common level" of their race. Whipper's invocations of the past exposed another conceptual flaw. It was illogical to claim that a history of oppression rendered colored men unfit for high attainments. Wagoner acknowledged that a lack of opportunities created a presumption against fitness for lofty public service, but presumptions were not facts, and disadvantages did not necessarily translate into "positive inferiority." Anyone seeking proof could observe the celebrated orator Frederick Douglass, whose career as a reformer was rooted in slavery, or President Grant, who was a tanner and a soldier before rising to the highest level of American statesmanship. Whipper's proposition was all the more pernicious because the effects of chaining progress to colored people's lowest attainments and past experiences of oppression would likely extend beyond the pursuit of a cabinet post. For Wagoner, who was one year away from a consular clerk commission at the US embassy in Paris, it was an ill-conceived prescription that threatened ambition and political advancement.[187]

No defense or apology for the proposal appeared in the press. Whipper might have deemed a rejoinder unnecessary once it became clear that there would be no cabinet appointment, or maybe he took the young man's criticism to heart. Whatever the case, one month later, reframed his concept in terms of legislative measures. Instead of presenting class in ways that placed a ceiling on Black aspirations, he deployed it as a basis for demanding rights and securing resources. The plan hinged on a belief that Reconstruction statutes discarded the taxonomy of racial hierarchy, thereby toppling the nation's "aristocracy of the skin."[188] As a result, legislative measures had to rest on circumstances, not complexion. This stipulation convinced him of the utility and validity of pressing for "class legislation" to facilitate progress by targeting specific segments of the population. He perceived it as radically different from state actions that deprived colored people of constitutional protections. It bore no resemblance to the discriminatory statutes he complained about when he joined the delegation seeking President Andrew Johnson's support for suffrage.

Class nomenclature was not simply a euphemism for racial designations. Unlike practices that upheld notions of biological sameness, difference, or rank, Whipper's conception of class was a function of social exigencies and political interests. It no longer attempted to corral the entire Black population into a single cluster. Congressional actions that constituted discrete groups of people as distinct classes of Americans illustrated the arrangement he envisioned and showed that it was consistent with the country's democratic ideals and structures. The liberty secured by the Thirteenth Amendment, Freedmen's Bureau assistance for the South's former slaves and poor White people, constitutional recognition of birthright citizenship, the Freedman's Bank, and the franchise for colored men were all "species of class legislation" that improved civil conditions for individuals. These "trophies of modern civilization" were comparable to enactments that had long been part of the nation's social fabric, he argued, adding that, since the founding of the republic, the "white race have had the benefit of class legislation."[189]

Dire conditions among emancipated slaves rendered them a discrete class. While the ideal of race love forged bonds between them and reformers, it did not require ignoring divergent historical trajectories, experiences, and needs. Whipper imagined a scenario in which a Southern congressional representative, perhaps a son of slaves, motivated by "love of race and fired with patriotism," would successfully demand an appropriation for loans that would enable Southern freed people to obtain and develop land. Such an initiative would revive Southern agriculture and be a boon to the nation's economy. It would be comparable to railroad and steamship subsidies and

226 RELUCTANT RACE MEN

federal assistance for handling the chaos and destruction stemming from the 1871 Chicago fire.[190]

The significance of Whipper's interpretation of class in reform discourse was twofold. On one hand, the premise that the federal government no longer sanctioned the use of race classifications in acknowledging rights undergirded his focus on individuals. As president of an 1874 Philadelphia campaign to press for passage of civil rights legislation, he represented a group effort to extend protections to all citizens. Speeches by William Forten, Isaiah Wears, and other young reformers launched the delegation's attempts to rally support for justice on behalf of one-sixth of the nation's population, whose civil rights were being denied. They argued that the government had an obligation to protect the "individual pursuit of happiness," which was a divinely ordained right acknowledged at the nation's founding. Moreover, Republicans had a duty to demand laws to protect the civil rights of "each citizen."[191]

Whipper's most prominent Reconstruction undertaking also reflected his class concept. While struggling to formulate clear conceptual bases for reform, he maintained a solid grip on managing the Philadelphia branch of the Freedman's Savings and Trust Company—a product of "class legislation." He assumed the position in 1870, within months of outlining his principle of race love and despite the fact that, as Wagoner wryly observed, Negro history had been "anything but a school for cashiers."[192] For Whipper, aiding people forced into the lowest stratum of society fulfilled a "solemn sense of duty" to the colored race, the nation, modern civilization, and humanity.[193] Yet noble aims and high regard for his management skill did not shield him from allegations that the bank was at odds with the spirit of the times. Critics disparaged it as an institution that was "founded on caste" for allegedly shepherding freed people into an untried economic venue. His defense rested on the project's meritorious goals—a justification he had once dismissed. The bank functioned largely as a "philanthropic and moral" entity, he explained. It offered practical lessons on the virtues of thrift to "dispel poverty, vice and degradation"—typical facets of slavery.[194] It was thus a crucial aspect of efforts to reconstruct the lives of freed people.

The bank's failure in the summer of 1874 outraged and distressed Whipper. He responded to the announcement with a letter of protest to the trustees on behalf of the 1,600 men, women, and children who deposited a half million dollars in Philadelphia's branch and patrons of the other thirty-six branches.[195] He understood that the institution faced a deficit and had become financially unstable from the impact of a depression, mismanagement by directors, and speculative investments. Reorganization efforts by Frederick Douglass, who accepted the presidency without realizing that failure was imminent, could not salvage the institution.[196] Nevertheless, Whipper was convinced that pecuniary factors alone were insufficient grounds for abandoning the enterprise and opposed its dissolution without consultations with depositors. He supported restructuring or replacing the institution, but he deemed it unconscionable to abolish an entity so vital to Black people's destiny. His protest drew support, but it was insufficient and came too late.[197]

Whipper limited his activism after carrying out the dismal task of closing accounts with depositors, who, if national averages applied, received no more than three-fifths of their investment values.[198] He continued to serve on AME Church publishing committees, but he issued no further declarations in the press about race practices. Decades of wrestling with the phenomena had led him to a settled position that colored people could and should organize and identify themselves in social and political blocs without fear of fostering contrived notions of innate difference or hierarchy. Aging, dispirited, and at the end of his reform career, he prepared his will. All of his bequests were personal, naming only family members and a few friends. He entrusted his legacy to a young grandnephew, William Whipper Purnell, with a request that the boy honor him by dropping his surname. Only traces of his political commitments remained visible; he hoped his namesake would grow up to be a "loyal citizen," and he named fellow Philadelphia reformer Isaiah Wears as a co-executor of his estate.[199] Yet some observers perceived a deep and abiding dedication to progress in his death. When he succumbed to a lingering illness two years after the dissolution of the Freedman's Bank, *Christian Recorder* correspondents wondered whether his despair over the institution's closure had proved fatal.[200]

Although entrusted with executing his friend's personal bequests, Isaiah Wears was an unlikely heir to Whipper's reform legacy. Conceptually his views aligned with Whipper's early race challenges, but they showed no capacity for the love or sympathy that guided Whipper's latter efforts to frame reform initiatives. His proposals following Whipper's death nevertheless illustrate experiments with new conceptions and configurations of reform on the unfamiliar terrain of freedom.

228 RELUCTANT RACE MEN

Wears's description of the basis for suffrage demands at the 1869 National Labor Convention expressed his thoughts on race. He declared that manhood, not color, established the group's claims. An environmentalist interpretation of complexional differences explained his position, which befitted efforts to unite Black and White workers. He speculated that the complexions of both populations were deviations "from the natural and original color of the human species."[201] Thus, boundaries distinguishing the populations could not be clearly delineated, and neither was a standard of normalcy. He complained that the entire idea of "races" was vague and entailed "labyrinths of ethnological uncertainties where arbitrary classifications hold sway."[202] This observation, combined with political philosophy and social factors, grounded his rejection of all attempts to treat colored people as a fixed group or stamp them with a "permanent classification." Moreover, he argued that consigning colored people to any "complexional class" would limit individual progress.[203] He knew of numerous well qualified men and women whose status as part of a group whose collective achievements were miniscule justified refusals to appoint them. A shameful historical record further highlighted the irrationality of trying to function as a race or class. He cited the "ease" with which European slave traders took Africans into captivity; generations of "stupid submission" to bondage; slave loyalty to families of Confederate soldiers fighting to strengthen the shackles of servitude; and, in the years since emancipation, barely a "ripple of resentment" over the "tens of thousands of causeless assassinations" of Black people exercising their rights as citizens. Atrocities that demanded "torch and blood" had elicited only wailing and "sentimental appeals." Such scathing judgments led to the conclusion that there was nothing of value in the "Negro" label. There were no grounds for race pride. The only way forward was to trust individual effort and acknowledge the uselessness of the "idea of '*our people*,' '*our race*.'"[204]

The collective doom Wears associated with functioning "as a class" did not void the necessity for stopgap cooperative measures to contend with caste structures. Even as he imagined a future in which individual worth and humanity governed social and political relations, he formulated a proposal for political advancement that echoed Whipper's call for "class legislation."[205] The aborted work of the Freedmen's Bureau supplied a point of departure for explaining the problem he identified and its remedy. In 1869, when Congress required the organization to dismantle programs that provided education, food, clothing, support for family unification and marriages, medical care, oversight of labor conditions, and shelter, destitute freed people were left to fend for themselves in the face of brutal state-sanctioned White supremacy. "The government threw them overboard," Wears observed, "to save the ship."[206] Because nothing replaced the withdrawn resources, he reasoned from the standpoint of necessity. "If the colored man must act and operate in this country as a separate class, I hold that the most efficient basis for him is to turn his attention with systematic uniformity to labor."[207] His plan did not encompass the entire colored populace. Like Whipper, he focused on the welfare of former slaves in the South struggling with the transition to liberty. An intervention was necessary because official actions that released people from bondage were not tailored to promote justice. They banned most forms of involuntary servitude without creating secure paths to liberty and well-being. As he surveyed the ragged contours of freedom, he observed that slavery had not merely been a set of regulations that maintained a legal institution; its operations and power hinged on "the relative material conditions of the capitalist and the laborer."[208] If government policies did not engage this facet of "the new order of things," the masses of colored people, "as a class," would be perpetually indigent. They would be forever vulnerable to "confidence men" peddling promises of utopia in emigration and colonization ventures.[209] Even if such schemes failed to entice significant numbers, they spread the injurious message that colored people lacked the capacity to thrive among White people. They also encouraged speculators to lure White immigrant workers who would increase labor competition and lower wages for all.[210]

Wears detailed his aims to ensure that his class idea did not replicate racial hierarchies and was suited to problems arising from actions of "the so-called superior race."[211] He was no supplicant; he warned that there could be no progress if pleading guided the work of reform. He envisioned a program that would enable Southern workers to experience liberty's benefits. In targeting this group, he explained, he was not endorsing "that spirit of caste" that used "complexional hue" to label and separate individuals and their interests. Instead, he sought to assist people whose material and political conditions reduced them to "objects of commiseration and pity."[212] The US Constitution assured him that "class legislation" was consistent with American political norms. He interpreted the preamble's stipulation that the government was responsible for "the general welfare" to mean that taxpayer dollars could finance benefits for "a particular class" of the citizenry.[213] Thus, a dedicated tax could support a new "Bureau or Department of the Freedmen" to provide homesteads for freedmen heading households.

230   RELUCTANT RACE MEN

The undertaking would expand on the proposal to distribute the proverbial "forty acres and a mule" linked to William Tecumseh Sherman's 1865 Special Field Order, No. 15—a program Congress attempted to develop but Andrew Johnson blocked.

Precedent showed that such an intervention would not be exceptional. Abraham Lincoln's 1862 initiative to aid farmers by creating the Department of Agriculture gave Wears a decisive example. Another case suggested that moral rectitude was not required to render a group worthy of federal assistance. A racist tirade explaining his claim gave lie to his anti-caste principles. "Witness the Indians," he began, making no mention of government removal, subjugation, or policies aimed at smothering self-determination. Assuming that the "Indian Bureau" was an institutional benefactor, he decried the "millions of dollars" in appropriations it received for agents and supplies to distribute among Native peoples. He bitterly observed, "The black man is compelled to pay his proportion . . . for a people savage, indolent and almost worthless as a class—a people who respect neither Christianity nor our civilization, rearing the walls of their tribal economy against everything but material aid."[214] The point of the bigoted rant was clear. It aimed to invalidate moral arguments against government aid for Black people.

Wears hoped colored congressional representatives would feel an obligation to designate freed people as a class of beneficiaries, but he also wanted support for benefits from a grassroots base of civic-minded Americans who organized "without regard to profession or complexion."[215] He believed their demands to politicians would validate targeted assistance in the realm of public opinion and advance the work of emancipation even as Reconstruction continued to falter.

———

Wears was no more successful than Whipper had been in configuring "class" measures that could function as a viable basis of reform. Sympathy for the idea was hard to find. In Congress, the will to implement programs benefitting Black people had passed. Before the demise of the Freedman's Bank, politicians intent on reforming the Republican Party broadcast the message that it was time for Negroes to fend for themselves. The declaration signaled the end of alliances that had generated crucial Reconstruction amendments and inspired unprecedented optimism about prospects for advancement.[216]

Singling out colored citizens for "class" or "special" measures also ran counter to reform currents. For some, such terms remained associated with discrimination. Targeted statutes about schooling, for example, meant substandard public education for colored children. Cincinnati, Ohio, activists sought to end "special legislation" in order to secure equal education via racially mixed public schools.[217] In a bid to integrate Delaware schools, Theophilus Steward organized a convention whose delegates insisted on "no special legislation" in favor of "legislation for the people."[218] From a different standpoint, his brother William held that the class idea was at odds with the common citizenship wrought by emancipation and rights. It represented an invalid means of making distinctions among American citizens even for beneficial purposes. When the Supreme Court declared the 1875 Civil Rights Act unconstitutional in 1883, there were loud cries about yet another assault on Black freedom. Henry McNeal Turner denounced the decision as a betrayal; it made a mockery of reformers who trusted and boasted of American citizenship. In contrast, William Steward assailed the premise of the overturned legislation, expressing disdain for "special" provisions. He viewed the court's decision as an object lesson on illegitimate measures. His commentary on the front page of the *Christian Recorder* read, "The bane of the negro is legislation 'especially for the negro.'"[219] He offered this principle as essential to the work of American reform with the conviction that citizenship meant Negroes needed nothing more than what was politically necessary for their White counterparts. .

Freedom and citizenship appeared to promise radical revisions in American configurations of race that would alter the terms of public and private association. However, the course of Reconstruction variously strengthened the significance of race constructions and complicated their meanings. Amid the chaos of change, qualms, conflicts, and commitments concerning the ethics and utility of employing racial categories as bases of association intensified. Unsettled questions kept misgivings and contest over race integral to reform endeavors, ensuring them an enduring role in efforts to map progress in a rapidly changing and increasingly hostile social and political climate. Churchmen, their institutional resources, their allies, critics, and ideas would continue to play pivotal roles in this process. Concerns that gave rise to Reconstruction-era reform initiatives would persist as Jim Crow's expansion overshadowed the hopeful prospects of freedom. Furthermore, a willingness among once ardent race critics and rising reformers to rethink the ethics of race practices would echo through expanded attempts to reconcile misgivings with a need for sound bases of collective advancement for colored Americans.

6

"Race-ship"

Citizenship and Imperatives of Progress

Frederick Douglass was bereft when Henry Highland Garnet died. He displayed his sorrow in the pages of the New York *Globe*. "In view of his death," he declared, "I am oppressed with a sense of loneliness."[1] He was not grieving the loss of a cherished ally. Garnet had been an adversary for more than four decades. In 1840, the men chose opposing sides in abolitionist conflicts over women's activism and political antislavery. When Garnet's 1843 convention address called for slave resistance, Douglass successfully lobbied to exclude the speech from the published proceedings. He praised Garnet for endorsing his *North Star*. However, the expression of gratitude contrasted his non-sectarian and antigovernment abolitionism with Garnet's fellowship with slaveholders in the Presbyterian Church. Before switching his own allegiance and newspaper to align with political antislavery forces, he denounced Garnet's Liberty Party commitment as a pro-slavery alliance. For his part, Garnet berated Douglass for belittling the religious convictions of people he purported to represent and scorned him as a "bitter unrelenting enemy" of his African emigration and civilization causes.[2]

Careers diverged as sharply as opinions. Douglass's prominence steadily rose over the years. He commanded an honorarium of one hundred dollars per lecture during Reconstruction. In contrast, Garnet struggled for public recognition. By 1881, he was in poor health and dispirited by a growing sense of obscurity and low-paying church positions. He had become an officer in the American Colonization Society when President James Garfield offered him a consular appointment to Liberia. He accepted. He explained to his old friend Alexander Crummell that he did not want to fade away among "ungrateful" Americans who ignored his lifelong service on their behalf. Douglass joined the well-wishers who saw Garnet off to Monrovia, where he died less than two months after arriving.[3]

Garnet's death marked the imminent passing of a generation that shaped the milieu in which Douglass evolved as a reformer. The *Globe*

Reluctant Race Men. Joan L. Bryant, Oxford University Press. © Oxford University Press 2024.
DOI: 10.1093/oso/9780195312966.003.0007

234 RELUCTANT RACE MEN

lament concluded with a roll call of other men with whom he had variously competed, debated, and allied himself over the course of his career. "Ward, Remond, Beman, Pennington, Doctor Smith, Gaines, Whipper, Watkins, and others," he recounted sadly, "have gone to rest."[4] The familiar reform circles that had given him mooring were broken.

Douglass was left to witness the aftermath of changes that had promised to stabilize Black citizenship. He had commended Reconstruction amendments as the "last step" in the journey to freedom. Constitutional reforms had seemed to guarantee Negroes' claims to "every single right, privilege, and power" that belonged to Americans. However, the era had collapsed by the time Garnet died. It gave way to Jim Crow—a period ushered in with enterprises reminiscent of developments that had diminished antebellum freedom. White citizens' groups, legislatures, and courts worked to reconfigure citizenship to narrow the rights of Negroes. They reinvigorated traditional connections between exclusion and African descent. States instituted grandfather clauses, poll taxes, vagrancy laws, and other measures to circumvent the Fifteenth Amendment's expansion of the franchise. The Supreme Court's 1873 *Slaughterhouse* decision curtailed the scope of national citizenship under the Fourteenth Amendment by ceding control over most citizenship rights to states. Three years later, the *Cruikshank* decision undermined the federal government's authority to protect individual rights from infringement by other citizens, namely Ku Klux Klan members and similar White terrorists. Lynching soared. By century's end, White perpetrators lynched an annual average of 150 Black people without penalty. Change culminated in the Compromise of 1877. It solidified southern Democrats' "redemption" of former Confederate states and expanded their national political influence. The noxious combination of civil and political exclusion, rampant mob violence, economic hardship, and derogatory cultural images earned the post-Reconstruction era its designation as the "nadir" of African American history.[5]

Douglass was not alone on this shifting reform terrain. Robert Purvis, who had also fought for change since the antebellum period, remained active in Philadelphia. The aged men reached a rapprochement three decades after Douglass named Purvis and Charles Remond among his "bitterest enemies" for supporting William Lloyd Garrison's *Liberator* over his own paper. Reconciliation with Purvis, who opposed race practices throughout his career, coincided with Douglass's increasing outspokenness against them. Joining these veteran critics were individuals whose reform activism developed after emancipation. John Sampson, Theophilus Steward, Benjamin

Tanner, and Isaiah Wears, among others, aired their own misgivings about race. Douglass also continued to enjoy widespread esteem. In 1894, he was, according to Reconstruction senator Blanche K. Bruce, "the recognized leader of the Colored Race in this Country."[6] The honorific reflects his enduring renown. Yet it is an unreliable index of his influence over late nineteenth-century reform activities. None of the diverse initiatives that flourished through the period's newspapers, conventions, churches, or leagues offered him a base from which to lead the colored population. Moreover, his disparaging viewpoints on race failed to hold sway over a rising generation of reformers that increasingly avoided blanket repudiations of the construct. Race men tried to redefine the imperatives of progress. Such divergent activists as Booker T. Washington and W. E. B. Du Bois advocated race practices to advance the status of Negroes. Thus, in the last decade of his life, Douglass could not keep step with developing trends. He faced the waning currency of precepts that were critical to his reform vision.

Death, political reversals, and a rising generation's interpretations of progress suggested the demise of race challenges. However, Douglass and others continued to contest the concept as they faced uncertainties about the colored population's prospects. Concerns about the future coalesced around the theme of disappearance. In renewed debates over whether colored people should leave the country, emigrationists and their critics reflected on the meaning of ancestry and destiny in mapping progress. The lingering specter of polygeny and questions about how the colored population would evolve in America inspired competing theories about the development of racial taxonomies. The spread of Jim Crow restrictions drew disparate reformers together to rethink the bases of their push for progress and the terms of their collective identity as they pondered how and whether they could be a race in America.

Engaging these issues entailed ongoing queries into the validity of categories that denoted supposed inherent differences. They prompted appeals to species unity and a common humanity to contest claims about Negro capacity, the rules and customs of race assignment, and barriers to equal citizenship. Although Douglass, the "Old Man Eloquent," was the most prominent of the disparate individuals contesting race, opposition did not die with him in 1895. The decline of his generation gave way to race men. They fostered broader conceptions of practicing race, but they did not altogether abandon the tradition of contesting the construct.

236 RELUCTANT RACE MEN

Henry Highland Garnet's departure for Liberia coincided with renewed popular interest in abandoning the United States. It signaled a blurring of long-held distinctions between colonization and emigration that linked the former project to White coercion. Reformers grappled with divergent perspectives on where the future of colored people lay amid speculations about their ability to thrive in America. They brought competing notions of race to bear on deliberations about whether some portion of the population would or should resettle in Africa for opportunities or as bearers of Western civilization.

The promise of emigration was visible in 1878, when thousands of spectators joined Martin Delany at a Charleston dock to consecrate the *Azor* before it sailed to Liberia. A celebratory launch of the ship carrying more than two hundred passengers forecast success for the Liberian Exodus Joint Stock Steamship Company that Delany and other Charlestonians founded. The project was not simply a business enterprise. Delany founded it on a theory of race that delineates ethical warrants for Black Americans to resettle in Africa. His 1879 treatise *The Origin of Races and Color* links emigration to fulfillment of a divine mandate for human progress. It argues that God created races to carry out the work of advancement. Emigration promised to reconstitute and preserve the original races.[7]

From the outset, Delany took pains to distinguish his ideas from both polygenesis and "the Darwinian development theory." He declared that he would not try to rebut Nott and Gliddon's arguments about "Three Creations." Apparently, others had given them due scrutiny, so he could disregard them. Nevertheless, he diligently contrasted his views with polygeny by situating the origin of races in God's response to the Tower of Babel. He concluded that, until that biblical event, there was just "One Race" because all people had descended from a single creation. The "Unity of the Human Race" expressed itself in a single language and a common basis for skin color. There were differences in the complexions of Noah's three sons, however, because they possessed varying concentrations of red pigmentation. These original variations in skin color had been of no consequence, Delany argued, because no one perceived them as "a mark of distinction." Hence, "races were unknown."[8]

The "confusion of tongues" at Babel changed this scenario. It enabled people to discern differences in skin complexions, which sparked preferences within differently colored groups for "their kind." The Genesis 11:8 account of God scattering people throughout the world showed the results of this development. Noah's sons and their descendants migrated to Africa, Asia, and

Europe, each group equipped with its own language and, "in all reasonable probability," its own distinctive complexion. Hence, "the Origin of Races" produced migrations that fulfilled God's aim of peopling the entire earth.[9]

Tracing the manner in which races developed helped Delany distance his ideas from Darwinian theory while continuing to reject polygeny. It was essential to show that new units of humanity emerged from existing life forms and were everlasting. In Darwin's evolutionary framework, races could disappear. However, for Delany, their importance persisted after they fulfilled their original purpose. Because they were providential, the races originating at Babel created a divinely inspired "race affinity" that united members of each group in a discrete destiny. The observation that the races "permanently and forever" severed ties with each other strengthened the justifications for African emigration. It predicted ongoing separation that would facilitate the restoration of "the three original sterling races." The process would contribute to world progress by regenerating the African race. Peopling the continent with Christian Negroes from America would deliver it from "superstition and ignorance" and foster the development of a "godly civilization."[10]

Despite auspicious beginnings and clear conceptual foundations, the emigration project was short lived. The company collapsed after its first voyage, dashing the hopes of individuals who had already registered for the second trip. Delany's dreams also floundered as he spent the remaining six years of his life seeking a government post to finance his own emigration dreams.[11]

Henry McNeal Turner gave the benediction at the Charleston launch of the *Azor*. Thereafter, he praised Delany's treatise as a "great work on ethnology."[12] Although his vision developed along different lines, he embraced Africa as a fatherland and set out to carry the emigration campaign forward. A Georgia legislator during Reconstruction, he reported spending "many years" as a "stern opposer" of colonization and emigration schemes. Repeat conversions led him to take up the emigrationist mantle—when he heard Alexander Crummell lecture on Liberia, watched Reconstruction's halting development, and witnessed its piecemeal collapse. Even before making a full-fledged commitment, he praised individuals who exercised their "God-given rights" to settle wherever they pleased instead of waiting to be "driven, forced, or expatriated."[13] In recognition of his outspoken support, the American Colonization Society, which was sending approximately one hundred people per year to Liberia in the decade following Reconstruction, designated him an honorary vice president for life.

238 RELUCTANT RACE MEN

After his election to the AME bishopric in 1880, Turner spearheaded his own initiatives and emerged as one of the most ardent proponents of migrating to Africa. He framed his campaign with a concept of Negro "Americanship," making emigration part of American Negro destiny to spread Christianity in Africa. He was convinced that it would help fulfill a divine plan that enabled Africans to endure American slavery. As a mechanism through which Negroes became Christians, the peculiar but "providential" institution had supposedly prepared them to bring redemption to their ancestral land. Accordingly, Africa was not to be the home for all Negroes. Turner envisioned a decade in which five to ten thousand migrants per year would make their way to Africa to Christianize it instead of languishing in prisons or facing lynch mobs. He steered clear of the old ACS argument that nature endowed Negroes with traits uniquely suited for life on the continent. Such a claim would have been misplaced in light of reports of illness and death among new immigrants in Liberia. Instead, he defended emigration with the argument that human beings are "cosmopolitan" by nature. Accordingly, Negroes were physically capable of living in any part of the world.[14]

Talk of a small-scale missionary enterprise vanished when Turner tried to communicate the urgency of leaving America. This message called for the rhetoric of extinction. Emigration became necessary to Negro survival; "is not self preservation the first law of nature?" he asked. Images of doom dramatized his contention that Negroes needed Africa as a refuge. In contrast to Delany, for whom races were inextinguishable, Turner suggested that bigotry and discrimination could result in American Negroes disappearing. Post-Reconstruction conditions were warning signs that White people were intent on destroying the population they had already excommunicated from the nation's social and political spheres. When the Supreme Court voided the 1875 Civil Rights Act, Turner advised Negroes to leave for Africa "or get ready for extermination." A decade later, his call for a national convention to organize "African repatriation" cautioned that the annihilation of Negroes was "only a question of time." Emigration would replace the threat of death with the promise of progress. It would foster a grand "evolution" producing nationhood that would generate respect for all Negroes. The race would not even deserve respect, he argued, until it demonstrated that it could create and maintain an autonomous government. A separate nation would enable Negroes to experience equality as God intended.[15]

Edward Blyden symbolized ACS success. A native of the former Danish West Indies educated by missionaries in Liberia, he went on to a career as a Presbyterian minister, government official, and professor and president at Liberia College. The organization sponsored him on US tours to market its project among Negroes and politicians.[16] He shared a popular expectation that emigration would spread Christianity in Africa. It thus seemed logical, if not obligatory, for him to recruit several million individuals to promote a Christian civilization. Although he conceived of his plan as a repatriation initiative, on its own, the act of return failed to capture his sense of the venture's importance. He was convinced that emigration would lift Negroes to a higher stage of spiritual evolution. Return would herald a "new phase of humanity," he argued, whereby Negroes would experience the divine with a "new racial spirit." Paradoxically, race consciousness was itself a prerequisite to achieving this result. Blyden believed that emigration demanded "distinct race perception and entire race devotion."[17] Right motivations required more than an acknowledgment of physical similarities between American Negroes and Africans. Migrants needed to feel instinctual ties to the continent and its peoples.

Thousands of poor southerners heeded calls to resettle in Africa. The proliferation of emigration clubs, the estimated 2,500 would-be emigrants who camped in Atlanta in 1891 awaiting ships that never materialized, a group of more than 230 disappointed individuals stranded in New York City, and the 3,000 people who paid three dollars each for worthless tickets to Africa hint at the mass appeal of emigration after Reconstruction.[18] Nevertheless, prospects for a large-scale or long-term exodus were nil. Federal legislation to finance emigration went nowhere, and successive private schemes failed even when they were not outright scams. Although denunciations were not necessary to foil initiatives that faltered on their own, their popularity inspired vocal opposition. Turner's fellow Methodists took leading roles in denouncing the idea of resettlement. The influential AME *Christian Recorder* published a steady stream of letters and editorials attacking the proposals even as it allowed emigration proponents to air their views. Turner griped that colored newspapers and conventions throughout the country reviled him for daring to promote emigration. A sympathizer, Bishop Richard Cain, protested that the *Recorder* was flooded with condemnations from individuals who opposed well-intentioned efforts to civilize Africa. AME officials and their AMEZ Church counterparts issued declarations of disapproval. Excessive financial and logistical burdens and potential threats to progress in the United States were standard themes. Detractors saw the project as an ill-conceived diversion of attention and resources from efforts

240 RELUCTANT RACE MEN

to improve the collective welfare of Black people in America. Such opponents were among the eight hundred convention delegates who responded to Henry McNeal Turner's 1893 call to formulate emigration plans. Their objections blocked a pivotal resolution declaring Africa the "only hope of the Negro race as a race."[19] They thus succeeded in muting the central purpose of the gathering. It adjourned with a modest commitment to investigate conditions facing American Negroes.

Veteran and novice opponents of colonization and emigration questioned the notion that natural forces tied American Negroes to Africa. Critics took issue with the suggestion that colored people belonged in Africa by virtue of ancestry or physical characteristics. Their opposition echoed the logic of antebellum anti-colonization arguments. They concurred with New York Age editor T. Thomas Fortune that the population was not African because its habitation, language, and Christian identity bespoke an American nationality.[20]

Not surprisingly, this reasoning was the point of departure for Robert Purvis and Frederick Douglass. Purvis treated emigration initiatives as indistinguishable from the colonization efforts he and his old allies had repudiated. He placed them in the same moral category as post-Reconstruction mob violence and caste. All were oppressive and relied on misrepresentations of Black people. An 1886 anti-lynching assembly gave him an opportunity to condemn pervasive problems of discrimination and distortion. He reluctantly chaired the event after pleas of infirmity were ignored. He took aim at ACS representatives, the "superannuated fossils" who chanted "Africa for Africans" with renewed vigor. He believed the legal fact of national citizenship discredited the idea that Black people were Africans and, therefore, belonged on the continent. Birth made an even more compelling case. "We are to the manner born," he declared. The logic that rendered "native Americans" Africans remained as bankrupt as it had been in antebellum days. Africans were people born in Africa. Purvis thus confidently concluded that there was "not a single African" in America.[21]

Douglass was similarly frustrated with "native land talk." He, too, subsumed emigration under colonization, but he saw no real danger in the renewed campaigns. He was sure that "the masses" would never leave America. The problem was that the initiatives were absurd. Like Purvis, he distinguished race designations from nationality and boasted that the United States was the only "native land" of American Negroes. Hence, the insistence that they owed Africa anything was baseless. Bodies manifested the natal and citizenship ties that bound the population to the nation. "His bones, his muscles, his sinews," he argued, "are all American." Colonizationists' refusal to accept this biological reality compromised Negroes' experience of citizenship.[22]

Critics within Turner's denomination shared some of the same views that Purvis and Douglass expressed. Chief among them were that American citizenship superseded ancestral connections to Africa and that race designations could not alter nationalities established by birth. They were recurring themes in church-sponsored speeches and publications that questioned the existence of natural ties between Negroes and Africa. An Episcopal Address from church bishops succinctly summarized why a majority opposed emigration. "Though deeply interested in the welfare of Africa," the group stated in an Independence Day issue of the *Christian Recorder*, "we are citizens of the United States."[23] Reverend Thomas Knox enlarged on the point, noting that citizenship meant American Negroes had "an American destiny." He used Turner's assertion that American slavery was providential to explain. If God allowed Negroes to be brought here, God would suffer them to remain here, in their "native country."[24]

Popular interest in emigration disturbed *Christian Recorder* editor Benjamin Lee. He believed it was misguided and aimed to discredit and discourage it. He complained that the ACS misrepresented American Negro identity when its *African Repository* reported that Black southerners did not see the United States as their home. To the extent that this observation had any validity, which he doubted, he considered the sentiment unnatural. Terror, harassment, and deception led southern citizens to look to Africa for sanctuary. Making no mention of his fellow bishop's emigration campaign, he spotlighted Blyden to teach potential migrants to distinguish between African and American phenomena. Readers should be on their guard, he warned, to avoid being "bewitched" by Blyden's "African fallacy."[25] Blyden was free to analyze things from an "African standpoint" because his training and career bound him to Liberia. Americans, however, were not versed in such thinking; they had to reason as Americans.

A tour of the South, in early 1890, led William Derrick to agree with Lee's assessment of southern perceptions. He returned to his New York congregation convinced that a national policy of Negro removal was untenable. Federal legislation to finance emigration defied common sense. Derrick oversaw foreign missions for the AME Church; he was interested in Christianizing Africa. However, he assessed emigration using a different

242 RELUCTANT RACE MEN

calculus and determined that proposals to send American Negroes to Africa were foolish. The initiative he had in mind was a US Senate bill recently introduced by Matthew Butler of South Carolina and ardently supported by Alabama senator John Morgan. The legislation authorized federal funds to pay transportation costs for Negroes who left the South intent on renouncing their American citizenship to become citizens of other countries.[26] Morgan identified the Congo Free State—the personal possession of Belgium's King Leopold II—as the ideal destination. It promised to reduce "race aversion" in America, thwart slave trading in the Congo region, Christianize Africans, and promote commercial ties with Leopold. Derrick urged a Long Island audience to ask Congress to ignore such proposals and leave Black people alone. An emigration program was ridiculous because Negroes were solely American. Their connections to Africa were no greater than Morgan's ties were. Comparisons illustrated the point. Derrick observed that German American citizens eagerly shared tales of their "fatherland"; French Americans extolled "LaBelle France"; and Italian Americans praised "sunny Italy." In contrast, he reported, the Negro says, "America is my home." "Africa is as strange and foreign to him as Lapland."[27]

Attacks directed at Turner and Blyden resonated with ideas other emigration opponents expressed. Indiana minister James Embry, who managed the *Christian Recorder*'s business wing under Benjamin Lee's editorship, bewailed preposterous claims about what emigration could accomplish. Proponents offered no credible evidence that it could actually improve the lot of migrants or that the "penniless and illiterate" individuals targeted for such ventures could build a nation. It was also ludicrous to expect the US government to finance the enterprise. Like Lee, he attributed zeal over emigration to pessimism over prospects in the United States. It was understandable that a "small minority" believed it would take centuries for Afro-Americans to advance here. It was reasonable to distrust the "Christian civilization" of people who believed that all the worth and dignity that God imparted to humanity existed solely for them. Emigration fervor represented a desire to escape this suffocating context and experience sovereignty. It showed no "special longing or affection for Africa." His scorn for a continent hobbled by "moral weakness . . . slavery and shame" made it hard for him to understand its draw. He saw no natural connections between would-be emigrants and Africa, but he conceded that any region suitable for civilization could become the "rightful home" of any people. This reasoning also explained the permanent presence of "the African race" in North America. Echoing a common refrain, he maintained that Afro-Americans were just as "at home" here as were other races.[28]

Forbearance gave way to censure as Embry scrutinized Turner's emigration project. He delineated its defects in an open letter published in the *Recorder*. Turner's status as a bishop did nothing to mitigate the intensity of criticism from someone occupying a lower ecclesiastical rank. The sincerity of Turner's hopes for Africa and her "exiled" American children had fallen prey to a faulty vision. "Your outlook seems always backward," Embry observed as he highlighted the flaws in Turner's plan. The idea that American slavery was providential for Africans lacked "practical value." It did not mean that the descendants were qualified to be missionaries or that they should abandon their homes. Turner's reasoning also betrayed a reliance on feelings to assess issues requiring "the coldest, clearest reason." The ever-present "race-pride" of White Americans exemplified the dangers of depending on sentiment. The vicious emotion not only robbed Black people of justice, Embry lamented; "it kills us all the day long." Reason would enable people to appreciate color differences as merely the product of refracted and absorbed light. Embry believed that such an understanding could help reduce the turmoil linked to variations in human appearance. Despite comparing Turner's ideas to bigotry among White people, he did not think sentiment was necessarily hazardous. It could be associated with virtuous or evil actions. Turner's sentiment regarding Africa's redemption was noble. Because it lacked logical coherence, however, it was an unsound basis for a viable enterprise. Furthermore, the emigration plan created risks. It offered fodder to "despicable whites" who wanted Black people to disappear from America.[29] It sent a message to Black people to flee in the face of injustice instead of agitating for their rights.

John Sampson entered the fray over emigration when he returned to the ministry after an eclectic career as a New York City teacher, editor of Cincinnati's *Colored Citizen*, lecturer, and lawyer. The North Carolina native lectured on social and scientific questions for twenty years before publishing his talks in an 1881 treatise entitled *Mixed Races: Their Environment, Temperament, Heredity, and Phrenology*. The collection won praise as an accomplished scientific work that bestowed credit on the race and deserved patronage from "all colors."[30] Sampson's anti-emigration position reflected his broader stand against actions premised on the existence of races. He despised the "narrow-minded spirit" of such endeavors and, in an 1883 letter to the *Christian Recorder*, boasted of crushing them. Some twenty years earlier,

244 RELUCTANT RACE MEN

he had joined forces with others to trounce an outbreak of "Negro exodus African fever." Now, "Blydenism" was peddling the "same old race ideas." The new emigration campaign proceeded as if race were an inherent quality of the blood, Sampson argued. Its champions used this idea to create seemingly natural bases for social divisions and to impute "superior humanity" to Negroes. Like Embry, he belittled sentiment. He disparaged Blyden's appeals as illogical conceptions of advancement. Only weak individuals, Sampson averred, depended on arousing feelings; those who were truly strong appealed to intellect and ethics. Incoherent connections between racial designations and nationality showcased defects. Echoing others, he criticized emigrationists' assumptions that appearance was a sign that people naturally belonged in Africa. "A man's color," he concluded, "is no evidence of his nationality." A postscript to his denunciations noted that he did not oppose missionary initiatives in Africa. The "anti-Americanization" talk of emigrationists compelled him to insist on the inalienable right of colored Americans to remain in their country.[31]

A scientific lens turned the issue of disappearance into questions about survival. Enduring polygenist assumptions about difference and newer speculations about how Negroes would fare in evolutionary contests cast doubt on their physical capacity to endure. Would the "mixed" portion of the group disappear because it combined purportedly different species and thereby compromised its reproductive capacity? Would the entire race ultimately die out in America because it was unfit for freedom and incapable of competing with the White population for life's resources? Reformers confronted such issues by attacking the theoretical underpinnings and evidence used to substantiate polygeny and predictions that Negroes could become extinct.

Polygenist speculations about origins remained important to concerns about the Negro's past. North Carolina principal and historian Edward Johnson introduced his "School History" of Negroes with an account of their beginnings. He contrasted writers who consigned Negroes to a "separate creation" to pander to popular prejudice with the best scholars who acknowledged one human creation of common blood. His concerns had less to do with proving species unity than with showing Negro children a glorious past. His account of origins highlighted the fallacy of the "Color Theory" linking

"RACE-SHIP" 245

dark skin to Noah's drunken curse and tried to demonstrate that Negroes had inhabited Eden and great Egyptian empires.[32] A more comprehensive consideration of polygenist claims and their bearing on questions of disappearance appeared in George Washington Williams's 1882 examination of Negro history. His aim was to hasten the day when there would be "no Black, no White"; everyone would simply be "American citizens." The army veteran, Baptist minister, lawyer, and former newspaper editor devoted the entire first chapter of his two-volume study to the unity of the human species. He ended the work insisting that Negroes would not disappear. Although the *History of the Negro Race in America from 1619 to 1880* begins with the observation that few people still subscribed to the proposition that Negroes are not part of the human family, the next ten pages refute the theory, and the following chapter explores the causes of differences in human appearance. After citing biblical evidence to establish that all the world's human populations evolved from one creation, the book traces the emergence of physical differences to Babel. The "racial peculiarities" evident in the different complexions and hair textures among the scattered populations reflected climatic forces in their various destinations. The diversity had no bearing on the essential unity of human beings; all groups remained physically connected by a common origin.[33]

A glimpse into the future further guided Williams in contending with claims originating in the past. He apprised readers of a new warning that Negroes might lack the capacity to survive amid the White population. However, he referenced antebellum American School predictions that death awaited mulattoes. He saw little difference between challenges to Negro fitness for survival and charges that "mixed" populations had diminished reproductive capacity. His evidence of the threat was a Civil War–era commentary on 1850 and 1860 census returns by then-superintendent Joseph C. K. Kennedy. By Kennedy's own admission, the data on Black and mulatto reproduction were insufficient grounds for definitive conclusions. Nevertheless, he maintained that they showed that extensive "mingling" sapped the colored population's "vitality." They predicted with "unerring certainty" that ongoing contact with the "dominant race" would result in the group's extinction. Williams initially downplayed the predictions because the data came from a bygone era of servitude. Even if they were credible, he decided that "pure sociological laws" governing freedom guaranteed that the population would persist with full reproductive powers. Complacency would have been premature, however, as American School race science continued to shape the census. The "Mulatto"

246 RELUCTANT RACE MEN

and "Black" categories of earlier censuses remained on 1870 and 1880 census forms. Although Williams did not mention the origins of the practice, he challenged the logic that gave rise to counting mulattoes. The work of French naturalist Jean Louis Armand de Quatrefages armed him with ways to refute claims that "mixture" impaired fecundity. Quatrefages pointed out that the "mixed" people comprising many of the world's populations experienced no reduction in their reproductive capability. Morphological differences had no bearing on basic physiological functions. Accordingly, Williams reminded readers of the unity of the human species and assured them that colored and White populations had the same capacity to procreate and survive.[34]

Government use of census data to determine whether some or all segments of the colored population faced extinction continued through 1920. In the 1890 census, Congress authorized more detailed racial designations, supplementing the "Mulatto" category on census forms with "Quadroon" and "Octoroon." The goal of measuring reproductive capacity in the "mixed" population remained tethered to polygenist assumptions. Commissioner of Labor Carroll Wright, who lobbied for the changes and became the acting superintendent for this census, explained, "Whether the mulattoes, quadroons, and octoroons are disappearing and the race becoming more purely Negro ... must be settled by statistics."[35] Yet, as Melissa Nobles argues, refining the data served no practical purpose. The Census Bureau acknowledged that the figures were worthless bits of misinformation. Its reports focused instead on the fate of colored people as a whole. The general conclusion was that they were unable to keep up with White population growth.[36]

The news vexed James Embry. Low population growth allegedly foretold the Negro's extinction. This was the conclusion of a preliminary analysis by Francis Walker, president of the Massachusetts Institute of Technology and former census superintendent. Embry partially discounted the growth disparities because he believed the numbers failed to account for European immigration in White population increases. He bluntly dismissed the conclusion that Negro survival was in jeopardy. If the forecasts had any validity, he reasoned, the populations of France, Switzerland, Norway, Scotland, and England, which grew at rates comparable to American Negro growth, were also becoming extinct. The experiences of those countries suggested that the real lesson in the data was that the Negro population would increase slowly but decisively.[37]

Race remained a factor in prospects for survival because the nation's caste system continued to thrive on ideas about "race variety and color."

The persistence of this structure forced Embry to weigh the possibility of an "extermination war" on Negroes. That educated men like Walker voiced no outright hatred for them but "hopingly" spread the news that they would disappear raised his anxiety. Faith shored up his confidence. He reasoned that providence surely included Negroes in the nation's destiny. Moreover, nature equipped them with the same capacity other human beings possessed to inhabit the earth. Equal access to freedom and rights would enhance their ability to survive as American citizens.[38]

Notions of mulatto weakness and Negro extinction came under John Sampson's scrutiny as he tried to theorize about progress in light of human development and difference. An explanation of causes of human variation built the groundwork for his inquiry. It entailed expanding on conventional environmentalist thinking to include heredity and spontaneity as factors in physical, mental, and moral development. Heredity, he observed, not immutable race traits, explained why individuals resembled their progenitors. Yet climatic factors often modified inherited characteristics and caused variations in individual appearance. Environmental influences on temperament, constitution, and mental activity could trump hereditary tendencies. Sampson repeated the argument that environment could alter physical characteristics of races, reasoning that it was the initial cause of variations. Its effects helped explain why populations displayed differences in spite of the fact that "OF ONE BLOOD GOD CREATED ALL HUMAN BEINGS."[39]

This monogenist starting point led Sampson to conclude that the unity of the species, along with climate-induced differences and heredity, proved that "mixed races" were not doomed to die. Claims to the contrary stemmed from misguided efforts to deduce essential differences from surface identities. Such correlations were merely myths. Observational data showed that reproduction and longevity among "mixed" populations were the same as they were for other groups.[40] Health laws and quality of life were equally significant for all people.

The counterpart of mulatto survival was that extinction posed no threat to the broader colored population. The principle of spontaneity guaranteed that all groups remained intact, even if they appeared "degenerate." This inexplicable "involuntary force" countered the constricting tendencies of heredity and environment. It imparted a will to thrive. It thus enabled humanity to flourish amid enslavement and discrimination. Because its effects were easier to illustrate than to explain, Sampson cited the intellectual prowess of Daniel Payne and the pluck of Benjamin Tucker Tanner as signs of spontaneity's

248 RELUCTANT RACE MEN

handiwork. The mental powers of such men displayed its ability to help individuals transcend inherited and environmental limitations. It ensured that less gifted individuals would at least survive.[41]

———

The fortunes of colored people who demonstrated the capacity to endure in the United States were unclear. Concerns about how they would exist loomed large as racial theories circulated about their future in America. Amalgamation, absorption, modified associations, reconfigured assignment rules, and new taxonomies marked the landscape race critics explored as they mapped progress. Their explorations raised questions about the permanence of racial groups, the logic of classification methods, and the stability of race categories.

Two hundred "representative intelligent colored men and women" in the South gave the public a glimpse of their ideas regarding race and progress. In 1887, they responded to a query from the New York *Independent* asking their opinions on the conditions and prospects of their race. The last of seven articles in the series, The Negro on the Negro, marveled at the seriousness and "deep moral purpose" with which these individuals engaged the issues. It reported that they were unanimous in their certitude that the entire race would continue to advance. Nevertheless, the prevailing view held that "the black race" was disappearing. Respondents explained that colored men commonly chose women with light complexions as partners. Thus, they expected "pure" Africans in the United States to become rare among future generations. As Negroes advanced, this segment of the population would be "doomed to extinction."[42]

Visions of progress among northern-based reformers also included cases of disappearing Negroes. Like their southern counterparts, northerners found reasons to be sanguine about possibilities for betterment despite the fate of Reconstruction. The state of affairs in the early 1880s made John Sampson hopeful. He conjectured that popular use of "COLORED" signaled improved social relations. It showed respect that he found missing from the terms "negro" and "darky." He predicted that, in time, further improvements of this sort would alter how colored people related among themselves and with others. Genuine bases of association would become possible. At present, he observed, they banded together for rights because a "natural sympathy" arose from shared experiences of prejudice. When rights ceased to be a problem, however, they would separate. Common interests and preferences would then guide their choices about relationships. Sampson stopped short of challenging the existence of races as he had done in his anti-emigration screed. Instead, he questioned the logic that assigned a diverse set of individuals to the Negro race. Doubts about the basis of racial groupings bolstered his confidence that colored people would cease to function as a social entity. Ultimately, they would associate "without regard to race identity," he explained, because they were "no more of one race than other citizens."[43]

The varied ancestral lines Negroes possessed also made Benjamin Tanner dubious about unity within the group. "The fact is," he declared, "our whole makeup is heterogeneous." Instead of being "of one blood," American Negroes possessed English, French, and German ancestry. Dissension was a product of this heterogeneity; it bred antipathy because Negroes inherited character traits of diverse nationalities. Like Sampson, Tanner believed the common heritage of slavery along with "present proscription" helped keep the population working together. He hoped awareness of the source of discord would ultimately help to alleviate it.[44]

Despite trying to reduce conflict, Tanner had no interest in seeing Negroes as a permanently identifiable race. Such an outcome clashed with his understanding of the future of races in America. World history led him to anticipate changes that were far more comprehensive than the modifications Sampson envisioned. He expected the nation's entire race taxonomy to become obsolete because Negroes and other groups would cease to exist as discrete races in North America. An "American" race would replace them.[45]

Political developments and natural history foretold the changes Tanner anticipated. The Civil War offered political lessons. It showed the impossibility of trying to operate two distinct governments within the country's geographic boundaries. Tanner argued that even topography conspired against it—an idea he gleaned from John Draper's *History of the American Civil War*. This "truth" indicated that the nation could accommodate only one race. "The one is the corollary of the other," he reasoned, "one government, one race, and both purely American."[46] His vision reframed the "social ethics" of Jim Crow segregation. Tanner warned a National Educational Assembly convention that hierarchy and division rooted in "accidents" of complexion and illogical race designations were unsustainable. The edict of the "'color' line" flouted the principle of free association accepted throughout Christendom. Its restrictions on common liberties fostered enough hatred and contempt to spark war. In view of this threat, Tanner insisted that Americans must

250 RELUCTANT RACE MEN

become "one people" if the Union were to be truly whole. There was no way to encompass "antagonistic races" in the republic.[47]

Political history also provided preliminary clues about the characteristics of the new American race. Just as the government of the independent republic did not simply mirror Europe, the physical traits of the people would be unique. Natural history offered a decisive key to their makeup. Science charted the protracted processes through which continental forces—atmosphere, water, food, and other natural elements—imparted distinctive shapes, colors, and spiritual characters to their inhabitants. As an adherent of environmentalist thought, Tanner believed nature created the original differences among African, European, and Asian populations. The coming American race would develop in a similar fashion. The population's long-term exposure to North America's physical and social influences would eradicate all "foreign" characteristics, "whether of bone or flesh, or even spirit."[48] Heterogeneous descendants of transplanted Europeans, Africans, and Asian would become a homogeneous race.

Although Tanner thought environmental forces could alter a population's entire physiognomy, the transformation he envisioned went beyond its environmentalist premise. It required "a change of blood," which could be achieved only through amalgamation. The result would be a race "truly identified with the continent."[49] Despite talk of continental forces, his vision required unexplained human interactions. When he advised his Bethel Literary and Historical Association audience that amalgamation entailed moral obligations, listeners might well have expected him to encourage them to intermarry. Instead, he admonished them to acquiesce to mixture as if it would occur without their agency. He was convinced of its inevitability; there was no need to advocate it. Declarations sufficed, for he was simply a messenger. "To use the parlance of the street," he quipped, "'the case is up with us.'"[50] Fusion was a foregone conclusion. Surrender was the sole option. It meant accepting the disappearance of a distinct Negro population that would be absorbed into the "oneness in color" of a "mixed" American race. A river analogy summarized the inescapable outcome. "Distinct race lines can no more be preserved in a country like ours, than can the waters of our Ohio be preserved when emptied into the Mississippi. Inter-mixture is to be the practice of the country within the next fifty years."[51] Somehow, European ancestry would predominate, overshadowing the African and Asian presence on the continent. By Tanner's reckoning, the coming American would have the blood quanta of an octoroon and possess a yellow tinge.[52]

"RACE-SHIP" 251

Tanner's timetable was a moving target. On some occasions, he predicted that it might take more than a century for absorption to come to pass because it could not begin until colored people made substantial progress. Clear signs of advancement could appear by the year 2000. He imagined that, by then, women would have voting rights and colored people occupying governors' offices, judgeships, and US Senate seats would wield power in numerous states. Fifty years later, the frequency of interracial marriages would increase and receive federal recognition.[53]

Broader discussions on the topic situated Tanner's vision. The ideas of White Methodist theologians and pundits who saw amalgamation as part of the nation's destiny made their way into the *Christian Recorder*. Commentaries from John W. Hamilton, founder of Boston's People's Church; Abel Stevens; Daniel Curry; and E. V. Smalley all corroborated Tanner's prediction that Negroes would blend with the White population and fade away as a discrete identifiable race.[54] Tanner was, nevertheless, aware of dissenting opinions, and he shared them with readers. In the final weeks of his sixteen-year editorial term at the *Recorder*, he presented the views of a Presbyterian colleague who rejected the idea that progress consigned Negroes to absorption. The challenger was John Reeve, pastor of Philadelphia's Central Presbyterian Church. The Long Island native had been a young parishioner in Henry Highland Garnet's church, graduated from New York Central College, and was the first colored person to earn a degree from Union Theological Seminary in New York. His reputation as a student of Greek and Hebrew earned him accolades as one of the era's "most scholarly" clerics. He lectured for Washington's Bethel Literary and Historical Association two weeks after Tanner addressed the group.[55] The venue became an occasion to critique his friend's analysis and present alternate interpretations of unity and the future.

Reeve's speech situated concerns about the Negro's prospects in a long history of queries about relations between people of African descent and White Americans. It noted that emancipation established the fact that Negro citizens were not destined to subjection. The issues Tanner considered called for further exploration. Was it necessary to have a "dead uniformity" in skin color to demonstrate the essential unity and equality of human beings? Must the matter be settled in "purely physical" terms? Reeve argued that relations between the Irish and the English and the social structure in India demonstrated that near-uniform complexions did not preclude systems of hatred and caste. He envisioned a "truer unity" that did not entail eliminating phenotypic diversity. Moreover, he found insufficient evidence and a lack of

252 RELUCTANT RACE MEN

cogency in the historical and scientific foundations of Tanner's conclusions. Reeve believed the developments that produced races among "heathen" peoples in Africa, Europe, and Asia were unreliable predictors of outcomes in North America. Natural forces might have controlled the former, but "modern man" exercised reason, ethics, and religion to restrain such powers. It was thus unrealistic to expect influences that shaped continents in the past to continue to hold sway. Why, he asked, would Negroes be unable to stave off factors pushing them to absorption?[56]

The views of the men Tanner cited to validate his prediction further undermined its legitimacy. Reeve discerned "the old poison" in their ideas about absorption, namely, the belief that Negroes were inherently inferior. Curry, for instance, found the phenomenon's inevitability mortifying. Abel Stevens eschewed the biblical truth of "one blood" in favor of "inferior and superior blood." Hamilton described mixture with a metaphor of unequal rivers; Negroes comprised the smaller Missouri River that ultimately merged into the larger Mississippi. Reeve maintained that an accurate account of the Negro's future required a different understanding of waterways. He advised his audience to look southward to Gulf Stream waters and observe the permanency of their color; they remained darker than surrounding currents. This example of "constancy in nature," a principle borrowed from Francis Bacon's philosophical idea of the constancy of matter, illustrated the status of Negroes. It explained their ongoing "distinctive influence" in American society. The chemistry principle of catalysis, describing "the action of presence" further elucidated the outcome Reeve anticipated: "The mere presence of a certain substance among the atoms of another substance produces . . . extensive changes upon those atoms, and yet the body thus operating is itself unchanged." Science thus ruled out absorption. Providence, moreover, mandated the enduring presence of American Negroes to carry out a divine mission of helping fellow citizens understand and accept the common humanity of all people. This endeavor, Reeve thought, could be more arduous than the missionary work colonizationists advocated. The difference reminded him of the contrast between difficulties Jesus experienced with Jerusalem's pious Pharisees and his acceptance among Galilee's sinners. Ongoing instruction in the essential unity of human beings was necessary for truth to prevail. Hence, Negroes could not disappear. Neither colonization nor absorption would eradicate them.[57]

As he succeeded Tanner at the helm of the *Recorder*, Benjamin Lee expressed similar doubts about disappearance through absorption. He maintained that physical differences among humans would endure even as he supported the legal right of interracial marriage. His familial roots in a clan of racially "mixed" people in southern New Jersey equipped him with anecdotal evidence about amalgamation. In the absence of a scientific theory of heredity—Mendel's insights on genetic inheritance would not circulate among American scientists until 1900—he shared his observations of the physical traits resulting from intermarriage. There is a "persistency of type," he told a Bethel Literary and Historical Association audience. Over the course of many generations, physical characteristics of distant ancestors constantly reappeared. This factor ruled out the idea that Negroes would fade into the White population. Despite their persistence, such differences were of little significance to Lee. He praised the end of a ban on intermarriage when his ministerial colleague Benjamin Arnett, a member of the Ohio General Assembly, succeeded in a campaign to repeal the state's Black Codes. Lee believed the state had no legitimate basis for interfering with natural affinities that led people to marry. Moreover, if White and colored people lacked the capacity for mutual affinity, as some people claimed, then legal prohibitions were unnecessary. The fundamental issue was that anti-miscegenation statutes displayed a flawed understanding of human difference. "The fact is," Lee argued, "miscegenation with reference to human beings is a misnomer."[58] The dissimilarities it purported to signify were no more salient than variations in eye color. Differences, however slight, would resist eradication in the face of amalgamation.

The AME Church issued no formal endorsements of interracial marriage as a denomination. Yet other high-ranking church officials showed the same sympathy for the practice that Lee, Tanner, and Arnett exhibited. One such leader was Lee's cousin Theodore Gould, pastor of the denomination's flagship Mother Bethel in Philadelphia. In the spring of 1882, he made news for officiating at the marriage of a White British widower and a young Black woman. This was not a routine pastoral obligation. The groom was not an AME Church member, and neither partner was a Philadelphia resident. The couple lived in Delaware, which banned interracial marriages. The ceremony took place at the *Christian Recorder* office. Senior bishop Daniel Payne and Levi Coppin, another prominent minister, were among the witnesses. The Philadelphia *Press* criticized the clerics and ridiculed the "parti-colored" lovers.[59]

Because absorption was a potential outgrowth of amalgamation, Alexander Crummell saw no reason to anticipate it. He believed that universal laws of

254 RELUCTANT RACE MEN

nature made fusion impossible. An Episcopal priest educated at New York's African Free Schools, the Oneida Institute, Yale Theological Seminary, and Cambridge University's Queens' College, he returned from twenty years of Liberian missionary work in 1873 and turned his attention to elevating Negroes in the United States. As he explained at an 1888 Episcopal Church Congress, his certitude about amalgamation sprang from his knowledge of how life forms evolved. Nature, he asserted, progressed from homogeneity to heterogeneity. Accordingly, wholesale amalgamation, or "blood unity," could not occur because it would create homogeneity, blurring differences between races. This rule was the reason "a new type of man" had yet to appear in America. It affirmed "the principle of race" as among "the most persistent of all things in the constitution of man." For Crummell, race was a "structural" facet of human nature. Maintaining the integrity of racial boundaries was thus a matter of instinct. These divisions had been violated under American slavery, which fostered rampant sexual exploitation of Black women. However, expert evidence convinced him that this "base process" of mixture significantly declined after emancipation. He was thus confident that races would remain intact as discrete entities.[60]

Reeve's arguments, Lee's observations, and Crummell's race principle failed to settle the matter. The scale of change that Tanner envisioned for the nation's race taxonomy might have seemed exceptional; however, its core idea was not unusual. Other reformers shared his sense that some degree of amalgamation lay ahead. Tanner presented some of their views after assuming the job of editing the *A.M.E. Church Review* in 1884. Boston's George Ruffin, the first northern colored judge to hold such a position, expressed views that were nearly identical to Tanner's outlook. He argued that the fate of Negroes was set; they would be "swallowed up and merged" into the larger White population. Despite the likelihood of resistance from both Black and White people, merger was inevitable.[61] George Downing modified prior claims about Negro absorption and considered the effects of environment and social factors on Black and White people alike. "Climate, habits, diet, intercourse, and miscegenation," he concluded, were making changes in appearance that could be observed at any gathering of colored people. "African peculiarities" were diminishing. At the same time, however, complexions of White Americans appeared to be darkening. In time, these mutual transformations would likely lead to a "common type" of American—an outcome he believed would solidify natural bonds among human beings. It would thus solve the nation's "color question."[62]

A fictionalized exchange between a *Recorder* correspondent, H.T.K., and a White interlocutor also presented amalgamation as part of the inexorable march of progress. It satirized the fear it inspired. H.T.K. assured his conversation partner that large-scale intermarriage would not occur in his lifetime. God deferred it, he explained, upon seeing that the gentleman could not bear it. The man could be certain, however, that his grandsons would not only witness the development; they might even help to advance it. It was useless to place faith in the alleged preventive powers of "natural antagonism" between races. Facts proved its unreliability. Moreover, science showed that, as colored people became more enlightened, educated, and wealthy, apparent physical distinctions separating them from White people would vanish through mixture.[63]

Frederick Douglass lent a prominent voice to reform discourse on amalgamation and intermarriage. His periodic reflections on the Negro's future in the *Recorder* and for a broader readership of the *North American Review* cited amalgamation as a logical outcome. It was an integral part of advancement. He shared the view of progress as a gradual process. The effects of slavery, which deformed bodies and traumatized psyches, would take years to overcome. Two decades after emancipation, he could still see the anguished faces of abused slave women on the distorted features of their descendants. Nevertheless, he believed Negroes would escape the destruction suffered by groups he deemed "weak races," including Jews, Moors, Chinese, and Native Americans. Annihilation was as implausible as mass emigration. Negroes would comprise a lasting part of the population; however, they might not be visible as such because they would not remain a "separate and distinct race." Even as he sidestepped the language of extinction, Douglass concluded that absorption would meld people into a "blended race."[64] Several factors convinced him of this prospect. The history of miscegenation in slavery predicted more of the same in freedom. Ignoring the domination and violence that characterized sexual encounters between slaves and White people, he mused that colored people had been "sufficiently attractive" when they were "degraded" and "ignorant" slaves to produce an "intermediate race" of a million people. Education and prosperity would no doubt result in the continued expansion of this population. Unification was consistent with the course of human history, which affirmed the common humanity of all people. Thus, the process would endure, continuously changing the "races and varieties" comprising the human family.[65]

Despite the connection he saw between amalgamation and progress, Douglass followed Tanner's example and presented his views as predictions.

256   RELUCTANT RACE MEN

He was merely "a prophet," he argued; he neither advocated nor disparaged interracial marriage. Many people thought otherwise when, after nearly two years as a widower, he married Helen Pitts, a White woman, in 1884. Controversy over the union raised political and ethical questions about intermarriage, advancement, and leadership.[66]

For Alexander Crummell and John Cromwell, it presented an occasion for further commentary on amalgamation. An editorial in the *Independent* lent urgency to the matter. An unidentified journalist praised Douglass's action as an example other Negro men should follow. "It is the best thing that could happen to the race in America," the writer declared. Crummell withheld judgment, stating that it would be rude to comment on private matters. He was incensed, however, by the journal's suggestion that "cultured" Black men should subscribe to a policy of amalgamation, effectively severing "the ties of race" and abandoning Black women. Such a policy would be injurious to a people whose need for unity would endure for years to come. Worse, perhaps, was the exaggerated value the writer attached to "the white man's blood" while disparaging the worth of Negro blood. In the face of such a degrading scenario, Crummell averred that it would be better for Negroes simply to "die out" than for amalgamation to provide the solution to the "*moral* monstrosity" of caste.[67]

John Cromwell's comments were more measured. The editorial in his *People's Advocate* did not condemn Douglass or interracial marriage. Yet his plaintive query "Must We Intermarry?" urged colored men not to heed the *Independent*'s call to follow the eminent man's example. It was not the time to make such a choice, he believed, because colored women were becoming lovelier and more cultured. In answer to the title of his commentary, he determined that amalgamation was a poor reform tool because it was useless against White bigotry. "Obliterating the color-line by absorption . . . simply rids the country of the Negro," he declared. It would do nothing to mitigate anti-Negro sentiment. Anyone who could not conceal the taint of "Negro blood" would still feel discrimination. He thought that a policy of intermarriage would betray a lack of faith in Negro capacity. Nevertheless, he did not rule out the practice as a future outcome. In fact, like Douglass and others, he predicted, "*intermarriages will come*" after Negroes developed themselves further and acquired power.[68] A flawed mechanism of progress would thus become a sure indicator of improvement.

The marriage was a dispiriting blow for observers who perceived it as a backward step. Disgruntled commentators took direct aim at Douglass.

"MOSES GONE OVER TO THE EGYPTIANS," shrieked the headline of one Baptist paper. It portrayed Douglass's choice as evidence of the depths to which colored people had fallen and signaled a need for change. If the leader preferred "Egyptians" to his "own race," he was not a fit representative. For some, his apparent lack of "race pride" proved that the race should no longer take pride in him.[69] The sense of betrayal was acute for Philadelphia politician Gilbert Ball. He believed Douglas had insulted colored women and harmed all colored people. They could not trust him. His stature had begun to decline before the misstep of intermarriage. Ball reported that young people were paying less attention to Douglass's views and appreciated Richard Greener as a prospect for a leadership position because he was "up to the times" and presented "more advanced ideas." Greener, who had cast himself as Douglass's rival, said little about the controversy. Yet his doubts about the wisdom of the marriage were evident in his quip, "Reason ceases when love begins."[70]

Defenders saw the marriage as a personal affair and attributed the uproar about it to unseemly American race practices. Purvis, Isaiah Wears, and others reminded critics of Douglass's lineage. Wears, a longtime friend and sometime critic, thought that Douglass's White ancestry made it illogical for him to rule out interracial marriage. Purvis, whose second wife was White, dismissed assaults on Douglass's character as prejudice. Tanner decided that the marriage reflected broader views about human difference that Douglass had expressed in recent years. It was an example of future developments that deeply pleased him.[71] Commentators in the *Afro-American* and other colored periodicals defended the marriage as consistent with Douglass's history of praiseworthy activism, which overlooked differences in order to aid all human beings. A Cleveland editorial speculated that Douglass viewed Pitts "not as a white lady . . . but simply as an American lady whom he loved." It charged critics with hypocrisy, recalling that, less than a year earlier, thousands had cheered when Douglass called amalgamation a force that moved civilization. The writer thus scoffed at the "ignorant prejudiced masses" who now expressed outrage that Douglass had acted on his principles.[72]

Douglass was loath to defend his relationship in public or to link it to predictions of amalgamation. He was wary of media curiosity about a personal family matter. The ceremony had been private. Francis Grimké, pastor of the Washington, DC, Fifteenth Street Presbyterian Church, performed it in his home. "I can give no explanation," Douglass told a *Washington Post* reporter. "I can make no apology."[73] He downplayed the reality of races when confronted with the charge that his marriage was inconsistent with his leadership and insulting to colored women. The claim that the union was at odds with his professed reform principles was baseless, he argued. His work on behalf of colored people stemmed from his commitment to justice. It was a matter of manhood and not about his designation as a Negro. Any pride he took in Negroes' accomplishments arose from his identification with downtrodden people. He refused to structure his identity using categories he excoriated. Privately, he confessed principles that framed his decision. A letter to Elizabeth Cady Stanton explained: "I could never have been at peace with my own soul or held up my head among men had I allowed the fear of popular clamor to deter me from following my convictions as to this marriage. I should have gone to my grave a self-accused and self-convicted moral coward."[74] Public outcry was all the more illogical to him because Pitts was merely "a few shades lighter" than he was. He felt certain that no one would have grumbled had he married a woman with dark skin. Yet the complexional disparity would have been the same as it was with his new wife. Exasperated, he told the *Post* reporter, "You may say that Frederick Douglass considers himself a member of the one race." There was "no division of races," he added, because "God Almighty made but one race."[75]

The terse assertion did not convey the depth of Douglass's sentiment about the principle of a common humanity or his ideas on racial classifications. A diary entry about visiting Areopagus (Mars Hill) with Pitts while touring Greece records his experience of being stirred by a reading of the apostle Paul's speech at the site from Acts 17. He tried to imagine the emotions of the ancient Athenians as they listened to Paul describe a god who created all nations "of one blood." Douglass's belief in the existence of a single human race inspired a vision of a future with physical manifestations of oneness. Reactions to his marriage deepened his conviction that amalgamation would continue until all the races of the human family "blended into one."[76] In an effort to promote this development, he sought to discredit false notions of difference with new rules of race assignment that eliminated the "one-drop rule" whereby any Negro ancestry rendered a person a Negro. In theory, this was an uncomplicated matter. However, the bigotry at the root of classification practices posed a formidable barrier to reform. He explained to *North American Review* readers that the rigid laws and customs designating people of "mixed blood" as Negroes aimed to "humiliate and degrade" them. They enforced hierarchies stemming from specious notions of White purity and superiority by forcing such people beneath "an arbitrary and hated color line." Despite this tradition, he believed change was possible and would foster moral progress. New assignment rules would mean that Americans would no longer "pervert" language; they would use terms that communicated truth. He did not specify how a revised classification scheme would label "mixed" people. The critical point was that they would not be Negroes.[77]

There was precedent for Douglass's position. Richard Greener and Martin Delany had previously expressed similar opinions. Both men perceived the nation's race assignment practices as unethical. Their common solution involved removing people from the Negro population by narrowing the category. Greener called for the revision when the *North American Review* asked him to predict the Negro's future. He abandoned the stance on the durability of racial classifications he espoused when working to develop the Negro American Society during Reconstruction's decline. Then he had insisted that physical features suggesting African ancestry, however imperceptible—a "kink in the hair, a tinge on the cheek, a low facial angle or a trace of prognathous"—created a moral imperative for individuals to identify and act as Negroes.[78] Now he argued for reclassification that would make "mixed bloods" part of the White population, where, he believed, they belonged. Such individuals would have "disappeared" from Negro rosters long ago, he conjectured, were it not for the "caste-prejudice" that policed racial boundaries.[79] Delany prescribed a remedy in his treatise on race permanence. He, too, criticized American conventions that designated individuals who possessed any degree of African ancestry as Negroes. To account for miscegenation, he proposed a rule in which the preponderance of "blood" determined one's classification. His plan was to alter the meanings of "quadroon" and "octoroon" so they would no longer refer to degrees of Negro ancestry. Instead, there would be Black and White quadroons and octoroons. The terms would indicate the extent to which a person was "removed" from any "pure" race. Thus, "black quadroon" named a person whose ancestry was 75 percent Black, whereas 75 percent of a "white quadroon's" ancestors were White. This majority rule proposition held that any quadroon or octoroon was "either a white or black person and should be classed as such." The adjustment was a rubric he had used for at least two decades and had seen in other parts of the world. The United States rejected change, he argued, to maintain practices that systematically debased people of African descent.[80]

260   RELUCTANT RACE MEN

Neither generations of amalgamation nor new assignment rules were necessary to reconfigure the country's racial schema. Because it was an invention, its foundations could be manufactured anew. This logic guided Theophilus Steward's conception of colored people's future in America. His proposal for constructing a new "race-ship" looked beyond physical phenomena and considered the importance of ideas in making races. Less of a prediction of what would occur, it warned of change that must come for the republic to survive. Benjamin Tanner printed the essay on the *Recorder's* front page. However, the political orientation and scope, which are evident in the title, target a broader audience. Although "The Modifications in the Race Idea Suggested by the Necessities of Modern Politics" follows reform conventions in its reliance on history, Steward's interpretation and critique of race are novel.[81] Seeds for the essay's ideas had percolated for some time. During his second appointment to an AME congregation in Wilmington, Delaware, he resumed earlier protests against segregation in the state's public education system. He assailed contrived notions of difference that incited opposition to "mixed schools." The term was meaningless in light of religious, philosophical, and scientific proof that there were no essential differences among human beings; all possessed the same capacity to learn. It might have made sense with reference to combining students of different national or religious identities. However, he observed that even differences in skin color, if reported truthfully, offered no logical basis for distinguishing all students of African descent from children classified as White.[82]

The piece he published six months later explicated the logic of color distinctions and explained why they should be eradicated. He argued that the nation was still using the conception of race it inherited from the founders of the republic. Those men had enlarged the "race-idea" by creating a classification scheme based on color. The result was a "composite race" of Europeans representing "various and antagonistic races—inferior and superior, subordinate and dominant." Together, they became "one great white race." This expansion suited a government that excluded Black and Native peoples from participation, for history showed that a republic could progress only to the extent that its "race idea" was compatible with its basis of political membership.[83]

Reconstruction had set the nation in conflict with this rule. The "white-race-idea" on which the government was founded was incompatible with post-emancipation political developments. Steward thus foresaw a crisis. "If the races of men are essentially distinct from one another, and each race permanent and unalterable, then a government necessitating the social and political blending of these races is out of harmony with nature, and consequently doomed to speedy overthrow."[84] Since the Fourteenth and Fifteenth Amendments and the 1875 Civil Rights Act effected such blending, there were just two alternatives. The government must abandon Reconstruction principles of inclusion, Steward argued, or relinquish false notions of essential difference between the White population and other Americans. If it chose the latter option, it would be able to devise a different "race-ship"—a lexicon of membership that was "co-extensive" with the constitution's parameters of citizenship.[85]

Prospects for a new taxonomy appeared to be sound despite government reversals of Reconstruction enactments. Steward's hopes were buoyed by popular use of the term "the American people" to refer to all citizens and by the existence of an "intermediate population" linking the extremes of dark and light complexions. Such developments were not solutions. Unlike Tanner, he put little stock in the idea that altering Negroes' physical features was the key to progress. The changes were significant because they suggested that Americans might be open to modified race constructs and willing to embrace a taxonomy that affirmed "the oneness of the entire species."[86] He was still hopeful five years later, even as he complained about race practices in religious circles. The invention of individuals "technically referred to . . . as white people" had corrupted religion by equating Christianity with Anglo-Saxon supremacy. The popular work, *Our Country: Its Possible Future and Its Present Crisis*, exemplified the problem. The author, Congregational minister Josiah Strong, argued that God was preparing the "Anglo-Saxon race" for victory in "the final competition of races." Biblical prophecy convinced Steward that the color-based "clan principle" in Strong's treatise would ultimately die. The disintegration of "race-bonds" would enable true Christianity to flourish.[87]

———

The hostile milieu of the century's final decades was an unlikely incubator for the hopefulness that sustained race challenges. How did reformers remain optimistic about progress amid dire circumstances? Characterizations of the era's oppressive conditions as aberrant helped foster faith in future progress. History showed Douglass, for example, that bigotry was an acute "moral disorder" that invented specious grounds for its existence. He observed that, centuries after Saxons rose to greatness from their lowly status as a "subject race," the descendants of Norman invaders continued to ascribe "all sorts of odious peculiarities" to their former conquests. A vacuous "race pride" thrived on fantasies of their own prowess and Saxon inferiority. He believed that the "color line" regulating America's caste system functioned in a similar illogical fashion. It reflected no intrinsic aspects of "human nature" because antipathy was not universal in encounters between White people and Negroes. Embry, for one, rejected claims that caste sentiment was instinctive; it was instead an unnatural "social disease." Tanner mocked the "'color' line" as a uniquely American phenomenon that bore no resemblance to "universally understood" lines—"the horizontal line, the equinoctial line, the battle line, the defense line, [and] the dip line." He longed to eradicate this abnormal "death-line," which, he believed, was incomprehensible outside the nation's sphere of influence.[88]

Douglass was further convinced that, because Jim Crow was out of sync with the natural order, it would ultimately yield to forces of progress. The "problem business," as he dubbed popular claims about Negroes, would go the way of Britain's "Jewish problem." He believed the "race problem" had been resolved because emancipation and the Fourteenth and Fifteenth Amendments appeared to eradicate the logic of practices that structured bondage and political exclusion.[89] Despite post-Reconstruction reversals, he was confident that it could never be reinstated. Such was his thinking in 1890, during his term as the US consul general to Haiti. He took stock of the political and moral condition of Negroes and the changes he had witnessed over the course of his career and declared himself hopeful. Belief in the natural unfolding of progress nurtured his confidence. Years earlier, he confessed "evolutionist" leanings. The theory enabled him to interpret setbacks as logical but temporary. He cautioned colored people that their status might sometimes appear to deteriorate. This was to be expected because atypical circumstances arising from the Civil War had placed them in positions that did not match their collective accomplishments. Premature elevation was unsustainable. Now, however, they would climb "naturally and gradually."[90]

Evolution, as he understood it, also meant that each successive generation improved on the achievements of its predecessors. However, he was unwilling to cede his own stature and authority to younger reformers. He acknowledged that some observers scorned him as an old man who was content with limited freedoms and rights. He advised them to trust the wisdom and patience he had gained from experience. "One by one," he recalled, "I have seen obstacles removed, errors corrected, prejudices softened, proscriptions relinquished, and my people advancing."[91] He believed in the nation's power, justice, and advancement and tried to inspire faith in the ultimate triumph of humanity.

Similar concerns about young people who ignored lessons from elders marked Mary Ann Shadd Cary's final reform endeavors. She had moved back to the United States with the Union army's Civil War victory. Douglass, one of the few news editors who supported her efforts to reestablish domestic reform networks, published her commentaries in his *New National Era*. Historian Jane Rhodes concludes that their long careers ultimately fostered mutual respect. Yet, Cary did not share Douglass's positive outlook or his views on race. She espoused new concepts to navigate the era's political landscape as she campaigned for women's rights, denounced lynching, and criticized Black American disunity. The premium she had placed on overcoming racial distinctions as an emigrationist gave way to calls for race conscious measures for collective advancement. One of her last reform speeches before she turned her attention to building a law practice in the closing years of her life was titled "Race Pride and Cooperation."[92]

Although Douglass's qualms about race persisted, his optimism faltered. The change appeared in what historian Philip Foner identified as the final great speech of his career. "The Lessons of the Hour," first presented late in 1893 and repeated throughout 1894, reflected a shift in his understanding of lynching. In 1892, he acknowledged that he had accepted propaganda as fact and, thus, believed lynching victims were rapists. He abandoned this position after reading analyses of lynching by Ida B. Wells. Seen through a new lens, this hallmark of Jim Crow became the most disquieting situation Douglass had encountered since slavery. His hope that mob violence would subside had been in vain. The "savage extravagance" had intensified, and its reach had extended beyond the South.[93]

Familiar reform arguments guided his attempts to tackle the new development. Although mobs targeted individuals, he saw lynching as a danger to the entire colored population; everyone had to contend with the threat of brutality. Moreover, misrepresentations that legitimized White attacks applied to the entire group. They were part of the machinery of Jim Crow, designed to sully Negro character. Attackers and their defenders targeted the "color" of their victims, he argued. They ascribed collective guilt in an effort to depict Negroes as categorically unfit citizens and humans, thereby justifying segregation, disenfranchisement, and even death.[94]

Past practices and appeals to a common humanity challenged the popular claim that lynching guarded the virtue of White women against a Negro menace. Black servitude and service throughout American history made it implausible that Black men were suddenly a monstrous threat to the safety and sanctity of White households. Moreover, Douglass insisted, as a class, Negroes were like all other human beings. As such, they possessed no greater propensity for sexual assaults than "any other variety of the human family." In contrast, lynch mobs were not ordinary people. Their actions demonstrated that they failed to comprehend the sacred character of human life that normal people possessed. The habit of wielding abusive and arbitrary power had corrupted their humanity.[95]

The remedy was clear. Change would come if the nation stopped violating the Constitution and began heeding citizens' rights. The "old trick" of misrepresenting things blocked this straightforward solution. Douglass was convinced that framing physical, social, and political persecution as "the Negro problem" absolved perpetrators of their crimes.[96] It made Negroes responsible for a national injustice.

Indicators for change were not encouraging. "American caste" was conspicuous even at the 1893 World's Columbian Exposition. Douglass had expected this global venue to display "human brotherhood." He was sorely disappointed to find it stocked with disparaging representations of Negroes. The era's hideous social and political facts eroded his faith in American freedom. They undermined his hope that the nation was "too great" to further subjugate a population it had enslaved for generations. After years of positively forecasting the Negro's prospects, he advised audiences not to ask about the outcome of the "so-called negro problem." He could no longer tell them.[97]

Douglass's death the following year coincided with the rising prominence of Booker T. Washington and W. E. B. Du Bois, whose views have come to represent the turn-of-the-century reform initiatives of "race men." Despite the antipathy between them, Washington and Du Bois factions stood on common ground in trying to press beyond the tradition of questioning race. Whereas Douglass and other race critics equated race classifications with erroneous claims of inherent difference, rank, and sameness, emerging reformers invoked the designations to denote and promote a shared identity among people of African descent. This shift threatened to eclipse race resistance.

Change began swiftly. Months after Douglass died, Washington's injunction "Cast down your bucket where you are" dramatically summed up his platform of accommodation in the Atlanta Cotton Exposition speech that propelled him into the role of Negro leader. He enlarged on Douglass's suggestion that the political positions Black men held during Reconstruction marked an unnatural path to advancement. The sentiment helped to justify his program of elevation through self-help, which departed from Douglass's longstanding protest politics. Although Washington defended Negroes against charges of innate inferiority, he did not take up the task of refuting race distinctions or questioning the idea that race categories marked natural differences and hierarchies. Indeed, the imagery of his "Atlanta Compromise" endorsed distinctions. The insistence that, socially, races should be "as separate as the fingers" affirmed the significance of discrete races for his southern White audience, echoing words Rutherford B. Hayes had uttered at the Hampton Institute fifteen years earlier. Hayes had committed himself to keeping the nation's discrete populations "separate as the fingers are." He acknowledged the utility of uniting to advance the public good; however, unity did not obliterate race distinctions. Fundamental "differences of nature" among races must be upheld, he argued, because they reflected a divine purpose and nature's laws.[98]

Washington's rhetoric mirrored his conception of the terms of advancement. Both privileged race. His reform program rested on a belief in laws of development that "all races" were required to follow. Although he confessed ignorance about Darwin's theory of evolution, he invoked it as a metaphor to explain progress. Races that became strong, he argued, had advanced "one step at a time through . . . grades of industrial, mental, moral, and social development."[99] The collective character of progress, in which races were the units of change, was as important as the content of individual stages.

Prominent reformers who criticized Washington's political compromises and commitment to industrial training nonetheless shared the idea that races were the appropriate bases of human progress. They valued the very things he was credited with achieving. According to his Tuskegee successor, Robert Moton, Washington's leadership among Negroes developed "their race pride, their race consciousness, and their race integrity."[100] Du Bois and other rising race men promoted the same ideals. Faced with circumstances that inspired Douglass to denounce race, emerging reformers embraced it as essential to American Negro progress. They worked to transform race into a basis of collective identity as they encouraged people of African descent to identify themselves as and with members of a distinct racial population.

The American Negro Academy (ANA) provided a venue for this effort. Founded in 1897, it reflected and promoted changes in perceptions of race in a rising generation of reformers. The organization was an exclusive self-styled intellectual vanguard. Membership, which was by invitation and limited to men, was capped at fifty. It drew accomplished professionals—journalists, clergy, academics, and attorneys. John Cromwell, Benjamin Lee, Theophilus Steward, Benjamin Tanner, Howard University sociology professor Kelly Miller, Wilberforce University classicist William Scarborough, and Francis Grimké along with his brother Archibald, an attorney and diplomat, were among the initial members. Booker T. Washington declined the group's invitation. There was some interest in inviting Richard Greener, who was gaining broad recognition in Republican Party politics and remained a popular speaker. He and Alexander Crummell had once been friends and reform allies. However, rumors that he had spent several years living as a White man in New York City crushed his membership prospects.[101]

The launch of the ANA was one of the final reform initiatives Crummell undertook before his death in 1898. As a founder and first president of the group, he, along with Du Bois, shaped the meaning of race in the organization's agenda. Crummell touted the project as unique, for it approached the task of elevation in a way he had never before witnessed. It confronted matters that had concerned him for years. He had long despaired of the dearth of race consciousness and pride among American Negroes. In the period following his return to America, he included this deficiency among the "heresies" that hindered advancement. The notion that colored people should ignore differences and "*forget, as soon as possible, that they ARE colored people*" galled him.[102] Its corollary, that they should abandon distinguishing reform endeavors as "colored," was equally disturbing. He tried to counter such ideas by insisting on the persistence of race and the permanence of "Race-life." However, his definition of a race—a "homogeneous population of one blood, ancestry, and lineage"—suggests that races could die out, or, at the very least, lose members whose bloodlines became tainted by outsiders.[103] Like Martin Delany, he tried to guard against transience by investing the phenomena with divine origins; races were "the organisms and the ordinance of God."[104] These ideas shaped his hopes for the ANA. A letter to John Cromwell shortly after the group formed expressed his concerns about misguided perceptions of race and American identity that the group had to confront. It tacitly admitted the ineffectiveness of his past efforts to instill consciousness with the claim that race was an indestructible instinct. "We have as yet no wide, stable basis of race feeling to work upon; it has got to be created. . . . Take the average Black man in America, & you will find that he thinks that the creation of race was a superfluous act on the part of the Almighty; & that that superfluity is to be corrected in America."[105]

Despite his belief in the need for the academy, Crummell initially questioned the feasibility of creating such an organization. Richard R. Wright Sr. and William Crogman approached him with the idea in 1894, as he was retiring from ministry. Wright was a former Georgia slave educated at Atlanta University, the University of Chicago, Harvard, Columbia, and Oxford. In 1891, he became president of the Georgia State Industrial College for Colored Youth. Crogman, a Saint Martin native and Wright's Atlanta University classmate, was a classics professor at Clark College. The men appealed to Crummell to help develop the organization they hoped would function as an intellectual clearinghouse for the race. Historian Wilson Moses suggests that Crummell demurred because he likely realized the project would need Douglass's imprimatur to gain legitimacy, and it would not be forthcoming.[106] Such an outlook was reasonable given Douglass's inability to abide "complexional pride." It was at odds with his belief in a common humanity. He blamed it for sustaining Jim Crow. The Supreme Court's 1883 repeal of the Civil Rights Act, for instance, was a "concession to race pride" that upheld the national caste system.[107] Evils of this sort made him wary. In 1889, as he observed growing appeals for Black people to nurture the feeling, he cautioned a Bethel Literary and Historical Association audience to eschew it.

> One of the few errors to which we are clinging most persistently . . . has come into great prominence of late. It is the cultivation and stimulation of a sentiment which we are pleased to call race pride. I find it in all our books, papers, and speeches. . . . I see no benefit to be derived from this everlasting exhortation. . . . It is building on a false foundation. Besides, what is the thing we are fighting against, . . . the lion in the way of our progress? What is it, but American race pride?[108]

Douglass's death enabled ANA founders to relegate such qualms to a bygone era. Crummell had long thought that Douglass's orientation was backward looking. He had ridiculed what he considered an irrational attachment

268 RELUCTANT RACE MEN

to memories of slavery and its legacy of wrongs. A truncated timeline of polygenist influence showed that it was time to move forward. He recalled that Gliddon and Nott rose to prominence in the 1820s with their "so-called physiological work" that defined the Negro as "a different species from the white man."[109] He believed that, by 1835, the currency of this school of thought had declined. It was thus inconceivable that it posed a threat at the end of the century. Crogman's *Progress of a Race, or the Remarkable Advancement of the Afro-American Negro* also associated the theory with the past, declaring, "In this age, such a preposterous idea does not receive countenance." The "assimilation of all the races" in Frederick Douglass and other individuals proved the existence of a single human race.[110] There was no need to defend an established fact. Polygeny warranted discussion only as a historical artifact to give young people an example of circumstances that prevailed before emancipation.

Du Bois shared Crummell's judgment that Negroes misunderstood the necessary role of race identity in effecting progress. He, too, was certain that the threat of polygenist claims had waned. He believed Darwin established scientific foundations for "human brotherhood" by acknowledging that similarities among races outweighed differences. Yet science failed to provide warrants for treating the oneness of humanity as a social reality. This situation was not simply the fault of post-Reconstruction exigencies. Du Bois admonished Negroes that, in planning their development, they must not confine their focus to the discrimination and lynching that defined Jim Crow because such matters comprised relatively minor facets of race.[111] In contrast, race identity was a moral imperative. To explain, Du Bois took up Douglass's misgivings about race pride. "If I strive as a Negro," he asked in his ANA inaugural address, "am I not perpetuating the very cleft that threatens and separates black and white America?"[112] History answered with a decisive no. It revealed advancement among races, he argued, not individuals. Attempts to evade "the race idea" were thus tantamount to trying to void a universal construct at the center of human history. It was a concept he valorized as the "vastest and most ingenious invention for human progress" that ever existed.[113] He shared Washington's conviction that denouncing it ran counter to the tenets of human development. "We cannot reverse history," he argued; "we are subject to the same natural laws as other races."[114]

The quest for a coherent basis of race identity left Du Bois to work through ideas on his own. Washington had little to offer him on this front. Crummell's position that races were biologically homogeneous was not tenable. Du Bois believed that "mere physical distinctions" did not account for "the deeper differences—the cohesiveness and continuity" of races over time. Only spiritual and psychological sensibilities could explain them. These admittedly intangible phenomena demonstrated the ability of race to bind diverse groups together, including, for example, Europe's Teutonic race of German, Scandinavian, and Dutch peoples. Their potency trumped the significance of "blood, color and cranial measurements." A reliance on sentiment enabled Du Bois to extend conceptions of race beyond physical difference and see commonalities within races without tethering them to "blood." This shift grounded his conception of race identity. It was of no great concern that spiritual and psychical divisions might not yield groupings that possessed "common blood" and phenotypic likeness. His new rule of race membership was not bound to a standard of physical similarity. It privileged affective forces that could not generate the kinds of empirical data natural sciences measured. Nevertheless, they "silently but definitely . . . divided human beings into races," generating results that were discernable to social scientists.[115]

The historical function of races further refined Du Bois's vision. As if echoing James McCune Smith and John Reeve, he observed that each race presented a unique contribution to civilization. Yet Negroes had not fully delivered their gifts. In keeping with precedent, they had to embrace a collective race identity to preserve themselves as a race. Only then could they develop distinctive gifts. The imperatives of progress thus ruled out "absorption by white Americans." The destiny of Negroes lay in being a race. The distinctiveness that Smith and Reeve assumed would endure by virtue of scientific principles became an obligation that required adherence to natural law. Race pride was key to ensuring observance. Du Bois cautioned that no race that had ever made its mark had done so while wishing it were something else. Race men had to be vigilant in fanning the flames of "race spirit."[116]

The role of race identity in fostering progress was twofold. It was a tool for elevating Negroes, and it promised to redirect the race. Both Crummell and Du Bois saw it as an engine of moral reform. Crummell believed reform initiatives undertaken by colored men "as colored men" were essential. "The whole of our future on this soil," he admonished, hinged on race conscious initiatives that would build character and foster moral and intellectual advancement. Race identity was essential to "moral and mental reconstruction" needed to fulfill the Negro's destiny.[117] Du Bois was similarly keen on reform, identifying it as paramount for the ANA. Initially, this would be a task of remediation to eradicate the lingering "immorality, crime, and laziness" that were legacies of slavery. This undertaking required collective action premised on a shared identity and a sense of mutual obligations. It called for "race solidarity," which, Du Bois maintained, was a tighter bond than the unity required for protest. Like Washington, he was convinced that moral reform was more valuable in the post-Reconstruction era than campaigns for rights. Collective "self-reformation," he concluded, would garner "more credit and benefit" for the race than "a thousand . . . Civil Rights bills."[118]

Mutual appreciation for the moral virtues of promoting race identity did not translate into a shared conception of the future. Generational differences were evident in the divergent ways Crummell and Du Bois situated race in their respective visions of progress. They held competing interpretations of how the ideal of a common humanity would be realized. Despite his assertions about the divine character of race, Crummell harbored misgivings that made race-conscious reform a provisional imperative for changing the meanings of blackness. He believed the moral elevation Negroes achieved through separate reform efforts would compel others to see them as equals. Blackness would thus no longer signify inferiority or difference. This achievement would erode hierarchies built and sustained through race practices and thereby destroy caste. His logic mirrored the bargain White abolitionists attempted to strike with antebellum reformers when they promised to reward Black elevation with color-blindness. Crummell expanded the idea. Moral improvement among Negroes would make White Americans "forget all the facts and theories of race," he declared. Accordingly, it would annihilate "all race distinctions."[119] A society free of racial stratification and differences would realize his dream of progress.

Race consciousness was embedded in the ideal of "human brotherhood" Du Bois sought to realize. His aim in espousing race as a site of identity was to give people assigned to the Negro category power over its meaning. He believed, with Crummell, that their experiences and ideas could become a basis for reinterpreting what it meant to be a Negro. The parallel between the two projects ended here. Du Bois did not follow Crummell's lead in equating new meanings with the end of race divisions in this world. Having imbued the distinctions with spiritual and psychological import, he made race categories loci of shared identity and culture. This reconfiguration aimed to give race greater significance. As a "unifying ideal," race represented his hope for solidarity that would foster the talents Negroes could contribute to American civilization. A new appreciation of the gifts of each race created would promote brotherhood.[120]

Du Bois presented race as congruent with the unity of the human species. His credo thus embraced a popular reform doctrine of oneness, but he modified it with a reference to races instead of nations. It simultaneously affirmed friendship among races and race pride.

> I BELIEVE in God who made of one blood all races that dwell on earth. I believe that all men, black and brown and white, are brothers, varying, through Time and Opportunity, in form and gift and feature, but differing in no essential particular, and alike in soul and in the possibility of infinite development. . . . I believe in pride of race.[121]

Given this stance, how did Du Bois contend with assumptions about race difference that plagued the older generation of reformers and now shaped Jim Crow? Like antebellum reformers who distinguished their race practices from the discriminatory intent of legislatures that upheld caste categories, he appealed to differences in logic and purpose. His "Marriage Credo," which confronted laws restricting interracial marriage, offered opponents of amalgamation practical warrants for ending Jim Crow separation without lodging a categorical assault on race distinctions. It underscored the incongruity of assailing distinctions and stratification while invoking race in the name of collective advancement, thus abandoning the imperative of a wholesale attack on race. He confessed that neither science nor revelation offered compelling bases for legislating "race purity." Ancient and recent history demonstrated that "race blending" could have advantageous outcomes. Egyptians, British peoples, Alexander Pushkin, and Frederick Douglass were proof; he may well have included himself. Judgments about interracial unions thus had to rest on situational factors. Sanctions against such marriages were appropriate when their purpose was to uphold morality, protect the "transmission of culture," and facilitate the development of a group's ideals. In other words, practices intended to foster collective race identity complemented his reform project and were valid. In contrast, objectionable race restrictions on "sacredly personal" choices sought to inscribe permanent social differences and halted the march to brotherhood. Such practices were indefensible, he argued, because they intended to separate people into hermetically sealed quarters and arbitrarily limit attachments.[122]

Du Bois's commitments guided him from contingent bases of judging racial practices to alternative ways of preserving races. He posited that elevation and the freedom to associate "without artificial stimulus or attempted segregation" would somehow secure "the integrity and individuality" of the

272 RELUCTANT RACE MEN

world's races. Such conditions would inexplicably enable them to endure. Each group would thus be able to devote its energies to refining its distinctive ideals.[123] Like Crummell, he imagined a time beyond the existence of races. The creed he proposed for the ANA admonished Negroes to nurture their identity as a race until "human brotherhood" became a realistic possibility. The unity of the species created the potential for this outcome. However, it lay in a distant future. In his vague postmillennial vision, the cultivation of race identity and solidarity culminated in a civilization reflecting the ideals of all races. It would bring about "that 'one far off Divine event'"—the millennium, when "the perfection of human life" would finally be realized.[124]

"The Comet," a short story in Du Bois's 1920 collection, *Darkwater: Voices from within the Veil*, illustrates the impossibility of realizing personhood without races in the course of human history. A poor Black man and a rich White woman at the center of the tale glimpse life without the idea of different races when they survive destruction caused by a comet they believe has killed everyone else in the world. As they navigate the ruins of New York City thinking that they are the only people alive, the woman perceives the man as "very human." She has a flash of insight about the fallacy of races that defined life before the catastrophe and muses, "How foolish our human distinctions seem—now." The man agrees, adding, "I was not—human, yesterday." The comet created a utopian moment, enabling the characters to abandon conventional notions of difference and rank. Ennobled by a "race-ship" that allows her to recognize a shared humanity, the woman is poised to undertake the work of building the world anew. She gains a new sense of self that renders her "neither high nor low, white nor black, rich nor poor. She was primal woman; mighty mother of all men to come." An acute awareness of the "vigorous manhood" of her fellow survivor leads her to transform his identity as well. He is "no longer a thing apart, a creature below, a strange outcast of another clime and blood, but her Brother Humanity incarnate . . . All-Father of the race to be."[125]

Reality intrudes before the pair can act out new identities and begin the work of repopulating the earth. A crowd finds them and Jim Crow relations promptly resume. Some White men in the group are intent on lynching the "nigger," assuming he made sexual advances toward a White woman. Her explanation that he was her rescuer quiets them. Nevertheless, as she awkwardly departs with her lover and the grateful father, the man has ceased to her "Brother.". His miraculous reunion with his wife, who inexplicably escaped Harlem's destruction, brings the tale to a dismal close. Although her survival is cause for tears of joy, they embrace with their dead infant in her arms—perhaps a symbol of foreclosed possibilities.

Although the Negro Academy billed itself as an intellectual vanguard of reform, the sense that race consciousness and pride were necessary to progress became increasingly common in the post-Reconstruction era. The expansion of Jim Crow helped explain their importance. A Louisiana correspondent to the *Christian Recorder*, one Reverend J. E. Iford, suggested that Negroes had no choice: "If the color-line is not wiped out, what must the negro do, he is here and can't leave just now? I answer, let the negro come out and stand upon the golden platform of race pride as does the white man."[126] Reverend Samuel Barrett echoed this sentiment while bemoaning the persistence of "different races and classes" in a supposedly democratic nation. He urged leaders to heed the inescapable fact that Afro-Americans comprised "a distinct class" and promote "race pride" as the only sound route to advancement.[127] Fearful that Negroes were being "unraced" by people intent on trying to "get away from the race," Hiram Archer, president of the African Methodist Payne University, placed the development of "race pride" among the chief virtues of Negro Christian colleges. In contrast to secular schools that trained students primarily for material gain, their focus helped the Negro "get acquainted with himself" and his "Christian manhood."[128] Promoters of race pride set aside the misgivings of Isaiah Wears and others, who continued to worry that the enterprise detracted from individual development needed to navigate the modern world. John Cromwell explained the situation to a Bethel Literary and Historical Association audience. "The material defect in the individual development theory is that the white people will not let you get rid of the idea of race. Attempt to follow out the theory of ignoring racial affinity and the restrictions of society . . . act as a constant reminder."[129] Cultivating pride was necessary and held out the promise of strengthening Black people's capacity to confront and transcend discrimination.

———

The drive for group consciousness broadened conceptions of race practices. Reformers increasingly invoked race designations to promote a sense of commonality among Americans of African descent. Visions of a new generation of reformers increased possibilities for race to become a positive feature of American citizenship, disentangled from stratification, subjugation, exclusion, discrimination, and emigration. This prospect promised to foster claims to being a race that did not reinscribe caste or cede claims to

American citizenship. Nevertheless, the conventions of opposing race did not suddenly vanish. At the close of the century, efforts to configure race practices that could foster a proud collective identity among Black people developed alongside ongoing condemnations of stratification and questions about the logic of racial classifications for citizens.

7

"The Whole Question of Race"

Jim Crow and the Problem of Consciousness

As Booker T. Washington's platform of accommodating civil and political inequality gained prominence, a group of Louisiana reformers prepared to dispute the legality of Jim Crow racial divisions. Twenty men—members of the Citizens' Committee to Test the Constitutionality of the Separate Car Law—organized to end segregated rail transportation. They took aim at Louisiana's Railway Accommodations Act, which required companies operating trains within the state to provide "equal but separate accommodations for the white and colored races."[1] Their initiative began in 1890, spearheaded by lawyers Louis Martinet and Rodolphe Desdunes, co-editors of the New Orleans *Crusader*, a daily that gave the committee its public voice. During legislative debates, the group condemned the bill as "Class Legislation" that was "unconstitutional, un-American, unjust, dangerous and against sound public policy."[2] Once Act 111 became law, proposals for a rail boycott failed—an outcome Martinet attributed to a popular misconception that the Supreme Court legalized discrimination when it dismantled the 1875 Civil Rights Act. He was convinced that opponents of equality circulated a lie to thwart Black progress. Refusing to give up, the committee launched a legal challenge to the statute in 1892. It lost and, on appeal, faced defeat again. In 1896, seven months after Washington delivered his "Atlanta Compromise" speech, the group's final appeal, *Plessy v. Ferguson*, appeared on the Supreme Court's spring calendar.[3]

Challenging race distinctions was critical to the strategy of the *Plessy* case. The endeavor relied on a long-standing reform claim that the nation's illogical racial taxonomy sustained a caste structure that conferred unwarranted privilege upon some individuals while wrongfully condemning others to subjection. Martinet complained that Act 111 used illegitimate criteria—"ethnical origins of color"—to circumscribe the rights of citizens.[4] This reasoning guided Albion Tourgée's approach in representing Homer Plessy, the Citizens' Committee member who volunteered to be arrested for

Reluctant Race Men. Joan L. Bryant, Oxford University Press. © Oxford University Press 2024.
DOI: 10.1093/oso/9780195312966.003.0008

violating the Separate Car Act by sitting in a rail car designated for White people. Two of the case's central claims targeted race. One assailed the logic of race assignment. Tourgée insisted that the law violated Plessy's Fourteenth Amendment right not to be deprived of property without due process. In barring him from the car reserved for White people, Louisiana refused to recognize seven-eighths of his ancestry, thereby denying his legitimate claim to whiteness. The statute was unjust because the racial classification rules on which it rested were illogical and erroneous; they did not accurately reflect the facts of his lineage. The related argument addressed historical functions of racial nomenclature. Tourgée asserted that Act 111 hinged on a classification scheme that violated the Thirteenth Amendment's slavery prohibition. Distinguishing people as Negroes had helped maintain a slave-eligible population. It followed that the state's requirement to sort individuals in rail cars "on the line of race" aimed to "perpetuate the caste distinctions on which slavery rested." Affirmation came from Justice John Harlan, the lone dissenter in the court's decision to reject Plessy's claims. He declared that "the arbitrary separation of citizens" mandated by the Separate Car Act imposed "a badge of servitude wholly inconsistent with the civil freedom . . . established by the Constitution."[5]

Plessy's defeat in the Supreme Court is emblematic of the political climate shaping African American reform efforts at the turn of the century. The judgment that the constitution sanctioned "separate but equal" facilities was consistent with broader post-Reconstruction reversals and symptomatic of a flourishing Jim Crow regime. Still, writer and lawyer Charles Chesnutt found the decision "epoch-making" for intensifying the institutionalization of "racial caste." The court stabbed rights to death, he argued, and tossed the bloody corpse at the feet of "the comprehensive Negro," which included people with "black, brown, yellow, and white" complexions.[6] Citizens' Committee leaders viewed the result as proof of national indifference to justice. Rodolphe Desdunes lamented that the seeming boundlessness of Jim Crow oppression overwhelmed him and his colleagues. They believed it would be useless and perhaps perilous to continue their activism. Disheartened and fearful, the group ended protests against segregated rail cars. It also abandoned campaigns against anti-miscegenation laws, jury exclusion, and segregated churches and shut down the *Crusader*'s printing press.[7]

Although the outcome of the case was consistent with broader political developments, the race challenges that framed it were out of sync with increasingly popular platforms for social change. As the Citizens' Committee disbanded, proponents of Booker T. Washington's program quickly assumed leadership positions in New Orleans reform networks and relegated protest to the sidelines.[8] An expanding push for race consciousness signaled further shifts in the orientation of activism. W. E. B. Du Bois issued no public comment when the court rendered the *Plessy* decision several days after his wedding. A year later, he specifically excluded Citizens' Committee concerns from the priorities outlined in his inaugural American Negro Academy address. He admonished that Negroes must sometimes look beyond such "pressing, but smaller" issues as segregated rail cars to develop a philosophical outlook on "the whole question of race."[9]

The competing reform currents surrounding *Plessy* hint at the complexity of interrogating race practices in an era marked by Jim Crow. Discriminatory cultural, economic, intellectual, political, and social developments nurtured ongoing attacks on constructions of human difference, sameness, and hierarchy. Efforts to make race a site of collective consciousness created an additional impetus to probe the logic and utility of racial categories. The queries were familiar. To what extent did espousing race classifications affirm false notions of innate difference and sameness? What were the ethics of structuring group identities with categories denoting physical likeness? What was the appropriate nomenclature for referencing discrete collective identities among American citizens? Race men had to contend with such concerns in trying to develop a discourse that would enable Black individuals to function as a people on terms they defined. Jim Crow made it clear to reformers of all persuasions that freedom and citizenship were not enough to place Black Americans on common ground or equal footing with White people. This cluttered landscape made it impossible to draw a clear line between race men and race critics. It complicated efforts to map group progress and transform conceptions of race at the dawn of the twentieth century.

———

Although Du Bois dismissed misgivings about race as he highlighted the necessity of consciousness, reformers in the American Negro Academy played leading roles in contesting the construct. Jim Crow injustices made it untenable to simply abandon the tradition. ANA organizers William Crogman and Alexander Crummell questioned the need to continue the practice because they believed polygenist theories were passé. Their cofounder, Richard Wright Sr. agreed that legitimate scientists disproved claims that Negroes

278   RELUCTANT RACE MEN

were a distinct and innately inferior species; however, he, Du Bois, and others considered it essential to refute such ideas as long as they remained prevalent. Accordingly, attacks on the scientific validity of race persisted.[10]

An 1896 study, *Race Traits and Tendencies of the American Negro*, was a conspicuous example of the enduring cachet of race science. It was the work of Frederick Hoffman, a self-taught statistician for the Prudential Insurance Company of America. His undertaking demonstrated that, even if polygenesis no longer defined research agendas of the most respected scholars, its claims and aims still captured American imaginations. Practitioners in the natural sciences and the developing social sciences, clerics, politicians, and self-styled public intellectuals like Hoffman kept polygenist notions alive.[11]

As the subject of the ANA's first published essay, Hoffman's study helped divert attention away from the race consciousness that Crummell and Du Bois placed at the forefront of the organization's agenda. Issues they hoped to transcend—problems of misrepresentation and discrimination—were features at the inaugural meeting alongside Du Bois's address on race preservation. The critique of Hoffman thus launched the organization's twenty-one Occasional Papers, followed by Du Bois's treatise. Kelly Miller, who earned a doctorate in mathematics at Howard University after abandoning graduate study at Johns Hopkins, delivered the assessment of Hoffman. His lengthy critique came on the heels of a shorter review Du Bois published in *Annals of the American Academy of Political and Social Sciences*.[12]

Hoffman's theme was not new. It addressed a recurring topic of the Negro's approaching demise. Theophilus Steward wearily reported that the issue surfaced periodically with "a great wail" alongside denunciations of Negro shiftlessness. He encountered it in religious and medical garb when southerners sounded alarms about Negroes' "tendency" for immorality and "disposition" toward consumption. His response to ominous scenarios of southern urban life was the simple observation that Negroes were not becoming extinct. High urban death rates failed to prove immorality or predict imminent death. Taking clues from antebellum environmentalists, he explained that these outcomes reflected the dire circumstances of former slaves who began their lives as free people "with nothing."[13] Anecdotal evidence, such as achievements of Black students at Ivy League colleges and of Black soldiers he observed in his work as a chaplain with the Twenty-Fifth US Colored Infantry, showed Negroes making decisive advances. Furthermore, Haitians demonstrated that Negroes, as such, were not doomed to death by urban life. Having briefly lived in Haiti on an aborted missionary assignment, Steward conjectured that conditions in the Haitian capital of Port au Prince were undoubtedly less favorable than Charleston's environment. Nevertheless, the island nation's population had doubled in the two previous decades. In contrast, consumption was rampant in Charleston and Savannah, where White authorities were responsible for public health conditions. The lesson was clear: as Negroes progressed, they were better able to secure their own welfare.[14]

Hoffman's methods called for scrutinizing the question of mortality. Du Bois and Miller both viewed his study as a pivotal development because it offered a statistical analysis of the "Negro Question." Miller considered it the most significant commentary on the matter since *Uncle Tom's Cabin* and predicted that it would inspire further interest in precise scientific inquiry.[15] Although historian George Frederickson defines Hoffman as an exemplar of "racial Darwinism," the insurance study displays both evolutionist and polygenist assumptions. As George Stocking argues in his analysis of anthropology history, Hoffman's social and biological speculations about Negroes and mulattoes rest on polygeny. It is difficult to miss the book's ideological underpinnings. Faced with stark disparities between Hoffman's data and arguments, Miller surmised at the start that "*a priori* considerations" were the guiding force behind the author's claims. The data were part of a poor attempt to justify an established position. Nevertheless, he and Du Bois carefully analyzed Hoffman's methods and evidence to assess the validity of his conclusion that race traits doomed Negroes to extinction.[16]

Defective methods riddled the study. Du Bois and Miller focused on problems with the urban death rates Hoffman used from the 1890 census. Du Bois pointed out that, according to Hoffman's figures, urban Negroes in the South comprised no more than 11 percent of the total Negro population, and 75 percent of all Negroes lived outside of large cities. Hoffman thus needed to explain how he could draw conclusions about an entire population using data that reflected the unique social conditions of only a small segment. Miller tried to demonstrate that location mattered by citing a report on the prior census stressing wide differences in Black mortality rates for rural and urban populations due to the "evils and vices of civilization."[17] Hoffman also failed to interpret Black urban death rates in the context of death rates for total urban populations. Miller observed that Hoffman's data showed that White urban death rates before 1890 exceeded Black mortality rates. Such details exposed the limitations of using only recent and isolated death rates to argue that race traits foretold the Negro's extinction. Furthermore,

280 RELUCTANT RACE MEN

they highlighted the problem of ignoring how class and living conditions impinged on the quality and duration of people's lives. Hoffman rejected the explanatory power of such contingent factors. "It is not in the *conditions of life*," he asserted, "but in the *race traits and tendencies* that we find the causes of the excessive mortality."[18] Living conditions mattered only to the extent that they mirrored the "immense amount of immorality" among Negroes; this, Hoffman argued, was "the root of the evil." It was a "race trait." Both reviewers seized upon this claim to underscore Hoffman's faulty logic. Du Bois called on Hoffman to explain how and why race traits took effect only after 1880. What explained a century of apparent dormancy? Moreover, assuming that one could legitimately attribute a population's death rates to race traits, the reviewers noted that 1880 death rates among Black urban dwellers were comparable to and sometimes lower than rates for cities in Germany, from which Hoffman had migrated. Miller asked, "If race traits are playing such havoc with Negroes in America, what direful agent of death . . . is at work in the cities of his own fatherland?" He similarly countered the charge that degradation in southern "black belts" doomed the race to death by asking whether documented "depravity" among poor White Appalachians was also a race trait.[19]

The familiar charge of Black mental inferiority pushed Miller to confront race science. He added his voice to attacks on the idea that facial angle and cranial capacity indicated superior intelligence among White people and mulattoes. His effort to repudiate this claim reflects the challenge of sorting through the din of the era's race discourse. First, he sought support from Columbia University economist William Ripley. Craniometry helped Ripley identify "primitive types" whose hereditary transmission of traits established their status as "true" races. According to George Stocking, Ripley's ideas sustained American polygeny at the turn of the century despite his avowed evolutionism. Nevertheless, Miller saw utility in Ripley's report that head measurements captured "merely race" rather than mental capacity. The conclusion guided his criticism of Hoffman's hierarchy of intelligence without compromising the ANA goal of developing a distinctive Black race identity. Claims about human difference were perhaps less pressing than arguments about innate rank. For the moment, he apparently felt free to ignore Ripley's attempts to prove the existence of essential race types.[20]

In theory, the alleged mental inferiority of Negroes was not an essential part of Hoffman's undertaking because his employers, who commissioned the study, had other concerns. Hoffman rose to prominence in the 1890s amid insurance industry struggles against state anti-discrimination laws that prohibited companies from providing Black policyholders with fewer benefits than White customers received for the same price. Prudential hired him to help fight these laws based on his previously published predictions about the Negro's extinction. His new task was to do more of the same. The study aimed to demonstrate that a Black/White insurance premium differential was an actuarial decision instead of a concession to Jim Crow etiquette of bigotry.[21]

This agenda minimized the significance of claims about Negro mental capacity. Hoffman downplayed his evidence that the brains of soldiers deemed half or three-fourths White were heavier than brains of "pure" Negroes. As a presumed indicator of higher intelligence, this measure purported to reflect a tendency for contact between "lower" and "superior" races to affect such "ornamental" traits as heel shape and facial angle. However, a superficial resemblance to White people did not compensate for damage to physical and moral characteristics needed for survival. Having devolved into a "hopelessly mixed" people, Negroes occupied a position inferior to "the pure black" person, deemed a rarity in America. The "infusion of white blood" was thus, for Hoffman, the primary barrier to Negro progress. It was the single most important factor in explaining the population's "excessive and increasing" death rate and its social inferiority. The calamitous results supposedly manifested themselves in widespread syphilis, scrofula, consumption, and low birth rates, proving that mixing between the White and Negro races violated "natural law." More importantly, they showcased factors that justified making distinctions in insurance policies. Although the harm was allegedly irreversible, Hoffman prescribed "race purity" to fortify Negroes for life's ongoing struggles.[22]

Du Bois's conviction that conserving races was a necessary element of advancement tempered the assault on Hoffman's claims about "mixture." He and Miller were understandably mute about his premise, as criticism might raise questions about the logic of ANA objectives. Yet concurring with Hoffman's call for purity might appear to sanction his conception of human difference. Du Bois was silent about the commentary on Black progress. Miller observed only that further scientific inquiry might clarify the true physical and moral effects of amalgamation.[23]

282 RELUCTANT RACE MEN

The Hoffman critique was the only ANA publication dedicated to polygenist notions of difference. However, individual academy members and recruits created other venues and opportunities to attack race practices. Their voices contributed to broad interrogations of the science of race, the logical and ethical bases of racial identity, race integrity and notions of sameness, and the meanings of race names. Their inquiries, along with the thriving regime of Jim Crow, placed efforts to cultivate race consciousness on a complicated and unstable terrain.

With zeal, Benjamin Tucker Tanner continued his campaign of questioning the logic and ethics of race. His conceptions of humanity were not conducive to the agenda of promoting race consciousness and pride. As plans for the ANA took shape, he reflected on what Frederick Douglass's life and death revealed about race in a short book, *The Color of Solomon—What?* On its face, the monograph celebrated Negro achievement. He had grown weary of the monopoly White people presumed to hold on greatness. In his mind, assertions that dark-skinned, crispy-haired Egyptians were White exemplified the blithe manner in which scientists distorted facts. Biblical scholars were similarly guilty. A new translation of the Bible rendered the wise King Solomon "white and ruddy." Tanner set out to dismantle the argument using ethnological, philological, genealogical, and exegetical analyses that led him to conclude that Solomon likely possessed tan skin and very curly hair, evidence of "Semitic and Hamitic extraction." There was nothing to suggest descent from Noah's son Japheth, commonly linked to European peoples. In short, Solomon was not White.[24]

Tanner's concerns suggest an interest in promoting race pride to disrupt the homage to whiteness. Indeed, the volume's dedication explains that he sought to "vindicate the colored races of the earth and save them from the delusion: 'The leading race in all history has been the white race.'"[25] Praise for Frederick Douglass's accomplishments as a man of color was a fitting component of this undertaking. The mutual respect the men developed after years of conflict would have made such an addition apropos. However, Tanner marked the loss of his colleague by bemoaning race practices. He was angry and disheartened by the ways that whiteness seemed to grant automatic access to political, economic, social, and religious opportunities. Douglass was a prime example of the extent to which it outweighed the worth of manhood, scruples, and intellect. An editorial excerpted from a Philadelphia newspaper illustrated his point. The unidentified writer speculated about the honors Douglass likely would have attained had he lived in any other civilized nation in the world. Knighthood in England and election to the French Academy were among the imagined possibilities. Whatever the case, it was certain that Douglass would not have been fettered by Jim Crow mores that circumscribed Negro life in America.[26]

Tanner's quarrel with race pressed beyond discrimination to confront classifications. In a sarcastic commentary on his quest for Solomon's color, he ventured that a thousand or even ten thousand years hence, there would be no ambiguity about the race or color of any significant figure of any class in America. Only here, he observed, was a person's color "a subject worthy of consideration." Douglass's death illuminated the national obsession. To Tanner's disgust, secular and religious news outlets took pains to identify Douglass as "the 'mulatto'" or as "colored." This labeling tradition stood in sharp contrast to practices he observed in the ancient world. Pagans, he argued, appreciated achievement without feeling a need to tag it with color designations or references to mixture. He doubted whether their vocabulary included such terms as "Mulatto, . . . Quarteroon, or Quinteroon, or Octoroon"—modern inventions to reference blending of "the common blood of the common race."[27]

There was ultimately little to celebrate in Solomon's status as a man of color. Tanner disparaged "race pride" because it fueled unfounded claims to all things great and blinded White people to the inherent worth of all human beings. His investigation ridiculed the preoccupation with color for its ties to a more fundamental problem. Claims to Solomon's whiteness went hand in hand with theological questions about the place of Negroes in biblical history. Just as White Christian clerics had used scripture to abet slavery, his contemporaries could be relied on to "practice caste." An 1891 letter from the unchurched Douglass substantiated this judgment. American Christianity was wholly unlike the "Christianity of Christ," Douglass had observed. It was the "man-degrading and Negro-hating" brand. Tanner unearthed its roots in alliances between White theologians and pseudoscience that denied the unity of the human race. The connection reared its head when editors of an MEC Sunday school publication speculated that Negroes were not descendants of Ham. This doubt was tantamount to banishing people of African descent "beyond the pale of a common humanity."[28] William Scarborough's introduction to the volume tied the sentiment directly to polygenesis and denounced the pre-Adamite theory that relegated Negroes to a non-biblical creation. The proposition was contrary to Christian teachings about human origins.

Tanner revisited the question of Hamitic lineage in his treatise *The Descent of the Negro*, the first pamphlet in a series planned by the AME Publishing House to feature the best of its writers. He used the occasion to interrogate fellow Methodists' skepticism about the Negro's place in biblical renderings of humanity. The conclusion of his argumentative and sardonic analysis was unsurprising. "Is Europe Japhetic? Is Asia Shemitic? Then Africa is Hamitic." The Bible attested to this genealogy, and philology confirmed it. Individuals who rejected Negroes' Hamitic origins and rendered Negroes "Pre-Adamites" betrayed polygenist ideas. The stakes of such claims within religious circles were high for Tanner. Referencing the most prominent Methodist purveyor of the theory, Alexander Winchell, Syracuse University's first chancellor, he called on younger men to contest his charges of innate Negro inferiority. He took aim at Winchell's "infidel pen," which dismissed the Bible's authority in establishing the foundations of human relations. The proposition that its account of human history did not include Negroes implied that alternative conceptions of humanity were valid. It diminished the applicability of the biblical narrative in favor of a theory that had lost its cachet even among respected scientists. Only the Bible, Tanner argued, explained human origins and "the rise of races." Christians who questioned and disregarded its status were not fit arbiters of truth.[29]

Polygenist assumptions in popular culture provoked the same ire and sarcasm found in religious circles. Thomas Dixon's tirade about Black inferiority and amalgamation in *The Leopard's Spots* was a noteworthy case. It elicited a twenty-one page rejoinder from Kelly Miller. The novel was the first part of the pro–Ku Klux Klan trilogy that inspired D. W. Griffith's *Birth of a Nation*. The tale's degrading images of Negroes tapped into White fears about equal rights. Such a scenario, it argued, would lead to dangerous mixing between "two antagonistic races."[30] Miller used his response to belittle the logic behind Dixon's amalgamation talk and his assault on Black capacity. He looked beneath the former Baptist preacher's anxieties, hatred, and disparagement to expose false accounts of the human species. Rants against amalgamation had come rather late, given estimates that approximately 60 percent of the Negro population had White ancestry. The mere existence of the group undermined assumptions about purportedly natural race barriers. Intermingling had been so extensive that Afro-Americans, as Miller preferred to call them, barely counted as Negroes. He assured Dixon that they harbored no fantasies about sex and marriage with White people. As beings with human qualities, their consensual interracial relationships were consistent with the laws of nature.

"THE WHOLE QUESTION OF RACE" 285

The social climate indicated that a wholesale "blending of the races" was an unlikely probability at that moment.[31] Nevertheless, the unity of the species made it a future possibility. He could not fathom how various populations of the human family could live together without mingling.

Dixon's enterprise appeared to be little more than a feeble attempt to revive the pro-slavery science of the American School that, Miller believed, had lost all credibility. Enlightened individuals rejected the idea that the size and shape of Negroes' heads limited their intelligence and made them incapable of civilization. They found no credibility in the idea that racial taxonomies mirrored variations in intellectual capacity. Miller drove home the point that, even apart from its noxious bigotry, Dixon's project rested on incoherent foundations. It was impossible to conceive of a single coherent classification that could accurately encompass all White people and exclude all Negroes.[32]

An unshakable repugnance toward claims of species difference fueled Theophilus Steward's quest for evidence to challenge the idea in all its forms. In 1897, while serving as an army chaplain, he reported the latest military statistics to repudiate fallacies about Negroes' propensity for disease and death. Eight years earlier, the US Army's surgeon general had reported higher rates of illness and death among colored troops than their White counterparts showed under similar conditions. Officials interpreted this finding as proof that Negroes possessed a "race proclivity to disease and death." Long-term data undermined this conclusion, however. *Christian Recorder* editor Henry T. Johnson declared that Steward's information fully refuted the claim that "constitutional inferiority" doomed Afro-Americans to elevated morbidity and mortality rates. Steward delighted in observing that, over the course of a decade, colored and White troops experienced comparable rates of illness, disability, and death. The data effectively disposed of "the 'proclivity' assumption."[33]

The army's report supplemented Steward's own evidence. His desire to demonstrate that there was no physical basis for dividing humans into discrete races led him to explore whether there were significant variations in the range of shoe sizes supplied to Black regiments and to White units. His request for data from the US Quartermaster General indicated that he needed them for "scientific purposes."[34] The response that there was no difference in shoes for colored and White troops was surely no surprise to a man who refused to accept the "color line" as a reflection of physical phenomena. He understood that the race purity the line purported to guard did not exist. The one-drop rule was proof. It showed that the construction and maintenance

286 RELUCTANT RACE MEN

of racial distinctions depended on Negroes being "kicked, cuffed, and shot out of the white race," regardless of the White ancestry many of them possessed.[35] He relished this outcome and predicted doom for those who policed racial distinctions to uphold whiteness as he imagined a future when it would be safer to be on the darker side of the fictional color boundary.

Scholarly speculations about mulatto mortality elicited a similarly caustic response. Steward found the views of Harvard geologist Nathaniel Southgate Shaler especially irksome. This teacher of Du Bois and protégé of Louis Agassiz argued that each race possessed distinctive traits that were nearly primordial. Shaler shared Hoffman's judgment that a union between a Negro and a White person produced physically compromised offspring. Evidence allegedly showed such people to be deficient in vitality and character; Shaler cited physicians who attested to the rarity of mulatto survival beyond age fifty. During Reconstruction, he ventured that the "mixed race" would probably die out in freedom. He continued to caution against "kinship in blood" while affirming the legitimacy of civil equality. The strictures of nature, as he understood them, imposed an obligation upon both races to avoid such interactions. Steward countered this position with proof, supplying a list of mulattoes as old as age seventy to disprove the conclusion that they invariably died young.[36]

Claims about race difference riled Steward until the end of his life. More than thirty years after his encounter with Shaler, he chastised another Harvard scholar for relying on his views. William McDougall, who cited Shaler in his book *Is America Safe for Democracy?*, alleged that mulattoes were mentally superior to "pure" Negroes. A psychologist who explored heredity and eugenics, he repeated Shaler's assertion that, with one unnamed exception, American Negroes who possessed any significant capabilities demonstrated the intellectual benefits of White ancestry. Steward prefaced his criticism by identifying himself as a colored man who traced his "mixed" lineage over the course of five generations. He boasted of two sons who graduated from Harvard. He was proud of the heritage that he and his brother documented in the 1913 history of their southern New Jersey community of Gouldtown. Nevertheless, he resented Shaler's presumption that his African ancestry diminished his mental ability and ridiculed the dissemination of dubious conjectures as knowledge. He observed that facts had ruled against Shaler in 1891 and asked derisively, "Are they with him now?"[37]

Global developments in the early years of the twentieth century inspired hope in future progress. Steward discerned flourishing civilizations displaying rapid scientific, social, and technological changes and governments that increasingly seemed to function on behalf of their populations. He perceived a growing spiritual awareness of a "common race with common rights" that affirmed human "oneness." International endeavors, such as the 1911 London conference to promote accord among races and growing interest in using Esperanto as a universal language, were concrete signs of advancement. Yet this rudimentary change tempered his enthusiasm. It suggested that Americans were indeed destined for unity, but formidable forces that impinged on human freedom hindered this outcome. Gender inequality was a chief obstacle. Although he had called for excluding women from the ANA, his observation echoed an unsuccessful campaign early in his ministerial career for women's voting in AME Church affairs. The influence of his recently deceased second wife, Susan McKinney, the first Black woman physician in New York, might have also informed his stance. Whatever the impetus, the widowed Wilberforce University instructor insisted on equal social and political rights for women and denounced their sexual commodification. Although women's suffrage was expanding, a second impediment was more intractable. As he had argued more than three decades earlier, the founders who restricted their vision of human rights to White men had made race an American trait. Because the fallacy of race was embedded in the nation's foundations, he did not believe piecemeal legislative measures could uproot it and yield justice. Extinguishing the hate at the core of this "obsolete Americanism" required people to act on conscience. They had to establish "HUMAN rights" by replacing race practices with respect, sympathy, and a broadening of hearts that united Americans into a cohesive family.[38] With the eyes of a cleric, he saw that this outcome could be realized only through divine intervention.

The surge of lynching intensified Steward's sense of urgency about eradicating American race practices. The phenomenon graphically illustrated the "false base" on which the society operated. It exhibited the alignment of racial notions of hierarchy and the structure of terror. He decried outlandish ideas that gave the erroneously named "white race" license to perpetuate a dangerous scam of superiority. By restricting the membership of citizens, he argued, the "night-mare" of race excluded Negroes from everything that "Americanism and American people" should encompass.[39] It facilitated the dehumanization of Black lives, making them vulnerable to mob violence. The charged situation led Steward to revisit the predicament he presented in the wake of Reconstruction's collapse. In 1883, he postulated

288 RELUCTANT RACE MEN

that the republic could not thrive unless it modified its conception of race to correspond to the Constitution's parameters of citizenship. Lynching demonstrated that, despite Black people's legal standing, the founders' race-ship of color continued to hold sway, upholding whiteness as the basis of political and social belonging. Justice John Harlan illustrated this scenario when he justified barring members of "the Chinese race" from citizenship on the grounds that they were "so different" from "white citizens."[40] Maintaining this racial landscape was not an option in the new century. Steward believed that, if the nation's conscience did not compel it to heed the anthropological fact and theological truth that "the human race is one," a revolution would ultimately force adherence. His certitude reflected the depth of his conviction that race practices violated the natural order. Such wrongs were not sustainable. Sanctioning them was tantamount to declaring that nature lied about what it meant to be human.[41]

The belief that Negroes had a vital equal role to play in American advancement laid the groundwork for Charles Roman's confrontation with race science. It framed his efforts to show that race was a defective mechanism for conceiving of human difference. Roman appeared to be better equipped for this task than most race critics. A physician trained at Meharry Medical College, he was a former president of the National Medical Association, a professional society for African American doctors, and editor of its journal. Yet his early twentieth-century treatise on progress echoed previous reform commentaries. He perceived the ongoing search for immutable differences in human bodies, ideas, and actions as nothing more than an attempt to legitimize a "doctrine of human inequality." The quest extended the long-standing problem of misrepresentation, which topped his list of the adversities that plagued Negroes. His project entailed assessing alleged differences in body parts and bodily functions to challenge ideas concerning race difference. He determined that skulls, facial angles, noses, genitals, ears, blood, skin, and hair offered no warrants for dividing and ranking people into races. Even the term "race," he concluded, was ill chosen because the differences it supposedly signified were not innate or fixed. They were "superficial, transitory, and environmental." Variations within the Negro population further defied the coherence of race classifications. Differences among Negroes were so extensive that they challenged the logic of classifying and treating them as a homogeneous entity. He noted further that features purportedly distinguishing any race became less distinct as people procreated with other populations. The long history of such activities meant "all races" were "crossed." This ordering of evidence issued a negative answer to the question of whether there were any "permanently inferior or superior races." It exposed flaws to discredit "the science of races." There were no scientific grounds for inequality. To the contrary, science validated Negroes' right to equal treatment as individual citizens because it identified the common traits shared by all "human varieties." It demonstrated the existence of one human species. He believed the country's founders affirmed this unity by creating a framework for equal citizenship and unfettered participation that had yet to be realized.[42]

The assumption that people assigned to a given race are fundamentally alike was a corollary of the idea that racial categories connote essential human differences. The truism that individuals comprising a race possess a common blood, embody a discrete type, and share fundamental sensibilities affirmed the alleged distinctiveness of races. Proponents of race integrity or "the fetish of Race Purity," as Charles Chesnutt dubbed it, aimed to preserve supposed sameness. He pilloried the popular initiative as "a modern invention of the white people to perpetuate the color line."[43] Bigots, reformers, and race men rallied to promote it.

Wilberforce University president William Scarborough, hailed as one of the era's most accomplished scholars, reviled the enterprise. There is "no such thing as 'Race Integrity,'" he charged and denounced the "abominable and intolerable stupid dogma" for spreading false ideas about the formation of races.[44] Malicious rhetoric and spurious arguments were obvious candidates for scorn. Thomas Dixon's racist diatribes made him an easy target. He headed a list of figures who trafficked in vitriolic speech, including such preachers of White supremacy as South Carolina senator Ben Tillman, Mississippi governor James Vardaman, and Georgia Populist Tom Watson. A Tulane University mathematician was, perhaps, a less obvious target. Yet William B. Smith also put himself squarely in the line of attack with his 1905 work, *The Color Line: A Brief on behalf of the Unborn*. The book served as a warning about the dangers future generations would face if Americans compromised "Caucasian race integrity." His reliance on the supposed fate of mulattoes to prove his point betrayed polygenist assumptions. The evidence, consisting of popular notions about hybridity, came from familiar sources. Physicians reportedly documented the overwhelming propensity for mulatto degeneracy, citing limited lung capacity and high rates of scrofula and tuberculosis

290 RELUCTANT RACE MEN

as signs of the constitutional weaknesses of "mixture." Observations from James McCune Smith's nemesis, Ephraim Squirer, and Steward's adversary, Nathaniel Shaler, linked the alleged constitutional frailty of mulattoes to death. Squirer's encyclopedia entry about Honduras referenced the rapid disappearance of its "mixed" Indian and Negro population. This development matched mortality data about "hybrids" throughout South America and Japan. Shaler's estimate of a sixty-year maximum lifespan suggested a pattern of mulatto death in the United States. The speculation that interracial marriage diminished fertility and happiness punctuated the claims. William Smith perhaps knew that his evidence was tenuous. He insisted that race integrity was necessary even if the premise that Negroes were "organically" inferior to Caucasians was wrong and mulattoes were not actually degenerate. Without decisive proof that Black and White populations are equal, he reasoned, even the "negrophilist" would have to admit the wisdom of strict separation.[45]

Other figures were more astute and less antagonistic. Like Negro race men, former Episcopal priest Edgar Gardner Murphy placed physical conceptions of race at the foundation of identity. According to social gospel historian Ralph Luker, Murphy promoted race integrity with "genteel American racism." His stance did not rule out humanitarian and just causes. For instance, he spearheaded an anti-lynching protest in Paris, Texas, after a mob tortured and burned rape and murder suspect Henry Smith before some ten thousand witnesses. Moreover, his account of the practical virtues of race integrity privileged Negro advancement and self-determination. He praised Negro efforts to promote race pride because it could play a pivotal role in sustaining racial separation. Discrimination and subjection undermined these endeavors, he reasoned, because "social differentiation" and opportunities for class mobility within the race were required to nurture pride. A race constantly forced to "go outside of itself" to experience the richness of life would be "perpetually tempted . . . to desert its own distinctive life." It was unreasonable to expect people to dedicate themselves to preserving a "race world" beset with deficiency and want. Negro race integrity thus necessitated "race sufficiency."[46]

An alternative perspective on White reformers' race purity agenda came from linguist William Pickens. The recent Yale University graduate teaching at Talladega College shared Murphy's insight that racial stratification was a barrier to Negro race integrity. It was logical for mulattoes to live as White people because doing so could lead to advantages. Yet he was unconvinced that simply expanding opportunities for Negroes would settle the issue. Such a program would have to be supplemented with new social and political conceptions of race categories—specifically, a change in the meaning of whiteness. Revision meant divesting it of the privilege that Homer Plessy and others understood they had lost by being designated "Negro." Putting the matter succinctly, Pickens advised, "Take the premium from white skin" and stop treating it as "capital."[47]

Calls for self-sufficiency resonated with established Black and White reformers. Indeed, the content and style of Murphy's message won praise from such diverse figures as Josiah Strong, Booker T. Washington, and Socialist Mary White Ovington, who would become a founder of the National Association for the Advancement of Colored People. Scarborough said nothing about Murphy, but he shared one of his goals. He preached "racial organization" and its potential to foster self-help. Such work assured internal development, which, he believed, was the only sound basis for growth.[48] The utility of collective action did not alter his judgments about race, however. It was common sense to this former Georgia slave for oppressed people to unite in order to develop themselves. Cooperation was all the more important as Negroes faced novel forms of brutality and discrimination, yet unity did not hinge on claims of an intrinsic sameness. Such an argument was baseless for any race.[49]

Scarborough directed his harshest accusations at bigots. He imagined that they would use the rhetoric of "race integrity" and "social equality" to harm Negroes to the point of annihilation. They seemed driven to such measures by the diverse appearance of Negroes, which was living testimony against the lie of White purity. His reference was surely to Dixon and others of his ilk. However, Murphy's views also qualified him for inclusion. Although he avoided malevolent speech, he shared Dixon's ideas about the supposed natural antipathy between races, declaring it a boon to his mission of separation.[50] Disparities between races gave urgency to Murphy's cause. He acknowledged that humans might have been similar in the past and might become equal in the future. Such conditions, however, did not alter his understanding of a present in which races were different and unequal in every way. The differences, which upheld his segregationist vision, were physical, premised on the idea that race was a biological fact that determined individual and collective realities. "The deepest thing about any man," he declared, "is his race."[51] Preserving it was critical, for it defined individual's humanity. Despite eschewing dire predictions of infertility and death from

292 RELUCTANT RACE MEN

amalgamation, he shared polygenists' aversion to the prospect and declared that he would prefer to witness the extermination of a race than to see its purity compromised.

The enmity that inspired race integrity campaigns perturbed Scarborough. However, charitable initiatives were no more acceptable. He prayed that Negroes would avoid all such endeavors, but he knew his plea was in vain. Reformers with diverse political agendas, from Booker T. Washington to new champions of Pan-Africanism, rallied under the banner of preserving "race individuality."[52] Du Bois sometimes appeared to perceive it as an end in itself, arguing that the destruction of Jim Crow was the only way to guarantee the maintenance of "race integrity . . . through race pride."[53] Scarborough had been a dissenter at the ANA's inaugural meeting and irked Alexander Crummell by questioning the viability of preserving race identity. It was disturbing for him to see his fellow reformers continuing to seek advancement on a path he believed led to hell. He was convinced that all proponents of race integrity imbibed and perpetuated the same defective ideas. They were trying to preserve something that "did not exist in the past, does not exist today, and cannot exist in the future."[54] Two lines of thought outlined the errors in thinking otherwise. The first was a traditional one cited by other race critics. The very idea of race purity, he observed, either ignored or misunderstood "the unity of the human race." It unwittingly accepted the premise that there were multiple "centers of creation," despite scientific research showing that all races were "identical in species."[55] The second argument was a novel extension of the first point. It challenged attempts to match discrete races to distinct regions, as if racial populations were autochthonous. In Scarborough's schema, the very existence of conventionally accepted races—the "so-called Mongolian," Negro, and White—depended on mixture. Races were, by definition, impure. They represented the effects of changing environments on the bodies of migrating peoples and the mixing that migrations occasioned among increasingly varied groups. He explained that, as "primitive" humans migrated out of their original location in Africa or Asia, environmental changes gave rise to populations that differed in "color, form, and language." Mingling among continuously moving and changing peoples culminated in the commonly recognized races. The processes that produced these outcomes were indistinct. It was impossible to reconstruct the logic and sequence of transformations and interactions. He imagined following such a trail. "On the route we are carried insensibly from center to extreme, not being able to mark the differences in the links of the chain that binds all these people into one. Everywhere neighboring races have blended. . . . No race is indigenous to the soil—unmixed, pure."[56] If migrations and blending meant that no population was native, there was no strict correspondence between race and place.

The historical mechanisms of making races thwarted prospects for integrity. Subsequent movements and conquests wrought additional changes. Thus, attempts to match current races with original examples were futile. Scarborough argued that not a single "pure specimen" remained of the Caucasians Blumenbach ranked above other races. The same could be said of the African race. Varied populations had long inhabited the continent, including "every complexion" in Egypt and in Ethiopia. If there was no purity in the ancient world, there was even less in his era. "It is very doubtful," he conjectured, "whether the type brought from Africa can today be found here unmixed." In fact, Negroes might represent the most mixed group in the world. Ongoing fusions made it even more difficult to group American Negroes into a single coherent color or cultural class. As he reckoned with "all the different bloods running in our veins," he felt compelled to conclude, "We are not a Negro race."[57] He speculated that a true accounting of Americans' ancestry would more than double the population numbered in the Negro category. Inevitable future mixtures made the rhetoric of preservation ludicrous.

The identity of Jews presented an opportunity for Scarborough to verify his conclusions. They were the only people who could point to a coherent basis for claiming race integrity because religious precepts tried to shield them from "foreign blood." It was apparent from the start, however, that Judaic tenets had limited effectiveness. The biblical record showed him a "long, long list of unions with idolators." The roster included, among others, "Jebusites, Amorites, Girgashites, Hittites, Hivites, and Perrizites."[58] The legendary Solomon and his Egyptian wife, both of whom failed the test of purity, were part of this history of mixing. Jews had intimate ties with many outsiders, and "Semitic blood" ran through the veins of many populations. This trend was sure to continue in America's diverse society.

Anxieties about mixture were lost on Scarborough. He understood that the language of "blood" denoted ancestral connections. However, he could fathom nothing about a Negro's blood to distinguish it from the blood of an individual assigned to any other race. He rejected the belief, popularized in fiction, that Negro ancestry, however remote, produced features typically ascribed to Negroes. The latest scientific research validated his position.

It disproved a notion that a tell-tale darkness at the cuticle of fingernails exposed otherwise undiscernible Negro blood. Charles Chesnutt ridiculed the idea as one of many superstitions about racial differences. Yet Pearce Kintzing, a surgeon at Maryland Medical College of Baltimore, decided to test it. He found that the fingernails of more than five hundred mixed-race subjects failed to betray Negro ancestry. Scarborough reviewed the evidence and concluded that, notwithstanding the old adage, blood did not always tell.[59]

Despite concerns about the pervasive nefarious race integrity campaigns, Scarborough shared the hopefulness of other reformers. He envisioned a time when everyone would be fully incorporated into the nation's polity. However, like Tanner, he saw this political outcome arising from physical processes. More than twenty-five years of marriage to Sarah Bierce, a White teacher, perhaps reflected and reinforced his positive outlook on the "union of races." In any case, he was convinced that the mingling that had continued unabated since European expansion into the Americas was bound to persist. Interracial domestic ties would thus produce a "typical American" who would render prevailing race classifications meaningless.[60]

———

The practical value of asserting a common identity to foster social and political advances did not diminish misgivings about race. Concerns about the logic, ethics, and mechanics of utilizing a lexicon of dubious conceptions of innate difference, hierarchy, and sameness endured. In questioning the conceptual grounds of race consciousness, reformers underscored challenges of trying to disentangle racial concepts from their historical role in framing American inequity and injustice.

John Sampson wrestled with this problem as he tried to navigate tensions between recognizing race designations as useful bases of collective action and opposing their connotations about human difference. He confronted the dilemma in urging White Methodists to support Christian education among Black people. Need was the guiding principle of his appeal. He advised his audience that its first obligation should be to "the race" needing the most help. Yet he took great pains to ensure that his plea was not mistaken for a belief in the existence of discrete physical races. He qualified his reference by asserting, "But for environments, there is but one race—the human race."[61] He suggested further that racial differences presented no barriers to mutuality. Indeed, an idealized vision of America as a "homogenous nation" encompassing "all races" created an obligation to aid the neediest race. He went further. Despite the ostensible purpose of his speech, he felt compelled to caution that, just as physical differences offered no grounds for dividing individuals, they provided no basis for uniting them. Circumstances required collaboration along racial lines. He acknowledged the political expediency of racial unity while rejecting the idea of race difference. He concluded, "We should be race men in the sense of rights, not blood, for of one blood God made all races."[62]

A desire for a comprehensive understanding of the conceptual grounds for race consciousness preoccupied Kelly Miller. The aim shaped his effort to determine the future. His essay "The Physical Destiny of the American Negro" presents race as a construct that signifies human difference while also functioning as a site of collective identity. The dual focus enabled him to explore the logic of the color line and the viability of race consciousness. Both issues made him optimistic about prospects for progress.[63] His hopes rested on a belief that discrimination was fraught with erroneous ideas and relied on unsustainable fallacies. "It must be taken for granted in the final outcome of things that the color line will be wholly obliterated," he concluded.[64] This vision framed his view of Negro destiny. It stemmed from a conviction that biological factors connecting human beings at creation remained "more fundamental" than alliances founded on race classifications. Despite the outcome's perceived inevitability, it could be fulfilled only in a distant future. As Daniel Payne had done, he likened it to biblical prophecy and projected it into the millennium. His generation thus had to contend with the "inspirited race consciousness" among White Americans who remained wedded to a "superficial distinction of color." The imperatives stemming from this reality were clear; Black people had to follow suit. "The negro race," Miller argued, "must become one with itself."[65] Only then could it truly be part of the nation's people.

This perspective differed from the stance Miller took upon hearing Du Bois's inaugural ANA address on race conservation. He had endorsed the speech, insisting that Negroes, like Jews, must preserve the physical basis of their peculiar identity in order to contribute their distinct gifts to humanity. Yet he saw nothing natural or positive about their racial status. The solidarity he discerned arose from "external compulsion." It was not a choice but a consequence of circumstances they did not create or control.[66] Miller's problem was that the terms on which Negroes could function as a race were ambiguous.

296   RELUCTANT RACE MEN

"The American Negro, as he is called, does not constitute a race in the sense of a compact, ethnic group, imbued with a common spirit and impelled by a common impulse. There is no solidified physical basis . . . for emergence of a common consciousness."[67] Dissimilarity was not an insurmountable bar. He observed that the White population functioned as a "homogeneous type" even as it routinely absorbed immigrants from diverse European nations. The "Jewish race" persisted as a discrete people for centuries despite infusions of blood from many nations that made it impossible to invoke purity as the foundation of its peoplehood. Religious convictions gave coherence to the group's claim to a singular "physical identity." In short, Jews constituted a race by virtue of traditions and beliefs that molded their consciousness as a people. American Negroes were similarly heterogeneous, encompassing a sizeable subset of people with African and European ancestry. Although he could not explain its source, Miller perceived a slow but decisive growth of "ethnic solidarity" among these individuals. This development signaled their potential to function and identify as a race despite divergent characteristics.[68]

The complexities and ethical implications of grounding identities and relationships in racial categories received careful scrutiny from Charles Chesnutt. The author won the esteem of Du Bois for identifying with Black people based on recognition of "a more or less remote Negro ancestor." He was recruited for membership in the American Negro Academy, but he declined the invitation.[69] Race consciousness occupied a complicated space in his reform endeavors. He perceived that, "under pressure," the phenomenon was growing among Negroes and deepening their appreciation for the power of "concerted action." For instance, protest crippled southern streetcar companies whose custom was to "jim-crow" Negroes. It also blocked performances of *The Clansman* in major cities. Boycotts withheld labor from southern planters who were complicit in wage fraud and lynching. Such acts, which he interpreted as expressions of race consciousness, were praiseworthy for the decisive role they could play in resolving the "Race Problem."[70] They illustrated how configuring race in terms of commonality via shared experiences—not biological sameness—could enhance possibilities for Negroes to work together for mutually beneficial ends.

Other speeches and essays looked to the future to rethink the contours of race. Like Benjamin Tanner's visions of amalgamation, nonfiction works locate the key to correcting distorted conceptions of humanity in an ultimate fusion of populations. They outlined a "theory of a future American race" that rested on the "the unity of the human race" and the natural history of progress. Evidence of longevity and fecundity among individuals born through "race crossing" supported the principle of unity. Europe's historical development offered lessons in progress. Chesnutt observed that scientists rejected the fallacy that a "pure Aryan, Indo-European race" shaped the continent and, instead, linked its progress to "racial heterogeneity."[71] He reasoned thus: "There is a tendency in nature toward the preservation of types, . . . and society tends to accentuate this tendency, especially when it involves the perpetuation of privilege. But every student of Darwin knows that all progress in nature comes through departure in types."[72] Anti-miscegenation statutes and other proscriptions on social interactions were impediments to fusion. However, they did not void prospects for future change. Chesnutt predicted that, as American expansion incorporated "dark races" into the nation's territories, the prominence of whiteness would decrease. In time, this outcome would help minimize the significance of color differences.[73] His inability to detail the logistics of all the obscure processes of change failed to diminish his faith in ultimate amalgamation. He was convinced that the laws of nature made it inevitable.

Fiction was Chesnutt's preferred arena. Du Bois would ultimately eulogize him as the "dean of Negro literature." When he pondered the possibilities of authorship, he envisioned writing for the "high and holy purpose" of reforming White Americans because their "unjust spirit of caste" thwarted the nation's "moral progress." He crafted literary works with an eye toward fomenting a "moral revolution."[74] Interrogating the character of social identities founded on race categories was part of this process. Literature enabled him to imagine complex scenarios in which individuals contested and renounced roles and relationships dictated by racial designations.

A short story, "The Wife of His Youth," helped launch Chesnutt's exploration. The tale centers on a moral dilemma. As it opens, the main character, Mr. Ryder, worries about preserving the integrity of the Blue Veins—a northern social organization of elites whose members find common ground and cause in the complexions and hair textures that signal their ancestry of "mixed blood." His reflections elucidate ethical and conceptual dimensions of facilitating their racial survival and progress—the type of enterprise shouldered by the era's race men. As the society's standard-bearer, Ryder bemoans lapses that occasionally allowed people with dark skin to participate in its affairs. Such errors threaten its adherence to the "natural" law of "self-preservation." Improvement requires members to be vigilant in refusing entreaties to identify with Negroes. An alliance of that sort would be a "backward step" and lead to "extinction." A forward-looking man, Ryder hopes to advance the Blue Veins by increasing the chances that White Americans will ultimately embrace them. He seeks for the Blue Veins the sort of fusion with White people Chesnutt believed would encompass all Americans and unfold naturally. A personal step Ryder is about to take promises to accelerate the process. He is on the verge of proposing marriage to a new society member, Mrs. Dixon, a widowed teacher who displays the physical traits, refinement, and social status the group values. The prospect of a committed romance with the charming young woman thrills him after his many years of living as "a single man." Anticipating the union also bolsters his vision of "absorption" into the White population.[75]

By the end of the story, Ryder has abandoned the preservation doctrine along with the assumption that blood and phenotype are natural and appropriate bases of loyalty. The imperatives of Blue Vein integrity and advancement have been eclipsed by an act that breaches the boundaries of the group's identity. Instead of proposing marriage at a ball he organized for the occasion, Ryder announces his ties to another woman, 'Liza Jane, who arrived at his door hours before the event. He prefaces the news with a narrative of the constancy that sustained her on a twenty-five-year quest to find a man named Sam Taylor—her husband before emancipation. Her devotion exemplifies true womanhood. She is "the wife of his youth."[76]

The use of a biblical reference to introduce 'Liza Jane signals the irony of her relationship to Ryder. Details about the pair sharply contrast her status with descriptions of such wives in scripture. Her "mincing" gait cannot mask the marks of a "laborious life." She is not the "graceful doe" of the wife in Proverbs whose charms can inspire a husband's everlasting delight in waters from his "own well." Furthermore, Ryder is not like the wayward Israelite men the prophet Malachi chastises for abandoning the Jewish wives of their youth for pagans. He has not forsaken a partner who shares his identity to seek sexual pleasure or social status with women alien to his people.[77] Other particulars about the couple's history and differences reinforce the irony. They stand in contrast to scriptural configurations of Hebrew peoplehood as a sacred standard for affinity. Their past lacks obligatory ties that would make 'Liza Jane Ryder's "companion . . . by covenant" because they had no legal marriage. Moreover, her inability to recognize that Ryder is Sam Taylor makes it impossible for her to assert her identity as his wife. Invocations of sameness that make Israelite relationships sacrosanct set the characters' dissimilarities in sharp relief. She has "very black" skin and wooly hair, while he is light with hair that is "almost straight." When they labored together in slavery, they did not share the same legal status. She was a slave, and he was free. She was a widow when they married; he was an orphan, apprenticed to a slaveholder until he reached adulthood. When he neared the end of his indenture, he fled to the North to escape an illegal sale that would have reduced him to chattel. She was sold down the proverbial river for warning him of the scheme, and he had been unable to learn her whereabouts. While she wandered the country searching for him after emancipation, he eluded the designs of women who tried to "capture" him in marriage and devoted himself to "upward struggle." In time, he became "as different from the ignorant boy who ran away . . . as the day is from the night."[78]

This chronicle of differences traces the contours of Ryder's dilemma. It lays the ethical foundation for his acknowledgment of ties to 'Liza Jane. He characterizes the decision as a matter of personal integrity—adherence to the injunction of Shakespeare's Polonius: "to thine own self be true." He thus closes his account of her quest by reintroducing himself to his friends. "I am the man," he says. It is a declaration about his present identity as he introduces her.[79] Although readers do not learn the aftermath of this denouement, it is apparent that presenting 'Liza Jane as part of his life changes the self he can project even if he fails to fulfill her dream of resuming marital happiness. Acknowledging her fidelity to the husband he was as an untutored youth unsettles the identity of the man who has become "dean of the Blue Veins."[80] His gesture is at once a matter of being true and an act of self-denial that promises to thwart prospects for marrying the woman he loves and pressing on toward whiteness. The decision, symbolized in the "expression of renunciation" he directs at Mrs. Dixon after telling 'Liza Jane's story, is, moreover, a tacit repudiation of the premise of Blue Vein identity and morality. He abandons conceptions of affinity and consciousness rooted in similarities of "blood" and phenotype.[81] His thanks to the members, all of whom echo Mrs. Dixon's insistence that he should acknowledge 'Liza Jane, cites their hearts as the guiding factor in their collective judgment. He thereby shifts the basis of their solidarity from external characteristics to inner qualities. Just as he asserts honor in disclosing his ties to 'Liza Jane and highlights her faithfulness in rendering her the epitome of womanhood, he relocates Blue Vein collective identity in shared virtue. These attempts to look beyond appearance and status for traits that link human beings and determine their worth leave readers to reflect on the ethics and limitations of using physical conceptions of likeness and hierarchy to demarcate parameters of belonging. They are

300 RELUCTANT RACE MEN

occasions to ponder the terms and implications of constituting a self through relationships with others.[82]

A tale of a ruined marriage exposes different sorts of tensions surrounding devotion and race consciousness. "White Weeds" features the grim consequences of embracing racial categories as morally necessary foundations of identity and affection. It is a fictional elaboration of Chesnutt's critique of "the fetish of Race Purity" that did not reach his contemporaries. It appeared posthumously because the *Atlantic Monthly* rejected the 1904 submission.[83]

The story features a White couple whose emotional bonds disintegrate on the night of their wedding because the husband fears that his intelligent and beautiful wife might possess "Negro blood." Hours before the event, Professor Carson, a native southerner at a northern college, receives an anonymous letter presenting the allegation. He is skeptical about the claim and feels obliged to honor the marriage contract. However, after the ceremony, he wants his new spouse, Marion, to assure him that she is White. "How white" must a person be, she asks, to be eligible for "Southern chivalry?"[84] Carson, the son of a slaveholder, explains that there are "no degrees." People who are "not all white are all black." Moreover, he feels that "the touch of a Negress" would pollute his White identity.[85] Indignant, Marion, whose ancestors all lived as White people, will not confirm or deny the accusation. She refuses to allow racial classifications to determine her desirability and worthiness of her husband's love. She feels no pity for him as doubt and dread consume him, making her a widow within a year of their unconsummated marriage. He committed "the unpardonable sin" of espousing a prejudice that reduced her to an extension of his whiteness instead of engaging her for who she was.[86] In the end, the professor's certainty about his race purity remains intact, but it costs him his life.

The irrationality of race classifications and identities is a common topic in Chesnutt's commentaries. He shared the perspective of other race critics that the prevailing rules of race assignment twisted reality. The idea of "mixed blood" highlighted it. He observed that "only a social fiction" could make a Negro out of a man whose ancestry was seven-eighths White.[87] Yet he was not satisfied with simply exposing the logistical flaws of race regimes. On its own, questioning classification conventions failed to reach the core issue regarding concepts of difference and rank that structured inequality. Paul Marchand, the central character in a novel Chesnutt wrote late in his career, makes this point. He is a quadroon in antebellum Louisiana who experienced manhood while studying in Paris and dreams of preaching "the doctrine of human equality" upon returning to New Orleans. When he grasps the impracticality of such an undertaking on American soil, he finds temporary solace in the "weaker position" that his preponderance of White blood meant he should be White instead of living the degradation tied to an "undistinguishable drop of blood." Chesnutt detested literary characterizations that failed to press beyond this stance. He ridiculed the "white negroes" who embodied this shortcoming in Albion Tourgée's fiction. He complained to writer George Washington Cable about their incessant bemoaning of "the drop of black blood that 'taints'—I hate that word, it implies corruption— their otherwise pure blood."[88]

Paul Marchand, F.M.C., one of six novels Chesnutt was unable to publish, extends his reflections on the bases and significance of racial identity. It presents a sharp critique of the flaws associated with founding identities on biological conceptions of race. Although he completed the manuscript in 1921, as literary scholar Matthew Wilson argues, it reflects nineteenth-century sensibilities about equality and progress. Publishers might have found its historical setting and its themes anachronistic. Nevertheless, it illuminates the range of ideas that sustained opposition to race at the turn of the century.[89] The novel's plot and ethical considerations revolve around Paul's experiences of freedom, wealth, and education that secure his elite status in New Orleans society. However, as a man of color, he suffers indignities and insults at the hands of White men. The news that he is White creates opportunities to confront the complicated meanings of race. To process his newly ascribed status, he reflects on the multifaceted ways that biological notions of race twist reality.

Family ties display the most glaring distortions. Warped relations are set in motion at Paul's birth, when a legal mistake, complicated by worries over illegitimacy and respectability, leads a wealthy White couple to place their infant in the care of a colored woman. When the distressed mother dies, her husband, Pierre Beaurepas, decides to continue the silence about his identity as the boy's father. He secretly pays for the child's care and education and monitors his development through an attorney while raising five orphaned nephews in his home. On his deathbed, he names his secret son as his heir, allowing the quadroon Marchand to become Paul Beaurepas, a White man. He stipulates that the son marry the daughter of an indebted friend and assume the position of family patriarch overseeing the cousins and the slaves. The father trusts the power of blood to create a new identity and establish new relationships.[90]

The novel explores the terms and implications of racial identity against this backdrop. Paul's parentage fails to settle the question of whether he can be White as scripted by his father. Characters with a vested interest in his racial status weigh the possibilities. The cousins doubt his capacity. They consider his identity in light of speculations about nature versus nurture and wonder whether his years of being "trained to subordination" irreparably damaged his ability to display the dignity they associate with the Beaurepas name. They had routinely contributed to this training by abusing the man they knew as a quadroon. When they learn that he maintains a written record of insults and abuses, they deem it proof of "his purity of race" because such a keen concern about honor is "foreign to quadroon nature." Nevertheless, they worry that his behavior might eventually betray some Negro trait or "mawkish negrophile sentiment." The father's friend and his daughter, the designated wife, feel similarly. The friend declares Paul "alien to our race and caste." Despite discerning no evidence of "Negro blood," he is convinced that Paul remains a Negro at heart. His daughter concurs. Because of his upbringing, the new "white-quadroon" or "quadroon-white" must feel and reason "as a Negro," she muses. It would be impossible to be certain about him.[91]

The attorney charged with carrying out the father's wishes views Paul's prospects for being a White Beaurepas differently. His concern is that Paul acts on feeling rather than rational self-interest. The former quadroon had to be cautioned about inappropriate denunciations of slavery, and he espouses the "radical doctrine of the *Rights of Man*," declaring that it applies to all men. These factors, combined with his devotion to his quadroon wife and their children raise fears that his new patron might refuse to play the role of the White man he has become.[92]

The father's trust in blood was misplaced. His experiment fails because invocations of biological purity cannot void or displace the identity established through social interactions. After manumitting the Beaurepas slaves, Paul renounces his ties to the family. The decision he communicates to his would-be cousins delivers an indictment of race. He explains that "race consciousness" required for him to assume a new role is not a product of "blood"; it is a social phenomenon forged through relationships.[93] He cannot live as a Beaurepas because he never experienced such connections with his parents, cousins, or other White people. The fallacy that transformed a quadroon into a White man is part of the same constellation of ideas and social practices that rendered a quadroon Black. The narrator explains the equally loathsome phenomena together.

By a legal fiction, which grew into a habit of thought that would last for generations to come, a man was black for all social purposes, so long as he acknowledged or was known to carry in his veins a drop of black blood. By his accession to the white race, Paul Beaurepas, formerly Marchand, f.m.c. became, *ipso facto*, an unmarried man . . . [and] an eligible aspirant for the hand of any unmarried white woman in Louisiana.[94]

The prospect of losing his identity as a husband is untenable. It would be dishonorable to follow his parents' example and consign his wife and children to a nameless future. Yet the law that deems him White makes such a course of action acceptable. Indeed, it requires it, rendering his wife "nothing—a light woman, a *milatresse*." She can never be his lawful spouse. His children are now illegitimate, merely "a gentleman's byblows." Paul understands that the outcome he perceives as vile and unnatural is normal in a world whose rules of race allow respectable men to father their own slaves and dispose of them for profit. Such was the case for one of the Beaurepas cousins, who sold a slave as she was about to give birth to his child so he could pay gambling debts.[95]

The racial customs that threaten Paul's family ties drive him from the country. He decries the fact that he lives in a society where "a man must be of one caste or another." He does not fit. He is legally White, but he lacks the consciousness needed to practice whiteness. He knows life as a quadroon and rejects a cousin's suggestion that this identity has disappeared. Despite his education, wealth, loving family, and access to the rank of White manhood, he faces a calamity of being "without a race" in a land structured by the doctrine that races are necessary categories of human existence and relations. It provides "no place for the individual" outside of this construct.[96] In defiance of social conventions, Paul refuses to allow the ancestry that renders him a member of the White race to dictate his affective bonds. To maintain his identity as a husband, he plans to return to France, where he believes his family ties will go unquestioned. The consciousness and commonality he forged and sustained through relationships will be free of the imperatives of bloodlines.

The experiences and perspectives of central characters in the three stories—Ryder, Marian, and Marchand—complicate and question the reliance on racial taxonomies to dictate emotional bonds. The scenarios they navigate challenge the coherence of race consciousness by probing the social, psychological, and ethical implications of basing human interactions

304 RELUCTANT RACE MEN

on "blood." The distorted familial and communal relationships they feature raise doubts about possibilities of forging racial identities that overcome flawed notions of difference, sameness, hierarchy, and love.[97]

———

The convergence of Jim Crow and campaigns for race consciousness reinvigorated questions about how to represent people of African descent. The resurgence of the topic highlighted the personal stakes associated with naming, a crucial facet of constructing identity. New concerns extended beyond the antebellum problem of determining how to present free people of color as a population facing similar social and political circumstances. The issue's significance was also broader than the focus on organizational titles. The question "Who are we?" connected names to efforts to cultivate a collective consciousness among the diverse individuals comprising Chesnutt's "comprehensive Negro." It tethered group titles to private identities, thus imbuing names with the power to signify individuals' sense of themselves and the people with whom they identified.

Benjamin Tanner issued the query to *Christian Recorder* readers as Reconstruction faltered. John Wesley Bowen, a professor at Gammon Theological Seminary and editor of *Voice of the Negro*, presented it at the dawn of the twentieth century amid declarations from Booker T. Washington and others that a New Negro was emerging.[98] The question and the arguments it inspired reflected ongoing efforts to contend with race and navigate citizenship. The failure of claims to a common humanity to unite people of African descent with other Americans made it clear to attorney D. Augustus Straker and others that a concrete "national or race identity" was necessary to the work of improving their lot.[99] Attempts to foster group identity with a shared name showcased divergent interpretations of African origins, bloodlines, nativity, habitation, physical traits, nationality, and ethnology. Straker was unconvinced that the distinctions competing stakeholders made among various designations amounted to meaningful differences. Nevertheless, individual attachment to particular labels and the absence of common assessment criteria generated a new contest over names at the turn of the century. The likelihood that it would fail to settle concerns about the terms of a collective consciousness did nothing to diminish its fervor.

Tanner's inquiry appeared in the aftermath of his defense of retaining the title of the AME Church. In the middle of a lecture on the necessity of "Colored

Organization," he abandoned his topic in an apparent effort to distinguish collective action from group identity. He declared that colored people in the United States were "neither Africans nor Negroes." The former term ignored their citizenship, and the latter stemmed from the Latin word for "black," which did not match the variety of complexions he observed.[100] He reasoned further that adherence to custom meant designating populations according to their place of habitation. Thus, he concluded, "we are Americans." The adjective "Colored" could be added for those who demanded specificity about appearance. It had the benefit of indicating "both the fact and [the] truth" that the complexions of Americans of African descent ranged "from the whitest white to the blackest black."[101]

Diverse kinds of arguments led *Christian Recorder* readers to concur with a designation that referenced citizenship. P. C. Hall of Mississippi pled indifference to racial terminology and cited recognition of Black men's humanity as the chief priority. Reaching this goal, however, required identifying the group as American agents of progress who possessed "souls, reason, intellect, [and] taste."[102] Correspondent John Bagwell complained about the inconsistent use of terms—"Africans, Negroes, Negro Americans, American Negroes, Blacks, and Colored people." This ambiguity threatened civil and political progress. A ready solution lay in an appeal to nationality, which made all individuals grouped under these diverse titles "simply Americans." Nativity and legal standing settled the matter for Augustus Hodges. After tracing four generations of his Virginia family to an African-born great grandfather, he insisted that birth and constitutional amendments made him and other people of African descent in the United States Americans. Just as European ancestry did not diminish the national identity of "the white American," he reasoned, "Africa has no claim upon us."[103]

Dissenters pinpointed flaws in arguments against "Negro." Targeting Tanner, John Cromwell, editor of the Washington, DC, *People's Advocate* and a founding member of the defunct Negro American Society (NAS), explained that "Negro" was apt because it derived from the Portuguese word *nigro*, meaning people "descended from a black."[104] Hence, colored Americans were Negroes. As NAS president, Richard Greener had affirmed Cromwell's critique. Appealing to ethnology, he had insisted that, "by birth," some Negroes were Americans and others were Africans. "By race," however, African natives as well as their descendants, "wherever scattered and however nearly bleached out, were designated Negroes." His commitment to the principle that individuals had a duty to use this naming custom in identifying themselves lapsed with the failure of the NAS.[105]

306 RELUCTANT RACE MEN

Tanner refused to engage the issue on ethnological grounds despite his interest in the field. As part of his biblical studies, he traced a natural history of people of African descent in his book *The Negro's Origins; and is the Negro Cursed?* to disprove claims that God ordained subjugation. Prevailing racial categories were a different matter, however. They were so embedded in the vocabulary of condescension and discrimination that even dictionary definitions illustrated the problem. A Negro, he explained, was commonly a member of "the black woolly-headed, flat-nosed and thick lipped race of men inhabiting Africa"—a description that did not apply to many US residents he observed. A "Negress" was a "wench," a word that was an affront to colored women. It was futile to try to transform such "terms of reproach" into respectable designations.[106] He accepted the descriptor "American negroes" for people in the United States with very dark complexions; however, capitalizing "Negro" suggested a nationality without a corresponding nation on the African continent. There were "no such things as American Negroes," he reasoned, because there was no Negro nation and colored Americans did not constitute a "nationality within a nationality."[107] He argued further that efforts to bind colored Americans to Africa equated American identity exclusively with whiteness. When Cromwell reminded him that maps of West Africa displayed an area designated "Negroland," Tanner conceded that "Negro" would apply to groups inhabiting that region. Yet this logic also reinforced his claim that colored people in the United States were "simon-pure American."[108] Organizations where he maintained affiliations—the AME Church and the American Negro Academy—were exempt from his naming protocol. Tradition justified keeping the title of the former and deference to "the imperial Alexander Crummell" shielded the latter from condemnation. Tanner believed that a change in the word order might make the ANA title more acceptable. Negro American Academy was preferable, he argued, because it would make the noun "American" an affirmation of Negro citizenship.[109]

A call for applying sound conceptual approaches in assessing names and racial categories prefaced Bowen's defense of "Negro." He relied on logical arguments in his study of historical theology and perceived danger in flawed methodologies. The work of his late Methodist colleague Alexander Winchell in trying to map "Adamic and non-Adamic races" illustrated his concern; it was an enterprise wholly "innocent of reason."[110] The illogical project and subsequent attempts to replicate it demonstrated the need for reliable anthropological and philosophical modes of analysis to push research beyond individual prejudices. Although Bowen also valued ethnology and etymology, he urged caution in using them to address the complexities of Negro history and identity.

A process of elimination led to the conclusion that "Negro" was the accurate choice. "African," which represented natal or ancestral origins, was the starting point of his assessment. It did not qualify as an appropriate race name because a reference to a continent did not capture "raceality." There was no evidence, Bowen argued, to demonstrate that an ancient North African cleric like Augustine of Hippo was racially the same as Alexander Crummell or Kahma, a famous southern African chief in the region that is now Botswana. The physical heterogeneity of the continent's populations and their scattered descendants meant that "African" could not designate any single race. Similar reasoning disqualified "Colored" and "Afro-American." The former term was merely a "rhetorical platitude" highlighting a physiological feature that marked several populations as "Not White." In addition to the fact that, historically, there was no discrete "colored race," Negroes had no basis for exercising a monopoly over the term. The "hybridity" of the "Afro-American" label—a sign of "adultery" between philology and history—was a liability that added to its failure to specify a race.[111] Bowen argued that there was no way to determine whether it named an African-born people of American parentage or an American-born people of African parentage. In either case, he reasoned, the individuals might be "white," "black," or members of a racial grouping in Africa. Furthermore, the designation muddled the issue of nationality by fusing references to a sovereign country and a continent that encompassed "multitudinous tribal kingdoms, governments and peoples."[112]

A commitment to analytic precision did not shield Bowen from pitfalls. An attempt to trace a history of "Negro" resulted in a sketch of its evolution from a philological term to an ethnological category. He argued that "philologically speaking," the word originally referenced dark complexions, but it had "no ethnological significance." It described sun-darkened individuals in a wide range of populations, including Egyptians, Moors, Filipinos, and Hawaiians, without consigning them to "The Negro Race." Usage had transformed the meaning, creating an ethnological term that extended beyond complexion to encompass "every species of African or of Negro descent." This expansion referenced "blood," not appearance. "Black skin, wooly hair and swollen lips," Bowen argued, "are not now the universal characteristics of Negroes; we must go to blood."[113] He struggled to explain how grounding "Negro" in "blood" differed from labels that referenced African roots. His observation that America's "Negro race" was "not a black race" seemed to confirm his conclusion. Yet his point that widespread "admixture" or a "complexity of bloods" explained the diversity that marked the population's physical characteristics raised questions about why a name should reference only one of many bloodlines. The rationale for his espousal of a "one-drop rule" lay in his observations that descendants of people deemed mulattoes and octoroons "*invariably* revert to the Negro" across generations by developing dark complexions.[114] He knew of no theory that explained this apparent atavism, but he believed that it was a fact and a sign of the enduring power of Negro "blood." Scientific accuracy in naming people who descended from a Negro thus required retaining the ancestral title. It followed that descendants themselves, regardless of their appearance, should identify themselves in anticipation of future generations whose ancestry would ultimately appear in dark skin philologically associated with Negroes.[115]

The term "Afro-American" offered opponents of "Negro" a capacious alternative for naming people of varied complexions. As its use spread, Tanner embraced it even though he preferred having no qualifications on claims to American identity and clung to the tenet "continents make their own people." He still believed North America would generate a population "peculiar to itself" from its various inhabitants.[116] However, "Afro-American" met demands for a distinctive name in his lifetime because it was consistent with practices among Americans of European descent and had a beautiful sound.

Contempt for "Negro" led to T. Thomas Fortune's defense of the hyphenated term. As editor of the New York *Sun* and a cofounder of the Afro-American League, he complained that "Negro" drew a new color line because it ignored mulattoes who helped constitute the race. He had tried to engage "all classes and types of people of African origin" when he co-published the New York *Globe* and billed it as a journal "for colored people of the United States."[117] Bowen's editorial presented him with an opportunity to refine his thinking. He opposed "Negro" because it treated Africa as an exception by ignoring the standard practice of grouping people by geopolitical location or in a way that signaled "race affinities and unities." Unlike these concrete bases of commonality that referenced populations in other parts of the world, "Negro" labeled people "by color, by hirsute texture and by cranial and facial conformation." Treating the term as a "race designation" was a misguided attempt to dignify a word that could never function as an accurate "geographical or political classification of race."[118] The same reasoning framed his abandonment of "colored." It also lacked geopolitical substance and was overly broad. He discerned cowardice in individuals who insisted on using it and belittled them for refusing to acknowledge the value of specific racial ties. "Afro-American" had the virtue of applying to "black and colored people" of African descent. Although, like Tanner and Chesnutt, Fortune believed the group would ultimately fade away as a discrete population and become part of a new American "race type," destiny did not eliminate the need to inscribe the term in the national lexicon as a proper race name.[119] Principle demanded that individuals identify as "African in origin and American in birth." This nexus paved the foundations for a "classification of race" to accompany the "habitation, language, and religion" that grounded their American citizenship.[120]

AME bishop James Embry shared the judgment that "Afro-American" was the only appropriate title for the race. The inappropriateness of using a "race-name" derived from a color led him to refuse ANA membership. He insisted that Christian scholars had a duty to uphold accurate speech and that "Negro" was "not the language of science, nor the voice of religion and fraternity." Its usage was "puerile."[121] Archeological research that rendered Africa the "mother of the oldest civilization, the oldest science, and the oldest art" demonstrated the value of referring to it in a name. A poem by Benjamin Lee's wife Mary further justified "Afro-American." Embry praised the work "Afmerica," which urged readers not to celebrate freedom by mimicking captive Israelites who hung up their lyres in despair. It likened a refusal to embrace the African past with an attempt to live "with no identity" or personality. As evidence of the literary virtue in "Afro-American," the poem added to the term's historical and scientific merit as a proper name. Lee's husband espoused the name without contributing to its defense. He simply cited the inability of the "Negro" label to function as a proper index of nationality or race. Unreliability sufficed to disqualify it.[122]

A diverse lot questioned the coherence of "Afro-American." It was too African for some and not American enough for others. Louis Martinet took the latter position in mocking the Afro-American League. Hyphenation, he mused, "keeps the 'Afro' always just so far from the 'American.'" He was convinced that the better class of New Orleanians would shun advocates of the name for fear that they accepted "the color line." One Louis Post complained that the term shortchanged American citizenship by failing to acknowledge the full birthright of Negroes—a name he also opposed. It was an undignified pretension to use a name that implied that colored people were Americans

310   RELUCTANT RACE MEN

"only by adoption." George Henderson, a Straight University theology professor who joined the ANA in spite of its name, concurred with Post. He thought that the degree to which "Afro-American" discounted citizenship gave it even less merit than "Negro," which he dismissed as "no more a race designation than the word 'white.'" The hyphenated label also lacked scientific utility because it failed to account for the totality of colored people's racial and national origins. This was especially true for individuals who, like him, claimed the "blood of nearly all races" and traced their ancestry to all countries. He reasoned that, if accuracy was the goal, the applicable designations would include "English-Afro-, Franco-Afro-, Germanico-Afro-, Italico-Afro-, Spanico-Afro-, Dutch-Irish-Afro-, Russo-Afro-, or in some cases, English-Franco-Germanico-Spanico-Scotch-Irish-Afro-American!" The only way to clarify the confusing situation was to identify all citizens as Americans and, when necessary, reference their color as "Negro," for dark people, and "brown," "mulatto," or "quadroon" for individuals with lighter complexions.[123] In contrast, Edward E. Cooper, publisher of the *Colored American*, a weekly billed as a "National Negro Newspaper," accepted "Afro-American" as a legitimate parallel to such designations as "Irish-American" or "German-American." This similarity did not change the fact that it was dubious on "strictly ethnological grounds" because it did not reference "any distinct species of Negroes." Although he worked through the Afro-American Council to ameliorate "the condition of the Afro-American race," he questioned the term's advantages over "Negro" and "black." Despite his apparent catholic stance on names, he wished "colored American" could stand as the "correct and comprehensive designation."[124] John Edward Bruce, a regular contributor to the paper through his Bruce Grit editorials, had no tolerance for the term because it evaded established racial taxonomies. He invoked Benjamin Disraeli's fictional Baron Sergius to explain that race was "the key of history." Sergius also subscribed to a principle that "blood" was the only thing that "makes a race." Bruce used this standard to declare "Afro-American" an "ethnological monstrosity." He imagined that it was the invention of a coward who believed freedom and rights created "an entirely new species of Negroes."[125]

Although "Negro" and "Afro-American" were prominent options, there were outlier titles. *Christian Recorder* reader J. H. Scott represented one such a case. Repugnance toward the "mean grammar" of "Negro" led him to privilege African origins. Ancestral roots pointed to a name with unambiguous

"THE WHOLE QUESTION OF RACE" 311

historical foundations. Making a continental homeland a racial phenomenon, he argued that the legal rights of American citizenship could not sever bonds of race, which made permanent Africans of US natives.[126] The ancient past and geography also grounded the name choice for Harvey Johnson, a prominent Baptist minister in Baltimore. He understood the racial taxonomy that produced both "negro" and "Caucasian" as part of an implausible theory intent on subverting the unity of the species to establish "the superiority of one branch of the human race over the other." The role of "negro" in the caste structure and its reference to anything black "whether cat, dog, horse, or what not" made it irredeemable.[127] "Colored" appealed to him as a race term that could function in a variety of local regions because of its broad scope. He would ultimately use it in guiding the organization of Maryland's Colored Baptist Convention. Yet if he were not bound by practical considerations, he would use "Hamite." It was his ideal because it designated a documented biblical history, referenced countries that became home to Ham's descendants, and acknowledged ancestral connections among population groups throughout the world who comprised the Hamitic people. In contrast, Negro Academy member William Ferris used the future to explain that, while "colored" was suitable to acknowledge Anglo-Saxon "blood" in the Negro population, "Negrosaxon" reflected the requirements of race advancement. It captured the need for Negroes to become Anglo-Saxon "in mind and character and disposition" to gain equal access to the political resources of American civilization.[128]

For some, debates over names were simply evidence of the bankruptcy of race practices. There was no accurate racial label. Irritated by squabbles over titles, Theophilus Steward ridiculed the popular options. He observed that, legally, "Negro" encompassed such a broad swath of people, "many of them white," that it was devoid of "ethnographic or ethnological value." However, it had utility as an unambiguous signifier of "social caste." Kelly Miller expressed similar sentiments without issuing a wholesale condemnation. He noted that the label was deficient as a marker of physical likeness among people it purported to describe, but it was a potent signifier of the servility imposed on descendants of American slaves. Steward expanded on the political import of "Negro": it "spells exclusion." It could apply to any people "unfellowshipped" from the nation's social compact. They did not need to be of African descent. American Jews, Native Americans, and Asian immigrants were Negroes for all practical purposes because they were singled out as

312   RELUCTANT RACE MEN

targets of discrimination.[129] "Afro-American" was not much better. Many White people did not believe the latter part of the term encompassed colored people, and many colored people did not perceive the former part as relevant to their lives. For Steward, the moniker was "a sign without significance" because it failed to inspire any sentiments or traditions.[130] He lost all patience with labeling when he encountered school textbooks that repeated the polygenist argument that Caucasians constituted the only "historic race." His initial impulse was to dispense with ethnographic classifications altogether and invoke simple commonsense distinctions between "pigmented and non-pigmented" skin. He acknowledged that this practice might leave some bodies unclearly classified but reasoned that separating humans into races was a necessarily flawed enterprise because it attempted to split what God created as a singular phenomenon. Unwilling to leave another defective scheme unquestioned, he dissected a textbook that showed Caucasians encompassing the Hamitic race, defined as Egyptian; the Semitic race included Jews and Arabs; and the Aryan race encompassed Europeans. There was no place in the account for Negroes. He ventured that, since freedom delivered the "poor 'niggers'" from Noah's curse of servitude, history teachers were intent on severing their Hamitic roots. The only logical course of action for the "so-called colored pupils" suffering under the fetish of White race pride was to hold fast to Ham and follow him into the Caucasian race. "No matter if they are as black as people can be," Steward admonished, they should declare themselves "white."[131]

Few people found race names more disturbing than Philadelphian Isaiah Wears. In addition to rejecting the idea that there was a physical basis for grouping people into discrete races, he bristled at designations that appeared to diminish American citizenship. The depth of his conviction was evident in a battle with Everett J. Waring, a young Baltimore attorney who claimed credit for coining "Afro-American" in 1878, when he was eighteen years old. Waring explained that, on ethnological grounds, the label was superior to the "Negro" name because the latter encompassed Africans and was thus meaningless in the United States. Wears belittled the proposal as another illogical "race-badge" that confused ethnological factors with political matters. He asked, "Does he not know that to be an American citizen involves no consideration of blood, and that it is entirely a legal and political relation?"[132] Yet ethnological accuracy was not Wears's real concern in debating race names. In principle, he continued to reject all notions of innate racial difference. Like race men, however, he wanted to define a sound basis for progress.

His commitment to unfettered individual advancement ruled out the option of mapping it in racial terms, and he believed many people shared his viewpoint.

> The great mass of the ordinarily intelligent of our people have arrived at the conclusion that INDIVIDUAL advancement and personal success are the winning cards in this great game of civil progress; it is not a conflict of races, hence we want no distinct name. . . . There is therefore no work for distinct races, and I may add no physical ground for the theory of distinct races.[133]

Conflicts over names obscured the premise of equality that Wears espoused. The only racial concept he was willing to promote recognized "one human race." He had no tolerance for "arbitrary classifications" that sent Black people "parading . . . as a race."[134] Others in his AME Church network apparently saw things differently. A conflict that played out for months in the *Christian Recorder* ended with a triumphant Waring proclaiming himself "god-father to my race." His parting message dismissively counseled that Wears was free to call himself an American "and thus pass for a white man."[135] However, the aged reformer should exhibit a degree of modesty in light of the term's reception and endorsement among prominent figures.

The death of Robert Purvis, in 1898, brought Wears back to the issue of race names. Tuberculosis left him too frail to attend the memorial service, so he submitted written remarks. Remembering his friend created another occasion to denounce racial categories. As he praised Purvis for refusing to campaign for human rights on the "low and marshy" platform of race, Wears could not help but distinguish him from the rising generation of "race-shriekers." Purvis's virtue was evident in his insistence that there was "but one race." His inspiring principles separated him from the wearisome "latter-day saints" who were dominating reform arenas. Wears did not understand why they insisted on lugging a profane attachment to race into civil and political venues. As he reflected on fifty years of laboring for equal rights, he bewailed the "semi-barbarous" prefix "Afro" affixed to the name "American" because it diminished claims to national identity, consigning Black people to a "qualified" version of citizenship.[136]

A query at the end of his acrimonious exchanges with Waring reflected his sense of frustration and defeat. "We thought," he lamented, "we had advanced beyond the consideration of mere race names." He could not understand how such matters could silence the pressing question of whether "such

314 RELUCTANT RACE MEN

entities as distinct races" even exist.[137] As he lionized Purvis for a lifetime of steadfast race challenges, it was disquieting for him to think that decades of earnest and scrupulous efforts had come to this end. The scenario suggested that whims concerning labels had undone a principled reform tradition.

———

The story of race challenges is not a tale of losers. Although Wears despaired of changes that came with the passing of reform generations, opposition to racial constructions did not simply cease. Old questions persisted, and Jim Crow dangers that heightened the need to unite also highlighted ongoing practices that structured invalid hierarchies and contrived notions of difference and sameness. Nineteenth-century initiatives paved foundations for future efforts to develop parameters for commonality and collective action on a hostile social and political terrain. A broad array of endeavors and principles held lessons about the politics, ethics, logic, science, and nomenclature of race that continued to configure citizenship, manhood, and humanity. They offered resources for conceptualizing the nexus of race and reform for new eras of American freedom and inequality.

Conclusion

"Along the Color Line"

Vexed by the inequality and tyranny that ushered Negroes into a new century, W. E. B. Du Bois sought a vantage point from which to contest violent and discriminatory race practices while nurturing race consciousness. He set out to work "along the color line." The venue for his enterprise was the *Horizon*, a periodical he launched in 1907 with two civil rights allies from the fledgling Niagara movement—Lafayette Hershaw, a land examiner for the Department of the Interior, and Freeman Henry Morris Murray, a printer and War Department clerk.[1] Subtitled *A Journal of the Color Line*, the monthly paved the way for broadening conceptions of the despised boundary that Du Bois identified seven years earlier as "the problem of the Twentieth Century."[2]

A cover design showing a woman looking toward the line that seemed to separate sea and sky illustrated the editors' efforts to discern Negroes' prospects. Surveying the horizon entailed comprehensive appraisals of current affairs and media discourse in three regular sections—The Over-Look, The Outlook, and the In-Look. Accounts of diverse viewpoints and actions among reformers, scholars, government officials, and "Negro haters" complemented Niagara movement battles against "the outer enemy" and "inner racial indifference."[3] A section entitled Along the Color Line identified the location that made it possible to assess national and international landscapes from multiple angles. It provided the editors with a perspective from which to distinguish the flawed reasoning and unjust treatment that sustained racialized exclusion and subjection from activities that displayed and fostered race consciousness and advancement. Repurposing the line enabled the men to reconcile ongoing denunciations of race with visions of a modern racial identity for Negroes.

Challenges to race appeared in reports of scholarly opinions and political developments that exposed the color line's artificial underpinnings. For instance, an excerpt from anthropologist Franz Boas's commentary on race

Figure C.1 Cover of the *Horizon: A Journal of the Color Line* 3:6 (June 1908).

suggested that the line's foundations were unstable. Boas ventured that anatomical differences between Negroes and Europeans made the existence of intellectual variations plausible. However, there was "no proof whatever" that physical divergences reflected "appreciable" inferiority.[4] The view from the line thus spotlighted defective logic in positing an innate mental hierarchy that placed populations labeled "white" above everyone else. International developments provided an occasion to ridicule the line's reliance on specious classifications. South Africa's discriminatory policies illustrated the flaws. Reports that new laws limited voting rights to people "of European descent" prompted Du Bois to ask how and where officials would "draw the Color Line." He questioned whether the restriction excluded the half million people designated as "colored," the thousands of Boers with "Negro blood," or a prominent government official and his spouse widely believed to be mulattoes or quadroons.[5] He shared the doubts of a London commentator who found it impossible to fathom a legally enforceable distinction. The situation underscored the fallacy of differentiating people as discrete unequal

CONCLUSION 317

races and thus highlighted the arbitrary boundaries the line supposedly policed. Noting that the South Africa case was just one instance of the "inevitable fusion of races," Du Bois left readers to make their own comparisons to American notions of White racial purity and superiority.[6]

Laudable reform endeavors and achievements enabled the editors to take stock of the agency that fueled race progress and pride. They commended opportunities the Niagara movement created for Negroes to participate in "the greatest moral battle of modern times"—the fight to abolish the color line.[7] Recommendations of worthy articles and books in Negro periodicals directed *Horizon* readers to works by the editors, as well as by such prominent figures as Washington, DC, educator Anna Julia Cooper. A tribute to the late Augustus Straker highlighted his accomplishments as a lawyer, judge, and politician in the Reconstruction South and the urban North. An exemplar of Black pride, he refused to assume the servile demeanor White southerners demanded of Negroes.[8] A list of developments viewed from the line in 1909 showed noteworthy progress in the face of Jim Crow. Among the year's "Credits" were Matthew Henson's ascent to the North Pole, the publication of one hundred books and articles about American Negroes, the circulation of three hundred newspapers and journals published by Negroes, and boxer Jack Johnson's victories over "all white men who dare to fight him." These advances withstood the year's devastating "Debits"—the presidency of William Taft, the ongoing White patronage enjoyed by Booker T. Washington, and the ninety-eight known Negro victims of lynching.[9]

Efforts to repurpose the color line survived the *Horizon's* demise in the summer of 1910. They resumed later that year with the founding of the National Association for the Advancement of Colored People (NAACP) and its periodical, *The Crisis: A Journal of the Darker Races*, which Du Bois edited. Along the Color Line was the lead item in the inaugural edition's contents. It was a regular section for the next six years and appeared periodically thereafter.[10] A drawing of surveyors that sometimes illustrated the segment represented the ongoing work of generating multidimensional accounts of practices that maintained the line and of the ideas, achievements, and experiences of the people it aimed to circumscribe.

A broad array of occurrences comprised the section. Reports of lynch mobs, poverty, labor strife, discrimination cases, legal setbacks, and urban ills appeared alongside boasts about educational and professional attainments, society news, political and legislative gains, church activities, reform initiatives, civil rights advances, and cultural events. Stories of varied

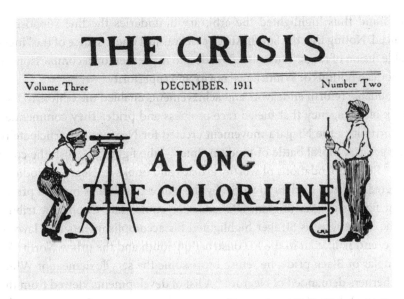

Figure C.2 Along the Color Line, *Crisis* 3:2 (December 1911): 51.

issues scrutinized from the color line shed light on its complexity and impact. They provided a resource with which people suffering under oppression and scorn could transcend the experience Du Bois famously called "double-consciousness." A legacy of slavery that Jim Crow reinforced, the phenomenon distorted the perspectives of Negroes who perceived the gaze of "amused contempt and pity" from White people as a mirror of Black identity and worth.[11] Views from the line sought to nurture self-definition by showcasing Black agency and providing critical perspectives on White condescension and aggression.

This orientation took root as race men promoted racial identification among Black people while leading the charge against Jim Crow race practices. Unlike reformers in nineteenth-century contexts, they were free of pressures to defend themselves against accusations of complicity in perpetuating a tyrannical fiction. They could denounce practices that engineered false differences and rankings without diminishing the virtues of a shared sense of identity grounded in a common racial designation.

Reformers with varied perspectives sought to balance race consciousness and race challenges. Kelly Miller was among those who juggled the task with nineteenth-century experience in questioning the logic of race. He faced developments of the new century using a principle he called "Race

CONCLUSION 319

Statesmanship." On one hand, it denoted a commitment to fostering group loyalty premised on the "race ideal."[12] His 1913 "Oath of Afro-American Youth," for example, stemmed from and sought to encourage race fidelity. Taking the oath meant pledging to resist despair in the face of bigotry and refrain from behaviors that might dishonor the race. It entailed a promise to inculcate "racial duty" in others and to strive to "uplift the race," ennobling everyone associated with it by "ties of blood."[13] After publishing the pledge in *Crisis*, Miller distributed it as a five-cent card that youth could carry or display on the family mantel as a reminder of their obligations. In appreciation, Howard University's Class of 1915 dedicated its yearbook to Miller, dean of the College of Arts and Sciences, citing the oath as a symbol of his edifying race loyalty and leadership.[14]

Duty to the race also compelled Miller to continue opposing notions of racial difference. It inspired a pamphlet in his Race Statesmanship Series entitled *Is Race Difference Fundamental, Eternal, and Inescapable?* The occasion for interrogating the matter was a 1921 speech by President Warren G. Harding celebrating the semi-centennial of Birmingham, Alabama. The event was an opportunity to present the official stance of the White House on the nation's "race problem." The address drew insights from Lothrop Stoddard's *The Rising Tide of Color: The Threat against White World Supremacy* and from Frederick Lugard, a British colonial official who advised each race to follow its own traditions and preserve its purity. Harding sought to establish social arrangements that would allow White and colored races to enjoy full citizenship. While maintaining that "permanent differentiation" was unnecessary in political and economic affairs, he insisted that progress for both races hinged on their ability to heed the "fundamental, eternal, and inescapable difference" between them. This recognition would yield "natural segregations," with Negro and White populations developing as separate races.[15]

Writing a month after the Birmingham speech, Miller acknowledged that his letter was overdue. However, a belated reply was better than silence given the potential threat the strategy posed to equality. Another likely motivation was that, immediately following the address, Black Nationalist reformer Marcus Garvey sent Harding a congratulatory telegram that appeared in the *New York Times* with the heading "Negroes Endorse Speech." The cable thanked the president on behalf of the "negroes of the world" for a policy that promised to establish human "brotherhood." It assured him that "true negroes" concurred with the opinion that "races should develop on their own social lines."[16] Miller tried to mute the endorsement by proclaiming that he knew of no instance in which any Negro, Garvey included, would accept a categorical proposition that race difference is "fundamental, inescapable, and eternal."[17] The pledge of Garvey's Universal Negro Improvement Association (UNIA) to fight forced segregation, even as it advocated self-segregated communities, seemed to support his observation.[18]

Past experiences guided Miller's assault on the "essential illogicality" of the "doctrine of eternal racial differences."[19] He reasoned that the premise of Negroes' claims to equal civil and political rights was the common humanity they shared with all other Americans. Harding purported to affirm such rights while denying their basis. For Miller, the assumption that equal rights could rest on the idea of race difference was as dangerous as building a house on sand. He noted that Harding did not need to mention a racial hierarchy for his southern audience to understand that he advocated it. "In the vocabulary of the South," he observed, "race difference means Negro inferiority. It would not be fair . . . to suppose that you would employ words which would convey to your hearers strange and unusual meaning."[20] Familiar arguments exposed the "fallacious foundation" of claims to essential race difference. Noting that the scientific data were inconclusive, Miller shared his confidence that divergent "racial attributes" reflected only "marginal dissimilarities." He ventured that Germans were "more phlegmatic" than the French, Celts "more hysterical" than Teutons, the Chinese "more stolid" than the Japanese, and Negroes more patient and forgiving than any other race.[21] Yet he perceived such qualities, along with physical differences, as merely variations in degree that undoubtedly resulted from custom and environmental conditions. Accordingly, they were unsound grounds for a policy of separate race development.

The Atlantic slave trade and "race promiscuity" raised questions about the character and distinctiveness of the racial traditions and ideals Harding sought to encourage. Miller noted that most American Negroes had no experience of African cultures. In addition, if "blood" determined cultural sensibilities, it was unclear which types of racial rituals would prevail among the "mixed breed" of Negroes.[22] Furthermore, in the modern era, it was impossible for any race or nation to practice its culture as a hermetically sealed phenomenon. Scientific, ethical, and social forces were pushing and pulling the entire human race "toward unity, not diversity."[23] This set of factors discredited efforts to premise national or group progress on the supposition that race designations were coherent markers of human difference.

CONCLUSION   321

Miller's ideas circulated widely. In addition to cultivating a readership as a prolific pamphleteer, by 1930, he was a syndicated columnist with access to readers of more than one hundred newspapers.[24] Yet engaging a mass audience did not ensure him a stable place among the era's race men. Harvard-educated philosopher Alain Locke, his junior colleague at Howard University, shed light on the situation in an eloquent introduction to Miller's final essay collection, which reproduced the Harding letter. He expressed respect for Miller's efforts, but he harbored doubts about their capacity to effect relevant change. At the outset, he acknowledged the scientific rigor with which Miller tackled social and political developments that impinged on Negro life. Miller had done the race a great service by dismantling the logic of obstructions in "the racial path."[25] Defending the race made him adept at shifting from one topic to the next to respond to attacks from multiple positions and address rapidly changing circumstances. Yet his concentration on "transitory" facets of the "race problem" limited his ability to offer a comprehensive analysis of race that might clarify and resolve the quandary.[26] It seemed that Miller's wholesale reliance on reason to challenge Jim Crow race practices was a throwback to a style of inquiry utilized by eighteenth-century rationalists. Locke thus doubted its utility in the work of developing a way forward. Moreover, the admirable race loyalty that sustained Miller's endeavors was a "feudal" sort of devotion that might be unable to inspire racial identity for a modern era.[27]

Locke's assessment appeared just a year before he edited *The New Negro: An Interpretation*—a collection of works by novelists, playwrights, poets, artists, scholars, and reformers. His lead essay, "The New Negro," marked a departure from the orientation he ascribed to Miller as it announced the emergence of a new race consciousness and pride. He rejected the reform narrative that cast Negroes as "a social problem" requiring sociologists, humanitarians, and "the Race-leader" to expend energy on resolving conflicts. He sought to move beyond the tradition of treating the Negro as "a something to be argued about, or . . . defended, or . . . 'helped up.'"[28] Whereas Miller implored youth to fight the despondency that could result from routine encounters with injustice, Locke surveyed the rising generation and declared the Negro mind free from the "inner grip of prejudice" and "the tyranny of social intimidation."[29] He perceived a new racial identity emerging in cities as they drew vast numbers of Negro migrants. He marveled at New York's Harlem—a new home to Negroes of all classes, outlooks, and backgrounds from the rural South, the Caribbean, and Africa. Although unique, it was a prophetic symbol of the impact of mass transplantation on "race sympathy" and solidarity among diverse peoples. "Hitherto, it must be admitted," he argued,

> that American Negroes have been a race more in name than in fact. . . . The chief bond between them has been that of a common condition rather than a common consciousness; a problem in common rather than a life in common. In Harlem, Negro life is seizing upon its first chances for group expression and self-determination.[30]

The groundwork for his idea that a coherent racial status required cultivating a shared consciousness developed years before his essay earned him the reputation of dean of the emergent Harlem Renaissance. It stemmed from challenges to race he had lodged a decade earlier, when, as a scholar committed to basing reform on logic, he insisted that the only rational conception of race was one that perceived it as a strictly social phenomenon.[31] This conclusion was part of a lecture series he launched in 1915, in which he refuted claims that race had biological foundations.[32] "Race Contacts and Interracial Relations" began with the observation that race refers to a "social inheritance" that has attempted to pass as a biological one. Races were thus "ethnic fictions" that grouped people together who lacked the purity of "blood" and consistency of "type" that racial designations purported to register.[33] He found that theories of race superiority, race purity, race permanence, and separate race development, all of which used social and political phenomena as proxies for biological race traits, also failed to meet the standard of rationality.[34]

Having summarized the fallacies of conventional race ideas, Locke considered the implications of his exercise. They would have been obvious to antebellum reformers who sought to eliminate race practices. However, men like Theophilus Steward, who assailed prevailing practices in order to reconfigure them, might have been sympathetic. Locke feared that the old reform impulse was still prevalent. He complained that "too many people in the world . . . feel that race is so odious a term that it should be eradicated from our thinking and from our vocabulary."[35] This outlook was imprudent, he explained, because the concept of race had the power to designate significant categories of human existence. Furthermore, its meaning was mutable. History demonstrated that the composition and identities of races varied and interpretations of the term could change. Just as the label "Christian" had evolved from a name of reproach to one that believers proudly embraced, "race," he predicted, would be altered by progressive practices.[36]

CONCLUSION   323

Although the lectures lack a clear account of how change was to proceed, they suggest a basis for transformation. They sketch elements of a theory aimed at reconciling Locke's critique of race with his quest for a modern identity. His vision offered a new conception of double consciousness that recognized American Negro identity as an equal part of the society it helped to define and a phenomenon that also thrived on separate ties to people of African descent based on common interests. Building on the conviction that race is strictly a social phenomenon, he revised the rules of comprising them. He appeared to propose what Theophilus Steward had called for—a new "race-ship." He reasoned that individuals who shared common principles and allegiance to the same social system belonged to the same "social kind." They were part of the same "social race," even if they were ethnically dissimilar.[37] People whose customs, values, and beliefs marked them as American thus shared membership in a common American race. Widespread misunderstanding of the country's civilization and of the factors that constituted races blocked recognition of this commonality.

In lieu of delineating the process through which Negroes would forge and maintain a discrete racial sensibility while comprising a race with White Americans, Locke explained why it was necessary. He was convinced that a "secondary race consciousness" would ensure the distinctiveness of Negroes' contributions to the nation's "social culture." It would, in turn, help fend off the disappearance of a clearly discernable Negro identity.[38] Cultural gifts would accord Negroes recognition and respect as part of American society on terms they valued and defined. He cautioned that the collective action needed to cultivate culture did not involve "race isolation" or "race integrity." Instead, the endeavors in his "theory of social conservation" reflected and developed "social solidarity out of heterogeneous elements."[39] They entailed sustained engagement with non-Negroes because recognition required that gifts be exhibited in ways that others could understand. Race consciousness and the cultural agency it would foster thus had the potential to promote a type of homogeneity—one of the historical functions of race. They would advance "culture-citizenship," which would enable Negroes to engage other people as equals in a diverse cultural milieu they helped create.[40]

Cultural production linked to the New Negro of the 1920s fortified Locke's conviction that race consciousness could thrive without reinscribing biological fictions that upheld the color line. The flourishing of literature, visual art, and music reinvigorated his belief in the possibility of culture-citizenship. It promised to generate a wholesale reappraisal of the Negro by Black and

324 RELUCTANT RACE MEN

White Americans alike. He believed it fostered a growing "feeling of race" that was enabling Negroes to develop "a right conception" of themselves and demonstrating that "race co-operation" was becoming "the mainspring of Negro life."[41] It distinguished Negroes as purposeful contributors to the nation's civilization. These developments were harbingers of what he envisioned as a "new democracy in American culture."[42]

Even as the Great Depression impinged on the cultural dynamism of the New Negro, a sense of urgency and optimism about race consciousness and unity persisted alongside ongoing critiques of the logic of race. Du Bois stressed the utility of race pride amid the calamitous economic and social landscape of the 1930s. New Deal policies that left masses of Black domestic and agricultural laborers harmed or unprotected inspired him to formulate a new "racial philosophy" that encompassed the Pan-African unity he espoused at the beginning of the century. He also reinstated Along the Color Line as a regular *Crisis* segment that featured international events.[43] These steps highlighted the global scope and significance of "the Negro problem" by connecting it to issues facing people of African descent around the world. He posited that, as a united front against common experiences of economic discrimination, inequality, and exploitation, an international coalition fueled by race pride could transform Negroes into citizens of a modern economic world.[44]

Against the backdrop of Locke's concept of "social race" that posited an interracial American race, Du Bois insisted that it was imperative for American Negroes to understand that their economic situation trumped cultural and social connections to their fellow White citizens. They had more in common with "dark people" in radically different cultural milieus, he argued, than with the Americans, whose customs and values they shared. He explained that if the nation's race configurations were logical and racial identity was solely about attitudes and thought, the common cultural outlook of Negroes and White Americans could unite them as a common race. Many Negroes he encountered failed to understand that race was not a matter of logic and ventured that they and White people comprised the same race. They had to accept the fact that political realities placed them on common ground with other Negroes around the world.[45] The "race-ship" Locke proposed was not a viable option.

Implementation posed a problem for Du Bois just as it had for Locke. He was uncertain about how to realize his vision of transnational race allegiances. "If we seek new group loyalty, new pride of race, new racial

CONCLUSION 325

integrity," he asked, "how, where, and by what method shall these things be attained?" In contrast to the "fatuous propaganda" he associated with Marcus Garvey's UNIA, he endeavored to cultivate sensibilities that would support economic and political unity.[46] He envisioned disparate peoples of African descent being bound together by "spiritual sympathy and intellectual co-operation" to promote "freedom of the human spirit."[47]

Jim Crow practices complicated the development of race conscious unity. The hierarchy that labeled everyone designated "Negro" as innately inferior and worthy of insult and discrimination made it counterintuitive for some people to ground their identities in the category. Du Bois observed that being treated "as a Negro" was especially demoralizing to accomplished individuals. The experience of having a racial designation void achievements and self-respect provoked indignation, shame, and a reluctance to identify with the masses of impoverished Negroes. It inspired elites to dispute any correlation between physical appearance and social status. Wary of race categories that labeled them as one with uneducated and destitute folk, they objected to being designated as " 'Negro' or even 'Afro-American' or any such term."[48] He lamented that such protestations accompanied a misguided longing for "the disappearance of 'race' " from the nation's lexicon.[49]

The task for modern reformers entailed changing what it meant to be la-beled "Negro." Echoing the concerns of Locke and others about rectifying Negroes' self-understanding, Du Bois stressed the necessity of disseminating accurate accounts of historical developments that could discredit Jim Crow's pejorative representations of their racial position.[50] This work differed from appeals to a glorious past that challenged the premise of Negro inferiority in order to eradicate race. It was not designed to convince White people that their assumptions about Negroes were erroneous. Instead, the aim was to reinterpret the meaning of "Negro" among Negroes. It was to inculcate identities that avoided rendering Black people as a homogeneous group, an innately inferior population, or as people essentially different from other humans. Accordingly, promoting race consciousness and pride was, in its own right, a way of continuing race challenges.

By the mid-twentieth century, the coexistence of endeavors that contested the rational basis of race practices and supported the cultivation of race consciousness had become commonplace. For example, there was no ap-parent inconsistency when journalist Roi Ottley framed his account of Black people's place in post–World War II America with a critique of race assign-ment and rank, along with praise for race identification. First, he observed

326   RELUCTANT RACE MEN

that the label "Negro" was a product of an illogical classification system. The physical traits of the people the term was supposed to describe were so wide ranging that attempts to synthesize them would strain the skills of the most erudite anthropologists. "Negro," he argued, did not identify a biologically distinct population; it was the product of a distorted mindset—a "badge of social and racial inferiority" that grouped disparate people into a caste. The Negro was "the American untouchable."[51] On the heels of deriding the race rules of sameness and hierarchy that scaffolded Jim Crow, he offered a complimentary appraisal of a competing mindset. He commended "new racial sentiments and loyalties" being forged within the confines of subjection and the rising "racial morale" with which increasing numbers of urban Negroes engaged modernity.[52] These divergent race constructions—sameness, stratification, and a shared consciousness—grounded the story of Negroes' ongoing American odyssey.

In addition to continuing the tradition of race challenges, race men paved the way for broadening the scope of contest over race. Decades after they began promoting race consciousness, it gained unprecedented popularity amid mass civil rights and Black Power protests of the 1960s and 1970s. A new generation of activists assailed Jim Crow practices that sustained discriminatory structures of difference, hierarchy, and sameness while intensifying efforts to develop a racial basis for collective identity that would reframe what it meant to be Black. Divergent and conflicting ideas about how to practice blackness occasioned new ways of contesting race. They did not challenge the existence of racial categories. Instead, they inspired debates over how individuals classified as Black should act, look, or think in order to signify blackness. This development further complicated the racial discourse that shaped the course of reform.

———

The diverse formulations and interpretations of race in the history of African American reform endeavors gain a measure of clarity in historian Evelyn Higginbotham's paradigm that presents the phenomenon as a double-voiced discourse. She characterizes constructions of collective identity among race men as "romantic racialism"—the sorts of innocuous appeals to distinctiveness that George Frederickson observed among nineteenth-century reformers. She supplements this interpretation with linguist M. M. Bakhtin's conception of discourse, explaining that race has served the aims

CONCLUSION 327

of people committed to Black subjugation as well as the objectives of African Americans who deployed it as a tool of resistance.[53] In theory, divergent intentions make the racial discourse of Black liberation substantively different from that of Black oppression.

Although intent forms the conceptual basis of distinguishing Black activists' assertions of racial identity from a racial hierarchy based on presumed biological traits, Higginbotham draws a bright line between the two types of phenomena by expanding on Barbara Fields's insistence that Black people developed themselves as a nation rather than as a race. Higginbotham likens Black racial discourse to notions of race that developed in fifteenth-century Europe with the emergence of nation-states. In an analogous fashion, she argues, African Americans registered an imagined kinship by constructing a "black nation with racially-laden meanings of blood ties."[54] Her effort to differentiate between Black racial identity and White racial domination suggests that the diverse ends advanced by appeals to racial discourse are not merely reflections of differences in intent. Instead, making sense of varied functions of race requires an understanding of the multiple ways it has been constituted.

The trajectory of challenges to race traced in his book sets the mutability of racial discourse in sharp relief. The analysis of reformers' engagement with disparate ideas and practices that structured human difference, hierarchy, sameness, and consciousness explains diverse configurations, functions, and meanings of race. It chronicles a long race history through misgivings, debates, justifications, refutations, and theories that marked the nation's social, scientific, religious, and political landscapes. This map of Black reform endeavors thus elucidates assorted practices that have constituted American phenomena called "race."

Notes

Introduction

1. W. E. B. Du Bois, *The Conservation of Races* (Washington, DC: Occasional Papers of the American Negro Academy, 1897), 5, 7.
2. See Felicia R. Lee, "CNN Trains Its Lens on Race," *New York Times*, July 23, 2008. Also see Correspondents of the *New York Times*, *How Race Is Lived in America* (New York: Times Books, Henry Holt, 2001). For an analysis of debates over racial categories in the US Census, see Melissa Nobles, *Shades of Citizenship: Race and the Census in Modern Politics* (Stanford, CA: Stanford University Press, 2000).
3. Du Bois, *The Conservation of Races*, 1–3.
4. Barbara J. Fields offers a different perspective on how to understand race in the United States. She describes race as an epiphenomenon of American slavery; it has no reality apart from its status as an "ideological medium" for explaining slavery and its long aftermath. While she ably explains how race has functioned as an ideology of oppression of Black Americans, she pays scant attention to racial discourses among Black Americans. Fields justifies her omission with the assertion that nineteenth-century Black Americans were not the ones "who invented themselves as a race." Fields's argument is consistent with the ideas of David Brion Davis, Winthrop Jordan, and Edmund Morgan, who root race in the evolution of American slavery. Barbara J. Fields, "Ideology and Race in American History," in *Region, Race, and Reconstruction: Essays in Honor of C. Vann Woodward*, ed. J. Morgan Kousser and James McPherson (New York: Oxford University Press, 1982), 143–147, 168–169; Fields, "Slavery, Race and Ideology in the United States of America," *New Left Review* 181 (May/June 1990): 114–115; David Brion Davis, *The Problem of Slavery in the Age of Revolution, 1770–1823* (Ithaca, NY: Cornell University Press, 1975); Winthrop D. Jordan, *White over Black: American Attitudes toward the Negro, 1550–1812* (Chapel Hill: University of North Carolina Press, 1968); Edmund Morgan, *American Slavery, American Freedom: The Ordeal of Colonial Virginia* (New York: W. W. Norton, 1975). See Ira Berlin, *Many Thousands Gone: The First Two Centuries of Slavery in North America* (Cambridge, MA: Harvard University Press, 1998), prologue. Also see Joanne Pope Melish, "The 'Condition' Debate and Racial Discourse in the Antebellum North," *Journal of the Early American Republic* 19 (Winter 1999): 671. My analysis of Black Americans' identity contrasts with Melish's conclusion of that, after 1800, the notion of a "nonracial identity" among Black Americans was "an oxymoron."
5. US Census Data, accessed October 4, 2001, http://fisher.lib.virginia.edu/cgi-local/censusbin; Simeon Moss, "The Persistence of Slavery and Involuntary Servitude in a Free State," *Journal of Negro History* 35 (1950): 303; Leon Litwack, *North of Slavery: The*

330　NOTES TO PAGES 4–5

Negro in the Free States, 1790–1860 (Chicago: University of Chicago Press, 1961) 14; Carter G. Woodson, *Free Negro Heads of Families in the United States in 1830, Together with a Brief Treatment of the Free Negro* (Washington, DC: Association for the Study of Negro Life and History, 1925), iii and passim.

6. Ira Berlin, *Slaves without Masters: The Free Negro in the Antebellum South* (New York: Oxford University Press, 1974).

7. David Roediger argues that the barriers to the political and civil participation that antebellum free people of color faced were so decisive that blackness "almost perfectly predicted a lack of the attributes of a freeman." Accordingly, they were "anticitizens." David Roediger, *The Wages of Whiteness: Race and the Making of the American Working Class* (New York: Verso Press, 1991), 56.

8. In the ongoing creation of the nation's race taxonomy, "multiracial" is one of the newest proposed classifications. Individuals who file suits to change their official race designation engage in the second type of challenge that questions rules of race assignment. Race practices related to identity are comparable to gender constructions of manliness or womanliness, which need not accurately reflect actions or experiences of people defined as men and women. For an analysis of the process of ascription in defining races, see Rogers Smith, *Civic Ideals: Conflicting Visions of Citizenship in U.S. History* (New Haven, CT: Yale University Press, 1997).

9. For studies that explore race by analyzing shifting cultural, economic, and legal parameters of whiteness, see Noel Ignatiev, *How the Irish Became White* (New York: Routledge, 1995); Ian Lopez, *White by Law: The Legal Construction of Race* (New York: New York University Press, 1996); Matthew Frye Jacobson, *Whiteness of a Different Color: European Immigrants and the Alchemy of Race* (Cambridge, MA: Harvard University Press, 1998); Roediger, *The Wages of Whiteness*. For studies that focus on Black Americans, see Mia E. Bay, *The White Image in the Black Mind: African American Ideas about White People, 1830–1925* (New York: Oxford University Press, 2000); Patrick Rael, *Black Identity and Black Protest in the Antebellum North* (Chapel Hill: University of North Carolina Press, 2002); Sterling Stuckey, *The Ideological Origins of Black Nationalism* (Boston: Beacon Press, 1972); Stuckey, *Slave Culture: Nationalist Theory and the Foundations of Black America* (New York: Oxford University Press, 1987); Wilson Moses, *The Golden Age of Black Nationalism, 1850–1925* (Hamden, CT: Archon, 1978); Kevin Gaines, *Uplifting the Race: Black Leadership, Politics, and Culture in the Twentieth Century* (Chapel Hill: University of North Carolina Press, 1996); George M. Frederickson, *The Black Image in the White Mind: The Debate of Afro-American Character and Destiny, 1817–1914* (New York: Harper & Row, 1971), chapter 4. Studies of "racialization" recognize race as part of broader historical processes. See Michael Omi and Howard Winant, *Racial Formation in the United States from the 1960s to the 1980s* (New York: Routledge and Kegan Paul, 1986); and Yehudi Webster, *The Racialization of America* (New York: St. Martin's Press, 1992).

10. Mia Bay's analysis of nineteenth-century Black American ideas about "the white race" offers the most sustained consideration of Black racial thought to date. She argues that, in denouncing white supremacy, Black Americans "challenged the meaning of

NOTES TO PAGES 5–11   331

race itself." However, in questioning the "innate moral character" of White people, they sometimes fell prey to the "audacious fiction" of race they sought to undermine. She deploys George Frederickson's notion of "romantic racialism" to distinguish Black Americans' apparent belief in the existence of permanently different races from racist ideologies they rejected. Patrick Rael draws similar conclusions about the antebellum period. He assumes that Black Americans grounded their collective identity in the concept of race. Sterling Stuckey provides the most extensive analysis of nineteenth-century conflicts over race terms. In his view, it reflects competing liberation strategies. He concludes that challenges to race constructions were a symptom of spiritual and psychological confusion and misgivings about race were a sign of false consciousness. See Bay, *White Image in the Black Mind*, 9, 39, 53–55, 221; Frederickson, *The Black Image in the White Mind*, 101–102; Rael, *Black Identity and Black Protest*, 249–252. Stuckey, *Slave Culture*, 244 and chapter 4.

11. For a critique of the "separation-integration dichotomy," see George A. Levesque, "Interpreting Early Black Ideology: A Reappraisal of Historical Consensus," *Journal of the Early Republic* (Fall 1981): 269–287.

12. William Ellery Channing, *The Works of William Ellery Channing* (Boston: American Unitarian Association, 1875), 138–149. Associations played pivotal roles in advancing the agendas of church leaders and political officials throughout the nineteenth century. See Robert T. Handy, *A Christian America: Protestant Hopes and Historical Realities*, 2nd edition (New York: Oxford University Press, 1984), 37–47; Jon Butler, *Awash in a Sea of Faith: Christianizing the American People* (Cambridge, MA: Harvard University Press, 1990), 268, 273–274, 287; R. Laurence Moore, "Religion, Secularization, and the Shaping of the Culture Industry in Antebellum America," *American Quarterly* 41 (June 1989): 218–219; Peter Dobkin Hall, "Religion in the Origins of Voluntary Associations in the United States," Working Papers of the Program on Non-Profit Organizations, #213 (New Haven, CT: Yale Institute for Social and Policy Studies, 1994).

13. *National Reformer*, September 1838; *Colored American*, April 4, 1837; February 10, 1838.

14. *Colored American*, March 29, 1838; *National Reformer*, November 1838, November 1839, December 1839; *Anglo-African Magazine*, October 1859, 309; *Frederick Douglass' Paper*, May 12, 1854. Patrick Rael argues that these antebellum reformers put "misplaced" faith in the power of public sentiment because they assumed that a rational "marketplace of ideas" could trump White people's "racial prejudice." See Rael, *Black Identity and Black Protest*, 206–208.

15. *Frederick Douglass' Paper*, May 27, 1852; January 12, 1855; June 29, 1855.

Chapter 1

1. *Freedom's Journal*, March 16, 1827.
2. *Freedom's Journal*, March 16, 1827; March 30, 1827.

332 NOTES TO PAGES 11–13

3. *Freedom's Journal*, August 17, 1827. Edward Clay's "Life in Philadelphia" broadsides depicting grotesque caricatures of free people of color offer a popular visual manifestation of the problem of misrepresentation. For examples, see Emma Jones Lapsansky, "'Since They Got Those Separate Churches': Afro-Americans and Racism in Jacksonian Philadelphia," *American Quarterly* 32 (Spring 1980): 65–67.

4. *Freedom's Journal*, February 14, 1829; March 7, 1829; September 28, 1827. Seven months after the paper's founding, Cornish resigned his senior editorial post to work with the New York African Free Schools. He continued to serve as an agent for the paper. Two months after *Freedom's Journal* collapsed, Cornish began editing the short-lived *Rights of All*, which also promised to render a "correct representation" of free people of color. Bella Gross, "*Freedom's Journal* and the *Rights of All*," *Journal of Negro History* 17 (July 1932): 242, 248; *Rights of All*, May 29, 1929.

5. The fact that colonization was officially voluntary and had limited success in sending people of color to Africa suggests that it posed no serious threat to those who viewed America as their rightful home. Colonization Society data indicate that free people of color comprised 38 percent of the 11,909 people it settled in Liberia between 1820 and 1866. (This figure does not include 314 people whose status was unknown or 1,227 people sent by the Maryland Colonization Society when it functioned as an independent body.) Bell Wiley, ed., *Slaves No More: Letters from Liberia, 1833–1869* (Lexington: University Press of Kentucky, 1980), 311n2. See *African Repository and Colonial Journal* 43 (1867): 109–117. The society's *Eleventh Annual Report* indicates that it hoped to send at least thirty thousand people to Africa each year. *Eleventh Annual Report of the American Society for Colonizing Free People of Colour of the United States* (Washington, DC: James C. Dunn, 1828), 13.

6. *Minutes of the Fourth Annual Convention for the Improvement of the Free People of Colour, in the United States, Held by Adjournments in the Asbury Church, New York* (New York, 1834), in Howard Bell, ed., *Minutes of the Proceedings of the National Negro Conventions, 1830–1864* (New York: Arno Press and the New York Times, 1969), 4. Bell's volume organizes the minutes in chronological order with their original pagination.

7. Thomas Jefferson, *Notes on the State of Virginia* (1784; Chapel Hill: University of North Carolina Press, 1955), 137–143; P. J. Staudenraus, *The African Colonization Movement, 1816–1865* (New York: Columbia University Press, 1961), 1–3. See Douglas R. Egerton, "'Its Origin Is Not a Little Curious': A New Look at the American Colonization Society," *Journal of the Early Republic* 5 (Winter 1985): 463–480. For examples of early interest in "returning" to Africa among free people of African descent, see Dorothy Sterling, ed., *Speak Out in Thunder Tones: Letters and Other Writings by Black Northerners, 1787–1865* (New York: Da Capo Press, 1998), 4–12.

8. See F. Freeman, *A Plea for Africa, Being Familiar Conversations on the Subject of Slavery and Colonization.* 2nd edition (Philadelphia: J. Whetham, 1837), 201; Cyrus Edwards, *Address Delivered at the State House, in Vandalia on the Subject of Forming a State Colonization Society; auxiliary to the American Colonization Society* (Jacksonville, IL: James G. Edwards, 1831), 4.

NOTES TO PAGES 13-15   333

9. *Proceedings of a Meeting Held in Princeton, New Jersey, July 14, 1824, to Form a Society in the State of New-Jersey, to Cooperate with the American Colonization Society* (Princeton, 1824), in *Freedom Not Far Distant: A Documentary History of Afro-Americans in New Jersey*, ed. Clement Price (Newark, NJ: New Jersey Historical Society, 1980), 100–104; Staudenraus, *The African Colonization Movement*, 85.

10. F. Freeman, *A Plea for Africa*, 173.

11. William McMurray, DD, *A Sermon preached in behalf of the American Colonization Society in the Reformed Dutch Church in Market Street, New York, July 10, 1825* (New York: J Seymour, 1825), 20–21.

12. *True American*, September 3, 1825; September 17, 1825. Lucius Elmer was a vice president of the American Colonization Society from 1843 until his death in 1883. Elmer was so adamant about the alien character of free people of color that he defended measures rescinding their rights, even when they appeared to violate New Jersey's constitution. For a sketch of Elmer's political career, see William Dayton, *Biographical Encyclopedia of New Jersey in the Nineteenth Century* (Philadelphia: Galaxy, 1877), 119–120. See also John P. Durbin, *Address Delivered in the Hall of the House of Representatives, Harrisburg, PA, on Tuesday Evening, April 6, 1852* (Philadelphia: Pennsylvania Colonization Society, 1852), 39; *Sixty-Seventh Annual Report of the American Colonization Society with the Minutes of the Annual Meeting and the Board of Directors, January 15 and 16, 1884*, printed in *The Annual Reports of the American Society for Colonizing the Free People of Colour of the United States*, vols. 64–91, *1881–1910* (New York: Negro Universities Press, 1969).

13. F. Freeman, *A Plea for Africa*, 223. Also, see William Lloyd Garrison, *Thoughts on African Colonization; or an Impartial Exhibition of the Doctrines, Principles and Purposes of the American Colonization Society. Together with the Resolutions, Addresses, and Remonstrances of the Free People of Color* (Boston: Mathew Carey, 1832), part 1, 139.

14. See *African Repository* 3 (n.d.), as quoted in Garrison, *Thoughts on African Colonization*, part 1, 135.

15. Emphasis is in the original. Garrison, *Thoughts on African Colonization*, part 1, 135, 137–138. F. Freeman, *Yaradee; A Plea for Africa, in Familiar Conversations on the Subject of Slavery and Colonization* (1836; repr., New York: Negro Universities Press, 1969), 170–171; *African Repository* 5 (November 1829): 278, as quoted in David Streifford, "The American Colonization Society: An Application of Republican Ideology to Antebellum Reform," *Journal of Southern History* 45:2 (May 1979): 211; American Colonization Society, *Seventh Annual Report* (1824), as quoted in Streifford, "The American Colonization Society," 211.

16. *True American*, September 3, 1925.

17. McMurray, *A Sermon preached in behalf of the American Colonization*, 20–21; Richard Fuller, *Our Duty to the African Race: An Address Delivered at Wash, D.C., Jan 21, 1851* (Baltimore, 1851), 12, 4, 6.

18. *Fifteenth Annual Report of the American Colonization Society*, as quoted in Garrison, *Thoughts on African Colonization*, part 1, 138.

19. *African Repository and Colonial Journal* 1 (1825).

334   NOTES TO PAGES 15–18

20. See *Freedom's Journal*, December 5, 1828 and December 12, 1828.

21. Although colonization was a private endeavor, Congress and state legislatures in Maryland, Missouri, New Jersey, Pennsylvania, and Virginia appropriated funds for the Colonization Society. Staudenraus, *The African Colonization Movement*, 243–244.

22. Lott Cary is quoted in Staudenraus, *The African Colonization Movement*, 109.

23. F. Freeman, *A Plea for Africa*, 1837, 221; *Eleventh Annual Report*, 13; James Hall, *An Address to the Free People of Color of the state of Maryland* (Baltimore, 1859), 3–4. See M. R. Delany, *Official Report of the Niger Valley Exploring Party* (New York: Thomas Hamilton, 1861), 57–62.

24. Fuller, *Our Duty to the African Race*, 12; McMurray, *A Sermon Preached in behalf of the American Colonization*, 16–17, 22.

25. *True American*, September 3, 1925; September 17, 1925; Presbyterian Church of the U.S.A. Synod of New York and New Jersey, *An Address to the Public on the Subject of the African School* (New York, 1816), in Price, *Freedom Not Far Distant*, 96; *National Enquirer and Constitutional Advocate of Universal Liberty*, September 14, 1837; F. Freeman, *A Plea for Africa*, 286–287.

26. Peter Williams, "A Discourse Delivered in St. Philip's Church, for the Benefit of the Colored Community of Wilberforce, in Upper Canada, on the Fourth of July, 1830," as quoted in Garrison, *Thoughts on African Colonization*, part 2, 65. For the complete speech, see Carter G. Woodson, ed. *Negro Orators and their Orations* (Washington, DC: Association for the Study of Negro Life and History, 1925), 77–86.

27. Bettye J. Gardner, "William Watkins: Antebellum Black Teacher and Anti-Slavery Writer," *Negro History Bulletin* 39 (September–October 1976): 625.

28. Garrison, *Thoughts on African Colonization*, part 2, 9–13, 62–63. Forten is quoted in Julie Winch, *A Gentleman of Color: The Life of James Forten* (New York: Oxford University Press, 2002), 191. Also see Julie Winch, *Philadelphia's Black Elite: Activism, Accommodation, and the Struggle for Autonomy, 1787–1848* (Philadelphia: Temple University Press, 1988), 34–48; Carol George, *Segregated Sabbaths: Richard Allen and the Emergence of Independent Black Churches, 1760–1840* (New York: Oxford University Press, 1973), 151–153.

29. Garrison, *Thoughts on African Colonization*, part 2, 62–63. Floyd Miller, *The Search for a Black Nationality: Black Emigration and Colonization, 1787–1863* (Urbana: University of Illinois Press, 1975), 48.

30. *Freedom's Journal*, February 21, 1829; David Walker, *David Walker's Appeal, in Four Articles; together with a Preamble, to the Coloured Citizens of the World, but in Particular, and Very Expressly, to those of the United States of America* (New York: Hill and Wang, 1999).

31. James Forten to William Lloyd Garrison, February 23, 1831, in Sterling, *Speak Out in Thunder Tones*, 59. See also Samuel E. Cornish and Theodore S. Wright, *The Colonization Scheme Considered, in Its Tendency to Uphold Caste-In Its Unfitness for Christianizing and Civilizing the Aborigines of Africa, and for Putting a Stop to the African Slave Trade* (Newark, NJ: Aaron Guest, 1840).

NOTES TO PAGES 18–20   335

32. Robert Purvis, *Remarks on the Life and Character of James Forten, Delivered at Bethel Church, March 30, 1842* (Philadelphia: Merrihew and Thompson, 1842), 14–15; *African Repository*, May 1842, quoted in Winch, A Gentleman of Color, 330.

33. Local anti-colonization meetings coincided with William Lloyd Garrison's lecture tour denouncing the ACS in Connecticut, Delaware, the District of Columbia, Maryland, Massachusetts, New Jersey, New York, Pennsylvania, and Rhode Island. Garrison, *Thoughts on African Colonization*, part 2, 13–51; *A Remonstrance Against the Proceedings of a Meeting, held November 23rd, 1831 at Upton's, in Dock Street, Philadelphia* (Philadelphia, 1832).

34. Historians James and Lois Horton link the rejection of Africa to "racist interpretations of Africans" that became increasingly popular in antebellum America. They suggest that the free population imbibed "typically 'American'" images of Africa as memories of the continent faded. They insist, however, that free people did not abandon their African identity; the colonization threat "forced" them to stress participation in American life. Patrick Rael concludes that, in the absence of the "nefarious rhetoric" of the ACS, free people "likely would have woven a return to Africa far more thoroughly into their public speech." Floyd Miller and Sterling Stuckey also stress fear of forced deportation as a decisive factor in anti-colonization. See James Horton and Lois Horton, *In Hope of Liberty: Culture Community and Protest among Northern Free Blacks, 1700–1860* (New York: Oxford University Press, 1997) 198–202; Rael, *Black Identity and Black Protest*, 276; Floyd Miller, *The Search for a Black Nationality*, 48–49, 54; Stuckey, Slave Culture, 202. See St. Clair Drake, "The Meaning of Negritude: The Negro's Stake in Africa," *Negro Digest* 13:8 (June 1964): 39. In his innovative analysis of nationalism in the early republic, David Waldstreicher argues that free people of African descent used speeches, parades, and pamphlets to create a distinct Black nationalism and nationality that mirrored the white nationalism of the ACS. Although there may be evidence to support this interpretation before 1830, it is difficult to make the case for the persistence of a distinct nationalism into the 1830s. See Waldstreicher, *In the Midst of Perpetual Fetes: The Making of American Nationalism, 1776–1820* (Chapel Hill, University of North Carolina Press, 1997), 308–344.

35. "James Forten to William Lloyd Garrison, May 6, 1832, in *Black Abolitionist Papers*, vol. 3, ed. C. Peter Ripley, (Chapel Hill: The University of North Carolina Press, 1991), 86–87.

36. Garrison, *Thoughts on African Colonization*, part 2, 16, 44.

37. Garrison, *Thoughts on African Colonization*, part 2, 37.

38. Emphasis is in the original. *Colored American*, September 1, 1838; Staudenraus, *The African Colonization Movement*, 180.

39. *Liberator*, June 4, 1831.

40. David Walker, *Appeal*, 50–51.

41. Garrison, *Thoughts on African Colonization*, part 2, 30, 31, 38, 34–35, 44, 70.

42. Garrison, *Thoughts on African Colonization*, 19–20.

43. *Black Abolitionist Papers*, vol. 3, 225n; Peter Williams Jr. *A Discourse, Delivered on the Death of Capt. Paul Cuffe, Before the New-York African Institution, In the African Methodist Episcopal Zion Church October 21, 1817* (Nendeln, Switzerland: Kraus

336 NOTES TO PAGES 20–24

Reprint, 1970) 15–16; Paul Cuffe to Peter Williams, August 30, 1815, in Sterling, *Speak Out in Thunder Tones*, 20–21.

44. *Freedom's Journal*, November 2, 1827; Garrison, *Thoughts on African Colonization*, part 2, 16, 47–48, 65.

45. Garrison, *Thoughts on African Colonization*, 15, 38, 47, 51.

46. *Liberator*, February 12, 1831; Garrison, *Thoughts on African Colonization*, part 2, 58–59.

47. Garrison, *Thoughts on African Colonization*, part 2, 14–15.

48. Garrison, *Thoughts on African Colonization*, part 2, 19, 36–37.

49. Garrison, *Thoughts on African Colonization*, part 2, 52–53.

50. Garrison, *Thoughts on African Colonization*, part 2, 37.

51. Garrison, *Thoughts on African Colonization*, part 2, 27, 30–34, 36, 41, 43.

52. Garrison, *Thoughts on African Colonization*, part 2, 30–31.

53. Garrison, *Thoughts on African Colonization*, part 2, 35.

54. The Boyer government promised to provide passage, free land, and supplies to each household. Disillusionment on the part of settlers and the government halted the program, which was fraught with religious, cultural, and class conflicts, as well as corruption. Haitian reports indicate that a third of the settlers left the island within one year. Julie Winch, "American Free Blacks and Emigration to Haiti" (paper presented at the Eleventh Caribbean Congress of the Caribbean Institute and Study Center for Latin America of Inter American University, August 1988), 14; Winch, *Philadelphia's Black Elite*, 52–61; Floyd Miller, *The Search for a Black Nationality*, 76–82; Staudenraus, *The African Colonization Movement*, 81–85; John Baur, "Mulatto Machiavelli, Jean Pierre Boyer, and the Haiti of His Day," *Journal of Negro History* 32 (July 1947): 325–328.

55. David Walker, *Appeal*, 56; Garrison, *Thoughts on African Colonization*, part 2, 26, 33, 42, 43, 46; Peter Williams, *A Discourse delivered in St. Philip's Church*.

56. Mathew Carey, *Reflections on the Causes that led to the Formation of the Colonization Society* (Philadelphia, 1832), 16; Staudenraus, *The African Colonization Movement*, 83–85.

57. For analyses of class standing and power struggles among convention participants, see Winch, *Philadelphia's Black Elite*, chapters 1 and 5; Harry A. Reed, *Platform for Change: The Foundations of the Northern Free Black Community, 1775–1865* (East Lansing: Michigan State University Press, 1994), 127–128, 154–158; and Rael, *Black Identity and Black Protest*.

58. Jane and William Pease share Sterling Stuckey's conclusion that Whipper simply heeded directives of white benefactors. The principle of moral suasion that William Lloyd Garrison championed clearly informed Whipper's thinking, just as it influenced such prominent abolitionists as Frederick Douglass, William Cooper Nell, Charles Remond, and Robert Purvis. However, while their reform careers evolved in alliances with Garrison and other white abolitionists, Whipper's perspectives developed squarely within Black reform arenas. Jane H. Pease and William Pease, *They Who Would Be Free: Blacks' Search for Freedom, 1830–1861* (Urbana: University of Illinois, 1990), 121–122; Stuckey, *Slave Culture*, 203.

NOTES TO PAGES 24–26   337

59. Fourteen non-delegates participated in the meeting as "honorary members." *Constitution of the American Society of Free Persons of Colour, for Improving their Condition in the United States; for the Purchasing of Lands; and for the Establishment of a Settlement in Upper Canada; also the Proceedings of the Convention, with their Address to the Free Persons of Colour in the United States* (Philadelphia: J. W. Allen, 1831), in Bell, *Proceedings*, 4–5, 9.

60. "Institutions for Mutual Relief," in *A Documentary History of the Negro People in the United States*, ed. Herbert Aptheker (New York: Citadel Press, 1990), 112–114.

61. *Constitution of the American Society of Free Persons of Colour* (1831), 10.

62. Historians Julie Winch and Harry Reed interpret the first convention as an ad hoc intervention on behalf of Ohio residents. However, the crisis that began for them in 1829 had abated by the time the convention met in September of the following year. As historian Robin Winks recounts, Indiana and Ohio Quakers had already purchased a parcel of land in Upper Canada that fostered the beginnings of a small settlement. Others had secured land on their own outside of the Wilberforce Colony. Furthermore, the mayor of Cincinnati, concerned about the loss of workers, had urged people to stay while he sought the repeal of the Black Codes. Although the codes remained in effect until 1838, only a fraction of Cincinnati's nearly three thousand colored residents left the city. Fewer than one thousand individuals had migrated to Upper Canada by the end of 1830; approximately half were from Cincinnati. Winch, *Philadelphia's Black Elite*, 91–93, 107; Harry A Reed, *Platform for Change*, 136–139; Robin Winks, *The Blacks in Canada: A History*, 2nd edition (New Haven, CT: Yale University Press, 1971), 155–157; "Meeting of February, 1830," in Aptheker, *A Documentary History of the Negro People in the United States*, vol. 1, 102–103; *Constitution of the American Society of Free Persons of Colour* (1831), 9, 10.

63. "The First Colored Convention," *Anglo-African Magazine*, October 1859. The debate Grice describes is not part of the 1830 convention proceedings. The omission marks the start of a common practice of excluding debates and positions from convention proceedings and minutes. Joseph Willson, a convention observer, reported that publication committees altered accounts of proceedings and presented their positions as the prevailing sentiments. He knew of cases in which decisions carried by the majority were "totally misrepresented before the public, by an alteration of the proceedings before . . . publication." [Joseph Willson, *Sketches of the Higher Class of Colored Society in Philadelphia by a Southerner* (Philadelphia: Merrihew & Thompson, 1841), 89–90; Winch, *Philadelphia's Black Elite*, 94–107.

64. Allen reportedly called the convention to prevent New Yorkers from meeting first. He also restricted attendance and participation in the proceedings. It is unclear why nearly one-third of the men in attendance were not counted as delegates. For a delegate's recollections of what inspired the convention, see "The First Colored Convention," *Anglo-African Magazine*, October 1859.

65. *Liberator*, May 28, 1831.

66. *Minutes and Proceedings of the First Annual Convention of the People of Colour, Held by Adjournments in the City of Philadelphia* (Philadelphia, 1831), 10, in Bell, *Proceedings*;

338   NOTES TO PAGES 26-31

Liberator, July 2, 1831; Martin Dann, ed. *The Black Press, 1827-1890: The Quest for National Identity* (New York: G. Putnam's Sons, 1971) 41-42.

67. *Minutes and Proceedings of the First Annual Convention*, 14, 4, 5, 12, 15.

68. *Minutes and Proceedings of the First Annual Convention*, 7-9.

69. Winch, *Philadelphia's Black Elite*, 94-107.

70. *Minutes and Proceedings of the First Annual Convention*, 4, 8.

71. *Minutes and Proceedings of the First Annual Convention*, 14, 4.

72. *Minutes and Proceedings of the First Annual Convention*, 5-7, 14; Garrison, *An Address Delivered before the Free People of Color in Philadelphia, New-York and Other Cities* (Boston, 1831), 13, in Garrison, *Thoughts on African Colonization*, n p; Philip Foner and George E. Walker, eds., *Proceedings of the Black State Conventions, 1840-1865*, vol. 2 (Philadelphia: Temple University Press, 1980) 86. See Paul Goodman, "The Manual Labor Movement and the Origins of Abolitionism," *Journal of the Early Republic* 13 (1993): 355-388.

73. *Minutes and Proceedings of the First Annual Convention*, 14-15.

74. *Minutes and Proceedings of the First Annual Convention*, 4-5, 10; See Garrison, *An Address*, 8.

75. *Minutes and Proceedings of the Second Annual Convention, For the Improvement of the Free People of Color in these United States Held by Adjournments in the City of Philadelphia* (Philadelphia, 1832), 6, in Bell, *Proceedings*, 9, 11, 6.

76. *Minutes and Proceedings of the Second Annual Convention*, 8.

77. *Liberator*, April 21, 1832.

78. *Minutes and Proceedings of the Second Annual Convention*, 10; Winks, *The Blacks in Canada*, 156-157.

79. Steward quit the settlement in 1837. *Minutes and Proceedings of the Second Annual Convention*, 9-11, 13-19, 20, 26; Austin Steward, *Twenty Years a Slave and Forty Years a Freeman* (Syracuse, NY: Syracuse University Press, 2002).

80. *College for Colored Youth: An Account of the New-Haven City Meeting and Resolutions: With Recommendations of the College, and Structures upon the Doings of New-Haven* (New York: The Committee, 1831).

81. Emphasis is in the original. *Minutes and Proceedings of the Second Annual Convention*, 5-6, 23-25, 32, 35-36. See Rael, *Black Identity and Black Protest*, chapter 5 and passim; Harry A. Reed, *Platform for Change*, 158. For an early articulation of this interpretation of moral suasion, see Howard Bell, "National Negro Conventions of the Middle 1840s: Moral Suasion vs. Political Action," *Journal of Negro History* 42 (October 1957): 247-260.

82. *Minutes and Proceedings of the Second Annual Convention*, 27.

83. *Minutes of the Third Annual Convention for the Improvement of the Free People of Colour, in the United States, Held by Adjournments in the City of Philadelphia* (New York, 1833) in Bell, *Proceedings*, 35-36.

84. *Minutes of the Third Annual Convention*, 34-35.

85. *Minutes of the Third Annual Convention*, 31.

86. *Minutes of the Third Annual Convention*, 22-23.

NOTES TO PAGES 32–37   339

87. *Minutes of the Third Annual Convention*, 8, 25, 15–19. For an extended discussion of the strategic character of appeals to respectability, see Rael, *Black Identity and Black Protest*, 206–207 and passim.

88. *Minutes of the Third Annual Convention*, 29.

89. Minutes of the Fourth Annual Convention, 3–7.

90. *Minutes of the Fourth Annual Convention*, 21–23; *Minutes and Proceedings of the Second Annual Convention*, 12–13.

91. *Minutes of the Fourth Annual Convention*, 16, 17.

92. *Minutes of the Fourth Annual Convention*, 15, 18, 26, 27.

93. *Minutes of the Fourth Annual Convention*, 12.

94. *Minutes of the Fourth Annual Convention*, 15, 24, 14–17.

95. *Minutes of the Fourth Annual Convention*, 15, 18, 20, 24, 27; Winch, *Philadelphia's Black Elite*, 171n12; John Runcie, "'Hunting the Nigs' in Philadelphia: The Race Riot of August 1834," *Pennsylvania History* 39 (April 1972): 187–218; Lapsansky, "'Since They Got Those Separate Churches'"; David Grimstead, "Rioting in Its Jacksonian Setting," *American Historical Review* 77 (April 1971): 361–397; Linda Kerber, "Abolitionists and Amalgamators: The New York City Race Riots of 1834," *New York History* 48 (1967): 28–39; John Werner, *Reaping the Bloody Harvest: Race Riots in the United States during the Age of Jackson, 1821–1849* (New York, 1986).

96. *Colored American*, June 9, 1838.

97. Whipper might not have heard Hamilton's speech because he arrived after the convention began. He seems to have drafted the Declaration of Sentiment before proposing that the convention formulate such a document. *Minutes of the Fourth Annual Convention*, 23; *Colored American*, June 9, 1838.

98. *Minutes of the Fourth Annual Convention for the Improvement of the Free People of Colour*, 27–28.

99. *Minutes of the Fourth Annual Convention*, 29–31.

100. *Minutes of the Fourth Annual Convention*, 31.

101. *Liberator*, June 21, 1834; June 28, 1834; July 5, 1834.

102. Whipper linked slavery and intemperance by citing Thomas Clarkson's observation that slave traders used alcohol to induce Africans to sell "their brethren." *Liberator*, June 21, 1834; June 28, 1834; July 5, 1834."

103. Wm. Whipper, "Moral Reform," Philadelphia, December 11, 1834, Amy Matilda Cassey Album, Library Company of Philadelphia.

104. Subsequent criticisms of the Reform Society emphasized the fact that convention delegates never authorized an "American" society. *Minutes of the Fifth Annual Convention for the Improvement of the Free People of Colour in the United States, Held by Adjournments, in the Wesley Church, Philadelphia, From the First to the Fifth of June, Inclusive, 1835* (Philadelphia, 1835), in Bell, *Proceedings*, 4, 5, 8–9, 11; *Colored American*, September 23, 1837.

105. It is unclear whether proponents of the Reform Society intended to displace the conventions altogether. Whipper's opponents clearly envisioned future convention gatherings. Whipper's position is ambiguous. He and Robert Purvis recommended that a committee name the Conventional Board for the next year, and he was chosen

340   NOTES TO PAGES 37–41

to serve on this selection committee. Evidence of the machinations surrounding the formation of the American Moral Reform Society appear in the preamble of its constitution drafted by Whipper, Stephen Smith, Augustus Price, New Yorker Edward Crosby, and William Powell of New Bedford. The document, which became part of the convention minutes, maintains that the society came into being at the 1834 convention. Although Whipper and John Jackson of Newtown, New York, had proposed such an action, there is no evidence that the convention considered it. *Minutes of the Fifth Annual Convention,* 5, 15, 31. *Minutes of the Fourth Annual Convention,* 35.

106. *Minutes of the Fifth Annual Convention,* 29. William and Jane Pease argue that the American Moral Reform Society's "all-embracing" program was its critical flaw and evidence of white abolitionist influence. Patrick Rael argues that moral reform endeavors stemmed from Black activists' limited options. Pease and Pease, *They Who Would Be Free,* 121–122; Rael, *Black Identity and Black Protest,* 206–207.

107. *Freedom's Journal,* December 26, 1828; *Colored American,* February 6, 1841; "Maryland Free Colored People's Convention, July 27 28, 1852," in Foner and Walker, *Proceedings,* vol. 2, 43, 47.

108. *Minutes of the Fifth Annual Convention,* 17, 12, 6, 14.

109. *Minutes of the Fifth Annual Convention,* 10–11, 14–15. The vote to eliminate "African" in institutional titles was taken on the final afternoon of the five-day convention. A unanimous vote might reflect the fact that many delegates had already left.

110. *Minutes of the Fifth Annual Convention,* 6, 7, 11, 18.

111. *Minutes of the Fifth Annual Convention,* 28, 27. Subsequent publications of the convention address name Whipper as the sole author. See *Minutes and Proceedings of the First Annual Meeting of the American Moral Reform Society Held at Philadelphia,* (Philadelphia: Merrihew and Gunn, 1837) in *Early Negro Writing, 1760–1837,* ed. Dorothy Porter (Boston: Beacon Press, 1971), 204–209.

112. *Minutes of the Fifth Annual Convention,* 26, 30, 27.

113. *Minutes of the Fifth Annual Convention,* 30, 27, 14.

114. For a detailed analysis of power struggles among New Yorkers and Philadelphians in the conventions, see Winch, *Philadelphia's Black Elite,* chapter 5.

Chapter 2

1. *Colored American,* April 1, 1837; *Zion's Herald,* April 26, 1837; *Colored American,* August 25, 1838; December 29, 1838; *National Enquirer,* August 3, 1827; August 31, 1837; August 3, 1837.

2. John Cook preached in African Methodist churches in the 1830s and was ordained as a Presbyterian in 1843. Daniel Payne and Morris Brown would later become AME Church bishops. Alexander Wayman, *Cyclopedia of African Methodism* (Baltimore: Methodist Episcopal Book Depository, 1882), 46, 67; *Black Abolitionist Papers,* vol. 3, 454n; Daniel Payne, *Recollections of Seventy Years* (1885; reprint, New York: Arno Press and the New York Times, 1969), 65; *Colored American,* May 13, 1837; Winch, *Philadelphia's Black Elite,* 108–109; Howard Bell, "The American

NOTES TO PAGES 41–46 341

Moral Reform Society, 1836–1841." *Journal of Negro Education* 27 (Winter 1958): 22, 39–40; Minutes of the Fifth Annual Convention, 10, 27, 29.

3. William Whipper and Robert Purvis did not formally affiliate with any religious denominations. Whipper maintained congenial ties to the AME Church, in which his business partner Stephen Smith was a preacher. Near the end of his life, Purvis developed connections with Unitarians. *Christian Recorder*, March 16, 1876; Margaret Hope Bacon, *But One Race: The Life of Robert Purvis* (Albany: State University of New York Press, 2007), 205, 208.

4. Sherri Burr, "Aaron Burr Jr. and John Pierre Burr: A Founding Father and His Abolitionist Son," Princeton & Slavery Project, accessed January 5, 2021, https://slavery.princeton.edu/stories/john-pierre-burr#ref-41; Minutes and Proceedings of the First Annual Meeting of the American Moral Reform Society (Philadelphia: Merrihew and Gunn, 1837), 211, 225–241; *Minutes of the Fifth Annual Convention*, 26; *Freedom's Journal*, March 16, 1827; William Watkins, *Address Delivered before the Moral Reform Society in Philadelphia, August 8, 1836* (Philadelphia: Merrihew & Gunn, 1836) in Porter, *Early Negro Writing, 1760–1837*, 158–159, 161, 165–166.

5. *Minutes of the Fifth Annual Convention*, 29.

6. *Colored American*, September 9, 1837; September 16, 1837; September 23, 1837; September 30, 1837.

7. *Genius of Universal Emancipation*, May 1831; *Liberator*, April 5, 1834; Benjamin Quarles, *Black Abolitionists* (New York: Oxford University Press, 1969), 75; Bacon, *But One Race*, 97; *National Enquirer*, August 24, 1836; November 12, 1836; Lawrence B. Glickman, "'Buy for the Sake of the Slave': Abolitionism and the Origins of American Consumer Activism," *American Quarterly* 56:4 (December 2004): 900–904.

8. Emphasis is in the original. *National Enquirer*, November 12, 1836.

9. Jacob Oson, *A Search for Truth; or An Inquiry for the Origin of the African Nation: An Address, Delivered at New-Haven in March, and at New-York in April 1817* (New York, 1817), 3. See Luke 10:27 (RSV).

10. *National Enquirer*, December 3, 1836.

11. *National Enquirer*, December 3, 1836.

12. *National Enquirer*, December 3, 1836. The biblical reference to "one blood" is in Acts 17:26.

13. For descriptions of the issues that the Moral Reform Society considered each year, see Winch, *Philadelphia's Black Elite*, 109–128; and Bell, "The American Moral Reform Society," 34–39.

14. *Colored American*, July 29, 1837; August 19, 1837; May 20, 1837.

15. The proceedings identified thirty-one delegates and seventy other members. *Minutes and Proceedings of the First Annual Meeting of the American Moral Reform Society*, 224, 225. *Colored American*, September 16, 1837.

16. Frederick Hinton insisted that the change came about through deception because the matter was put to another vote when "the more sensible and reflecting men" were not present. The issue prompted such an overwhelming response that Samuel Cornish refused to print all the letters sent to the *Colored American*. *Minutes and*

342 NOTES TO PAGES 46–56

Proceedings of the First Annual Meeting of the American Moral Reform Society, 217–219, 221, 223, 231, and passim; *Colored American*, September 2, 1837; September 9, 1837.

17. *Colored American*, September 9, 1837.

18. Sterling Stuckey interprets conflicts over the Reform Society's position as a fight between separatists and integrationists. Stuckey, Slave Culture, 208; *Colored American*, September 2, 1937; September 23, 1937; *Minutes and Proceedings of the First Annual Meeting of the American Moral Reform Society*, 216.

19. Emphasis is in the original. *Colored American*, September 2, 1837.

20. *Colored American*, August 26, 1837; March 15, 1838; August 19, 1837; March 4, 1837; March 29, 1838; September 9, 1837.

21. Emphasis is in the original. *Rights of All*, August 14, 1829 as quoted in Floyd Miller, *The Search for a Black Nationality*, 89.

22. Emphasis is in the original. *Colored American*, August 19, 1837; March 4, 1837.

23. *Colored American*, March 15, 1838. Emphasis is in the original. Oson, *A Search for Truth*, 10.

24. John Fanning Watson, *Annals of Philadelphia, Being a Collection of Memoirs, Anecdotes, and Incidents of the City and its Inhabitants from the Days of the Pilgrim Founders* (Philadelphia: Author, 1830), 479.

25. *Colored American*, March 15, 1838.

26. *Colored American*, November 11, 1837.

27. *Colored American*, November 11, 1837.

28. *Freedom's Journal*, February 29, 1828.

29. *Colored American*, March 3, 1838; September 16, 1837.

30. *Colored American*, September 9, 1837.

31. *National Enquirer, and Constitutional Advocate of Universal Liberty*, September 14, 1837.

32. *Colored American*, February 10, 1838; *National Reformer*, November 1838.

33. *Colored American*, March 29, 1837

34. *Colored American*, June 19, 1839.

35. *National Reformer*, September 1838; *Colored American*, August 26, 1837; November 11, 1837; February 10, 1838; January 29, 1838; *Freedom's Journal*, June 20, 1828.

36. *Colored American*, March 3, 1838.

37. *Colored American*, August 25, 1838; March 29, 1838.

38. *Colored American*, March 29, 1838; March 13, 1841.

39. *National Enquirer*, September 14, 1837.

40. *Liberator*, April 14, 1832.

41. *Colored American*, September 16, 1837.

42. *Colored American*, March 29, 1838; September 16, 1837.

43. Leonard Sweet incorrectly reports that all antebellum free people believed that "condition" caused prejudice. He argues that they "correctly" understood that, if color were the cause, "prejudice would have been a white problem . . . which most likely would have been solved only by colonization." He characterizes the claim that color caused prejudice as "the white argument" and maintains that Whipper rejected race

NOTES TO PAGES 56–62   343

categories "in deference to white sensibilities." See Leonard Sweet, *Black Images of America, 1784–1870* (New York: W. W. Norton, 1976), 101, 108. Sterling Stuckey insists that Whipper was ashamed of his African ancestry. See Stuckey, *Slave Culture*, 210–211. Patrick Rael likens Whipper's views to that of colonizationists and insists that Whipper believed that "blackness itself" and White people's abhorrence of it caused the degradation of colored people. See Rael, *Black Identity and Black Protest in the Antebellum North*, 181. For further discussion of the "condition-color" debate, see Joanne Pope Melish, *Disowning Slavery: Gradual Emancipation and Race" in New England, 1780–1860* (Ithaca, NY: Cornell University Press, 1998).

44. *Colored American*, March 29, 1839; July 28, 1838; March 4, 1837.
45. *Colored American*, October 7, 1838; March 22, 1838; February 10, 1838.
46. *Colored American*, August 26, 1837; October 27, 1838; February 16, 1839; *National Inquirer*, September 14, 1837. For an explanation of White abolitionists' support for the idea that free people of color had to improve their moral condition in order to eliminate prejudice, see Frederickson, *The Black Image in the White Mind*, 37–42.
47. Richard R. Wright Jr., *Centennial Encyclopaedia of the African Methodist Episcopal Church Containing Principally the Biographies of the Men and Women, Both Ministers and Laymen, Whose Labors during a Hundred Years, Helped Make the A.M.E. Church What It Is* (Philadelphia: Book Concern of the A.M.E. Church, 1916), 255; *Colored American*, December 2, 1837; December 9, 1837; February 10, 1838.
48. *Colored American*, January 29, 1838; January 19, 1839; *Review of Pamphlets on Slavery and Colonization. First Published in the Quarterly Christian Spectator, for March 1833* (New Haven, CT: A. H. Maltby, 1833), 20. Floyd Miller identifies Lewis Woodson as "Augustine." For his analysis of Woodson's career and opinions, see "The Search for a Black Nationality: Martin R. Delaney and the Emigrationist Alternative" (Ph.D. dissertation, University of Minnesota, 1970), 12–39; and "The Father of Black Nationalism: Another Contender," *Civil War History* 17 (December 1971): 310–319. See Byron Woodson Sr., *A President in the Family: Thomas Jefferson, Sally Hemings, and Thomas Woodson* (Westport, CT: Praeger, 2001).
49. *Colored American*, December 9, 1837.
50. *Colored American*, January 27, 1838; November 4, 1837; February 17, 1838; May 3, 1838; July 28, 1838; *Philanthropist*, October 13, 1837; *Freedom's Journal*, January 31, 1829.
51. *Colored American*, August 25, 1838.
52. *Colored American*, July 28, 1838.
53. *Colored American*, July 28, 1838; June 23, 1838; March 22, 1838.
54. *Colored American*, December 29, 1838.
55. *Colored American*, March 22, 1838.
56. *Colored American*, August 11, 1838.
57. *Colored American*, February 10, 1838.
58. *Colored American*, May 3, 1838; June 23, 1838.
59. *Colored American*, May 3, 1838; June 23, 1838.
60. *Colored American*, April 22, 1837; March 22, 1838.

344 NOTES TO PAGES 62–69

61. *National Reformer*, October 1838; *Colored American*, June 10, 1837; *Black Abolitionist Papers*, 3, 252–253. See David McBride, "Black Protest against Racial Politics: Gardner, Hinton, and Their Memorial of 1838," *Pennsylvania History* 46 (April 1979):149–162.

62. Minutes of the Fifth Annual Convention, 10, 27; *National Reformer*, September 1838; *Colored American*, March 29, 1838. The *National Reformer* appeared from September 1838 to December 1839. There was a lapse from May through August in 1839. A one-year subscription cost $1.00, compared to the *Colored American*'s $2.00. Arthur Tappan subsidized the *Colored American* throughout its six-year run.

63. *Colored American*, December 22, 1838; December 29, 1838; August 25, 1838.

64. *Colored American*, August 25, 1838; *National Reformer*, September 1838.

65. *Colored American*, September 15, 1838; August 25, 1838.

66. *National Reformer*, October 1838.

67. *National Reformer*, September 1838; Benjamin Bacon and Charles W. Gardner, *The Present State and Condition of the Free People of Color of the City of Philadelphia.* (Philadelphia, 1838) in *Black Abolitionist Papers*, reel 2:315–338; *National Enquirer*, August 3, 1837.

68. *Colored American*, September 1, 1838; September 15, 1838; January 29, 1838; March 29, 1838; February 6, 1841; January 19, 1839; *National Reformer*, September 1838; March 1839.

69. *National Reformer*, October 1838.

70. Emphasis is in the original. *National Reformer*, October 1838.

71. *National Reformer*, November 1838.

72. *National Reformer*, October 1838; November 1838; January 1839.

73. *National Reformer*, December 1838; November 1839; November 1838.

74. *National Reformer*, November 1838; December 1838; November 1839.

75. *National Reformer*, September 1839.

76. *National Reformer*, September 1839; December 1838.

77. *Colored American*, December 29, 1838; *National Enquirer*, August 3, 1837; August 31, 1837; *National Reformer*, October 1838.

78. *National Reformer*, January 1839; September 1839.

79. Paul Finkelman, "Prelude to the Fifteenth Amendment: Black Legal Rights in the Antebellum North," *Rutgers Law Journal* 17 (Spring/Summer 1986): 415–482; Rhonda Freeman, *The Free Negro in New York City in the Era before the Civil War* (New York: Garland Press) 1994, 92–93; Marion Thompson Wright, "Negro Suffrage in New Jersey, 1776–1875," *Journal of Negro History* 33 (1948):182–184. See also Litwack, *North of Slavery*.

80. *National Reformer*, November 1838; September 1838; January 1839.

81. Eric Foner, "The Meaning of Freedom in the Age of Emancipation," *Journal of American History* 81 (September 1994): 443.

82. *Colored American*, March 13, 1841; Michael R. Winstone, "The Quest for Freedom: Selected Documents Illustrative of Some Aspects of the Life of Blacks between 1774 and 1841," *Journal of Negro History* 61 (January 1976): 92. See also Eric Foner, *Reconstruction: America's Unfinished Revolution, 1863–1877* (New York: Harper & Row, 1988); Roediger, *The Wages of Whiteness*. For broader analysis of the

NOTES TO PAGES 69–78   345

politics of antebellum citizenship, see Rogers Smith, *Civic Ideals*; James H. Kettner, *The Development of American Citizenship, 1608–1870* (Chapel Hill: University of North Carolina Press, 1978), part 4.

83. *National Reformer*, December 1839.

84. Morel also became an agent for the *National Reformer*. *National Reformer*, October 1838; November 1839; *Colored American*, June 13, 1840; September 5, 1840; January 30, 1841; February 13, 1841; February 20, 1841.

85. *National Reformer*, December 1839.

Chapter 3

1. *Colored American*, October 30, 1841; and December 4, 1841; *Convention of the Colored Inhabitants of the State of New York, August 18–20, 1840*, in Foner and Walker, Proceedings, vol. 1, 9, 16.

2. *Colored American*, May 2, 1840; March 13, 1841; June 6, 1840; August 15, 1840.

3. The names of Whipper, Robert Purvis, James Bias, and John Burr, all members of the American Moral Reform Society, were included in David Ruggles's convention announcement. The reactions of Whipper and Purvis indicate that they did not actually sign the call. The "colored citizens of New Haven" reported that the convention announcement included names of people who opposed the convention. They denounced the proposal citing general opposition and a lack of preparation and consultation. The convention never materialized. *Colored American*, July 25, 1840; August 1, 1840; *National Anti-Slavery Standard*, September 10, 1840; *Liberator*, September 25, 1840.

4. *Colored American*, September 30, 1837; Quarles, Black Abolitionists, 34; *New York Daily Tribune*, January 25, 1858; *Liberator*, September 8, 1854; *Frederick Douglass' Paper*, May 4, 1854.

5. *National Anti-Slavery Standard*, June 18, 1840; July 2, 1840; August 20, 1840; September 10, 1840; October 1, 1840.

6. *Colored American*, August 15, 1840; July 18, 1840; Quarles, *Black Abolitionists*, 154.

7. *New England Colored Citizens' Convention, Boston, August 1, 1859*, in Philip S. Foner and George E. Walker, eds. *Proceedings of the Black State Conventions, 1840–1865*, vol. 2 (Philadelphia: Temple University Press, 1980), 207–208.

8. *Colored American*, August 15, 1840. See *Colored American*, August 8, 1840.

9. *Colored American*, August 15, 1840; May 2, 1840.

10. *Colored American*, September 10, 1840; January 30, 1841; October 1841. *Convention of the Colored Inhabitants of the State of New York, August 18–20, 1840*, 8.

11. *Colored American*, January 30, 1841.

12. *Colored American*, February 20, 1841; *Convention of the Colored Inhabitants of the State of New York, August 18–20, 1840*, 8, 12. See also *Colored American*, October 31, 1840; January 2, 1841; January 9, 1841.

13. *Convention of the Colored Inhabitants of the State of New York, August 18–20, 1840*, 8; James McCune Smith to Gerrit Smith, December 28, 1846, Gerrit Smith Papers.

346 NOTES TO PAGES 78–83

14. *Convention of the Colored Inhabitants of the State of New York, August 18–20, 1840*, 21.

15. *Colored American*, December 5, 1840; December 4, 1841.

16. *New York State Convention of Colored Citizens, Troy, August 25–27, 1841*, in Foner and Walker, *Proceedings*, vol. 1, 27. See also *National Anti-Slavery Standard*, September 23, 1841; *New York State Free Suffrage Convention, September 8, 1845*, in Foner and Walker, *Proceedings*, vol. 1, 38; *Colored Men's State Convention of New York, Troy, September 4, 1855*, in Foner and Walker, *Proceedings*, vol. 1, 89; *Suffrage Convention of the Colored Citizens of New York, Troy, September 14, 1858*, in Foner and Walker, *Proceedings*, vol. 1, 99.

17. *Proceedings of the Connecticut State Convention of Colored Men held at New Haven on September 12th and 13th, 1849*, in Foner and Walker, *Proceedings*, vol. 2, 29, 30.

18. *Proceedings of the Connecticut State Convention of Colored Men held at New Haven on September 12th and 13th, 1849*, 31–32, 27.

19. *Proceedings and Address of the Coloured Citizens of N.J. Convened at Trenton, August 21st and 22nd, 1849 for the Purpose of Taking the Initiatory Measures for Obtaining the Right of Suffrage in This Our Native State*, in Foner and Walker, *Proceedings*, vol. 2, 5; Thomas Shourds, *History and Genealogy of Fenwick's Colony, New Jersey* (Bridgeton, New Jersey: G. F. Nixon, 1876), 384; *North Star*, October 20, 1848.

20. *Proceedings and Address of the Coloured Citizens of N.J. Convened at Trenton, August 21st and 22nd, 1849*, 3, 5.

21. Emphasis is in the original. *North Star*, February 8, 1850.

22. *Memorial of John Mercer Langston for Colored People of Ohio to General Assembly of the State of Ohio, June, 1854*, in Foner and Walker, *Proceedings*, vol. 2, 298–299.

23. *Proceedings of the State Convention of Colored Men, Held in the City of Columbus, Ohio, Jan. 16th, 17th & 18th, 1856*, in Foner and Walker, *Proceedings*, vol. 2, 310–311.

24. Despite state voting prohibitions, Black Ohioans could hold elective office. In 1855, Langston won the election for town clerk of Brownhelm, Ohio. Paul Finkelman, "The Strange Career of Race Discrimination in Antebellum Ohio," *Case Western Reserve Law Review* 55:2 (2004): 377n18, 381, https://scholarlycommons.law.case.edu/casel rev/vol55/iss2/5.

25. *Proceedings of the State Convention of Colored Men, Held in the City of Columbus, Ohio, Jan. 16th, 17th & 18th, 1856*, vol. 2, 311.

26. *Colored American*, February 20, 1841.

27. *Colored American*, March 6, 1841; March 13, 1841.

28. *Colored American*, July 3, 1841.

29. *Colored American*, July 3, 1841; September 25, 1841; *Proceedings of the State Convention of the Colored Freemen of Pennsylvania, held in Pittsburgh, on the 23d, 24th, and 25th of August, 1841, for the Purpose of Considering their Condition and the Means of Improvement*, in Foner and Walker, *Proceedings*, vol. 1, 111.

30. *Proceedings of the State Convention of the Colored Freemen of Pennsylvania, held in Pittsburgh, on the 23d, 24th, and 25th of August, 1841, for the Purpose of Considering their Condition and the Means of Improvement*, 106, 107, 109.

NOTES TO PAGES 83–86   347

31. *Proceedings of the State Convention of the Colored Freemen of Pennsylvania, held in Pittsburgh, on the 23d, 24th, and 25th of August, 1841, for the Purpose of Considering their Condition and the Means of Improvement*, 115.

32. *Proceedings of the State Convention of the Colored Freemen of Pennsylvania, held in Pittsburgh, on the 23d, 24th, and 25th of August, 1841, for the Purpose of Considering their Condition and the Means of Improvement*, 109, 110, 112–116.

33. *Proceedings of the First Convention of the Colored Citizens of the State of Illinois, Convened at the City of Chicago, Thursday, Friday, and Saturday, October 6th, 7th, and 8th, 1853*, in Foner and Walker, *Proceedings*, vol. 2, 60–61; *Proceedings of the First Convention of the Colored Citizens of the State of California, Held at Sacramento, Nov. 20th, 21st, and 22nd in the Colored Methodist Church, 1855*, in Foner and Walker, *Proceedings*, vol. 2, 117–118.

34. *National Anti-Slavery Standard*, August 21, 1845; *National Reformer*, September 1839.

35. *Minutes of the State Convention of the Coloured Citizens of Pennsylvania, Convened at Harrisburg, December 13th and 14th, 1848*, in Foner and Walker, vol. 1, 122, 133–134.

36. In his autobiography, Gibbs reported acting on his new consciousness "as early as 1845" by joining Isaiah Wears, John Bowers, and others in a delegation charged with presenting Philadelphians' suffrage appeals the state legislature. No other extant record of an 1845 suffrage delegation could be located. For an account of broad reform dynamics among Philadelphians in 1848, see Winch, *Philadelphia's Black Elite*, chapter 8. *Minutes of the State Convention of the Coloured Citizens of Pennsylvania, Convened at Harrisburg, December 13th and 14th, 1848*, 119, 122; Elizabeth McHenry, *Forgotten Readers: Recovering the Lost History of African American Literary Societies* (Durham, NC: Duke University Press, 2002), 52; Harry C. Silcox, "The Black 'Better Class' Political Dilemma: Philadelphia Prototype Isaiah C. Wears," *Pennsylvania Magazine of History and Biography* 113 (January 1989): 47; Mifflin Wistar Gibbs, *Shadow and Light: An Autobiography with Reminiscences of the Last and Present Century* (Washington, DC, 1902), 11, 22.

37. *Minutes of the State Convention of the Coloured Citizens of Pennsylvania, Convened at Harrisburg, December 13th and 14th, 1848*, 122.

38. *Minutes of the State Convention of the Coloured Citizens of Pennsylvania, Convened at Harrisburg, December 13th and 14th, 1848*, 123, 125.

39. *Minutes of the State Convention of the Coloured Citizens of Pennsylvania, Convened at Harrisburg, December 13th and 14th, 1848*, 124.

40. Robert Purvis became acutely aware of the fact that the federal government did not recognize colored people as citizens when he applied for a passport. After receiving a "special form" of a passport identifying his American birth as a "person of color," not a citizen, he convinced Philadelphia abolitionist and colonizationist Roberts Vaux to intervene and secured a replacement designating him a US citizen. Roberts Vaux to Louis McLane, Secretary of State, May 16, 1834, in Rebecca Sharp, "A Rare Find: Passport Applications of Free Blacks," Rediscovering Black History, July 22, 2020, National Archives, https://rediscovering-black-history.blogs.archives.gov/2020/07/22/a-rare-find-passport-applications-of-free-blacks/.

348   NOTES TO PAGES 86–92

41. *Minutes of the State Convention of the Coloured Citizens of Pennsylvania, Convened at Harrisburg, December 13th and 14th, 1848,* 126.
42. *Minutes of the State Convention of the Coloured Citizens of Pennsylvania, Convened at Harrisburg, December 13th and 14th, 1848,* 126–127.
43. *Minutes of the State Convention of the Coloured Citizens of Pennsylvania, Convened at Harrisburg, December 13th and 14th, 1848,* 127–128.
44. *Minutes of the State Convention of the Coloured Citizens of Pennsylvania, Convened at Harrisburg, December 13th and 14th, 1848,* 128–129.
45. *Minutes of the State Convention of the Coloured Citizens of Pennsylvania, Convened at Harrisburg, December 13th and 14th, 1848,* 130–131.
46. *Minutes of the State Convention of the Coloured Citizens of Pennsylvania, Convened at Harrisburg, December 13th and 14th, 1848,* 131–132.
47. New Yorkers dominated both of these renewed national conventions, comprising more than three-fifths of the 1843 delegation and two-thirds of the 1847 delegation. *Minutes of the National Convention of Colored Citizens Held at Buffalo, on the 15th, 16th, 17, 18, and 19th of August, 1843 for the Purpose of Considering their Moral and Political Condition as American Citizens,* in Bell, *Proceedings,* 10; *Proceedings of the National convention of the Colored People and their Friends, held in Troy on the 8th and 9th of October, 1847,* in Bell, *Proceedings,* 7, 19, 17.
48. *Report of the Proceedings of the Colored National Convention, held at Cleveland, Ohio, on Wednesday, September 6, 1848,* in Bell, *Proceedings,* 18–20.
49. *Proceedings of the Colored National Convention, held in Rochester, July 6th, 7th, and 8th, 1853,* in Bell, *Proceedings,* 12–15.
50. *Proceedings of the Colored National Convention, held in Rochester, July 6th, 7th, and 8th, 1853,* 40; "Anti-Colonization and Woman's Rights Ticket," Broadside, in *Black Abolitionist Papers,* vol. 3, ed. C. Peter Ripley (Chapel Hill: University of North Carolina Press, 1991) , 45; *Proceedings of the New York State Council of Colored People, January 2, 1854,* in Foner and Walker, *Proceedings,* vol. 2, 80–81; *Liberator,* March 5, 1855; Pease and Pease, *They Who Would Be Free,* 251–255.
51. Jane and William Pease attribute the council's demise to "parochialism," personal squabbles, and "insufficient theoretical underpinnings." Pease and Pease, *They Who Would Be Free,* 254–255.
52. *Frederick Douglass Paper,* December 16, 1853; *Colored Men's State Convention of New York, Troy, September 4, 1855,* 91; *Proceedings of the Colored National Convention, held in Franklin Hall, Sixth Street below Arch, Philadelphia, October 16th, 17th, and 18th, 1855,* 30–33, in Bell, *Proceedings,* 10; *Frederick Douglass' Paper,* November 9, 1855.
53. *North Star,* February 2, 1849, in *Minutes of the State Convention of the Coloured Citizens of Pennsylvania, Convened at Harrisburg, December 13th and 14th, 1848,* 134–135; *North Star,* June 22, 1849.
54. *Liberator,* February 25, 1842.
55. Benjamin Roberts, *Argument of Charles Sumner, Esq., against the Constitutionality of Separate Colored Schools, in the case of Sarah C. Roberts vs. The City of Boston* (1849), as quoted in *North Star,* February 8, 1850. See *Roberts v. City of Boston,* 59

NOTES TO PAGES 92–99   349

Mass. (5 Cush.) 198 (1850). For broader historical analysis of the Boston school case, see Donald Jacobs, "The Nineteenth Century Struggle over Segregated Education in Boston Schools," *Journal of Negro Education* 39 (Winter 1970): 76–85.

56. *North Star*, March 23, 1849.

57. *North Star*, August 17, 1849; December 21, 1849.

58. *Proceedings of the State Convention of Colored People held in Albany, New York, on the 22nd 23rd, and 24th of July 1852*, in Foner and Walker, *Proceedings*, vol. 1, 57–59.

59. *Proceedings of the Colored National Convention, held in Rochester, July 6th, 7th, and 8th, 1853*, 22–23, 25; Horton and Horton, *In Hope of Liberty*, 218; "Charles L. Reason to Editor, Philadelphia *Daily Register*, 24 January 1854," in *Black Abolitionist Papers*, vol. 4, 193n7.

60. *Proceedings of the Colored National Convention, held in Franklin Hall, Sixth Street below Arch, Philadelphia, October 16th, 17th, and 18th, 1855*, 11–12, 25–27; *Provincial Freeman*, April 15, 1854.

61. *National Reformer*, September 1839; September 1838; December 1838; January 1839; *North Star*, August 25, 1848; October 13, 1848; April 27, 1848; November 16, 1849; June 15, 1849; December 14, 1849; Winch, *Philadelphia's Black Elite*, 149–150; *Minutes of the State Convention of the Colored Citizens of Ohio, Convened at Columbus, January 9th, 10th, 11th, and 12th, 1850*, in Foner and Walker, *Proceedings*, vol. 2, 253; *Colored American*, June 13, 1840; June 20, 1840; July 11, 1840; August 29, 1840.

62. Benjamin Tucker Tanner, *An Apology for African Methodism* (Baltimore: Author, 1867), 313.

63. David Smith, *Biography of the Rev. David Smith, of the A.M.E. Church, Being a Complete History, Embracing over Sixty Years' Labor in the Advancement of the Redeemer's Kingdom on Earth* (Freeport, NY: Books for Libraries Press, 1971), 53.

64. Payne, Recollections of Seventy Years, 50–51, 85; *Colored American*, October 17, 1837; Daniel Payne, *History of the African Methodist Episcopal Church* (1891; New York: Arno Press and the New York Times, 1969), 237, 239.

65. Memorial of the Trustees of the African Methodist Episcopal Church called Bethel, (1807) in Elmer Clark, ed., *Journal and Letters of Francis Asbury*, vol. 3 (Nashville, TN: Abingdon Press, 1958), 367.

66. *Proceedings of the National Convention of the Colored People and their Friends, held in Troy on the 8th and 9th of October, 1847*, 16; *Minutes of the National Convention of Colored Citizens: Held at Buffalo, on the 15th, 16th, 17, 18, and 19th of August 1843*, 15.

67. *Colored American*, April 22, 1837; April 15, 1837; April 29, 1837; October 27, 1838; June 19, 1839.

68. *North Star*, November 23, 1849.

69. *National Reformer*, September 1839; September 1838; December 1838; *North Star*, September 1, 1848; November 10, 1848; *Colored American*, March 29, 1838; June 19, 1839.

70. *North Star*, September 29, 1848; November 10, 1848.

71. *National Reformer*, November 1839; *Colored American*, February 20, 1841; February 6, 1841; *Colored American*, January 30, 1841; *National Reformer*, April 1839.

72. *Liberator*, January 9, 1852.

350   NOTES TO PAGES 99–103

73. Emphasis is in the original. *Colored American*, February 6, 1841; January 30, 1841; *National Reformer*, January 1839.

74. Thomas James, *Life of Rev. Thomas James, by Himself* (Rochester: Post Express Printing, 1886), 8, electronic edition, North American Slave Narratives: Documenting the American South, University of North Carolina, 2000, http://docsouth.unc.edu/neh/jamesth/jamesth.html. See Joan Bryant, "Race and Religion in Nineteenth-Century America," in *Perspectives on American Religion and Culture*, ed. Peter Williams (Cambridge: Blackwell, 1999), 246–258.

75. *North Star*, February 25, 1848; March 24, 1848.

76. *North Star*, February 25, 1848; March 24, 1848; February April 7, 1848; March 23, 1849.

77. *Colored American*, October 27, 1838.

78. I am grateful to David Grinnell, Coordinator of Archives and Manuscripts at the University of Pittsburgh Library System, for alerting me about Lewis Woodson's Wesleyan Methodist Church affiliation. Woodson's ties with other reformers fractured during this period. Frederick Douglass, John Vashon, and Martin Delany raised questions about his character. Vashon and Delany accused him of disavowing his acquaintances with colored people. Luther Lee and E. Smith, *Debates of the General Conference of the M.E. Church, May, 1844* (New York: O. Scott, 1845), 469, 478; Payne, *History of the African Methodist Episcopal Church*, 286, 296; *Christian Recorder*, February 7, 1878; *True Wesleyan*, December 28, 1844. *Liberator*, September 6, 1850; August 16, 1850; *North Star*, October 24, 1850.

79. *North Star*, March 24, 1848.

80. *Proceedings of the State Convention of the Colored Freemen of Pennsylvania, held in Pittsburgh, on the 23d, 24th, and 25th of August, 1841, for the Purpose of Considering their Condition and the Means of Improvement*, 114; *Report of the Proceedings of the Colored National Convention, held at Cleveland, Ohio, on Wednesday, September 6, 1848*, 20.

81. *Aliened American*, April 9, 1853.

82. *North Star*, January 7, 1848; January 19, 1849.

83. *North Star*, January 7, 1848; January 19, 1849.

84. *National Reformer*, October 1838; February 1839; Benjamin Tucker Tanner, *An Outline of Our History and Government for African Methodist Churchmen, Ministerial and Lay, In Catechetical Form* (Philadelphia: Grant, Faires, & Rodgers, 1884), appendix, 170; *Journal of the Proceedings of the Sixty-Eighth Convention of the Protestant Episcopal Church of the diocese of New-York* (New York: Daniel Dana, Jr. 1851), appendix A, 57; *Mirror of Liberty*, January 1839. See also *Colored American*, March 4, 1837; February 6, 1841; *North Star*, April 17, 1851.

85. James Oliver Horton, *Free People of Color: Inside the African American Community* (Washington, DC: Smithsonian Institution Press, 1993), 159; George Hogarth to P. Loveridge (n.d.), in Tanner, *An Outline of Our History and Government*, appendix, 170–171.

86. *Colored American*, December 5, 1840; *Repository of Religion and Literature*, July 1858, 54.

NOTES TO PAGES 104–109   351

87. *Colored American*, November 9, 1841; Norwood, *The Story of American Methodism*, 173–174; David Smith, *Biography*, 66–67. See David Bradley, *A History of the A.M.E. Zion Church*, part 1, *1796–1872* (Nashville, TN: Parthenon Press, 1956).

88. Ruth Bogin, "'Liberty Further Extended': A 1776 Antislavery Manuscript by Lemuel Haynes," *William and Mary Quarterly* 40 (January 1983): 94, 96; *Colored American*, March 11, 1837; Ottobah Cuguano, *Thoughts and Sentiments on the Evil and Wicked Traffic of the Slavery and Commerce of the Human Species*, in *Pioneers of the Black Atlantic: Five Slave Narratives from the Enlightenment, 1772–1815*, ed. Henry Louis Gates Jr. and William L. Andrews (Washington, DC, 1998), 107, 118; Thomas Clarkson, *Essay on the Slavery and Commerce of the Human Species* (London, 1786); Olaudah Equiano, *The Interesting Narrative of the Life of Olaudah Equiano, or Gustavus Vassa, the African, Written by Himself*, ed. Robert Allison (New York: Bedford Books, 1995), 43–44.

89. *Proceedings of the Colored National Convention, held in Franklin Hall, Sixth Street below Arch, Philadelphia, October 16th, 17th, and 18th, 1855*, 30–33.

90. Henry Highland Garnet, *Walker's Appeal, with a Brief Sketch of His Life. By Henry Highland Garnet, and also Garnet's Address to the Slaves of the United States of America* (New York: J. H. Tobitt, 1848), 90, 93, 95. For similarities between Garnet's address and an abolitionist address to slaves delivered a short time earlier, see *Address of the New England Anti-Slavery Convention to the Slaves of the United States* (Boston: Oliver Johnson, 1848).

91. Cynthia S. Hamilton, "Hercules Subdued: The Visual Rhetoric of the Kneeling Slave," *Slavery & Abolition: A Journal of Slave and Post-Slave Studies* 34:4 (2013): 631–633.

92. *Slave's Friend* 8 (1836): 5–6.

93. *Liberator*, February 22, 1834.

94. *National Reformer*, November 1839.

95. *Mirror of Liberty*, August 1838.

96. Gerrit Smith to Gen. John H. Cooke, December 11, 1840, Gerrit Smith Papers; *Impartial Citizen*, April 11, 1849.

97. Bacon, *But One Race*, 137.

98. *Colored American*, October 14, 1837.

99. *Minutes of the State Convention of the Coloured Citizens of Pennsylvania, Convened at Harrisburg, December 13th and 14th, 1848*, 27; *Black Abolitionist Papers*, vol. 3, 183–186.

100. *Report of the Proceedings of the Colored National Convention, held at Cleveland, Ohio*, 5–6, 13, 19; *Provincial Freeman*, May 17, 1856.

101. *Colored American*, April 11, 1840; January 16, 1841.

102. The emphasis is in the original. *New England Colored Citizens' Convention, Boston, August 1, 1859*, 211. The convention drew participants from Massachusetts, Rhode Island, Connecticut, Maine, New York, New Jersey, Pennsylvania, Illinois, and Canada.

103. *Weekly Anglo-African*, May 11, 1861.

104. Jane Rhodes, *Mary Ann Shadd Cary: The Black Press and Protest in the Nineteenth Century* (Bloomington: Indiana University Press, 1998), 138; Dorothy Sterling,

352 NOTES TO PAGES 109–113

The Making of an Afro-American: Martin Robison Delany, African Explorer, Civil War Major, & Father of Black Nationalism (New York: Da Capo Press, 1996), 161; M. R. Delany, *Official Report of the Niger Valley Exploring Party*, in *Martin R. Delany: A Documentary Reader*, ed. Robert S. Levine (Chapel Hill: University of North Carolina Press, 2003), 348–351; Moses, *The Golden Age of Black Nationalism, 1850–1925*, 45–48.

105. Mary A. Shadd, *A Plea for Emigration, or Notes of Canada West, in its Moral, Social, and Political Aspect, with Suggestions Respecting Mexico, W. Indies and Vancouver Island, for the Information of Colored Emigrants*, ed. Richard Almonte (1852; repr., Toronto: Mercury Press, 1998), 74, 76, 59; Nobles, *Shades of Citizenship*, 25–45; Winks, *The Blacks in Canada*, appendix: "How Many Negroes in Canada?," 484–486.

106. For two years, Shadd masked the fact that a woman was editor of the paper by signing editorials with her initials. She finally revealed her identity in 1854, after receiving compliments as a "colored man" publishing the paper. *Provincial Freeman*, August 26, 1854; September 2, 1854; Rhodes, *Mary Ann Shadd Cary*, 102–117, 128.

107. Rhodes, *Mary Ann Shadd Cary*, 96–97, 114–115, 121; *Provincial Freeman*, March 25, 1854; April 22, 1854; Shadd, *A Plea for Emigration*, 87.

108. *Proceedings of the Convention, of the Colored Freemen of Ohio, held in Cincinnati, January 14, 15, 16, 17, and 19, 1852*, in Foner and Walker, *Proceedings*, vol. 1, 279; Floyd Miller, *The Search for a Black Nationality*, 52.

109. *Provincial Freeman*, April 25, 1857.

110. *Provincial Freeman*, April 25, 1857; August 19, 1854; October 28, 1854; July 19, 1856; May 30, 1857. The group also opposed migration from Canada to the West Indies.

111. Mary Ann Shadd Cary to George Whipple, November 27, 1851, in *Black Abolitionist Papers*, vol. 2, 184–185. (Despite the reference to "Cary," Shadd was not married when she wrote the letter.) Winks, *The Blacks in Canada*, 368; Shadd, *A Plea for Emigration*, 61-64; *Provincial Freeman*, August 19, 1854; October 28, 1854.

112. As a teacher in New York City, Shadd had been part of colored reform circles, where she became acquainted with Ray, Samuel Cornish, James McCune Smith, and Charles Reason. She cited these men as references when she sought AMA funding for her school in Canada. Mary Ann Shadd Cary to George Whipple, November 27, 1851, in *Black Abolitionist Papers*, vol. 2, 185.

113. *Colored American*, February 6, 1841; Winks, *The Blacks in Canada*, 178–204; *Provincial Freeman*, November 3, 1855; Rhodes, *Mary Ann Shadd Cary*, 106–108.

114. When defending Canadian emigration against colonizationists claims that Africa was the appropriate home for colored people, Wilson understated the significance of bigotry in Canada West, calling it a mere annoyance to colored migrants. He argued that the "equitable and impartial" laws of the province removed the "edge" from the prejudice exhibited by White Canadians. *Colored American*, February 25, 1841; March 20, 1841; *National Era*, April 8, 1847.

115. *Provincial Freeman*, July 19, 1856; *Frederick Douglass' Paper*, July 4, 1856.

116. *Provincial Freeman*, July 19, 1856.

NOTES TO PAGES 114–118   353

117. *Provincial Freeman*, July 19, 1856; August 19, 1854; May 30, 1857; Rhodes, *Mary Ann Shadd Cary*, 52. Abraham Shadd's political activism led to his election to the Town Council in Raleigh, West Canada, in 1859.

118. Martin Delany, "Political Destiny of the Colored Race on the American Continent," in Levine, *Martin R. Delany*, 252, 251.

119. Delany, "Political Destiny of the Colored Race on the American Continent," 252, 251. See *Proceedings of the National Emigration Convention of the Colored People, Held in Cleveland Ohio, on Thursday, Friday, and Saturday, the 24th, 25th, and 26th of August, 1854* (Pittsburgh: A. A. Anderson, 1854), 33–70.

120. Richard K. MacMaster, "Highland Garnet and the African Civilization Society," *Journal of Presbyterian History* 48:2 (Summer 1970): 105–106, 108; *Frederick Douglass' Paper*, July 22, 1859.

121. Quoted in Victor Ullman, *Martin R. Delany: The Beginnings of Black Nationalism* (Boston: Beacon Press, 1971), 60–61.

122. Miller, *The Search for a Black Nationality*, 151–152.

123. Delany, "Political Destiny of the Colored Race," 250–251.

124. Delany, "Political Destiny of the Colored Race," 250–251.

125. Delany, "Political Destiny of the Colored Race," 250–252.

126. Carla Peterson argues that Delany's patriarchal nationalist rhetoric was too complicated in the 1850s to be reduced to "raciality." Martin Delany, *The Condition, Elevation, Emigration, and Destiny of the Colored People of the United States, Politically Considered* (Baltimore: Black Classic Press, 1993), 214, 202; Carla L. Peterson, *"Doers of the Word": African-American Women Speakers & Writers in the North (1830–1880)* (New Brunswick, NJ: Rutgers University Press, 1998), 114–115; Martin Delany, *Official Report of the Niger Valley Exploring Party* (New York: Thomas Hamilton, 1861), in Levine, *Martin R. Delany*, 356.

127. Delany's fears that the United States would annex the British provinces disqualified them as sites for permanent asylum. Delany, "Political Destiny of the Colored Race," 249, 275; Moses, *The Golden Age of Black Nationalism*, 32–55; Sterling, *The Making of an Afro-American*, 159–166.

Chapter 4

1. *National Reformer*, January 1839.

2. James McCune Smith delivered lectures on phenology upon returning to New York after receiving his medical degree in Scotland. Some of Whipper's other reform allies shared the popular fascination with phrenology, including Philadelphia dentist James Bias, who helped sponsor anti-phrenology presentations before becoming a practitioner. Phrenologists capitalized on curiosity surrounding the *Amistad* captives by publishing a profile of the group's leader, Joseph Cinque, and determined that he was intellectually superior to "most persons belonging to his race." *Colored American*, September 23, 1837; September 27, 1837; September 30, 1937; December 23, 1837; *Liberator*, August 15, 1831; October 22, 1831; *North Star*, December 22,

354 NOTES TO PAGES 118–121

1848; *Voice of the Fugitive*, April 22, 1852; *Provincial Freeman*, June 23, 1855; L. N. Fowler, "Phrenological Developments of Joseph Cinquez, Alias Ginqua," *American Phrenological Journal and Miscellany*, 2 (1840): 136–138; See J. J. G. Bias, *Synopsis of Phrenology* (Philadelphia, 1859).

3. *National Reformer*, January 1839.

4. *National Reformer*, November 1839; November 1838.

5. J. Theodore Holly, "Thoughts on Hayti," *Anglo-African Magazine*, June 1859, 185–187; *Liberator*, December 26, 1835.

6. Garrison, *Thoughts on African Colonization*, part 2, 61; *Liberator*, June 4, 1831; *North Star, October 12, 1849; Proceedings of the Colored National Convention, held in Rochester, July 6th, 7th, and 8th, 1853*, 8; *National Reformer*, November 1838; *North Star*, December 22, 1848.

7. For alternative interpretations of how African American reformers engaged ethnology, see Bay, *White Image in the Black Mind*, 39, 53–55, 221; and Rael, *Black Identity and Black Protest*, 249–252.

8. *North Star*, February 25, 1848.

9. William Stanton insists that Morton "never equated cranial capacity and intelligence." However, he quotes Morton's comments about brain size and superior mental attributes that explicitly make this correlation. Moreover, the connection seemed evident to Morton's colleagues. Stanton also argues that Nott did not promote race science to justify slavery, but he viewed slavery as a solution for the problem of having different species occupying one nation. William Stanton, *The Leopard's Spots: Scientific Attitudes toward Race in America, 1815–1859* (Chicago: University of Chicago Press, 1960), 35, 41, 45, 141, 160; Stephen Jay Gould, *The Mismeasure of Man* (New York: W. W. Norton, 1996), 74–85; C. Loring Brace, *"Race" Is a Four-Letter Word: The Genesis of the Concept* (New York: Oxford University Press), 81, 90–91. Also see Samuel George Morton, *Crania Americana; or a Comparative View of the Skulls of the Various Aboriginal Nations of North and South America* (Philadelphia: J. Dobson, 1839); Morton, *Crania Aegyptiaca, or Observations in Egyptian Ethnography, Derived from Anatomy, History, and the Monuments* (Philadelphia, 1844); Louis Agassiz, "Diversity of Origins of the Human Races," *Christian Examiner* 49 (July 1850): 110–145; J. C. Nott and George R. Gliddon, eds., *Types of Mankind or Ethnological Researches Based upon the Ancient Monuments, Paintings, Sculptures, and Crania of Races*, 7th edition (Philadelphia: Lippincott, Grambo, 1855); Reginald Horsman, *Josiah Nott of Mobile: Southerner, Physician, and Racial Theorist* (Baton Rouge: Louisiana State University Press, 1987).

10. Paul Erikson, "The Anthropology of Charles Caldwell, M.D.," *Isis* 72 (June 1981): 253, 254, 256; See Charles Caldwell, MD, *Phrenology Vindicated and Antiphrenology Unmasked* (New York: Samuel Colman, 1838); Caldwell, *Thoughts on the Original Unity of the Human Race* (New York: E. Bliss, 1830), 74, 77, 131, 171–173, and passim. Prichard's *Researches into the Physical History of Mankind* appeared in 1813, 1826, 1838, and 1851.

NOTES TO PAGES 121-125   355

11. Gould, *The Mismeasure of Man*, 71; Bachman is quoted in Brad Hume, "Quantifying Characters: Polygenist Anthropologists and the Hardening of Heredity," *Journal of the History of Biology* 41 (2008): 142.

12. Gould, *The Mismeasure of Man*, 71; Frederickson, *The Black Image in the White Mind*, 72; James Forten Jr., *An Address Delivered before the Ladies' Anti-Slavery Society of Philadelphia, On the Evening of the 14th of April, 1836* (Philadelphia, 1836), in *Black Abolitionist Papers*, 3, 161; *Colored American*, September 16, 1837; Samuel Stanhope Smith, *An Essay on the Causes of the Variety of Complexion and Figure in the Human Species* (Cambridge, MA: Harvard University Press, 1965), 57-58; Benjamin Rush is quoted in Ronald Takaki, *Iron Cages: Race and Culture in 19th-Century America* (New York: Oxford University Press, 1990), 32; Erikson, "The Anthropology of Charles Caldwell, M.D.," 254. Benjamin Rush, "Observations Intended to Favor a Supposition that the Black Color (as it is called) of the Negroes is Derived from Leprosy. Read at a Special Meeting July 14, 1797," *Transactions of the American Philosophical Society* 4 (1799): 295. For an analysis of the broader phenomenon of "Negroes turning white" in the late eighteenth century, see Melish, *Disowning Slavery*, 140-146. An examination of the environmentalist ideas of Smith and Rush appears in Jordan, *White over Black*, 509-525 and passim.

13. Frederick Douglass, "The Claims of the Negro Ethnologically Considered: An Address before the Literary Societies of Western Reserve College, July 12, 1854," in *The Frederick Douglass Papers, Series One: Speeches, Debates, and Interviews*, vol. 2, *1847-54*, ed. John Blassingame (New Haven, CT: Yale University Press, 1982), 507.

14. *Colored American*, February 10, 1838; June 9, 1838; December 15, 1838; May 2, 1840; January 13, 1838; February 6, 1841; December 23, 1837; *Freedom's Journal*, December 26, 1828; *Liberator*, January 21, 1837; *Minutes of the New England Conference of the African Methodist Episcopal Church Held in the City of New Bedford, Mass. from June 10th to the 21st, 1852* (New Bedford: Press of Benjamin Lindsey, 1852), 5; "Maryland Free Colored People's Convention, July 27-28, 1852," in Foner and Walker, Proceedings, vol. 2, 43, 47; *Elevator*, November 17, 1865; Maria Stewart, "An Address Delivered at the African Masonic Hall, Boston, February 27, 1833," in *Maria W. Stewart, America's First Black Political Writer: Essays and Speeches*, ed. Marilyn Richardson (Bloomington: Indiana University Press, 1987), 57; *North Star*, June 13, 1850. Although their analysis focuses on responses to race science between 1870 and 1920, Nancy Stepan and Sander Gilman suggest that antebellum Black reformers were uncomfortable and unfamiliar with the terms of scientific argument and authority. See Nancy Leys Stepan and Sander Gilman, "Appropriating the Idioms of Science: The Rejection of Scientific Racism," in *The Bounds of Race: Perspectives on Hegemony and Resistance*, ed. Dominic La Capra (Ithaca, NY: Cornell University Press, 1991), 72-103.

15. See Agassiz, "Diversity of Origins of the Human Races," 142; Nott and Gliddon, *Types of Mankind*, 48-50; Josiah Nott, "The Negro Race," *Anthropological Review* 4 (July 1866):103-106.

16. *Freedom's Journal*, April 18 and May 9, 1828; Gould, *The Mismeasure of Man*, 71, 405; Samuel Stanhope Smith, *Essay*, 187-212.

356   NOTES TO PAGES 125-129

17. *Freedom's Journal*, April 13, 1827; April 6, 1827; Wilson Jeremiah Moses, *Afrotopia: The Roots of African American Popular History* (Cambridge: Cambridge University Press, 1998), 51–52.

18. Russwurm's genealogy follows the example of an 1825 essay, "Observations on the Early History of the Negro Race," which he reprinted from the American Colonization Society's *African Repository and Colonial Journal. Freedom's Journal*, April 13, 1827; April 6, 1827; December 5, 1828. For similar genealogical appeals to Egypt, see *Freedom's Journal*, August 12, 1827. Noah's biblical curse on Canaan is in Genesis 9:20–27 (RSV). See Pliny, *Natural History*, trans. H. Rackham (Cambridge, MA: Harvard University Press, 1949). For analyses of Canaan's curse, see Benjamin Braude, "The Sons of Noah and Constructions of Ethnic and Geographical Identities in the Medieval and Early Modern Periods," *William and Mary Quarterly* 54 (January 1997): 103–142; and William McKee Evans, "From the Land of Guinea: The Strange Odyssey of the Sons of Ham," *American Historical Review* 85 (1980): 15–43. For a study of the significance of Egypt in nineteenth-century racial discourse, see Scott Trafton, *Egypt Land: Race and Nineteenth-Century American Egyptomania* (Durham, NC: Duke University Press, 2004).

19. *Freedom's Journal*, April 13, 1827.

20. *Freedom's Journal*, April 13, 1827.

21. Pechlin is quoted in Sidney N. Klaus, "A History of the Science of Pigmentation," in *The Pigmentary System: Physiology and Pathophysiology*, ed. James J. Norland (New York: Oxford University Press, 1998), 6. Pechlin regretted that his experiments were limited to cadavers owing to "evil on the part of the Negroes" who refused to participate in his research.

22. Moses, *Afrotopia*, 53–55; *Freedom's Journal*, April 20, 1827.

23. *Freedom's Journal*, April 18, 1828; May 9, 1828; September 19, 1828; Samuel Stanhope Smith, *Essay*, 29, 93–97, 103; T. H. Gallaudet, *A Statement with regard to the Moorish Prince, Abduhl Rahahman* (New York: Daniel Fanshaw, 1828). See Terry Alford, *Prince among Slaves: The True Story of an African Prince Sold into Slavery in the American South* (New York: Oxford University Press, 1986).

24. *Liberator*, August 27, 1831. The biblical reference to skin turning white as punishment is an erroneous description of Numbers 12:1–10 (RSV), in which Miriam becomes leprous and "as white as snow" after she and Aaron criticize their brother Moses for marrying a Cushite woman.

25. *Liberator*, August 27, 1831.

26. *Liberator*, August 27, 1831.

27. Bruce Dain, *A Hideous Monster of the Mind: American Race Theory in the Early Republic* (Cambridge, MA: Harvard University Press, 2002) 170; Hosea Easton, *A Treatise on the Intellectual Character, and Civil and Political Condition of the Colored People of the U. States; and the Prejudice Exercised towards Them* (Boston: Isaac Knapp, 1837); "Convention of the Colored Citizens of Massachusetts, August 1, 1858," 105n6; *Liberator*, March 12, 1831; May 28, 1831; October 22, 1831; July 7, 1832; January 21, 1837; *Minutes and Proceedings of the Second Annual Convention*, 4; *Minutes and*

NOTES TO PAGES 129–134   357

Proceedings of the Third Annual Convention, 4. *Minutes and Proceedings of the Fourth Annual Convention*, 8.

28. Easton, *A Treatise*, 5, 37, 38.

29. Easton, *A Treatise*, 37–38.

30. Easton, *A Treatise*, 5–6, 8, 14, 18, 20, 22. See Mia Bay for an interpretation of Easton's historical analysis as a "theory of racial development." Bay, *White Image in the Black Mind*, 47.

31. Easton, *Treatise*, 20; Albert J. Raboteau, *A Fire in the Bones: Reflections on African American Religious History* (Boston: Beacon Press, 1995), 41, 51.

32. Easton, *A Treatise*, 21.

33. Easton, *A Treatise*, 22–23.

34. Easton, *A Treatise*, 24. See Ron Eyerman, *Cultural Trauma: Slavery and the Formation of African-American Identity* (Cambridge: Cambridge University Press, 2002).

35. Marcy is quoted in Klaus, "A History of the Science of Pigmentation," 8.

36. Easton, *A Treatise*, 24, 25. See Genesis 30: 25–39 (RSV). It is not clear whether Easton was familiar with Heliodorus's ancient Greek novel, the *Aethiopica*, in which Queen Persinna of Aethiopia attributes the light complexion of her newborn daughter to the fact that she was gazing at a painting of the white-skinned Andromeda when she conceived the child. Thanks to Michele Ronnick for bringing this connection to my attention. See Michele Valerie Ronnick, "Heliodorus," *Oxford Encyclopedia of African Thought*, vol. 1, ed. Abiola Irele and Biodun Jeyifo (New York: Oxford University Press, 2010), 440–442.

37. Easton, *A Treatise*, 22, 24, 25, 26. See Pietro Corsi, *The Age of Lamarck: Evolutionary Theories in France, 1790–1830* (Berkeley: University of California Press, 1988).

38. Easton, *A Treatise*, 47–48, 52–53.

39. "Convention of the Colored Citizens of Massachusetts, August 1, 1858," 98–99.

40. *Liberator*, July 14, 1837.

41. *Colored American*, February 27, 1841; R. J. M. Blackett, *Beating against the Barriers: The Lives of Six Nineteenth-Century Afro-Americans* (Ithaca, NY: Cornell University Press, 1989), 6–11; Garrison, *Thoughts on African Colonization*, 23–24; James W. C. Pennington, *The Fugitive Blacksmith; or Events in the History of J. W. C. Pennington, Pastor of a Presbyterian Church, New York, formerly a Slave in the State of Maryland, United States*, electronic ed., North American Slave Narratives, Documenting the American South, University of North Carolina at Chapel Hill, 2001, http://docsouth.unc.edu/neh/penning49/penning49.html.

42. Emphasis is in the original. James W. C. Pennington, *A Text Book of the Origin and History, &c. &c. of the Colored People* (Hartford, CT: L. Skinner, 1841), 46–47; Blackett, *Beating against the Barriers*, 17–18, 20.

43. Pennington, *A Text Book*, 9–12, 21–23, 32–33, 35, 37. For examples of appeals to African achievements and the greatness of ancient Egypt and Ethiopia that appeared in the reform press, see *Colored American*, March 18, 1837; July 7, 1838; *Liberator*, March 26, 1839.

44. Jefferson, *Notes on the State of Virginia*, 178, 180.

358   NOTES TO PAGES 135–140

45. Pennington, *A Text Book*, 45, 49–52; Henri Gregoire, *On the Cultural Achievements of Negroes*, trans. Thomas Cassirer and Jean-Francois Briere (Amherst: University of Massachusetts Press, 1996), 83–112. The 1810 English translation that would have been available to Pennington appeared under the title *An Inquiry Concerning the Intellectual and Moral Faculties and Literature of Negroes*. Allison Blakely, *Blacks in the Dutch World: The Evolution of Racial Imagery in a Modern Society* (Bloomington: Indiana University Press, 1993).

46. Pennington, *A Text Book*, 54–58.

47. Pennington, *A Text Book*, 64–65.

48. Pennington, *A Text Book*, 36–37, 66.

49. *Pennsylvania Freeman*, May 16, 1850; *Frederick Douglass' Paper*, October 22, 1852; Henry Highland Garnet, *A Memorial Discourse; Delivered in the Hall of the House of Representatives, Washington, City, D.C. on Sabbath, February 12, 1865, with an Introduction by James McCune Smith, MD* (Philadelphia: Joseph M. Wilson, 1865), 23; Garnet, *The Past and Present Condition of the Colored Race*, in *"Let Your Motto be Resistance": The Life and Thought of Henry Highland Garnet*, ed. Earl Ofari (Boston: Beacon Press, 1972), appendix, 161–162, 166–167; Jefferson, *Notes on the State of Virginia*, 177.

50. *Pennsylvania Freeman*, May 16, 1850.

51. *Voice of the Fugitive*, February 26, 1851.

52. *Voice of the Fugitive*, February 26, 1851.

53. *Voice of the Fugitive*, February 26, 1851; See [Robert Chambers], *Vestiges of the Natural History of Creation* (London, 1844), electronic ed., Project Gutenburg, 86, https://www.gutenberg.org/cache/epub/7116/pg7116-images.html.

54. *Voice of the Fugitive*, February 26, 1851.

55. John Lewis, *The Life, Labors, and Travels of Elder Charles Bowles, of the Free Will Baptist Denomination, by Eld. John W. Lewis. Together with an Essay on the Character and Condition of the African Race by the Same.* , electronic ed., North American Slave Narratives. Documenting the American South, University of North Carolina at Chapel Hill, 2000, 227, 243–245, 249, 257–259, 263–264. http://docsouth.unc.edu/neh/lewisjw/lewisjw.html; *Liberator*, July 7, 1832; *Black Abolitionist Papers*, vol. 3, 354n; *Colored American*, March 18, 1837; July 7, 1838.

56. For a comprehensive analysis of Douglass's address, see Waldo Martin, *The Mind of Frederick Douglass* (Chapel Hill: University of North Carolina Press, 1984), 229–238.

57. Douglass, "The Claims of the Negro" 501–502, 510, 515, 517, 519.

58. Douglass, "The Claims of the Negro," 521.

59. Morton is quoted in Hume, "Quantifying Characters," 136–137. See Samuel George Morton, *Letter to the Rev. John Bachman, D. D. on the Question of Hybridity in Animals, Considered in Reference to the Unity of the Human Species* (Charleston, NC: Walker and James, 1850) 14, 17.

60. Louis Agassiz, "Diversity of Origins of the Human Races," 110–111, 116, 120, 124–125, 135; Morton, *Crania Americana*, 31; Stanton, *The Leopard's Spots*, 39, 50–51, 70, 97. In 1830, Caldwell made a similar argument that Noah and his family were Caucasian. Caldwell, *Thoughts on the Original Unity*, 72–73.

NOTES TO PAGES 140–147   359

61. Josiah C. Nott, "Physical History of the Jewish Race," *Southern Quarterly* 1 (July 1850): 429, 432–433, 434, 436, 446; *Frederick Douglass' Paper*, September 8, 1854.

62. Nott, "Physical History of the Jewish Race," 447–449.

63. Miriam Claude Meijer, "Petrus Camper on the Origin and Color of Blacks," *History of Anthropology Newsletter* 24 (December 1997): 3, 4, 5, 6. The article contains Meijer's translation of Camper's 1764 lecture, "On the Origin and Color of Blacks"; Nott and Gliddon, *Types of Mankind*, xxxi.

64. For an example of White Christian criticism of polygeny, see "Josiah C. Nott, On the Diversity of Origin of the Human Races," *Princeton Review* 22 (October 1850): 603–642.

65. Pennington, *A Text Book*, 5–6.

66. Garnet, *The Past and Present Condition*, appendix, 160–161, 173; *North Star*, June 16, 1848.

67. *Pennsylvania Freeman*, May 16, 1850; Milton Sernett, *North Star Country: Upstate New York and the Crusade for African American Freedom* (Syracuse, NY: Syracuse University Press, 2002), 63.

68. *Frederick Douglass' Paper*, January 27, 1854.

69. Ward identified Simeon as Black despite scholarly interpretations of "Niger" as a reference to hair color. See Acts 13:1 (RSV) for the biblical reference to Simeon and other early Christian teachers. *Frederick Douglass' Paper*, January 27, 1854; *Pennsylvania Freeman*, May 16, 1850; Pennington, *A Text Book*, 17–18; Samuel Ringgold Ward, *Autobiography of a Fugitive Negro* (1855; repr., New York: Arno Press and the New York Times, 1968), 271, 273.

70. John Lewis, *The Life, Labors, and Travels*, 230, 235–237.

71. Douglass, "The Claims of the Negro," 502, 520, 522.

72. James McCune Smith, *The Destiny of the People of Color, A Lecture Delivered before the Philomathean Society and Hamilton Lyceum* (New York, 1841), 8, 16, appendix A. I am grateful to Michele Ronnick for translating Smith's Latin passage.

73. Caldwell, *Thoughts on the Original Unity*, 42; Hume, "Quantifying Characters," 134; Stanton, *The Leopard's Spots*, 141.

74. Nott, "Physical History of the Jewish Race," 448; Josiah C. Nott, "The Mulatto a Hybrid," *American Journal of the Medical Sciences* 6 (July 1843): 252–256; and *Boston Medical and Surgical Journal* 29 (August 1843): 29–32; Nobles, *Shades of Citizenship*, 37–39, 40–41; *North Star*, December 7, 1849; "Black and Mulatto Populations of the South," *DeBow's Review* 8 (June 1850):587–588.

75. *New York Spectator*, September 21, 1837; *Colored American*, September 23, 1837; September 30, 1937; *Philanthropist*, October 17, 1837.

76. *Frederick Douglass' Paper*, March 25, 1852; April 15, 1852; December 24, 1852; September 9, 1853.

77. *Frederick Douglass' Paper*, April 15, 1852.

78. Jordan, *White over Black*, 505–506; James McCune Smith, "On the Fourteenth Query of Thomas Jefferson's *Notes on Virginia*," *Anglo-African Magazine* 1 (August 1859): 227–228.

79. James McCune Smith, "On the Fourteenth Query," 225–227, 229.

360 NOTES TO PAGES 147-153

80. John Lewis, *The Life, Labors, and Travels*, 237, 245.

81. Pennington, *A Text Book*, 92–95. Also see James Pennington , "A Review of Slavery and the Slave Trade," *Anglo-African Magazine* 1 (May 1859): 158–159.

82. *Proceedings of the Colored National Convention, held in Rochester, July 6th, 7th, and 8th, 1853*, 55.

83. *Frederick Douglass' Paper*, February 5, 1852.

84. *Frederick Douglass' Paper*, April 20, 1855; George Levesque, "Boston's Black Brahmin: Dr. John S. Rock," *Civil War History* 26 (1980): 329.

85. S.S.N., "Anglo-Saxons and Anglo-Africans," *Anglo-African Magazine* I (August 1859): 247–249.

86. S.S.N. "Anglo-Saxons and Anglo-Africans," 247–249.

87. Smyth's critique of Agassiz came just after Agassiz presented his polygenist stance at the third meeting of the American Association for the Advancement of Science in Charleston. S.S.N. "Anglo-Saxons and Anglo-Africans," 250; Brian Wallis, "Black Bodies, White Science: Louis Agassiz's Slave Daguerreotypes," *American Art* 9 (Summer 1995): 44. See Augustin Calmet, Charles Taylor, and Edward Robinson, *Calmet's Dictionary of the Holy Bible*, rev. (New York: Jonathan Leavitt, 1832); Thomas Smyth, DD, *The Unity of the Human Races Proved to be the Doctrine of Scripture, Reason, and Science. With a Review of the Present Position and Theory of Professor Agassiz* (New York: George Putnam, 1850); Nicholas Wiseman, DD, *Twelve Lectures on the Connection between Science and Revealed Religion. Delivered in Rome* (Andover, MA: Gould and Newman, 1837), 135.

88. S.S.N. "Anglo-Saxons and Anglo-Africans," 240–251.

89. James McCune Smith, "On the Fourteenth Query," 233–236; James Cowles Prichard, *Researches into the Physical History of Mankind*, 4th edition (London: Houlston and Stoneman, 1851), 220–227.

90. James McCune Smith, "On the Fourteenth Query," 234–235

91. James McCune Smith, "On the Fourteenth Query," 236.

92. *Anglo-African Magazine* 1 (April 1859): 97–100; (May 1859): 142–144.

93. James McCune Smith, "On the Fourteenth Query," 230–232.

94. James McCune Smith, "On the Fourteenth Query," 237.

95. Delany, *The Condition, Elevation, Emigration, and Destiny of the Colored People of the United States*, 110–111; *New York Herald*, February 15, 1845; March 3, 1845; *New York Daily Tribune*, February 19, 1845; James McCune Smith, "Civilization: Its Dependence on Physical Circumstances," *Anglo-African Magazine* 1 (January 1859): 5, 11–12. Bruce Dain argues that Smith failed to directly challenge American School ethnological clams and that his theory of progress mimicked and fell victim to polygeny. See Dain, *A Hideous Monster*, 229, 239, 256–263.

96. Smith reported that he wrote his essay on civilization in 1844 and "slightly" revised it for publication in 1859. Portions of the essay also appear in a letter to Horace Greeley published in *Frederick Douglass' Paper* on September 25, 1851. Frederick Douglass cites one of its arguments in his 1854 speech "The Claims of the Negro" (522). Smith's article on climate and longevity was initially an unsuccessful submission to an 1845 Harvard University essay contest. It was also published as a

NOTES TO PAGES 153–158   361

Merchants' Magazine article before appearing as a pamphlet. *Liberator*, December 19, 1845; James McCune Smith, "On the Fourteenth Query," 237; James McCune Smith, *Dissertation on the Influence of Climate on Longevity* (New York: Office of Merchants' Magazine, 1846), 3.

97. James McCune Smith, *Dissertation on the Influence of Climate*, 3–4, 28–29; James McCune Smith, "Civilization," 12; James McCune Smith, "On the Fourteenth Query," 237. Smith consulted Lambert Adolphe Quetelet and Edouard Smits, *Recherches sur la reproduction et la mortalite de l'homme aux differens ages, et sur la population de la Belgique* (Brussels: Chez Louis Hauman et Cie Libraires, 1832). See Henry Thomas Buckle, *History of Civilization in England*, vol. 1, 2nd London edition (New York: D. Appleton, 1862), 29–108.

98. James McCune Smith, "Civilization," 6; James McCune Smith, *Dissertation on the Influence of Climate*, 13.

99. James McCune Smith, "Civilization," 7–8; James McCune Smith to Gerrit Smith, December 18, 1846, and May 12, 1848, Gerrit Smith Papers, Special Collections Research Center, Syracuse University Library.

100. James McCune Smith, "Civilization," 12–13.

101. James McCune Smith, "On the Fourteenth Query," 229–230.

102. James McCune Smith, "On the Fourteenth Query," 12–14; *Frederick Douglass' Paper*, September 25, 1851.

103. James McCune Smith, "Civilization," 15; *Frederick Douglass' Paper*, September 25, 1851.

104. James McCune Smith, "On the Fourteenth Query," 237–238.

105. Stanton, *The Leopard's Spots*, 160; Nott and Gliddon, *Types of Mankind*, 53.

106. Nott, "Physical History of the Jewish Race," 448; James McCune Smith, "Toussaint L'Ouverture and the Haytian Revolutions," in *Masterpieces of Negro Eloquence: The Best Speeches Delivered by the Negro from the Days of Slavery to the Present Time*, ed. Alice Moore Dunbar (New York: Johnson Reprint, 1970), 26; *Frederick Douglass' Paper*, September 25, 1851; J. Theodore Holly, "Thoughts on Hayti. Number III," *Anglo-African Magazine* 1 (August 1859): 242.

107. James McCune Smith, "The German Invasion," *Anglo-African Magazine* 1 (March 1859): 86; *Frederick Douglass' Paper*, September 25, 1851; James McCune Smith, "Civilization," 12.

108. *Frederick Douglass' Paper*, September 25, 1851; James McCune Smith, "Civilization," 15–16; Hume, "Quantifying Characters," 142.

109. James McCune Smith, *The Destiny of the People of Color*, 7, 9–10, 15–16.

110. The idea that Negroes and White people are constitutionally different does not appear in Child's popular antislavery text where she classifies Negroes with other human beings. James McCune Smith, *The Destiny of the People of Color*, 7, 8, 16–17, appendix A; Lydia Maria Child, *An Appeal in Favor of that Class of Americans Called Africans* (Boston, 1833).

111. James McCune Smith, "Civilization," 5; *Frederick Douglass' Paper*, September 25, 1851; Henry James, "Morality and the Perfect Life," in *Moralism and Christianity,*

362   NOTES TO PAGES 158–164

or Man's Experience and Destiny. In Three Lectures (New York: J. S. Redfield, 1850), 108–109.

112. Frederick Douglass' Paper, March 4, 1852; William G. Allen, A Short Personal Narrative, in The American Prejudice against Color, ed. Sarah Elbert (Boston: Northeastern University Press, 2002), 99–105; William G. Allen, The American Prejudice against Color. An Authentic Narrative, in Elbert, The American Prejudice against Color, 42; William Hall Jr. to Gerrit Smith, October 16, 1839, Gerrit Smith Papers; Gerrit Smith to General John H. Cooke, December 11, 1840, Gerrit Smith Papers; William G. Allen to Gerrit Smith, May 15, 1845, Gerrit Smith Papers.

113. Frederick Douglass' Paper, May 20, 1852.

114. Frederick Douglass' Paper, May 20, 1852.

115. Frederick Douglass's report on Allen's anti-colonization lectures reveals another instance in which Allen used James McCune Smith's idea of progress. Frederick Douglass' Paper, June 10, 1852; July 30, 1852.

116. Frederick Douglass' Paper, July 16, 1852; August 6, 1852?

117. Frederick Douglass' Paper, July 30, 1852.

118. Frederick Douglass' Paper, April 29, 1852; May 20, 1852; July 30, 1852; William G. Allen, Wheatley, Banneker, and Horton (Boston: Press of Daniel Laing, Jr., 1849)

119. Frederick Douglass' Paper, July 19, 1852; July 30, 1852; August 13, 1852.

120. Frederick Douglass' Paper, April 1, 1852; August 13, 1852; October 22, 1852; November 5, 1852; Stanton, The Leopard's Spots, 37.

121. William G. Allen, The American Prejudice against Color, 54–82; Aliened American, April 9, 1853; Leeds Times, December 10, 1853 in Black Abolitionist Archive, Doc 14543, University of Detroit Mercy, https://libraries.udmercy.edu/archives/special-collections/index.php?collectionSet=all&collectionCode=baa&record_id=1085.

122. Frederick Douglass' Paper, December 24, 1852.

123. Emphasis in the original. Such perceptions of Morton have been the focus of enduring scholarly debate. Stephen Jay Gould's analysis of Morton's data on skulls affirms the type of distortions that Douglass condemned. He concludes that Morton fudged data to match his convictions. Gould has been accused of being swayed by his own biases against Morton. After remeasuring some of Morton's skulls, a team of anthropologists concluded that Morton's adherence to scientific methods protected his measurements from "cultural biases." C. Loring Brace also charges Gould with bias against Morton. He attributes discrepancies in Morton's comparisons to "home-made measuring equipment" instead of bias. Douglass, "The Claims of the Negro," 507–509, 510–511, 514. See Gould, The Mismeasure of Man, 85–86, 100–101; Jason E. Lewis, David DeGusta, Marc R. Meyer, Janet M. Monge, Alan E. Mann, et al. "The Mismeasure of Science: Stephen Jay Gould versus Samuel George Morton on Skulls and Bias," PloS Biol 9:6 (June 2011): e1001071, doi:10.1371/journal.pbio.1001071, http:/www.plosbiology.org; Brace, "Race" Is a Four-Letter Word, 88–90.

124. Douglass, "The Claims of the Negro," 523–524.

125. James McCune Smith, Destiny of the People of Color, 7–8.

126. New York Daily Tribune, May 8, 1844; Black Abolitionist Papers 3, 433, 436; Nott and Gliddon, Types of Mankind, 50–51. For full accounts of controversy over errors

NOTES TO PAGES 164–181   363

in the 1840 census, see Stanton, *The Leopard's Spots*, 60–64; and Litwack, *North of Slavery*, 40–45.

127. Stanton, *The Leopard's Spots*, 192–193.

128. *Frederick Douglass' Paper*, January 8, 1852.

129. *Frederick Douglass' Paper*, March 25, 1852; James McCune Smith, "On the Fourteenth Query," 230, 236–237.

130. *Frederick Douglass' Paper*, March 25, 1852.

131. James McCune Smith, "A Word for the 'Smith Family,'" *Anglo-African Magazine* (March 1860): 80. See Eric D. Anderson, "Black Responses to Darwinism, 1859–1915," in *Disseminating Darwinism: The Role of Place, Race, Religion, and Gender*, ed. Ronald L. Numbers and John Stenhouse (Cambridge: Cambridge University Press, 1999), 247–266.

132. James McCune Smith, "A Word for the 'Smith Family,'" 79.

133. James McCune Smith, "A Word for the 'Smith Family,'" 79.

134. Stanton, *The Leopard's Spots*, 180–182, 185–187; Louis Menand, *The Metaphysical Club: A Story of Ideas in America* (New York: Farrar, Straus and Giroux, 2001), 124–128.

135. *Christian Recorder*, February 23, 1861; June 22, 1861.

136. Louis Agassiz, *A Journey in Brazil, by Professor and Mrs. Louis Agassiz* (Boston: Ticknor and Fields, 1868), 296–297.

137. *Proceedings of the National Convention of Colored Men, held in the City of Syracuse, N. Y. October 4, 5, 6, and 7, 1864*, 41–42.

Chapter 5

1. Foner, Reconstruction, 288; Pauli Murray, *Proud Shoes: The Story of an American Family* (New York: Harper & Row, 1987), 166–175.

2. Theophilus Gould Steward, *Fifty Years in the Gospel Ministry: From 1864 to 1914* (Philadelphia: A.M.E. Book Concern, 1914), 31. Although the text of Delany's lecture is not extant, the title suggests that it was an early version of the opening argument in his 1879 treatise, *The Origin of Races and Color*. The work affirmed commonality among human beings based on a single creation (see chapter 6). See Martin Delany, *The Origin of Races and Color* (Baltimore: Black Classic Press, 1991), 9 and passim.

3. *New National Era*, August 31, 1871; Foner, *Reconstruction*, 288; Robert S. Levine, ed. *Martin R. Delany: A Documentary Reader* (Chapel Hill: University of North Carolina Press, 2003), 378; Robert S. Levine, *Martin Delany, Frederick Douglass, and the Politics of Representative Identity* (Chapel Hill: University of North Carolina Press, 1997), 219–220.

4. *Congressional Record*, 43rd Congress, First Session, (May 22, 1874), appendix 316, quoted in Michael O'Malley, "Specie and Species: Race and the Money Question in Nineteenth-Century America," *American Historical Review* 99 (April 1994): 381.

5. *Christian Recorder*, February 27, 1869.

364 NOTES TO PAGES 182–185

6. *Christian Recorder*, February 27, 1869; Edwin S. Redkey, *Black Exodus: Black Nationalist and Back-to-Africa Movements, 1890–1910* (New Haven, CT: Yale University Press, 1969), 31, 40; Ronald Lewis, "Reverend T. G. Steward and 'Mixed' Schools in Delaware, 1882," *Delaware History* 19 (1981): 54; William Seraile, *Fire in His Heart: Bishop Benjamin Tucker Tanner and the A.M.E. Church* (Knoxville: University of Tennessee Press, 2003), 56.

7. Garnet, A Memorial Discourse, 65.

8. James McCune Smith to Gerrit Smith, February 17, 1865, Gerrit Smith Papers, Special Collections Research Center, Syracuse University Libraries; Garnet, *A Memorial Discourse*, 65.

9. *Christian Recorder*, February 22, 1862.

10. *Christian Recorder*, February 22, 1862; March 29, 1862; July 22, 1862.

11. Abraham Lincoln, "Address on Colonization to a Deputation of Negroes," in *Collected Works of Abraham Lincoln*, vol. 5, ed. Roy P. Basler (New Brunswick: Rutgers University Press, 1953), 371–375, *Christian Recorder*, September 20, 1862; *Liberator*, September 12, 1862; Purvis, "Speech of Robert Purvis at the Annual Meeting of the American Anti-Slavery Society in 1860," in *Speeches and Letters by Robert Purvis, Published by the Request of the "Afro-American League"* (Philadelphia, n.d.), 21, 19. For divergent interpretations of the duration of Lincoln's support for colonization, see George Frederickson, "A Man but Not a Brother: Abraham Lincoln and Racial Equality," *Journal of Southern History* 40 (1975): 39–58; Michael Vorenberg, "Abraham Lincoln and the Politics of Black Colonization," *Journal of the Abraham Lincoln Association* 14 (Summer 1993): 23–45; James McPherson, *Battle Cry of Freedom* (New York: Oxford University Press, 1988).

12. *Liberator*, August 22, 1862.

13. *Proceedings of the National Convention of Colored Men, held in the City of Syracuse, NY, 1864*. Boston: J. S. Rock, George Ruffin, 1864, in Bell, *Proceedings*, 9.

14. *Proceedings of the National Convention of Colored Men, held in the City of Syracuse, NY, 1864*, 14, 52.

15. *Proceedings of the National Convention of Colored Men, held in the City of Syracuse, NY, 1864*, 33.

16. *Proceedings of the National Convention of Colored Men, held in the City of Syracuse, NY, 1864*, 41, 22.

17. *Proceedings of the National Convention of Colored Men, held in the City of Syracuse, NY, 1864*, 41–42.

18. *Christian Recorder*, February 24, 1866; April 28, 1866; February 17, 1866.

19. *Christian Recorder*, February 17, 1866.

20. *Christian Recorder*, July 22, 1865 and February 17, 1866.

21. Italics are in the original. *Christian Recorder*, February 17, 1866.

22. *Proceedings of the State Convention of the Coloured Men of the State of New Jersey, Held in the City of Trenton, N.J., July 13th and 14th, 1865 with a Short Address to the Loyal People of New Jersey, Together with the Constitution of the Equal Rights League of the State of New Jersey*, in Foner and Walker, Proceedings, 13, 15; *Christian Recorder*, August 26, 1865; September 2, 1865; February 17, 1866.

NOTES TO PAGES 185–189 365

23. Robert Purvis to Parker T. Smith, February 22, 1867, Leon Gardiner Collection, Historical Society of Pennsylvania.

24. *Christian Recorder*, July 22, 1865; April 21, 1866; Robert Purvis to Parker T. Smith, February 22, 1867.

25. Robert Purvis to Parker T. Smith, February 22, 1867; *New York Herald*, January 18, 1867.

26. Richard McCormick, "William Whipper: Moral Reformer," *Pennsylvania History* 43 (January 1976): 39–40; *Colored American*, September 9, 16, and 23, 1837; William Still, *The Underground Rail Road* (1871; repr., Chicago: Johnson, 1970) 766–767; *Titusville Morning Herald*, May 27, 1870.

27. Ancestry.com, 1860 United States Federal Census (Provo, UT: Ancestry.com Operations, 2009); *Provincial Freeman*, July 22, 1854; April 14, 1855; September 22, 1855; November 3, 1855; Marie Carter, "William Whipper's Lands along the Sydenham," in *The Promised Land: History and Historiography of the Black Experience in Chatham-Kent's Settlements and Beyond*, ed. Boulou Ebanda de B'béri, Nina Reid-Maroney, and Handel Kashope Wright (Toronto: University of Toronto Press, 2014), 81–84.

28. William Whipper to Gerrit Smith, April 22, 1856, Gerrit Smith Papers, Special Collections Research Center, Syracuse University Libraries.

29. Whipper did not question Smith's reference to "black men," but his insistence on bracketing the term with quotation marks throughout his letter flagged qualms about its appropriateness. William Whipper to Gerrit Smith, April 22, 1856, Gerrit Smith Papers.

30. McCormick, "William Whipper," 40; *Christian Recorder*, February 16, 1861.

31. *Christian Recorder*, February 27, 1869.

32. *Christian Recorder*, March 13, 1869.

33. *Frederick Douglass' Paper*, November 9, 1855; *Douglass' Monthly*, March 1859; Mary A. S. Cary to Benjamin Coates, November 20, 1858, Benjamin Coates African Colonization Collection, Special Collections, Haverford College Library.

34. MacMaster, "Henry Highland Garnet and the African Civilization Society," 95–112. Benjamin Coates, *Cotton Cultivation in Africa, Suggestions on the Importance of the Cultivation of Cotton in Africa in Reference to the Abolition of Slavery in the United States through the Organization of an African Civilization Society* (Philadelphia: C. Sherman & Son, 1858), 8.

35. *Douglass' Monthly*, March 1859.

36. William Whipper to Benjamin Coates, February 24, 1859, Benjamin Coates African Colonization Collection.

37. Benjamin Coates to William Coppinger, September 26, 1868, and April 6, 1867, in Emma J. Lapsansky-Werner and Margaret Hope Bacon, eds., *Back to Africa: Benjamin Coates and the Colonization Movement in America, 1848–1880* (University Park: Pennsylvania State University Press, 2005), 249, 207–209.

38. Benjamin Coates to William Coppinger, September 26, 1868, in Lapsansky-Werner and Bacon, *Back to Africa*, 249–250; Coates to Joseph Tracy, March 8, 1869, in Lapsansky-Werner and Bacon, *Back to Africa*, 288–289.

366   NOTES TO PAGES 189–192

39. Emphasis is in the original. *Christian Recorder*, August 28, 1869.

40. *New York Herald*, January 18, 1867; *Christian Recorder*, July 22, 1865.

41. William Whipper et al., *Address of the Stockholders of Liberty Hall, Nos. 716 and 718 Lombard Street* (Philadelphia: Rev. Elisha Weaver, Agent African Methodist Episcopal Book Concern, 1866), 7, 8, 10, 11. Liberty Hall had been the site of the Institute for Colored Youth, which moved to a new building. Whipper's name headed the list of the stockholders who initiated the purchase. It included William Still, Rev. Stephen Smith, Robert Allen, William Warrick Jr., Henry Jones, Rev. J. J. Clinton, Rev. Elisha Weaver, Robert Adger, and James W. Purnell.

42. *Christian Recorder*, August 3, 1872; *Proceedings of the National Convention of the Colored Men of America, Held in Washington, D.C., January 13, 14, 15, and 16, 1869*, in Foner and Walker, *Proceedings*, 373; *Catalogue of the Officers and Students of Howard University* (Washington, DC: Judd & Detweiler, 1869), 3; *Catalogue of the Officers and Students of Howard University*, (Washington, DC: Judd & Detweiler, 1870), 2; *Catalogue of the Officers and Students of Howard University*, (Washington, DC: Judd & Detweiler, 1871), 4; *Catalogue of the Officers and Students of Howard University*, (Washington, DC: Reed & Woodward, 1872), 4; *Christian Recorder*, July 31, 1869.

43. *Christian Recorder*, August 31, 1872; April 25, 1863; May 12, 1866; January 2, 1873; January 29, 1874; April 8, 1875; August 31, 1872; June 2, 1866.

44. Emphasis is in the original. Whipper et al., *Address of the Stockholders of Liberty Hall*, 6, 7.

45. Whipper, et al., *Address of the Stockholders of Liberty Hall*, 7, 10.

46. *Christian Recorder*, March 13, 1869. Whipper's unexplained reference to "hybrids" raises questions about the degree to which his new perspective included an attempt to attribute his past rejection of race to his birth designation as "a Mulatto or Mustee"— terms referring to African, European, and possibly Native American ancestry. Although the meaning of his label is ambiguous, it signals the extent to which he tried to reinterpret human difference to navigate new parameters of freedom. For details of Whipper's birth record, see Cory James Young, "A Just and True Return: A Dataset of Pennsylvania's Surviving County Slave Registries," *Magazine of Early American Datasets 46 McNeil Center for Early American Studies*, 2021, https:repository.upenn.edu; J. B. Eshleman, "Record of Returns Made in Writing . . . As Clerk . . . by Possessors of Negro or Mulatto Children Born after March 1, 1780 . . . John Hubley, Clerk, June 7, 1788," *Lancaster History*, 29.

47. *Christian Recorder*, March 13, 1869.

48. *Christian Recorder*, November 4, 1865; August 31, 1872; April 20, 1872; June 16, 1866.

49. *Christian Recorder*, March 13, 1869.

50. *Christian Recorder*, March 6, 1869.

51. *Christian Recorder*, February 13, 1873; March 20, 1969.

52. *Christian Recorder*, June 2, 1866.

53. The American Equal Rights Association held its last convention in 1869 and formally dissolved in 1870. *Christian Recorder*, July 22, 1865; January 6, 1866; April 21, 1866.

54. *Christian Recorder*, September 29, 1866.

55. *Christian Recorder*, March 13, 1869.

NOTES TO PAGES 192–197   367

56. *Proceedings of the National Convention of the Colored Men of America, Held in Washington, D.C., January 13, 14, 15, and 16, 1869*, 364, 379, 380.

57. *Christian Recorder*, March 20, 1869.

58. *Proceedings of the National Convention of the Colored Men of America, Held in Washington, D.C., January 13, 14, 15, and 16, 1869*, 361, 365.

59. *Proceedings of the National Convention of the Colored Men of America, Held in Washington, D.C., January 13, 14, 15, and 16, 1869*, 359, 365; *Christian Recorder*, May 4, 1867.

60. *Christian Recorder*, March 20, 1869 and June 16, 1866.

61. *Proceedings of the National Convention of the Colored Men of America, Held in Washington, D.C., January 13, 14, 15, and 16, 1869*, 346.

62. Judith Giesberg, *"A Great Thing for Our People": Institute for Colored Youth in the Civil War Era*, digital exhibition, February 9, 2015, Falvey Memorial Library, Villanova University, https://exhibits.library.villanova.edu/institute-colored-youth/graduates/harriet-c-johnson.

63. *Proceedings of the Colored National Convention, held in Franklin Hall, Sixth Street below Arch, Philadelphia, October 16th, 17th, and 18th, 1855*, 10,; *Proceedings of the National Convention of the Colored Men of America, Held in Washington, D.C., January 13, 14, 15, and 16, 1869*, 353, 354.

64. *Proceedings of the National Convention of the Colored Men of America, Held in Washington, D.C., January 13, 14, 15, and 16, 1869*, 367.

65. *Proceedings of the National Convention of the Colored Men of America, Held in Washington, D.C., January 13, 14, 15, and 16, 1869*, 372.

66. *Proceedings of the National Convention of Colored Men, held in the City of Syracuse, NY, 1864*, 29, 36–39.

67. *Proceedings of the National Convention of the Colored Men of America, Held in Washington, D.C., January 13, 14, 15, and 16, 1869*, 345, 354, 366; Silcox, "The Black 'Better Class' Political Dilemma: Philadelphia Prototype Isaiah C. Wears," 47–48.

68. *Proceedings of the National Convention of the Colored Men of America, Held in Washington, D.C., January 13, 14, 15, and 16, 1869*, 368.

69. *Proceedings of the National Convention of the Colored Men of America, Held in Washington, D.C., January 13, 14, 15, and 16, 1869*, 368, 370, 373, 374.

70. Silcox, "The Black 'Better Class' Political Dilemma: Philadelphia Prototype Isaiah C. Wears," 60; *Proceedings of the National Convention of the Colored Men of America, Held in Washington, D.C., January 13, 14, 15, and 16, 1869*, 384–385.

71. *Proceedings of the National Convention of the Colored Men of America, Held in Washington, D.C., January 13, 14, 15, and 16, 1869*, 384–385.

72. Emphasis is in the original. William D. Forten to Charles Sumner, February 1, 1869, as quoted in Winch, *A Gentleman of Color*, 368–369.

73. Winch, *A Gentleman of Color*, 369.

74. *Christian Recorder*, April 9, 1870.

75. *Christian Recorder*, February 19, 1870, April 9, 1870, April 27, 1867; *New Brunswick Weekly Fredonian*, May 27, 1970, in Price, Freedom Not Far Distant, 140–141; Daniel Payne, *The Moral Significance of the XVth Amendment. Sermon delivered at the Ohio*

368 NOTES TO PAGES 197–202

Annual Conference of the African Methodist Episcopal Church, May 8, 1870 (Xenia, OH: Xenia Gazette, 1870), 6, 8.

76. *New National Era*, October 19, 1871.

77. "State Convention of the Colored Voters of New York, Syracuse, October 1870," in Foner and Walker, *Proceedings*, 422; *Proceedings of the National Convention of the Colored Men of America, Held in Washington, D.C., January 13, 14, 15, and 16, 1869*, 353.

78. *New National Era*, March 28, 1872.

79. Geo. T. Downing et al., circular letter, February 1869, Gerrit Smith Papers.

80. *Elevator*, April 14, 1865.

81. *New National Era*, September 8, 1870; October 6, 1870; Ben Perley Poore, *Congressional Directory* (Washington, DC: Government Printing Office, 1872), 138.

82. For the first nine months of operations, Douglass was corresponding editor of the *New Era*, and Martin served as chief editor. When Martin abandoned the project, Douglass became the sole editor and changed the title to *New National Era*. *New Era*, March 17, 1870; January 13, 1870; January 17, 1870; June 23, 1870.

83. *Christian Recorder*, August 14, 1869.

84. *Proceedings of the National Convention of the Colored Men of America, Held in Washington, D.C., January 13, 14, 15, and 16, 1869*, 356.

85. Eric Foner, *Freedom's Lawmakers: A Directory of Black Officeholders during Reconstruction*, rev. edition (Baton Rouge: Louisiana State University Press, 1995), xx–xxi; Eric Foner, *Reconstruction*, 282–283.

86. *Congressional Record*, 43rd Congress, First Session, (January 24, 1874): 902–903. See William Shakespeare, *The Merchant of Venice*, ed. Jay L. Halio (New York: Oxford University Press, 1993), act 3, scene 1.

87. Philip Foner, *Frederick Douglass*, 2nd edition (New York: Citadel Press, 1969), 269–271; Frederick Douglass to William Whipper, June 9, 1870, Leon Gardiner Collection, Historical Society of Pennsylvania; *New National Era*, October 6, 1870. Despite his scorn, Douglass published substantial accounts of religious celebrations of the Fifteenth Amendment in his *New Era* newspaper. See *New Era*, April 7, 1870.

88. Philip Foner, *Frederick Douglass*, 269–271; *Christian Recorder*, June 25, 1870.

89. Reginald F. Hildebrand, *The Times Were Strange and Stirring: Methodist Preachers and the Crisis of Emancipation* (Durham, NC: Duke University Press, 1995), xvi, 31–32, 38–41.

90. Payne, *Recollections*, 41, 65. 74. *Christian Recorder*, June 3, 1865.

91. *Christian Recorder*, June 3, 1865; April 20, 1867.

92. *Christian Recorder*, June 3, 1865; July 22, 1865; April 20, 1867. *Journal of the 18th Session and 17th Quadrennial Session of the General Conference of the African Methodist Episcopal Church, in the World, 1884* (Philadelphia, 1884), 41. See also William Gravely, "The Social, Political and Religious Significance of the Formation of the Colored Methodist Episcopal Church," *Methodist History* 17 (October 1979): 17.

93. Smith is quoted in Hildebrand, *The Times Were Strange*, 95–96.

NOTES TO PAGES 203–206   369

94. Emphasis is in the original. James Lynch to Matthew Simpson, May 28, 1867, in William B. Gravely, "The Decision of A.M.E. Leader, James Lynch, To Join The Methodist Episcopal Church: New Evidence at the Old St. George's Church, Philadelphia," *Methodist History* 15 (July 1977): 267, 265.

95. James Lynch to Matthew Simpson, May 28, 1867, in Gravely, "The Decision of A.M.E. Leader, James Lynch, To Join The Methodist Episcopal Church," 265.

96. Lynch opposed colored conventions on similar grounds. "The Freedmen of Georgia: Minutes of and Interview between the Colored Ministers and Church Officers at Savannah with the Secretary of War and Major Gen. Sherman, Jan. 12 1865," *National Freedman: Monthly Journal of the National Freedman's Relief Association* 1 (April 1, 1875): 99; Lynch to Matthew Simpson, May 28, 1867, 265–266; Ralph Morrow, *Northern Methodism and Reconstruction* (East Lansing: Michigan State University Press, 1956), 138–139; *Christian Recorder*, August 18, 1866; January 16, 1873.

97. William B. Gravely, "Hiram Revels Protests Racial Separation in the Methodist Church (1876)," *Methodist History* 8 (April 1970): 14; H. R. Revels, "We Ought not to Separate," *Southwestern Advocate*, May 4, 1876, in Gravely, "The Decision of A.M.E. Leader, James Lynch, To Join The Methodist Episcopal Church," 17–20.

98. Hildebrand, *The Times Were Strange*, 114; William Gravely, "Hiram Revels Protests Racial Separation in the Methodist Church (1876)," 14.

99. Gilbert Haven is quoted in Morrow, *Northern Methodism*, 183.

100. Revels, "We Ought not to Separate," 17–20.

101. J. W. E. Bowen, *An Appeal for Negro Bishops, But No Separation* (New York: Eaton & Mains, 1912), 66, 74–75, 87–88; Hildebrand, *The Times Were Strange*, 116–117.

102. Morrow, *Northern Methodism*, 136–137.

103. Officials of the Methodist Episcopal Church, North decided to permit elections of Negro bishops in 1920. The denomination representative W. T. McDowell explained the change as a sign that the organization was no longer accepting "a race church" and was abandoning "race consciousness" in favor of embracing "human consciousness." McDowell's announcement is quoted and summarized in *Competitor* 1:5 (June 1920): 5.

104. "The Cook Family in History," *Negro History Bulletin* 9 (June 1946): 214; John H. Cook to Oliver Otis Howard, December 1, 1867, Oliver Otis Howard Papers, George J. Mitchell Department of Special Collections & Archives, Bowdoin College Library, Brunswick, Maine.

105. Charles B. Boynton, *The Duty which the Colored People Owe to Themselves: A Sermon Delivered at Metzerott Hall, Washington, D.C.* (Washington, DC: Office of the Great Republic, 1867), Daniel Murray Pamphlet Collection, Library of Congress, https://www.loc.gov/item/ca25001511/; Cook to Oliver Otis Howard, December 1, 1867.

106. Boynton, *The Duty which the Colored People Owe to Themselves*, 3, 1. The biblical reference to Moses choosing to identify with the Israelites instead of with Pharaoh's daughter is in Hebrews 11:23–25 (RSV).

107. Boynton, *The Duty which the Colored People Owe to Themselves*, 4.

108. Boynton, *The Duty which the Colored People Owe to Themselves*, 3–5.

370 NOTES TO PAGES 206–211

109. Boynton, *The Duty which the Colored People Owe to Themselves*, 4.

110. Boynton, *The Duty which the Colored People Owe to Themselves*, 6–8.

111. Emphasis is in the original. Oliver Otis Howard, *Autobiography of Oliver Otis Howard*, vol. 2 (New York: Baker & Taylor, 1907), 426, 425; Frederick Douglass to O. O. Howard, 1870 July 13, ALS, Oliver Otis Howard Papers, Bowdoin College Library, Brunswick, Maine.

112. "True Position 1868," First Congregational Church, Washington, DC, Book 2, Digital Howard @University, http://dh.howard.edu/ooh_fc/2; "Proceeding of an Ex Parte Council Held at the First Congregational Church, Nov. 1868," O. O. Howard Collection, First Congregational Church, Washington, DC, Book 1, Digital Howard @University, http://dh.howard.edu/ooh_fc/1; Howard, *Autobiography of Oliver Otis Howard*, vol. 2, 435.

113. W.R.H., "The Color Line in Churches," *American Missionary* 37:9 (September 1883): 271–272.

114. D. M. Wilson, "It Decides Nothing," *American Missionary* 37:9 (September 1883): 270.

115. Washington Gladden, "The Christian League of Connecticut," *Century Magazine* 25 (November 1882): 50–60; Joan Bryant, "Race and Religion in Nineteenth-Century America," 246–258.

116. Clark charged African Methodist leaders with inconsistency in attacking him for supporting separate schools for colored children. He reasoned that there was no difference between the need for colored churches and the need for colored schools. *Christian Recorder*, April 17, 1884; October 25, 1877.

117. *New Era*, March 17, 1870; August 18, 1870.

118. *Christian Recorder*, February 24, 1866; February 13, 1864; *New Era*, May 5, 1870.

119. *Christian Recorder*, August 26, 1875.

120. *Christian Recorder*, December 13, 1877; See James M. O'Toole, *Passing for White: Race, Religion, and the Healy Family, 1820–1920* (Amherst: University of Massachusetts Press, 2003).

121. *Christian Recorder*, December 13, 1877.

122. *Christian Recorder*, June 2, 1887.

123. *Christian Recorder*, September 6, 1883.

124. *Christian Recorder*, September 20, 1883.

125. Tanner, An Outline of Our History and Government for African Methodist Churchmen, 138; *Christian Recorder*, July 17, 1873.

126. Steward, *Fifty Years in the Gospel Ministry*, 188–189.

127. Jeremiah H. Pierce, *A Brief Statement of the Public School Contest. J. H. Pierce, vs. The Union District Trustees of Burlington County, New Jersey as Brought before the Supreme Court, June 13, 1883, and Decided, Feb. 21, 1884, by Said Court, Containing all Arguments, Pro and Con* (Philadelphia: "Christian Recorder" Print No. 631, 1884).

128. Benjamin William Arnett and J. A. Brown, Ohio General Assembly, House of Representatives, , *The Black Laws! Speech of Hon. B. W. Arnett of Greene County and Hon. J. A. Brown of Cuyahoga County, in the Ohio House of Representatives*

NOTES TO PAGES 211–217   371

(Columbus, OH: Ohio State Journal, 1886), Daniel Murray Pamphlet Collection, Library of Congress, https://www.loc.gov/item/91898104/, 9, 14.

129. Arnett et al., *The Black Laws!* 16.

130. Tanner, *An Outline of Our History*, 138.

131. *Christian Recorder*, January 31, 1878.

132. Benjamin F. Lee, "Organic Union Symposium," *A.M.E. Church Review* 9 (1892): 234–235.

133. *Christian Recorder*, September 27, 1894.

134. *Christian Recorder*, February 13, 1890

135. *Christian Recorder*, November 3, 1866; November 10, 1866.

136. The biblical reference is to Micah 4:4 (RSV).

137. *Christian Recorder*, July 17, 1873.

138. Bishop J. W. Hood, "The Necessity of a Separate Church for Africans," *Independent*, September 18, 1884. Also see C. L. Goodell, "White and Colored Churches," *Independent*, May 24, 1883; and Sandy Dwayne Martin, *For God and Race: The Religious and Political Leadership of AMEZ Bishop James Walker Hood* (Columbia: University of South Carolina Press, 1999).

139. *Christian Recorder*, November 26, 1885.

140. Benjamin F. Lee, "Organic Union Symposium," 236–237; J. T. Jenifer, "Why I Am An African Methodist," *A.M.E. Church Review* 7 (1891): 291; Tanner, An Apology for African Methodism, 112; Tanner, *An Outline of Our History*, 10, 137.

141. *Christian Recorder*, October 25, 1877.

142. Theophilus Gould Steward, "Missionary Sermon Delivered before the Georgia Annual Conference Missionary Society, in Americus, Georgia, June 31st 1870," in *Pioneer Echoes: Six Special Sermons* (Baltimore: Hoffman 1889), 11–12.

143. Theophilus Gould Steward, "The Centre of Power in the Work of Social Reform" (n.d.), in *Fifty Years in the Gospel Ministry*, 100.

144. Theophilus Gould Steward, "Missionary Sermon Delivered before the Georgia Annual Conference Missionary Society, in Americus, Georgia, June 31st 1870," in *Pioneer Echoes*, 11–12.

145. Steward, "Missionary Sermon Delivered before the Georgia Annual Conference Missionary Society, in Americus, Georgia, June 31st 1870," 11–12.

146. The segment of Joseph's story that Steward referenced is in Genesis 37: 1–16 (RSV).

147. Theophilus Gould Steward, "Inaugural Sermon, Beaufort, S.C. June 18, 1865," in *Fifty Years in the Gospel Ministry*, 43–44, 46.

148. Steward, "Inaugural Sermon," 44.

149. Steward, "Inaugural Sermon," 50.

150. *Christian Recorder*, August 3, 1870; February 20, 1869; April 17, 1869.

151. *Christian Recorder*, July 6, 1870.

152. *Christian Recorder*, April 9, 1864.

153. *Christian Recorder*, November 21, 1863.

154. *Christian Recorder*, April 9, 1864; November 21, 1863.

155. *Christian Recorder*, March 25, 1865.

156. *Christian Recorder*, May 6, 1865.

372 NOTES TO PAGES 217–221

157. *Christian Recorder*, June 24, 1865.

158. *Christian Recorder*, January 23, 1864.

159. *Christian Recorder*, June 24, 1865.

160. *Christian Recorder*, January 23, 1864; June 24, 1865.

161. "Communication from Pittsburgh Annual Conference," in *Sixteenth Session, and the Fifteenth Quadrennial Session of the General Conference of the African Methodist Episcopal Church, Atlanta, Georgia, from May 1st to 18th, 1876* (Philadelphia, 1876), 226–227.

162. "Communication from Pittsburgh Annual Conference," 227, 229.

163. Emphasis is in the original. "Communication from Pittsburgh Annual Conference," 227–228.

164. "Communication from Pittsburgh Annual Conference," 228.

165. "Communication from Pittsburgh Annual Conference," 228.

166. *Christian Recorder*, April 28, 1881.

167. *Christian Recorder*, April 28, 1881.

168. Emphasis is in the original. *Christian Recorder*, April 28, 1881.

169. *Christian Recorder*, August 20. 1870.

170. H. C. C. Astwood, "Shall the Name of the African Methodist Episcopal Church be Changed to that of the Allen Methodist Church?," *A.M.E. Church Review* 4 (1888): 319–322.

171. *Christian Recorder*, February 20, 1869.

172. Jenifer, "Why I Am An African Methodist," 287.

173. *Christian Recorder*, April 8, 1865.

174. *Christian Recorder*, April 1, 1865; July 23, 1870. Ultimately, concerns about missions and aiding destitute freed people led Stanford to forge an alliance with the ACS and migrate to Liberia, but not before severing ties with the church, where he had edited the *Christian Recorder* and led the publishing unit, in order to serve in the Methodist Episcopal Church. *Christian Recorder*, July 23, 1870; Wayman, *Cyclopedia of African Methodism*, 153; Adell Patton, Jr. "The 'Back-to-Africa' Movement in Arkansas," *Arkansas Historical Quarterly* 51 (Summer 1992): 164–177.

175. *Christian Recorder*, February 20, 1869.

176. *Christian Recorder*, August 27, 1870; September 17, 1870.

177. Emphasis is in the original. J. T. Jenifer, "Has African Methodism Been a Success in New England?," in *The Budget: Containing the Annual Reports of the General Officers of the African M. E. Church of the United States of America, 1881–1887*, ed. Benjamin Arnett, 211–212; Benjamin F. Lee, "Organic Union Symposium," 237; *Christian Recorder*, September 17, 1870.

178. Tanner, *An Outline of Our History*, 11; *Journal of the 17th Session and 16th Quadrennial Session of the General Conference of the African Methodist Episcopal Church, in the United States.* (Xenia, OH, 1882) 26; Tanner, *An Apology for African Methodism*, 112, 115–116.

NOTES TO PAGES 222–229   373

179. Daniel Payne, *A Treatise on Domestic Education* (Cincinnati, OH: Cranston and Stowe, 1885), 77, 81–82, 88–89.
180. Daniel Payne, *Semi-Centenary of the A.M.E. Church* (1866; repr., Freeport, NY: Books for Libraries Press, 1972), 19–20.
181. Tanner, *An Outline of Our History*, 138–139; *Journal of the 17th Session and 16th Quadrennial Session of the General Conference of the African Methodist Episcopal Church* (1882), 26; Tanner, *An Apology for African Methodism*, 116.
182. Theophilus Gould Steward, *Fifty Years in the Gospel Ministry*, 70.
183. Emphasis is in the original. Daniel Payne, "Thoughts on the Past, the Present and the Future of the African M. E. Church," *A.M.E. Church Review* 1 (July 1884): 3, 6.
184. Foner, *Frederick Douglass*, 309, 285, 288—293.
185. *New National Era*, November 28, 1872; *Christian Recorder*, November 30, 1872.
186. *New National Era*, November 28, 1872; *Christian Recorder*, November 30, 1872.
187. *Christian Recorder*, December 14, 1872; *New National Era*, December 19, 1872; *Christian Recorder*, April 11, 1878.
188. *New National Era*, December 12, 1872.
189. *New National Era*, December 12, 1872.
190. *New National Era*, December 12, 1872.
191. *New National Era*, March 19, 1874.
192. *Christian Recorder*, January 15, 1870; March 30, 1876; December 14, 1872.
193. *Christian Recorder*, July 9, 1874.
194. *New Era*, June 23, 1870; January 17, 1870.
195. *Christian Recorder*, July 9, 1874; February 27, 1873; December 7, 1872.
196. Foner, *Frederick Douglass*, 309–311.
197. *Christian Recorder*, July 9, 1874; *National Republican*, July 13, 1874.
198. Foner, *Reconstruction*, 532.
199. The initial connection between the two men might have been established when Wears was a young apprentice in Columbia, Pennsylvania. Will of William Whipper, Philadelphia, 1876, 229, Ancestry.com; Tanner, *An Apology for African Methodism*, 199–204.
200. *Christian Recorder*, March 30, 1876; March 16, 1876.
201. *Proceedings of the Colored National Labor Convention: held in Washington, D.C., on December 6th, 7th, 8th, 9th and 10th, 1869* (Washington, DC: Printed at the Office of the New Era), 13.
202. *Christian Recorder*, April 18, 1878.
203. *Christian Recorder*, April 18, 1878.
204. Emphasis is in the original. *Christian Recorder*, April 18, 1878.
205. *New Era*, May 5, 1870; *Christian Recorder*, April 18, 1878.
206. *Christian Recorder*, June 6, 1878.
207. *Christian Recorder*, May 5, 1878.
208. *Christian Recorder*, May 5, 1878.
209. *Christian Recorder*, May 5, 1878.
210. *Christian Recorder*, May 5, 1878.
211. *Christian Recorder*, May 5, 1878.

374 NOTES TO PAGES 229–235

212. *Christian Recorder*, May 5, 1878.
213. *Christian Recorder*, June 20, 1878.
214. *Christian Recorder*, June 6, 1878.
215. *Christian Recorder*, May 5, 1878; June 20, 1878.
216. Eric Foner, *Reconstruction*, 503, 510.
217. *New Era*, November 28, 1872.
218. *Proceedings of the Conventions of Colored People, Held in Dover, Del.* (Dover, DE, 1873). See also, Ronald Lewis, "Reverend T. G. Steward and the Education of Blacks in Reconstruction Delaware," *Delaware History* 19 (1981): 156–178.
219. *Christian Recorder*, November 1, 1883, November 8, 1883.

Chapter 6

1. *Christian Recorder*, March 23, 1882.
2. *North Star*, February 11, 1848; Joel Schor, "The Rivalry between Frederick Douglass and Henry Highland Garnet," *Journal of Negro History* 64 (Winter 1979): 30–38. Henry Highland Garnet to Benjamin Coates, September 9, 1859, Benjamin Coates African Colonization Collection. In 1851, Douglass reversed his position on political antislavery and merged the *North Star* with Gerrit Smith's *Liberty Party Paper* to create *Frederick Douglass' Paper*.
3. Philip S. Foner, *Frederick Douglass*, 116, 327; Alexander Crummell, "Eulogium on Henry Highland Garnet, D. D. before the Union Literary and Historical Association; Washington D.C. May 4th, 1882," in *Africa and America: Addresses and Discourses* (1891; repr., New York: Negro Universities Press, 1969), 303–304; William Seraile, "The Brief Diplomatic Career of Henry Highland Garnet," *Phylon* 46 (1st Quarter, 1985): 74, 76, 78; *Sixty-Fourth Annual Meeting of the American Colonization Society with the Minutes of the Annual Meeting and of the Board of Directors, January 18 and 19, 1881* (Washington City: Colonization Building, 1881), 3; *Christian Recorder*, May 18, 1882.
4. *Christian Recorder*, March 23, 1882. The surnames on Douglass's list refer to Samuel Ringgold Ward, Charles Lennox Remond, Amos Gerry Beman, James W. C. Pennington, James McCune Smith, John J. Gaines, William Whipper, and William Watkins Jr.
5. "The New Law," *New Era*, June 9, 1870; Eric Foner, Reconstruction, 504–505, 529, 530–533; August Meier, *Negro Thought in America, 1881–1915: Racial Ideologies in the Age of Booker T. Washington* (Ann Arbor: University of Michigan Press, 1963), 19–21. See Rayford Logan, *The Negro in American Life and Thought: The Nadir, 1877–1901* (New York: Dial Press, 1954).
6. Purvis described Douglass as "meanly ambitious." *Frederick Douglass' Paper*, August 12, 1853; *Liberator*, September 16, 1853; Bacon, *But One Race*, 185–186; Frederick Douglass, *Address by Hon. Frederick Douglass, Delivered in the Metropolitan A.M.E. Church, Washington, D.C. Tuesday, January 9th, 1894, on The Lessons of the Hour* (Baltimore: Thomas & Evans, 1894), cover page; Moses, *Afrotopia*, 176.

NOTES TO PAGES 236–243   375

7. Redkey, *Black Exodus*, 22; Dorothy Sterling, *The Making of an Afro-American*, 319–320; Alfred B. Williams, *The Liberian Exodus. An Account of Voyage of the First Emigrants in the Bark "Azor," and Their Reception at Monrovia, with a Description of Liberia—Its Customs and Civilization, Romances and Prospects* (Charleston, 1878), electronic edition, Documenting the American South, University of North Carolina, 2000, http://docsouth.unc.edu/church/williams/williams.html, 31–32; Delany, *The Origin of Races and Color*, 15.

8. Delany, *The Origin of Races and Color*, 9, 18, 23–24, 30, 32, 35.

9. Delany, *The Origin of Races and Color*, 17, 19, 27.

10. Delany, *The Origin of Races and Color*, 9, 14–16, 19, 26–27, 37, 91, 94–95.

11. Redkey, *Black Exodus*, 22; Levine, Martin Delany, Frederick Douglass, and the Politics of Representative Identity, 236.

12. Redkey, *Black Exodus*, 30; *Christian Recorder*, February 22, 1883.

13. Redkey, *Black Exodus*, 28–30; *Christian Recorder*, November 24, 1866.

14. Redkey, *Black Exodus*, 31, 34–36.

15. *Christian Recorder*, June 16, 1881; September 29, 1881; February 22, 1883; December 13, 1883; February 14, 1889; Redkey, *Black Exodus*, 38, 184; Henry McNeal Turner, "The American Negro and his Fatherland," in *Africa and the American Negro: Addresses and Proceedings of the Congress on Africa*, ed. J. W. E. Bowen (Atlanta, GA: Gammon Theological Seminary, 1896), 195–196.

16. Redkey, *Black Exodus*, 30, 47, 55; Edward W. Blyden, LLD, "The African Problem and the Method of Its Solution," *A.M.E. Review* 7:2 (October 1890): 205, 211–213.

17. Blyden, "The African Problem and the Method of Its Solution," 205, 216–218.

18. Redkey, *Black Exodus*, 31, 40, 103–106, 115–116, 150–161, 171, 175.

19. Redkey, *Black Exodus*, 59, 68, 188–189, 193–194, 228–230; *Christian Recorder*, July 12, 1883; December 13, 1883.

20. T. Thomas Fortune, "Will the Afro-American Return to Africa?," *A.M.E. Church Review* 8 (April 1892): 389.

21. Purvis is quoted in Bacon, *But One Race*, 194–196.

22. *Christian Recorder*, June 26, 1884; Frederick Douglass, *Address by Hon. Frederick Douglass, Delivered in the Metropolitan A.M.E. Church, Washington, D.C. on The Lessons of the Hour*, 25–26.

23. The signatories to the bishops' address included Benjamin Arnett, Wesley J. Gaines, James Handy, Benjamin F. Lee, Moses B. Salter, Benjamin Tucker Tanner, and Alexander Wayman. *Christian Recorder*, July 4, 1895.

24. *Christian Recorder*, May 15, 1890.

25. *Christian Recorder*, January 23, 1890.

26. Redkey, *Black Exodus*, 59–63, 71.

27. See Adam Hothschild, *King Leopold's Ghost: A Story of Greed, Terror, and Heroism in Colonial Africa* (New York: Houghton Mifflin, 1998). *Christian Recorder*, February 6, 1890.

28. *Christian Recorder*, December 20, 1877; Charles Smith, *A History of the African Methodist Episcopal Church* (1922, Reprint. New York: Johnson Reprint, 1968), 214;

376 NOTES TO PAGES 243–252

J. C. Embry, DD, "The Declaration of Independence and the Race Problem," *A.M.E. Church Review* 8 (October 1891): 161–162.

29. *Christian Recorder*, February 14, 1889; February 21, 1889; January 2, 1896.

30. John Sampson, *Mixed Races: Their Environment, Temperament, Heredity, and Phrenology* (Hampton, VA: Normal School Steam Press, 1881), n.p.; Joseph H. Morgan, *Morgan's History of the New Jersey Conference of the A.M.E. Church, From 1872 to 1887, and of the Several Churches, as far as possible, From Date of Organization* (Camden, NJ: S. Chew, 1887), 44; *Christian Recorder*, September 29, 1881.

31. *Christian Recorder*, January 18, 1883.

32. Edward A. Johnson, *A School History of the Negro Race in America, from 1819 to 1890, With a Short History as to the Origin of the Race; Also a Short Sketch of Liberia* (Raleigh, NC: Edwards and Broughton, 1890), 7–8, 12–13, electronic edition, Documenting the American South, University of North Carolina at Chapel Hill, 2000, http://docso uth.unc.edu/church/johnson/johnson.html.

33. George Washington Williams, *History of the Negro Race in America from 1619 to 1880*, vol. 1 (New York: Putnam, 1883), x, 1, 3, 5, 19–21. See John Hope Franklin, *George Washington Williams: A Biography* (Chicago: University of Chicago Press, 1985).

34. Williams, *History of the Negro Race in America*, vol. 2, 549–551.

35. Wright is quoted in Nobles, *Shades of Citizenship*, 58.

36. Nobles, *Shades of Citizenship*, 57–60.

37. Rev. J. C. Embry, D. D. "The Declaration of Independence and the Race Problem," 160–163.

38. Embry, D. D. "The Declaration of Independence and the Race Problem," 160–163.

39. Sampson, *Mixed Races*, 12–13.

40. Sampson, *Mixed Races*, 37.

41. Sampson, *Mixed Races*, 19.

42. "The Negro on the Negro, VII," *Independent* 39 (February 24, 1887): 7.

43. Sampson, *Mixed Races*, 26.

44. *Christian Recorder*, August 17, 1882.

45. *Christian Recorder*, August 16, 1883; May 15, 1884.

46. *Christian Recorder*, August 16, 1883.

47. *Christian Recorder*, August 16, 1883; August 23, 1883.

48. *Christian Recorder*, May 15, 1884.

49. *Christian Recorder*, May 15, 1884.

50. *Christian Recorder*, April 12, 1883.

51. *Christian Recorder*, August 11, 1881.

52. *Christian Recorder*, August 16, 1883; September 2, 1880.

53. *Christian Recorder*, March 22, 1883.

54. *Christian Recorder*, May 15, 1884; September 2, 1880; April 12, 1883; Seraile, *Fire in His Heart*, 90.

55. Seraile, *Fire in His Heart*, 19; *Christian Recorder*, June 12, 1884; *Commencement Exercises, N.Y. Central College, July 9, 1856*; *Crisis* 1:4 (February 1911): 13; *Crisis* 10:5 (September 1915): 221.

56. *Christian Recorder*, June 12, 1884.

NOTES TO PAGES 252-257   377

57. *Christian Recorder*, June 12, 1884; May 15, 1884. The principle of "action of presence" might have helped James McCune Smith explain his conviction that the distinctive features of populations did not disappear in the "stream" of civilization. See chapter 4.

58. *Christian Recorder*, June 12, 1884; March 18, 1886. For an account of Benjamin Lee's family background, see "The Lees from Gouldtown," *Negro History Bulletin* 10 (February 1947): 99–100, 108, 119. Lee's cousins also published a history of the clan. See William Steward and Theophilus Gould Steward, *Gouldtown, A Very Remarkable Settlement of Ancient Date* (Philadelphia: J. Lippincott, 1913).

59. Roger Lane, *William Dorsey's Philadelphia & Ours: On the Past and Future of the Black City in America* (New York: Oxford University Press, 1991), 38.

60. J. R. Oldfield, ed., introduction to *Civilization and Black Progress: Selected Writings of Alexander Crummell on the South* (Charlottesville: University Press of Virginia for Southern Texts Society, 1995), 2–6, 9; Wilson J. Moses, "Civilizing Missionary: A Study of Alexander Crummell," *Journal of Negro History* 60 (April 1975): 234–235, 240; Alexander Crummell, "The Race-Problem in America," in *Africa and America: Addresses and Discourses* (1891; repr., New York: Negro Universities Press, 1969), 42, 45, 47. Moses identifies 1873 as the year Crummell returned to the United States. Despite his own sojourn in Liberia, Crummell looked askance at calls for emigration and ridiculed emigrationist Henry McNeal Turner as a "turbulent screeching and screaming creature." Redkey, *Black Exodus*, 230.

61. George L. Ruffin, "A Look Forward," *A.M.E. Church Review* 2 (July 1885): 29; *Christian Recorder*, December 22, 1887; July 2, 1891.

62. George T. Downing, "The Africo-American Force in America," *A.M.E. Church Review* 1 (October 1884): 159, 160, 162; *Christian Recorder*, December 13, 1877.

63. *Christian Recorder*, February 21, 1884.

64. Charles A. Gardiner, John T. Morgan, Frederick Douglass, Z. B. Vance, Joel Chandler Harris, Richard T. Greener, Oliver Johnson, S. C. Armstrong, J. H. Walworth, and J. A. Emerson, "The Future of the Negro," *North American Review* 139 (July 1884): 84–86; *Christian Recorder*, June 26, 1884; Frederick Douglass, "The Future of the Colored Race," *North American Review* 142 (May 1886): 437–440.

65. Gardiner et al., "The Future of the Negro," 84–86; *Christian Recorder*, June 26, 1884; Douglass, "The Future of the Colored Race," 437–440.

66. Douglass, "The Future of the Colored Race," 439. Reverend Francis Grimké performed the private wedding ceremony in his home.

67. Emphasis is in the original. "Frederick Douglass's Marriage," *Independent* 36 (January 31, 1884): 6; Alexander Crummell, "A Protest against the Doctrine of Amalgamation," *Independent* 36 (February 21, 1884): 3.

68. Emphasis is in the original. *People's Advocate*, January 31, 1884.

69. *People's Advocate*, January 31, 1884.

70. *Christian Recorder*, February 7, 1884; February 21, 1884; May 31, 1883; *People's Advocate*, January 31, 1884. Greener is quoted in Waldo Martin, *The Mind of Frederick Douglass*, 99.

71. *Christian Recorder*, February 7, 1884.

72. *People's Advocate*, January 31, 1884.

378   NOTES TO PAGES 258–262

73. Francis J. Grimké, "The Second Marriage of Frederick Douglass," *Journal of Negro History* 19 (July 1934): 324–325; "God Almighty Made but One Race: An Interview Given in Washington, D.C. on 25 January, 1884," in John Blassingame and John McKivigan, eds. *Frederick Douglass Papers, Series One: Speeches, Debates, and Interviews*, vol. 5 (New Haven, CT: Yale University Press, 1992), 146–147.

74. Frederick Douglass, *Life and Times of Frederick Douglass, Written by Himself* (London: Collier Books, 1969), 534; Douglass, "The Nation's Problem: An Address Delivered in Washington, D.C., on 16 April 1889," in Blassingame and McKivigan, *Frederick Douglass Papers*, vol. 5, 413; "To Elizabeth Cady Stanton, Washington, D.C., May 30, 1884," in Philip Foner, *Frederick Douglass*, 694–695

75. "God Almighty Made but One Race: An Interview Given in Washington, D.C. on 25 January, 1884," 146–147.

76. Frederick Douglass Diary, Thursday, March 24, 1887, Frederick Douglass Papers, Library of Congress Manuscript Division, https://www.loc.gov/resource/mfd.01001/?sp=51; Douglass, "The Future of the Colored Race," 440.

77. Douglass, "The Future of the Colored Race," 439–440.

78. *Christian Recorder*, March 21, 1878.

79. Gardiner et al., "The Future of the Negro," 90.

80. Delany, *The Origin of Races and Color*, 25, 39, 93; Delany, *Official Report of the Niger Valley Exploring Party*, in M. R. Delany and Robert Campbell, *Search for a Place: Black Separatism and Africa, 1860* (Ann Arbor: University of Michigan Press, 1969), 90.

81. *Christian Recorder*, April 26, 1883.

82. William Seraile, *Voice of Dissent: Theophilus Gould Steward (1843–1924) and Black America* (Brooklyn: Carlson, 1991), 77, 80; *Christian Recorder*, December 7, 1882; Ronald Lewis, "Reverend T. G. Stewart and 'Mixed' Schools in Delaware, 1882," 53–58.

83. *Christian Recorder*, April 26, 1883.

84. *Christian Recorder*, April 26, 1883.

85. *Christian Recorder*, April 26, 1883.

86. *Christian Recorder*, April 26, 1883. William Seraile argues that Steward's proposal supports Tanner's amalgamation theory. See Seraile, *Fire in His Heart*, 90.

87. Josiah Strong, *Our Country: Its Possible Future and Its Present Crisis*, ed. Jurgen Herbst (Cambridge, MA: Belknap, 1963), 213–214; Theophilus Steward, *The End of the World, or, Clearing the Way for the Fullness of the Gentiles* (Philadelphia: A.M.E. Church Book Rooms, 1888), 73, 120, 126.

88. Frederick Douglass, "The Color Line," *North American Review* 132 (June 1881): 567–568, 570; Embry, "The Declaration of Independence and the Race Problem," 155–156; *Christian Recorder*, August 23, 1883 and July 12, 1883.

89. Frederick Douglass, *The Race Problem. Great Speech of Frederick Douglass, Delivered before the Bethel Literary and Historical Association in the Metropolitan A.M.E. Church, Washington, D.C. October 21, 1890* (1890), 11–12, 15–16.

90. Frederick Douglass, "'It Moves,' or the Philosophy of Reform: An Address Delivered in Washington, D.C., on 20 November, 1883," in Blassingame and McKivigan, Frederick Douglass Papers, vol. 5, 129; *Christian Recorder*, June 26, 1884. See Anderson, "Black Responses to Darwinism, 1859–1915," 248.

NOTES TO PAGES 263–266   379

91. Douglass, *The Race Problem*, 16.

92. Jane Rhodes, *Mary Ann Shadd Cary*, 207–208, 202, 208–209.

93. Philip S. Foner, *Frederick Douglass*, 365; Mark Elliott, *Color-Blind Justice: Albion Tourgée and the Quest for Racial Equality from the Civil War to Plessy v. Ferguson* (New York: Oxford University Press, 2006), 274.

94. Frederick Douglass, "Lessons of the Hour: An Address Delivered in Washington, D.C., on January 1894," in Blassingame and McKivigan, *Frederick Douglass Papers*, vol. 5, 575–576.

95. Douglass, "Lessons of the Hour," 575–576; Douglass, *Address by Hon. Frederick Douglass, Delivered in the Metropolitan A.M.E. Church, Washington, D.C. Tuesday, January 9th, 1894, on The Lessons of the Hour*, 3, 7, 8, 16, 14–15, 17–18.

96. Douglass, *Address by Hon. Frederick Douglass, Delivered in the Metropolitan A.M.E. Church, Washington, D.C. Tuesday, January 9th, 1894*, 29–31, 33.

97. Douglass, *Address by Hon. Frederick Douglass, Delivered in the Metropolitan A.M.E. Church, Washington, D.C. Tuesday, January 9th, 1894*, 19–20, 23.

98. For an example of Washington defending Negroes against charges of innate inferiority, see Booker T. Washington, "Education Will Solve the Race Problem. A Reply," *North American Review* 525 (August 1900): 221–233; Booker T. Washington, "Speech Before the Atlanta Cotton States and International Exposition, September 18, 1895, Atlanta, Georgia," in *The Booker T. Washington Papers*, vol. 3, edited by Louis R. Harlan (Urbana: University of Illinois Press, 1974), 583–587; Hayes is quoted in George Sinkler, *Racial Attitudes of American Presidents from Abraham Lincoln to Theodore Roosevelt* (Garden City, NY: Anchor Books, 1972), 204.

99. Anderson, "Black Responses to Darwinism," 249; Booker T. Washington, *Working with the Hands* (New York: Double, Page, 1904), 245; Washington, "Industrial Education for the Negro," in *The Negro Problem: A Series of Articles by Representative American Negroes of To-day*, ed. Booker T. Washington (1903; repr., New York: Arno Press, 1969), 9–10. For an example of a White commentator who shared Washington's view, see John Carlisle Kilgo, "Our Duty to the Negro," *South Atlantic Quarterly* 2 (October 1903): 375–376. Kilgo, president of Trinity College in Durham, North Carolina, argued, "In passing from a lower to a higher plane of life and manhood, the negro must travel the ordinary way of progress along which all other races have come."

100. Robert R. Moton, speech delivered at a memorial meeting in honor of Booker T. Washington, held in New York City, February 11, 1916, "A Life of Achievement," *BlackPast.org*, http://www.blackpast.org/1916-robert-r-moton-life-achievement.

101. Alfred Moss, *The American Negro Academy: Voice of the Talented Tenth* (Baton Rouge: Louisiana State University Press, 1981), 250, 23, 29–34, 36–38, 31–32, 290; Michael Robert Mounter, "Richard Theodore Greener: The Idealist, Statesman, Scholar, and South Carolinian" (PhD dissertation, University of South Carolina, 2002), 326–430. Moss reports that ANA membership never exceeded forty-eight individuals in a given year. Ninety-nine men joined the group over the course of its thirty-one-year career.

380   NOTES TO PAGES 266–269

102. Emphasis is in the original. Alexander Crummell, *Civilization the Primal Need of the Race, Inaugural Address, March 5, 1897 and The Attitude of the American Mind toward the Negro Intellect, First Annual Address, December 28, 1897* (Washington, DC: Occasional Papers of the American Negro Academy, 1898), 3, 8, 13; Alexander Crummell, "The Social Principle among a People and Its Bearing on Their Progress and Development," in Oldfield, *Civilization and Black Progress*, 35.

103. Crummell, "The Race-Problem in America," 47, 49.

104. Crummell, "The Race-Problem in America," 46.

105. Letter from Crummell to John Wesley Cromwell, October 5, 1897, as quoted in Oldfield, *Civilization and Black Progress*, 19.

106. Moss, *The American Negro Academy*, 18; Moses, *Afrotopia*, 176. Also see Wilson Jeremiah Moses, *Alexander Crummell: A Study of Civilization and Discontent* (New York: Oxford University Press, 1989), 259–261.

107. Frederick Douglass, "This Decision has Humbled the Nation: An Address Delivered in Washington, D.C., on 22 October 1883," in Blassingame and McKivigan, *Frederick Douglass Papers*, vol. 5, 121–122.

108. Douglass, "The Nation's Problem," 411–413.

109. Crummell, *Civilization the Primal Need of the Race*, 10.

110. Crummell, preface to *Africa and America*, iii–iv; H. F. Kletzing and W. H. Crogman, *Progress of a Race or the Remarkable Advancement of the Afro-American Negro* (Atlanta, GA: J. L. Nichols, 1900), 18–19.

111. Du Bois, *The Conservation of Races*, 5.

112. Du Bois, *The Conservation of Races*, 11.

113. Du Bois, *The Conservation of Races*, 7.

114. Du Bois, *The Conservation of Races*, 6, 7, 10.

115. Du Bois, *The Conservation of Races*, 6–8, 10–11. Wilson Moses interpreted Du Bois's ANA address as "a restatement" of Crummell's Christian stance on races as "the 'organisms and ordinance of God.'" Wilson J. Moses, "W. E. B. Du Bois's 'The Conservation of Races' and Its Context: Idealism, Conservatism and Hero Worship," *Massachusetts Review* 34 (Summer 1993): 284. Joel Williamson and Davis Levering Lewis attribute Du Bois's conception of race consciousness to his training in Hegel's philosophy of history at the University of Berlin. See Joel Williamson, "W. E. B. Du Bois as a Hegelian," in *What Was Freedom's Price?*, ed. David Sansing, (Jackson: University Press of Mississippi, 1978), 32–36 and passim; Williamson, *The Crucible of Race: Black-White Relations in the American South since Emancipation* (New York: Oxford University Press, 1984), 397–403; David Levering Lewis, *W. E. B. Du Bois: Biography of a Race, 1868–1919* (New York: Henry Holt, 1993), 139–140, 171. For claims that Du Bois aimed higher than he was able to reach in understanding race, see K. Anthony Appiah, "The Uncompleted Argument: Du Bois and the Illusion of Race," in *"Race," Writing, and Difference*, Henry Louis Gates, ed. (Chicago: University of Chicago Press, 1986), 21–37; and Appiah, *In My Father's House: Africa in the Philosophy of Culture* (New York: Oxford University Press, 1992), 28–46; Moses, *The Golden Age of Black Nationalism, 1850–1925*.

116. Du Bois, *The Conservation of Races*, 5, 7, 10, 12.

NOTES TO PAGES 269–276 381

117. Crummell, "The Social Principle among a People," 37, 39.
118. Du Bois, *The Conservation of Races*, 11, 12, 13, 15. David Levering Lewis argues that Du Bois and his ANA colleagues did not understand that their calls for race unity and purity were akin to warriors using boomerangs as weaponry. See Lewis, *W. E. B. Du Bois*, 173.
119. Crummell, "The Social Principle among a People," 37, 39, 40; Moses, *Afrotopia*, 125.
120. W. E. B. Du Bois, "Strivings of the Negro People," *Atlantic Monthly* 80 (August 1897), 197, electronic edition, TheAtlantic.com. https://www.theatlantic.com/magazine/archive/1897/08/strivings-of-the-negro-people/305446/. This essay became the basis of the first chapter of *The Souls of Black Folk*. See Du Bois, *The Souls of Black Folk* (1903; repr., New York: New American Library, 1982) 43–53.
121. W. E. B. Du Bois, "Credo," *Independent* 57 (October 6, 1904): 787.
122. W. E. B. Du Bois, "Marrying of Black Folk," *Independent* 69 (October 13, 1910): 812.
123. Du Bois, "Marrying of Black Folk," 812.
124. Du Bois, "Marrying of Black Folk," 812; Du Bois, *The Conservation of Races*, 15, 12, 9. Du Bois quotes Tennyson's poem to allude to the millennium. See Alfred Lord Tennyson, *In Memoriam* (Boston: Ticknor, Reed, and Fields, 1850).
125. W. E. B. Du Bois, "The Comet," in *Darkwater: Voices from within the Veil* (1920; repr., Mineola, NY: Dover, 1999), 157–158. For a full analysis of the story, see Ryan Schneider, "Sex and the Race Man: Imagining Interracial Relationships in W. E. B. Du Bois's Darkwater," *Arizona Quarterly* 59:2 (Summer 2003): 59–80.
126. *Christian Recorder*, May 20, 1886.
127. Samuel Barrett, *The Significance of Leaders in Afro-American Progress* (Newburgh, NY: News, 1909), 13.
128. *Quadrennial Report, Payne University, Selma, Ala. 1908–1912, to the Bishops & Members of the Twenty-fourth General Conference, Kansas City, MO, 1912* (Nashville, TN: A.M.E. Sunday School Union, 1912), 13, 15.
129. John W. Cromwell, *History of the Bethel Literary and Historical Association* (Washington, DC: R. L. Pendleton, 1896), 13–14.

Chapter 7

1. Elliott, *Color-Blind Justice*, 2; Sec. 1. Louisiana Railway Accommodations Act, 1890, No. 111, Louisiana Laws, Baton Rouge, Louisiana, 1890.
2. C. Van Woodward, *American Counterpoint: Slavery and Racism in the North-South Dialogue* (New York: Little Brown, 1971), 162.
3. Elliott, *Color-Blind Justice*, 250; Joseph Logsdon and Caryn Cossé Bell, "The Americanization of Black New Orleans, 1850–1900," in *Creole New Orleans: Race and Americanization*, ed. Arnold R. Hirsch and Joseph Logsdon (Baton Rouge: Louisiana State University Press, 1992), 254–257.
4. Elliott, *Color-Blind Justice*, 250.
5. Elliott, *Color-Blind Justice*, 290; U.S. Reports, Plessy v. Ferguson, 163 U.S. 537 (1896), 562.

382 NOTES TO PAGES 276–280

6. Charles Chesnutt, "The Courts and the Negro, c. 1908," in *Charles W. Chesnutt: Essays and Speeches*, ed. Joseph R. McElrath Jr. et al. (Stanford, CA: Stanford University Press, 1999), 266–267.

7. Logsdon and Bell, "The Americanization of Black New Orleans," 256-259; Rodolphe Rodolphe Lucien Desdunes, *Our People and Our History* (Baton Rouge: Louisiana State University Press, 1973) 146.

8. Washington questioned the *Plessy* ruling even as he endorsed social separation. He reasoned that if skin color regulated rail car seating, the courts could also separate bald riders from men with red hair. Although he viewed separate rail car policies as illogical, he wanted his White supporters to understand that colored people did not object to segregation; they simply opposed the unjust treatment of paying equal fares for subpar facilities. This was not a condemnation of Jim Crow trains. He reported that they merely created a "temporary inconvenience" for Negro travelers. The real potential for harm was to White people, whose morals and conceptions of justice could suffer permanent damage for tolerating a wrong. Desdunes, *Our People and Our History*, 147; Logsdon and Bell, "The Americanization of Black New Orleans," 259–260; Booker T. Washington, "Who Is Permanently Hurt?," *Boston Our Day*, June 1896, in *Plessy v. Ferguson: A Brief History with Documents*, ed. Brook Thomas (Boston: Bedford Books, 1997), 135.

9. David Levering Lewis, *W. E. B. Du Bois*, 178; Du Bois, *The Conservation of Races*, 5.

10. June O. Patton, "'And the Truth Shall Make You Free': Richard Robert Wright, Sr., Black Intellectual and Iconoclast, 1877–1897," *Journal of Negro History* 81 (Winter–Autumn 1996): 23–25.

11. Frederick Hoffman, *Race Traits and Tendencies of the American Negro* (New York: Macmillan, 1896).

12. Moss, *The American Negro Academy*, 51–52, 290; Kelly Miller, *A Review of Hoffman's Race Traits and Tendencies of the American Negro* (Washington, DC: Occasional Papers of the American Negro Academy, 1897); W. E. B. Du Bois, Review of *Race Traits and Tendencies of the American Negro, Annals of the American Academy of Political and Social Science* 9 (January 1897): 127–133.

13. T. G. Steward, "Negro Mortality," *Social Economist* 9 (October 1895): 204–207.

14. Theophilus Gould Steward, *Fifty Years in the Gospel Ministry*, 149–150; Steward, "Negro Mortality," 204–207.

15. Kelly Miller, *Review of Hoffman's Race Traits*, 1; Du Bois, Review of *Race Traits and Tendencies of the American Negro*, 127.

16. Frederickson, *The Black Image in the White Mind*, 250–251; George Stocking, *Race, Culture, and Evolution: Essays in the History of Anthropology* (New York: Free Press, 1968), 52–53; Miller, *Review of Hoffman's Race Traits*, 3; Alfred Moss, *The American Negro Academy*, 93–94.

17. Miller quoted Dr. John Billings's report on census data. Du Bois, Review of *Race Traits and Tendencies of the American Negro*, 128, 129; Miller, *Review of Hoffman's Race Traits*, 4.

18. Hoffman's emphasis is in the original. Miller, *Review of Hoffman's Race Traits*, 4; Hoffman, *Race Traits and Tendencies*, 95.

NOTES TO PAGES 280–286   383

19. Miller, *Review of Hoffman's Race Traits*, 4, 10, 13; Du Bois, Review of *Race Traits and Tendencies of the American Negro*, 129, 130.

20. George Stocking, *Race, Culture, and Evolution: Essays in the History of Anthropology* (New York: Free Press, 1968), 54, 60–64; Miller, *Review of Hoffman's Race Traits*, 15.

21. Megan J. Wolff, "The Myth of the Actuary: Life Insurance and Frederick L. Hoffman's *Race Traits and Tendencies of the American Negro*," *Public Health Reports* 121:1 (January/February 2006): 88–90, accessed August 14, 2009, http://www.ncbi.nlm. nih.gov/pmc/articles/PMC1497788/.

22. Hoffman, *Race Traits and Tendencies*, 177, 187–188, 197–198, 206.

23. Miller, *Review of Hoffman's Race Traits*, 20, 25.

24. Benjamin Tucker Tanner, *The Color of Solomon—What?* (Philadelphia: A.M.E. Book Concern, 1895), vi, 16–18, and *passim*.

25. Tanner, *The Color of Solomon*, 86.

26. Seraile, *Fire in His Heart*, 36-41; Tanner, *The Color of Solomon*, 14–15. See *Philadelphia Press*, February 24, 1895.

27. Tanner, *The Color of Solomon*, 14, 40–42.

28. Tanner, *The Color of Solomon*, vii, x–xii, 42.

29. *Christian Recorder*, September 20, 1883; Benjamin Tucker Tanner, *The Descent of the Negro* (Philadelphia: A.M.E. Publishing House, 1898), 10–11, 13–15, 18–19. See Alexander Winchell, *Adamites & Preadamites; or, A Popular Discussion concerning the Remote Representatives of the Human Species & their Relation to the Biblical Adam* (Syracuse, NY: J. T. Roberts, 1878).

30. Thomas Dixon Jr., *The Leopard's Spots* (New York: Doubleday, 1902), 201 and passim.

31. Kelly Miller, *As to "The Leopard's Spots": An Open Letter to Thomas Dixon, Jr.* (Washington, DC: Hayworth, 1905), 16, 17.

32. Miller, *As to The Leopard's Spots*, 5, 7.

33. *Christian Recorder*, January 21, 1897.

34. T. G. Steward to Quartermaster General, September 12, 1902, T. G. Steward Papers; *Colored American Magazine* 2 (April 1901): front matter, n.p. Steward's research was probably intended for his proposed work "The Story of the American Negro as Slave, Citizen and Soldier," which he advertised as "a thoroughly reliable and authentic account of the 'Race' in America." There is no evidence that he published the title. Instead, he issued *The Colored Regulars*, which offers a brief historical sketch of colored Americans, but focuses on soldiers in the Spanish American War. See Theophilus Gould Steward, *The Colored Regulars in the United States Army With a Sketch of the History of the Colored American, and an Account of His Services in the Wars of the Country, from the Period of the Revolutionary War to 1899* (1904; reprint, New York: Arno Press and the New York Times, 1969).

35. Steward to Quartermaster General, September 12, 1902; "Philippines" [1900], T. G. Steward Papers. See Steward, *Fifty Years in the Gospel Ministry*, 348.

36. Nathaniel Southgate Shaler, "Science and the African Problem," *Atlantic Monthly* 66 (July 1890): 37; *New Era*, July 14, 1870; Theophilus Steward to William McDougall,

384   NOTES TO PAGES 286–292

February 23, 1923, T. G. Steward Papers; Williamson, "W. E. B. Du Bois as a Hegelian," 38.

37. Steward to William McDougall; Theophilus Steward to Frank Steward, March 3, 1923; Steward and Steward, *Gouldtown*. Steward's sons Charles and Frank were 1896 graduates of Harvard. See Harvard University, *Quinquennial Catalogue of the Officers and Graduates of Harvard University, 1636–1905* (Cambridge, MA: John Wilson and Son, 1905), 33.

38. T. G. Steward, *Our Civilization* (Wilberforce, OH, 1919), 5–6, 10, 13–14, 17–19, 23–28. *Christian Recorder*, March 19, 1870; July 30, 1870; August 20, 1870; and May 10, 1900. See William Seraile, "Susan McKinney Steward: New York State's First African-American Woman Physician," *Afro-Americans in New York Life and History* 9:2 (July 1985): 27–44.

39. T. G. Steward, "The Race Issue, So-Called, a Social Matter Only," *Competitor* (March 1920): 6–7.

40. *Plessy v. Ferguson*, 561.

41. T. G. Steward, "The Race Issue," 6–7.

42. Charles V. Roman, *American Civilization and the Negro: The Afro-American in Relation to National Progress* (Philadelphia: F. A. Davis, 1916), 321, 322, 325, 327, 329, 344, 353, 365.

43. Charles Chesnutt, "Age of Problems, Speech to the Cleveland Council of Sociology, Cleveland, O., November 1906," in McElrath, 248; Chesnutt, "Race Prejudice: Its Causes and Cures, Speech to the Boston Literary and Historical Association, Boston, Mass., 15 June 1905," in McElrath et al., *Essays and Speeches*, 231–232.

44. *Free American*, March 19, 1887; William Scarborough, "Race Integrity," *Voice of the Negro* 4:4 (1907): 197, 202.

45. Scarborough, "Race Integrity," 197–199, William Benjamin Smith, *The Color Line a Brief in behalf of the Unborn* (New York: McClure, Phillips, 1905), 67–70, 74.

46. Ralph E. Luker, *The Social Gospel in Black and White: American Racial Reform, 1885–1912* (Chapel Hill: University of North Carolina, 1991), 282; Edgar Gardner Murphy, *Problems of the Present South; A Discussion of Certain of the Educational, Industrial, and Political Issues in the Southern States* (New York: Macmillan, 1904), 273–274.

47. Emphasis is in original. William Pickens, "Social Equality," *Voice of the Negro* 3 (January 1906): 26; William Pickens, *Bursting Bonds: The Heir of Slaves*, enlarged edition (Boston: Jordan and More Press, 1923), 134.

48. Luker, *The Social Gospel in Black and White*, 282; W. S. Scarborough, "The Negro's Program for 1906," *Voice of the Negro* 3 (January 1906): 49.

49. Scarborough, "The Negro's Program for 1906," 47; Scarborough, "Race Integrity," 200.

50. Scarborough, "Race Integrity," 201; Luker, *The Social Gospel in Black and White*, 285.

51. Murphy, as quoted in Luker, *The Social Gospel in Black and White*, 285, 287, 286.

52. Scarborough, "Race Integrity," 200, 201; S. E. F. C. V. Hamedoe, "The First Pan African Conference of the World," *Colored American Magazine* 1 (September 1900): 224.

53. Du Bois, "Marrying of Black Folk," 812; Moss, *The American Negro Academy*, 50–51.

54. Scarborough, "Race Integrity," 197, 200.

NOTES TO PAGES 292–296   385

55. Scarborough, "Race Integrity," 197, 200.
56. Scarborough, "Race Integrity," 198.
57. Scarborough, "Race Integrity," 199, 200; Michele Valerie Ronnick, ed., *The Autobiography of William Sanders Scarborough: An American Journey from Slavery to Scholarship* (Detroit, MI: Wayne State University, 2005), 158.
58. Scarborough, "Race Integrity," 199; Scarborough, introduction to Tanner, *The Color of Solomon*, vi–viii.
59. Charles Chesnutt, "The Future American: A Stream of Dark Blood in the Veins of the Southern Whites, Essay published in the *Boston Evening Transcript*, 25 August 1900," in McElrath et al., *Essays and Speeches*, 127; Scarborough, "Race Integrity," 200; Pearce Kintzing, "On the Persistence of Certain Racial Characteristics," *American Medicine* (July 1904): 204–205. For a literary example of the idea that fingernails betray race identity, see Mark Twain, *Pudd'nhead Wilson and Those Extraordinary Twins* (1894; repr., New York: Penguin Books, 1986), 158.
60. Scarborough, "Race Integrity," 201; Ronnick, *Autobiography of William Sanders Scarborough*, 15–16.
61. John Patterson Sampson, *Address of Rev. J. Sampson, D. D. Presiding Elder of the New England Conference of the A.M.E. Church, at the 46th Annual Convention of the Monmouth County Sunday School Association, Ocean Grove, New Jersey* (1905), 3.
62. Sampson, *Address of Rev. J. Sampson*, 4, 7.
63. Kelly Miller, "Physical Destiny of the American Negro," in *Out of the House of Bondage* (1914; reprint, New York: Schocken Books, 1971), 42–59. August Meier and Bernard Eisenberg map inconsistencies in Miller's perspectives on education, labor, urban life, lynching, and Booker T. Washington. However, they do not explore his ideas about the concept of race. August Meier, "The Racial and Educational Philosophy of Kelly Miller, 1895–1915," *Journal of Negro Education* 29 (Spring 1960): 121–127; Bernard Eisenberg, "Kelly Miller: The Negro Leader as a Marginal Man," *Journal of Negro History* 45 (July 1960): 182–197.
64. Miller, "Physical Destiny of the American Negro," 45.
65. Miller, "Physical Destiny of the American Negro," 43–44, 45, 50.
66. Moss, *The American Negro Academy*, 51; Miller, "Physical Destiny of the American Negro," 50.
67. Miller, "Physical Destiny of the American Negro," 47.
68. Miller, "Physical Destiny of the American Negro," 47, 49–50.
69. W. E. B. Du Bois, "Postscript," *Crisis*, January 1933, 20; Moss, *The American Negro Academy*, 76; Chesnutt reportedly referred to himself as a "voluntary negro." See Charles Hackenberry, introduction to *Mandy Oxendine*, by Charles W. Chesnutt (Urbana: University of Illinois Press, 1997), xxiv.
70. Chesnutt, "The Age of Problems, Speech to the Cleveland Council of Sociology, Cleveland, O., November 1906," in McElrath et al., *Essays and Speeches*, 248, 239.

386 NOTES TO PAGES 297–301

71. Chesnutt, "The Future American: What the Race is Likely to Become in the Process of Time, Essay published in the *Boston Evening Transcript*, 18 August 1900," in McElrath et al., *Essays and Speeches*, 122–123.

72. Chesnutt, "The Age of Problems," 248.

73. Chesnutt, "The Future American: A Complete Race-Amalgamation Likely to Occur, Essay published in the *Boston Evening Transcript*, 1 September 1900," in McElrath et al., *Essays and Speeches*, 134–135.

74. Richard Broadhead, ed. *The Journals of Charles Chesnutt* (Durham, NC: Duke University Press, 1993), 139–140.

75. Charles Chesnutt, "The Wife of His Youth," in *The Wife of His Youth and Other Stories of the Color Line* (New York: Houghton, Mifflin, 1899); repr., Ann Arbor: University of Michigan Press, 1968), 5, 7–8.

76. Chesnutt, "The Wife of His Youth," 22.

77. Earle V. Bryant, "Scriptural Allusion and Metaphorical Marriage in Charles Chesnutt's 'The Wife of His Youth,'" *American Literary Realism* 33 (Fall 2000): 57–64. I draw on Earle Bryant's explanation of linkages between the title of the story and biblical injunctions requiring an Israelite man's devotion to "the wife of his youth" as a sign of loyalty to Yahweh and his people. However, I see no basis for his conclusion that Chesnutt used the story to create a "moral imperative to acknowledge and accept one's blackness" (60). Chesnutt, "The Wife of His Youth," 17, 22; Proverbs 5: 15, 18–19; Malachi 2:14–15 (RSV).

78. Malachi 2:14 (RSV); Chesnutt, "The Wife of His Youth," 10, 4, 22, 5, 21.

79. Chesnutt, "The Wife of His Youth," 12, 21–24; William Shakespeare, *Hamlet*, ed. Mark Norfolk (London: Aurora Metro Books, 2017), act 1, scene 4, line 33.

80. Chesnutt, "The Wife of His Youth," 14, 21, 22, 1.

81. Chesnutt, "The Wife of His Youth," 23.

82. For literary criticism on class, race, and moral themes in "The Wife of his Youth," see Andreá N. Williams, *Dividing Lines: Class Anxiety and Postbellum Black Fiction* (Ann Arbor: University of Michigan Press, 2013), 144–150 and passim.

83. William L. Andrews, *The Literary Career of Charles W. Chesnutt* (Baton Rouge: Louisiana State University Press, 1980), 131–132; Charles Chesnutt, "White Weeds," in *The Short Fiction of Charles W. Chesnutt*, ed. Sylvia Lyons Render (Washington, DC: Howard University Press, 1981).

84. Chesnutt, "White Weeds," 402.

85. Chesnutt, "White Weeds," 402.

86. Chesnutt, "White Weeds," 403.

87. Chesnutt, "The Future American: A Complete Race-Amalgamation Likely to Occur," 134.

88. Charles Chesnutt, *Paul Marchand, F.M.C.* (Jackson: University Press of Mississippi, 1998), 129–30; Chesnutt to George Washington Cable, June 13, 1890, in *"To Be an Author": Letters of Charles W. Chesnutt, 1889–1905*, ed. Joseph R. McElrath Jr. and Robert C. Leitz III (Princeton, NJ: Princeton University Press, 1997), 65–66.

89. Matthew Wilson, introduction to Chesnutt, *Paul Marchand, F.M.C.*, xxvii.

90. Chesnutt, *Paul Marchand*, 75–80.

NOTES TO PAGES 302–308   387

91. Chesnutt, *Paul Marchand*, 85, 102, 119–120, 138.

92. Chesnutt, *Paul Marchand*, 83–84.

93. Chesnutt, *Paul Marchand*, 138.

94. Chesnutt, *Paul Marchand*, 131.

95. Chesnutt, *Paul Marchand*, 85, 138.

96. Chesnutt, *Paul Marchand*, 139.

97. Black women writers helped popularize the ideal of race consciousness through fiction. A common feature is the ethical choice characters make upon discovering Negro blood in their veins. Questions about acknowledging ancestry and the ethics of racial affiliation are resolved in voluntary association and identification with the race. For examples of this literature, see Frances E. W. Harper, *Iola Leroy, or Shadows Uplifted*, 2nd edition (1893; repr., New York: Oxford University Press, 1988); Jessie Fauset, "Emmy," in *Short Fiction by Black Women, 1900–1920*, comp. Elizabeth Ammons (New York: Oxford University Press, 1991), 437–475; M. Louise Burgess-Ware, "Bernice, The Octoroon" (1903), in Ammons, *Short Fiction by Black Women, 1900–1920*, 250–275; Sarah A. Allen, pseud. [Pauline Hopkins], "The Test of Manhood: A Christmas Story" (1902), in Ammons, *Short Fiction by Black Women, 1900–1920*, 205–217.

98. *Christian Recorder*, December 23, 1880; J. W. E. Bowen, "Who Are We? Africans, Afro-Americans, Colored People, Negroes, or American Negroes?, *Voice of the Negro* 3 (January 1906): 32–36; Bowen, An Appeal for Negro Bishops, But No Separation, 33 Booker T. Washington, *A New Negro for a New Century* (Chicago: American, 1900).

99. *Christian Recorder*, May 2, 1878.

100. *Christian Recorder*, January 31, 1878; November 29, 1877.

101. *Christian Recorder*, February 14, 1878.

102. *Christian Recorder*, February 3, 1881.

103. *Christian Recorder*, December 23, 1880; March 3, 1881.

104. *People's Advocate*, February 9, 1878.

105. *Christian Recorder*, March 21, 1878.

106. *Christian Recorder*, March 21, 1878; March 14, 1878; March 28, 1878.

107. *Christian Recorder*, March 21, 1878; March 14, 1878; March 28, 1878; *Peoples Advocate*, March 23, 1878.

108. *Christian Recorder*, March 28, 1878.

109. Alfred Moss, *The American Negro Academy*, 38; "A Minuscule," *A.M.E. Church Review* 21 (October 1904): 136.

110. Bowen, "Who Are We?," 31.

111. Bowen, "Who Are We?," 32, 34.

112. Bowen, "Who Are We?," 33.

113. Bowen, "Who Are We?," 34, 35.

114. Emphasis is in the original. Bowen, "Who Are We?," 34, 35.

115. Bowen, "Who Are We?," 35.

116. "A Minuscule," 130–131.

388   NOTES TO PAGES 308–315

117. T. Thomas Fortune, "The Latest Color Line," *Liberia* 11 (November 1897): 60–65; *New York Globe*, January 13, 1883; I. Garland Penn, *The Afro-American Press, and Its Editors* (1891, repr., Salem, NH: Ayer, 1988), 134.

118. T. Thomas Fortune, "Who Are We? Afro-Americans, Colored People, or Negroes?," *Voice of the Negro* 3 (March 1906): 197.

119. Fortune, "Who Are We?," 197.

120. Fortune, "Who Are We?," 197–198.

121. Moss, *The American Negro Academy*, 38; J. C. Embry, "The Afro-American Christian Scholar," *A.M.E. Church Review* 9 (1892): 180–181; *Christian Recorder*, October 14, 1897.

122. Mary Lee's poem alludes to Psalms 137: 1–4. M. E. Lee, "Afmerica," *A.M.E. Church Review* 2 (July 1885): 54–55; *Christian Recorder*, February 16, 1893; "A Minuscule," 137.

123. Martinet quoted in Elliott, *Color-Blind Justice*, 251–252; *Liberia* 27 (November 1905): 85–86; Moss, *The American Negro Academy*, 73; "A Minuscule," 134–136.

124. *Colored American*, March 19, 1898; December 17, 1898; April 2, 1898.

125. *Colored American*, March 12, 1898; December 15, 1898; Benjamin Disraeli, Endymion, vol. 2 (London: Longmans, 1880), 202, 205.

126. *Christian Recorder*, December 23, 1880; February 3, 1881.

127. Harvey Johnson, *The Hamite* (Baltimore, 1889), 8, 7.

128. Johnson, *The Hamite*, 7; William Ferris, *The African Abroad, or His Evolution in Western Civilization* (New Haven, CT: Tuttle, Morehouse, and Taylor Press, 1913), 303–304.

129. Theophilus Gould Steward, "How the Colored Man Sees the War," n.d., Theophilus Gould Steward Papers; Miller, *Out of the House of Bondage*, 47.

130. Steward, "How the Colored Man Sees the War."

131. T. G. Steward, "History and the Races," *A.M.E. Church Review* 19 (July 1902): 423–425.

132. *Christian Recorder*, January 19, 1893; Cromwell, History of the Bethel Literary and Historical Association, 22.

133. *Christian Recorder*, February 2, 1893.

134. *Christian Recorder*, March 9, 1893.

135. *Christian Recorder*, January 12, 1893; February 16, 1893.

136. Isaiah Wears to Members of the American Negro Historical Society, 1898, Leon Gardiner Collection of American Negro Historical Society Records, Historical Society of Pennsylvania.

137. *Christian Recorder*, March 9, 1893.

Conclusion

1. Murray's brother F. Morris Murray served as the magazine's business manager, and the family's printing company, variously located in Arlington, Virginia, and in the District of Columbia, published it. To keep the journal afloat, the editors tried unsuccessfully to make it the official organ of the Niagara movement. Susanna Ashton,

NOTES TO PAGES 315–320   389

"Du Bois's *Horizon*: Documenting Movements of the Color Line," *MELUS* 26 (December 2001): 3–23; "Lafayette McKeene Hershaw," *Journal of Negro History* 30 (October 1945): 462–464; Mitchell to Du Bois, July 22, 1910, *Niagara Movement*, Special Collections and University Archives, University of Massachusetts Amherst, https://credo.library.umass.edu/view/full/mums312-b004-i226; Charles E. Bentley to Du Bois, November 5, 1909, *Niagara Movement*, Special Collections and University Archives, University of Massachusetts Amherst.

2. W. E. B. Du Bois, "To the Nations of the World" (Pan-African Conference, 1900), in Alexander Walters, *My Life and Work* (New York: Fleming H. Revell, 1917), 257.

3. The cover design changed several times over the course of the journal's tenure. *Horizon* 5 (September 1908): 2; Murray to Comrade, August 2, 1907, *Niagara Movement*, Special Collections and University Archives, University of Massachusetts Amherst.

4. W. E. B. Du Bois, "Niagara Movement," *Horizon* 5 (November 1909): 9; Franz Boas, "Race Problems in America," *Horizon* 5 (November 1909): 9; Boas, "Race Problems in America," *Science* 29 (May 1909): 839–849.

5. W. E. B. Du Bois, "The Color Line," *Horizon* 5 (December 1909): 1.

6. Du Bois, "The Color Line," 1; W. E. B. Du Bois, "Mulattoes," *Horizon* 3 (March 1908): 8.

7. "Niagara Movement," *Horizon* 4 (September 1908): 1.

8. "Our Magazines," *Horizon* 3 (May 1908): 17; "Our Magazines," *Horizon* 4 (September 1908): 17; "Straker," *Horizon* 3 (March 1908): 6.

9. "1909," *Horizon* 5 (January 1910): 3.

10. The segment's title changed to The Horizon in 1916. The content remained the same. *Crisis* (November 1910): cover; *Crisis*, August 1916, 194.

11. Du Bois, "Strivings of the Negro People," 194.

12. "Oath of Afro-American Youth" (advertisement), in Kelly Miller, *Segregation: The Caste System and the Civil Service* (Washington, DC, 1914), n. p.

13. Kelly Miller, "An Oath of Afro-American Youth," *Crisis* (June 1913): 92.

14. Howard University, *NIKH: 1915 Howard University Yearbooks*, book 95 (1915), 6–9, http://dh.howard.edu/bison_yearbooks/95.

15. Warren G. Harding, *Address of the President of the United States at the Celebration of the Semi-Centennial of the Founding of the City of Birmingham, Alabama, October 26, 1921* (Washington, DC: Government Printing Office, 1921), 6–8. See Lothrop Stoddard, *The Rising Tide of Color: The Threat against White World Supremacy* (New York: Charles Scribner's Sons, 1920).

16. *New York Times*, October 27, 1921.

17. Kelly Miller, *Is Race Difference Fundamental, Eternal, and Inescapable? An Open Letter to President Warren G. Harding* (Washington, DC: Austin Jenkins, 1921), 1, 10.

18. Marcus Garvey, *Message to the People* (Dover, MA: Majority Press, 1986), 30, 34; "UNIA Declaration of Rights of the Negro Peoples of the World, New York, August 13, 1920," in *The Marcus Garvey and Universal Negro Improvement Papers*, vol. 2, ed. Robert Hill (Berkeley, University of California Press, 1983), 571–580.

19. Miller, *Is Race Difference Fundamental, Eternal, and Inescapable?*, 10, 8.

20. Miller, *Is Race Difference Fundamental, Eternal, and Inescapable?*, 9, 11–12.

390　NOTES TO PAGES 320–324

21. Miller, *Is Race Difference Fundamental, Eternal, and Inescapable?*, 14, 11.
22. Miller, *Is Race Difference Fundamental, Eternal, and Inescapable?*, 18–21.
23. Miller, *Is Race Difference Fundamental, Eternal, and Inescapable?*, 11, 17–18.
24. Eisenberg, "Kelly Miller," 182–183.
25. Alain Locke, introduction to *The Everlasting Stain*, by Kelly Miller (Washington, DC: Associated, 1924), ix, x.
26. Locke, introduction to *The Everlasting Stain*, ix, x.
27. Locke, introduction to *The Everlasting Stain*, xii, x. Locke was far less charitable when he and W. E. B. Du Bois praised the rising generation of writers who would come to symbolize the cultural advances of the New Negro. They contrasted the literary prowess and promise of such figures as novelist Jessie Fauset and poets Langston Hughes and Countee Cullen with the misguided activities of Kelly Miller. See W. E. B. Du Bois and Alain Locke, "The Younger Literary Movement," *Crisis* 27 (February 1924): 161.
28. Alain Locke, "The New Negro," in *The New Negro: An Interpretation*, ed. Alain Locke (1925; repr., New York: Simon & Schuster, 1992), 3–4. Miller's examination of Howard's prospects appeared in the volume. See Kelly Miller, "Howard: The National Negro University," in Locke, *The New Negro*, 332.
29. Locke, "The New Negro," 4.
30. Locke, "The New Negro," 6, 7.
31. Alain Locke, *Race Contacts and Interracial Relations: Lectures on the Theory and Practice of Race*, ed. Jeffrey C. Stewart (1916; repr., Washington, DC: Howard University Press, 1992), 88.
32. Locke developed the lectures for a Howard University seminar, but the administration rejected his course proposal. He delivered them under the auspices of Howard University's NAACP and Social Science Club. Jeffrey C. Stewart, introduction to Locke, *Race Contacts and Interracial Relations*, xx.
33. Locke, *Race Contacts and Interracial Relations*, 12, 11.
34. Locke, *Race Contacts and Interracial Relations*, 74–76.
35. Locke, *Race Contacts and Interracial Relations*, 84.
36. Locke, *Race Contacts and Interracial Relations*, 100, 84–85.
37. Locke, *Race Contacts and Interracial Relations*, 79.
38. Locke, *Race Contacts and Interracial Relations*, 96–99.
39. Locke, *Race Contacts and Interracial Relations*, 98–99.
40. Locke, *Race Contacts and Interracial Relations*, 99–100.
41. Locke, "The New Negro," 11, 15; Locke, *Race Contacts and Interracial Relations*, 97.
42. Locke, "The New Negro," 9.
43. Du Bois's complaint about New Deal inequalities noted that, in just four months after its passage, the National Industrial Recovery Act depressed wages and increased joblessness for Negroes. Southern employers sought government sanction for New Deal disparities by lobbying Congress for lower minimum wage requirements for Negro employees to account for their "inherent irradicable element of incapability." W. E. B. Du Bois, "Pan-Africa and New Racial Philosophy," *Crisis* 40 (November 1933): 247; Juan F. Perea, "The Echoes of Slavery: Recognizing the Racist Origins of

NOTES TO PAGES 324–327   391

the Agricultural and Domestic Worker Exclusion from the National Labor Relations Act," *Ohio State Law Journal* 72 (2011): 105; "Along the Color Line," *Crisis* 37 (February 1930): 57–61.

44. DuBois, "Pan-Africa and New Racial Philosophy," 247; W. E. B. Du Bois, "On Being Ashamed of Oneself: An Essay on Race Pride," *Crisis* 40 (September 1933): 200.

45. DuBois, "Pan-Africa and New Racial Philosophy," 247.

46. Du Bois, "On Being Ashamed of Oneself," 199.

47. DuBois, "Pan-Africa and New Racial Philosophy," 247.

48. Du Bois, "On Being Ashamed of Oneself," 199–200.

49. Du Bois, "On Being Ashamed of Oneself," 199.

50. Du Bois, "On Being Ashamed of Oneself," 200.

51. Roi Ottley, *Black Odyssey: The Story of the Negro in America* (New York: Charles Scribner's Sons, 1948), 1, 5.

52. Ottley, *Black Odyssey*, 5.

53. Evelyn Brooks Higginbotham, "African-American Women's History and the Metalanguage of Race," *Signs* 17 (Winter 1992): 267

54. Higginbotham, "African-American Women's History and the Metalanguage of Race," 268–270; Fields, "Slavery, Race and Ideology in the United States of America," 114–115.

Bibliography

Primary Sources

Manuscript Sources

Papers of the American Missionary Association, Yale University, Manuscripts and Archives

Amos G. Beman Scrapbooks, I–IV, 1838–1857, Beinecke Library, Yale University

Minutes of the Bethel Literary and Historical Association, Moorland-Spingarn Research Center, Howard University

Mary Ann Shadd Carey Papers, Moorland-Spingarn Research Center, Howard University

Mary Ann Shadd Carey Papers, Ontario Provincial Archives, Toronto

Amy Matilda Cassey Album, Library Company of Philadelphia

Benjamin Coates African Colonization Collection, Special Collections, Haverford College Library

Leon Gardiner Collection, Historical Society of Pennsylvania

Kelly Miller Papers, Manuscript, Archives, and Rare Book Library, Emory University

Gerrit Smith Papers, Special Collections Research Center, Syracuse University Libraries

Theophilus Gould Steward Papers, Schomburg Research Center, New York Public Library

Benjamin Tucker Tanner Papers, Yale University, Manuscripts and Archives

Newspapers and Periodicals

Aliened American (Cleveland, OH)

A.M.E. Church Review

Anglo-African Magazine

Christian Recorder (Philadelphia)

Colored American (New York and Philadelphia)

Colored American (Washington, DC)

Colored American Magazine

Competitor

Elevator

Frederick Douglass' Paper (Rochester, NY)

Free American (Columbus, OH)

Freedom's Journal (New York)

Genius of Universal Emancipation

Independent

Liberator (Boston)

Liberia

Mirror of Liberty

National Anti-Slavery Standard

National Enquirer and Constitutional Advocate of Universal Liberty

394 BIBLIOGRAPHY

National Era
National Reformer (Philadelphia)
New Era (Washington, DC)
New York *Globe*
North Star (Rochester, NY)
Pennsylvania Freeman
People's Advocate (Washington, DC)
Provincial Freeman (Canada)
Repository of Religion and Literature, and of Science and Art
Voice of the Fugitive (Canada)
Weekly Anglo-African
Zion's Herald

Published Works

Address of the New England Anti-Slavery Convention to the Slaves of the United States.
Boston: Oliver Johnson, 1848.

Agassiz, Louis. "Diversity of Origins of the Human Races." *Christian Examiner* 49 (July 1850): 110–145.

Agassiz, Louis. *A Journey in Brazil, by Professor and Mrs. Louis Agassiz*. Boston: Ticknor and Fields, 1868.

Allen, Richard. *The Life Experiences and Gospel Labors of the RT. Reverend Richard Allen.* Nashville, TN: Abingdon Press, 1960.

Allen, William G. *The American Prejudic Against Color. An Authentic Narrative.* London: W. and F. G. Cash, 1853. In *The American Prejudice Against Color*. edited by Sarah Elbert, 35–92, Boston: Northeastern University Press, 2002.

Allen, William G. *A Short Personal Narrative*. Dublin: William Curry, 1860. In *The American Prejudice against Color*. edited by Sarah Elbert, 95–119, Boston: Northeastern University Press, 2002.

Allen, William G. *Wheatley, Banneker, and Horton*. Boston: Press of Daniel Laing, Jr., 1849.

Andrews, William L. ed. *From Fugitive Slave to Free Man: The Autobiographies of William Wells Brown*. New York: Mentor Books, 1993.

The Annual Reports of the American Society for Colonizing the Free People of Colour of the United States. Vols. 64–91, *1881–1910*. New York: Negro Universities Press, 1969.

Arnett, Benjamin, ed. *The Budget: Containing the Annual Reports of the General Officers of the African M.E. Church of the United States of America, 1881–1887.*

Arnett, Benjamin William, and J. A. Brown, Ohio General Assembly, House of Representatives. *The Black Laws! Speech of Hon. B. W. Arnett of Greene County and Hon. J. A. Brown of Cuyahoga County, in the Ohio House of Representatives.* Columbus, OH: Ohio State Journal, 1886. Daniel Murray Pamphlet Collection, Library of Congress, https://www.loc.gov/item/91898104/.

Articles of Association of the African Methodist Episcopal Church of the City of Philadelphia, in the Commonwealth of Pennsylvania. Philadelphia: Rhistoric, 1969.

Astwood, H. C. C. "Shall the Name of the African Methodist Episcopal Church be Changed to That of the Allen Methodist Church?" *A.M.E. Church Review* 4 (1888): 319–322.

Barrett, Samuel. *The Significance of Leaders in Afro-American Progress*. Newburgh, NY: News, 1909.

BIBLIOGRAPHY 395

Bell, Howard H., ed. *Minutes of the Proceedings of the National Negro Conventions, 1830–1864*. New York: Arno Press, 1969.

"Black and Mulatto Populations of the South." *DeBow's Review* 8 (June 1850): 587–588.

Blassingame, John ed. *Frederick Douglass Papers*, Series One, vol. 2, New Haven, CT: Yale University Press, 1982.

Blassingame, John and John McKivigan, eds. *Frederick Douglass Papers*, Series One, vol. 5 New Haven, CT: Yale University Press, 1992.

Blyden, Edward W. "The African Problem and the Method of Its Solution." *A.M.E. Review* 7:2 (October 1890): 205–218.

Boas, Franz, "Race Problems in America," Horizon 5 (November 1909):9–10.

Boas, Franz, "Race Problems in America," *Science* 29 (May 1909): 839–849.

Bowen, J. W. E. *An Appeal for Negro Bishops, But No Separation*. New York: Eaton & Mains, 1912.

Bowen, J. W. E. "Who Are We? Africans, Afro-Americans, Colored People, Negroes, or American Negroes? *Voice of the Negro* 3 (January 1906): 32–36.

Boynton, Charles B. *The Duty which the Colored People Owe to Themselves: A Sermon Delivered at Metzerott Hall, Washington, D.C.* Washington, DC: Office of the Great Republic, 1867.

Broadhead, Richard, ed. *The Journals of Charles Chesnutt*. Durham, NC: Duke University Press, 1993.

Brown, William Wells. *The Rising Son, or the Antecedents and Achievements of the Colored Race*. Boston: S. G. Brown, 1874.

Buckle, Henry Thomas. *History of Civilization in England*. Vol. 1. 2nd London edition. New York: D. Appleton, 1862.

Burgess-Ware, M. Louise. "Bernice, The Octoroon." (1903) in *Short Fiction by Black Women, 1900–1920*. Compiled by Elizabeth Ammons, 250–275. New York: Oxford University Press, 1991.

Caldwell, Charles. *Phrenology Vindicated and Antiphrenology Unmasked*. New York: Samuel Colman, 1838.

Caldwell, Charles. *Thoughts on the Original Unity of the Human Race*. New York: E. Bliss, 1830.

Calmet, Augustin, Charles Taylor, and Edward Robinson. *Calmet's Dictionary of the Holy Bible*. Rev. New York: Jonathan Leavitt, 1832.

Carey, Mathew. *Reflections on the Causes that Led to the Formation of the Colonization Society*. Philadelphia, 1832.

Catalogue of the Officers and Students of Howard University. Washington, DC: Judd & Detweiler, 1869.

Catalogue of the Officers and Students of Howard University. Washington, DC: Judd & Detweiler, 1870.

Catalogue of the Officers and Students of Howard University. Washington, DC: Judd & Detweiler, 1871.

Catalogue of the Officers and Students of Howard University. Washington, DC: Reed & Woodward, 1872.

[Chambers, Robert]. *Vestiges of the Natural History of Creation*. London, 1844. Electronic ed., Project Gutenberg. https://www.gutenberg.org/cache/epub/7116/pg7116-images.html.

Channing, William Ellery. *The Works of William Ellery Channing*. Boston: American Unitarian Association, 1875.

396   BIBLIOGRAPHY

Chesnutt, Charles. *Paul Marchand, F.M.C.* Jackson: University Press of Mississippi, 1998.

Chesnutt, Charles. "What Is a White Man?" *Independent* 41 (May 30, 1889): 5.

Chesnutt, Charles. *The Wife of His Youth and Other Stories of the Color Line.* New York: Houghton, Mifflin, 1899. Reprint, Ann Arbor: University of Michigan Press, 1968.

Chesnutt, Charles. *The Short Fiction of Charles* W. Chesnutt. edited by Sylvia Lyons Render. Howard University Press,Washington, DC, 1981.

Child, Lydia Maria. *An Appeal in Favor of that Class of Americans Called Africans.* Boston, 1833.

Clark, Elmer, ed. *Journal and Letters of Francis Asbury.* Vol. 3. Nashville, TN: Abingdon Press, 1958.

Clarkson, Thomas. *Essay on the Slavery and Commerce of the Human Species.* London, 1786.

Coates, Benjamin. *Cotton Cultivation in Africa, Suggestions on the Importance of the Cultivation of Cotton in Africa in Reference to the Abolition of Slavery in the United States, through the Organization of an African Civilization Society.* Philadelphia: C. Sherman & Son, 1858.

College for Colored Youth: An Account of the New-Haven City Meeting and Resolutions: With Recommendations of the College, and Structures upon the Doings of New-Haven . New York: The Committee, 1831.

Coker, Daniel. *Journal of Daniel Coker, A Descendant of Africa.* Baltimore: Edward J. Coale, 1820. In *Paul Cuffee, Peter Williams, Daniel Coker, Daniel H. Peterson, Nancy Prince.* Nendeln, Switzerland: Kraus Reprint, 1970.

Coker, Daniel. *Sermon Delivered Extempore in the African Bethel Church in the City of Baltimore, on the 21st of January, 1816, to a Numerous Concourse of People, on Account of the Coloured People Gaining their Church (Bethel) in the Supreme Court of the State of Pennsylvania, by the Reverend D. Coker, Minister of Said Church. To which is Annexed a List of the African Preachers in Philadelphia, Baltimore, &c Who have Withdrawn from under the Charge of the Methodist Bishops of the Conference, (BUT ARE STILL METHODISTS).* In *Documentary History of the Negro People in the United States,* edited by Herbert Aptheker, 67–69. New York: Citadel Press, 1969.

"The Cook Family in History." *Negro History Bulletin* 9 (June 1946): 195–196, 213–215.

Cooper, Anna Julia. *A Voice from the South.* Xenia, OH: Aldine Printing House, 1892. Reprint, New York: Oxford University Press, 1988.

Cornish, Samuel E., and Theodore S. Wright. *The Colonization Scheme Considered, in Its Tendency to Uphold Caste—In Its Unfitness for Christianizing and Civilizing the Aborigines of Africa, and for Putting a Stop to the African Slave Trade.* Newark, NJ: Aaron Guest, 1840.

Cosey, A. B. *The Negro from A to Z.* Washington, DC, 1897. African American Perspectives: Pamphlets from the Daniel A. Murray Collection, 18181907, American Memory, Library of Congress. Accessed January 16, 2001. http://lcweb2.loc.gov/ammem/aap/aaphome.html.

Crummell, Alexander. *Civilization the Primal Need of the Race, Inaugural Address, March 5, 1897 and The Attitude of the American Mind toward the Negro Intellect, First Annual Address, Dec. 28, 1897.* Washington, DC: Occasional Papers of the American Negro Academy, 1898.

Crummell, Alexander. "Eulogium on Henry Highland Garnet, D. D. before the Union Literary and Historical Association; Washington D.C. May 4th, 1882." In *Africa and*

BIBLIOGRAPHY   397

America: Addresses and Discourses, 269–305. Springfield, MA: Wiley & Co. 1891. Reprint, New York: Negro Universities Press, 1969.

Crummell, Alexander. "A Protest against the Doctrine of Amalgamation." *Independent* 36 (February 21, 1884): 3.

Crummell, Alexander. "The Race-Problem in America." In *Africa and America: Addresses and Discourses*, 35–54. Springfield, MA: Wiley & Co. 1891. Reprint, New York: Negro Universities Press, 1969.

Crummell, Alexander. "The Social Principle among a People and Its Bearing on Their Progress and Development." In *Civilization and Black Progress: Selected Writings of Alexander Crummell on the South*, edited by J. R. Oldfield, 29–42. Charlottesville: University Press of Virginia for Southern Texts Society, 1995.

Cuffe, Paul. *A Brief Account of the Settlement and Present Situation of the Colony of Sierra Leone, in Africa*. NY: Samuel Wood, 1812. In *Paul Cuffee (sic), Peter Williams, Daniel Coker, Daniel H. Peterson, Nancy Prince*. Nendeln, Switzerland: Kraus Reprint, 1970.

Cuguano, Ottobah. *Thoughts and Sentiments on the Evil and Wicked Traffic of the Slavery and Commerce of the Human Species*. In *Pioneers of the Black Atlantic: Five Slave Narratives from the Enlightenment, 1772-1815*. edited by Henry Louis Gates Jr. and William L. Andrews, 82–180. Washington, DC: Civitas, 1998.

Davenport, Charles B. "The Effects of Race Intermingling." *Proceedings of the American Philosophical Society* 56 (1917): 364–368.

Davis, Daniel Webster. *The Life and Public Services of Reverend William Washington Browne, Founder of the Grand Fountain U. O. of True Reformers and Organizer of the First Distinctive Negro Bank in America, With an Introduction by the Rt. Reverend Benjamin F. Lee*. Philadelphia: A.M.E. Book Concern, 1910.

Delany, Martin. *The Condition, Elevation, Emigration, and Destiny of the Colored People of the United States, Politically Considered*. Philadelphia: Author, 1852.

Delany, Martin. "Political Destiny of the Colored Race on the American Continent." In *Martin R. Delany: A Documentary Reader*, ed. Robert S. Levine. 245–279. Chapel Hill: University of North Carolina Press, 2003.

Delany, Martin. *The Origin of Races and Color*. 1879. Reprint, Baltimore: Black Classic Press, 1991.

Delany, M. R. *Official Report of the Niger Valley Exploring Party*. New York: Thomas Hamilton, 1861. In *Martin R. Delany: A Documentary Reader*. edited by Robert S. Levine, 336–357, Chapel Hill: University of North Carolina Press, 2003.

Desdunes, Rodolphe Lucien. *Our People and Our History*. Baton Rouge: Louisiana State University Press, 1973.

Dewees, Jacob. *The Great Future of America and Africa; An Essay Showing Our Whole Duty to the Black Man, Consistent with Our Own Safety and Glory*. Philadelphia: H. Orr, 1854.

Disraeli, Benjamin. *Endymion*. London: Longmans, 1880.

Dixon, Thomas, Jr. *The Leopard's Spots*. New York: Doubleday, 1902.

The Doctrines and Discipline of the A.M.E. Church. Philadelphia, 1817.

Douglass, Frederick. *Address by Hon. Frederick Douglass, Delivered in the Metropolitan A.M.E. Church, Washington, D.C. on The Lessons of the Hour*. Baltimore: Thomas & Evans, 1894.

Douglass, Frederick. "The Claims of the Negro Ethnologically Considered: An Address before the Literary Societies of Western Reserve College, July 12, 1854." In *The Frederick

398 BIBLIOGRAPHY

Douglass Papers, Series One: Speeches, Debates, and Interviews, vol. 2, *1847–54*. edited by John Blassingame, 497–525. New Haven, CT: Yale University Press, 1982.

Douglass, Frederick. "The Color Line." *North American Review* 132 (June 1881): 567–577.

Douglass, Frederick. "The Future of the Colored Race." *North American Review* 142 (May 1886): 437–440.

Douglass, Frederick. *Life and Times of Frederick Douglass, Written by Himself*. London: Collier Books, 1969.

Douglass, Frederick. *The Race Problem. Great Speech of Frederick Douglass, Delivered before the Bethel Literary and Historical Association in the Metropolitan A.M.E. Church, Washington, D.C. October 21, 1890*. Washington?, 1890.

Downing, George T. "The Africo American Force in America." *A.M.E. Church Review* 1 (October 1884): 157–162.

Du Bois, W. E. B. "Americanization." *Crisis* 24 (August 1922): 154.

Du Bois, W. E. B. "The Comet." In *Darkwater: Voices from within the Veil*. New York: Harcourt, Brace and Howe, 1920, 149–160. Reprint, Mineola, NY: Dover, 1999.

Du Bois, W. E. B. "The Color Line." *Horizon* 5 (December 1909): 1.

Du Bois, W. E. B. *The Conservation of Races*. Washington, DC: Occasional Papers of the American Negro Academy, 1897.

Du Bois, W. E. B. "Credo." *Independent* 57 (October 6, 1904): 787.

Du Bois, W. E. B. *Dusk of Dawn: An Essay toward An Autobiography of a Race Concept*. New York: Schocken Books, 1968.

Du Bois, W. E. B. "Marrying of Black Folk." *Independent* 69 (October 13, 1910): 812.

Du Bois, W. E. B. "Mulattoes." *Horizon* 3 (March 1908): 7–8.

Du Bois, W. E. B. "Niagara Movement," Horizon 5 (November 1909): 9.

Du Bois, W. E. B. "On Being Ashamed of Oneself: An Essay on Race Pride." Crisis 40 (September 1933): 199–200.

Du Bois, W. E. B. "Pan-Africa and New Racial Philosophy." *Crisis* 40 (November 1933): 247, 262.

Du Bois, W. E. B. "Postscript." *Crisis*, January 1933, 20–22.

Du Bois, W. E. B. Review of *Race Traits and Tendencies of the American Negro. Annals of the American Academy of Political and Social Science* 9 (January 1897): 127–133.

Du Bois, W. E. B. *The Souls of Black Folk*. 1903. Reprint, New York: New American Library, 1982.

Du Bois, W. E. B. "Strivings of the Negro People," *Atlantic Monthly* 80 (August 1897): 194–198. Electronic edition. TheAtlantic.com.https://www.theatlantic.com/magazine/archive/1897/08/strivings-of-the-negro-people/305446/

Du Bois, W. E. B. "To the Nations of the World" (Pan-African Conference, 1900). In Alexander Walters,*My Life and Work*, 257–260. New York: Fleming H. Revell, 1917.

Du Bois, W. E. B., and Alain Locke. "The Younger Literary Movement." *Crisis* 27 (February 1924): 161–163.

Durbin, John P. *Address Delivered in the Hall of the House of Representatives, Harrisburg, PA, on Tuesday Evening, April 6, 1852*. Philadelphia: Pennsylvania Colonization Society, 1852.

Easton, Hosea. *A Treatise on the Intellectual Character and the Civil and Political Condition of the Colored People of the United States*. Boston: Isaac Knapp, 1837.

BIBLIOGRAPHY   399

Edwards, Cyrus. *Address Delivered at the State House, in Vandalia on the Subject of Forming a State Colonization Society; auxiliary to the American Colonization Society.* Jacksonville, IL: James G. Edwards, 1831.

Eleventh Annual Report of the American Society for Colonizing Free People of Colour of the United States. Washington, DC: James C. Dunn, 1828.

Embry, J. C. "The Afro-American Christian Scholar." *A.M.E. Church Review* 9 (1892): 180–182.

Embry, J. C. "The Declaration of Independence and the Race Problem." *A.M.E. Church Review* 8:2 (October 1891): 154–163.

Embry, James C. *Ethnology: "Our Father's House" and Family.* Philadelphia: AME Book Concern, 1893.

Equiano, Olaudah. *The Interesting Narrative of the Life of Olaudah Equiano, or Gustavus Vassa, the African, Written by Himself.* edited by Robert Allison. New York: Bedford Books, 1995.

Faduma, Orishatukeh. *The Defects of the Negro Church.* Washington, DC: Occasional Papers of the American Negro Academy, 1904.

Fauset, Jessie. "Emmy." In *Short Fiction by Black Women, 1900–1920.* Compiled by Elizabeth Ammons, 437–475. New York: Oxford University Press, 1991.

Ferris, William. *The African Abroad, or His Evolution in Western Civilization.* New Haven, CT: Tuttle, Morehouse, and Taylor Press, 1913.

Foner, Philip, and Walker, George, eds. *Proceedings of the Black State Conventions, 1840–1865.* Vols. 1, 2. Philadelphia: Temple University Press, 1979–1981.

Foner, Philip, and Walker, George, eds. *Proceedings of the Black State Conventions, 1865–1900.* Philadelphia: Temple University Press, 1986.

Fortune, T. Thomas. "The Latest Color Line." *Liberia* 11 (November 1897): 60–65.

Fortune, T. Thomas. "Who Are We? Afro-Americans, Colored People, or Negroes? *Voice of the Negro* 3 (March 1906): 195–198.

Fortune, T. Thomas. "Will the Afro-American Return to Africa?" *A.M.E. Church Review* 8 (April 1892): 387–391.

Fowler, L. N. "Phrenological Developments of Joseph Cinquez, Alias Ginqua." *American Phrenological Journal and Miscellany* 2 (1840): 136–138.

"The Freedmen of Georgia: Minutes of and Interview between the Colored Ministers and Church Officers at Savannah with the Secretary of War and Major Gen. Sherman, Jan. 12 1865." *National Freedman: Monthly Journal of the National Freedman's Relief Association* 1 (April 1, 1875): 99.

Freeman, F. *A Plea for Africa, Being Familiar Conversations on the Subject of Slavery and Colonization.* Revised and enlarged 2nd edition. Philadelphia: J. Whetham, 1837.

Freeman, F. *Yaradee; A Plea for Africa, in Familiar Conversations on the Subject of Slavery and Colonization.* 1836. Reprint, New York: Negro Universities Press, 1969.

Fuller, Richard. *Our Duty to the African Race: An Address Delivered at Wash, D.C., Jan. 21, 1851.* Baltimore: W. M. Innes, 1851.

Gallaudet, T. H. *A Statement with regard to the Moorish Prince, Abduhl Rahahman.* New York: Daniel Fanshaw, 1828.

Gardiner, Charles A., John T. Morgan, Frederick Douglass, Z. B. Vance, Joel Chandler Harris, Richard T. Greener, Oliver Johnson, S. C. Armstrong, J. H. Walworth, and J. A. Emerson. "The Future of the Negro" *North American Review* 139 (July 1884): 78–99.

400 BIBLIOGRAPHY

Gardner, Bettye J. "William Watkins: Antebellum Black Teacher and Anti-Slavery Writer," *Negro History Bulletin* 39 (September–October 1976): 623–625.

Garnet, Henry Highland. *A Memorial Discourse; Delivered in the Hall of the House of Representatives, Washington, City, D.C. on Sabbath, February 12, 1865, with an Introduction by James McCune Smith, MD.* Philadelphia: Joseph M. Wilson, 1865.

Garnet, Henry Highland. *The Past and Present Condition of the Colored Race.* In *"Let Your Motto Be Resistance": The Life and thought of Henry Highland Garnet,* edited by Earl Ofari, appendix, 160–183. Boston: Beacon Press 1972.

Garnet, Henry Highland. *Walker's Appeal, with a Brief Sketch of His Life. By Henry Highland Garnet, and also Garnet's Address to the Slaves of the United States of America.* New York: J. H. Tobitt, 1848.

Garrison, William Lloyd. *Thoughts on African Colonization: Or An Impartial Exhibition of the Doctrines, Principles and Purposes of the American Colonization Society. Together with the Resolutions, Addresses and Remonstrances of the Free People of Color.* Boston: Mathew Carey, 1832.

Garvey, Marcus. *Message to the People.* Dover, MA: Majority Press, 1986.

Gladden, Washington. "The Christian League of Connecticut." *Century Magazine* 25 (November 1882): 50–60.

Gibbs, Mifflin Wistar. *Shadow and Light: An Autobiography with Reminiscences of the Last and Present Century.* Washington, DC, 1902.

Goodell, C. L. "White and Colored Churches." *Independent* 35 (May 24, 1883): 1.

Gregoire, Henri. *On the Cultural Achievements of Negroes.* Translated by Thomas Cassirer and Jean-Francois Briere. Amherst: University of Massachusetts Press, 1996.

Grimké, Francis J. "The Second Marriage of Frederick Douglass." *Journal of Negro History* 19 (July 1934): 324–329.

Gurley, R. R. *Letter to the Hon. Henry Clay, President of the American Colonization Society, and Sir Thomas Fowell Buxton, Chairman of the General Committee of the African Civilization Society, on the Colonization and Civilization of Africa.* London: Wiley and Putnam, 1841.

Hagood, L. M. *The Colored Man in the Methodist Episcopal Church.* 1890. Reprint, Westport, CT: Greenwood Press, 1970.

Hall, James. *An Address to the Free People of Color of the State of Maryland.* Baltimore: John D. Toy, 1859.

Hamedoe, S. E. F. C. V. "The First Pan African Conference of the World." *Colored American Magazine* 1 (September 1900): 223–231.

Harding, Warren G. *Address of the President of the United States at the Celebration of the Semi-Centennial of the Founding of the City of Birmingham, Alabama, October 26, 1921.* Washington, DC: Government Printing Office, 1921.

Harper, Frances E. W. *Iola Leroy, or Shadows Uplifted.* 2nd edition. 1893. Reprint, New York: Oxford University Press, 1988.

Harvard University. *Quinquennial Catalogue of the Officers and Graduates of Harvard University, 1636–1905.* Cambridge, MA: John Wilson and Son, 1905.

Hoffman, Frederick. *Race Traits and Tendencies of the American Negro.* New York: Macmillan, 1896.

Holly, J. Theodore. "Thoughts on Hayti." *Anglo-African Magazine* (June 1859): 185–187.

Holly, J. Theodore. "Thoughts on Hayti. Number III." *Anglo-African Magazine* 1 (August 1859): 241–242.

BIBLIOGRAPHY 401

Hood, J. W. "The Necessity of a Separate Church for Africans." *Independent* 36 (September 18, 1884): 3.

Hopkins, Pauline [Sarah A. Allen, pseud.]. "The Test of Manhood: A Christmas Story." In *Short Fiction by Black Women, 1900–1920*. Compiled by Elizabeth Ammons, 205–217. New York: Oxford University Press, 1991.

Howard, Oliver Otis. *Autobiography of Oliver Otis Howard*. Vol. 2. New York: Baker & Taylor, 1907.

Howells, William Dean. *An Imperative Duty*. Boston: Harper & Brothers, 1891.

Hunt, Benjamin. *Remarks on Hayti as a Place of Settlement for Afric-Americans; and on the Mulatto as a Race for the Tropics*. Philadelphia: T. B. Pugh, 1860.

James, Henry. "Morality and the Perfect Life." In *Moralism and Christianity, or Man's Experience and Destiny. In Three Lectures*, 97–184. New York: J. S. Redfield, 1850.

James, Thomas. *Life of Rev. Thomas James, by Himself* (Rochester: Post Express Printing, 1886), 8, electronic edition, North American Slave Narratives: Documenting the American South, University of North Carolina, 2000, http://docsouth.unc.edu/neh/jamesth/jamesth.html

Jefferson, Thomas. *Notes on the State of Virginia*. 1784. Reprint, Chapel Hill: University of North Carolina, 1955.

Jenifer, J. T. "Why I Am An African Methodist." *A.M.E. Church Review* 7 (1891): 277–292.

John, Edward, A. *A School History of the Negro Race in America, from 1819 to 1890, With a Short History as to the Origin of the Race; Also a Short Sketch of Liberia*. Raleigh, NC: Edwards and Broughton, 1890. Electronic edition. Documenting the American South. Chapel Hill: University of North Carolina at Chapel Hill, 2000. http://docsouth.unc.edu/church/johnson/johnson.html.

Johnson, Harvey. *The Hamite*. Baltimore: J.F. Weishampel, 1889.

Journal of the 17th Session and 16th Quadrennial Session of the General Conference of the African Methodist Episcopal Church, in the United States. Xenia, OH, 1882.

Journal of the 18th Session and 17th Quadrennial Session of the General Conference of the African Methodist Episcopal Church, in the World, 1884. Philadelphia, 1884.

Journal of the Proceedings of the Sixty-Eighth Convention of the Protestant Episcopal Church of the diocese of New-York. New York: Daniel Dana, Jr. 1851.

Kennedy, Randall. "My Race Problem and Ours." *Atlantic Monthly* (May 1997): 55–66.

Kilgo, John Carlisle. "Our Duty to the Negro." *South Atlantic Quarterly* 2 (October 1903): 369–385.

Killian, Charles, ed. *Sermons and Addresses, 1853–1891, Bishop Daniel A. Payne*. New York: Arno Press, 1972.

Kintzing, Pearce. "On the Persistence of Certain Racial Characteristics." *American Medicine* (July 1904): 204–205.

Kletzing, H. F., and W. H. Crogman. *Progress of a Race or the Remarkable Advancement of the Afro-American Negro*. Atlanta: J. L. Nichols, 1900.

Lapsansky-Werner, Emma J., and Margaret Hope Bacon, eds. *Back to Africa: Benjamin Coates and the Colonization Movement in America, 1848–1880*. University Park: Pennsylvania State University Press, 2005.

Lee, Benjamin F. "Organic Union Symposium." *A.M.E. Church Review* 9 (1892): 234–235.

Lee, Benjamin F., Jr. "Selection, Environment, and the Negro's Future." *A.M.E. Church Review* 20:4 (1904): 388–390

Lee, M. E. "Afmerica," *A.M.E. Church Review* 2 (July 1885): 55–59.

402   BIBLIOGRAPHY

Lee, Luther, and E. Smith. *Debates of the General Conference of the M.E. Church, May, 1844*. New York: O. Scott, 1845.

Levine, Robert S. ed. *Martin R. Delany: A Documentary Reader*. Chapel Hill: University of North Carolina Press, 2003.

Lewis, John. *The Life, Labors, and Travels of Elder Charles Bowles, of the Free Will Baptist Denomination, by Eld. John W. Lewis. Together with an Essay on the Character and Condition of the African Race by the Same*. Electronic edition, North American Slave Narratives. Documenting the American South, University of North Carolina at Chapel Hill, 2000, https://docsouth.unc.edu/neh/lewisjw/lewisjw.html.

Lewis, Robert Benjamin. *Light and Truth; Collected from the Bible and Ancient and Modern History, containing the Universal History of the Colored and Indian Race, from the Creation of the World to the Present Time*. Boston: Benjamin F. Roberts, 1844.

Lincoln, Abraham. "Address on Colonization to a Deputation of Negroes." In *Collected Works of Abraham Lincoln*, vol. 5, edited by Roy P. Basler, 371–375. New Brunswick, NJ: Rutgers University Press, 1953.

Locke, Alain. Introduction to *The Everlasting Stain*, by Kelly Miller. Washington, DC. Associated, 1924.

Locke, Alain. "The New Negro." In *The New Negro: An Interpretation*, edited by Alain Locke, 3–16. 1925. Reprint, New York: Simon & Schuster, 1992.

Locke, Alain. *Race Contacts and Interracial Relations: Lectures on the Theory and Practice of Race*. edited by Jeffrey C. Stewart. 1916. Reprint, Washington, DC: Howard University Press, 1992.

Matthews, Victoria Earle. "The Value of Race Literature: An Address. Delivered at the First Congress of Colored Women of the United States, at Boston, Mass., July 30th, 1895." *Massachusetts Review* 27 (1986): 170–185.

McElrath, Joseph R., Jr., Robert C. Leitz, III, and Jesse S. Crisler eds. *Charles W. Chesnutt: Essays and Speeches*. Stanford, CA: Stanford University Press, 1999.

McElrath, Joseph R., Jr. and Robert C. Leitz III, eds. *"To Be an Author": Letters of Charles W. Chesnutt, 1889–1905*. Princeton, NJ: Princeton University Press, 1997.

McMurray, William, DD. *A Sermon Preached in Behalf of the American Colonization Society in the Reformed Dutch Church in Market Street, New York, July 10, 1825*. New York: J Seymour, 1825.

Miller, Kelly. *As to "The Leopard's Spots": An Open Letter to Thomas Dixon, Jr*. Washington, DC: Hayworth, 1905.

Miller, Kelly. "Howard: The National Negro University." In *The New Negro: An Interpretation* ed. Alain Locke. 1925. Reprint, New York: Simon & Schuster, 1992.

Miller, Kelly. *Is Race Difference Fundamental, Eternal, and Inescapable? An Open Letter to President Warren G. Harding*. Washington, DC: Austin Jenkins, 1921.

Miller, Kelly. *Out of the House of Bondage*. 1914. Reprint, New York: Schocken Books, 1971.

Miller, Kelly. "Physical Destiny of the American Negro." In *Out of the House of Bondage*. 1914, 42–59. Reprint, New York: Schocken Books, 1971.

Miller, Kelly. *The Primary Needs of the Negro Race. An Address Delivered before the Alumni Association of the Hampton Normal and Agricultural Institute, by Professor Kelly Miller, June 14, 1899*. Washington, DC: Howard University Press, 1899

Miller, Kelly. *Race Adjustment and The Everlasting Stain*. New York: Arno Press and the New York Times, 1968.

Miller, Kelly. *A Review of Hoffman's Race Traits and Tendencies of the American Negro*. Washington, DC: Occasional Papers of the American Negro Academy, 1897.

BIBLIOGRAPHY   403

Miller, Kelly. "Social Equality." *National Magazine* 21 (February 1905). Internet Archive. http://www.archive.org/stream/socialequality00mill/socialequality00mill_djvu.txt.

Minutes and Proceedings of the First Annual Meeting of the American Moral Reform Society Held at Philadelphia in *Early Negro Writing, 1760–1837*. edited by Dorothy Porter, 200–248. Boston: Beacon Press, 1971.

Minutes of the Four Last Annual Conferences of the African Methodist Episcopal Church Held at Pittsburgh, (Pa.,) Washington, (D.C.,) Philadelphia, and New York, 1833–4. Philadelphia: Joseph M. Corr, General Book Steward , 1834, in *Early Negro Writing, 1760–1837*, edited by Dorothy Porter, 182–199. Boston: Beacon Press, 1971.

Minutes of the New England Conference of the African Methodist Episcopal Church Held in the City of New Bedford, Mass. from June 10th to the 21st, 1852. New Bedford, NJ: Press of Benjamin Lindsey, 1852.

Morton, Samuel George. *Crania Aegyptiaca, or Observations in Egyptian Ethnography, Derived from Anatomy, History, and the Monuments*. Philadelphia: John Pennington, 1844.

Morton, Samuel George. *Crania Americana; or a Comparative View of the Skulls of the Various Aboriginal Nations of North and South America*. Philadelphia: J. Dobson, 1839.

Morton, Samuel George. *Letter to the Rev. John Bachman, D.D. on the Question of Hybridity in Animals, Considered in Reference to the Unity of the Human Species*. Charleston, NC: Walker and James, 1850.

Murphy, Edgar Gardner. *Problems of the Present South; A Discussion of Certain of the Educational, Industrial, and Political Issues in the Southern States*. New York: Macmillan, 1904.

"The Negro on the Negro." *American Missionary* 41 (April 1887): 106–108.

"The Negro on the Negro, VII." *Independent* 39 (February 24, 1887): 7.

Nott, Josiah C. "The Mulatto a Hybrid—Probable Extermination of the Two Races if the Whites and Blacks are Allowed to Intermarry." *American Journal of the Medical Sciences* 6 (July 1843): 252–256.

Nott, Josiah C. "The Negro Race." *Anthropological Review* 4 (July 1866): 103–106.

Nott, Josiah C. "On the Diversity of Origin of the Human Races." *Princeton Review* 22 (October 1850): 603–642.

Nott, Josiah C. "Physical History of the Jewish Race." *Southern Quarterly* 1 (July 1850): 426–451.

Nott, Josiah C. *Two Lectures on the Natural History of the Caucasian and Negro Races*. Mobile, AL: Dade and Thompson, 1850.

Nott, J. C., and George R. Gliddon, eds. *Types of Mankind or Ethnological Researches Based upon the Ancient Monuments, Paintings, Sculptures, and Crania of Races*. 7th edition. Philadelphia: Lippincott, Grambo, 1855.

Oson, Jacob. *A Search for Truth; or An Inquiry for the Origin of the African Nation: An Address, Delivered at New-Haven in March, and at New-York in April 1817*. New York, 1817.

Ottley, Roi. *Black Odyssey: The Story of the Negro in America*. New York: Charles Scribner's Sons, 1948.

Payne, Daniel. *First Annual Address to the Philadelphia Annual Conference of the African Methodist Episcopal Church*. Philadelphia, 1853.

Payne, Daniel. *The Moral Significance of the XVth Amendment. Sermon delivered at the Ohio Annual Conference of the African Methodist Episcopal Church, May 8, 1870*. Xenia, OH: Xenia Gazette, 1870.

404 BIBLIOGRAPHY

Payne, Daniel. *Recollections of Seventy Years.* 1888. Reprint, New York: Arno Press and the New York Times, 1969.

Payne, Daniel. *Semi-centenary of the A.M.E. Church.* 1866, Reprint, Freeport, NY: Books for Libraries Press, 1972.

Payne, Daniel. "Thoughts on the Past, the Present and the Future of the African M.E. Church." *A.M.E. Church Review* 1 (July 1884): 1–5.

Payne, Daniel. *A Treatise on Domestic Education.* Cincinnati, OH: Cranston and Stowe, 1885.

Pennington, James. *The Fugitive Blacksmith; or Events in the History of J. W. C. Pennington, Pastor of a Presbyterian Church, New York, Formerly a Slave in the State of Maryland, United States.* London: Charles Gilpin, 1849. Electronic edition. University of North Carolina, Documenting the American South, North American Slave Narratives. 2001. Accessed May 3, 2002. http://docsouth.unc.edu/neh/penning49/penning49.html.

Pennington, James. "A Review of Slavery and the Slave Trade." *Anglo-African Magazine* 1 (May 1859): 155–159.

Pennington, James W. C. *A Text Book of the Origin and History, &c. &c. of the Colored People.* Hartford, CT: L. Skinner, 1841.

Pickens, William. *Bursting Bonds: The Heir of Slaves.* Enlarged edition. Boston: Jordan and More Press, 1923.

Pickens, William. "Social Equality." *Voice of the Negro* 3 (January 1906): 26.

Pierce, Jeremiah H. *A Brief Statement of the Public School Contest. J. H. Pierce, vs. The Union District Trustees of Burlington County, New Jersey as Brought before the Supreme Court, June 13, 1883, and Decided, Feb. 21, 1884, by Said Court, Containing all Arguments, Pro and Con.* Philadelphia: Christian Recorder Print No. 631, 1884.

Plecker, W. A. "Virginia's Effort to Preserve Racial Integrity." In *A Decade of Progress in Eugenics: Scientific Papers of the Third International Congress of Eugenics held at American Museum of Natural History, New York, August 21–23, 1932, 105–112.* Baltimore: Williams & Wilkins,1934. Reprint, New York: Garland Press, 1984.

Pliny. *Natural History.* Translated by H. Rackham. Cambridge, MA: Harvard University Press, 1949.

Poore, Ben Perley. *Congressional Directory.* Washington, DC: Government Printing Office, 1872.

Presbyterian Church of the U.S.A. Synod of New York and New Jersey. *An Address to the Public on the Subject of the African School.* New York, 1816.

Price, Clement, ed. *Freedom Not Far Distant: A Documentary History of Afro-Americans in New Jersey.* Newark, NJ: New Jersey Historical Society, 1980.

Proceedings of the Colored National Labor Convention: held in Washington, D.C., on December 6th, 7th, 8th, 9th and 10th, 1869. Washington, DC: Printed at the Office of the New Era.

Proceedings of the Conventions of Colored People, Held in Dover, Del. Dover, DE, 1873.

Proceedings of the National Emigration Convention of the Colored People, Held in Cleveland Ohio, on Thursday, Friday, and Saturday, the 24th, 25th, and 26th of August, 1854. Pittsburgh, PA: A. A. Anderson, 1854.

Prichard, James Cowles. *Researches into the Physical History of Mankind.* 4th edition. London: Houlston and Stoneman, 1851.

Purvis, Robert. *Remarks on the Life and Character of James Forten, Delivered at Bethel Church, March 30, 1842.* Philadelphia: Merrihew and Thompson, 1842.

BIBLIOGRAPHY 405

Purvis, Robert. *Speeches and Letters by Robert Purvis, Published by the Request of the "Afro-American League."* Philadelphia, n.d.

Quadrennial Report, Payne University, Selma, Ala. 1908–1912, to the Bishops & Members of the Twenty-fourth General Conference, Kansas City, MO, 1912. Nashville, TN: A.M.E. Sunday School Union, 1912.

Redkey, Edwin S., ed. *Respect Black: The Writings and Speeches of Henry McNeal Turner.* New York: Arno Press, 1971.

A Remonstrance against the Proceedings of a Meeting, held November 23rd, 1831 at Upton's, in Dock Street, Philadelphia. Philadelphia, 1832.

Redkey, Edwin S., ed. *Respect Black: The Writings and Speeches of Henry McNeal Turner.* New York: Arno Press, 1971.

Reuter, Edward. *The Mulatto in the United States.* Chicago: University of Chicago, 1913.

Review of Pamphlets on Slavery and Colonization. First Published in the Quarterly Christian Spectator, for March 1833. New Haven, CT: A. H. Maltby, 1833.

Ripley, C. Peter, ed. *Black Abolitionist Papers,* 5 vols. Chapel Hill: University of North Carolina Press, 1985–1992.

Roberts v. City of Boston, 59 Mass. (5 Cush.) 198 (1850).

Roman, Charles V. *American Civilization and the Negro: The Afro-American in Relation to National Progress.* Philadelphia: F. A. Davis, 1916.

Ronnick, Michele Valerie, ed. *The Autobiography of William Sanders Scarborough: An American Journey from Slavery to Scholarship.* Detroit, MI: Wayne State University, 2005.

Ruffin, George L. "A Look Forward." *A.M.E. Church Review* 2 (July 1885): 29–33.

Rush, Benjamin. "Observations Intended to Favor a Supposition that the Black Color (as it is called) of the Negroes is Derived from Leprosy. Read at a Special Meeting July 14, 1797." *Transactions of the American Philosophical Society* 4 (1799): 295.

Sampson, John Patterson. *Address of Rev. J. Sampson, D. D. Presiding Elder of the New England Conference of the A.M.E. Church, at the 46th Annual Convention of the Monmouth County Sunday School Association, Ocean Grove, New Jersey.* 1905.

Sampson, John Patterson. *Mixed Races: Their Environment, Temperament, Heredity, and Phrenology.* Hampton, VA: Normal School Steam Press, 1881.

Scarborough, William. *The Educated Negro and His Mission.* Washington, DC: Occasional Papers of the American Negro Academy, 1903.

Scarborough, William. "The Negro's Program for 1906." *Voice of the Negro* 3 (January 1906): 47–49.

Scarborough, William. "Race Integrity." *Voice of the Negro* 4 (May 1907): 197–202.

Shadd, Mary Ann. *A Plea for Emigration, or Notes on Canada West, in its Moral, Social, and Political Aspect, with Suggestions Respecting Mexico, W. Indies and Vancouver Island, for the Information of Colored Emigrants.* Edited by Richard Almonte. Toronto: Mercury Press, 1998.

Shaler, Nathaniel Southgate. "Science and the African Problem." *Atlantic Monthly* 66 (July 1890): 36–45.

Sixteenth Session, and the Fifteenth Quadrennial Session of the General Conference of the African Methodist Episcopal Church, Atlanta, Georgia, from May 1st to 18th, 1876. Philadelphia, 1876.

Sixty-Fourth Annual Meeting of the American Colonization Society with the Minutes of the Annual Meeting and of the Board of Directors, January 18 and 19, 1881. Washington, D.C. City: Colonization Building, 1881.

406 BIBLIOGRAPHY

Sixty-Seventh Annual Report of the American Colonization Society with the Minutes of the Annual Meeting and the Board of Directors, January 15 and 16, 1884, printed in *The Annual Reports of the American Society for Colonizing the Free People of Colour of the United States*. Vols. 64–91, *1881–1910*. New York: Negro Universities Press, 1969.

Smith, David. *Biography of the Rev. David Smith, of the A.M.E. Church, Being a Complete History, Embracing over Sixty Years' Labor in the Advancement of the Redeemer's Kingdom on Earth. Including "The History of the Origin and Development of Wilberforce University."* Freeport, NY: Books for Libraries Press, 1971.

Smith, James McCune. "Citizenship." *Anglo-African Magazine* 1 (May 1859): 144–150.

Smith, James McCune. "Civilization: Its Dependence on Physical Circumstances." *Anglo-African Magazine* 1 (January 1859): 5–17.

Smith, James McCune. *The Destiny of the People of Color, A Lecture Delivered before the Philomathean Society and Hamilton Lyceum, in January 1841*. New York, 1843.

Smith, James McCune. *Dissertation on the Influence of Climate on Longevity*. New York: Office of Merchant's Magazine, 1846.

Smith, James McCune. "The German Invasion." *Anglo-African Magazine* 1 (February 1859): 44–52, and (March 1859): 83–86.

Smith, James McCune. "On the Fourteenth Query of Thomas Jefferson's *Notes on Virginia*." *Anglo-African Magazine* 1 (August 1859): 225–238.

Smith, James McCune. "Toussaint L'Ouverture and the Haytian Revolutions." In *Masterpieces of Negro Eloquence: The Best Speeches Delivered by the Negro from the Days of Slavery to the Present Time*, edited by Alice Moore Dunbar, 19–32. New York: Johnson Reprint, 1970.

Smith, James McCune. "A Word for the 'Smith Family.'" *Anglo-African Magazine* (March 1860): 77–83.

Smith, Samuel Stanhope. *An Essay on the Causes of the Variety of Complexion and Figure in the Human Species*. Cambridge, MA: Harvard University Press, 1965.

Smith, William Benjamin. *The Color Line a Brief in behalf of the Unborn*. New York: McClure, Phillips, 1905.

Smits, Edouard. *Recherches sur la reproduction et la mortalite de l'homme aux differens ages, et sur la population de la Belgique*. Brussels: Chez Louis Hauman et Cie Libraires, 1832.

Smyth, Thomas, DD. *The Unity of the Human Races Proved to be the Doctrine of Scripture, Reason, and Science. With a Review of the Present Position and Theory of Professor Agassiz*. New York: George Putnam, 1850.

S.S.N., "Anglo-Saxons and Anglo-Africans," *Anglo-African Magazine* I (August 1859): 247–251.

Steward, Austin. *Twenty Years a Slave and Forty Years a Freeman*. Syracuse, NY: Syracuse University Press, 2002.

Steward, Theophilus Gould. *A Charleston Love Story; or, Hortense Vanross*. New York: F. Tennyson Neely, 1899.

Steward, Theophilus Gould. *The Colored Regulars in the United States Army, With a Sketch of the History of the Colored American, and an Account of His Services in the Wars of the Country, from the Period of the Revolutionary War to 1899*. 1904. Reprint, New York: Arno Press and the New York Times, 1969.

Steward, Theophilus Gould. *The End of the World, or, Clearing the Way for the Fullness of the Gentiles*. Philadelphia: A.M.E. Church Book Rooms, 1888.

Steward, Theophilus Gould. *Fifty Years in the Gospel Ministry: From 1864 to 1914*. Philadelphia: A.M.E. Book Concern, 1914.

BIBLIOGRAPHY 407

Steward, Theophilus Gould. *Genesis Re-Read; or the Latest Conclusions of Physical Science Viewed in Their Relation to the Mosaic Record.* Philadelphia: A.M.E. Book Room, 1885.

Steward, Theophilus Gould. "History and the Races." *A.M.E. Church Review* 19 (July 1902): 423–426.

Steward, Theophilus Gould. *How the Black St. Domingo Legion Saved the Patriot Army in the Siege of Savannah, 1799.* Washington, DC: Occasional Papers of the American Negro Academy, 1899.

Steward, Theophilus Gould. *Memoirs of Mrs. Rebecca Steward, Containing a Full Sketch of Her Life with Various Selections from Her Writings.* Philadelphia: Publication Dept. of the A.M.E. Church, 1877.

Steward, Theophilus Gould. "Negro Mortality." *Social Economist* 9 (October 1895): 204–207.

Steward, Theophilus Gould. *Our Civilization.* Wilberforce, OH, 1919.

Steward, Theophilus Gould. *Pioneer Echoes: Six Special Sermons.* Baltimore: Hoffman, 1889.

Steward, Theophilus Gould. "A Plea for Patriotism." *Independent* 50 (September 29, 1898): 887.

Steward, Theophilus Gould. "The Race Issue, So-Called, a Social Matter Only." *Competitor* 1 (March 1920): 6–7.

Steward, William, and Theophilus Gould Steward. *Gouldtown, A Very Remarkable Settlement of Ancient Date.* Philadelphia: J. Lippincott, 1913.

Stewart, Maria. "An Address Delivered at the African Masonic Hall, Boston, February 27, 1833." In *Maria W. Stewart, America's First Black Political Writer: Essays and Speeches,* ed. Marilyn Richardson, 56–64. Bloomington: Indiana University Press, 1987.

Stoddard, Lothrop. *The Rising Tide of Color: The Threat against White World Supremacy.* New York: Charles Scribner's Sons, 1920.

Strong, Josiah. *Our Country: Its Possible Future and Its Present Crisis.* New York: Baker and Taylor, 1885. Edited by Jergen Herbst. Cambridge, MA: Belknap, 1963.

Sumner, Charles. *The Question of Caste,* African-American Pamphlet Collection, 1824–1909. Library of Congress, American Memory Project. Accessed February 12, 2001. http://memory.loc.gov/cgi-bin/query.

Tanner, Benjamin Tucker. *An Apology for African Methodism.* Baltimore: Author, 1867.

Tanner, Benjamin Tucker. *The Color of Solomon—What?* Philadelphia: A.M.E. Book Concern, 1895.

Tanner, Benjamin Tucker. *The Descent of the Negro.* Philadelphia: A.M.E. Publishing House, 1898.

Tanner, Benjamin Tucker. *The Negro's Origins; and is the Negro Cursed?* Philadelphia: Author, 1869.

Tanner, Benjamin Tucker. *An Outline of Our History and Government for African Methodist Churchmen, Ministerial and Lay, in Catechetical Form.* Philadelphia: Grant, Faires, & Rodgers, 1884.

Turner, Henry McNeal. "The American Negro and His Fatherland." In *Africa and the American Negro: Addresses and Proceedings of the Congress on Africa,* edited by J. W. E. Bowen, 195–198. Atlanta, GA: Gammon Theological Seminary, 1896.

Turner, Henry McNeal. *The Genius and Theory of Methodist Polity, or the Machinery of Methodism. Practically Illustrated through a Series of Questions and Answers.* Northbrook, IL: Metro Books, 1972.

Twain, Mark. *Pudd'nhead Wilson and Those Extraordinary Twins.* 1894. Reprint, New York: Penguin Books, 1986.

408 BIBLIOGRAPHY

"UNIA Declaration of Rights of the Negro Peoples of the World, New York, August 13, 1920." In *The Marcus Garvey and Universal Negro Improvement Papers*, vol. 2, edited by Robert Hill, 571–580. Berkeley: University of California Press, 1983.

Walker, David. *David Walker's Appeal, in Four Articles; together with a Preamble, to the Coloured Citizens of the World, but in Particular, and Very Expressly, to those of the United States of America*. 1829. Reprint, New York: Hill and Wang, 1999.

Ward, Samuel Ringgold. *Autobiography of a Fugitive Negro*. 1855. Reprint, New York: Arno Press and the New York Times, 1968.

Washington, Booker T. "Education Will Solve the Race Problem. A Reply." *North American Review* 525 (August 1900): 221–233.

Washington, Booker T. *Frederick Douglass*. Philadelphia: George W. Jacobs, 1907.

Washington, Booker T. "Industrial Education for the Negro." In *The Negro Problem: A Series of Articles by Representative American Negroes of To-day*, edited by Booker T. Washington, 9–29. 1903. Reprint, New York: Arno Press, 1969.

Washington, Booker T. *A New Negro for a New Century*. Chicago: American, 1900.

Washington, Booker T. "Speech before the Atlanta Cotton States and International Exposition, September 18, 1895, Atlanta, Georgia." In *The Booker T. Washington Papers*, vol. 3, edited by Louis R. Harlan, 583–587. Urbana: University of Illinois Press, 1974.

Washington, Booker T. *Working with the Hands*, New York: Double, Page, 1904.

Watkins, William. *Address Delivered Before the Moral Reform Society in Philadelphia, August 8, 1836*. In *Early Negro Writing, 1760–1837*, edited by Dorothy Porter, 155–166. Boston: Beacon Press, 1971.

Watson, John Fanning. *Annals of Philadelphia, Being a Collection of Memoirs, Anecdotes, and Incidents of the City and its Inhabitants from the Days of the Pilgrim Founders*. Philadelphia: Author, 1830.

[Watson, John Fanning.] *Methodist Error, or Friendly Christian Advice to those Methodists who Indulge in Extravagant Emotions and Bodily Exercises, by a Wesleyan Methodist*. Trenton: D. & E. Fenton, 1819.

Wayman, Alexander. *The Life of Rev. James Alexander Shorter, One of the Bishops of the African M.E. Church*. Baltimore: J. Lanahan, 1890.

Wayman, Alexander. *My Reflections of African M.E. Ministers*. Philadelphia: A.M.E. Book Room, 1881.

Whipper, William, William Still, Stephen Smith, Robert Allen, William Warrick, Jr., Henry Jones, J. J. Clinton, Elisha Weaver, Robert Adger, and James W. Purnell. *Address of the Stockholders of Liberty Hall*. Philadelphia: Elisha Weaver, African Methodist Episcopal Book Concern, 1866.

Wiley, Bell, ed. *Slaves No More: Letters from Liberia, 1833–1869*. Lexington: University Press of Kentucky, 1980.

Williams, Fannie Barrier. "After Many Days: A Christmas Story." In *Short Fiction by Black Women, 1900–1920*. Compiled by Elizabeth Ammons, 218–238. New York: Oxford University Press, 1991.

Williams, George Washington. *History of the Negro Race in America from 1619 to 1880*. 2 vols. New York: Putnam, 1883.

Williams, Peter Jun. *A Discourse, Delivered on the Death of Capt. Paul Cuffe, Before the New-York African Institution, In the African Methodist Episcopal Zion Church October 21, 1817*. New York, 1817. In *Paul Cuffee (sic), Peter Williams, Daniel Coker, Daniel H. Peterson, Nancy Prince*. Nendeln, Switzerland: Kraus Reprint, 1970.

BIBLIOGRAPHY   409

Williams, Peter Jun. "A Discourse Delivered in St. Philip's Church, for the Benefit of the Colored Community of Wilberforce, in Upper Canada, on the Fourth of July, 1830." In *Negro Orators and their Orations*, edited by Carter G. Woodson, 77–86. Washington, DC: Association for the Study of Negro Life and History, 1925.

[Willson, Joseph.] *Sketches of the Higher Class of Colored Society in Philadelphia by a Southerner*. Philadelphia: Merrihew & Thompson, 1841.

Wilson, D. M. "It Decides Nothing." *American Missionary* 37:9 (September 1883): 270.

Winchell, Alexander. *Adamites & Preadamites; or, A Popular Discussion concerning the Remote Representatives of the Human Species & their Relation to the Biblical Adam*. Syracuse, NY: J. T. Roberts, 1878.

Wiseman, Nicholas, DD. *Twelve Lectures on the Connection between Science and Revealed Religion. Delivered in Rome*. Andover, MA: Gould and Newman, 1837.

Woodson, Byron, Sr. *A President in the Family: Thomas Jefferson, Sally Hemings, and Thomas Woodson*. Westport, CT: Praeger, 2001.

Woodson, Carter G. *Free Negro Heads of Families in the United States in 1830, Together with a Brief Treatment of the Free Negro*. Washington, DC: Association for the Study of Negro Life and History, 1925.

Wright, Richard R., Jr., *Centennial Encyclopaedia of the African Methodist Episcopal Church Containing Principally the Biographies of the Men and Women, Both Ministers and Laymen, Whose Labors during a Hundred Years, Helped Make the A.M.E. Church What It Is*. Philadelphia: Book Concern of the A.M.E. Church, 1916.

Wright, Theodore S., Charles Ray, and James McCune Smith. *An Address to the Three Thousand Colored Citizens of New-York Who are Owners of the One Hundred and Twenty Thousand Acres of Land, in the State of New-York, Given to Them by Gerrit Smith, Esq. of Peterboro*. New York, 1846.

Secondary Sources

Adeleke, Tunde. *Without Regard to Race: The Other Martin Robinson Delany*. Jackson: University Press of Mississippi, 2003.

Alford, Terry. *Prince among Slaves: The True Story of an African Prince Sold into Slavery in the American South*. New York: Oxford University Press, 1986.

Anderson, Eric, D. "Black Responses to Darwinism, 1859–1915." In *Disseminating Darwinism: The Role of Place, Race, Religion, and Gender*, edited by Ronald L. Numbers and John Stenhouse, 247–266. Cambridge: Cambridge University Press, 1999.

Andrews, William L. *The Literary Career of Charles W. Chesnutt*. Baton Rouge: Louisiana State University Press, 1980.

Angell, Stephen. *Bishop Henry McNeal Turner and African-American Religion in the South*. Knoxville: University of Tennessee Press, 1992.

Angell, Stephen W. and Anthony B. Pinn, eds. *Social Protest Thought in the African Methodist Episcopal Church, 1862–1939*. Knoxville: University of Tennessee Press, 2000.

Appiah, Kwame. "The Conservation of 'Race.'" *Black American Literature Forum* 23 (Spring 1989): 37–60.

Appiah, Kwame Anthony. *In My Father's House: Africa in the Philosophy of Culture*. New York: Oxford University Press, 1992.

410   BIBLIOGRAPHY

Appiah, K. Anthony. "The Uncompleted Argument: Du Bois and the Illusion of Race." In *"Race," Writing, and Difference*, edited by Henry Louis Gates, 21–37. Chicago: University of Chicago Press, 1986.

Appiah, K. Anthony, and Amy Gutman, *Color Conscious: The Political Morality of Race*. Princeton, NJ: Princeton University Press, 1996.

Aptheker, Herbert, ed. *A Documentary History of the Negro People in the United States*. New York: Citadel Press, 1990.

Ashton, Susanna. "Du Bois's *Horizon*: Documenting Movements of the Color Line." *MELUS* 26 (December 2001): 3–23.

Bacon, Margaret. *But One Race: The Life of Robert Purvis*. Albany: State University of New York Press, 2007.

Bacon, Margaret. "'One Great Bundle of Humanity': Frances Ellen Watkins Harper (1825–1911)." *Pennsylvania Magazine of History and Biography* 113 (January 1989): 21–44.

Balibar, Etienne, and Wallerstein, Immanuel. *Race, Nation, Class: Ambiguous Identities*. New York: Verso Press, 1991.

Bardolph, Richard. "Social Origins of Negroes, 1770–1865," *Journal of Negro History* 40 (July 1955). 244–240.

Barnes, Kenneth C. *Journey of Hope: The Back-to-Africa Movement in Arkansas in the Late 1800s*. Chapel Hill: University of North Carolina Press, 2004.

Baur, John. "Mulatto Machiavelli, Jean Pierre Boyer, and the Haiti of His Day." *Journal of Negro History* 32 (July 1947): 307–353.

Bay, Mia E. *The White Image in the Black Mind: African American Ideas about White People, 1830–1925*. New York: Oxford University Press, 2000.

Bell, Howard. "The American Moral Reform Society, 1836–1841." *Journal of Negro Education* 27 (Winter 1958): 34–40.

Bell, Howard. "Expressions of Negro Militancy in the North, 1840–1860." *Journal of Negro History* 45 (January 1960): 11–20.

Bell, Howard. "Free Negroes in the North, 1830–1835: A Study in National Cooperation." *Journal of Negro Education* 26 (1957): 447–455.

Bell, Howard. "National Negro Conventions of the Middle 1840's: Moral Suasion vs. Political Action." *Journal of Negro History* 42 (October 1957): 247–260.

Berlin, Ira. *Many Thousands Gone: The First Two Centuries of Slavery in North America*. Cambridge, MA: Harvard University Press, 1998.

Berlin, Ira. *Slaves without Masters: The Free Negro in the Antebellum South*. New York: Oxford University Press, 1974.

Berzon, Judith. *Neither White nor Black: The Mulatto Character in American Fiction*. New York: New York University Press, 1978.

Blackett, R. J. M. *Beating against the Barriers: The Lives of Six Nineteenth-Century Afro-Americans*. Ithaca, NY: Cornell University Press, 1989.

Blackett, R. J. M. "William G. Allen, the Forgotten Professor." *Civil War History* 26 (March 1980): 39–52.

Blakely, Allison. *Blacks in the Dutch World: The Evolution of Racial Imagery in a Modern Society*. Bloomington: Indiana University Press, 1993.

Blight, David W. "In Search of Learning, Liberty, and Self Definition: James McCune Smith and the Ordeal of the Antebellum Black Intellectual." *Afro-Americans in New York Life and History* 9 (July 1985): 7–25.

Bogin, Ruth. "'Liberty Further Extended': A 1776 Antislavery Manuscript by Lemuel Haynes." *William and Mary Quarterly* 40 (January 1983): 85–105.

BIBLIOGRAPHY   411

Brace, C. Loring. *"Race" Is a Four-Letter Word: The Genesis of the Concept*. New York: Oxford University Press, 2005.

Bradley, David. *A History of the A.M.E. Zion Church*. Part 1, *1796–1872*. Nashville, TN: Parthenon Press, 1956.

Braude, Benjamin. "The Sons of Noah and Constructions of Ethnic and Geographical Identities in the Medieval and Early Modern Periods." *William and Mary Quarterly* 54 (January 1997): 103–142.

Brubaker, Rogers, and Frederick Cooper. "Beyond Identity." *Theory and Society* (Dortrecht) 29 (February 2000): 1–47.

Bryant, Earle V. "Scriptural Allusion and Metaphorical Marriage in Charles Chesnutt's 'The Wife of His Youth.'" *American Literary Realism* 33 (Fall 2000): 57–64.

Bryant, Joan. "Colored Conventions and the American Race Problem." In *Colored Conventions in the Nineteenth Century Colored and the Digital Age*, edited by Gabrielle Foreman, Jim Casey, and Sarah Lynn Patterson, 167–178. Chapel Hill: University of North Carolina. Press, 2021.

Bryant, Joan. "Race and Religion in Nineteenth-Century America." In *Perspectives on American Religion and Culture*, edited by Peter Williams, 246–258. Cambridge: Blackwell, 1999.

Bryant, Joan. "Les Réformateurs Africains-Américains et la Lutte contre la Marginalisation Raciale." In *Histoire en Marges: Les Périphéries de L'Histoire Globale*, edited by Hélène Le Dantec-Lowry, Marie-Jeanne Rossignol, Matthieu Renault, et Pauline Vermeren, 49–73. Presses Universitaires François-Rabelais de Tours, 2018.

Bullock, Penelope L. *The Afro-American Periodical Press, 1836–1909*. Baton Rouge: Louisiana State University Press, 1981.

Butler, Jon. *Awash in a Sea of Faith: Christianizing the American People*. Cambridge, MA: Harvard University Press, 1990.

Carter, Marie. "William Whipper's Lands along the Sydenham." In *The Promised Land: History and Historiography of the Black Experience in Chatham-Kent's Settlements and Beyond*, edited by Boulou Ebanda de B'béri, Nina Reid-Maroney, and Handel Kashope Wright, 73–90. Toronto: University of Toronto Press, 2014.

Chaddock, Katherine Reynolds. *Uncompromising Activist Richard Greener: First Black Graduate of Harvard*. Baltimore: Johns Hopkins University Press, 2017.

Cooper, Frederick. "Elevating the Race: The Social Thought of Black Leaders, 1827–1850." *American Quarterly* 24 (December 1972): 604–625.

Coppin, Levi. *Unwritten History*. Philadelphia, 1919.

Correspondents of the *New York Times*. *How Race Is Lived in America*. New York: Times Books, Henry Holt, 2001.

Corsi, Pietro. *The Age of Lamarck: Evolutionary Theories in France, 1790–1830*. Berkeley: University of California Press, 1988.

Cox, Lewis. *Pioneer Footsteps*. Cape May, NJ: Star and Wave Press, 1917.

Crew, Spencer. "Black New Jersey before the Civil War: Two Case Studies." *New Jersey History* 99 (1981): 67–86.

Cromwell, John, W. *History of the Bethel Literary and Historical Association*. Washington, DC: R. L. Pendleton, 1896.

Dain, Bruce. *A Hideous Monster of the Mind: American Race Theory in the Early Republic*. Cambridge, MA: Harvard University Press, 2002.

Dann, Martin, ed. *The Black Press, 1827–1890: The Quest for National Identity*. New York: G. Putnam's Sons, 1971.

412 BIBLIOGRAPHY

Davis, David Brion. *The Problem of Slavery in the Age of Revolution, 1770–1823*. Ithaca, NY: Cornell University Press, 1975.

Davis, David Brion. "Reconsidering the Colonizationist Movement: Leonard Bacon and the Problem of Evil." *Intellectual History Newsletter* 14 (April 1992): 3–16

Davis, Hugh. "Northern Colonizationists and Free Blacks, 1823–1837: A Case Study of Leonard Bacon." *Journal of the Early Republic* 17 (Winter 1997): 651–675.

Davis, James. *Who Is Black? One Nation's Definition*. University Park: Pennsylvania State University Press, 1991.

Dayton, William. *Biographical Encyclopedia of New Jersey in the Nineteenth Century*. Philadelphia: Galaxy, 1877.

Dean, David M. *Defender of the Race. James Theodore Holly, Black Nationalist Bishop*. Boston: Lambeth Press, 1979.

Del Pino, Julius. "Blacks in the United Methodist Church from Its Beginning to 1968." *Methodist History* 19 (October 1980): 3–20.

Drake, St. Clair. "The Meaning of Negritude: The Negro's Stake in Africa." *Negro Digest* 13:8 (June 1964): 33–48.

Du Bois, W. E. B. *Black Reconstruction in America, 1860–1880*. New York: Athenaeum, 1935.

Du Bois, W. E. B., ed. *The Negro Church*. Atlanta: Atlanta University Press, 1903.

Dvorak, Katherine. *An African-American Exodus: The Segregation of the Southern Churches*. New York: Carlson, 1991.

Egerton, Douglas R. "'Its Origin Is Not a Little Curious': A New Look at the American Colonization Society." *Journal of the Early Republic* 5 (Winter 1985): 463–480.

Eisenberg, Bernard. "Kelly Miller: The Negro Leader as a Marginal Man." *Journal of Negro History* 45 (July 1960): 182–197.

Elliott, Mark. *Color-Blind Justice: Albion Tourgée and the Quest for Racial Equality from the Civil War to "Plessy v. Ferguson."* New York: Oxford University Press, 2006.

Erikson, Paul. "The Anthropology of Charles Caldwell, M.D." *Isis* 72 (June 1981): 252–256.

Ernest, John. "Liberation Historiography: African American Historians before the Civil War." *American Literary History* 14 (Fall 2002): 413–443.

Ernest, John. *Liberation Historiography: African American Writers and the Challenge of History, 1794–1861*. Chapel Hill: University of North Carolina Press, 2004.

Ernst, Robert. "Negro Concepts of Americanism." *Journal of American History* 39 (July 1954): 206–219.

Essah, Patience. "Slavery and Freedom in the First State: The History of Blacks in Delaware from the Colonial Period to 1865." PhD dissertation, University of California, Los Angeles, 1985.

Evans, William McKee. "From the Land of Guinea: The Strange Odyssey of the Sons of Ham." *American Historical Review* 85 (1980): 15–43.

Eyerman, Ron. *Cultural Trauma: Slavery and the Formation of African-American Identity*. Cambridge: Cambridge University Press, 2002.

Fagan, Benjamin, *The Black Newspaper and the Chosen Nation*. Athens: University of Georgia Press, 2016.

Fields, Barbara Jean. "Ideology and Race in American History." In *Region, Race, and Reconstruction: Essays in Honor of C. Vann Woodward*, edited by J. Morgan Kousser and James McPherson, 143–177. New York: Oxford University Press, 1982.

Fields, Barbara Jean. "Slavery, Race and Ideology in the United States of America." *New Left Review* 181 (May/June 1990): 95–118.

BIBLIOGRAPHY   413

Finkelman, Paul. "Prelude to the Fifteenth Amendment: Black Legal Rights in the Antebellum North." *Rutgers Law Journal* 17 (Spring/Summer 1986): 415–482.

Finkelman, Paul. "The Strange Career of Race Discrimination in Antebellum Ohio." *Case Western Reserve Law Review* 55:2 (2004): 373–408, https://scholarlycommons.law.case. edu/caselrev/vol55/iss2/5.

Fishman, George. "The Struggle for Freedom and Equality: African Americans on New Jersey, 1624–1849/50." PhD dissertation, Temple University, 1990.

Foner, Eric. *Freedom's Lawmakers: A Directory of Black Officeholders during Reconstruction.* Rev. edition. Baton Rouge: Louisiana State University Press, 1995.

Foner, Eric. "The Meaning of Freedom in the Age of Emancipation." *Journal of American History* 81 (September 1994): 435–460.

Foner, Eric. *Reconstruction: America's Unfinished Revolution, 1863–1877.* New York: Harper & Row, 1988.

Foner, Eric. *The Story of American Freedom.* New York: W. W. Norton, 1998.

Foner, Philip. *Frederick Douglass.* 2nd edition. New York: Citadel Press, 1969.

Fordham, Monroe. *Major Themes in Northern Black Religious Thought, 1800–1860.* Hicksville, NY: Exposition Press, 1975.

Foucault, Michel. *The Archeology of Knowledge.* Translated by A. M. Smith. New York: Pantheon Books, 1972.

Franklin, John Hope. *George Washington Williams: A Biography.* Chicago: University of Chicago Press, 1985.

Franklin, John Hope. "George Washington Williams and the Beginnings of Afro-American Historiography." *Critical Inquiry* 4 (1978): 657–672.

Frazier, E. Franklin. *The Negro Church in America.* New York: Schocken Books, 1974.

Frederickson, George M. *The Black Image in the White Mind: The Debate of Afro-American Character and Destiny, 1817–1914.* New York: Harper & Row, 1971.

Frederickson, George. "A Man but Not a Brother: Abraham Lincoln and Racial Equality." *Journal of Southern History* 40 (1975): 39–58.

Freeman, Rhonda. *The Free Negro in New York City in the Era before the Civil War.* New York: Garland Press, 1994.

Fulop, Timothy. "'The Future Golden Day of the Race': Millennialism and Black Americans in the Nadir, 1877–1901." *Harvard Theological Review* 84 (1991): 75–99.

Gaines, Kevin. *Uplifting the Race: Black Leadership, Politics, and Culture in the Twentieth Century.* Chapel Hill: University of North Carolina Press, 1996.

Gates, Henry Louis, Jr. "The Trope of the New Negro and the Reconstruction of the Image of the Black," *Representations* 24 (Fall 1988): 129–155.

Gatewood, Willard. *Aristocrats of Color: The Black Elite, 1880–1920.* Bloomington: Indiana University Press, 1990.

George, Carol. *Segregated Sabbaths: Richard Allen and the Emergence of Independent Black Churches, 1760–1840.* New York: Oxford University Press, 1973.

Glaude, Eddie S. *Exodus! Religion, Race, and Nation in Early Nineteenth-Century Black America.* Chicago: University of Chicago Press, 2000.

Glickman, Lawrence B. "'Buy for the Sake of the Slave': Abolitionism and the Origins of American Consumer Activism." *American Quarterly* 56:4 (December 2004): 899–912.

Goodman, Paul. "The Manual Labor Movement and the Origins of Abolitionism." *Journal of the Early Republic* 13 (1993): 355–388.

Gossett, Thomas. *Race: The History of an Idea in America.* New York: Oxford University Press, 1963.

414   BIBLIOGRAPHY

Gotanda, Neil. "A Critique of 'Our Constitution Is Color-Blind.'" In *Critical Race Theory*, edited by Kimberlé Crenshaw, Neil Gotanda, and Gary Peller, 257–275 (New York: New Press, 1995).

Gould, Stephen Jay. *The Mismeasure of Man*. New York: W. W. Norton, 1993.

Gravely, William B. "African Methodism and the Rise of Black Denominationalism." In Rethinking *Methodist History*, edited by Russell Richey and Kenneth Rowe, 239–263. Nashville, TN: United Methodist Publishing House, 1985.

Gravely, William B. "The Decision of A.M.E. Leader, James Lynch, to Join the Methodist Episcopal Church: New Evidence at the Old St. George's Church, Philadelphia." *Methodist History* 15 (July 1977): 263–269.

Gravely, William B. "The Dialectic of Double Consciousness in Black American Freedom Celebrations, 1808–1863." *Journal of Negro History* 67 (1982): 302–317.

Gravely, William B. *Gilbert Haven: Methodist Abolitionist; A Study in Race, Religion, and Reform, 1850–1880*. New York: Abingdon Press, 1973.

Gravely, William B. "Hiram Revels Protests Racial Separation in the Methodist Church (1876)." *Methodist History* 8 (April 1970): 13–20.

Gravely, William D. "James Lynch and the Black Christian Mission during Reconstruction." In *Black Apostles at Home and Abroad*, edited by David W. Wills and Richard Newman, 40–61. Boston: G. K. Hall, 1982.

Gravely, William B. "The Rise of African Churches in America (1786–1822): Re-examining the Contexts." *Journal of Religious Thought* 41 (Spring/Summer 1984): 58–73.

Gravely, William B. "The Social, Political and Religious Significance of the Formation of the Colored Methodist Episcopal Church." *Methodist History* 17 (October 1979): 3–25.

Grimstead, David. "Rioting in its Jacksonian Setting." *American Historical Review* 77 (April 1971): 361–397.

Gross, Bella. *Clarion Call: The History and Development of the Negro People's Convention Movement in the United States from 1817 to 1840*. New York: Author, 1947.

Gross, Bella. "*Freedom's Journal* and the *Rights of All*." *Journal of Negro History* 17 (July 1932): 241–286.

Hackenberry, Charles. Introduction. Charles W. Chesnutt, *Mandy Oxendine*, edited by Charles Hackenberry, i–xxvii. Urbana: University of Illinois Press, 1997.

Hall, Stephen G. *A Faithful Account of the Race: African American Historical Writing in Nineteenth-Century America*. Chapel Hill: University of North Carolina Press, 2009.

Haller, John S., Jr. *Outcasts from Evolution: Scientific Attitudes of Racial Inferiority, 1859–1900*. Carbondale: Southern Illinois University Press, 1971.

Hamilton, Cynthia S. "Hercules Subdued: The Visual Rhetoric of the Kneeling Slave." *Slavery & Abolition: A Journal of Slave and Post-Slave Studies* 34:4 (2013): 631–652.

Handy, James. *Scraps of African Methodist Episcopal History*. Philadelphia: A.M.E. Book Concern, n.d.

Handy, Robert T. *A Christian America: Protestant Hopes and Historical Realities*. 2nd edition. New York: Oxford University Press, 1984.

Harris, Leslie M. *In the Shadow of Slavery: African-Americans in New York City, 1626–1863*. Chicago: University of Chicago Press, 2003.

Harris, Robert. "Early Black Benevolent Societies, 1780–1830." *Massachusetts Review* 20 (Autumn 1979): 603–625.

Hegeman, Susan. "Franz Boas and Professional Anthropology: On Mapping the Borders of the 'Modern.'" *Victorian Studies* 41 (Spring 1998): 455–484.

BIBLIOGRAPHY   415

Higginbotham, Evelyn Brooks. "African-America Women's History and the Metalanguage of Race." *Signs: Journal of Women in Culture and Society* 17 (Winter 1992): 251–274.

Hildebrand, Reginald F. *The Times Were Strange and Stirring: Methodist Preachers and the Crisis of Emancipation*. Durham, NC: Duke University Press, 1995.

Hite, Roger William. "The Search for an Alternative: The Rhetoric of Black Emigration, 1850–1860." PhD dissertation, University of Oregon, 1971.

Horsman, Reginald. *Josiah Nott of Mobile: Southerner, Physician, and Racial Theorist*. Baton Rouge: Louisiana State University Press, 1987.

Horton, James Oliver. *Free People of Color: Inside the African American Community*. Washington, DC: Smithsonian Institution Press, 1993.

Horton, James Oliver, and Lois Horton. *In Hope of Liberty: Culture Community and Protest among Northern Free Blacks, 1700–1860*. New York: Oxford University Press, 1997.

Horton, Lois. "From Class to Race in Early America: Northern Post-Emancipation Racial Reconstruction." *Journal of the Early Republic* 19 (Winter 1999): 629–650.

Hothschild, Adam. *King Leopold's Ghost: A Story of Greed, Terror, and Heroism in Colonial Africa*. New York: Houghton Mifflin, 1998.

Hume, Brad. "Quantifying Characters: Polygenist Anthropologists and the Hardening of Heredity." *Journal of the History of Biology* 41 (2008): 119–158.

Hutton, Frankie. *The Early Black Press in America, 1827 to 1860*. Westport, CT: Greenwood Press, 1993.

Ignatiev, Noel. *How the Irish Became White*. New York: Routledge, 1995.

Jacobs, Donald. "The Nineteenth Century Struggle over Segregated Education in Boston Schools." *Journal of Negro Education* 39 (Winter 1970): 75–85.

Jacobson, Matthew Frye. *Whiteness of a Different Color: European Immigrants and the Alchemy of Race*. Cambridge, MA: Harvard University Press, 1998.

Jason, William C., Jr. "The Delaware Annual Conference of the Methodist Church, 1864–1965." *Methodist History* 4 (July 1966): 26–40.

Jones, Jacqueline. *A Dreadful Deceit: The Myth of Race from the Colonial Era to Obama's America*. New York: Basic Books, 2013.

Jones, Martha S. *Birthright Citizens: A History of Race and Rights in Antebellum America*. Cambridge, UK: Cambridge University Press, 2018.

Jordan, Winthrop D. *White over Black: American Attitudes Toward the Negro, 1550–1812*. Chapel Hill: University of North Carolina Press, 1968.

Kennedy, Randall. "Finding a Proper Name to Call Black Americans." *Journal of Blacks in Higher Education* 46 (Winter 2004–2005): 72–83.

Kerber, Linda. "Abolitionists and Amalgamators: The New York City Race Riots of 1834." *New York History* 48 (1967): 28–39.

Kettner, James H. *The Development of American Citizenship, 1608–1870*. Chapel Hill: University of North Carolina Press, 1978.

Kinshasha, Kwando. *Emigration vs. Assimilation: The Debate in the African American Press, 1827–1861*. Jefferson, NC: McFarland, 1988.

Klaus, Sidney N. "A History of the Science of Pigmentation." In *The Pigmentary System: Physiology and Pathophysiology*, edited by James J. Norland, 1–10. New York: Oxford University Press, 1998.

Lane, Roger. *William Dorsey's Philadelphia & Ours: On the Past and Future of the Black City in America*. New York: Oxford University Press, 1991.

Lapsansky, Emma. "'Since They Got Those Separate Churches': Afro-Americans and Racism in Jacksonian Philadelphia." *American Quarterly* 32 (Spring 1980): 54–78.

416 BIBLIOGRAPHY

"The Lees from Gouldtown," *Negro History Bulletin* 10 (February 1947): 99–100, 108, 119.

Levesque, George. *Black Boston: African American Life and Culture in Urban America, 1750–1860*. New York: Garland Press, 1994.

Levesque, George. "Boston's Black Brahmin: Dr. John S. Rock." *Civil War History* 26 (December 1980): 326–334.

Levesque, George. "Interpreting Early Black Ideology: A Reappraisal of Historical Consensus." *Journal of the Early Republic* 1 (Autumn 1981): 269–287.

Levine, Robert S. *Martin Delany, Frederick Douglass, and the Politics of Representative Identity*. Chapel Hill: University of North Carolina Press, 1997.

Lewis, David Levering. *W. E. B. Du Bois: Biography of a Race, 1868–1919*. New York: Henry Holt, 1993.

Lewis, David Levering. *W. E. B. Du Bois: The Fight for Equality and the American Century, 1919–1963*. New York: Henry Holt, 2000.

Lewis, Jason E., David DeGusta, Marc R. Meyer, Janet M. Monge, Alan E. Mann, et al. "The Mismeasure of Science: Stephen Jay Gould versus Samuel George Morton on Skulls and Bias." *PloS Biol* 9:6 (June 2011): https://doi.org/10.1371/journal.pbio.1001071. http./www.plosbiology.org.

Lewis, Ronald L. "Reverend T. G. Steward and the Education of Blacks in Reconstruction Delaware." *Delaware History* 19 (1981): 156–178.

Lincoln, C. Eric, and Lawrence Mamiya. *The Black Church in the African American Experience*. Durham, NC: Duke University Press, 1990.

Little, Lawrence. *Disciples of Liberty: The African Methodist Episcopal Church in the Age of Imperialism, 1884–1916*. Knoxville: University of Tennessee Press, 2000.

Litwack, Leon. *Been in the Storm So Long: The Aftermath of Slavery*. New York: Alfred Knopf, 1979.

Litwack, Leon. *North of Slavery: The Negro in the Free States, 1790–1860*. Chicago: University of Chicago Press, 1961.

Logan, Rayford. *The Betrayal of the Negro from Rutherford B. Hayes to Woodrow Wilson*. New York: Macmillan, 1965.

Logan, Rayford. *The Negro in American Life and Thought: The Nadir, 1877–1901*. New York: Dial Press, 1954.

Logsdon, Joseph, and Caryn Cossé Bell. "The Americanization of Black New Orleans, 1850–1900." In *Creole New Orleans: Race and Americanization*, edited by Arnold R. Hirsch and Joseph Logsdon, 201–261. Baton Rouge: Louisiana State University Press, 1992.

Lopez, Ian. *White by Law: The Legal Construction of Race*. New York: New York University Press, 1996.

Loury, Glenn C. "Racial Justice: The Superficial Morality of Colorblindness." Unpublished paper presented at the Institute on Race and Social Division, Boston University, September 2000.

Luker, Ralph E. *The Social Gospel in Black and White: American Racial Reform, 1885–1912*. Chapel Hill: University of North Carolina, 1991.

MacMaster, Richard K. "Highland Garnet and the African Civilization Society." *Journal of Presbyterian History* 48:2 (Summer 1970): 105–106.

Maffly-Kipp, Laurie. *Setting Down the Sacred Past: African-American Race Histories*. Cambridge, MA: Harvard University Press, 2010.

Malcomson, Scott L. *One Drop of Blood: The American Misadventure of Race*. New York: Farrar, Straus & Giroux, 2000.

BIBLIOGRAPHY   417

Martin, Sandy Dwayne. *For God and Race: The Religious and Political Leadership of AMEZ Bishop James Walker Hood.* Columbia: University of South Carolina Press, 1999.

Martin, Waldo. *The Mind of Frederick Douglass.* Chapel Hill: University of North Carolina Press, 1984.

McBride, David. "Black Protest against Racial Politics: Gardner, Hinton, and Their Memorial of 1838." *Pennsylvania History* 46 (April 1979): 149–162.

McCormick, Richard. "William Whipper: Moral Reformer." *Pennsylvania History* 43 (January 1976): 23–46.

McHenry, Elizabeth. *Forgotten Readers: Recovering the Lost History of African American Literary Societies.* Durham, NC: Duke University Press, 2002.

McPherson, James. *Battle Cry of Freedom.* New York: Oxford University Press, 1988.

Meier, August. *Negro Thought in America, 1881–1915: Racial Ideologies in the Age of Booker T. Washington.* Ann Arbor: University of Michigan Press, 1963.

Meier, August. "The Racial and Educational Philosophy of Kelly Miller, 1895–1915." *Journal of Negro Education* 29 (Spring 1960): 121–127.

Meijer, Miriam Claude. "Petrus Camper on the Origin and Color of Blacks." *History of Anthropology Newsletter* 24 (December 1997): 3–9.Melish, Joanne Pope. "The 'Condition' Debate and Racial Discourse in the Antebellum North." *Journal of the Early Republic* 19 (Winter 1999): 651–672.

Melish, Joanne Pope. *Disowning Slavery: Gradual Emancipation and Race" in New England, 1780–1860.* Ithaca, NY: Cornell University Press, 1998.

Menand, Louis. *The Metaphysical Club: A Story of Ideas in America.* New York: Farrar, Straus and Giroux, 2001.

Miller, Albert G. *Elevating the Race: Theophilus G. Steward, Black Theology, and the Making of African-American Civil Religion, 1865–1924.* Knoxville: University of Tennessee Press, 2003.

Miller, Floyd. "The Father of Black Nationalism: Another Contender." *Civil War History* 17 (December 1971): 310–319.

Miller, Floyd. *The Search for a Black Nationality: Black Emigration and Colonization, 1787–1863.* Urbana: University of Illinois Press, 1975.

Miller, Floyd. "The Search for a Black Nationality: Martin R. Delaney and the Emigrationist Alternative." Ph.D. dissertation, University of Minnesota, 1970.

Miller, Kelly. "An Oath of Afro-American Youth." *Crisis* (June 1913): 92.

Miller, Kelly. *Segregation: The Caste System and the Civil Service.* Washington, DC, 1914.

Moore, R. Laurence. "Religion, Secularization, and the Shaping of the Culture Industry in Antebellum America." *American Quarterly* 41 (June 1989): 216–242.

Moreno, Paul. "Racial Classifications and Reconstruction Legislation." *Journal of Southern History* 61 (May 1995): 271–304.

Morgan, Edmund. *American Slavery, American Freedom: The Ordeal of Colonial Virginia.* New York: W. W. Norton, 1975.

Morgan, Joseph H. *Morgan's History of the New Jersey Conference of the A.M.E. Church, From 1872 to 1887* Camden, NJ: S. Chew, 1887.

Morrow, Ralph. *Northern Methodism and Reconstruction.* East Lansing: Michigan State University Press, 1956.

Moses, Wilson J. *Afrotopia: The Roots of African American Popular History.* Cambridge: Cambridge University Press, 1998.

Moses, Wilson J. *Alexander Crummell: A Study of Civilization and Discontent.* New York: Oxford University Press, 1989.

418　BIBLIOGRAPHY

Moses, Wilson J. "Civilizing Missionary: A Study of Alexander Crummell." *Journal of Negro History* 60 (April 1975): 229–251.

Moses, Wilson J. *The Golden Age of Black Nationalism, 1850–1925*. Hamden, CT: Archon Books, 1978.

Moses, Wilson J. "W. E. B. Du Bois's 'The Conservation of Races' and Its Context: Idealism, Conservatism and Hero Worship." *Massachusetts Review* 34 (Summer 1993): 275–294.

Moss, Alfred. *The American Negro Academy: Voice of the Talented Tenth*. Baton Rouge: Louisiana State University Press, 1981.

Moss, Hilary J. "Education's Inequity: Opposition to Black Higher Education in Antebellum Connecticut." *History of Education Quarterly* (Spring, 2006) 46: 16–35.

Moss, Simeon. "The Persistence of Slavery and Involuntary Servitude in a Free State." *Journal of Negro History* 35 (1950): 289–314.

Mounter, Michael Robert. "Richard Theodore Greener: The Idealist, Statesman, Scholar, and South Carolinian." PhD dissertation, University of South Carolina, 2002.

Murray, Pauli. *Proud Shoes: The Story of an American Family*. New York: Harper & Row, 1987.

Nash, Gary. *Forging Freedom. The Formation of Philadelphia's Black Community, 1720–1840*. Cambridge, MA: Harvard University Press, 1988.

Nelson, William. *New Jersey Biographical and Genealogical Notes*. Newark: New Jersey Historical Society, 1916.

Nobles, Melissa. *Shades of Citizenship: Race and the Census in Modern Politics*. Stanford, CA: Stanford University Press, 2000.

Norwood, Frederick. *The Story of American Methodism*. Nashville, TN: Abingdon Press, 1974.

Oldfield, J. R., ed. *Civilization and Black Progress: Selected Writings of Alexander Crummell on the South*. Charlottesville: University Press of Virginia for Southern Texts Society, 1995.

O'Malley, Michael. "Specie and Species: Race and the Money Question in Nineteenth-Century America." *American Historical Review* 99 (April 1994): 369–395.

Omi, Michael, and Howard Winant. *Racial Formation in the United States from the 1960s to the 1980s*. New York: Routledge and Kegan Paul, 1986.

O'Toole, James M. *Passing for White: Race, Religion, and the Healy Family, 1820–1920*. Amherst: University of Massachusetts Press, 2003.

Patton, Adell, Jr. "The 'Back-to-Africa' Movement in Arkansas." *Arkansas Historical Quarterly* 51 (Summer 1992): 164–177.

Patton, June O. " 'And the Truth Shall Make You Free': Richard Robert Wright, Sr., Black Intellectual and Iconoclast, 1877–1897." *Journal of Negro History* 81 (Winter–Autumn 1996): 17–30.

Payne, Daniel. *History of the African Methodist Episcopal Church*. 1891. New York: Arno Press and the New York Times, 1969.

Pease, William H., and Jane H. Pease. *Bound with Them in Chains: A Biographical History of the Antislavery Movement*. Westport, CT: Greenwood Press, 1972.

Pease, William H., and Jane H. Pease. "Negro Conventions and the Problem of Black Leadership." *Journal of Black Studies* 2 (1971): 29–44.

Pease, William H., and Jane H. Pease. "The Negro Convention Movement." In *Key Issues in the Afro-American Experience*, vol. 1, edited by Nathan Huggins, Martin Kilson, and Daniel M. Fox, 191–205. New York: Harcourt Brace Jovanovich, 1971.

BIBLIOGRAPHY 419

Pease, William H., and Jane H. Pease. *They Who Would Be Free: Blacks' Search for Freedom, 1830–1861*. Urbana: University of Illinois Press, 1990.

Penn, I. Garland. *The Afro-American Press, and Its Editors*. 1891. Reprint. Salem, NH: Ayer, 1988.

Perea, Juan F. "The Echoes of Slavery: Recognizing the Racist Origins of the Agricultural and Domestic Worker Exclusion from the National Labor Relations Act." *Ohio State Law Journal* 72 (2011): 95–138.

Pernot, M., ed. *After Freedom*. Burlington, NJ: Burlington County Historical Society, 1987.

Peterson, Carla L. *"Doers of the Word": African-American Women Speakers & Writers in the North (1830–1880)*. New Brunswick, NJ: Rutgers University Press, 1998.

Pingeon, Frances. "An Abominable Business: The New Jersey Slave Trade, 1818." *New Jersey History* 109 (Fall/Winter 1991): 15–35.

Quarles, Benjamin. *Black Abolitionists*. New York: Oxford University Press, 1969.

Raboteau, Albert J. *A Fire in the Bones: Reflections on African American Religious History*. Boston: Beacon Press, 1995.

Raboteau, Albert J. "Exodus, Ethiopia, and Racial Messianism: Texts and Contexts of African American Chosenness." In *Many Are Chosen: Divine Election and Western Nationalism*, edited by William R. Hutchison and Hartmut Lehmann, 175–195. Minneapolis: Fortress Press, 1994.

Rael, Patrick. *Black Identity and Black Protest in the Antebellum North*. Chapel Hill: University of North Carolina Press, 2002.

Raybold, G. A. *Annals of Methodism, or Sketches of the Origin and Progress of Methodism in Various Portions of West Jersey*. Philadelphia: T. Stokes, 1847.

Redkey, Edwin. S. *Black Exodus: Black Nationalist and Back-to-Africa Movements, 1890–1910*. New Haven, CT: Yale University Press, 1969.

Reed, Adolph. "'Double Consciousness': Race, American Identity and American Political Thought." Paper presented at Conference on Political Identity in America Thought, Yale University, April 19–21, 1991.

Reed, Harry A. *Platform for Change: The Foundations of the Northern Free Black Community, 1775–1865*. East Lansing: Michigan State University Press, 1994.

Rhodes, Jane. *Mary Ann Shadd Cary: The Black Press and Protest in the Nineteenth Century*. Bloomington: Indiana University Press, 1998.

Richards, Leonard. *"Gentlemen of Property and Standing": Anti-abolition Mobs in Jacksonian America*. New York: Oxford University Press, 1970.

Richardson, Harry. *Dark Salvation: The Story of Methodism as It Developed among Blacks in America*. Garden City, NY: Anchor Press, 1976.

Richardson, Joe. *Christian Reconstruction: The American Missionary Association and Southern Blacks, 1861–1891*. Athens: University of Georgia Press, 1986.

Roediger, David. "The Pursuit of Whiteness: Property, Terror, and Expansion, 1790–1860." *Journal of the Early Republic* 19 (Winter 1999): 579–600.

Roediger, David. *The Wages of Whiteness: Race and the Making of the American Working Class*. New York: Verso Press, 1991.

Ronnick, Michele Valerie. "Heliodorus." In *Oxford Encyclopedia of African Thought*, vol. 1, edited by Abiola Irele and Biodun Jeyifo, 440–442. New York: Oxford University Press, 2010.

Runcie, John. "'Hunting the Nigs' in Philadelphia: The Race Riot of August 1834." *Pennsylvania History* 39 (April 1972): 187–218.

420 BIBLIOGRAPHY

Rusert, Britt. *Fugitive Science: Empiricism and Freedom in Early African American Culture America and the Long 19th Century*. New York: New York Press, 2017.

Said, Edward. *The World, the Text, and the Critic*. Cambridge, MA: Harvard University Press, 1983.

Schiebinger, Londa. "The Anatomy of Difference: Race and Sex in Eighteenth-Century Science." *Eighteenth-Century Studies* 23 (Summer 1990): 387–405.

Schneider, Ryan. "Sex and the Race Man: Imagining Interracial Relationships in W. E. B. Du Bois's Darkwater." *Arizona Quarterly* 59:2 (Summer 2003): 59–80.

Schor, Joel. "The Rivalry between Frederick Douglass and Henry Highland Garnet." *Journal of Negro History* 64 (Winter 1979): 30–38.

Scott, James C. *Domination and the Arts of Resistance: Hidden Transcripts*. New Haven, CT: Yale University Press, 1990.

Seraile, William. "The Brief Diplomatic Career of Henry Highland Garnet." *Phylon* 46 (1st Quarter 1985): 71–81.

Seraile, William. *Bruce Grit: The Black Nationalist Writings of John Edward Bruce*. Knoxville: University of Tennessee Press, 2003.

Seraile, William. *Fire in His Heart: Bishop Benjamin Tucker Tanner and the A.M.E. Church*. Knoxville: University of Tennessee Press, 2003.

Seraile, William. "Susan McKinney Steward: New York State's First African-American Woman Physician." *Afro-Americans in New York Life and History* 9:2 (July 1985): 27–44.

Seraile, William. *Voice of Dissent: Theophilus Gould Steward (1843–1924) and Black America*. New York: Carlson, 1991.

Sernett, Milton. *North Star Country: Upstate New York and the Crusade for African American Freedom*. Syracuse, NY: Syracuse University Press, 2002.

Shakespeare, William. *Hamlet*. edited by Mark Norfolk. London: Aurora Metro Books, 2017.

Shakespeare, William. *The Merchant of Venice*. Edited by Jay L. Halio. New York: Oxford University Press, 1993.

Shklar, Judith N. *American Citizenship: The Quest for Inclusion*. Cambridge, MA: Harvard University Press, 1991.

Shourds, Thomas. *History and Genealogy of Fenwick's Colony, New Jersey*. Bridgeton, NJ: G. F. Nixon, 1876.

Silcox, Harry C. "The Black 'Better Class' Political Dilemma: Philadelphia Prototype Isaiah C. Wears." *Pennsylvania Magazine of History and Biography* 113 (January 1989): 45–66.

Sinkler, George. *Racial Attitudes of American Presidents from Abraham Lincoln to Theodore Roosevelt*. Garden City, NY: Anchor Books, 1972

Smedley, Audrey. *Race in North America: Origin and Evolution of a Worldview*. Boulder, CO: Westview Press, 1993.

Smith, Charles S. *A History of the African Methodist Episcopal Church*. 1922. Reprint. New York: Johnson Reprint, 1968.

Smith, Rogers. *Civic Ideals: Conflicting Visions of Citizenship in U.S. History*. New Haven, CT: Yale University Press, 1997.

Spires, Derrick R. *The Practice of Citizenship: Black Politics and Print Culture in the Early United States*. Philadelphia: University of Pennsylvania Press, 2019.

Stanton, William. *The Leopard's Spots: Scientific Attitudes toward Race in America, 1815–1859*. Chicago: University of Chicago Press, 1960.

Staudenraus, J. *The African Colonization Movement, 1816–1865*. New York: Columbia University Press, 1961.

BIBLIOGRAPHY 421

Stauffer, John. *The Black Hearts of Men: Radical Abolitionists and the Transformation of Race*. Cambridge, MA: Harvard University Press, 2001.

Stephenson, Gilbert Thomas. *Race Distinctions in American Law*. 1910. Reprint, New York: Johnson Reprint, 1970.

Stepan, Nancy Leys, and Sander Gilman. "Appropriating the Idioms of Science: The Rejection of Scientific Racism." In *The Bounds of Race: Perspectives on Hegemony and Resistance*, edited by Dominic La Capra, 72–103. Ithaca, NY: Cornell University Press, 1991.

Sterling, Dorothy. *The Making of an Afro-American: Martin Robison Delany, African Explorer, Civil War Major, & Father of Black Nationalism*. New York: Da Capo Press, 1996.

Sterling, Dorothy, ed. *Speak Out in Thunder Tones: Letters and Other Writings by Black Northerners, 1787–1865*. New York: Da Capo Press, 1998.

Stewart, James Brewer. "The Emergence of Racial Modernity and the Rise of the White North, 1790–1840." *Journal of the Early Republic* 18 (Spring 1998): 181–217.

Stewart, James Brewer. "'Modernizing Difference:' The Political Meanings of Color in the Free States, 1776–1840." *Journal of the Early Republic* 19 (Winter 1999): 691–712.

Still, William. *The Underground Rail Road*. 1871. Reprint. Chicago: Johnson, 1970.

Stocking, George. *Race, Culture, and Evolution: Essays in the History of Anthropology*. New York: Free Press, 1968.

Streifford, David. "The American Colonization Society: An Application of Republican Ideology to Antebellum Reform." *Journal of Southern History* 45:2 (May 1979): 201–220.

Stuckey, Sterling. *The Ideological Origins of Black Nationalism*. Boston: Beacon Press, 1972.

Stuckey, Sterling. *Slave Culture: Nationalist Theory and the Foundations of Black America*. New York: Oxford University Press, 1987.

Sweet, Leonard. *Black Images of America, 1784–1870*. New York: W. W. Norton, 1976.

Takaki, Ronald. *Iron Cages: Race and Culture in 19th-Century America*. New York: Oxford University Press, 1990.

Tennyson, Alfred, Lord. *In Memoriam*. Boston: Ticknor, Reed, and Fields, 1850.

Thomas, Brook, ed. *Plessy v. Ferguson: A Brief History with Documents*. Boston: Bedford Books, 1997.

Trafton, Scott. *Egypt Land: Race and Nineteenth-Century American Egyptomania*. Durham, NC: Duke University Press, 2004.

Ullman, Victor. *Martin R. Delany: The Beginnings of Black Nationalism*. Boston: Beacon Press, 1971.

US Census Bureau. *Negro Population in the United States, 1790–1915*. 1918. New York: Arno Press and the New York Times, 1968.

Van Woodward, C. *American Counterpoint: Slavery and Racism in the North-South Dialogue*. New York: Little, Brown, 1971.

Vorenberg, Michael. "Abraham Lincoln and the Politics of Black Colonization." *Journal of the Abraham Lincoln Association* 14 (Summer 1993): 23–45.

Waldstreicher, David. *In the Midst of Perpetual Fetes: The Making of American Nationalism, 1776–1820*. Chapel Hill: University of North Carolina Press, 1997.

Walker, Clarence, E. *A Rock in a Weary Land: The African Methodist Episcopal Church during the Civil War and Reconstruction*. Baton Rouge: Louisiana State University Press, 1982.

Wallis, Brian. "Black Bodies, White Science: Louis Agassiz's Slave Daguerreotypes." *American Art* 9 (Summer 1995): 44.

422 BIBLIOGRAPHY

Walters, Ronald. *American Reformers, 1815–1860*. New York: Hill and Wang, 1978.

Walters, Ronald. *The Antislavery Appeal: American Abolitionism after 1830*. New York: W. W. Norton, 1978.

Washington, Jack. *In Search of a Community's Past: The Black Community in Trenton, New Jersey, 1860–1900*. Trenton, NJ: Africa World Press, 1990.

Wayman, Alexander. *Cyclopedia of African Methodism*. Baltimore: Methodist Episcopal Book Depository, 1882.

Webster, Yehudi. *The Racialization of America*. New York: St. Martin's Press, 1992.

Werner, John. *Reaping the Bloody Harvest: Race Riots in the United States during the Age of Jackson, 1821–1849*. New York: Garland Press, 1986.

Williams, Andreá N. *Dividing Lines: Class Anxiety and Postbellum Black Fiction*. Ann Arbor: University of Michigan Press, 2013.

Williamson, Joel. *The Crucible of Race: Black-White Relations in the American South since Emancipation*. New York: Oxford University Press, 1984.

Williamson, Joel. *New People: Miscegenation and Mulattoes in the United States*. New York: New York University Press, 1984.

Williamson, Joel. "W. E. B. Du Bois as a Hegelian." In *What Was Freedom's Price?*, edited by David Sansing, 21–49. Jackson: University Press of Mississippi, 1978.

Wills, David W. "Aspects of Social Thought in the African Methodist Episcopal Church, 1884–1910." PhD dissertation, Harvard University, 1975.

Wills, David W. "Womanhood and Domesticity in the A.M.E. Tradition: The Influence of Daniel Alexander Payne." In *Black Apostles at Home and Abroad*, edited by David W. Wills and Richard Newman, 133–146. Boston: G. K. Hall, 1982.

Winch, Julie. "American Free Blacks and Emigration to Haiti." Paper presented at the Eleventh Caribbean Congress of the Caribbean Institute and Study Center for Latin America of Inter American University, August 1988.

Winch, Julie. *A Gentleman of Color: The Life of James Forten*. New York: Oxford University Press, 2002.

Winch, Julie. *Philadelphia's Black Elite: Activism, Accommodation, and the Struggle for Autonomy, 1787–1848*. Philadelphia: Temple University Press, 1988.

Winks, Robin. *The Blacks in Canada: A History*. 2nd edition. New Haven, CT: Yale University Press, 1971.

Winstone, Michael R. "The Quest for Freedom: Selectd Documents Illustrative of Some Aspects of the Life of Black between 1774 and 1841." *Journal of Negro History* 61 (January 1976): 88–97.

Wolff, Megan J. "The Myth of the Actuary: Life Insurance and Frederick L. Hoffman's *Race Traits and Tendencies of the American Negro*." *Public Health Reports* 121:1 (January/February 2006): 88–90.

Sweet, John Wood. *Bodies Politic: Negotiating Race in the American North, 1730–1830*. Baltimore: Johns Hopkins University Press, 2003.

Woodard, Helena. *African British Writings in the Eighteenth Century: The Politics of Race and Reason*. Westport, CT: Greenwood Press, 1999.

Wright, Marion Thompson. "Negro Suffrage in New Jersey, 1776–1875." *Journal of Negro History* 33 (1948): 168–224.

Wright, Richard C. "The Economic Conditions of Negroes in the North, III, Negro Communities in New Jersey." *Southern Workman* 37 (1908): 385–393.

Yacovone, Donald. "The Transformation of the Black Temperance Movement, 1827–1854." *Journal of the Early Republic* 8 (Fall 1988): 281–297.

Yee, Shirley J. *Black Women Abolitionists: A Study in Activism, 1828–1860*. Knoxville: University of Tennessee, 1992.

Young, Cory James. "A Just and True Return: A Dataset of Pennsylvania's Surviving County Slave Registries," *Magazine of Early American Datasets 46* McNeil Center for Early American Studies, 2021. https:repository.upenn.edu.

Index

For the benefit of digital users, indexed terms that span two pages (e.g., 52–53) may, on occasion, appear on only one of those pages.

African Methodist Episcopal (AME)
  Church, 41, 191–92, 199, 221–23,
  239–40, 253, 304–5
  Bethel Literary and Historical
    Association, 250, 251, 252–53, 273
  defense of existence, 112, 209–10, 211–
    12, 213–14
  denominational defections, 202–4
  missions to freed people, 201, 214–15
  name, 103, 215–17, 218, 219–21
  political work, 17, 22–23, 25–26, 94–95,
    180, 185, 197, 200, 210–11
African Methodist Episcopal Zion
  (AMEZ) Church, 99, 103–4, 212–
  13, 239–40
African Civilization Society, 114–15
Afro-American Council, 309–10
Agassiz, Louis, 120–21, 139–40
Allen, Richard, 17–23, 24–26, 190–91
Allen, William G., 159–62
amalgamation, 118, 121, 250, 251, 252–56,
  257–59, 284–85, 296–97
American Colonization Society
  biological justifications, 12–13, 14–
    16, 188–89
  comparison with emigration, 114–15,
    187–88, 236, 237
  Liberia, 11–12, 17
  opposition, 12, 17–22, 30–31, 38,
    44–45, 48–49, 53, 59–60, 80–81, 99–
    100, 240–41
  religious basis, 11–14, 15–16, 80, 187
American Missionary Association, 111–
  12, 201
American Moral Reform Society (AMRS).
  See also Whipper, William
  conflicts, 41, 45, 46–48, 53–54, 56, 57–
    58, 65, 78

demise, 70
founding, 36–37, 40
membership, 41, 46, 63–64, 67–68
National Reformer, 62–63, 64–65
reform principles, 42–45, 51–53, 54–55,
  64, 66–67
religious foundations, 41–42, 43, 52–53
views on race, 41–42, 45, 50–52,
  66, 69–70
American Negro Academy, 1, 266–
  67, 276–78
American School of ethnology (American
  School)
  craniology, 140
  Gliddon, George, 120–21
  Morton, Samuel, 120–21, 139–40
  Nott, Josiah, 120–21, 140, 145
  polygenesis, 118, 120–21, 127, 128–29,
    244–45, 267–68
  resurgence in Pre-Adamite
    theory, 283–84
antislavery, 104–7
  American Anti-Slavery Society,
    75, 105–6
  Free produce, 43, 66
Arnett, Benjamin, 213–14
Astwood, H. C. C., 219–20

Baptists, 93–94, 103, 310–11
Bell, Phillip, 53, 198–99
Bias, James, 85, 89–90
Bibb, Henry, 96, 99, 100, 107–8, 136–37
biblical authority and imagery, 15, 50, 58–
  59, 142–43, 144, 205–6, 214–15, 219,
  257–59, 298–99
Black Nationalism, 109. *See also*
  emigration; Langston, John Mercer;
  Delany, Martin

426 INDEX

Blyden, Edward, 238–39, 241, 243–44
Bowen, Henry Chandler, 212–13
Bowen, John Wesley, 304, 306–8
Boynton, Charles, 205–7
Bruce, John, 309–10
Burr, Hester, 43, 67
Burr, John, 42–43

Cain, Richard, 200, 201
Caldwell, Charles, 144
Campbell, Jabez, 200
Camper, Petrus, Camper scale, 140–42
Canada, 111–12. *See also* emigration
Cary, Mary Ann Shadd, 90, 96, 99, 109–14,
    194, 262–63
    *Plea for Emigration or Notes on Canada
    West, A,* 110
Catholic Church, 208–9
Catto, William, 80
Census, U.S. 145, 164, 245–46
Chesnutt, Charles
    amalgamation, 296–98
    Jim Crow, 276, 296
    Paul Marchand, F.M.C., 301–3
    race as biological difference, 293–
        94, 300
    race classifications, 300–1
    race consciousness, 296, 299–300, 301,
        302, 303
    race integrity, 289, 297–98, 302
    reform literature, 297
    whiteness, 300
    "White Weeds," 300
    "Wife of His Youth, The," 297–300
Child, Lydia Maria, 157–58
citizenship, 28, 33, 38–39, 51–53, 132,
    195–98, 218–19, 234, 240–41, 260–
    61, 273–74, 287–89, 304–5, 306, 308–
    9, 310–11, 323–24
Civil Rights Act, 1875, 180–81, 200, 226
Civil War and emancipation, 183–
    84, 249–50
Clark, Molson, 212
Clark, Peter, 208
Coates, Benjamin, 187–88
Collins, Leonard, 99, 101
Cook, John Hartwell, 205, 206–7
Congregational Church, 57, 205–7

Conventions, County (1841)
    Albany, 78–79
    New York, 72
Conventions, National
    1830, 24–26
    1831, 26–28
    1832, 28–30
    1833, 30–32
    1834, 32–34
    1835, 36–40
    1847, 96
    1853, 88–89
    1855, 94
Conventions, State and Regional
    California (1855), 83–84
    Illinois (1853), 83–84
    New England, 75–76, 108–9
    New Jersey (1849), 80
    New York (1841, 1851, 1852), 76, 78,
        92–93, 148
    Ohio (1856), 81–82
    Pennsylvania (1841, 1848), 82–83,
        84–88, 91
Cornish, Samuel, 46–47, 48–54, 56, 59–60,
    62, 63, 64–65, 67–68, 96–97
Crogman, William, 277–78
Cromwell, John, 256, 305–6
Crummell, Alexander, 189, 253–54, 256,
    266–68, 270
Cuff, Reuben, 46
Cuguano, Ottobah, 104–5

Day, William Howard, *Aliened American*
    (newspaper), 101–2
Desdunes, Rodolphe, 275–76
Delany, Martin
    Black Nationalism, 115–16
    Canada, 116–17
    emigration as divine racial plan,
        236–37
    labor, 107–8
    Origin of Races and Color, 236
    "Political Destiny of the Colored
        Race on the American Continent,
        The," 114
    race challenges, 115, 259
    race traits and difference, 114, 115, 116
Derrick, William, 241–42

INDEX 427

Dickerson, William, "Reasons for the Existence and Continuance of Race Churches, The," 212

Dixon, Thomas, 284–85, 289–90

Douglass, Frederick
amalgamation, 255
defense of race practices, 101–2
lynching, 263–64
marriage controversy, 255–59
race challenges, 138, 144
against race pride, 267
religious practices, 94, 96, 97, 99–100, 198–99, 200
women reformers, 90, 113, 263

Douglas, H. Ford, 107–8, 111

Downing, George, 108–9, 184, 193, 198–99, 208–9, 254

Du Bois, William Edward Burghardt
challenging extinction, 278, 279–80
"Comet, The," 272
Conservation of Races, The, 1–2
Crisis, 317, 324
Horizon, 315, 317
Pan-African philosophy of race, 324–25
race identity and integrity, 1–2, 271–72, 276–78, 281, 292–93, 325
race pride and species unity, 265–66, 268–70, 271, 325
reconceptualizing the color line, 315–18

Duffin, James, W., 61

Easton, Hosea, 128–32
education, 27–28, 30, 92, 93–94, 189–90
Embry, James, 242–43, 246–47, 309
emigration
Africa, 109, 116
Canada 22–23, 25, 29, 31, 109–14
compared to colonization, 23
Haiti, 22–23
opposition to, 31, 241–42, 243–44
environmentalism, 121–22, 125–26, 127–28, 154
Episcopalians, 94–95, 102–3, 208–9
Equal Rights League, 185, 195–96
Ethiop. See Wilson, William
evolution
Darwinism, 166

Lamarckian thought, 131, 161
as progress 262–63, 265
extinction, 145, 238, 246, 247, 248, 255, 279–80, 297–98

Ferris, William, 310–11
Fields, Barbara, 327
Forten, James, Sr., 41, 46, 51, 53, 55, 63–64
Forten, James, Jr., 42–43
Forten, William, 195–97
Fortune, T. Thomas, 240, 308–9
Frederickson, George, 5, 326–27

Garnet, Henry Highland, 53–54, 82, 104–5, 114–15, 135–36, 142–43, 197–98, 215–16, 220–21
Garrison, William Lloyd, 97, 99, 195–96
Garvey, Marcus Universal Negro Improvement Association (UNIA), 319–20, 324–25
Gibbs, Mifflin, 83–84, 85
Gladden, Washington, "The Christian League of Connecticut," 207
Greener, Richard, 256–57, 259
Grice, Hezekiah, 25, 30

Hamilton, John, 108
Hamilton, William, 12, 29–30, 32–33
Handy, James, 201, 215–16
Harding, Warren G., 319–20
Harris, Andrew, 63–64, 66
Haven, Gilbert, 204
Haynes, Lemuel, 104–5
Herodotus, 125–27, 135–36
Hershaw, Lafayette, 315
Higginbotham, Evelyn, 326–27
Hinton, Frederick, 46, 48, 62
Hoffman, Frederick, Race Traits and Tendencies of the American Negro, 278–81
Holly, James Theodore, 119, 219
Hood, James, 212–13
Howard, O. O., 206–7

interracial marriage, 252–53, 255, 256–57, 284–85

Jefferson, Thomas, 12–13, 165–66

428 INDEX

Jenifer, J. T., 213–14, 221
Jewish race, 140, 160–61, 255, 293, 295–96
Jim Crow, 234, 235, 249–50, 262, 263, 271, 273, 325, 326
Johnson, Andrew, 184–85, 191–92, 229–30
Johnson, Edward, 244–45
Johnson, Harriet, 194
Johnson, Harvey, 310–11

Langston, John Mercer, 115
Lee, Benjamin, 209–10, 211–12, 221, 241, 252–53
Lee, Mary, *Afmerica*, 309
Lewis, John, 137–38, 147
Lincoln, Abraham, 183, 230
Locke, Alain, 321–24
Locke, Ishmael, 80
Lynch, James, 201, 202–3, 204, 216, 217
lynching, 234, 263, 268

Martin, Sella, 198–99
Martinet, Louis, 275–76, 309–10
Menard, John W., 194
Methodist Episcopal Church North 201–2, 204, 222–23
Methodist Episcopal Church South, 202–3, 222–23
Miller, Kelly
    miscegenation, 252–53, 254, 255, 259
    names, 284–85, 311–12
    race challenges, 279–80, 284–85, 319–20
    race consciousness, 295–96
    race leadership, 318–19, 321
Mitchell, John G., 218–19
monogenism, 121, 156–57, 247
moral improvement, need for, 56
    as cause of discrimination, 56–57
Morel, Junius, 50, 53, 70, 102–3
Morris, Robert, 92
Moses, Wilson, 126–27, 267
mulattoes, 144–45, 166
Murphy, Edgar Gardner, 290, 291–92
Murray, Freeman Henry Morris, 315

National Council of the Colored People, 89–90, 93–94

Native Americans
    oppression compared, 18–19
    racist ideas about, 191–92, 230
Niagara movement, 315, 317

Oson, Jacob, *Search for Truth; or An Inquiry for the Origin of the African Nation, A*, 44–45, 49
Ottley, Roi, 325–26

Pan-Africanism, 292–93. *See also* Du Bois, William Edward Burghardt
Payne, Daniel, 41, 46, 67, 201–2, 219, 221–23
Peck, David Jones, 85
Peck, John, 29, 32, 94
Pennington, James W. C., 134–35, 142–43, 147–48
Pickens, William, 290–91
Pierce, Jeremiah, 197, 210–11
Plessy v. Ferguson, 275–76
Presbyterians, 41, 251
Prichard, James Cowles, 121, 150–51, 154–55
Purvis, Charles, 195–96
Purvis, Robert, 41–42, 43, 47–48, 55, 66, 89–90, 102–3, 106, 183, 185–86, 234–35, 240, 257

Quakers, 58–59, 106, 166, 187–88

race categories, 147–48, 149–51
race integrity, 289–90, 292–93
racial designations
    African, 102–3, 215–16, 219, 307
    Afric-American, 18, 22
    Afro-American, 284–85, 308–10
    Anglo-African, 149
    colored, 64–66, 102–3, 307, 308–9
    Hamite, 310–11
    Negro, 48–49, 305, 306–12
    Negrosaxon, 310–11
    white, 55, 309, 311–12
Ray, Charles, 57, 70, 72, 75–78, 93–95, 112–13
Reason, Charles, 93–94
Reconstruction
    "class" measures, 225, 231

Civil Rights Act, 1875 180–81, 231
Fifteenth Amendment, 180, 196–98, 262
Fourteenth Amendment, 181–82, 262
Freedmen's Bureau, 205, 206–7, 228–30
Freedman's Savings and Trust Company, 225, 226, 227, 230
Thirteenth Amendment, 180, 183–84
Reeve, John, 251–52
Remond, Charles, 90, 91–92, 208–9
Revels, Hiram 203–4
Roberts v. the City of Boston, 92
Roberts, Joseph Jenkins, 192–93
Rock, John, 80–81, 148, 182–83
Roman, Charles, 288–89
Ruffin, George, 254
Ruggles, David, 74, 102–3, 106
Russwurm, John, 11–12, 124–27

Sampson, John, 243–44, 247–49, 294–95
Scarborough, William, 283, 289–90, 291–94
segregation, 58–60, 61, 62
   churches, 94–97
   conventions, 75–76
   schools, 92–94, 112, 210–11. *See also Roberts v. the City of Boston*
Shadd, Abraham, 21–22, 26–27, 30, 85, 109–10
Shakespeare, William
   Polonius (*Hamlet*), 299–300
   Shylock (*Merchant of Venice*), 183, 200
Sigourney, Lydia H., 105–6
Smith, Charles, 202
Smith, Gerrit, 186–87, 189–90
Smith, James McCune, 74–75, 76, 104–5
   bigotry, 164–65
   blood, 144
   census errors, 164
   craniology, 145–47
   Darwinism, 166
   emancipation, 182
   environmentalism, 154
   "On the Fourteenth Query of Jefferson's Notes on Virginia," 165–66
   polygenesis, 144–45, 166
   "Word for the 'Smith Family,' A," 166

Smith, John Augustine, 146
Smith, Samuel Stanhope, 127
Smith, Stephen, 36–37, 186–87, 197
Smith, William B., *Color Line: A Brief on behalf of the Unborn. The*, 289–90
Squirer, Ephraim, 164–65, 289–90
Stanford, Anthony, 201, 220–21
Steward, Barbara Ann, 90
Steward, Susan McKinney, 286–87
Steward, Theophilus
   human unity, 286–87
   lynching and race fictions, 287–88
   missions and race, 201, 214–15
   myths of Negro disposition and mulatto mortality, 278–79, 286
   race concept, 260–61
   race names, 311–12
   research on race difference, 285–86
   women's rights, 286–87
Steward, William, 185
Stewart, Maria, 123
Stowe, Harriet Beecher, 113
Straker, D. Augustus, 304, 317
Sumner, Charles, 92, 195–97
suffrage. *See* voting rights

Tanner, Benjamin Tucker, 210, 211–12, 221, 222–23, 249–51, 257, 282–84, 304–6, 308
Turner, Henry McNeal, 194, 217–18, 237, 238
temperance, 27–28, 31–32, 36

voting rights. *See also* Fifteenth Amendment
   disenfranchisement, 62, 68–69
   suffrage campaigns, 72, 74, 78, 184, 185–86, 194–97

Wagoner, Henry, Jr., 224
Wagoner, H. O., Sr., 88–89
Walker, David, *Appeal to the Coloured Citizens of the World*, 18, 19–20, 22–23
Walker, William, 197–98, 208

430 INDEX

Ward, Samuel Ringgold, 73, 106, 112–13, 135–36, 143
Waring, Everett, 312–13
Washington, Booker T., 265, 304
Watkins, William, 64–65, 98–99
Wears, Isaiah, 193, 194, 196, 227–30, 312–13
Whipper, William. *See also* American Moral Reform Society
    church relations, 94–95, 96, 97–99, 189–90, 227
    class legislation, 224–26
    conventions. *See* Conventions, National; Conventions, State and Regional
    death, 227
    early reform vision and debates, 34–36, 46–47, 52–53, 77, 89–90
    emigration, 186–87

Freedman's Savings and Trust Company (Freedman's Bank), 226–27
    philanthropy, 187, 189–90
    race challenges, 51, 55–56, 69–70
    race love, 190–91
Whipple, George, 111–12
whiteness, 55, 66–67, 98, 105–6, 190–92, 260–61, 275–76
Williams, George Washington, 244–46
Williams, Peter, 17, 20, 22–23
Wilson, William J., 90
Winchell, Alexander, Pre-Adamite theory, 284, 306–7
women's rights, 90, 194, 286–87
Woodson, Lewis, 57–59, 61–62, 82–83, 89–90, 96, 100–1
Wright, Richard R., Sr., 277–78
Wright, Theodore, 78, 106–7

Printed in the USA/Agawam, MA
October 18, 2024

874657.003